THE LAW IN CONTEXT SERIES

Since 1970 the Law in Context series has been at the forefront of the movement to broaden the study of law. It has been a vehicle for the publication of innovative scholarly books that treat law and legal phenomena critically in their social, political, and economic contexts from a variety of perspectives. The series particularly aims to publish scholarly legal writing that brings fresh perspectives to bear on new and existing areas of law taught in universities. A contextual approach involves treating legal subjects broadly, using materials from other social sciences, and from any other discipline that helps to explain the operation in practice of the subject under discussion. It is hoped that this orientation is at once more stimulating and more realistic than the bare exposition of legal rules. The series includes original books that have a different emphasis from traditional legal textbooks, while maintaining the same high standards of scholarship. They are written primarily for undergraduate and graduate students of law and of other disciplines, but most also appeal to a wider readership. In the past, most books in the series have focused on English law, but recent publications include books on European law, globalisation, transnational legal processes, and comparative law.

Books in the Series

Anderson, Schum & Twining: *Analysis of Evidence*

Ashworth: *Sentencing and Criminal Justice*

Barton & Douglas: *Law and Parenthood*

Beecher-Monas: *Evaluating Scientific Evidence: An Interdisciplinary Framework for Intellectual Due Process*

Bell: *French Legal Cultures*

Bercusson: *European Labour Law*

Birkinshaw: *European Public Law*

Birkinshaw: *Freedom of Information: The Law, the Practice and the Ideal*

Brownsword & Goodwin: *Law and the Technologies of the Twenty-First Century*

(continued after Index)

Evidence Matters

Science, Proof, and Truth in the Law

SUSAN HAACK
University of Miami

CAMBRIDGE
UNIVERSITY PRESS

32 Avenue of the Americas, New York, NY 10013-2473, USA

Cambridge University Press is part of the University of Cambridge.

It furthers the University's mission by disseminating knowledge in the pursuit of education, learning, and research at the highest international levels of excellence.

www.cambridge.org
Information on this title: www.cambridge.org/9781107698345

First published 2014

Printed in the United States of America

A catalog record for this publication is available from the British Library.

Library of Congress Cataloging in Publication data
Haack, Susan, author.
Evidence matters : science, proof, and truth in the law / Susan Haack.
pages cm – (Law in context)
Includes bibliographical references and index.
ISBN 978-1-107-03996-4 (hardback) – ISBN 978-1-107-69834-5 (paperback)
1. Evidence (Law) 2. Admissible evidence. 3. Science and law. I. Title.
K2261.H32 2014
347′.06–dc23 2013048953

ISBN 978-1-107-03996-4 Hardback
ISBN 978-1-107-69834-5 Paperback

Until lately the best thing I was able to think of in favor of civilization ... was that it made possible the artist, the poet, the philosopher, and the man of science.... Now I believe that ... the chief worth of civilization is that it makes the means of living more complex, that it calls for great and combined intellectual efforts, instead of simple, uncoordinated ones.... Because more complex and intense intellectual efforts mean a fuller and richer life.

–Oliver Wendell Holmes (1900)

Contents

Acknowledgments

"Epistemology and the Law of Evidence: Problems and Projects"–the most recent of these essays–is based on a talk given at a 2012 workshop on legal epistemology organized by Rachel Herdy in the law faculty at the Universidade Federal do Rio de Janeiro, Brazil. It was also presented, in an abridged form and under the title "Problems and Projects in the Theory (and Practice) of Evidence Law," as an after-dinner speech at the 2013 conference of the Canadian Institute for the Administration of Justice.

"Epistemology Legalized: Or, Truth, Justice, and the American Way" was my Olin Lecture in Jurisprudence at the Notre Dame Law School, and appeared in the *American Journal of Jurisprudence* 49 (2004): 43–61.

"Legal Probabilism: An Epistemological Dissent" was first presented in 2011, at a workshop on standards of proof and scientific evidence organized by Jordi Ferrer Beltrán and his colleagues in the faculty of law at the University of Girona, Spain; and was one of the series of lectures I gave the following year in the faculty of law at the Universidad Externado de Colombia in Bogotá. It appeared, in Spanish translation by María José Viana and Carlos Bernal, in Carmen Vázquez, ed., *Estándares de prueba y preuba científica: Ensayos de epistemología jurídica* (Barcelona: Marcial Pons, 2013), 65–98.

"Irreconcilable Differences? The Troubled Marriage of Science and Law" has proved especially popular since it was first presented at a 2007 meeting in Bretton Woods, New Hampshire, organized by David Michaels and his colleagues at the Project on Scientific Knowledge and Public Policy (SKAPP). In 2008 it was presented in the faculty of law at the University of Alicante, Spain, and at Amherst College; in 2010 it was the basis of my talk at a joint conference of the School of Medicine and the College of Law at Florida International University; in 2011 it was presented in the department of philosophy at the University of Western Ontario, Canada, and in the faculty of law at the Pontifical Catholic University of Rio de Janiero (PUC-Rio); in 2012 it was presented at the Universidad Externado de Colombia; and in 2013 a modified version was given at the VI Congreso internacional de derecho procesal in Cartagena, Colombia. This essay was first published in *Law & Contemporary Problems* 72, no.1 (2009): 1–24; and also appeared, in Spanish translation by Orión Vargas, in *Proceso judicial y cultura*, ed. Mónica Bustamente Ruaz (Medellín, Colombia: Universidad de Medellín, 2013), 109–96.

"Trial and Error: Two Confusions in *Daubert*"–the earliest of these essays–was first presented at the 2003 SKAPP meeting in Coronado, California, and later at law school colloquia at the University of Montana (2003), George Mason University, the University of Pennsylvania, University College London (2004), and the University of Florida (2005). It was first published (under the title "Trial and Error: The Supreme Court's Philosophy of Science") in the *American Journal of Public Health* 95 (2005): S66–73; was reprinted in the *International Barristers Quarterly* 41, no.2 (2006): 376–91; and also appeared, in Italian translation by Giovanni Tuzet, in *Ars Interpretandi: Annuario I ermaneutica guiridica* 11 (2006): 303–25.

"Federal Philosophy of Science: A Deconstruction–and a Reconstruction," written at the invitation of the then editor-in-chief, appeared in the *NYU Journal of Law & Liberty* 5, no.2 (2010): 394–435. This paper is based on a shorter talk entitled "Popper on Trial: A Brief History of a Big Muddle," given at a 2009 conference on Popper organized by the Max Weber Program at the European University Institute in Fiesole, Italy. It was first presented in its full form, in the same year, at the China University of Politics and Law in Beijing; then in 2010 in the faculty of law at the University of Girona and at a colloquium of the Center for Conceptual and Historical Foundations of Science at the University of Chicago; and in 2011 at PUC-Rio.

"Peer Review and Publication: Lessons for Lawyers" grew out of a shorter talk I gave at a 2006 meeting of the National Institute of Justice in Tampa, Florida; and appeared in the *Stetson Law Review* 36, no.3 (2007): 789–819–after which it served as the basis for an invited presentation on the same subject at the Committee on Science, Technology, and Law at the National Academies of Science (2008).

"What's Wrong with Litigation-Driven Science?" was first presented at the 2006 SKAPP meeting in New York; and was published (with the subtitle "An Essay in Legal Epistemology") in the *Seton Hall Law Review* 38, no.3 (2008): 1053–83.

"Proving Causation: The Weight of Combined Evidence," written at the invitation of the editors, first appeared (under the title "Proving Causation: The Holism of Warrant and the Atomism of *Daubert*") in the *Journal of Biomedical and Health Law* IV, no.2 (2008): 253–89. It was presented in the

School of Law at the University of Minnesota and at a conference organized by the department of mathematics at Iowa State University (2009); in the faculties of law at the University of Girona and at Universidad de Caldas, Colombia, and as the keynote lecture at the annual meeting of the Society of University Neurosurgeons (2010); and at PUC-Rio (2011).

"Correlation and Causation: The 'Bradford Hill Criteria' in Epidemiological, Legal, and Epistemological Perspective" was first presented at a 2012 workshop on causation in mass torts organized by Diego Papayannis in the faculty of law at the University of Girona and, later the same year, was aired to an audience of public-health professionals at the Fundação Oswaldo Cruz in Rio de Janeiro. It appears here for the first time.

"Risky Business: Statistical Proof of Specific Causation," written in 2010 at the invitation of Jordi Ferrer Beltrán, will appear, in Spanish translation by Nicola Muffato, in Diego Papayannis, ed., *Causalidad y atribución de responsibilidad* (Barcelona: Marcial Pons, forthcoming). It has been presented in legal colloquia at Uppsala University (Sweden), the University of Girona, the University of British Columbia, and Wayne State University (2011); in the law faculties at the Universidad Externado de Colombia and the University of Medellín (2012); and in the law faculty at the Jagiellonian University in Kraków, Poland (2013). It appears here for the first time in English.

"Nothing Fancy: Some Simple Truths about Truth in the Law" was written in 2010 at the invitation of Jorge Cerdio and Germán Sucar in the department of law at the Instituto Tecnológico Autónoma de México (ITAM), for inclusion in a three-volume series entitled *Verdad y Derecho* to be published by Marcial Pons, where it will appear in Spanish translation by Ramón Ortega García. In 2012 it was presented in the School of Law at the University of San Francisco and in the law faculties at the University of Girona and the University of Medellín; and in 2013 it was presented at the Osgoode Law School at York University in Toronto and in the philosophy department at Universität Paderborn, Germany. It appears here for the first time in English.

~

This book has been a decade in the making; and a great many people have helped me in a great variety of ways. I am grateful to all those who invited me to participate in relevant events and publications, especially to David Michaels and the other organizers of SKAPP and to Jordi Ferrer Beltrán and his colleagues in legal philosophy at the University of Girona; to the audiences at the many fora and in the many countries where I have presented these papers over the years, and to the army of correspondents who, as always, also offered helpful comments and suggestions; to the students in my Law School class on scientific evidence, for their good questions; to my faculty assistant,

Beth Hanson, for capable and good-natured help of many kinds; to Pamela Lucken and all the other skilled and patient staff in the University of Miami Law Library who helped me find relevant material, check references, and get citations in the proper form; to Mark Migotti, who made ever-helpful comments on innumerable drafts; and to Howard Burdick, but for whom … well, but for whom.

Introduction: A Pragmatist Perspective on Science, Proof, and Truth in the Law

> To be master of any branch of knowledge, you must master those which lie next to it ....
>
> –Oliver Wendell Holmes[1]

Is truth in the law just plain truth–or is it something *sui generis*? Is a trial a search for truth–or is it something more, or something less, than that? Do the adversarial procedures of common-law systems promote factually sound verdicts? Do legal rules excluding relevant testimony enable the accurate determination of factual issues, or impede it? What bearing, if any, does the mathematical calculus of probabilities have on the degrees and standards of proof invoked in the law? What role can statistical evidence appropriately play in legal proof? How do the argument and counter-argument of adversarial proceedings differ from what scientists do as they seek out, sift, and weigh evidence? How can courts best handle the scientific testimony on which they now so often rely, and how are they to distinguish genuine science from pretenders–or reliable scientific testimony from unreliable hokum?

The dozen interdisciplinary essays collected here take up a whole nexus of such questions about science, proof, and truth in the law, bringing my work in epistemology and philosophy of science (and, from time to time, my work in philosophy of logic and language, metaphysics, etc.) to bear both on general questions about legal standards of proof and the relative merits of common-law and civil-law approaches to the handling of evidence, and on specific questions about the role of scientific testimony in legal proceedings. A key theme of my epistemology is that the structure of evidence can be understood by analogy with a crossword puzzle; and, just as this would lead you to expect, the

1 Oliver Wendell Holmes, "The Profession of the Law" (1886), in Sheldon Novick, ed., *Collected Works of Justice Holmes* (Chicago: University of Chicago Press, 1995), vol. 3, 471–73, 472.

arguments of these essays ramify, interlock, and loop up and back. The first three essays focus on evidence, evidentiary procedures, proof, and probability; the next five turn to the role of scientific testimony and legal efforts to domesticate it; then in the next three essays I look specifically at causation evidence in toxic tort litigation; and in the last piece I explore questions about truth in the law and its relation to truth in the sciences.

All of these essays are imbued with the spirit of the classical pragmatist tradition–influenced, that is, not only by Oliver Wendell Holmes's writings on the law, but also by the classical pragmatists' thinking about inquiry generally, and about scientific inquiry in particular. My understanding of the evolution of legal concepts and legal systems, for example, and my stress on the limits of formalism, align with Holmes's. My objective conception of truth is in the spirit of C. S. Peirce's observation that "truth is SO, whether you or I or anybody thinks it is so or not"; my distinction between genuine inquiry and advocacy research runs parallel to his distinction between real inquiry and sham reasoning; and my crossword analogy is inspired in part by his critique of Descartes's metaphor of a chain of reasons. In my conception of scientific inquiry as a human enterprise, thoroughly fallible but nevertheless capable of real advance, there are echoes not only of Peirce, but also of the other classical pragmatists. And my conceptions of law, morality, and the relations between them are shaped, in part, by William James's and John Dewey's ethical writings.

Unlike the usual fare of analytic legal philosophy–often preoccupied with its own internecine disputes, and operating at a sometimes dizzyingly high level of generality and abstraction–this work of mine is prompted by real-life legal issues: by disputes that have arisen in court, by debates over the desirability of this or that rule or procedure, and so on. The rules, procedures, cases, etc., come largely from US law; but most of the issues they raise are of much more than parochial interest, and so too, I believe, are the benefits of a sound philosophical approach to understanding and resolving them.

~

The first essay included here, "Epistemology and the Law of Evidence: Problems and Projects," sets the stage. I begin by explaining what I take epistemology to be, how I see it bearing on questions about evidence and evidentiary procedures in the law, and what pitfalls we need to avoid when we apply epistemological theory to legal practice. Next, I lay out my understanding of the differences between pseudo-inquiry and the real thing; of the nature and structure of evidence; and of the multiple determinants of evidential quality, and hence of degree of warrant–or, in legal terms, of proof. Then I can signal some of the ways this theoretical work can be applied in legal contexts:

to shed light on Peirce's critique of adversarialism, for example, and on Judge Kozinski's animadversions against "litigation-driven" science; to distinguish degrees of proof from mathematical probabilities, and at the same time explain what role statistical evidence can properly play; to understand the reasoning behind Jeremy Bentham's critique of exclusionary rules of evidence; to see how, when, and why a congeries of pieces of evidence may have greater weight than any of its components alone; and so on. Finally, as the title of this essay promises, I conclude with a list of "projects": i.e., of significant outstanding problems in legal epistemology; and with an argument that two-way traffic between legal practice and epistemological theory could greatly benefit not only legal thinking about evidence, but also the increasingly self-referential and narrowly-focused "niche" epistemology that, sadly, predominates today.

The second essay, "Epistemology Legalized: Or, Truth, Justice, and the American Way"–the earliest of the papers included here–focuses first on the adversarial character of US evidence law (evidence prepared and presented by the parties to a case, the witnesses for each side cross-examined by the attorneys for the other); and then on its reliance on exclusionary rules (rules limiting what evidence may be presented to a finder of fact). This essay explores two powerful epistemological criticisms of such an evidentiary régime: Peirce's, that the "hot and partisan debate" encouraged by adversarialism fosters a focus on victory rather than truth; and Bentham's, that rules limiting the admissibility of various kinds of testimony run contrary to the epistemological desideratum of comprehensiveness, the desirability of taking all the relevant evidence into account.

It can hardly be denied that the drawbacks Peirce and Bentham identified are real; nevertheless, I argue, neither Peirce's nor Bentham's critique is fatal to the idea that adversarialism and exclusionary rules *can* be a reasonable way to determine verdicts–given, that is, the inevitable limitations of time and resources. The real problem is that these common-law procedures can be defended only on certain assumptions, among them that resources are roughly equal on both sides; and that these assumptions are rarely true in practice–as I illustrate with some examples from the law governing scientific testimony, where prosecutors' resources are almost always greater than defenders', and manufacturer defendants' resources almost always greater than individual tort plaintiffs'.

In the introduction to "Epistemology Legalized" I note that epistemology should also help us make headway with some contested issues about degrees and standards of proof; and in the essay that follows, "Legal Probabilism: An Epistemological Dissent," I tackle some of these directly. The core argument is that probabilistic conceptions of degrees of proof and, in particular, the subjective Bayesianism still dismayingly prevalent among evidence scholars, are fatally flawed. The first step is to show that degrees and standards of proof are best construed epistemologically, as degrees to which a conclusion must be warranted by the evidence presented for the party with the burden of proof to prevail–as the reasons for having standards of proof at all, as well as jury instructions on how to interpret such standards, reveal. The next step, calling on my foundherentist epistemology,[2] is to show that degrees of epistemic warrant simply don't conform to the axioms of the standard mathematical calculus of probabilities; from which it follows that degrees of proof cannot plausibly be construed probabilistically.

Still, this doesn't yet show how, in the particular, probabilistic approaches fail, or how, specifically, my approach succeeds; this is the purpose of the second half of the essay. I first show that Kadane and Schum's well-known subjective-Bayesian account of the evidence in the notorious trial of Sacco and Vanzetti (two Italian immigrants convicted of a 1920 robbery and murder) is seriously flawed; and that my foundherentist account can do significantly better. Then–to make clear that, though it isn't probabilistic, my account is perfectly capable of accommodating statistical and probabilistic evidence appropriately–I show that Finkelstein and Fairley's well-known subjective-Bayesian analysis of the case of Janet and Malcolm Collins (convicted of robbery largely on the basis of purely statistical evidence) is also seriously flawed; and that here too my approach does significantly better. I note in passing that my analysis also sheds some light on the role of DNA identification evidence–and so, like the previous essay, raises some issues specifically about scientific testimony.

Ever since scientific witnesses began to appear in court on a regular basis, there have been complaints about them; as early as 1858 we find the US Supreme Court writing that "experience has shown that opposite opinions of persons professing to be experts may be obtained to any amount."[3] Still, even in Holmes's day, scientific testimony played a much smaller role than it does now. Nonetheless, the Holmesian insight that legal systems are local, social institutions needing constantly to adapt to new circumstances is very relevant to the papers that follow, which explore the ongoing efforts of the US legal system to devise better ways of handling the scientific testimony on which, in this technologically advanced age, it more and more relies.

[2] Susan Haack, *Evidence and Inquiry: Towards Reconstruction in Epistemology* (Oxford: Blackwell, 1993); expanded 2nd ed., *Evidence and Inquiry: A Pragmatist Reconstruction of Epistemology* (Amherst, NY: Prometheus Books, 2009).

[3] Winans v. N.Y. & Erie R.R. Co., 62 U.S. 88, 101 (1858).

The fourth piece here, "Irreconcilable Differences? The Troubled Marriage of Science and Law," opens a clutch of essays on scientific testimony. It begins with a sketch of the many and various interactions of the law with science–legal regulation of hazardous scientific work, lawmakers' and regulators' reliance on scientific advice, the prosecution of scientists accused of fraudulently using federal research funds, constitutional cases involving the teaching of evolution in public high schools, "cultural heritage" cases involving ancient human remains, and courts' increasing reliance on scientific evidence–and continues with a summary history of US law on expert testimony.

Because expert witnesses present scientific, technical, or other specialized knowledge not available to the average juror, they aren't confined to testifying as to what they witnessed, but are allowed to give opinions. This special class of witnesses includes experts of every kind, including, e.g., specialists in automotive or even tire design, in accident reconstruction, in construction practices and standards, in computing, in the valuation of real estate or antiques or art, in forensic accounting, etc., etc., as well as practitioners of just about every scientific (and quasi-scientific) specialty imaginable. For a long time US law required only that an expert be qualified in his field. But in 1923 the very brief ruling in *Frye v. United States*–excluding proffered expert testimony as to the results of a primitive lie-detector test that Mr. Frye had taken–added a new requirement on the content of such testimony: that novel scientific testimony is admissible only if "the principle or discovery" on which it is based is "sufficiently established to have gained general acceptance in the particular field in which it belongs."[4] Gradually, over many decades, courts around the country began to rely on *Frye*, until eventually the "*Frye* Rule" was accepted in the majority of jurisdictions. (It remains the law today in a number of states, among them New York, California, and Pennsylvania.)

But in 1975 the Federal Rules of Evidence (FRE) were enacted; and FRE 702, providing that expert testimony was admissible provided that it was relevant and not otherwise excluded by law, made no mention either of *Frye* or of "general acceptance." Had *Frye* been superseded, or not? The situation wasn't clarified until 1993, when the US Supreme Court made its ruling in *Daubert v. Merrell Dow Pharmaceuticals*[5]–the first time in the history of the Court that it had ruled on the standard of admissibility of expert testimony.

The core argument of "Irreconcilable Differences" is that the difficulties in handling scientific testimony arise in part from tensions between the practices and values of science and the culture of the US legal system: e.g., between

4 Frye v. United States, 293 F. 1013, 1014 (D.C. Cir. 1923).
5 Daubert v. Merrell Dow Pharm., Inc., 509 U.S. 579 (1993) ("*Daubert* III").

the investigative character of science and the adversarial culture of the law; between the open-endedness of scientific investigation and the legal concern for finality; between the atomistic tendencies of evidence law and the quasi-holism of warrant; between the informal, pragmatic character of scientific inquiry and the formal procedures of the law; and so on. These tensions reveal themselves both in the history of legal efforts to domesticate scientific testimony by rules of admissibility, and in recent small compromises of finality and modifications of adversarialism in dealing with such testimony–the latter representing a modest move in the direction of civil-law evidentiary procedures.

The next essay, "Trial and Error: Two Confusions in *Daubert*," turns specifically to the remarkable foray into philosophy of science in the Supreme Court's *Daubert* ruling. As I said, the question before the *Daubert* Court was whether the old *Frye* Rule had been superseded, in federal courts, by FRE 702. It had, the Court ruled; nevertheless, courts still have an obligation to screen proffered expert testimony not only for relevance, *but also for reliability*. This, Justice Blackmun's ruling continued, requires that they satisfy themselves that such evidence qualifies as *bona fide* "scientific ... knowledge."[6] Calling on the philosophy of Karl Popper, and throwing in a quotation from Carl Hempel for good measure, Justice Blackmun suggests that the mark of the genuinely scientific is falsifiability or testability; and, in line with this, the first of the indicia of reliability on the "flexible list" he offers by way of guidance to federal judges–now known as the "*Daubert* factors"–is whether the work on which supposedly scientific testimony is based "can be (and has been) tested."[7]

As the title of the essay suggests, these philosophical dicta of Justice Blackmun's are confused, in more ways than one. Casting around for a criterion of genuinely scientific, and hence reliable, expert testimony, he runs together two incompatible philosophies of science: Popper's falsificationism, and Hempel's confirmationism. He apparently doesn't realize that Popper's philosophy of science is singularly ill-suited for the purpose to which he put it, since–emphatically denying that scientific theories can ever be shown to be true or even probable–Popper deliberately eschews the notion of reliability; nor does he seem aware that Hempel's work provides neither a criterion of demarcation, nor any substantive help in assessing the reliability of complex scientific evidence. Moreover, when you think about it, it's clear that Justice Blackmun's approach was seriously misconceived from the get-go. He runs together "reliable" and "scientific"; but these are different not only in

6 *Id.*, 590.
7 *Id.*, 593.

meaning, but also in extension. Not all, and not only, scientific testimony is reliable.

Not surprisingly, in its subsequent rulings on expert testimony–in 1997, in *General Electric Co. v. Joiner*,[8] reaffirming that the standard of appellate review for such evidentiary rulings is abuse of discretion, and in 1999, in *Kumho Tire Co. v. Carmichael*,[9] holding that *Daubert* (but not necessarily those *Daubert* factors) applies to all expert testimony, not only to the scientific–the Supreme Court has quietly backed away from its earlier enthusiasm for philosophy of science. The result, however, has been to leave courts with wide discretion in screening expert testimony, but very limited guidance about how to do this.

Still, you have to wonder: where did the Supreme Court's allusions to Popper's philosophy of science come from, and what did federal courts make of the first *Daubert* factor, whether the proffered evidence "can be (and has been) tested"? The purpose of the next essay, "Federal Philosophy of Science: A Deconstruction–And a Reconstruction," is not only to answer these questions, but also to show exactly why Popper's falsificationism is so radically unsuited for the purpose to which Justice Blackmun put it; and to suggest a better understanding of science in its place.

I begin by presenting Popper's falsificationist philosophy of science in sufficient detail to show that, his rhetoric about "objective scientific knowledge" notwithstanding, his approach is so profoundly and so pervasively negative as to amount, in effect, to a covert skepticism; and so couldn't possibly provide a criterion of the reliability of scientific testimony. Next, I explain how Justice Blackmun misconstrues Popper's ideas, and identify some sources of his misunderstandings in the amicus briefs in *Daubert*, in the then-recent literature in the law reviews, and in Popper's own (very ambiguous) writings. Then I look in some detail at what federal courts have made of the Supreme Court's allusions to Popper. And finally, in the "reconstructive" part of this essay, I argue that, ironically enough, the interpretation most federal courts have given the first *Daubert* factor gestures towards a better epistemology of science than the flawed Popperian philosophy of science from which it ostensibly derives, but from which, in fact, it deviates quite radically; and that the account of the structure and quality of the evidence with respect to scientific claims developed in my *Defending Science–Within Reason*[10] provides the framework for understanding why.

8 Gen. Elec. Co. v. Joiner, 522 U.S. 136 (1997) ("*Joiner* III").

9 Kumho Tire Co. v. Carmichael, 526 U.S. 137 (1999).

10 Susan Haack, *Defending Science–Within Reason: Between Scientism and Cynicism* (Amherst, NY: Prometheus Books, 2003).

Among the indicia of reliability on the *Daubert* Court's "flexible list," besides "falsifiability," was "peer review and publication."[11] But, as I point out in the next essay, "Peer Review and Publication: Lessons for Lawyers," "peer review" may refer either to the process of *pre-publication* peer review, or to the long-run scrutiny of the relevant scientific community *after* publication. Looking at the evolution of the pre-publication peer-review process that became standard practice at scientific journals after World War II–and at how the system presently operates–it becomes very clear that there is no guarantee *either* that all work that survives such review is sound, *or* that all sound work survives such review. So if this *Daubert* factor is understood as suggesting that courts screening for reliability should focus on whether proffered scientific testimony is based on work that has survived pre-publication peer review, though this will be relatively easy for a judge to determine, it is a very poor indicator of reliability. And if, on the other hand, it is understood as suggesting that courts should focus on whether the work on which proffered scientific testimony is based will survive the long-run scrutiny of the scientific community–which would certainly be a better indication of reliability–the problem is that it is impossible even for scientists expert in the field concerned, let alone for judges, to predict what work will survive and what will in due course be discarded as untenable.

In 1995, making the final ruling in *Daubert* (on remand from the Supreme Court), Judge Kozinski introduced a new *Daubert* factor of his own, suggesting that if the work on which proffered testimony is based is "litigation-driven," this raises a red flag about its reliability.[12] Thinking about the merits of this idea soon has us facing some subtle issues about the differences between real investigation and "advocacy research," i.e., seeking out plausible-sounding evidence supporting a predetermined conclusion. These are tackled, with Peirce's help, in the next essay, "What's Wrong with Litigation-Driven Science?" It's true, as Judge Kozinski suggests, that research undertaken for the purposes of litigation may be less reliable than research undertaken independently–but so too may research undertaken for marketing purposes; and, contrary to the exception Judge Kozinski makes in a footnote,[13] the same is true of forensic science, almost always conducted for the police or the prosecution. Moreover, as we see from Judge Bernstein's ruling in a Pennsylvania case, *Blum v. Merrell Dow Pharmaceuticals*,[14] in the kinds of toxic tort case that have shaped US law on scientific testimony, not only the expert testimony offered by plaintiffs, but

11 *Daubert* III (note 5 above), 593.
12 Daubert v. Merrell Dow Pharm., Inc., 43 F.3d 1311 (9th Cir. 1995) ("*Daubert* IV").
13 *Id.*, 1317 n.5.
14 Blum v. Merrell Dow Pharm., Inc., 33 Phila. Cnty. Rep. 193 (1996) ("*Blum* IV").

also the expert testimony offered by defendants, may be based on advocacy research.

In *Daubert*, in *Blum*, and in many such toxic tort cases–notably in *Oxendine v. Merrell Dow Pharmaceuticals*,[15] in *Joiner*,[16] and more recently in *Milward v. Acuity Specialty Products*[17]–plaintiffs argue that the expert testimony they wish to present is sufficient, considered jointly, to establish causation "by a preponderance of the evidence," even though no part of it would be sufficient by itself; and defendants sometimes argue in response that a collection of pieces of evidence can never be any stronger than any of its components individually. The next paper, "Proving Causation: The Weight of Combined Evidence"–the first of a trio on questions of causation–draws on my epistemological theory to show that, *under certain conditions*, a combination of pieces of evidence none of which is sufficient by itself really *can* warrant a causal conclusion to a higher degree than any of its components alone can do.

When my account is applied to the very complex congeries of evidence typically proffered to prove general causation in toxic tort cases, it suggests answers to some frequently-disputed questions: Is epidemiological evidence essential for proof of causation? Should such evidence be excluded unless its results are statistically significant? Should animal studies be excluded on principle? And so on. Moreover, the argument of this paper reveals that (as I suggested in "Irreconcilable Differences"), by encouraging the practice of screening each item of expert testimony individually for reliability, the evidentiary atomism implicit in *Daubert* can actually stand in the way of an accurate assessment of the worth of complex causation evidence.

In assessing questions of general causation in toxic tort cases, courts sometimes rely on the so-called "Bradford Hill criteria," which the original version of "Proving Causation" discussed only briefly. But in the next paper, "Correlation and Causation: The 'Bradford Hill Criteria' in Epidemiological, Legal, and Epistemological Perspective," I look in detail at Hill's ideas, the role they have played in litigation, and the ways in which they have been misunderstood. The first stage (the "epidemiological perspective") looks closely at the famous lecture, "The Environment and Disease,"[18] in which Hill spelled out the nine factors he believes should be taken into account in determining whether a statistical correlation between exposure to some substance and the occurrence of some disease or disorder is likely causal, and his many caveats

[15] Oxendine v. Merrell Dow Pharm., Inc., 506 A.2d 1100 (D.C. 1986) ("*Oxendine* I").

[16] *Joiner* III (note 8 above).

[17] Milward v. Acuity Specialty Prods. Grp., Inc., 69 F.3d 11 (1st Cir. 2011).

[18] Austin Bradford Hill, "The Environment and Disease: Association or Causation?" *Proceedings of the Royal Society of Medicine* 58 (1965): 295–300.

about how these factors should be used. The next stage (the "legal perspective") is to show that courts have sometimes badly misunderstood these factors, and have applied them in ways Hill never envisaged, and probably wouldn't have endorsed. Then, putting Hill's ideas in epistemological perspective, I show that what he offers is best conceived as a kind of sketch-map of the much larger territory of evidence potentially relevant to causal claims–a sketch-map that, when superimposed on the more detailed epistemological map I have provided, is seen to be helpful so far as it goes, but partial and incomplete.

Hill himself was very clear that there can be no hard-and-fast rules for determining when epidemiological evidence indicates causation, and seems to have grasped the quasi-holistic character of the determinants of evidential quality. But the legal *penchant* for convenient checklists, and the atomistic tendencies of US evidence law, have encouraged legal players to misconstrue his factors as "criteria" for the reliability of causation testimony, and many courts have misread his partial sketch-map.

The next piece, "Risky Business: Statistical Proof of Specific Causation," draws attention to its pragmatist orientation from the start with its opening quotation from Holmes about the evolution of legal concepts and rules. In line with this, the essay begins with a brief history of the evolution of the concepts of causation, responsibility, negligence, etc., deployed in the US legal system, and of some of the social, technological, and other changes that prompted these adaptations: such as the rapid growth of the railroad system in the second half of the nineteenth century, and the subsequent rise in crossing accidents; and, later, the rise of massive drug and chemical companies whose products sometimes proved harmful–in some instances, decades after exposure.

But this paper focuses primarily on one recent development in particular: the rise of the idea that evidence showing that exposure to the defendant's product more than doubles the risk of some disease or disorder is key to establishing specific causation, i.e., to showing that *this plaintiff's* injury was caused by this product. The first stage is historical: tracing how this idea arose and how it spread, distinguishing the several ways it has been construed, and exploring the reasons some courts have given for accepting it and others for rejecting it. The next stage is epistemological: showing that evidence of more than doubled risk, though relevant, is *neither necessary nor sufficient* for proof of individual causation, and providing a more defensible account of the role such evidence *can* legitimately play. And the last stage is policy-oriented: arguing, first, that to require, as some courts have done, that a plaintiff's expert must produce evidence of more than doubled risk for his testimony to be even admissible imposes an unreasonable burden; and finally, that the more adequate understanding of the role of evidence of increased risk developed here would not only be epistemologically sounder, but also better serve the goals of tort law.

The concluding essay, "Nothing Fancy: Some Simple Truths about Truth in the Law," turns from proof to truth. I begin with the distinction between truth (the phenomenon) and truths (particular true claims); and the confusions that neglect of this distinction has fostered: e.g., that, because some truths are vague, truth itself must be a matter of degree; that, because some truths hold only at a given place, time, or jurisdiction, truth itself must be relative; and so on. Then, developing an understanding of truth along the lines of F. P. Ramsey's laconicism, I argue that, whatever the subject-matter of the proposition concerned, what it means to say that a proposition is true is the same: that it is the proposition that *p*, and *p*. Next, I look at the deceptively simple-seeming distinction between factual and legal truths, noting that there are many mixed and borderline cases–and, in passing, that the concept of legal reliability articulated in *Daubert* itself fudges the line somewhat. However, I continue, mixed and borderline cases aside, legal truths, i.e., truths about legal provisions, are a special sub-class of truths about social institutions; and, like many truths about a society, are socially constructed, made true by things people do–primarily by legislators' decisions, but also in part by judges' interpretations of statutes and precedents, and so forth.

And finally–anticipating the objection that, by focusing on truths *about* legal provisions to the neglect of the more vital issue of the truth *of* legal provisions, I have ducked the really hard questions–I turn specifically to the normative character of law. Legal systems, legal provisions, and legal decisions, I argue, may be morally better or worse, and the law *can* be an engine of moral progress; but legal norms cannot be assimilated to moral norms, and are not appropriately conceived as true or false representations of moral principles. And this, as I show, suggests a new and nuanced approach to an old but still daunting question: why the law should be obeyed.

~

These essays were written for publication in a wide variety of journals and books–some for US law reviews, one for the *American Journal of Public Health*, one for the *American Journal of Jurisprudence*, and others for publication in Spain, Mexico, and Brazil. So I have edited them to unify the style of references and trimmed them here and there to avoid annoying repetition. Inevitably, though, given their interlocking structure, certain themes recur: the multiple determinants of evidential quality, for example, the quasi-holistic character of warrant, the material character of relevance, the difference between genuine inquiry and advocacy research, the misguided search for the "scientific method," the constant evolution of the law and of legal concepts, and of US law on scientific testimony in particular.

Inevitably, also, while this editorial work was in process, there were various legal and other developments relevant to my arguments: for example, Bendectin, the drug at issue in *Daubert*, *Blum*, *Oxendine*, etc., returned to the US market (now made by a Canadian manufacturer and with a new name, "Diclegis"); and Florida, which had long been, at least officially, a *Frye* state, amended its Rule of Evidence 702 to correspond to the federal Rule 702 as modified in 2000 in light of the rulings in *Daubert*, *Joiner*, and *Kumho Tire*. I have given details of these changes in new footnotes. I have also included a glossary that will, I hope, be helpful to legal readers unfamiliar with the language of epistemology, to philosophical readers unfamiliar with the language of the law, and to any readers curious about the specifics of the diseases and disorders they read about in toxic tort cases; a table of cases cited, giving their histories; a list of the statutes, rules, etc., to which I refer; and, of course, a full bibliography.

July 2013

—1—

Epistemology and the Law of Evidence: Problems and Projects

> As for the philosophers, they make imaginary laws for imaginary commonwealths; and their discourses are as the stars, which give little light, because they are so high.
>
> —Francis Bacon[1]

Even today, more than four centuries later, Bacon's complaint still resonates. Now, as then, the writings of philosophers—even of philosophers of law, who might be expected to be a little more grounded in the real world—all too often "give little light, because they are so high." I will try to buck this trend by showing you that epistemological ideas really can illuminate real-life legal issues.

1 IDENTIFYING EPISTEMOLOGICAL ISSUES IN THE LAW

Every legal system needs, somehow, to determine the truth of factual questions. At one time, courts in England and continental Europe relied on in-court tests[2]—"proof" in the old meaning of the English word (a meaning that still survives in descriptions of liquor as "80% proof,"[3] and in the old proverb "the proof of the pudding is in the eating"). In trial by oath, a defendant would be asked to swear on the testament or on a reliquary that he was innocent, and "oath-helpers" or "con-jurors" might be called to swear that *his* oath wasn't

[1] Francis Bacon, *The Advancement of Learning* (1605), in Basil Montagu, ed., *The Works of Francis Bacon* (London: William Pickering, 1825), vol. II, 295.

[2] For more details of the history sketched here, see "Legal Probabilism: An Epistemological Dissent," pp. 47–77 in this volume, 48–50.

[3] The phrase refers to the strength of the liquor, calculated as twice the percentage of alcohol present; so, e.g., liquor that is "80% proof" would be 40% alcohol. Merriam Webster, *Webster's Ninth New Collegiate Dictionary* (Springfield, MA: Merriam-Webster Publishing, 1991), 942.

foresworn;[4] in trial by ordeal, a defendant might be asked, e.g., to pick up a ring from the bottom of a cauldron of boiling water, and his arm would later be checked to determine whether it had healed cleanly or had festered—which supposedly showed that he was guilty;[5] in trial by combat, the two parties to a case would literally fight it out.[6] The rationale for these procedures was, presumably, theological: God would strike a man who swore falsely, would ensure that an innocent defendant's wound healed cleanly, would see to it that the party in the right prevailed in combat; and these methods of proof (or "proof") were tolerated, presumably, because such theological assumptions were widely-enough accepted.

In continental Europe, in-court tests by oath and ordeal would gradually be replaced by canonical law and the Inquisition, and then by secular, national legal systems—which, however, still relied on torture to extract confessions.[7] In 1766 Voltaire, who had long criticized the use of torture to determine guilt, complained about the practice of courts in Toulouse, which acknowledged "not only half-proofs but also quarters [e.g., a piece of hearsay] and eighths [e.g., a rumor]"—and then added up these fractional proofs, so that "eight doubts could constitute a perfect proof." But by this time the system was already in trouble; and in 1808 it would be reformed under Napoleon's legal code.[8]

In England, in-court tests by oath and ordeal were gradually replaced by a nascent system of jury trials.[9] The first such trial was held in Westminster in 1220: five men accused of murder agreed "to submit to the judgement of twelve of their property-owning neighbors"; and, in a procedure recognizably descended from the older practice of calling on con-jurors, these jurymen swore that one of the accused was law-abiding, but that the other four (who

4 Lisi Oliver, *The Beginnings of English Law* (Toronto: University of Toronto Press, 2002), 174 ff.

5 Robert Bartlett, *Trial by Fire and Water: The Medieval Judicial Ordeal* (Oxford: Clarendon Press, 1986), 9 ff.

6 George Neilson, *Trial by Combat* (London: Williams and Norgate, 1890).

7 Sadakat Kadri, *The Trial: A History, from Socrates to O. J. Simpson* (New York: Random House, 2005), 39–45.

8 *Id.*, 67–68.

9 These early English jury trials were not, to be sure, the first-ever trials by jury. A (very different) kind of jury trial was found in ancient Athens, where in 399 B.C. Socrates was tried before 501 fellow-citizens. Kadri (note 7 above), 9. On ancient Greek legal procedure more generally, A. Andrewes, "The Growth of the Athenian State," in John Boardman and N. G. L. Hammond, eds., *Cambridge Ancient Histories* (Cambridge: Cambridge University Press, 1983), III Part 3, *The Expansion of the Greek World, Eighth to Sixth Centuries B.C.*, chapter 43, 360–91, 388; Mogens Herman Hansen, *The Athenian Democracy in the Age of Demosthenes: Structure, Principles, and Ideology*, trans. J. A. Cook (Oxford: Blackwell, 1991), chapter 8.

in due course were hanged) were thieves.[10] But it would take centuries for the full array of now-familiar common-law evidentiary procedures—witnesses, cross-examination, exclusionary rules of evidence—to evolve.[11]

Had the theological assumptions on which they rested been true, tests by oath, ordeal, and combat would have been epistemologically reasonable ways to determine facts at issue. But now, because we no longer believe those theological assumptions *are* true, we don't see those proof-procedures as epistemologically defensible. Still, even today some legal systems rely on practices reminiscent of the old provision in trial by oath that whether a defendant needed oath-helpers, and if so, how many, depended on his rank.[12] In traditional Sharia law, as presently practiced in, for example, Saudi Arabia, a man's testimony is given twice the weight of a woman's.[13] And even in modern, western legal systems there are occasional reminders of the older proof-procedures: for example—rather as the word of the king or a bishop was taken to be sufficient by itself, without his needing to swear a solemn oath or, *a fortiori*, to produce oath-helpers[14]—some courts in the US have held government websites to be self-authenticating.[15]

Modern western legal systems, however, don't use anything like those older in-court tests, but instead rely primarily[16] on the presentation of evidence: the testimony of witnesses, documentary evidence, and physical evidence such as the alleged murder weapon, the allegedly forged will, and so forth—"proof" in the current sense of the word, of showing some claim to be true, or likely true. Of course, the rationale for these practices *also* depends on certain presuppositions. This point can be made vivid by thinking about what the consequences would be for the law if these assumptions were false. If, for example,

[10] Kadri, *The Trial* (note 7 above), 70–71. (The defendants, Kadri reports, had been identified by a self-confessed murderer in hopes that, by informing on them, she would save her own life.)

[11] See e.g., Stephan Landsman, "Of Witches, Madmen, and Product Liability: An Historical Survey of the Use of Expert Testimony," *Behavioral Science and Law* **13**, no.2 (1995): 131–57.

[12] Oliver, *The Beginnings of English Law* (note 4 above), 174 ff.

[13] Hunt Janin and André Kahlmeyer, *Islamic Law: The Sharia from Muhammad's Time to the Present* (Jefferson, NC: McFarland and Company, 2007), 32.

[14] Oliver, *The Beginnings of English Law* (note 4 above), 174.

[15] Federal Rule of Evidence 902 provides that certain kinds of evidence, including documents bearing "a seal purporting to be [*sic*] that of the United States," are self-authenticating; and this has been interpreted as including government websites. See e.g., Estate of Gonzales v. Hickman, ED CV 05–660 MMM (RCx), 2007 WL 3237727, *2 (C.D. Cal. May 30, 2007); Paralyzed Veterans of Am. v. McPherson, No. C 06–4670 SBA, 2008 WL 4183981 (N.D. Cal. Sept. 9, 2008); Williams v. Long, 585 F. Supp. 2d 679, 685 (D. Md. 2008).

[16] The qualification "primarily" is intended to acknowledge, e.g., the role of legal presumptions.

Richard Rorty had been right to insist that the entire epistemological enterprise is misconceived,[17] if standards of what makes evidence stronger or weaker really were, as he professed to believe,[18] purely conventional—not universal, but local to this or that epistemic community, and not truth-indicative, but free-floating[19]—then what we optimistically call the "justice system" would really be nothing but a cruel kind of judicial theater.

As this thought-experiment reveals, modern evidentiary procedures (in both common-law and civil-law jurisdictions) presuppose that evidence may be objectively better, or worse; that the better a claim is warranted by the evidence, the likelier it is to be true; and that these or those legal rules and procedures are good-enough ways of ensuring that verdicts are factually sound. In fact, as I understand it, what we ask the finder of fact to do is precisely to determine whether the defendant's guilt or his liability has been established to the legally-required degree of proof by the evidence presented; and this is to make an *epistemological* judgment.

As I put it nearly a decade ago, the law is "up to its neck in epistemology,"[20] for even the briefest reflection on the rationale for evidentiary rules and procedures raises a host of questions of interest to an epistemologist. Are degrees and standards of proof best understood as degrees of credence on the part of the fact-finder, as mathematical probabilities, or as degrees of warrant of a claim by evidence? What *is* the relation of degrees of proof to the mathematical calculus of probabilities—and what role, if any, does that calculus have in legal proof?[21] And if, as I believe, degrees of proof are degrees of warrant, what determines how well this or that evidence warrants a claim? Must we choose between "fact-based" and "story-based" or "narrative" accounts of proof, or are

[17] Richard Rorty, *Philosophy and the Mirror of Nature* (Princeton, NJ: Princeton University Press, 1979). Rorty's critique of epistemology is, however, nothing but a farrago of confusions and equivocations—confusions and equivocations painstakingly disentangled in Susan Haack, *Evidence and Inquiry* (1993; 2nd ed., Amherst, NY: Prometheus Books, 2009) chapter 9, and revisited more briefly in Susan Haack, "Confessions of an Old-Fashioned Prig," in Haack, *Manifesto of a Passionate Moderate: Unfashionable Essays* (Chicago, IL: University of Chicago Press, 1998), 7–30, and in Susan Haack, "Coherence, Consistency, Cogency, Congruity, Cohesiveness, &c.: Remain Calm! Don't Go Overboard!" (2004), in Haack, *Putting Philosophy to Work: Inquiry and Its Place in Culture* (Amherst, NY: Prometheus Books, 2008, expanded ed., 2013), 69–82.

[18] I say "professed" because, I assume, when he needed to choose a medical treatment or find out whether the publisher's check had arrived, Rorty looked to the evidence, just as you or I would do.

[19] Rorty, *Philosophy and the Mirror of Nature* (note 17 above), chapter 5, §§5, 6.

[20] "Epistemology Legalized: or, Truth, Justice, and the American Way," pp. 27–46 in this volume, 28.

[21] The subject of "Legal Probabilism: An Epistemological Dissent," pp. 47–77 in this volume.

there other possibilities? Can combined evidence sometimes reach a higher degree of proof than any of its elements alone could do? When can we rely on the testimony of a witness, and when should we be suspicious of his honesty, or his competence, or both? Are there special difficulties when the witness is an expert? How are we to distinguish the genuine expert from the plausible charlatan? Is a group of people always, or sometimes, in an epistemologically stronger position than an individual—and if so, when, and why? Was C. S. Peirce right to complain that the adversarial procedures of common-law systems are poorly suited to discovering the truth?[22] Was Jeremy Bentham right to argue that, because they prevent relevant evidence from ever being heard, exclusionary rules are a clear impediment to arriving at the facts of a case, and mainly serve the interests of attorneys who benefit from their skill in gaming the system?[23] Etc., etc., etc.

2 CHARACTERIZING LEGAL EPISTEMOLOGY

The word "epistemology" is a relatively recent coinage, dating from the mid- to late-nineteenth century.[24] But epistemology, the philosophical theory of knowledge, is very old, dating back at least to Plato's efforts to distinguish genuine knowledge (*episteme*) from mere belief or opinion (*doxa*).[25]

In the course of its long history, epistemology has undertaken a whole range of projects: not only distinguishing genuine knowledge from mere belief or sheer opinion, but also offering definitions or explications of the concept of knowledge; proposing arguments to establish that knowledge is possible—or that it isn't; articulating the differences between knowing that p, knowing X, and knowing how to Φ; exploring the relations of knowledge, certainty, and probability; asking how we know mathematical truths, empirical truths, moral truths, religious truths, etc., etc.; reflecting on supposed sources of knowledge—intellectual intuition, sensory experience, introspection, memory, inference, testimony, revelation, religious experience?—and their

[22] C. S. Peirce, *Collected Papers*, eds. Charles Hartshorne, Paul Weiss, and (vols. 7 and 8) Arthur Burks (Cambridge, MA: Harvard University Press, 1931–58) 2.635 (1878); also in *Writings: A Chronological Edition*, ed., the Peirce Edition Project (Indianapolis, IN: Indiana University Press, 1982–present) 3:331. See also "Epistemology Legalized" (note 20 above), 33–39.

[23] Jeremy Bentham, *Rationale of Judicial Evidence* (1827; New York: Garland, 1978). See also "Epistemology Legalized" (note 20 above), 39–45.

[24] Merriam Webster, *Webster's Ninth New Collegiate Dictionary* (note 3 above), 419, dates the word to c.1856; but fifty years later we find Peirce complaining that it is "an atrocious translation of *Erkenntnislehre*." Peirce, *Collected Papers* (note 22 above), 5.494 (c.1906).

[25] See, e.g., Plato, *Republic*, trans. G. A. Grube, revised by C. D. C. Reeve (Indianapolis, IN: Hackett Publishing Company, 1992), Book 7.

interrelations; articulating the structure of evidence and the determinants of evidential quality; trying to understand what makes evidence relevant to a claim, and what it means to describe evidence as misleading; characterizing procedures of inquiry and what makes them better or worse; distinguishing genuine inquiry from pseudo-inquiry and "advocacy research"; exploring epistemological virtues, such as intellectual honesty, patience, and thoroughness, and epistemological vices, such as self-deception, hastiness, and carelessness; looking at the effects of the environment in which inquiry takes place on how well or poorly it is conducted; evaluating the effects of sharing information; suggesting how to assess the worth of testimony, and investigating social aspects of knowledge more generally; and so on and on.

And what, exactly, do I mean by "legal epistemology" or "epistemology legalized"? In my mouth these phrases refer, not to a specialized, peculiar *genre* of epistemology, but simply to *epistemological work relevant to issues that arise in the law.*

John Stuart Mill writes in the introduction to his *System of Logic* (1843) that "[t]he business of the magistrate, of the military commander, of the navigator, of the physician, of the agriculturalist is to judge of evidence and act accordingly." For they all "have to ascertain certain facts, in order that they apply certain rules...."[26] The word "epistemology" hadn't yet become current; but Mill's agreeably old-fashioned phrase, "judge of evidence," identifies what I take to be the *core* epistemological concern: to understand what evidence is, how it is structured, and what makes it better or worse, stronger or weaker. And, as Mill's putting "the magistrate" at the top of his list signals, it is precisely *this* aspect of epistemology that is most relevant to legal issues about proof and proof-procedures.

Relevance, however, is a matter of degree; some epistemological work is highly relevant to legal concerns, some relevant but less so, some only marginally relevant—and some not relevant at all. Moreover, not all legally-relevant epistemology will be helpful. What we need is not only epistemological theory *focused centrally on evidence and its evaluation* (though it may, to be sure, use other words, such as "data," "reasons," or "information"), but also epistemological theory *detailed enough* to get a serious grip on specific questions

[26] John Stuart Mill, *A System of Logic: Being a Connected View of the Principles of Evidence and the Methods of Scientific Investigation* (1843; 8th ed., London: Longman, Green, 1970), 7. Nowadays, we would probably say, not "judge of evidence," but "judge the weight [or the worth] of evidence"); but Mill's phrase is exactly apt—as is his addendum, "and act accordingly": the navigator must assess the evidence, that, say, a storm is coming, and do what is necessary to protect his ship, a physician must assess the evidence that, say, the patient is having a heart attack, and treat him appropriately, and so on.

raised by evidentiary procedures in the law; and, of course—well, *true* epistemological theory.

When I speak of the relevance of epistemology to the law, I refer to the field or discipline of epistemology, *not* to a professional specialism—which is by no means the same thing. Of late, philosophy has become hyper-professionalized and hyper-specialized,[27] so that by now there is a whole cadre of people self-identified as epistemologists. And these days many seem to use the word "epistemology" to refer to whatever those who identify themselves professionally as specialists in epistemology do. But this, while no doubt helpful to the careers of members of the guild, threatens to narrow the scope of the epistemological enterprise to issues that happen to be fashionable in the Analytic Epistemologists' Union (AEU).[28] Indeed, so severe is the hyper-specialization that the AEU seems, in turn, to have splintered into sub-groups—the virtue epistemologists, the feminist epistemologists, the social epistemologists, etc. Moreover, self-styled "social epistemologists" are sometimes thought, by themselves and others, to have the monopoly on legally-relevant epistemology.[29] But this, though again no doubt helpful to the careers of members of the guild, threatens to narrow the scope of the epistemological ideas brought to bear on the law even further, to the current preoccupations of this sub-group—which is particularly unfortunate when, as happens more often than one would like, social epistemology is conducted without benefit of a good understanding of evidence and its quality.[30]

Neither *all* the work of those specialists and sub-specialists in epistemology nor *only* the work of those specialists and sub-specialists is helpful in understanding the evidentiary issues with which the law deals. Some of the work of specialist-epistemologists (e.g., the seemingly endless attempts to refute the skeptic, those constantly-recycled "Gettier paradoxes,"[31] efforts to catalogue

[27] See Susan Haack, "Out of Step: Academic Ethics in a Preposterous Environment," in Haack, *Putting Philosophy to Work* (note 17 above), 251–68.

[28] My coinage, of course. See e.g., my "Foreword" to the 2nd ed. of *Evidence and Inquiry* (note 17 above), 23.

[29] For example, the only category acknowledged by the Philosophy Research Network (PRN: the relevant branch of SSRN, the Social Sciences Research Network) in which work on legal epistemology seems to belong is "Social Epistemology and Testimony."

[30] For example, to judge by the index, in Alvin I. Goldman, *Knowledge in a Social World* (Oxford: Clarendon Press, 1999) (an influential foray into "social epistemology") there are *no references to the concept of evidence*—except in the chapter on the law!

[31] Edmund Gettier, "Is Justified True Belief Knowledge?" *Analysis* 23 (1963): 121–23; reprinted in Louis J. Pojman, ed., *Theory of Knowledge: Classical and Contemporary Sources* (Belmont, CA: Wadsworth, 2nd ed., 1998), 142–43. In a paper I wrote in 1983 but didn't publish until 2009 (when a new wave of Gettierology was well under way), I had argued that these paradoxes arise from the mismatch between the concept of knowledge, which is categorical, and

and classify the epistemic virtues)[32] is irrelevant, or only marginally relevant, to legal concerns. Moreover, much work by specialist-epistemologists even on legally-relevant topics—e.g., about the evaluation of testimony, or the epistemological consequences of evidence-sharing—isn't detailed enough, or isn't detailed enough in the relevant respects, to be very helpful to an understanding of evidentiary issues in the law; and a good deal of the work of professional epistemologists (e.g., efforts to understand epistemic justification in terms of the truth-ratios of belief-forming processes)[33] is, to put it bluntly, just wrong-headed.[34]

Besides, before the current hyper-specialization set in, when philosophers felt somewhat freer to go where their intellectual bent and the task at hand took them, inductive logician L. J. Cohen had contributed significantly to issues in legal epistemology.[35] And there have long been legal scholars and judges who have made real contributions to epistemological issues in the law: I think, e.g., of Jeremy Bentham's battery of criticisms of exclusionary rules of evidence;[36] of John Wigmore's diagrammatic representations of the structure of evidence;[37] of Judge Learned Hand's diagnosis of the "logical anomaly" at the heart of expert-witness testimony;[38] and of Leonard Jaffee's reflections on the role of statistical evidence at trial[39]—to mention just a few. For that matter, there is a good deal of epistemology built into such routine legal materials

the concept of justification, which is gradational; and that in consequence there *can be no* definition of knowledge which doesn't *either* allow such paradoxes *or else* lead to skepticism. Susan Haack, "'Know' Is Just a Four-Letter Word," in Haack, *Evidence and Inquiry* (note 17 above), 2nd ed., 301–31. This diagnosis, I still believe, simply dissolves the supposed problem on which so much energy has been, and continues to be, wasted.

32 See e.g., Linda Zagzebski, *Virtues of the Mind* (New York: Cambridge University Press, 1996); Abrol Fairweather and Linda Zagzebski, eds., *Virtue Epistemology: Essays on Epistemic Virtue and Responsibility* (New York: Oxford University Press, 2001).

33 See e.g., Alvin I. Goldman, "What Is Justified Belief?", in George Pappas, ed., *Justification and Knowledge* (Dordrecht, the Netherlands: Reidel, 1979), 1–21; *Epistemology and Cognition* (Cambridge, MA: Harvard University Press, 1986); "Two Concepts of Justification," in James Tomberlin, ed., *Philosophical Perspectives, 2: Epistemology* (Atascadero, CA: Ridgeview, 1988), 51–70.

34 As I argued in excruciating detail in *Evidence and Inquiry* (note 17 above) chapter 7.

35 L. Jonathan Cohen, *The Provable and the Probable* (Oxford: Clarendon Press, 1977).

36 Bentham, *Rationale of Judicial Evidence* (note 23 above).

37 John Henry Wigmore, *The Principles of Judicial Proof as Given by Logic, Psychology, and General Experience as Illustrated in Judicial Trials* (1913; 5th American ed., Littleton, CO: Fred B. Rothman & Co., 1981).

38 Learned Hand, "Historical and Practical Considerations Regarding Expert Testimony," *Harvard Law Review* 15 (1901): 40–58.

39 Leonard R. Jaffee, "Of Probativity and Probability: Statistics, Scientific Evidence, and the Calculus of Chances at Trial," *University of Pittsburgh Law Review* 46 (1984–5): 925–1083.

as jury instructions on standards of proof,[40] and a good deal of epistemology implicit in judicial rulings.[41]

Thoughtful scientists have also made real epistemological contributions: Percy Bridgman,[42] for example, whose reflections on the pointless "ballyhoo" made about the "scientific method" and the need to get down, instead, to the nuts and bolts of scientific work reveal the naïveté of some judicial observations about the supposed method of science, notably Justice Blackmun's comments on "methodology" in *Daubert*;[43] or W. K. Clifford,[44] whose reflections on when and why it is appropriate to rely on experts' opinions, and when and why it is inappropriate, have a lot to teach us about expert testimony. And many novelists explore epistemological themes—often, to be sure, matters of epistemic character, with only indirect bearing on legal issues, as with Samuel Butler's remarkable portrayal of self-deception, hypocrisy, and sham inquiry in *The Way of All Flesh*;[45] but sometimes strikingly legally relevant. You can learn a lot about what makes evidence misleading from Michael Frayn's playful treatment in *Headlong*,[46] or (in a more directly legal way) from Scott Turow's exploration in *Reversible Errors*.[47] You can learn even from (good) *bad* novels, such as Arthur Hailey's *Strong Medicine*,[48] which is quite revealing

40 See §4, pp. 16–18 below.

41 See, for example (on the weight of combined evidence), Milward v. Acuity Specialty Prods. Grp., Inc., 639 F.3d 11 (1st Cir. 2011).

42 Percy W. Bridgman, "On 'Scientific Method'" (1949), in Bridgman, *Reflections of a Physicist* (New York: Philosophical Library, 2nd ed., 1955), 81–83, 81.

43 Daubert v. Merrell Dow Pharm., Inc., 509 U.S. 579, 589–95 (1993) ("*Daubert* III").

44 William Kingdon Clifford, "The Ethics of Belief" (1877) in Clifford, *The Ethics of Belief and Other Essays*, eds. Leslie Stephen and Frederick Pollock (London: Watts & Co., 1947), 70–96, 85 ff.

45 Samuel Butler, *The Way of All Flesh* (1903; New York: American Library, 1998). This semi-autobiographical *Bildungsroman* tells the story of a young man who grows from callow boy to self-deceived curate, and finally, after professional and personal disgrace, achieves intellectual adulthood. It is discussed at length in Susan Haack, "The Ideal of Intellectual Integrity, in Life and Literature" (2005), in Haack, *Putting Philosophy to Work* (note 17 above), 209–220.

46 Michael Frayn, *Headlong* (New York: Picador, 1999) tells the story of a hapless philosophy lecturer who, hoping to buy a painting cheaply from his financially stressed and artistically clueless aristocratic neighbor, uncovers evidence suggesting that the painting is, as he suspects, a missing Bruegel—no, that it isn't—yes, that it is—no, that it isn't, …, and so on and on through the whole book.

47 Scott Turow, *Reversible Errors* (New York: Warner Vision Books, 2002) tells the story of an attorney who, required by the court to take on the last-minute appeal of a death-row inmate, uncovers more and more evidence indicating that his client is guilty—until, at last, he finds the one piece of evidence that puts all the rest in a different light, and shows the client to be innocent after all.

48 Arthur Hailey, *Strong Medicine* (London: Pan Books, 1984) tells the story of a drug company's development of a drug against morning-sickness in pregnancy, a drug that turns out

about what can go wrong, epistemologically speaking, with a pharmaceutical company's trials of a drug.

Of course legal epistemology, like all legal philosophy, is inherently susceptible to certain pitfalls. One very real danger, foreshadowed in the quotation from Bacon with which I began, is ascending to so high a level of abstraction that you fail to engage in a meaningful way with any real-world legal system. And then there's the opposite danger, being so closely concerned with the evidentiary practices of a particular jurisdiction that you fail to engage with legal practices that are even slightly different—a danger Bacon also notes; though he attributes it to lawyers, who, he complains, "write according to the states where they live, what is received law."[49] It's also all too easy to confuse the epistemologically ideal with the best that's practically feasible—and it can be very hard to figure out what practical constraints we simply have to live with, and what could, and perhaps should, be overcome. And yet another problem is keeping clear which elements of the rationale for, or which elements of criticisms of, various evidentiary rules and procedures are truly epistemological, and which depend, rather, on concern for various policy objectives.

Then there's what I think of as the problem of "conceptual slippage": the small (and sometimes not-so-small) differences between legal and epistemological uses of the same terms. The concept of *evidence*—which in legal contexts includes physical evidence, rarely considered by epistemologists, is itself an example; then there's *reliability*—a technical term in reliabilist epistemology and, since *Daubert*, a very different technical term in US evidence law, and moreover one that doesn't, like the ordinary concept, come in degrees;[50] *causation*—which, as articulated over centuries of tort law, has diverged both from ordinary and from scientific usage;[51] and *knowledge*—which, as it appears in "*scienter*" requirements, e.g., that the defendant "knew or should

to cause terrible birth defects. (Bendectin, the drug at issue in *Daubert*, which the plaintiffs believed had caused their son's birth defect, was also prescribed for the treatment of morning-sickness.)

49 Bacon, *The Advancement of Learning* (note 1 above), 295.

50 *Daubert* III (note 43 above), 590 n.9. I should note that Federal Rule of Evidence 702 (which *Daubert* III was interpreting) was modified in 2000, coming into effect in its modified form in December that year; and was "restyled" in 2011; and now requires that expert testimony be "based upon sufficient facts or data," is "the product of reliable principles and methods," "which the witness has applied … reliably … to the facts of the case." The first of these three clauses may hint at a gradational understanding of "reliable"; but the second and third, like that footnote in *Daubert* III, suggest a categorical understanding.

51 See e.g., Lawrence M. Friedman, *A History of American Law* (New York: Simon and Schuster, 1973), 409 ff.

have known" that the goods he bought suspiciously cheaply were stolen,[52] seems quite far removed from most epistemologists' conceptions. Moreover, even when a concept is of interest both to legal scholars and to epistemologists, their focus is often very different. The AEU's interest in the definition of knowledge, for example, is often motivated by the hope of refuting skepticism or, more recently, with resolving a new rash of Gettier-type paradoxes; and epistemological interest in testimony is often focused on a (not always well-defined) idea of "social knowledge."

3 ARTICULATING LEGALLY-RELEVANT EPISTEMOLOGICAL IDEAS

The epistemological ideas developed in my *Evidence and Inquiry*[53] and later modified, refined, and amplified in chapter 3 of *Defending Science—Within Reason*[54] are focused centrally on the structure of evidence and its evaluation; and they interlock both with my ideas about the nature and conduct of inquiry,[55] and with my ideas about epistemological character.[56] They are worked out in greater-than-usual (though, inevitably, still far from perfect) detail; and they are at least approximately true—or so I believe: if I didn't, I'd drop them and start again! So, given the argument of the previous section, they should prove legally helpful; as, in fact, I believe they have. Setting

[52] The Model Penal Code explains the presumption of knowledge in such cases as requiring: (a) that a dealer be found in possession of stolen property from two or more persons on separate occasions; or (b) that he have received stolen property in another transaction within the year preceding the transaction charged; or (c) being a dealer in the type of property received, he acquired it for a consideration he knows is far below its reasonable value. Model Penal Code § 223.6(2) (ALI 1962), in 10A *Uniform Laws Annotated* 561 (West Group 2001). Statutes on receiving stolen property vary somewhat from state to state: e.g., the Minnesota statute speaks of the defendant's "knowing or having reason to know" that the property was stolen (Minn Stat Ann § 609.53 (West 2009)); the Missouri statute adds to the provisions of the Model Penal Code that the defendant knew the property to be stolen or acquired it "under such circumstances as would reasonably induce a person to believe the property was stolen" (Mo Ann Stat § 570.080 (Vernon 1999 & Supp 2012)); and the Delaware statute speaks of the defendant's "knowing that [the property] has been acquired under circumstances amounting to theft, or believing that it has been so acquired" (11 Del Code Ann § 851 (Mitchie Supp 2012)).

[53] Haack, *Evidence and Inquiry* (note 17 above); "A Foundherentist Theory of Empirical Justification," in Pojman, *Theories of Knowledge* (note 31 above), 2nd ed., 283–93.

[54] Susan Haack, *Defending Science—Within Reason* (Amherst, NY: Prometheus Books, 2003).

[55] See Susan Haack, "Preposterism and Its Consequences" (1996), in Haack, *Manifesto of a Passionate Moderate* (note 17 above), 188–204.

[56] See Haack, "The Ideal of Intellectual Integrity, in Life and Literature" (note 45 above), where I argue, *inter alia*, that epistemic virtues such as intellectual honesty concern a person's relation to evidence: e.g., his willingness to acknowledge, and adapt his beliefs in response to, contrary evidence.

questions of epistemic character aside (because, fascinating as they are, their relevance to the law is very indirect), I will focus here on questions about *inquiry* and its conduct, and about when and how evidence contributes to the *justification* of a belief or the *warrant* of a claim.

Inquiry and Pseudo-Inquiry: Inquiry, as I understand it, is an attempt to discover the truth of some question or questions; by which I mean, simply, that the goal of an inquiry into whether *p*, say, is to end up concluding that *p*, if *p*, and that not-*p*, if not-*p* (and that it's more complicated than a simple matter of whether *p* or not-*p*, if it *is* more complicated than that). Pseudo-inquiry, by contrast, is an attempt to make the best possible case for some conclusion determined in advance. So a genuine inquirer is motivated to seek out all the evidence he can; to judge as fairly as possible how strong it is, in what direction it points, and how clearly; and to draw a conclusion only when he judges that he has adequate evidence to do so. A pseudo-inquirer, by contrast, will seek out all the favorable evidence he can, and try to play down or explain away any evidence unfavorable to his predetermined conclusion. "Advocacy research" (as we might call, e.g., a trade union's efforts to find evidence in support of their demands) is a form of pseudo-inquiry.

In real life, of course, people's motives are usually mixed; and what we find is not so much a clean, sharp demarcation between pseudo-inquiry and the real thing as a continuum from less to more commitment to arriving at a predetermined upshot, from less to more openness to all the evidence. In line with this, how well inquiry is conducted depends, *inter alia*, on how honest, thorough, and competent the search for evidence is, and how honest, thorough, and competent the appraisal of its worth. And as this reveals, inquiry conducted in an environment in which there is pressure to reach a predetermined conclusion, or for that matter to reach *some* conclusion right away, is likely to be less well-conducted than inquiry free of such pressures.

Evidence and Warrant: My account of what makes a person justified in believing something, or what makes a claim warranted is, in brief, evidentialist, experientialist, gradational, foundherentist, quasi-holistic, and worldly; and, in its most developed form, it combines individual and social elements. Each of these points, obviously, requires considerable amplification and explanation.

My theory is *evidentialist*:[57] by which I mean that it rests on the assumption that whether, and if so to what degree, a person is justified in believing

[57] I first used the term in *Evidence and Inquiry* (note 17 above), 22, 118, 191, 194, 195, 271. After I had introduced it, I found it had already been used, with at least roughly the same meaning, in Richard Feldman and Earl Conee, "Evidentialism," *Philosophical Studies* 48 (1985): 15–34. (I gather from our correspondence that Prof. Goldman thinks evidentialism denies that there

something depends on how good his evidence is—"his evidence" including both his experiential evidence and his background beliefs or reasons. My theory is also, as this reveals, *experientialist*: i.e., it takes the evidence with respect to empirical claims to include a subject's sensory experience, his seeing, hearing, etc., this or that and his remembering seeing, hearing etc., this or that.[58] From a purely epistemological perspective, it is crucial to spell out what, exactly, experiential evidence is, and how, exactly, it contributes to justification;[59] but for present purposes I will set these issues aside, except to say that I conceive of experiential evidence as consisting, not of propositions believed, but of perceptual events, and of its causal role in bringing about beliefs as contributing to justification in virtue of the way language is learned.[60]

My theory is also *gradational*: i.e., it construes the quality of evidence (and hence of epistemic justification), not as categorical, but as a matter of degree: evidence with respect to a claim may be stronger, or weaker; a person may be more, or less, justified in believing something; and a claim or proposition may be warranted in greater, or in lesser, degree.[61]

And my theory is *foundherentist*: i.e., it is intermediate between the traditionally-rival families of theories of epistemic justification, foundationalism and coherentism—which, however, don't exhaust the options. Unlike coherentism, but like (some forms of) foundationalism, foundherentism allows a role for experiential evidence as well as for reasons; unlike foundationalism, but like coherentism, it allows pervasive relations of mutual support among beliefs.[62]

The foundherentist account of the structure of evidence is informed by an analogy with a crossword puzzle: experiential evidence is the analogue of the

is any connection between epistemic justification and likely truth; but as readers of the last chapter of *Evidence and Inquiry* will clearly see, in my case at any rate, this is egregiously false.)

58 I also include introspective evidence under "experiential evidence"; but have no theoretical account of such evidence to offer.

59 See Haack, *Evidence and Inquiry* (note 17 above), chapter 5 (but note that, when I turn to the explanation of what makes evidence better or worse, I rely on propositional proxies for experiential states); Haack, *Defending Science* (note 54 above), 61–63.

60 The picture I offer is of language as learned in part by ostension and in part by verbal definition, but with a gradualist twist: all language-learning involves both—the more observational a term, the greater the role of ostension, and the more theoretical the term, the greater the role of intra-linguistic connections. This is why a person's being in, say, the kind of perceptual state a normal person would be in when seeing a cardinal bird three feet away in good light gives support to his belief that there's a cardinal in front of him (how much depending also to some degree on other beliefs of his, e.g., about how normal his vision is). For a fuller account, see again Haack, *Defending Science* (note 54 above), 61–63.

61 Haack, *Evidence and Inquiry* (note 17 above), chapter 4.

62 *Id.*, chapter 1; see also Haack, "A Foundherentist Theory" (note 53 above).

clues, and reasons (a person's background beliefs, ramifying in all directions) the analogue of already-completed crossword entries. The same analogy also informs the foundherentist account of the determinants of evidential quality, of what makes evidence stronger or weaker, better or worse; which has three dimensions:

- how *supportive* the evidence is of the belief in question (analogue: how well a crossword entry fits with the clue and any completed intersecting entries);
- how *secure* the reasons are, independently of the belief in question (analogue: how reasonable those intersecting completed crossword entries are, independently of the one in question);
- how *comprehensive* the evidence is (analogue: how much of the crossword has been completed).

Because this theory of what makes evidence better or worse is multi-dimensional, it doesn't guarantee a linear ordering of degrees of justification; nor, *a fortiori*, does it offer anything like a numerical scale. And, as this suggests, it precludes identifying degrees of warrant with mathematical probabilities.[63]

Of course, each of the determinants of evidential quality needs to be spelled out in a lot more detail—much more detail than I can make room for here. But, briefly and roughly: how well a body of evidence supports a conclusion depends on the degree of explanatory integration of this evidence with that conclusion, i.e., how well evidence and conclusion fit together in an explanatory account.[64] How supportive a particular piece of evidence is depends on whether, and if so, how much, adding that piece of evidence enhances the explanatory integration of the whole. Evidence may be *positive* with respect to a claim, i.e., support it to some degree; or *negative*, i.e., undermine it to some degree; or it may be *neutral* with respect to the claim in question, neither supporting it nor undermining it—i.e., *irrelevant* to that claim.

How well evidence E justifies a belief is enhanced the *more* independently secure the positive reasons are, but the *less* independently secure the negative reasons are. I should also note that, while the independent security requirement might appear, at first glance, to be circular—since "secure" here is a synonym for "justified"—there is really no vicious circle, and no infinite regress. The independent security requirement applies only to reasons for a belief, not to the experiential evidence that ultimately grounds our beliefs about the

[63] This argument is made in much more detail in "Legal Probabilism" (note 21 above), 60–62.

[64] Hence the need for propositional proxies for experiential evidence (note 59 above): an explanatory account needs to be, as the phrase suggests, a set of propositions.

world; and this experiential evidence consists of events, not propositions, and so neither has nor stands in need of justification.

How comprehensive evidence is depends on how much of the evidence relevant (positively or negatively) to the proposition in question it includes.

My theory is *worldly*: i.e., its account of evidential quality isn't purely formal or syntactic, but material; it depends on facts about the world. Why so? First, the foundherentist understanding of supportiveness of evidence relies on the idea of degree of explanatory integration of evidence-plus-conclusion; and genuine explanation requires a vocabulary that picks out real kinds of thing or stuff.[65] Second, the foundherentist understanding of comprehensiveness relies on the concept of relevance; which, again, isn't a formal but a material matter. Is the way this job applicant loops the letter "g," for example, relevant to whether he can be trusted with the firm's money? It depends on whether graphology (the theory that handwriting is indicative of character) is true—i.e., on facts about the world.

My theory is *quasi-holistic*: i.e., it is neither atomistic (as foundationalist theories usually are), nor fully holistic (as coherentist theories usually are). The evidence relevant to a claim is usually complex and ramifying; but not everything is relevant to everything. So what I offer is a kind of articulated quasi-holism.

And, in its most fully-developed form, my theory *combines individual and social elements*. In *Evidence and Inquiry* I focused on *what makes an individual more or less justified* in believing something at a time; but by the time of *Defending Science* I was able to go beyond this to construct an account of *what makes a claim more or less warranted* at a time. (In ordinary English, of course, the words "justification" and "warrant" are more or less interchangeable; but I have adopted them as technical terms to represent these two different, though related, concepts.) *Evidence and Inquiry* focused on the evidence that actually leads someone to believe something at a time. The result was an account of justification that is personal (because it depends on the quality of the evidence that causes a person to have a certain belief), but not subjective (because how good a person's evidence is doesn't depend on how good he believes it to be).[66] *Defending Science* focused instead on the evidence a person possesses at a time, whether or not this is what causes him to have the belief in question at that time. This shift made it possible to construct, first, an account of how warranted a claim is for a person at a time; then an account of how warranted a claim is for a group of people at a time—which requires,

[65] Haack, *Defending Science* (note 54 above), chapter 5.

[66] Haack, *Evidence and Inquiry* (note 17 above), 58, 160.

inter alia, an understanding of what is involved epistemologically in relying on others' testimony; and finally, an account of how warranted the claim is by the evidence available at a time.[67]

4 APPLYING THESE EPISTEMOLOGICAL IDEAS TO EVIDENTIARY ISSUES

As I will show, these epistemological ideas illuminate a number of the issues about evidence and evidentiary procedure listed earlier. By way of preliminary, however, I need to articulate the epistemological dimensions of the legal concepts of burden, degree, and standard of proof.

US law assigns burdens of proof (also known as burdens of persuasion): i.e., it specifies which party has the obligation to establish the elements of a case; and it sets standards of proof: i.e., specifies to what degree those elements must be proven for the party that has the burden of proof to prevail. In criminal cases, the burden of proof falls on the prosecution, which is required to make its case "beyond a reasonable doubt";[68] in civil cases, the burden of proof falls on the plaintiff, who is normally required to make his case "by a preponderance of the evidence" or, as is sometimes said, "more probably than not"; and in a smaller class of cases, e.g., those involving issues of citizenship, an intermediate standard, "clear and convincing evidence," applies.[69]

[67] This is worked out in some detail in Haack, *Defending Science* (note 54 above) chapter 3. The reason for starting with the individual is simple, but crucial: the warrant of any empirical claim depends ultimately on experience, i.e., on sensory interactions with the world; and it is individuals who have such interactions. This point is not a new one; it is made, for example, in Bertrand Russell, *Human Knowledge, Its Scope and Limits* (New York: Simon and Schuster, 1948), 8; but the account I construct to accommodate it is not, so far as I know, to be found, even in embryo, elsewhere.

[68] "The requirement that guilt of a criminal charge be established by proof beyond a reasonable doubt dates at least from our early years as a nation." *In re* Winship, 397 U.S. 358, 362 (1970). "[The] demand for a higher degree of persuasion in criminal cases was recurrently expressed though ancient times, [though] its crystallization into the formula 'beyond a reasonable doubt' seems to have occurred as late as 1878." Charles T. McCormick, *Handbook of the Law of Evidence* (St. Paul, MN: West Publishing Co., 1954), 681–82.

[69] Kenneth S. Broun, et al., eds., *McCormick on Evidence* (St. Paul, MN: Thomson/West, 2006), vol. 2, 487–90. The details may differ, but my understanding is that approximately the same structure is found in many legal systems. Not in all, however: according to Jean-Sébastien Borghetti, "Litigation on Hepatitis B Vaccination and Demyelinating Disease in France: Breaking Through Scientific Uncertainty in France," in Diego Papayannis, ed., *Uncertain Causation in Tort Law* (Cambridge: Cambridge University Press, forthcoming), "[f]acts do not have to be established 'on the balance of probabilities', or 'beyond a reasonable doubt'. First and second instance judges freely decide if evidence is enough to consider a fact as established. Their appreciation is a matter of '*intime conviction*' and may not be challenged before the *Cour de cassation* or the *Conseil d'Etat*."

The different standards indicate that legal proof must be understood as coming in degrees, a matter of more and less; but there is disagreement about what, exactly, these degrees of proof are degrees *of*. Some (stressing the phrase "burden of persuasion") take them to be fact-finders' degrees of belief;[70] some (stressing the phrase "more probable than not") take them to be mathematical probabilities;[71] and some—the subjective Bayesians—combine the two: degrees of proof are to be construed as mathematical probabilities, and mathematical probabilities are in turn to be construed as subjective degrees of belief.[72] Others, myself among them, take degrees of proof to be *epistemological likelihoods*,[73] i.e., degrees of warrant of a claim by evidence.

How legal degrees of proof are best understood is not itself an epistemological question. It is, rather, a matter of understanding, for example, what is going on when standards of proof are spelled out in jury instructions and in instructions to judges about the circumstances in which they may preempt or override a jury verdict; and also requires reflection on why we need such standards at all. To keep things manageable, here I will comment, very briefly, only on jury instructions.[74]

Sometimes these instructions sound subjective, as if they referred simply to jurors' degrees of belief: Florida jury instructions in criminal cases, for example, contrast "an abiding conviction of guilt" with a conviction that "wavers and vacillates";[75] and federal jury instructions speak of "a settled conviction of

70 Broun et al., eds., *McCormick on Evidence* (note 69 above), vol. 2, 483.

71 See, e.g., David Kaye, "Do We Need a Calculus of Weight to Understand Proof Beyond a Reasonable Doubt?" in Peter Tillers and Eric D. Green, eds., *Probability and Inference in the Law of Evidence: The Uses and Limits of Bayesianism* (Dordrecht, the Netherlands: Kluwer, 1988), 129–45; Richard Lempert, "The New Evidence Scholarship: Analyzing the Process of Proof," 61–102 in the same volume.

72 See e.g., Michael O. Finkelstein and William B. Fairley, "A Bayesian Approach to Identification Evidence," *Harvard Law Review* 83, no.3 (1969–70): 489–517; David Schum, *Evidential Foundations of Probabilistic Reasoning* (New York: John Wiley and Sons, 1994); Jay Kadane and David Schum, *A Probabilistic Analysis of the Sacco and Vanzetti Evidence* (New York: Wiley and Sons, 1996). Both are criticized in detail in "Legal Probabilism" (note 21 above).

73 In ordinary English, of course, the words, "probability" and "likelihood," mean essentially the same thing; but I have adopted "likelihood" specifically for the epistemological meaning.

74 My treatment here will be very sketchy—just enough to get the epistemology in focus. In "Legal Probabilism" (note 21 above) I will give a much fuller discussion of jury instructions, of the circumstances in which a judge may grant JMOL (Judgment as a Matter of Law, the term now used to include both directed verdicts and judicial rulings overturning a jury verdict), and of the rationale for setting standards of proof.

75 *Florida Standard Jury Instructions in Criminal Cases* ([Tallahassee, FL?]: The Florida Bar/LexisNexis, 7th ed., 2009), § 3.7. ("Conviction," here, of course means "degree of belief, degree of confidence in the truth of a proposition.")

the truth of the charge."[76] But, as you see when you read on, what is intended can't plausibly be taken to be *simply* fact-finders' subjective degrees of belief: the Florida instructions continue with the warning that "*it is to the evidence introduced at this trial, and to this alone,*"[77] that jurors must look for proof; and the federal instructions explain that the "settled conviction" they refer to must be the result of "*weighing and considering all the evidence.*"[78] Jurors' degree of "conviction," in other words, should correspond appropriately to the strength of the evidence.

And sometimes these instructions sound probabilistic: federal jury instructions on the standard of proof in ordinary civil cases, for example, speak of the claim's being "more probably true than not true,"[79] and in explaining "clear and convincing" speak in terms of the claim's being "highly probable."[80] But degrees of proof can't plausibly be taken to be simple mathematical probabilities, either—as, again, you see when you notice that jurors are told that they must be "*persuaded by the evidence*"[81] that it is more probable than not, or highly probable, that the conclusion is true; which suggests what is intended is epistemic likelihood, degree of warrant of the claim by evidence, and not mathematical probability.

This brief analysis of jury instructions confirms that legal degrees of proof are best understood in epistemological terms. And if this is right, what we need to understand degrees of proof is an epistemological theory, an account of what makes evidence stronger or weaker, a claim more or less warranted. Only a gradational theory, obviously, will be helpful here: a significant point, given that many epistemologists assume, explicitly or implicitly, that warrant or justification is categorical (and even Alvin Goldman, whose project began with a gradational understanding, soon retreated to a categorical approach).[82] Moreover, given the frequent references in jury instructions to the need for

76 Kevin F. O'Malley et al., 2008, *Federal Jury Practice and Instructions: Criminal* (6th ed., Eagan, MN: Thomson/West, 2008) (and supplement 2010), vol. A, §12.10, 165 (citing United States v. Cleveland, 106 F.3d 1056, 1062–1063 (1st Cir. 1997)).

77 *Florida Standard Jury Instructions in Criminal Cases* (note 75 above), § 3.7.

78 O'Malley et al., *Federal Jury Practice and Instructions: Criminal* (note 76 above) 2008, 165 (my italics).

79 Kevin F. O'Malley et al., *Federal Jury Practice and Instructions: Civil* (Eagan, MN: West Group, 5th ed., 2000) (and supplement 2010), vol. 3, §101.41, 13.

80 *Id.*, §104.03, 143.

81 *Id.*, §101.41, 53 and §104.03, 143 (my italics).

82 See, e.g., Goldman, "What Is Justified Belief?" (note 33 above), 10, which acknowledges that justification is a matter of degree; and then notice that—as I pointed out in *Evidence and Inquiry* (note 17 above), 197—as soon as Goldman modifies his initial definition to take account of anticipated objections, he seems to have closed off the possibility of accommodating degrees of justification.

jurors to take account of the fact that potentially relevant evidence is missing, the evidence presented lacking in some relevant respect,[83] only a theory that goes beyond the supportiveness and independent security of the evidence at hand to appeal, in addition, to how comprehensive it is can be adequate to the task: another significant point, given that many epistemologists go no further than requiring that all the evidence currently available to a person or group of people be taken into account. So the foundherentist theory seems a strong candidate.

To deny that degrees of proof are mathematical probabilities is emphatically not to deny that statistical evidence—the random-match probabilities that by now are a routine part of DNA testimony, for example, or the epidemiological evidence common in toxic-tort cases, etc., etc.—plays a significant role in many cases. But how statistical evidence is best accommodated in a theory of legal proof has been the subject of long-running disputes in which Bayesian approaches of various stripes (objective and subjective) have been dominant. So you may be wondering whether my approach can handle such evidence satisfactorily.

First, just to be clear: we can't *identify* the statistical probability that a match between the defendant's DNA and DNA found at the crime scene isn't random with the degree of proof that the defendant is guilty, nor the relative risk that a person who has been exposed to this substance will develop this disorder with the degree of proof that this exposure caused the plaintiff to develop this disorder.[84] More generally, we can't equate statistical probabilities presented as evidence in a case with degrees of proof.

One very striking illustration of this point is the now-famous English case of Raymond Easton. Strong DNA evidence linked Mr. Easton to the crime of which he was accused; but he was so handicapped by advanced Parkinson's disease that he was physically incapable of having committed it.[85] Another way to illustrate the point would be by reference to cases like *Sargent* (1940)[86] and *Smith* (1945),[87] where there was evidence of a high statistical probability

[83] For example, in the Sixth Circuit juries are instructed that a reasonable doubt "may arise from the evidence, the lack of evidence, or the nature of the evidence." O'Malley et al., *Federal Jury Practice and Instructions: Criminal* (note 76 above), 174.

[84] As I argue in "Risky Business: Statistical Proof of Individual Causation," pp. 264–93 in this volume.

[85] Genewatch UK, *The Police National Database: Balancing Crime Detection, Human Rights and Privacy*, available at http://www.genewatch.org/uploads/f03c6d66a9b354535738483c-1c3d49e4/NationalDNADatabase.pdf (January 2005). See "Legal Probabilism" (note 21 above), 76–77 for my foundherentist analysis of the evidence in this case.

[86] Sargent v. Mass. Accident Co., 29 N.E.2d 825 (Mass. 1940).

[87] Smith v. Rapid Transit, Inc., 58 N.E.2d 754 (Mass. 1945).

that a bus on a certain route belonged to a certain company, and the question was whether this evidence was sufficient to establish that it was this company that operated the bus that caused an accident on this route. In both *Sargent* and *Smith* the courts ruled—correctly, in my opinion—that statistical evidence alone was *not* sufficient; and in *Smith*, we get a hint of why it isn't, in the court's observation that "[w]hile the defendant had the sole franchise for operating a bus line on Main Street, ... this did not preclude private or chartered buses from using this street."[88]

True, if the mathematical probability that a bus on this route was operated by company A is high, this *supports* the claim that it was a company-A bus that caused the accident—to what degree depending on how high the statistical probability is. (Why so? Because what the statistical evidence tells us is that almost all the licensed buses on this route are run by company A, and "Mrs. Smith was injured by a bus on Main Street; almost all the buses licensed to serve Main Street were company-A buses; Mrs. Smith was injured by a company-A bus" is quite a nicely integrated explanatory story.) But on my approach this is not sufficient to warrant Mrs. Smith's claim against company A. The statistical evidence may itself be more or less *independently secure*—more so if, e.g., it is based on a careful search of good records of what franchises were issued, less so if, e.g., it is based merely on the word of someone or other who answered a phone at the Town Hall. Moreover, as the court in *Smith* realized, if this is all the evidence we have, it is sadly lacking in *comprehensiveness*: we don't know, for instance, whether "gypsy" buses, not licensed by the municipality, also ply this route, and if so, how often; nor whether company-B buses, licensed on a different route, sometimes take a short-cut down this stretch of Main Street; nor whether company-A drivers were on strike the day of the accident; nor, ..., etc.[89]

The same argument goes, *mutatis mutandis*, for statistical DNA evidence, epidemiological evidence, etc. But of course I chose the old bus cases for a reason. The "blue bus hypothetical," based on *Smith*,[90] was a recurrent theme in what was known as the "New Evidence Scholarship,"[91] which

88 *Id.*, 755.

89 For a detailed foundherentist analysis of another famous "naked statistical evidence" case, *People v. Collins*, see "Legal Probabilism" (note 21 above), 71–76.

90 Charles Nesson, "The Evidence or the Event? On Judicial Proof and the Acceptability of Verdicts," *Harvard Law Review* 98, no.7 (1984–5): 1357–92, 1357 ff.

91 According to Lempert, "The New Evidence Scholarship" (note 71 above), 61, before the Federal Rules of Evidence were ratified in 1975, evidence scholarship in the US was pretty much moribund; but in the wake of the FRE there was first a wave of discussions of details of the Rules, and then a new interest in evaluative questions about proof, self-described as the "New Evidence Scholarship."

focused, for a while, on the contrast between "fact-based" and "story-based" approaches to proof. And as it happens, this was where I first got drawn into legal epistemology: a colleague interested in this debate, taking the fact-based vs. story-based distinction to be more or less equivalent to the epistemological dichotomy of foundationalism vs. coherentism, wondered if my foundherentism mightn't be a possible resolution.[92]

After a decade or so of work, I now see that my colleague was on the right track—though wrong on some of the details. Though neither was perfectly clear, the evidence scholars' and the epistemologists' distinctions were more different from each other than he may have realized. For one thing, "fact-based" seems to have referred to the various Bayesian approaches; for another, the "story-based" party, as represented by Prof. Allen,[93] proposed not only a distinctive narrative conception of proof, but also the revisionary idea that what should matter is the comparative merits of plaintiffs' and defendants' explanatory stories. This would amount to a significant shift in the burden of (civil) proof, since as things stand now the defendant doesn't need to *have* an alternative explanatory story, but will prevail so long as the plaintiff's story doesn't meet the standard of proof. But in a larger sense my colleague was right: as he suspected, (i) my approach falls *neither* into the "fact-based" (Bayesian, probabilistic, atomistic), *nor* into the "story-based" (narrative, revisionary, more holistic) category; and (ii) it can provide a better understanding of degrees of proof than either.

Moreover, as I showed in a 2008 paper,[94] my understanding of the key differences between real inquiry and pseudo-inquiry, and of the continuum of intermediate possibilities found in real life, suggests what is right about Judge Kozinski's argument that "litigation-driven" science is inherently less likely to be reliable than science conducted independently of litigation:[95] the desire to reach a predetermined conclusion (e.g., a pharmaceutical company's desire to reach the conclusion that its drug is harmless, or a plaintiff's desire to reach the conclusion that it was this drug that caused his child's birth defects, etc.) is, indeed, quite likely to threaten the honesty and thoroughness serious inquiry

[92] For a fuller version of the story, see Carmen Vázquez, "Entrevista a Susan Haack," *Doxa* 36(2013): 573–86.

[93] Ronald J. Allen, "A Reconceptualization of Civil Trials," *Boston University Law Review* 66 (1986): 401–437. Allen's proposal was restricted to civil cases; however, a recent paper by Michael Pardo proposes the same comparative approach to criminal proof, an even more radical kind of revisionism. Michael Pardo, "Estándares de prueba y teoría de prueba," in Carmen Vázquez, ed., *Estándares de prueba y prueba científica: Ensayos de epistemología jurídica* (Barcelona: Marcial Pons, 2013), 99–118.

[94] "What's Wrong with Litigation-Driven Science?", pp. 180–207 in this volume.

[95] Daubert v. Merrell Dow Pharm., Inc., 43 F.3d 1311, 1317 (9th Cir.1995) ("*Daubert* IV").

requires. However, the same applies to marketing-driven science, to university science funded by drug companies or other commercial outfits, *and* to the forensic sciences—for which Judge Kozinski expressly makes an exception.[96]

And, as we will see in "Epistemology Legalized,"[97] my account of inquiry, pseudo-inquiry, etc., also suggests both what is right about Peirce's critique of adversarial procedures, and what is wrong. What's true is that an adversarial process would be far from ideal as a way to go about figuring out, say, the truth of some scientific question. But what a legal fact-finder is asked to determine is *not* whether the defendant did it, but whether this proposition has been established to the required degree of proof by the evidence presented; and—unlike scientific inquiry, which takes the time it takes—legal decisions are made under significant constraints of time and resources and in light of competing desiderata and interests. Arguably, given those constraints and desiderata, an adversarial process that gives each side a strong incentive to seek out favorable evidence and to undermine, or find some different explanation for, apparently unfavorable evidence can be a good-enough way of arriving at factually sound verdicts given these exigencies. As I point out, however, this argument only works given certain assumptions, e.g., about how accurately plea-bargaining decisions reflect the likely upshot at trial—a matter which has subsequently been addressed by the US Supreme Court,[98] and has by now been the subject of a little empirical research;[99] and on the assumption that the two sides have roughly equal resources—which is rarely true in practice. Similarly, while it's true, as Bentham realized,[100] that comprehensiveness of evidence is an epistemological desideratum, it doesn't follow that exclusionary rules of evidence are simply epistemologically indefensible. For, again, it's arguable that, in the legal context, excluding certain kinds of evidence (e.g., the unnecessarily repetitive) may also be part of a good-enough way of arriving at factually sound verdicts[101]—though this obviously doesn't justify any

96 *Id.*, 1317, n.5. See also Susan Haack, "Técnicas forenses, ciencia impulsada por litígios y el problema de los incentivos perversos: Lecciones a partir de la saga *Ramirez*," in Monica María Bustamente Rúa, ed., *Derecho probatorio contemporáneo: Prueba cientifica y técnicas forenses* (Medellín, Colombia: Universidad de Medellín, 2012), 333–40.

97 See "Epistemology Legalized" (note 20 above), 33–39.

98 Lafler v. Cooper, 132 S. Ct. 1376 (2012) (granting a new trial because ineffective assistance of counsel resulted in rejection of a plea offer, and the defendant was convicted at trial and received a more severe sentence than he would have served had he accepted the plea bargain).

99 Lucian E. Dervan and Vanessa A. Edkins, "The Innocent Defendant's Dilemma: An Innovative Empirical Study of Plea Bargaining's Innocence Problem," *Journal of Criminal Law and Criminology*, **103**, no.1 (2013): 1–47.

100 Bentham, *Rationale of Judicial Evidence* (note 28 above), vol. 1, chapters IX, X.

101 "Epistemology Legalized" (note 20 above), 39–45.

particular exclusionary rule or set of such rules, which would each have to be argued on its merits.[102]

5 LOOKING FORWARD TO NEW PROJECTS

I hope this sketch has been enough to show you something of how my epistemological theory can contribute to our understanding of evidentiary issues in the law. I don't expect, however, to run out of work any time soon; for there are numerous juicy problems in legal epistemology to which, as yet, I have no very satisfactory solutions.

- **Testimony:** A very brief discussion in *Evidence and Inquiry*[103] acknowledged that much of what a person believes is the result of testimonial evidence, i.e., of the person's hearing or reading what someone else says or writes—combined with his belief that the someone else in question is well-informed, and has no incentive to deceit or concealment on the matter in question. Of course, I added, if he doesn't understand the other person's language, his reading what that person writes or hearing what he says won't contribute to his belief. The more sustained discussion of shared evidence in *Defending Science* suggested how to understand the degree of warrant of a claim for a group of people: start with the degree of warrant of that claim for a hypothetical individual whose evidence is the joint evidence of all the members of the group; but include the disjunctions (rather than the conjunctions) of disputed reasons; and then discount the degree of warrant by some measure of (i) the degree to which each member is justified in believing that the others are competent and honest and (ii) the degree of efficiency of communication within the group.[104] What light, I wonder, might all this shed on questions about the reliability of testimony that arise in legal contexts?
- **Expert Testimony:** Some of the special epistemological problems with evaluating the worth of expert testimony arise from the fact that much scientific and technical work requires its own distinctive, specialized vocabulary, comprehensible only to those who are familiar with its theoretical or technical context—a thought that extends the idea expressed above, that in general we can learn from others' testimony only if we understand it. But other special epistemological problems

[102] See, e.g., "Risky Business: Statistical Proof of Specific Causation," pp. 264–93 in this volume, 291

[103] *Evidence and Inquiry* (note 17 above), 124.

[104] Haack, *Defending Science* (note 54 above) 69–71.

with evaluating the worth of scientific testimony arise, probably, from the difficulty of recognizing, if you are unfamiliar with a scientific field, what is relevant to what. Are there, I wonder, instances where misjudgments of relevance have been legally crucial? And how exactly do these ideas interlock with Learned Hand's observation, long ago, that there is a paradox at the heart of expert testimony: that this is "setting the jury to decide, where doctors disagree"[105]—when it is precisely because they have knowledge not possessed by the average juror that we need experts in the first place?

- **The Misleading and the Unreliable:** FRE 403 (b) says that testimony is inadmissible if it would waste time or confuse or mislead the finder of fact. *Daubert* says that expert testimony is inadmissible if it is (irrelevant and/or) unreliable. At first blush, one might think the *Daubert* Court was trying to get at what makes expert testimony misleading; but on reflection it is clear that being misleading and being unreliable are *different* flaws. For one thing, evidence isn't misleading in and of itself, but only in the context of other evidence;[106] whereas "unreliable" doesn't have this contextual character. It would be helpful, I think, to articulate when, and why, even reliable testimony might, nevertheless, be misleading.
- **"Weight of Evidence Methodology":** In a recent US case, *Milward v. Acuity Special Products*,[107] where a federal appeals court revisits the issue of the weight of combined evidence, we find several different understandings of "weight of evidence methodology": (i) as suggested by Dr. Smith (the proffered plaintiff's expert toxicological witness, the admissibility of whose evidence was at issue), who said he was using the methodology proposed by Austin Bradford Hill;[108] (ii) as suggested by a self-described expert on scientific method; and (iii) as suggested by the court's own reasoning. Does any of these different understandings, I wonder, shed real light on the issue, and if so, which, and how?
- **International *Daubert*:** Since the US Supreme Court made its ruling on the standard of admissibility of expert scientific testimony, not only

105 Hand, "Historical and Practical Considerations Regarding Expert Testimony" (note 38 above), 54.

106 As I argued in "'Know' Is Just a Four-Letter Word" (note 31 above), 321–24.

107 *Milward* (note 41 above).

108 *Id.*, 17. See Austin Bradford Hill, "The Environment and Disease: Association or Causation?" *Proceedings of the Royal Society of Medicine* 58 (1965): 295–300; and, for a detailed discussion of Hill's contribution, Haack, "Correlation and Causation: the 'Bradford Hill Criteria' in Epidemiological, Epistemological, and Legal Context," pp. 239–63 in this volume.

has *Daubert* been adopted by many states in the US, but its influence has also been felt in other jurisdictions: in Canada,[109] for example, and in England and Wales;[110] and in some civil-law countries, including Italy,[111] Mexico,[112] and Colombia.[113] Each time, however, it seems to have been modified, subtly or not-so-subtly. The Colombian version, for example, replaces Justice Blackmun's quasi-Popperian references to "testability" by distinctly un-Popperian talk of "verification"; and the Law Commission for England and Wales proposes requiring that admissible expert evidence be not (as *Daubert* says) "reliable," but "reliable enough"—thus acknowledging, as *Daubert* did not, that reliability comes in degrees: insofar, an advance, but unfortunately also risking making the reliability requirement essentially vacuous. So there are interesting questions about which, if any, of these is epistemologically better, and which, and why.

Obviously, this list is by no means exhaustive; there are plenty of other legal-epistemological questions to which sound answers would be welcome. How, for example, should we think about physical evidence? (I'm not sure, exactly; but it strikes me that such evidence doesn't stand mute in court, but plays its role by way of attorneys' descriptions of relevant features—"look how neatly

109 R.v. J.-L. J., [2000] 2 S.C.R. 600 (Can.) interpreted R v. Mohan, [1994] 2 S.C.R. 9 (Can.) as requiring that novel scientific testimony meet a threshold reliability requirement, and listed indicia of reliability almost identical to the *Daubert* factors.

110 Law Commission Report No.325 on Expert Evidence in Criminal Proceedings, Feb. 21, 2011, urged that there be a "statutory reliability test," providing that experts' testimony is admissible only if it is "sufficiently reliable to be admitted," and that trial judges be provided with "a single list of generic factors to help them apply the reliability test." This recommendation has not yet been implemented, though Jamieson and Bader point out that it is already sometimes followed in practice. Allan Jamieson and Scott Bader, "Got a Match, Guv?" available at http://www.barristermagazine.com/archive-articles/issue49/got-a-match,-guv.html, 2011. There has also been criticism of the proposal: see, e.g., Adam Wilson, "The Law Commission's Recommendation on Expert Opinion Evidence: Sufficient Reliability?" *Web Journal of Current Legal Issues*, 3, 2011.

111 Cass. Pen., sez. IV, 13 Dicembre 2010, n. 43786 (acknowledging and amplifying ideas from *Daubert*).

112 Conocimientos Científicos. Características que deben tener para que pueden ser tomados en cuenta por el juzgador al momento de emitir su fallo, Suprema Corte de Justicia [SCJN] [Supreme Court], Semanario Judicial de la Federación y Su Gaceta, Novena Época, tomo XXV, Marzo de 2007, Tesis Aislada 1a. CLXXXVII/2006, Página 258 (Mex.) (arguing that admissible scientific testimony must be both relevant and reliable ["*fidedigna*"], and listing indicia of reliability strongly reminiscent of the *Daubert* factors).

113 Article 422 of the Código de Procedimiento Penal lists indicia of reliability strongly reminiscent of the *Daubert* factors, satisfaction of at least one of which is required for the admissibility of new scientific evidence and scientific publications. Código de Procedimiento Penal [CPP] art 422.

the head of this spanner matches the crack in the victim's skull," "see how utterly dissimilar this signature is from this other one, which we know is really X's," and so forth.) Or, again: can we say anything about whether, in general, a group of people, such as a jury, is likely to be better at assessing the weight of evidence than a single person, such as a judge? (I'm tempted to say no, that it depends on the particular jury and the particular judge; but it should be possible to say more about when a group might do better, and when not.) Or, again: can I shed any light on what it means to describe a jury as "impartial"? And so on.

~

The emphasis here has been on the usefulness of epistemology to the law; but I certainly don't mean to suggest that the law can't also be useful to epistemology. On the contrary: thinking about real-life evidentiary issues can be extremely helpful to an epistemologist—not least because philosophy so often confines itself to an unsatisfying diet of simplified, made-up examples, while the law provides ample illustration of just how complicated, ambiguous, tangled, and confusing real-life evidence can be. The "niche" epistemology fashionable today puts me in mind of John Locke's shrewd observation about "those who readily and sincerely follow reason, but … have not a full view." Such people "have a pretty traffic with known correspondents in some little creek," he comments, "but will not venture into the great ocean of knowledge."[114] A more robust two-way traffic between legal practice and epistemological theory, I believe, could benefit both parties.

[114] John Locke, *The Conduct of the Understanding*, in *Posthumous Works of Mr. John Locke* (London: A. and J. Churchill, 1706), 1–137, 9–10.

—2—

Epistemology Legalized: Or, Truth, Justice, and the American Way

> [T]he man of mere theory is in the practical sphere an useless and dangerous pedant.
>
> —F. H. Bradley[1]

1 TRUTH AND JUSTICE

The invitation to give the Olin Lecture in Jurisprudence at Notre Dame was quite unexpected: but perhaps I shouldn't have been too surprised to find myself called upon to play the role of jurisprude. I did, after all, once publish an essay entitled "Confessions of an Old-Fashioned Prig"[2]—an essay in which I tried to articulate why it matters whether you care about the truth, and what has gone wrong in the thinking of those, like Richard Rorty, who profess to believe that truth is "entirely a matter of solidarity,"[3] that the supposed ideal of concern for truth is a kind of superstition, and that standards of better and worse evidence are nothing but local, parochial conventions. And all this had a quite direct bearing on my present topic; for if Rorty & co. were right, we would surely stand in need of the most urgent and radical revision not only of our legal thinking, but of our legal system itself.

Jeremy Bentham's powerful metaphor of "Injustice, and her handmaid Falsehood"[4] reminds us, if we need reminding, that substantive justice requires not only just laws, and just administration of those laws, but also

[1] F. H. Bradley, *Ethical Studies* (London: Henry S. King and Co., 1876), 204.

[2] Susan Haack, "Confessions of an Old-Fashioned Prig," in Haack, *Manifesto of a Passionate Moderate: Unfashionable Essays* (Chicago: University of Chicago Press, 1998), 7–30.

[3] Richard Rorty, *Objectivity, Relativism and Truth* (Cambridge: Cambridge University Press, 1991), 32.

[4] Jeremy Bentham, *Rationale of Judicial Evidence* (London: Hunt and Clarke, 1827; New York: Garland, 1978), vol. 1, 22.

factual truth—objective factual truth; and that in consequence the very possibility of a just legal system requires that there be objective indications of truth, i.e., objective standards of better or worse evidence. Almost any case would illustrate the point, but the case of Kerry Kotler is especially vivid: in 1992, after serving 11 years of a twenty-five-to-fifty year sentence for rape, Mr. Kotler was released from prison when DNA evidence established that he was not the perpetrator; less than three years later, he was charged with another rape, and again convicted—this time on DNA evidence.[5] Unless there is an objective fact of the matter about which rape, or rapes, Kotler committed, and unless DNA evidence is objectively more truth-indicative than eyewitness testimony, etc., this would be, not justice, but a ghastly farce. Not to labor the point: the law is up to its neck in epistemology.

When Bentham published his *Rationale of Judicial Evidence* in 1827, the theory of evidence was, as he observed, largely unexplored and uncharted. By now, the territory is much traveled by legal scholars, and even visited by the occasional venturesome philosophical tourist. I can't hope to offer anything to rival the map Bentham himself drew, either in scope or in detail; nor can I aspire to a scholarly treatment of his remarkable treatise, let alone of the subsequent literature. My plan is, rather, to sketch some epistemological themes of mine, and explore their bearing on two familiar, radical epistemological criticisms of our legal system: (i) that an adversarial system is an epistemologically poor way of determining the truth; and (ii) that exclusionary rules of evidence are epistemologically undesirable. Neither criticism, I shall argue, is decisive; both, however, throw harsh light on disturbing aspects of the way our legal system functions in practice.

The task I have set myself requires coming to terms with the inevitable tensions between philosophical and legal thinking—epistemology being the part of philosophy to which it falls to articulate what evidence is and what makes it better or worse, the law of evidence a mesh of practices, procedures, and rules regulating the legal handling of evidence. Epistemology, like philosophy generally, is essentially universal; the law of evidence, like the law generally, varies from place to place and from time to time. Moreover, my task requires thinking about "the law(s) of evidence" in the broadest sense: i.e., not only about legal rules of admissibility and exclusion of evidence, burdens and standards of proof, and so forth, but also about the procedures and practices

5 Edward Connors, Thomas Lundgren, Neal Miller, and Tom McEwen, *Convicted by Juries, Exonerated by Science*, National Institute of Justice (NIJ) Research Report (June 1996). The victim in the earlier crime had identified Mr. Kotler both in a photo array and in a line-up. *Ibid.*

that structure legal efforts to determine the truth.[6] Additionally, the task requires discriminating those questions about the law of evidence that epistemology can reasonably be expected to illuminate, and those which, because they involve value judgments of other kinds, are beyond the reach of purely epistemological argument. On top of which, it requires an epistemology that is—well, *true*; for mistaken epistemology can only obscure, and not illuminate, legal issues. I will do what I can.

2 EVIDENCE AND INQUIRY[7]

Inquiry is something just about everyone engages in just about every day, when they want to know the source of a bad smell, the cause of a delayed flight, or whatever; and it is the professional occupation of scientists, historians, detectives, investigative journalists, of legal and literary scholars, and of philosophers, among others. Unlike such other human activities as cooking dinner, composing a symphony, dancing, debating, or pleading a case before the Supreme Court, inquiry is an attempt to discover the truth of some question or questions. To understand this, no elaborately articulated theory of truth is needed; it is sufficient that the concept of truth satisfy the Aristotelian Insight, that "to say of what is not that it is not, or of what is that it is, is true"—that a proposition be true just in case things are as it says. Someone who is trying to find out whether the butler did it, for example, wants to end up believing that the butler did it if the butler did it; that the butler didn't do it if the butler didn't do it; and that it's more complicated than that if it *is* more complicated than that.

Inquiry involves, first, being struck by a question. If the answer is to be found by means of some familiar routine, you simply do what is needed (look up the number in the phone book, or whatever). If the answer is not so easily found, however, the next step is to make a conjecture about what, if true, would answer the question at issue; figure out the consequences of your conjecture; check out how well those consequences stand up to any evidence you already have and any further evidence you can lay your hands on; and then

6 On broader and narrower conceptions of the law of evidence, see William Twining, "What Is the Law of Evidence?" in Twining, *Rethinking Evidence* (Oxford: Blackwell, 1990), 178–218.

7 I draw in this section on Susan Haack, *Evidence and Inquiry* (1993; 2nd ed., Amherst, NY: Prometheus Books, 2009), especially chapter 4; "Confessions of an Old-Fashioned Prig" (note 2 above); "The Same, Only Different" (2002), in Haack, *Putting Philosophy to Work: Inquiry and Its Place in Culture* (Amherst, NY: Prometheus Books, 2008), 47–52; *Defending Science—Within Reason: Between Scientism and Cynicism* (Amherst, NY: Prometheus Books, 2003), especially chapter 3.

use your judgment whether to stick with your conjecture, modify it, abandon it and start again, or suspend judgment until more evidence comes along. Inquiry is better conducted the more insightful, imaginative, and informed the conjectures, the more rigorous the reasoning, the more thorough the search for evidence, and the more scrupulously honest and (as we say) judicious the weighing of evidence. Strictly speaking, in fact, if you are trying to find evidence to support a foregone conclusion rather than following the evidence where it leads, you aren't really inquiring; which is why, when the government or our university institutes an Official Inquiry into this or that, some of us reach for our scare quotes.

An inquirer's business is to discover the true answer to his question; so his obligation is to seek out what evidence he can and assess it as fairly as possible. So, again strictly speaking, "disinterested, unbiased inquirer" is a kind of pleonasm, and "interested, biased inquirer" an oxymoron. But in real life, obviously, it's a lot messier. Probably nobody is of rock-solid, across-the-board intellectual integrity, and even the most honest inquirers have their prejudices and blind spots; and an advocate anxious to avoid being blindsided may inquire with scrupulous thoroughness.

The concepts of inquiry and of evidence are intimately intertwined. The evidence with respect to factual, empirical claims is a complex mesh in which experiential evidence, i.e., the evidence of the senses, and reasons, i.e., background beliefs, work together like the clues and ramifying intersecting entries in a crossword puzzle. How reasonable a crossword entry is depends on how well it is supported by the clue and any completed intersecting entries; how reasonable those other entries are, independent of the entry in question; and how much of the crossword has been completed. Similarly, how well a factual claim is warranted by evidence depends on how well it is supported by experiential evidence and background beliefs; how secure those background beliefs are, independent of the claim in question; and how much of the relevant evidence the evidence includes. Relevance is not a matter of logic, but depends on matters of fact. (Someone who believes in astrology may *think* that the astrological sign of an applicant for a position in the marketing department is relevant to whether he is assertive and forceful or timid and retiring; but whether it *is* relevant depends on whether the alignment of heavenly bodies at the time of his birth actually *does* determine his character).

How supportive evidence is of a claim depends on how well it anchors the claim in experience, and how well it integrates it into an explanatory account; i.e., on how good the circumstances of any relevant observations were, and how well the claim in question fits into an explanatory story with the other relevant facts presumed known. But supportiveness alone is not enough; the warrant of a claim also depends on how warranted the reasons that support it are, independent of the claim itself. This avoids a vicious circle: eventually we arrive at sensory evidence, which neither has nor stands in need of warrant; without leaving the whole mesh of evidence dangling in mid-air, for sensory evidence anchors it in the world. But even supportiveness and independent security together are not enough; the warrant of a claim also depends on how much of the relevant evidence the evidence includes—for however supportive and however secure the evidence is, it won't give strong warrant to the claim in question if it omits some essential facts. It is because comprehensiveness is one determinant of quality of evidence that thorough inquiry requires not only sifting and weighing the available evidence, but also, when necessary, seeking out additional evidence (which reminds me to remind you of the two meanings of "partial": "biased" and "incomplete").

Even working on some question alone, without benefit of collaborators or rivals, involves a kind of dialogue with yourself: trying out a conjecture, imagining possible objections, working out possible responses—or simply looking over what you typed yesterday, and asking yourself, "what *was* I thinking?" But life is short; and rather than seeking out evidence for ourselves, first-hand, most of the time we depend on what others tell us. I rely on an airline representative's answer to a question about plane schedules; a historian relies on a colleague's authentication of a document; astronomers rely on observations made by another team in another hemisphere, or on observations made in China a millennium ago. Often enough we interpret what others say, and take their competence and honesty for granted, without giving the matter serious thought; but sometimes we have to struggle to understand what they say or write, and sometimes we suspect they may be confused or misinformed, or may have reason to deceive us. And even when evidence-sharing seems effortless, it depends implicitly on the grounds each inquirer has for justified confidence in others' competence and honesty.

Both cooperation and competition can advance inquiry. Cooperation can enable productive division of labor and the pooling of evidential resources; competition can be a powerful incentive to intellectual effort, and to honesty. And of course the engagement of many people, whether cooperatively or competitively, extends the time available for seeking out and scrutinizing evidence. Indeed, one strength of natural-scientific inquiry is precisely that (even though research projects are doubtless sometimes rushed or cut short because a grant is running out, or because a publication deadline must be met, or … etc.) a question can be pursued by generation after generation of scientific workers until a solution is finally reached. Unfortunately, however, both cooperation and competition can turn sour and counter-productive.

Cooperation may be real mutual help; but it can turn into mere mutual support and boosterism. Competition may be honest mutual criticism or honest rivalry for priority; but it can breed mere rhetoric and counter-rhetoric, posturing and counter-posturing. And at its worst, competition gone sour can even lead to the misrepresentation, distortion, or concealment of evidence.

We sometimes describe disagreements among proponents of rival scientific theories or historical claims as "debates"; and participants in such controversies sometimes engage in something that looks a lot like advocacy. Moreover, eloquence and appeals to authority sometimes produce an artificial scientific consensus, at least temporarily. But disagreements among inquirers, unlike debates between rival advocates, can't be decided by a vote on the basis of rival presentations; they will settle on a conclusion only if and when the evidence brings the community of inquirers to a genuine, unforced consensus.

When we need the answer to some question in a hurry, we may be obliged to curtail our search for further evidence, as well as our scrutiny of the evidence already in hand—as we may choose to do when the question doesn't seem important enough to warrant the time and trouble a thorough search or scrutiny would take, or when an answer already seems well-enough warranted that additional effort would be a waste of time. And we are often faced with urgent practical problems—a medical emergency, say, when a decision about treatment must be made at once, and can't wait for new evidence to settle disagreement in the field; or an intelligence emergency, where some action must be taken now, on information known to be incomplete. In such circumstances, we have no choice but to decide what to do on the basis of whatever evidence we have—if we're wise, taking what backup precautions we can against the possibility that the evidence in hand is misleading.

All this has a quite direct bearing on legal determinations of truth. But as we leave the epistemological high ground for the legal bramble-patch, we encounter a dense tangle of questions. For example: To what extent do legal and epistemological conceptions of evidence coincide, and how, where, and why do they diverge? They coincide only partially, for the law focuses on evidence that can be produced in court: i.e., on testimony, and sometimes on physical things—photographs, weapons, etc.—which would more likely be classified by an epistemologist as the objects of sensory evidence. What could epistemology tell us about such legal notions as proof beyond a reasonable doubt, the weight of evidence, the preponderance of evidence? My epistemology, at any rate, has a good deal to say about what makes evidence better or worse, a claim more or less warranted, but much less about the specific grades of proof that are of peculiar legal concern; which—if Richard Posner's report that judges' estimates of what degree of probability represents "beyond a reasonable doubt" range from 75% to 95% is anything to go by[8]—seem to be quite vague. What could epistemology contribute to the debate between "fact-based" and "story-based" approaches in the "New Evidence Scholarship"?[9] Etc., etc. But here I will focus on two radical epistemological criticisms of common-law evidentiary procedure: C. S. Peirce's critique of adversarialism, and Jeremy Bentham's critique of exclusionary rules of evidence.

3 THE EPISTEMOLOGICAL CRITIQUE OF ADVERSARIALISM

"Some persons fancy that bias and counter-bias are favorable to the extraction of truth—that hot and partisan debate is the way to investigate. This is the theory of our atrocious legal procedure. But Logic puts its heel upon this suggestion"; thus C. S. Peirce, the greatest of American philosophers, in a discussion of the methods of inquiry.[10] Almost a century later, Judge Marvin Frankel would write that "[w]e proclaim to each other and to the world that the clash of adversaries is a powerful means for hammering out the truth.... [But d]espite our untested statements of self-congratulation, we know that others searching after facts—in history, geography, medicine, whatever—do not emulate our adversarial system."[11]

Advocacy is, indeed, a very different enterprise from inquiry. An advocate's business is to make the strongest possible case that this—his side's—answer is the true one; so he will be most effective if he selects and emphasizes whatever evidence favors the proposition in question, and ignores or plays down the rest. Moreover, Peirce was right to warn that when "it is no longer the reasoning which determines what the conclusion shall be, but the conclusion which determines what the reasoning shall be" the inevitable result will be "a rapid deterioration of intellectual vigor"—"man loses his conception of truth and of reason," and comes to think of reasoning as "merely decorative," until

8 Richard Posner, *Frontiers in Legal Theory* (Cambridge, MA: Harvard University Press, 2001), 367. However, I don't believe, as Posner apparently does, that legal degrees of proof can be equated with mathematical probabilities; see "Legal Probabilism: An Epistemological Dissent," pp. 47–77 in this volume, 56–64.

9 See Richard Lempert, "The New Evidence Scholarship," in *Probability and Inference in the Law of Evidence: The Uses and Limits of Bayesianism*, eds. Tillers and Green, 61–102; and "Epistemology and the Law of Evidence: Problems and Projects," pp. 1–26 in this volume, 20–21.

10 Charles Sanders Peirce, *Collected Papers*, eds Charles Hartshorne, Paul Weiss, and (vols. 7 and 8) Arthur Burks (Cambridge, MA: Harvard University Press, 1931–58), 2.635 (1878); also in *Writings: A Chronological Edition*, eds. Peirce Edition Project (Indianapolis, IN: Indiana University Press, 1982 –), 3: 331.

11 Marvin F. Frankel, "The Search for Truth: An Umpireal View," *University of Pennsylvania Law Review* 123, no.5 (1975): 1031–59, 1036.

"the truth for him is that for which he fights."[12] To allow a clash of "bias and counter-bias" to replace a search for and scrutiny of evidence in the sciences, history, etc., really would be, as Peirce insisted, a recipe for disaster (a disaster that presently constitutes a real threat to our academic, indeed our intellectual, culture).[13] However, Peirce's assumption that the theory of our legal procedure is that allowing rival advocates to have at it is a good way to inquire is, to say the least, a considerable over-simplification.

First: science is—or rather, the sciences are—best conceived as a loose federation of kinds of empirical inquiry; but a legal system might be better described as a set of rules and machinery for resolving disputes and making it possible for people to live together in some kind of order. Not that inquiry is irrelevant to the law; but the reason it is relevant is that we want, not simply resolutions, but substantively *just* resolutions. Moreover, legal inquiry operates under a kind of time constraint not relevant to physics, history, etc.; for, with good reason, the law seeks, in the words of Justice Blackmun, "quick, final and binding ... judgment"[14]—the desideratum of promptness imposing time constraints at one end of the process, and the desideratum of finality-and-bindingness at the other.

Second, our adversarial system isn't advocacy all the way down; a trial is only one stage of the process, after the investigations of the police or the FBI, the attorneys for each side and their investigators, after an indictment, and so on. Although in a sense (as the Supreme Court averred in a 1966 ruling) "[t]he basic purpose of a trial is the determination of truth,"[15] a trial is really quite unlike a scientific or historical investigation. Rather, it is a late stage of a whole process in which a decision is made as to a defendant's guilt or liability, the stage at which the finder of fact sifts through the evidence presented by the advocates for each side and assesses whether it establishes guilt or liability to the required degree of proof.[16] Moreover, legal determinations are constrained not only by the desire to arrive at factually correct verdicts, but also by other, non-truth-related desiderata: that citizens' constitutional rights must be respected; that it is much worse to convict an innocent man than to acquit a guilty one; and so on.

12 Peirce, *Collected Papers* (note 10 above), 1.57–8 (c.1896).

13 See Susan Haack, "Preposterism and Its Consequences" (1996), reprinted in Haack, *Manifesto of a Passionate Moderate* (note 2 above), 188–208; "Out of Step: Academic Ethics in a Preposterous Environment," in *Putting Philosophy to Work* (note 7 above), 251–68.

14 Daubert v. Merrell Dow Pharm., Inc., 509 U.S. 579, 597 (1993) ("*Daubert* III").

15 Tehan v. United States *ex rel.* Shott, 382 U.S. 406, 416 (1966).

16 "A late," rather than "the final" stage, since a full account would include the appeals process.

So the question is *not*, as Peirce apparently took for granted, simply whether "hot and partisan debate is the way to investigate"; rather, it is whether an adversarial trial conducted in accordance with the rules of evidence, in combination with pre-trial investigation itself undertaken in the knowledge that the trial will be conducted in this way and subject to these rules, and given the concern for promptness and finality as well as constitutional constraints and other non-epistemological desiderata, is a tolerably good way of arriving at verdicts that often enough find guilty defendants guilty and innocent defendants not guilty, and compensate deserving but not undeserving plaintiffs.

Obviously it is not within the competence of epistemology alone to tell us what weight to give considerations about efficiency in arriving at the truth and what to such other desiderata as promptness and finality; nor, therefore, to tell us how good an approximation to invariably true verdicts is "tolerably good," since this requires just such weighing of epistemological values against values of other kinds. As I see it, while justice delayed *is* justice denied, nonetheless late *is* better than never; so that, e.g., we certainly should be willing to consider revision of rules about the introduction of new evidence, etc., now that DNA analysis can reveal whether someone convicted of a long-ago crime was actually the perpetrator. But I want to concentrate here on the epistemological core of our question.

The best case that could be made for the epistemological efficacy of an adversarial system, given the special circumstances under which the legal search for truth is conducted, would run somewhat as follows. Since for good reason the legal process, unlike the process of scientific inquiry, has to be concluded within a relatively short time-frame, we need a way of ensuring that the search for and scrutiny of evidence are as thorough as that time-frame allows. An adversarial system is one way to do this. If everyone involved knows that eventually, at the trial stage, the determination will be made by an impartial jury weighing the evidence developed and presented by the parties, each subject to cross-examination by the other, this should encourage precisely the kind of thoroughness we are aiming to achieve. For an advocate's goal is to win; so counsel for each party is motivated to seek out evidence favoring his side of the case, and to bring out the flaws in evidence pointing the other way. To be sure, the process isn't perfect; but it is a reasonable substitute for the ideal, as something not dissimilar might be in the case of an urgent medical or intelligence decision.

This optimistic argument is right, up to a point: the adversarial process *can* enable thorough evidential search and scrutiny. However, the optimistic argument is right *only* up to a point: the adversarial process will enable thorough evidential search and scrutiny only if, for example, the resources available to each side for seeking out and scrutinizing evidence are adequate and comparable, if juries are willing and able to decide cases on the basis of the evidence, etc. And this obliges us to ask how well the adversarial process we actually have really works.

Our present trial system, with its very specific, formalized division of labor, is of course an artifact of history. In early medieval times English courts relied on in-court tests by oath and ordeal; and even when, later, jury trials became common, they differed significantly from jury trials today. For example, jurors might be specially chosen for their special expertise, or they might be allowed to go around the town investigating the alleged offense for themselves.[17] Certainly our present system is a better way of arriving at factually correct verdicts than trials by oath or ordeal; probably it is better than those early jury trials (though the specialized jury may have had its merits—after all, a panel of physicians would likely be better than a random selection of lay persons at assessing the evidence relevant to an emergency medical decision). But it certainly isn't perfect—as, if we could ask him, Thomas Barefoot might tell us.

After Mr. Barefoot was convicted of capital murder in the state of Texas, two psychiatrists testified at his sentencing hearing (as required by the Texas death-penalty statute) as to the likelihood that he would be dangerous in future. Neither had ever met him; and one, Dr. Grigson—who testified that there was a "*one hundred percent and absolute*" chance that Barefoot would commit future acts of violence[18]—was so notorious for his pro-prosecution testimony at such hearings that he had earned the nickname "Dr. Death." (Between 1973 and 1994 he testified in over 140 capital cases, in more than 90% of which the jury sentenced the defendant to death.)[19] Questioned by Mr. Barefoot's attorney about studies showing that psychiatric predictions of future dangerousness are wildly unreliable, Dr. Holbrook said he disagreed with their conclusion, and Dr. Grigson said he wasn't familiar with most of them, but in any case they were accepted by only a "small minority group" of psychiatrists. Mr. Barefoot was duly sentenced to death.

When the case found its way to the US Supreme Court, the American Psychiatric Association (APA) submitted an amicus brief acknowledging that

[17] Frederic William Maitland, *The Forms of Action at Common Law*, eds. A. H. Chaytor and W. J. Whittaker (Cambridge: Cambridge University Press, 1909), lecture II; Stephan Landsman, "Of Witches, Madmen, and Product Liability: An Historical Survey of the Use of Expert Testimony," *Behavioral Science and Law* 13, no.2 (1995): 131–57.

[18] Barefoot v. Estelle, 463 U.S. 880, 919 (1983) (Blackmun, J., dissenting).

[19] Thomas Regnier, "*Barefoot* in Quicksand: The Future of 'Future Dangerousness' Predictions in Death Penalty Sentencing in the World of *Daubert* and *Kumho*," *University of Akron Law Review* 37, no.3 (2004): 467–507, 481, n.80.

two out of three psychiatric predictions of future dangerousness are mistaken. However, in his ruling for the majority—observing that the APA didn't say that such predictions were wrong *all* the time, only *most* of the time—Justice White dismissed the argument that the jury should not have been allowed to hear this evidence; relevant federal and state law anticipates, he pointed out, that cross-examination and the presentation of contrary evidence are the appropriate means of unmasking dubious testimony.[20] This probably wasn't much comfort to Mr. Barefoot, who was executed in 1984.

To be sure, we don't have a definitive list of who is really guilty and who is not, who is really liable and who is not, against which to check whether our adversarial process results in jury verdicts that are usually, often, or rarely factually sound. Nevertheless, we have ample reason to think that the process fails dismayingly often: those DNA exonerations, for one thing—which are likely only the tip of the iceberg, since every innocent person exonerated by DNA was convicted on some evidence, probably evidence of a kind on which other innocent people were also convicted who *can't* be exonerated by DNA because there is no biological material to test; and the sometimes wildly inconsistent verdicts in tort cases involving the same chemicals, drugs, or devices and the same alleged damage, for another. On this point, I fear, Peirce only exaggerates: "We employ twelve good men and true to decide a question, we lay the facts before them with the greatest care, the 'perfection of human reason' presides over the presentment, they hear, they go out and deliberate, they come to a unanimous opinion, and it is generally admitted that the parties to the suit might almost as well have tossed up a penny to decide! Such is man's glory!"[21]

A hoary old joke defines a jury as "twelve people whose job it is to decide which side has the better lawyer." We laugh; but uneasily, for we know that the resources available to many criminal defendants are pitifully small, and that the contingency-fee system can't always redress the inequality of resources of an individual plaintiff and a mammoth corporate defendant. There are grounds for doubting even that the system ensures that evidential search and scrutiny is most thorough when there is most at stake.[22]

Again, we read that better-educated potential jurors are likelier to find ways to avoid jury-duty, and likelier to be challenged if they are empaneled. Besides

[20] *Barefoot* (note 18 above), 898.

[21] Peirce, *Collected Papers* (note 10 above), 1.626 (1898).

[22] At the time of Mr. Barefoot's conviction and sentencing, the sum available for an indigent Texas defendant in a death-penalty case for "investigation and experts" was $500; one wonders how much might have been spent at that time by the defense team for, say, a Hollywood celebrity accused of shoplifting, or a sports star accused of sexual assault.

the expensive jury consultants employed in high-profile cases, now there is demographically-based computer software to help attorneys identify which members of a jury pool may be expected to be sympathetic to their side, which to be sympathetic to the other, and which neutral.[23] We may even begin to lose our grip on what it means for a jury to be "impartial," and to wonder whether it isn't too much to ask that each juror be willing to go with the evidence; isn't it enough that a jury be fairly divided between those prejudiced in one direction and those prejudiced in the other? And now, after watching real jury deliberations on television,[24] I wonder how thoroughly jurors understand judges' instructions, how often one juror succumbs to pressure from the others to conform, and how often jurors compromise on a verdict which, rather than representing anyone's real opinion, simply gets things over with in a way all of them can more or less live with.

Moreover, in our overburdened system, the proportion of cases actually decided by a jury is quite small.[25] And even if, as it may be said, attorneys negotiating a plea bargain or a settlement agreement are simply relying on their assessment of the chances of success at a trial, the optimistic argument now requires a further assumption: that attorneys often enough can and do predict correctly what the result would be if a case were to go to a jury—i.e., it relies not only on the approximation of jury verdicts to the truth, but also on the approximation of attorneys' predictions to jury verdicts.[26]

On top of which, just as competition in inquiry sometimes does, the culture of adversarialism can turn sour and counter-productive. In fact, a central theme of Judge Frankel's now-classic paper was that exactly this was happening: while counsel "must not knowingly break the law or countenance fraud … [w]ithin these unconfining limits, advocates freely employ time-honored

23 Charles Nesson, "Peremptory Challenges: Technology Should Kill Them?" *Law, Probability and Risk* 3 (2003): 1–12, refers to SmartJury (now available only at http://web.archive.org/web/20030216122804/http://www.smartjury.com/).

24 In the series "In the Jury Room," shown on ABC in the summer of 2004.

25 According to a 2001 press report, only 4.3% of federal criminal cases and 1.4% of federal civil cases ended in a jury verdict. See William Glaberson, "Juries, Their Power Under Siege, Find Their Role Is Being Eroded," *New York Times*, March 2, 2001, A1. The same year this paper of mine was first published, a now-celebrated paper by Marc Galanter documented a significant decrease in the absolute number of trials, both federal and state: "Although virtually every other indicator of legal activity is rising, trials are declining not only in relation to cases in the courts but to the size of the population and the size of the economy." Marc Galanter, "The Vanishing Trial: An Examination of Trials and Related Matters in Federal and State Courts," *Journal of Empirical Legal Studies* 1, no.3 (November 2004): 459–570.

26 Now, almost a decade later, I should note the Supreme Court's decision in Lafler v. Cooper, 132 S. Ct. 1376 (2012). For more details, see "Epistemology and the Law of Evidence" (note 9 above), n.98.

tricks and stratagems to block or distort the truth." Attorneys manage strategically "to avoid too much knowledge"; they use the very devices that can test dishonest witnesses and help ferret out falsehoods to make honest witnesses look shifty and competent witnesses look confused; they shop for complaisant experts.[27] As a result, rather than engaging in the thorough search for and scrutiny of evidence that the optimistic argument assumes, they may actually impede it. It's hard to believe that Judge Frankel's reservations apply with any less force now than they did a quarter of a century ago.

In short: an adversarial system is not an inherently hopeless way to determine the truth under the inevitable time-pressures; but there is good reason to fear that the adversarial system we actually have, as it presently functions, is very far from optimal. It's a bit like the pre-publication peer-review system. Asking others in the field to read and comment on work submitted is not an inherently hopeless way to determine what work is worthy of publication.[28] But in philosophy at least, the peer-review system we actually have, as it presently functions—grossly overburdened as more and more people must publish to get tenure, or even to get on tenure-track, corrupted by the many willing to use their position to get friends' work published or to suppress rivals' work, and well-known to be the coach-class of professional publishing, shunned by those with enough frequent-flyer miles to be allowed into the first-class cabin of prestigious-publication-by-invitation—is far from optimal; so far, in fact, that no one really believes (whatever some university administrators profess) that peer review is either a necessary or a sufficient condition of good work.

4 THE EPISTEMOLOGICAL CRITIQUE OF EXCLUSIONARY RULES

In *Barefoot*, Justice Blackmun had written a strongly-worded dissent focused on the evidentiary issues: "The Court holds that psychiatric testimony about a defendant's future dangerousness is admissible, despite the fact that such testimony is wrong two times out of three ... because, it is said, the testimony is subject to cross-examination and impeachment.... [T]his is too much for me.... [W]hen a person's life is at stake, ... a requirement of greater reliability should prevail."[29] Cross-examination and impeachment may not be enough, he argued, when flimsy evidence is presented to jurors in the guise of science.

27 Frankel, "The Search for Truth" (note 11 above), 1038 ff.

28 On the history and current practices of scientific peer review, see "Peer Review and Publication: Lessons for Lawyers," pp. 156–79 in this volume, 158–72.

29 *Barefoot* (note 18 above), 915 (Blackmun, J., dissenting).

At the time, scholars were still debating whether the old *Frye* Rule, according to which novel scientific testimony is admissible only if it is generally accepted in the field to which it belongs,[30] had or hadn't been superseded with the passage of the Federal Rules of Evidence in 1975; for FRE 702 provided simply that the testimony of a qualified expert, including a scientific expert, is admissible if it is relevant and not otherwise excluded by law, and didn't mention *Frye*, or acceptance in the relevant community. The issue was resolved a decade later, in *Daubert*; and this time it was Justice Blackmun who wrote the ruling.

Describing *Frye* as an "austere standard, absent from, and incompatible with, the Federal Rules of Evidence," and acknowledging that "[v]igorous cross-examination, presentation of contrary evidence, and careful instruction on the burden of proof are the traditional and appropriate means of attacking shaky but admissible evidence,"[31] the Court ruled unanimously that the Federal Rules *had* superseded *Frye*. However, in a part of the ruling from which Justices Rehnquist and Stevens dissented, Justice Blackmun added that FRE 702 requires that courts screen proffered expert testimony not only for relevance *but also for reliability*. Though both sides could declare victory—the plaintiffs because *Frye* was set aside, the defendants because expert testimony must now be screened for reliability—the new standard was in some ways more stringent than the old. (One wonders whether Justice Blackmun was remembering *Barefoot*, and hoping that better standards of admissibility would keep out such flimsy evidence as Dr. Death's.)

This, however, brings us directly up against the second radical epistemological criticism of the Anglo-American legal system: that exclusionary rules are inherently at odds with the epistemological desideratum of completeness. This is the main theme of Bentham's treatise on evidence: "[t]he theorem to be proved" is that "merely with a view to rectitude of decision, … no species of evidence whatsoever … ought to be excluded."[32] For evidence to have probative force, it must be not only correct, but also complete; evidence which is true so far as it goes but which omits some essential point can be thoroughly misleading. So, Bentham argues, exclusionary rules are to be avoided; the right way to deal with misleading evidence is to put it in the context of *further* evidence, either by bringing out more details by interrogation, or by introducing other witnesses. By these standards, the English jurisprudence on the

30 Frye v. United States, 293 F. 1013 (D.C. Cir. 1923).

31 *Daubert* III (note 14 above), 596.

32 Bentham, *Rationale of Judicial Evidence* (note 4 above), vol. 1, 1.

subject of evidence, with its thicket of exclusionary rules, he continues, is "incompetent … to the discovery of truth, … incompetent, therefore, … to the purposes of justice"—as, Bentham adds, is almost every rule that has ever been laid down on the subject.[33]

But does Bentham's critique of English evidence law in 1827 have any relevance to US evidence law here and now? I shall set aside complications posed by the different rules in different states, the different rules for administrative courts, different arrangements for grand juries, etc., etc., and focus on the Federal Rules of Evidence. Rule 102 sounds like something of which Bentham would have approved: the Rules are to be construed so as "to secure fairness in administration, elimination of unjustifiable expense and delay, and … growth and development of the law of evidence to the end that the truth may be ascertained and proceedings justly determined"; and so does rule 402, providing that "all relevant evidence is admissible, except as otherwise provided [by law]…. Evidence which is not relevant is not admissible." Rule 106 even specifically requires completeness: when a written or recorded statement, or part of such a statement, is introduced by one party, the other may require the introduction of any other part or any other recorded statement which ought in fairness to be considered along with it.

Rule 403, however, provides that "[a]lthough relevant, evidence may be excluded if its probative value is substantially outweighed by the danger of unfair prejudice, confusion of the issues or misleading the jury, or by considerations of undue delay, waste of time, or needless presentation of cumulative evidence"; and in fact the mesh of rules intended to keep out confusing or misleading evidence is not so different, probably, from the English evidence law that Bentham had condemned so severely. True, Bentham allows that rules excluding evidence on grounds of "delay, vexation or expense" are justifiable, provided the non-truth-related evil they prevent outweighs the truth-related evil they cause.[34] But while he might have approved of some of our policy-related exclusionary rules, he specifically argued against spousal privilege[35]—which he describes as "grant[ing] to every man a license to commit all sorts of wickedness, in the presence and with the assistance of his wife";[36] and I doubt

33 *Id.*, vol. 1, 4.

34 *Id.*, vol. 1, 3.

35 See Charles Alan Wright and Peter J. Henning, *Federal Practice and Procedure* (Eagan. MN: Thomson Reuters, 2009), vol. 2A, §405, citing Trammel v. United States, 455 U.S. 40, 53 (1980): "the witness spouse alone has a privilege to refuse to testify adversely; the witness may be neither compelled to testify nor foreclosed from testifying."

36 Bentham, *Rationale of Judicial Evidence* (note 4 above), vol. 5, 340.

he would have approved of, e.g., Rule 407, providing that evidence of subsequent measures which, had they been taken sooner, might have prevented the damage for which the defendant is being sued, is not admissible to prove negligence, culpable conduct, etc.—presumably intended, among other things, to avoid discouraging landlords from fixing wonky steps and such.

More to the epistemological point, however, is Bentham's discussion of hearsay. Bentham classifies this as a species of "inferior evidence," because it is liable to "a characteristic fraud": the fact that the person whose words are reported cannot be cross-examined constitutes an incentive to lying. Nevertheless, he argues, "[w]hen standing by itself, this evidence, if false, is not at all dangerous; it would have nothing to support it, and would probably be falsified by ascertained circumstances." At the same time, "[i]n connection with other proofs, it may be necessary for explaining and completing a series of facts." As with "casual written evidence," "[i]ts exclusion may occasion the loss of information which cannot be obtained in any other way."[37] So he would admit such evidence unless the secondary witness is available to testify in person. This, of course, runs almost exactly contrary to the Federal Rules, which *exclude* hearsay evidence unless otherwise provided, but allow numerous exceptions—many of them applicable even if the out-of-court declarant is available as a witness. These exceptions—testimony as to secondary witnesses' statements of their sense impressions at the time they spoke, excited utterances, dying declarations, then-existing mental, emotional or physical conditions, as well as recorded recollections, etc., etc.—are allowed on the grounds that such hearsay supposedly satisfies adequate "indicia of reliability...."

Bentham is certainly correct in regarding completeness of evidence as an epistemological desideratum—though I would prefer to put the point gradualistically: comprehensiveness of evidence is one determinant of degree of warrant. However, it follows *neither*, as Bentham believes, that the best strategy is to let in all relevant evidence, *nor* that the best strategy is to try to exclude relevant but unreliable evidence. It doesn't follow that more evidence is always better than less, so that the policy should be to let it all in; for additional-but-still-incomplete evidence *may* lead us in the wrong direction, while the previously available even-more-incomplete evidence would have led us in the right direction. This is why Bentham reaches for those modal qualifiers as he argues that if hearsay evidence is false, other evidence will "probably" show it to be so, and that hearsay evidence "may be" necessary to fill in the gaps in

37 Jeremy Bentham, *A Treatise on Judicial Evidence*, ed. M. Dumont (1825; Littleton, CO: Fred B. Rothman and Co., 1981), 201, 202, 200.

other testimony. But it doesn't follow, either, that since we don't have all the evidence, the policy should be to exclude potentially unreliable stuff. This is why, when Judge Posner argues in favor of exclusionary rules, he too reaches for words like "may," and "probably."[38] Both strategies have benefits; both have drawbacks.

As even a brief exploration of the exclusionary strategy with respect to expert testimony as it plays out in *Daubert* and its progeny suggests, crafting effective rules specifying indicia of reliability is harder than it sounds. For one thing, while reliability is a matter of degree, an expert's testimony must either be admitted, or not. For another, if courts decide *with respect to each expert* whether his testimony should be admitted, in whole or in part, they may fail to recognize that the testimony of several experts might, in some instances, fit together in an explanatory story to give more credibility to a fact in issue than the testimony of any one would do. This is in effect an application of Bentham's point that additional evidence may change the complexion of the evidence we already have; and also a kind of corollary of my theory: as the way a crossword entry interlocks with others may reasonably raise our confidence that it is correct, the way that, e.g., an epidemiological study suggesting a weak correlation of substance S with disorder D interlocks with toxicological results suggesting a possible mechanism by which S might sometimes cause this or that physiological damage, may reasonably increase our confidence that the statistical results are not misleading.[39]

Moreover, as the Supreme Court has gradually modified and amplified what it said in *Daubert* about how to determine reliability, it has left more and more to courts' discretion. According to *Daubert*, courts are to look to a potential witness's methodology, not his conclusions, and may refer to such factors as falsifiability, the known or potential error rate, peer-review and publication, and general acceptance in the scientific community. In *Joiner*,[40] however—ruling that, even though excluding expert testimony may well be outcome-determinative, the standard of review for such evidentiary decisions is abuse of discretion, not some more stringent standard—the Supreme Court quietly

[38] Richard Posner, *Frontiers in Legal Theory* (note 8 above), chapters 11 and 12, *passim*; see e.g., p. 350: trial by jury "may" produce in Darwinian fashion a higher quality of lawyer than bench trials, in which a judge "may" seek to compensate for the inadequacies of the weaker lawyer.

[39] See Susan Haack, "An Epistemologist Among the Epidemiologists" (2004), reprinted in Haack, *Putting Philosophy to Work* (note 7 above), 195–98; "Correlation and Causation: The 'Bradford Hill Criteria' in Epidemiological, Legal, and Epistemological Perspective," pp. 239–63 in this volume, 258–61; and "Proving Causation: The Weight of Combined Evidence" pp. 208–38 in this volume, 206–38.

[40] Gen. Elec. Co. v. Joiner, 522 U.S. 136 (1997) ("*Joiner* III").

abandoned the distinction between methodology and conclusions on which it had relied in *Daubert*. And in *Kumho Tire*—ruling that *Daubert* applies to *all* expert testimony, not only the scientific—the Supreme Court noted that the factors on *Daubert*'s "flexible" list may or may not be apropos, depending on the kind of expertise involved; courts may use any, all, or none of them, or, where appropriate, others of their own devising.[41]

In a way, *Kumho*'s advice—in effect, that courts should use whatever indicators of reliability are appropriate in a particular case and with respect to a particular witness[42]—seems supremely sensible. (Think of the expert on police training techniques in *Berry*,[43] excluded for lack of peer-reviewed publications; of the forensic document examiner in *Starzecpyzel*,[44] admitted after a *Daubert* hearing the conclusion of which was that *Daubert* didn't apply; or of Mr. Carlson, the tire expert in *Kumho Tire*, with his "visual-inspection method"[45]—he looked at the tires.) On the one hand, readily applicable, specific criteria, such as whether the evidence has been published in a peer-reviewed journal, don't identify the reliable-enough reliably enough; but on the other hand, as the *Kumho* Court acknowledges, its much less specific advice relies heavily on courts' discretion—it's rather like advising someone to "do the right thing." In practice, it seems, while since *Daubert* federal courts have been tougher in excluding dubious expert testimony proffered by plaintiffs in tort cases, they have been less so with dubious forensic testimony in criminal cases.

And in Texas, apparently, *plus ça change, plus c'est la même chose.* After repeated reprimands for his irresponsible testimony in Texas capital cases, Dr. Grigson was expelled from the APA in 1995; but even after his expulsion he continued to testify for the state of Texas. The Texas rules of evidence are modeled on the Federal Rules; and in 1995 the Texas Supreme Court adopted *Daubert*.[46] In *Nenno*, a 1998 capital-murder case, the Texas Court of Criminal Appeals ruled that the testimony of a supervisor from the FBI Behavioral Science Unit that a person matching the description established

41 Kumho Tire Co. v. Carmichael, 526 U.S. 137, 141 (1999): "Daubert's list of specific factors neither necessarily nor exclusively applies to all experts or in every case."

42 "[W]e can neither rule out, nor rule in, for all cases and for all time the applicability of the factors mentioned in Daubert.... Too much depends upon the particular circumstances of the particular case at issue." *Id.*, 150.

43 Berry v. City of Detroit, 25 F.3d 1342 (6th Cir. 1994).

44 United States v. Starzecpyzel, 880 F. Supp. 1027 (S.D.N.Y. 1995).

45 *Kumho Tire* (note 41 above), 146.

46 E.I. du Pont de Nemours & Co. v. Robinson, 923 S.W.2d 549, 556 (Tex. 1995). The ruling in *Robinson* also introduced two additional "*Daubert*" factors of its own: whether the technique depends on subjective judgments, and whether it has non-judicial uses.

by evidence in the case "would be an extreme threat to society"[47] was admissible; arguing that the *Daubert* factors need not apply outside the context of "hard science"—and thus using the fact that predictions of future dangerousness are not "hard science" to justify a *lower* standard of admissibility.[48] This decision preceded *Kumho*: but so far as I can see, there is nothing in *Kumho Tire*—which was cited approvingly in Texas evidentiary case law just a month after it was decided[49]—that would have precluded it.

Because *Daubert* shifted some of the responsibility for determining the quality of evidence away from the jury, the traditional decider of fact, to the courts, it has prompted debate over whether judges or juries are likely to be better at assessing the worth of complex and perhaps arcane expert evidence. As I said in "Epistemology and the Law of Evidence," I think there is probably no good answer to this question, beyond "it depends on the judge, the jury, and the evidence in question."[50] The more important point is that our rules of evidence are not designed to compensate for failures of the adversarial system; for as the author of a text on the FRE observes, noting that except in egregious cases ("plain error") a potentially reversible exclusion will not be considered on appeal unless it was first brought to the attention of the trial court, "[t]he adversary system, based on party responsibility, is deeply engrained in our jurisprudence, *particularly in the field of evidence*."[51]

And now we see that, just as the inclusive strategy that Bentham urges would work poorly unless the advocates for the parties do a decent job of seeking out relevant evidence and of revealing the flaws in the dubious stuff admitted along with everything else, so too the exclusionary strategy built into our rules of evidence will also work poorly unless the parties do a decent job of challenging dubious stuff to get it excluded. And thinking, for example, of how much more feasible it is likely to be for a mammoth corporation than for an indigent criminal defendant to make a *Daubert* challenge to proffered expert testimony, we see that tweaking the rules of evidence is not the way to compensate for large discrepancies in the parties' resources.

~

Hence my conclusion: "The American Way"—the way of adversarialism and of exclusionary rules—isn't an inherently bad way to determine the truth in

47 Nenno v. Dretke, No. Civ.A.H 02 4907, 2006 WL 581271, *1 (S.D. Tex. Mar. 7, 2006) (quoting from the transcript of Mr. Nenno's trial).

48 Nenno v. State, 970 S.W.2d 549, 561 (Tex. Crim. App. 1998) (overruled on other grounds).

49 Godsey v. State, 989 S.W.2d 482, 490 (Tex. App. 1999).

50 "Epistemology and the Law of Evidence" (note 9 above), 26.

51 Michael Graham, *Federal Rules of Evidence in a Nutshell* (St. Paul, MN: West Publishing, 6th ed., 2003), 19.

legal disputes; but as it presently works it isn't nearly as good a way as we would ideally like it to be. In general, of course, what legal way of determining the truth will work best at a given place or time is likely to depend in complicated ways on matters of history, culture, economics, and social mores; and for our legal system to work significantly better would probably take changes not only within the system itself, but also in the larger social context in which it operates. But I'm not sure it's for a "person of mere theory" like myself to offer detailed proposals about how such improvements, so desirable from the point of view of justice, might be achieved

—3—

Legal Probabilism: An Epistemological Dissent

> [I]t is clear that some things are almost certain, while others are matters of hazardous conjecture. For a rational man, there is a scale of doubtfulness, from simple logical and arithmetical propositions and perceptive judgments, at one end, to such questions as what language the Myceneans spoke or "what song the Sirens sang" at the other.... [T]he rational man, who attaches to each proposition the right degree of credibility, will be guided by the mathematical theory of probability *when it is applicable*.... The concept "degree of credibility," however, is applicable much more widely than that of mathematical probability.
>
> —Bertrand Russell[1]

Russell's right. The mathematical calculus of probabilities is perfectly fine *in its place*; but that place is a limited one. In particular, this mathematical calculus sheds little or no light on the crucial concept Russell calls "rational credibility," and I call "warrant." One consequence, as I shall argue here, is that we can't look to probability theory for an understanding of degrees and standards of proof in the law, but must look, instead, to an older and less formal branch of inquiry: epistemology.

In §1, I argue in some detail why legal standards of proof are best understood in terms of the degree to which the evidence presented must warrant the conclusion (of the defendant's guilt or liability) for a case to be made. In §2, I show that it follows from my epistemological analysis that degrees of warrant cannot be identified with mathematical probabilities; and so, that "legal probabilism"—by which I mean the thesis that legal degrees of proof are to be identified with the probabilities that figure in the mathematical calculus of

[1] Bertrand Russell, *Human Knowledge, Its Scope and Limits* (New York: Simon and Schuster, 1948), 381. ("Perceptive," here, doesn't have its usual meaning, "insightful," but means, simply, "perceptual.")

probability—is misguided. These arguments are completely general, applying to any kind of legal probabilism. The rest of the paper, however, will focus specifically on one popular form of legal probabilism—subjective Bayesianism; and will show how subjective-Bayesian accounts fail, and my approach succeeds, in advancing our understanding of the evidence in two famous, and famously complicated, cases. In §3, I show that Kadane and Schum's subjective-Bayesian analysis of evidence in the Sacco and Vanzetti case is seriously flawed—and that my approach can do significantly better; and in §4, to make clear that, though it isn't probabilistic, my approach is nonetheless perfectly capable of accommodating statistical evidence appropriately, I turn to Finkelstein and Fairley's subjective-Bayesian analysis of the evidence in *Collins*, showing that it, too, is seriously flawed—and, again, that my approach can do significantly better.

1 STANDARDS OF PROOF ARE BEST UNDERSTOOD AS DEGREES OF WARRANT

Different legal systems have (or have had) very different ways of determining matters of fact. As I noted briefly in "Epistemology and the Law of Evidence,"[2] in early Anglo-Saxon times courts relied on trial by oath: a defendant would swear before God that he was not guilty, and "oath-helpers" (also known as "compurgators" or "con-jurors") might be required to back him up. Lisi Oliver's book on the history of early English law tells us that around 695 A.D. whether a defendant needed to swear an oath at all, and if so, whether his oath required the backing of oath-helpers, and if so, how many, depended on his rank: the word of the king or a bishop was sufficient without his having to swear an oath; a priest or a deacon had to swear an oath, but didn't need oath-helpers to back it up; a freeman's oath required the support of three oath-helpers of the same rank.[3] Sadakat Kadri's more popular book on the history of trial procedures tells us that in 899 Queen Uta of Germany was acquitted of a charge of adultery only after eighty-two knights swore that she was innocent.[4] Any formal defect in the procedure, Kadri continues—even if the witness himself had removed the sacred relic from the reliquary on which he swore!—excused perjury.[5] Frederic Maitland tells us that the practice of "Wager of Law,"

[2] "Epistemology and the Law of Evidence: Problems and Projects," pp. 1–26 in this volume, 1–3.

[3] Lisi Oliver, *The Beginnings of English Law* (Toronto: University of Toronto Press, 2002), 174 ff.

[4] Sadakat Kadri, *The Trial: A History, From Socrates to O. J. Simpson* (New York: Random House, 2005), 20.

[5] *Ibid.*

i.e., pledging oneself to swear an oath of innocence, wasn't formally abolished in England until 1833.[6]

According to Robert Bartlett, a whole variety of legal "ordeals" emerged during the reign of Charlemagne: trial by cold water, by the cauldron, by the cross, by walking on red-hot ploughshares, etc.[7] In a "trial by hot iron," for example, the defendant would be asked to take hold of a red-hot iron bar, and his wound would later be checked to see whether it had healed cleanly, or had festered—which was taken as a sign of guilt.[8] However, Bartlett continues, trial by ordeal was a last resort, used only when there was no other way to discover the truth.[9] The law of the town of Enns (Austria), granted in the year 1212, provided that in a case of rape the accused had the option of trial by ordeal if there were only two witnesses—but not if there were seven or more.[10] And by 1215, when the fourth Lateran Council forbade priests from taking part in legal ordeals, the practice was already dying out;[11] by 1300, Bartlett writes, it was "everywhere vestigial."[12]

According to George Neilson, trial by combat—in which the merits of a case were decided by physical combat between the parties—was introduced in England under William the Conqueror. An Englishman who chose to avoid the duel, Neilson continues, was subject to trial by ordeal; a Norman who chose not to duel, however, had the option of defending himself by oath.[13] By the time of Henry II, trial by combat had already been confined to a narrow class of cases, and its scope became even narrower as time passed.[14] But English law didn't officially abolish the practice until 1819, when the Appeal of Murder Act was passed—after Abraham Thornton had managed to weasel out of a conviction on a charge of murder by offering to defend himself "with his body."[15]

6 Frederic William Maitland, *The Forms of Action at Common Law*, eds. A. H. Chaytor and W. J. Whittaker (Cambridge: Cambridge University Press, 1909), 14.

7 Robert Bartlett, *Trial by Fire and Water: The Medieval Judicial Ordeal* (Oxford: Clarendon Press, 1986), 9 ff.

8 *Id.*, 21, 33; see also Maitland, *The Forms of Action at Common Law* (note 6 above), Lecture II; Kadri, *The Trial* (note 4 above), chapter 1.

9 Bartlett, *Trial by Fire and Water* (note 7 above), 27–28.

10 *Id.*, 29. (One wonders what happened if there were three, four, five, or six witnesses!)

11 Maitland, *The Forms of Action at Common Law* (note 6 above), Lecture II, suggests that the demise of trial by ordeal was the result of the decision by the fourth Lateran Council; but Michele Taruffo, *La semplice verità: Il guidice e la costruzzione de fatti* (Rome: Editora Laterza, 2009), chapter 1, shows that the Church's decision merely ratified a shift already taking place in legal practice.

12 Bartlett, *Trial by Fire and Water* (note 7 above), 34.

13 George Neilson, *Trial by Combat* (London: Williams and Norgate, 1890), 31–32.

14 *Id.*, 33–36.

15 *Id.*, 328–31.

At its most aggressive, the adversarial culture of US law is sometimes eerily reminiscent of trial by combat; and I have occasionally heard scientists of my acquaintance describe their unhappy experience as expert witnesses under cross-examination as "trial by cold water." And, of course, we still require witnesses to swear under oath to tell "the truth, the whole truth, and nothing but the truth" (though nowadays, I imagine, few seriously believe that lying under oath will provoke divine punishment); and, as I also noted in "Epistemology and the Law of Evidence," rather as in trial by oath the word of the king was held to be sufficient, recently some US courts have held government websites to be self-authenticating.[16]

But here I want to look in detail at burdens and standards of proof in modern legal systems. I will focus here on current US law, where "burden of proof" includes both principles about which party is obliged to produce evidence (also known as the "burden of production"), and principles about which party is obliged to establish the elements of the case to the required degree (also known as the "burden of persuasion").[17] Standards of proof specify the degree or level of proof that must be supplied in various kinds of case:[18] "beyond a reasonable doubt" in a criminal case; "by a preponderance of the evidence" or "more probably than not" in ordinary civil cases; and "clear and convincing" evidence in special circumstances such as commitment to a mental hospital, the termination of parental rights, denaturalization, the contents of a lost will, etc.[19] And then there's the "reasonable suspicion" or "probable cause" required for a search;[20] and the requirement in the Texas death-penalty statute that the

16 "Epistemology and the Law of Evidence" (note 2 above), 3 and note 15.

17 Michael Graham, *Evidence* (St. Paul: Thomson/West, 2nd ed., 2007), 577–79.

18 Like the common law generally, these standards have gradually evolved over time. One commentator suggests that the highest and most familiar standard, beyond a reasonable doubt, "has been embedded in Anglo-American law for at least seven hundred years, and perhaps well over a thousand years" (Loretta DeLoggio, "Beyond a Reasonable Doubt: A Historical Analysis," *New York State Bar Journal* (April 1986): 19–25, 25). Chadbourn, however, dates a "precise distinction" requiring proof beyond a reasonable doubt in criminal cases to the early 1700s (James H. Chadbourn, ed., *Wigmore on Evidence* (Boston: Little, Brown and Company, 1981), vol. 9, 405). According to Justice Brennan: "[t]he requirement that guilt of a criminal charge be established by proof beyond a reasonable doubt dates at least from our early years as a nation"; and as McCormick puts it, "[the] demand for a higher degree of persuasion in criminal cases was recurrently expressed through ancient times, [though] its crystallization into the formula 'beyond a reasonable doubt' seems to have occurred as late as 1798.'" *In re* Winship, 397 U.S. 358, 361 (1970) (citing McCormick, *Handbook of the Law of Evidence* [St. Paul, MN: West Publishing Co., 1954], 681–82.)

19 Kenneth S. Broun et al., eds., *McCormick on Evidence* (St. Paul, MN: Thomson/West, 2006), vol. 2, 488–89.

20 The terminology of "probable cause" derives from courts' interpretation of the Fourth Amendment to the US Constitution. US Const Amend IV (search and seizure clause).

jury may sentence a defendant to death only if it finds "beyond a reasonable doubt" that "there is a probability" that he will be dangerous in future[21]—"definitely maybe," as a student of mine once put it.

Some assignment of burdens and standards of proof (explicit or implicit)[22] is needed to ensure that a result is reached. And the rationale for the *particular* burdens and standards of proof, likewise, is grounded in policy considerations: most obviously, the requirement that a criminal charge be proven *by the prosecution* and *beyond a reasonable doubt* rests on the idea that it is much worse to convict someone of a crime he didn't commit than to fail to convict someone of a crime he did commit. In *Addington v. Texas* (1979), Chief Justice Burger wrote for the US Supreme Court that, in a typical civil case involving a monetary dispute, the "preponderance" standard ensures that "[t]he litigants … share the risk of error in roughly equal fashion"; while in a criminal case, because the defendant has so much at stake, we require proof "beyond a reasonable doubt" to ensure that "our society imposes almost the entire risk of error upon itself." [23] Such policy considerations are certainly not beyond the reach of philosophical reflection;[24] but they are not my present concern—which is, rather, to understand what these standards of proof amount to.

It's easy enough to order the standards from strongest to weakest: "beyond a reasonable doubt"; "clear and convincing evidence"; "by a preponderance of the evidence"; "reasonable suspicion."[25] None of them, however, is very precisely defined; nor, for that matter, is it clear that precise definitions would be desirable even if they were feasible. (Indeed, some federal circuits advise judges that they shouldn't try to define "reasonable doubt," but should let

Briefly and roughly, there is probable cause "where the known facts and circumstances are sufficient to warrant a man of reasonable prudence in the belief that contraband or evidence of a crime will be found." Ornelas v. United States, 517 U.S. 690, 696 (1996); see also Illinois v. Gates, 462 U.S. 213, 238 (1983).

[21] Texas Code of Crim Proc Ann art 37.071 (Vernon 2006 & Supp 2012).

[22] "Or implicit" because, as I mentioned in "Epistemology and the Law of Evidence" (note 2 above), n.69, I understand that in France, for example, there are no explicit standards.

[23] Addington v. Texas, 441 U.S. 418, 423–24 (1979).

[24] In this context I think of Percy Bridgman's shrewd comment about human beings' tendency to rationalize social institutions that arose in "hit or miss fashion"; "[a] dog is content to turn around three times before lying down, but a man would have to invent an explanation of it." Percy W. Bridgman, "The Struggle for Intellectual Integrity" (1933), in Bridgman, *Reflections of a Physicist* (New York: Philosophical Library, 2nd ed., 1955), 361–79, 368.

[25] Though it may be worth noting that the Appeals Court in *Winship* had suggested that there is only a "tenuous difference" between the reasonable doubt and the preponderance standards—a suggestion which, however, the Supreme Court very firmly rejected. *In re* Winship (note 18 above), 367.

jurors discern its meaning for themselves.)[26] But a more fundamental question really *does* require an answer: what exactly are degrees of proof degrees *of*?

In a concurring opinion in *Winship* (1970), Justice Harlan wrote that the function of standards of proof is to "instruct the factfinder concerning the *degree of confidence* our society thinks he should have in the correctness of factual conclusions for a particular type of adjudication."[27] The authors of the 2006 edition of a well-known textbook, *McCormick on Evidence*, are even more explicitly psychological: the "reasonable doubt" formula, they write, "points to what we are really concerned with, *the state of the jury's mind*"; whereas "preponderance of the evidence" and "clear and convincing evidence" are misleading, because they "*divert attention to the evidence*." But this, they continue, is a step removed from the essential thing, the degree of the juror's belief; the evidence is only "the instrument by which the jury's mind is influenced."[28]

I think this has things exactly backwards. Admittedly, the language in which standards of proof are expressed is in part psychological: at any rate, talk of the "burden of persuasion" sounds subjective, suggesting that the attorney's task is simply to induce a certain state of mind in the jurors; and so does "convincing." But the language of standards of proof is also in part epistemological: the "reasonable" in "beyond a reasonable doubt," like the "clear" in "clear and convincing," sounds objective, since it apparently refers to the quality of the evidence presented. And the epistemological aspect, I believe, is crucial. This is not to say that the fact-finder's degree of confidence in the conclusion is completely irrelevant; after all, a reasonable person will proportion his degree of belief at least approximately to the strength of the evidence—i.e., the better the evidence warrants p, the more confidence he will have that p is true. It *is* to say, however, that the fact-finder's degree of belief is a distinct, and distinctly secondary, matter; *the strength of the evidence is primary*.

A sampling of jury instructions on standards of proof confirms this epistemological understanding. I begin with Florida:

- The standard jury instructions in criminal trials provided by the Supreme Court of Florida contrast an "abiding conviction of guilt" with a conviction that "wavers and vacillates"; but are very clear that "it is to the evidence introduced in this trial, and to this alone, that you must look for proof," and that "[a] reasonable doubt as to the guilt of the

[26] Kevin F. O'Malley et al., eds., *Federal Jury Practice and Instructions: Criminal* (6th ed., Eagan, MN: Thomson/West, 2008, and Supplement 2010), vol. 1A, §12:10, 164.
[27] *In re* Winship (note 18 above), 370 (my italics).
[28] Broun et al., eds., *McCormick on Evidence* (note 19 above), vol. 2, 483.

defendant may arise from the evidence, conflict in the evidence, or the lack of evidence."[29]

- Florida instructions on the preponderance standard focus more centrally on degree of persuasion: "'[g]reater weight of the evidence' means the more persuasive and convincing force and effect of the entire evidence in the case."[30]
- Florida instructions on "clear and convincing evidence," however, again focus centrally on the epistemological: "'[c]lear and convincing' evidence is evidence that is precise, explicit, lacking confusion, and of such weight that it produces a firm belief or conviction, without hesitation, about the matter in issue."[31]

I turn next to federal guidelines—in which we find a good deal of implicit epistemology:

- Federal jury instructions on the criminal standard of proof contrast "reasonable doubt" with merely "possible" doubt: "[p]roof beyond a reasonable doubt ... must be proof of such a convincing character that a reasonable person would not hesitate to rely and act upon it in the most important of his or her affairs."[32] The first circuit has approved a formulation by Judge Keeton: "reasonable doubt may arise not only from the evidence produced but also from a lack of evidence. [It] exists when, after weighing and considering all the evidence, using reason and common sense, jurors cannot say that they have a settled conviction of the truth of the charge."[33] The third circuit has approved this formulation: "The doubt must be reasonable. It is not a mere possible or imaginary doubt.... A reasonable doubt is a fair doubt, based upon reason and common sense.... [A] defendant must never be convicted on mere assumption, conjecture, or speculation."[34] The sixth circuit adds that a reasonable doubt: "may arise from the evidence, the lack of evidence, or the nature of the evidence";[35] the eighth circuit writes that the

29 *Florida Standard Jury Instructions in Criminal Cases* ([Tallahassee, FL?]): The Florida Bar/ LexisNexis, 7th ed., 2009), § 3.7.

30 *Florida Standard Jury Instructions in Civil Cases* ([Tallahassee, FL?]: The Florida Bar/ LexisNexis, 2nd ed., 2010), § 401.3.

31 *Ibid.*

32 O'Malley, et al, *Federal Jury Practice and Instructions: Criminal* (note 26 above), vol. 1A, §12:10, 161.

33 *Id.*, 165 (citing United States v. Cleveland, 106 F.3d 1056, 1062 (1st Cir. 1997)).

34 *Id.*, 171 (citing United States. v. Isaac, 134 F.3d 199, 202 (3d Cir. 1998) (on rehearing)).

35 *Id.*, 174.

presumption of innocence "can be overcome only if the government proves, beyond a reasonable doubt, each essential element of the crime charged";[36] and the ninth that the verdict "may arise from careful and impartial consideration of all the evidence, or from lack of evidence."[37]

- Federal jury instructions on the standard of proof in ordinary civil cases, citing model jury instructions for the ninth circuit, explain that, to find that a case has been made by a "preponderance of the evidence," "you must be persuaded by the evidence that the claim … is more probably true than not true."[38]
- And federal jury instructions explain "clear and convincing evidence" as setting a higher standard than "preponderance of the evidence," requiring that the jury "be persuaded by the evidence that it is highly probable that the claim … is true."[39]

None of these, admittedly, is entirely transparent; but (with the possible exception of the Florida instruction on the "preponderance" standard) they all make it very clear that standards of proof should be understood, *not* as a simple psychological matter of the degree of jurors' belief, but as primarily an epistemological matter, the degree of belief *warranted by the evidence*.

Further confirmation can be found by looking at the circumstances in which a judge may direct or overturn a verdict. The *Manual of Federal Practice* tells us that a court may grant a motion for Judgment as a Matter of Law (JMOL) when either there is a complete absence of proof on one or more material issues, or "there are no controverted issues of fact on which reasonable persons could differ"; i.e., when, viewing the matter in the light most favorable to the party against whom the motion is made, "there can be only one reasonable conclusion." JMOL is improper, however, if the evidence is conflicting, or insufficient to make only one conclusion reasonable.[40] Federal Rule of Criminal Procedure 29 instructs a judge to direct a verdict of acquittal if "the evidence is insufficient to sustain a conviction."[41]

[36] *Id.*, 187.

[37] *Id.*, 189.

[38] Kevin F. O'Malley et al., eds., *Federal Jury Practice and Instructions: Civil* (Eagan, MN: West Group, 5th ed., 2000, and Supplement 2010), §101.41, 53.

[39] *Id.*, §104.03, 143.

[40] Richard A. Givens (updated by Kevin Shirey), *Manual of Federal Practice, 2010 Cumulative Supplement* (New Providence, NJ: Lexis Nexus, 2010), §7.51, 790–91. "JMOL" covers both directed verdicts (where a judge takes the verdict out of the jury's hands) and judgments *n.o.v.* or "notwithstanding the verdict" (where a judge overrides a verdict the jury has already brought in).

[41] Charles Alan Wright and Peter J. Henning, *Federal Practice and Procedure* (Eagan, MN: Thomson Reuters, 4th ed., 2009), Vol. 2A, §467, 362 (the quotation is from the authors' description, not from the text of the rule).

And the Florida Supreme Court has explained that "courts should not grant a motion for judgment of acquittal unless the evidence is such that no view which the jury may lawfully take of it favorable to the opposite party can be sustained under the law."[42]

A robustly epistemological understanding of degrees of proof is not only more faithful to the language of jury instructions and the like than a purely psychological understanding; it is also, and more fundamentally, integral to what is required by the role that standards of proof play in legal proceedings. Articulating what that role is, however, requires some subtlety.

In some trials (though not all) the key issue is a factual one: Did Mrs. Coppolino die of natural causes, or was she poisoned?[43] Was it the defendant, Robert Downing, or someone else, who posed as the Reverend Claymore to obtain goods by fraud?[44] Did Ethel Brownstone really sign the document ostensibly giving these valuables to her niece, or is the signature a forgery?[45] Was it Nicola Sacco and Bartolemeo Vanzetti, or the Morelli gang, who committed the payroll robbery and murder at the Slater and Morrill shoe factory?[46] Was it Janet Collins who knocked over the old lady in an alley and stole her purse, and Malcolm Collins who drove the getaway car, or two other people entirely?[47] Was it his exposure to leaking Toluene that caused Bob Moore's acute respiratory problems, or his history of heavy smoking and asthma?[48] Etc., etc.

In 1996, the Supreme Court wrote in *Tehan* that the "purpose of a trial is the determination of truth."[49] It's true that a verdict is substantively just only if the determination made is factually correct:[50] only, that is, if the defendant convicted of the crime really was the perpetrator, the defendant found liable for an injury really was responsible for causing it.[51] Nevertheless, a trial is very different from an open-ended scientific or scholarly investigation, sifting for as long as it takes through all the evidence that can be had; legal

42 Michael E. Allen, *Florida Criminal Procedure* (Eagan, MN: Thomson Reuters, 2010), §18:13, 750–751 (citing Fitzpatrick v. State, 900 So. 2d 495, 507 (Fla. 2005)).
43 Coppolino v. State, 223 So. 2d 68 (Fla. Dist. Ct. App. 1968).
44 United States v. Downing, 753 F.2d 1224 (3d Cir. 1985).
45 United.States v. Starzecpyzel, 880 F. Supp. 1027 (S.D.N.Y. 1995).
46 See below, §3, pp. 64–71.
47 See below, §4, pp. 71–77.
48 Moore v. Ashland Chem., Inc., 151 F.3d 269 (5th Cir. 1998).
49 Tehan v. United States *ex rel.* Shott, 382 U.S. 406, 416 (1966).
50 Of course, factual truth is only necessary for substantive justice, and not sufficient, which would also require just laws, and just administration of those laws.
51 Courts have sometimes deliberately made exceptions to this principle in civil cases. See "Risky Business: Statistical Proof of Specific Causation," pp. 264–93 in this volume, 268 and note 23.

determinations of fact are subject both to limitations of time and to constraints on how evidence may lawfully be obtained and what evidence may lawfully be presented.[52] What the legal finder of fact is asked to do is *not*, strictly speaking, to determine whether the defendant is guilty, or is liable, but—eschewing guesswork, whim, prejudice, and, as the third circuit puts it, "assumption, conjecture, or speculation"—to determine whether the evidence establishes the defendant's guilt or liability to the required degree.[53]

This obviously requires standards of proof to be understood, *not* simply in terms of the fact-finder's degree of confidence, regardless of whether or not this degree of confidence is appropriate given the evidence, but in terms of what it is *reasonable* to believe in light of the evidence presented. In short, the task of the finder of fact is a paradigmatically epistemological one: to "judge of evidence," in John Stuart Mill's exactly appropriate phase.[54] The fact-finder must determine, as Russell would have put it, whether the evidence presented makes the proposition(s) at issue rationally credible to the required degree; or, in my epistemological vocabulary, *whether the evidence presented warrants the proposition(s) at issue to the required degree.*[55]

2 DEGREES OF WARRANT AREN'T MATHEMATICAL PROBABILITIES

As Ian Hacking observes, throughout its history the concept of probability "has [had] two aspects": it has connections both with the notion of degree of

[52] As I was finishing this paper, Prof. Dershowitz wrote in an editorial on the trial of Casey Anthony (who had just been acquitted of the murder of her two-year-old daughter): "Scientists search for truth. Philosophers search for morality. A criminal trial searches only for … proof beyond a reasonable doubt." Alan M. Dershowitz, "Casey Anthony: The System Worked," *Wall Street Journal*, July 7, 2011, A15.

[53] Since I am speaking primarily about US law, this should, strictly speaking, read "by the *admissible* evidence presented." But I won't keep repeating this; from here on, it should be understood as implicit.

[54] John Stuart Mill, *A System of Logic, Ratiocinative and Inductive: Being a Connected View of the Principles of Evidence and Methods of Scientific Investigation* (1843; 8th ed., London: Longman, Green, 1970), 5.

[55] For a fuller statement of this, see "Epistemology Legalized: Or, Truth, Justice, and the American Way," pp. 27–46 in this volume, 34–35. I wouldn't go as far as Steve Martini's fictional attorney Harry Hines, who believes that "most victories in criminal courts are fashioned from the preponderance of perjury. You spin yours and they do theirs, and in the end the side that is most adept at invention wins"; and that "throughout history truth has withered and died of loneliness in most courtrooms." Steve Martini, *Undue Influence* (New York: G. P. Putnam, 1994), 420. But it is certainly no part of my argument that the legal system always *succeeds* in doing what it aspires to do, arriving at verdicts warranted to the required degree by the evidence presented.

belief warranted by evidence, and with the notion of a "tendency ... to produce stable relative frequencies."[56]

We commonly use the language of probability or likelihood when we talk about the credibility or warrant of a claim—about how probable or how likely is it, given this evidence, that the claim is true, or, unconditionally, about how probable or how likely the claim is. I talk this way myself: e.g., when I wonder how probable or how likely it is, given the evidence we now have, that there is any causal connection between vaccines and autism;[57] or how probable or how likely it is that Egypt will have a genuinely democratic government five years from now. The *Oxford English Dictionary* takes the usual sense of "probable" (in British English) to be "may in view of present evidence be reasonably expected to happen or be the case."[58] Similarly, *Merriam-Webster's Dictionary* gives as its first definition (for American English), "supported by evidence strong enough to establish presumption but not proof."[59]

Closely connected with this core usage is our habit, in conversational speech, of hedging what we say by "probably" when we are reluctant to commit ourselves categorically. When a colleague asks me, "will you be at the talk tomorrow?" and I expect to be, but don't want to be too firmly committed to making it, I may answer, "probably." More generally, we use "probably" and the like when we *think* something is so, but aren't sure: e.g., when I say that the leftovers in the fridge, though past their best, are probably still OK to eat. When the evidence that p is less than overwhelming, recognizing that p *might* turn out to be false, we use "probably" as a way to hedge our commitment.

And of course "probable," etc., also turn up in the language of legal standards of proof: one formulation of the "preponderance" standard is "more probable than not," one formulation of "clear and convincing" is "highly probable," and one formulation of "reasonable suspicion" is "probable cause." The natural and obvious way to understand these legal uses is in the usual, epistemological sense: how reasonable a claim is in the light of the evidence.

But "probable" and its cognates are also the characteristic idiom of gamblers, statisticians, and actuaries. In these uses, rather than hedging our degree of commitment to a claim, "probable" is part of the content of the claim itself:

56 Ian M. Hacking, *The Emergence of Probability* (Cambridge: Cambridge University Press, 1975), 1.

57 An issue discussed briefly in Susan Haack, "Erkendelsesteori: hvem har brug for det?" ("Epistemology: Who Needs It?"), *Kritik* 200 (2011): 26–35.

58 *Oxford English Dictionary Online*, http://www.oed.com.

59 *Merriam-Webster Dictionary Online*, http://www.merriam-webster.com/dictionary/probable.

that there is a 1% chance that a 55 year-old man will die in the next year, a 50% chance that the coin will come up heads, a more than doubled risk of Guillain-Barré Syndrome among those recently vaccinated against swine flu, etc.[60] This is the idiom regimented by the standard probability calculus, interpretable in terms of relative frequencies or propensities.

Many have hoped to shoehorn legal degrees of proof into this more formal mold. Leibniz, for example, called the theory of probability "natural jurisprudence";[61] and George Boole hoped to apply it to "the estimation of the probability of judgments."[62] More recently, legal probabilism has been the subject of prolonged debate among practitioners of the New Evidence Scholarship[63]—a debate that resurfaced in 2010 in the form of an exchange prompted by the recently proposed "restyling" of the Federal Rules of Evidence.[64] This time, it seems, the trigger was the explanation of relevance given in FRE 401: that evidence is relevant just in case it *either raises or lowers the probability* of some fact at issue. It should already be clear, however, that we shouldn't simply *assume*, just because the words "probable," "probably," and "probability" occur in legal contexts, that we are dealing with mathematical, rather than epistemological, probabilities.

Some critics of legal probabilism have expressed skepticism about the possibility of assigning numbers to degrees of proof. "That ... moral probabilities ... could ever be represented by numbers ... and thus be subject to numerical analysis," Thomas Starkie wrote in 1842, "cannot but be regarded as visionary

[60] My last example alludes to the history leading up to the adoption, by some US courts, of a more-than-doubled-risk criterion for specific causation in toxic-tort cases. See "Risky Business" (note 51 above), 270–74.

[61] John Locke, however, had denied that precise rules for calculating legal degrees of proof were possible. I rely on Hacking, *The Emergence of Probability* (note 56 above), 86–87.

[62] George Boole, *The Laws of Thought* (1854; reprinted New York: Dover, n.d.), chapter XXI; the quotation is from 376. On 382, however, Boole acknowledges that "*[f]rom the mere records of the decisions of a court ... it is not possible to deduce any definite conclusion respecting the correctness of the individual judgments of its members.*"

[63] John Kaplan, "Decision Theory and the Factfinding Process," *Stanford Law Review* 20 (1968): 1065–92. See also, e.g., Richard Lempert, "The New Evidence Scholarship: Analyzing the Process of Proof," in Tillers and Green, eds., *Probability and Inference in the Law of Evidence: Uses and Limits of Bayesianism*, 62–102; Roger Park and Michael Saks, "Evidence Scholarship Reconsidered: Results of the Interdisciplinary Turn," *Boston College Law Review* 47 (2005–06): 949–1031.

[64] Michael D. Risinger, et al., "Bayes Wars Redivivus—An Exchange," *International Commentary on Evidence* 8, no. 1, ISSN (Online) 1554–4567, DOI: 10.2202/1554–4567.1115 (November 2010) (a lengthy e-mail exchange among the "authors"). For the proposed "restyling" of the Federal Rules of Evidence, see Robert L. Hinkle, Chair, Advisory Committee on Evidence Rules, memorandum to Honorable Lee H. Rosenthal, Chair, Standing Committee on Rules of Practice and Procedure (May 6, 2009), United States Courts, available at http://www.uscourts.gov/uscourts/RulesAndPolicies/rules/proposed0809/EV_Report.pdf.

and chimerical."[65] Others have argued that precise calculation of probabilities, even if it were feasible, is usually undesirable: Laurence Tribe writes of "The Costs of Precision," such as "the dwarfing of soft variables," and suggests that, in criminal trials, a Bayesian approach may encourage a "presumption of guilt."[66] I agree: it isn't feasible to put precise numbers on degrees of proof; nor would it necessarily be desirable to do so even if we could. But my objection to legal probabilism is more fundamental: I think that identifying legal degrees of proof (which I take to be degrees of epistemic warrant) with mathematical probabilities is a kind of equivocation. On this, I'm with Richard von Mises, who long ago averred that "probability theory has nothing to do with such questions as, 'Is there a probability of Germany being at some time in the future at war with Liberia?'"[67]

There will be some overlap between my arguments and those of other critics of legal probabilism, such as L. Jonathan Cohen[68] (on the philosophical side) and Leonard Jaffee[69] and Ronald Allen[70] (on the legal side).[71] I won't, however, like Cohen, call on any kind of inductive logic, quasi-Baconian or otherwise; for the moral of the "grue" paradox,[72] I believe, is that there *can be no*

65 Thomas Starkie, *A Practical Treatise of the Law of Evidence* (Philadelphia, PA: T. & J. W. Johnson, 7th ed., 1842), vol. 1, 579.

66 Laurence Tribe, "Trial by Mathematics: Precision and Ritual in the Legal Process," *Harvard Law Review* 84 (1971): 1329–93, 1358 (the costs of precision), 1361 (the dwarfing of soft variables), and 1368 (presumption of guilt). This paper was in part a response to Michael O. Finkelstein and William B. Fairley, "A Bayesian Approach to Identification Evidence," *Harvard Law Review* 83, no. 3 (1969–70): 489–517, discussed at length in §4, pp. 71–77 below.

67 Richard von Mises, *Probability, Statistics and Truth* (London: Allen and Unwin, 2nd revised English edition, 1928), 9.

68 L. Jonathan Cohen, *The Provable and the Probable* (Oxford: Clarendon Press, 1977).

69 Leonard R. Jaffee, "Of Probativity and Probability: Statistics, Scientific Evidence, and the Calculus of Chances at Trial," *University of Pittsburgh Law Review* 46 (1984–85): 925–1083.

70 Ronald J. Allen, "A Reconceptualization of Civil Trials" (1986), in Peter Tillers and Eric D. Green, eds., *Probability and Inference in the Law of Evidence: The Uses and Limits of Bayesianism* (Dordrecht, the Netherlands: Kluwer, 1988), 21–60.

71 I note for the record, however, that my epistemological account was developed long before I read either Cohen or Allen.

72 On the "grue" paradox, see Nelson Goodman, "The New Riddle of Induction" (1954) in Goodman, *Fact, Fiction and Forecast* (1954; 2nd ed., Indianapolis, IN: Bobbs-Merrill, 1965), 59–83; on its consequences for the possibility of a syntactically-characterizable inductive logic, see Haack, *Defending Science—Within Reason: Between Scientism and Cynicism* (Amherst, NY: Prometheus Books, 2003), 84–86. It should be said, however, that—though Cohen makes no reference to "grue," and his only reference to Goodman (*The Provable and the Probable* [note 68 above], 184) is not relevant to the present point—one *might* find, reading between the lines of his discussion of "relevant variables" (133 ff.), an implicit acknowledgment that supportiveness is not, after all, wholly formal, but depends in part on material facts. But unfortunately, rather than pursuing the consequences of this key point, Cohen goes on to offer a "logical syntax of inductive probability," presupposing a list of relevant variables (chapter 17).

formal inductive logic. And while there is some distant affinity between the concept of explanatory integration that will play a role in my epistemological account and the "explanatory stories" that play a role in Allen's proposed "reconceptualization of civil trials," these are somewhat different concepts, with different roles in the two accounts—two accounts that, moreover, differ in their purpose.[73]

In brief summary:[74] how warranted a claim is depends on the quality of the evidence—experiential evidence and reasons—with respect to that claim. What makes evidence with respect to a claim better or worse is: (i) how supportive the evidence is; (ii) how secure the reasons are, independent of the claim at issue; and (iii) how comprehensive the evidence is, i.e., how much of the relevant evidence it includes. Evidence may support a claim, or undermine it, or do neither. The better the independent security of reasons supporting a claim, the more warranted the claim is; but the better the independent security of reasons undermining a claim, the less warranted it is; and more comprehensive evidence gives more warrant to a conclusion than less comprehensive evidence does provided that the additional evidence is at least as favorable as the rest.

Still briefly and roughly, whether and if so to what degree evidence is supportive of a claim depends on the contribution it makes to the explanatory integration of evidence-plus-conclusion—on how well the evidence and the conclusion fit together in an explanatory account. In line with this, whether and if so how much support a particular piece of evidence gives to a conclusion depends on whether and if so how much adding that piece of evidence contributes to the explanatory integration of the whole.[75] Think of a crossword

73 Allen, "A Reconceptualization of Civil Trials" (note 70 above), § III; Lempert, "The New Evidence Scholarship" (note 63 above), 84 ff. summarizes Allen's proposal. As his title indicates, Allen's approach is intended to apply only to civil trials—which itself reveals that his preoccupations are more legal than, like mine, epistemological; as does the fact that he gives no account of what makes a story better or worse. Moreover, because it relies on a comparative judgments of plaintiff's and defendant's explanatory stories, Allen's proposal is—again, as his title indicates—*revisionary*, apparently imposing a greater burden on defendants in civil cases than they presently bear. (Allen acknowledges [45] the possible objection that his account rests on the distinction between a simple denial of the plaintiff's case and an affirmative allegation of the defendant's case; and replies that he sees this, not as a categorical distinction, but as a matter of degree.)

74 Fuller details can be found in "Epistemology and the Law of Evidence" (note 2 above), 12–16.

75 My concept of explanatory integration differs from the more familiar concept of "inference to the best explanation" in two ways: it is not, like "inference to the *best* explanation," optimizing, but gradational; and it is, not, like "inference *to* the best explanation," one-directional, but goes up and back, conceiving of *explanans* and *explanandum* as mutually explanatory. And perhaps, to forestall any misunderstanding, I should reiterate that my

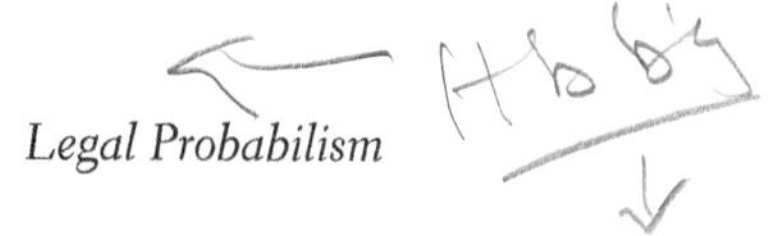

entry that fits snugly with its clue and other completed entries, but where one of those other entries in particular—perhaps the one with an "x" in the middle—is especially significant because, without it, the overall fit would be much looser; this is the analogue of a piece of evidence the support of which is particularly crucial with respect to some conclusion.

The determinants of evidential quality, and hence of warrant, are not entirely formal, but in part material.[76] In other words, whether evidence is relevant to a claim can depend on facts about the world: e.g., whether the defendant's wound's having healed cleanly is relevant to his guilt, as the practice of trial by hot iron presupposed, depends on whether it is true that God will protect the falsely accused from harm; whether the effect of this drug on rats is relevant to its effect on humans depends on whether rats are similar to humans in the salient physiological respects, whether the substance the rats are given is exactly the same as the drug humans will take, etc.[77] And so on.

As we saw, a piece of evidence is relevant to a conclusion iff it affects the degree of supportiveness of the evidence overall; i.e., iff adding it either contributes to or detracts from the explanatory integration of evidence-plus-conclusion—which, as I said, may depend on facts about the world. I note in this context that while the definition of relevant evidence found in the FRE (whether in the old or the "restyled" version)—as evidence that either raises or lowers the probability of some fact at issue—is silent on the material character of the concept, Rule 104 (Preliminary Questions) notes that the relevance of evidence may "depend[] on whether a fact exists"; and that when this is so, the court may admit the evidence on condition that proof of the fact in question be introduced later.

It should already be apparent that, if the concepts of quality of evidence and degree of warrant are as complex, as subtle, as multi-dimensional, and as worldly as this account suggests, the mathematical theory of probabilities couldn't possibly, by itself, constitute a theory of warrant. This isn't yet enough, however, to show that if we had an adequate theory of warrant in hand, the calculus of probabilities couldn't then serve as a way of computing degrees of warrant.

concept of explanatory integration plays its role in the explanation of supportiveness—which is, to repeat, only one dimension of warrant.

[76] See Susan Haack, *Defending Science—Within Reason* (Amherst, NY: Prometheus Books, 2003), 76–77.

[77] See also "Proving Causation: The Weight of Combined Evidence," pp. 208–38 in this volume, n.86 (on the catastrophically misleading animal studies of Thalidomide conducted by the manufacturer, Grünenthal).

But I don't believe it could, for at least three reasons:

(a) Mathematical probabilities form a continuum from 0 to 1; but because of the several determinants of evidential quality, there is no guarantee of a linear ordering of degrees of warrant.[78]

(b) The mathematical probability of (*p* and not-p) must add up to 1; but when there is no evidence, or only very weak evidence, either way, neither *p* nor not-*p* is warranted to any degree.

(c) The mathematical probability of (*p* & *q*) is the product of the probability of *p* and the probability of *q*—which, unless both have a probability of 1, is always less than either; but combined evidence may warrant a claim to a higher degree than any of its components alone would do.[79]

The second and third points have quite a direct bearing on issues that arise in the law.

The "preponderance of the evidence" standard can't be adequately understood in terms simply of which party produces *more* evidence; it's not a matter of counting the number of witnesses proffered, or hefting the weight of the documents presented, by each side. But the alternative form of words, "more probable than not," also requires careful handling. It's not enough that one party produce better evidence than the other; what's required is that the party with the burden of proof produce *evidence good enough to warrant the conclusion to the required degree.*[80] So, exactly as point (b) above would lead you

[78] After I had reached this conclusion, I found that this point was already made by John Maynard Keynes in *A Treatise on Probability* (London: MacMillan and Co., Ltd., 1921), 27–28—though not, of course, on the foundherentist grounds I give.

[79] After I had reached this conclusion (in "Proving Causation: The Weight of Combined Evidence," (note 77 above)), I found that the points about negation and conjunction were already made in Cohen, *The Provable and the Probable* (note 68 above), chapter 5 (conjunction) and chapter 7 (negation)—though again, of course, not on the foundherentist grounds I give.

[80] Prof. Pardo suggests that, if we interpret the "preponderance" standard probabilistically, as "more [mathematically] probable than not," this will require a verdict against the plaintiff even if, e.g., the probability of his theory of what happened is 0.4, while the probability of the defendant's theory is only 0.2. Michael Pardo, "Estándares de prueba y teoría de la prueba," in Carmen Vázquez, ed., *Estándares de prueba y preuba científica: Ensayos de epistemología jurídical* (Barcelona: Marcial Pons, 2013), 99–118, 112. But this is not really, as Pardo suggests, an argument against legal probabilism; it is an argument for reconstruing the preponderance standard (as Allen proposes; see note 70 above) as requiring, not that a plaintiff produce evidence making his claim more likely than not, but only that he produce evidence making his claim more likely than the defendant's story. Whether "likely," in this context, should be understood in terms of mathematical probabilities or in terms of degrees of warrant is an entirely independent question.

to expect, even the preponderance standard—which, in virtue of the formulation "more probable than not," sounds the most amenable to a probabilist interpretation—in fact resists it.

With respect to point (c) it's worth noting, first, that if legal degrees of proof *were* mathematical probabilities, jury instructions to the effect that each element of the case should be established to the required degree would seem to make it almost impossibly difficult to meet the standard of proof; as is obvious when you realize that—supposing for the sake of argument (though *only* for the sake of argument) that proof beyond a reasonable doubt requires a mathematical probability of 0.95—evidence establishing each of three independent elements to this degree would have a joint probability of only 0.85, well below the threshold, and evidence establishing each of three independent elements to a probability of 0.51 would have a joint probability of only 0.13.

In fact, a congeries of evidence can warrant a conclusion to a *higher* degree than any of its components alone would do. In "Proving Causation," I will develop this argument in the context of legal disputes in toxic-tort cases about so-called "weight of evidence methodology."[81] Briefly and roughly: combining evidence will raise the degree of warrant of a conclusion just in case it makes the evidence overall more supportive of the conclusion; and/or improves the independent security of component pieces of evidence; and/or introduces additional evidence which is no less favorable to the conclusion than the more restricted evidence. This won't invariably happen: the point isn't that combined evidence is *always* stronger than any of its components, but that it *sometimes* is. For example, epidemiological evidence of increased risk of disease or disorder D among those exposed to substance S may, or may not, interlock with other studies. If we also know that the same substance, S, in comparable doses, gives rise to the same kind of damage, D, in animals known to be physiologically similar to humans in the relevant respects, and that toxicology shows that chemical compounds closely similar to S are also associated with D, then the combined evidence may give us better reason to think that S causes

[81] "Proving Causation" (note 77 above), 216–26. See, e.g., Oxendine v. Merrell Dow Pharm. Inc., 506 A.2d 1100, 1108 (D.C. 1986) ("*Oxendine* I") ("[Dr. Done] conceded his inability to conclude that Bendectin was a teratogen on the basis of any of the individual studies which he discussed, but he also made clear that all of these studies must be viewed together and that, so viewed, they supported his conclusion"); Gen. Elec. Co. v. Joiner, 522 U.S. 136, 153 (1997) ("*Joiner* III") (Justice Stevens, dissenting) ("It is not intrinsically 'unscientific' for experienced professionals to arrive at a conclusion by weighing all available scientific evidence"); Milward v. Acuity Specialty Prods. Grp. Inc., 639 F.3d 11 (1st Cir. 2011) ("Dr. Smith's testimony was that a weighing of the Hill factors …, supported the inference that the association between benzene exposure and APL (Acute Promyelocytic Leukemia) is genuine and causal").

D than any of these pieces of evidence alone would do. Similarly, evidence that the defendant had a strong motive to want the victim dead may interlock with evidence that he owned a gun of the right caliber and evidence that he was seen fleeing the scene of the crime to give more warrant to the conclusion that he did it than any of these pieces of evidence alone would do.

If, as I have argued, legal degrees of proof are best construed as degrees of rational credibility or warrant and if, as I have also argued, degrees of rational credibility or warrant cannot be identified with mathematical probabilities, legal probabilism is misguided. Still, simply showing that legal probabilism is misguided doesn't by itself enable us to get a better grip on complex evidence; as the saying goes, the proof of the pudding is in the eating. So the next move is to put my epistemological approach to work, and to show its advantages over avowedly probabilistic—subjective-Bayesian—approaches to the evidence in two famous, or perhaps notorious, cases: *Commonwealth v. Sacco and Vanzetti*,[82] and *People v. Collins*.[83]

3 *COMMONWEALTH V. SACCO AND VANZETTI*: FOUNDHERENTISM TRUMPS SUBJECTIVE BAYESIANISM

From an epistemological perspective, subjective Bayesianism (which seems to be the predominant form of legal probabilism today), is the most challenging. Why so? Because it combines an emphasis on Bayes's Theorem (a.k.a. "Bayes' formula," or "Bayes' rule") with a subjective interpretation of probabilities, not as objective frequencies or propensities, but as subjective degrees of belief;[84] and construes the calculus of probabilities, so understood, as *constituting* an epistemological theory. The degrees of belief a person gives various propositions are rational, the argument goes, if they are consistent; and they are consistent if they satisfy the axioms of the calculus of probabilities. Moreover, the argument continues, Bayes's Theorem provides a way to adjust or "update" one's prior degrees of belief, or prior probabilities, as new evidence comes in (thus avoiding the supposed "conjunction problem"). So, subjective Bayesians

[82] For transcripts of the trial and subsequent proceedings see Anonymous, ed., *The Sacco and Vanzetti Case: Transcript of the Record of the Trial of Nicola Sacco and Bartolemeo Vanzetti in the Courts of Massachusetts and Subsequent Proceedings*, 1920–27 (Mamaroneck, NY: Paul P. Appel, 1969).

[83] People v. Collins, 438 P.2d 33 (Cal. 1968).

[84] The *locus classicus* for the subjective interpretation is Bruno de Finetti, "La prévision: Ses lois logiques, ses sources subjectives," *Annales de l'Institut Henri Poincaré* 7 (1927): 1–68. In English translation by Henry E. Kyburg, Jr., in Kyburg and Smokler, eds., *Studies in Subjective Probability*, 93–158. The idea was taken up in an influential book, Leonard J. Savage, *The Foundations of Statistics* (New York: Wiley, 1954).

conclude—since what legal standards of proof demand is, precisely, that the fact-finder have a certain degree of rational belief in the conclusion, and since degree of belief under probabilistic coherence constraints *is* degree of rational belief—legal degrees of proof can be identified with probabilities, understood as he proposes. This is (to judge by its popularity) heady stuff. But it is also potentially very confusing, so it will be helpful to back up a few steps.

The calculus of probabilities, originally designed to represent the odds in games of chance, is an uncontroversial bit of mathematics; and Bayes's Theorem (named after the Reverend Thomas Bayes, who proved it)[85] is an uncontroversial theorem of that calculus. This theorem is routinely used to calculate "inverse" probabilities: that is, when the probability of B given A and of B given not-A is known, to calculate the probability of A given B. To borrow the very simple example given in Max Black's article on probability in the 1967 MacMillan *Encyclopedia of Philosophy*: suppose we know that 90% of a certain set of men own an automobile, and 10% do not (the "prior" probabilities); that, among those who own an automobile, 10% also own a bicycle, and among those who do not own an automobile, 20% own a bicycle (the "conditional" probabilities); then Bayes's formula allows us to calculate the ("posterior") probability that a man in the set who owns a bicycle also owns a car.[86] So far, so straightforward.

For a subjective Bayesian, however, Bayes's Theorem represents something far more epistemologically ambitious: a way of calculating the posterior probability of a hypothesis H given evidence E from the prior probability of H and the conditional probabilities of E given H and of E given not-H. And so, as he sees it, Bayes's Theorem provides a precise way of adjusting one's degrees of belief in light of new evidence.

This is the theoretical background against which Jay Kadane and David Schum offer their analysis of the evidence presented in the trial of Nicola Sacco and Bartolemeo Vanzetti,[87] two Italian immigrants who were accused of a murder committed during a 1920 payroll robbery in South Braintree,

[85] Bayes himself, however, didn't publish the proof, which appeared in the *Philosophical Transactions of the Royal Academy*, after his death, in 1763, thanks to his executor Richard Price; and it was Price, and not Bayes, who suggested that the theorem might have broader implications. David Schum, *Evidential Foundations of Probabilistic Reasoning* (New York: John Wiley and Sons, 1994), 48–49.

[86] Max Black, "Probability," in Paul Edwards, ed., *The Encyclopedia of Philosophy* (New York: MacMillan Publishing Co., Inc., and the Free Press, 1967), vol. 6, 464–79, 471. I have deliberately chosen this older source to indicate how Bayes's theorem was routinely used before subjective Bayesianism became fashionable.

[87] Jay Kadane and David Schum, *A Probabilistic Analysis of the Sacco and Vanzetti Evidence* (New York: John Wiley and Sons, 1996).

Massachusetts. The central issue at trial was a factual one—whether they really were the perpetrators. The evidence presented was complicated to say the least; a hundred and fifty-eight witnesses testified—ninety-nine for the prosecution, and fifty-nine for the defense: some about having seen Sacco and/or Vanzetti at the scene of the crime, some about the reliability or otherwise of the alibis they gave, some about the likelihood that the fatal bullet was fired from Sacco's gun, others about a cap allegedly belonging to Sacco found at the scene, the getaway car, subsequent actions of the defendants that allegedly revealed their consciousness of guilt—and so forth and so on. The jury found Sacco and Vanzetti guilty, and they were sentenced to death. In August 1927, after numerous motions and appeals—all of them, including one based on Celestino Madeiros's confession that it was he and other members of the Morelli gang, not Sacco and Vanzetti, who committed the crime, unsuccessful—Sacco and Vanzetti were executed.[88]

Sacco and Vanzetti were anarchists; and at the time of the trial, after the Russian revolution, the US was in the grip of a "Red Scare." In 1918 Congress had passed the Sedition Act, making it a federal offense, when the country was at war, to "willfully utter, print, write, or publish any disloyal, profane, scurrilous, or abusive language about the form of government of the United States...."[89] Many thought that Sacco and Vanzetti had been scapegoated for their political views. In 1927, the year they were executed, Felix Frankfurter published a short book pointing out many flaws both in the evidence on which they were convicted and in the judge's rulings;[90] on the day of the execution, Upton Sinclair began writing *Boston*, a passionate novel based on the case;[91] the following year, Edna St. Vincent Millay wrote a poem inspired by the case, "Justice Denied in Massachusetts";[92] on the fiftieth anniversary of their execution, the then-governor of Massachusetts, Michael Dukakis, issued a proclamation acknowledging that "the atmosphere of [Sacco and Vanzetti's] trials and appeals was permeated by prejudice against foreigners and hostility toward unorthodox political views," and declaring August 23, 1977, "Nicola

88 For a brief history, see Michael Miller Topp, ed., *The Sacco and Vanzetti Case: A Brief History and Documents* (New York: Palgrave/Macmillan, 2005), "Introduction," 1–51, and "Chronology of Events Related to the Sacco and Vanzetti Case," 185–88. Madeiros was executed the same day as Sacco and Vanzetti, for a different murder. *Id.*, 188.

89 Pub L No 65–150, 40 Stat 553 (1918) (amendment to the Espionage Act of 1917). The Sedition Act was repealed in 1921. Pub Res No 66–64, 41 Stat 1359 (1921).

90 Felix Frankfurter, *The Case of Sacco and Vanzetti: A Critical Analysis for Lawyers and Laymen* (Boston: Little, Brown and Company, 1927).

91 Upton Sinclair, *Boston* (New York: A. C. Boni, 1928).

92 Edna St. Vincent Millay, "Justice Denied in Massachusetts," in *The Buck in the Snow and Other Poems* (New York: Harper and Brothers Publishers, 1928), 32–33.

Sacco and Bartolemeo Vanzetti Memorial Day."[93] The case continues to excite controversy to this day. So, if Kadane and Schum have really succeeded in shedding light on the evidence, this would be of more than theoretical interest.

In fact, however, Kadane and Schum's analysis is more confusing than illuminating. For one thing, their title, promising a "probabilistic analysis" of the Sacco and Vanzetti evidence, is misleading. Yes, they offer a breakdown of the evidence into component parts (represented by means of Wigmore diagrams);[94] but they do this, so to speak, entirely by hand—probability theory plays no role in their *analysis* of the evidence, only in its *synthesis* to draw conclusions.[95] For another, though Kadane and Schum are well aware of Cohen's objections to construing degrees of proof as standard mathematical probabilities, they offer no reply;[96] instead, after noting that the Federal Rules define relevant evidence as evidence that either raises or lowers the probability of some fact at issue,[97] they simply take for granted that legal degrees of proof are mathematical probabilities. Moreover, they offer no categorical conclusions, only various posterior probabilities that Sacco was involved in the crime, or that Vanzetti was, given various assignments of prior probabilities to various items of evidence and various assignments of conditional probabilities. After hundreds of pages of diagrams and calculations, this is disappointing, to say the least.

93 The text of this Proclamation is reprinted in Topp, *The Sacco and Vanzetti Case* (note 88 above), 182–84.

94 John Henry Wigmore, *The Principles of Judicial Proof as Given by Logic, Psychology, and General Experience as Illustrated in Judicial Trials* (1913; 5th ed., Littleton, CO: Fred B. Rothman & Co., 1981). For a summary account, see Jean Godwin, "Wigmore's Chart Method," *Informal Logic* 20, no. 3 (2000): 223–43.

95 An earlier book of Schum's had alluded to such concepts as missing evidence, relevance, and credibility but, so far as I can determine, didn't come even close to developing anything like a theory of warrant. Schum, *Evidential Foundations of Probabilistic Reasoning* (note 85 above), 15, 29 (on missing evidence), 69 ff. (on relevance), and 207 (on credibility).

96 Kadane and Schum, *A Probabilistic Analysis of the Sacco and Vanzetti Evidence* (note 87 above), 239–40. Earlier, Schum had discussed Cohen's approach in some detail: David Schum, "A Review of the Case against Blaise Pascal and His Heirs," *Michigan Law Review* 77 (1979): 446–63; and there are numerous references to Cohen in his *Evidential Foundations of Probabilistic Reasoning* (note 85 above). But I wasn't able to identify replies to Cohen's objections—only a suggestion, in the 1979 piece, that the benefits of Bayesianism are so significant that they somehow outweigh the problem of the "paradoxes" of negation, conjunction, etc.

97 Kadane and Schum, *A Probabilistic Analysis of the Sacco and Vanzetti Evidence* (note 87 above), 50. See also Schum, *Evidential Foundations of Probabilistic Reasoning* (note 85 above), 71–73, where Schum maintains that people's judgments of relevance depend on their "standpoint"; but seems to elide this into the very different claim that relevance itself is standpoint-relative.

But there are far worse problems. First: the fact that Kadane and Schum offer a whole range of very different conclusions, *all* of them probabilistically consistent, reveals that *probabilistic consistency is not sufficient to guarantee rational or reasonable degrees of belief*[98]—which would surely also require, if we are to speak in these terms at all, reasonable *prior* degrees of belief and reasonable *conditional* degrees of belief.

Second: Kadane and Schum acknowledge that the probabilities in which they traffic can be understood neither in terms of the doctrine of chances, nor in statistical terms; rather, they say, they are "personal, subjective, or [i.e., I presume, 'i.e.'] epistemic probabilities."[99] But "personal" doesn't mean the same as "subjective," and neither means the same as "epistemic"; and the verbal fudging here is symptomatic of a deeper issue. Suppose for the sake of argument (though *only* for the sake of argument) that the probabilities Kadane and Schum calculate *are* degrees of belief: *whose* degrees of belief are they? Their own, they reply, and some other scholars'.[100] As this reveals, Kadane and Schum are piggybacking on the epistemological judgment of people who have studied the case. The supposed identification of probabilities with these people's (subjective) degrees of belief is spurious; what we're really dealing with are *experts' opinions about* (objective) *epistemic likelihoods*.

And so, third: while Kadane and Schum's many pages of calculations may create the impression that the calculus of probabilities is doing serious epistemological heavy lifting, this is an illusion. The only epistemological work going on here is Kadane and Schum's entirely informal decomposition of the evidence into component elements, and their and other experts' entirely informal appraisals of the worth of the evidence. The mathematics, when it isn't downright misleading, is mostly decorative.

To show that my account does better (rather than provide the book-length treatment that would be needed if I were to look at *all* the evidence), I will take my cues from Frankfurter's discussion of the various elements of the evidence in the case. As I said before, the idiom of probability has both epistemological and mathematical/statistical uses; and when Frankfurter writes that "[e]very

98 *Qua* foundherentist, of course, I don't believe *any* kind of consistency or coherence, on its own, is sufficient for warrant. See Haack, *Evidence and Inquiry* (1993; 2nd ed., Amherst, NY: Prometheus Books, 2009), chapter 3; "Coherence, Consistency, Cogency, Congruity, Cohesiveness, &c.: Remain Calm! Don't Go Overboard!" (2004), in Haack, *Putting Philosophy to Work* (2008; expanded ed., Amherst, NY: Prometheus Books, 2013), 69–82.

99 Kadane and Schum, *A Probabilistic Analysis of the Sacco and Vanzetti Evidence* (note 87 above), 24, 120, 159. They even write that "[w]hat nonindependence means is that knowledge of one item of evidence *may influence our judgment* of the probative force of another." *Id.*, 129 (italics mine).

100 *Id.*, 239–40.

reasonable probability points away from Sacco and Vanzetti [and] every reasonable probability points toward the Morelli gang,"[101] it's quite clear that he is using "probability" in its epistemological sense. Moreover, as we will shortly see, his epistemological observations about the weaknesses in the evidence against Sacco and Vanzetti have—if you'll pardon the anachronism[102]—a decidedly foundherentist cast.

Frankfurter points out, for example, the numerous flaws in the eyewitness testimony placing Sacco at the scene. At trial, a year after the robbery and murder took place, Mary Splaine testified with great confidence that she had seen Sacco—whom she described in considerable (though, as we shall see, not entirely accurate) detail—at the scene of the crime. But she had seen the man she identified as Sacco—who was allegedly in a getaway car traveling at 15 to 18 miles an hour—only from a distance of 60 to 80 feet, and for only between one-and-a-half and three seconds. She emphasized that the man she saw had a "good-sized left hand, a hand that denoted strength"; but Sacco's hands were smaller than average. Moreover, she had earlier told police that she *couldn't* identify the person she saw, and at another time had identified a *different* man, who, however, turned out to have been in jail at the time of the crime; and she picked out Sacco only after she had seen him several times at the police station and in court.[103] Another eyewitness, Frances Devlin, who also claimed to have seen Sacco in the car, had also said earlier that she couldn't positively identify him.[104] Louis Pelzer said he had seen Sacco too; but fellow-workmen testified that he had been hiding under a bench at the time of the shooting.[105] Two other eyewitnesses, Ferguson and Pierce, who saw the crime from one floor above where Splaine and Devlin were standing, found it impossible to make any identification at all.[106] Etc., etc. In short, as I would say:

- *though, if it were true that Splaine, Pelzer, and Devlin saw Sacco in the getaway car, this would strongly support the proposition that Sacco was involved, this eyewitness testimony was, to say the least, sadly lacking in*

[101] Frankfurter, *The Case of Sacco and Vanzetti* (note 90 above), 101.

[102] Only the *term* is anachronistic, I should add: for my foundherentism was from the beginning intended in part as an articulation of the standards of better and worse evidence, more and less warranted belief, implicit in our everyday assessments of evidence. See especially *Evidence and Inquiry* (note 98 above), chapter 1. Imagining Justice Frankfurter reading my book, I think of Molière's M. Jourdain, who discovers to his amazement that he has "spoken prose for forty years, without knowing anything about it." Molière, *Le Bourgeois Gentilhomme* (1670), Act II, Scene VI.

[103] Frankfurter, *The Case of Sacco and Vanzetti* (note 90 above), 11–15; the quotation is from 11.

[104] *Id.*, 15.

[105] *Id.*, 17–18.

[106] *Id.*, 16.

> *independent security. There is a far better explanation of why Splaine identified Sacco than that he was in fact the man she saw at the crime scene—that she had seen him at the police station and in court; there is a far better explanation of why Pelzer identified Sacco than that he was the man he saw at the crime scene—that Pelzer didn't want to admit he had been hiding after he heard shots; and it seems likely that Devlin, who later insisted she had never had any doubt that Sacco was the man she saw, had grown more certain over time because of "the immensity of the crime and everything."*[107]

Frankfurter also looks in detail at the firearms testimony. Expert witness Captain William H. Proctor testified at trial that "bullet 3" was "consistent with" its having been fired from Sacco's pistol;[108] and Judge Thayer interpreted this to mean that "it was [Sacco's] pistol that fired the shot." However, not all of Proctor's evidence was given at trial; and in a subsequent affidavit he acknowledged that "[a]t no time was [he] able to find any evidence whatever which convinced [him] that [this bullet] came from Sacco's pistol."[109] "By prearrangement," Frankfurter comments, "the prosecution brought before the jury a piece of evidence apparently most damaging to the defendants, when in fact the *full* truth concerning this evidence was very favorable to them."[110] In short, as I would say:

- *the firearms testimony presented at trial was sadly lacking in comprehensiveness, so that the conclusion that one of the fatal bullets came from Sacco's gun was very poorly warranted.*

The lies Sacco and Vanzetti told at the police station were presented by the prosecution as indicating "consciousness of guilt"; but given that this was a period of wholesale arrests and deportations of aliens suspected of Communist sympathies, Sacco and Vanzetti may very well have lied, not because they were guilty of the Braintree crime, but because they thought they were in trouble over their political radicalism.[111] Moreover, Frankfurter points out, none of the stolen $16,000 was ever found in Sacco or Vanzetti's possession; and neither man went into hiding or left the country after the crime—both stayed in their old lodgings, and both continued to pursue their old work.[112] However,

[107] *Id.*, 15.

[108] Five other bullets were also found in the dead bodies at the scene; but the evidence excluded the possibility that any of these others had been fired by Sacco or by Vanzetti. *Id.*, 76.

[109] *Id.*, 76–79.

[110] *Id.*, 76.

[111] *Id.*, 35 ff.

[112] *Id.*, 35–36.

he continues, shortly after the crime Madeiros mysteriously came into possession of $2,800—roughly the amount one might expect to have been his share of the loot.[113] In short, as I would say:

- *the lies Sacco and Vanzetti told the police offer only very weak support to the conclusion that they were trying to hide their complicity in the Braintree crime; for the explanatory integration of this evidence with that conclusion is no better than its integration with the conclusion that they were trying to avoid being penalized for their political views. Moreover, the additional evidence about their subsequent behavior gives further support to the latter conclusion, while undermining the former.*

I could go on; but this is enough, I hope, to illustrate the advantages of the foundherentist approach over Kadane and Schum's impressively complicated, but ultimately baffling, "probabilistic analysis" of this evidence.

Well, yes, you may be thinking: but even if the foundherentist epistemological approach is, as you say, better *in this instance*, this really isn't the kind of case that best illustrates the virtues of legal probabilism. After all, the Sacco and Vanzetti case didn't involve any probabilistic or statistical evidence; but it is in handling such evidence, surely, that legal probabilism really comes into its own. I disagree; but to show why, I need to turn to my second illustration.

4 *PEOPLE V. COLLINS*: AGAIN, FOUNDHERENTISM TRUMPS SUBJECTIVE BAYESIANISM

There's no question that statistical and probabilistic evidence—from DNA analyses[114] in criminal cases to epidemiological studies in toxic-tort cases, actuarial calculations in wrongful-death suits, etc., etc.—plays a very significant role in the law; and quite properly so. And there is no question, either, that the mathematical calculus of probabilities (Bayes's Theorem of course included) is applicable to such evidence. It doesn't follow, however, that the calculus of probabilities can illuminate the epistemic role such evidence plays in the context of the larger body of evidence in a case; and, as we shall soon

[113] *Id.*, 114.

[114] Calculations of the probability of a random match with the defendant are mathematical extrapolations from empirical data. These aren't pure mathematics; but they aren't quite "statistical," either, if that is taken to mean "based on surveys of [DNA] patterns in the population." (See Colin Aiken, Paul Roberts, and Graham Jackson, *Fundamentals of Probability and Statistical Evidence in Criminal Proceedings: Guidance for Judges, Lawyers, Forensic Scientists and Expert Witnesses* [London: Royal Statistical Society, 2010] for an attempt to draw the distinctions needed here.)

see, it isn't true. On the contrary, in fact: by tempting us to confuse statistical probabilities with degrees of proof, legal probabilism can seduce us into forgetting that the statistical evidence in a case should be treated as *one piece of evidence among many*.

Here I am deliberately echoing an observation reported in *Landrigan* about the idea that epidemiological evidence of at least a doubled risk is sufficient to establish specific causation in a toxic-tort case: "a relative risk of 2.0 is not so much a password to a finding of causation as one piece of evidence, among others."[115] This gets the key epistemological point exactly right. And I am also deliberately setting myself against the words of the article on epidemiology in the first edition of the *Reference Manual on Scientific Evidence*, a couple of years before: "[t]he relative risk from an epidemiological study can be adapted to [the civil] 50% plus standard to yield a probability or likelihood that an agent caused an individual's disease."[116] This commits precisely the confusion against which I am warning.

But I will focus here on the evidence in another criminal case. *People v. Collins*, however, was hardly, like the Sacco and Vanzetti case, a *cause célèbre*; on the contrary, it was the kind of case only an evidence scholar could love—frankly piddling, except for a bizarre epistemological twist that led Finkelstein and Fairley to open what would become a key paper in the legal-probabilist literature, offering a "Bayesian approach to identification evidence," with a commentary on *Collins*.[117] But as we shall see, though Finkelstein and Fairley's effort has more philosophical merit than Kadane and Schum's, it is seriously flawed nonetheless.

But let me begin at the beginning: with the old lady who was knocked down in an alley and had her purse stolen. The victim described the robber as a young woman weighing roughly 145 pounds, with light blond hair in a ponytail; and another eyewitness said he had seen a blond woman run out of the alley and jump into a yellow car driven by a black man with a mustache and a

115 Landrigan v. Celotex Corp., 605 A.2d 1079, 1087 (N.J. 1992) (reporting an argument made by the defense on appeal). Compare this, from a 1997 English criminal case: "... the judge should have left it to the jury to weigh, on the one hand, the cogent DNA evidence coupled with the other evidence identifying the appellant as the potential assailant against, on the other, the defendant's evidence and that of his alibi witnesses." R v. Doheny, [1997] 1 Crim. App. 369 (Eng.).

116 Linda A. Bailey, Leon Gordis, and Michael D. Green, "Reference Guide on Epidemiology," in Federal Judicial Center, *Reference Manual on Scientific Evidence* (Washington, D.C.: Federal Judicial Center, 1990), 123–80, 168. (The articles on epidemiology in later editions of the *Reference Manual* (2000, 2011) gradually qualify this bold claim. See, again, "Risky Business" (note 51 above), 279, 285.)

117 Finkelstein and Fairley, "A Bayesian Approach to Identification Evidence" (note 66 above).

beard. Janet and Malcolm Collins were accused of the crime; Janet was white, with blond hair, Malcolm was black, and the couple drove a rickety old yellow car.[118] However, the victim couldn't positively identify Janet, and the other eyewitness's identification of Malcolm was shaky. So at trial, to shore up their not-very-strong case, the prosecution first introduced a mathematics instructor to testify—relying purely on a probabilistic argument itself based, not on statistical data, but on sheer assumption—that, given the "product rule," the odds against there being another such couple around (blond woman and black man with facial hair, in a yellow car) were an astronomical 1 in 12 million; and then told the jury that these made-up numbers were "conservative estimates," and that they had been given "mathematical proof" that the Collinses were guilty.[119] The jury duly convicted.

Janet served her time; but Malcolm appealed, and in 1968 was granted a new trial.[120] Justice Sullivan's argument in the ruling granting the new trial was two-pronged: first, that the statistics that apparently swayed the jury were invented, with no factual basis whatsoever; second, that even if they had been real, "no mathematical formula could ever establish ... that the prosecution's eyewitnesses correctly observed and accurately described the distinctive features ... linking the defendants to the crime."[121] The first point is undeniable; the second—while also, I believe, correct—raises questions about what role, exactly, statistical evidence plays in the identification of a specific perpetrator or perpetrators.

Statistical identification evidence, Finkelstein and Fairley agree, shouldn't normally be sufficient, but needs to be accompanied by other evidence forming the basis for a "'prior' estimate of identity." This answer, they continue, can be justified by Bayes's Theorem, which enables us to "translate" a statistical probability into "a probability statement that describes the probative force of that statistic."[122] Somehow, in short, Bayes's Theorem is to transform the mathematical sense of "probable" into the epistemic. Of course, no theorem of the probability calculus could possibly perform such a miracle of "translation."

118 Officer Kinsey, while driving home from work, saw the defendants in their yellow Lincoln, placed them under surveillance, and followed them home. The couple didn't, by the way, match the eyewitnesses' description exactly: Janet's hair was dark blond, and Malcolm didn't have a beard. *Collins* (note 83 above) 34.

119 *Collins* (note 83 above), 37 ("conservative estimates"), 41 ("mathematical proof").

120 However, the prosecution was unable to get the witnesses together a second time, so this new trial never took place. George Fisher, "Green Felt Jungle: The Story of *People v. Collins*," in Richard Lempert, ed., *Evidence Stories* (New York: Foundation Press, 2006), 7–28, 21–22.

121 *Collins* (note 83 above), 40.

122 Finkelstein and Fairley, "A Bayesian Approach to Identification Evidence" (note 66 above),498.

So it comes as no great surprise that, in fact, Finkelstein and Fairley bridge the gap between statistical and epistemic probabilities, *not* (as advertised) by applying Bayes's Theorem, but by tinkering with the interpretation of "probable." What Finkelstein and Fairley, like Kadane and Schum, mean by "subjective" probability is the (objective) probability assigned by some subject to the proposition in question. Unlike Kadane and Schum, however, Finkelstein and Fairley make an effort to explain what this objective-probability-assigned-by-some-subject amounts to: "the relative frequency of guilt over cases judged to be similar in the degree of belief they engender."[123]

I *think* what this means is that the "subjective" probability (i.e., the *objective* probability assigned by some subject *x*) that the defendant is guilty is the proportion of (presumably, possible-but-not-necessarily-actual) cases in which the facts are different from this one but in which *x* judges that his degree of belief in the defendant's guilt would be the same, in which the defendants *would* be guilty. Finkelstein and Fairley admit their gloss is "artificial";[124] but the fact is, it's close to unintelligible. What class of possible cases is a juror supposed to be imagining? How are these possible cases supposed to be individuated? How is a juror supposed to estimate the proportion of those possible cases in which the defendant would be guilty? And how is all this supposed to work when you extrapolate it from *x*'s judgment of the probability of the defendant's guilt to his assignments of prior probabilities, or of conditional probabilities?

To show that my account does better, let me begin with Justice Sullivan's observation—with which Finkelstein and Fairley agree—that statistical evidence is about a population and so, without other evidence, can't warrant a conclusion about an individual. Imagine a case like *Collins*, but with real, not invented, statistical evidence. It is almost, but perhaps not quite, too obvious to need saying that the statistics, by themselves, would have no bearing at all were it not for (i) the eyewitness evidence and (ii) the fact that the defendants fit the eyewitnesses' description of the perpetrators. Suppose, then, that this were all the evidence we had:

- E1: eyewitnesses identify the perpetrators as a blond woman and a black man with a mustache and beard, who drove away in a yellow car;
- E2: couples fitting this description are very rare (one in *n*) in the population in the area where the robbery took place;
- E3: the Collinses fit this description.

[123] *Id.*, 504.
[124] *Ibid.*

This evidence gives *some* degree of support to the conclusion that the Collinses were the perpetrators: that the Collinses committed the crime would explain what the eye-witnesses saw, and the statistical evidence indicates that relatively few other possible explanations are possible. Supportiveness alone, however, is not enough; and the degree of warrant this evidence gives the conclusion is obviously quite low. Not only is the degree of supportiveness less than overwhelming; there are also issues about independent security (e.g., the reliability of the eyewitnesses), and the comprehensiveness of the evidence is sadly lacking—i.e., there is a good deal of obviously relevant evidence missing.

Now imagine that we have some additional evidence:

- E4: the eyewitnesses aren't visually impaired, got a good look, have no reason to lie, etc.;
- E5: there is reason to believe the perpetrators were local;
- E6: the Collinses have no alibi;
- E7: the Collinses' subsequent behavior was evasive.

The addition of E4–E7 improves the explanatory integration of evidence-plus-conclusion appreciably: the conjunction of E1–E3 supports the conclusion that the Collinses committed the crime to a fairly modest degree, but the conjunction of E1–E7 supports it to a significantly higher degree. Moreover, some worries about independent security are resolved; and E1–E7 is significantly more comprehensive than E1–E3, and the additional evidence no less favorable to the conclusion. So E1–E7 warrants the conclusion to a significantly higher degree than E1–E3 alone.

But now imagine that we have, instead, this very different additional evidence:

- E4*: the eyewitnesses are visually impaired, and/or didn't get a good look, and/or have some motive to finger Janet and Malcolm Collins, and/or had seen them in handcuffs at the police station before they picked them out of the lineup, and/or . . ., etc.;
- E5*: there is reason to believe the perpetrators weren't local, but from another state;
- E6*: the Collinses offer an alibi, which has been confirmed;
- E7*: the Collinses produce documents (verified as legitimate) showing that they had bought their yellow car only *after* the crime took place.

E4*, E5*, E6*, and E7* *undermine* the conclusion that the Collinses were the perpetrators; so the conjunction of E1–E3 with E4*–E7* is better explanatorily integrated with, and hence supports, the conclusion that the Collinses were *not* the perpetrators, rather than the conclusion that they were. And the evidence that the alibi has been confirmed and the documents regarding the purchase of the car verified raises the degree of warrant of the conclusion that they were not the perpetrators by resolving some issues about the independent security of evidence undermining the conclusion that they were.

I could go on; but this is enough, I hope, to illustrate the advantages of a foundherentist approach over Finkelstein and Fairley's impressively clever, but ultimately baffling, probabilistic analysis. And if so—since Finkelstein and Fairley are concerned, not just with *Collins*, but with the role of statistical/probabilistic identification evidence generally—my approach should shed some light on this broader field.

When Finkelstein and Fairley's paper was published, DNA "fingerprinting" had not yet entered the legal system.[125] But cases involving this increasingly common kind of evidence can illustrate the general epistemological point particularly well. Let me return to the case of Raymond Easton, mentioned briefly in "Epistemology and the Law of Evidence."[126] Mr. Easton was arrested for a robbery on the basis of a DNA "cold hit"; the probability was very low that the match between Mr. Easton's DNA (on file after an earlier arrest for domestic violence) and DNA found at the crime scene was random. However, Mr. Easton suffered from Parkinson's disease; he was too weak to dress himself or to walk more than a few yards—let alone to drive to the crime scene, or to commit the crime.[127]

This is a case structurally much like my second imaginary extrapolation of *Collins*: probabilistic evidence seems to support the conclusion that Mr. Easton committed the crime (since Mr. Easton's being at the scene would explain this DNA's being there); but there is other evidence undermining this conclusion (since Mr. Easton was so physically impaired, we have no explanation of how he could have got to the crime scene, or how he could have committed the robbery). In short, the conjunction of the DNA evidence with the rest supports the conclusion that Mr. Easton *didn't* do it, and undermines the conclusion that he did. And so—assuming reasonable independent security (e.g., that a reputable doctor has confirmed that Mr. Easton really has Parkinson's), and assuming that no significant evidence is missing (e.g., that

[125] DNA identification evidence was first used in a criminal case in the US in 1987, in the Florida trial of Tommy Lee Andrews. Andrews v. State, 533 So. 2d 841 (Fla. Dist. Ct. App. 1988).

[126] "Epistemology and the Law of Evidence" (note 2 above), 19–20.

[127] Genewatch UK (January 2005), available at http://www.genewatch.org/uploads/f03c6d66a9b354535738483c1c3d49e4/NationalDNADatabase.pdf, 23.

Mr. Easton paid an accomplice to drive him to the crime scene)—the conclusion that he didn't do it is well warranted.

My argument is not, of course, restricted to criminal cases. After all, DNA evidence can play a key role in paternity or inheritance cases, epidemiological evidence plays a large role in toxic-tort litigation, and so on. In any case—do I really need to say this again?—my "epistemological dissent" from legal probabilism doesn't apply only to cases involving probabilistic or statistical evidence, but is quite general. The point is that, rather than enhancing our understanding of what legal degrees of proof are, probabilism impedes it—and that sound epistemology can help where legal probabilism hinders

—4—

Irreconcilable Differences? The Troubled Marriage of Science and Law

> In many respects [the scientific expert] seems to be a positive annoyance to lawyers, and even to judges at times, a sort of intractable, incompatible, inharmonious factor, disturbing the otherwise smooth current of legal procedure; too important or necessary to be ruled out, too intelligent and disciplined mentally to yield without reason to ordinary rules and regulations of the court, and at the same time possessing an undoubted influence with the jury that it is difficult to restrict by the established rules and maxims of legal procedure.
>
> —Charles F. Himes[1]

> It is often said, with good cause, that ... the goal of a trial and the goal of science are ... at odds.... As a general rule, courts don't do science very well.
>
> —Edward Humes[2]

1 GETTING STARTED

There wasn't much to be said for the miserable weeks after hurricanes Katrina and Wilma—except, perhaps, that all those hours spent sweating in the dark prompted some vivid thoughts about what life must have been like before electric light and power was available at the flick of a switch, and renewed my appreciation of the countless ways in which science now so thoroughly permeates modern life—including the legal system.

By now, legal proceedings rely far more on scientific testimony than they did when Dr. Himes wrote in 1893. And of course science and the law intertwine

1 Charles F. Himes, "The Scientific Expert in Forensic Procedure," *Journal of the Franklin Institute* 135, no. 6 (1893): 407–36, 411.

2 Edward Humes, *Monkey Girl: Evolution, Education, Religion, and the Battle for America's Soul* (New York: Ecco, 2007), 257.

in many other ways, too. Scientific advisers contribute to regulatory decision-making; and the law regulates potentially hazardous scientific research,[3] may get involved when fraud is alleged in scientific work funded by government grants,[4] and may be called on to resolve disputes between scientific interests and interests of other kinds—e.g., in "cultural heritage" cases such as the tussle over the fate of the 9,000-year-old skeleton of Kennewick Man,[5] or in constitutional cases over high-school biology teaching.[6]

I shall confine myself here largely to scientific testimony in litigation—which, from the beginning, has prompted complaints both about the venality and dishonesty of scientific witnesses, and about the scientific ignorance and credulity of jurors, attorneys, and judges. But some of what I have to say will also be relevant to the other contexts in which science interacts with the law; for the core of my argument will be that there are real tensions between the goals and values of the scientific enterprise and the culture of the law—especially, perhaps, the culture of the US legal system.[7] Science is investigative in character, for example, while the culture of our legal system is strongly adversarial; the sciences search for general principles, while the legal focus is on particular cases; the scientific enterprise is pervasively fallibilist—i.e., open to revision in the light of new evidence—while the law is concerned to arrive at prompt and final resolutions; the sciences push for innovation, while the legal system focuses on precedent; scientific investigation is informal, problem-oriented, and pragmatic, while the legal system relies on formal

3 See, e.g., Susan Haack, *Defending Science—Within Reason: Between Scientism and Cynicism* (Amherst, NY: Prometheus Books, 2003), 322–24 (on National Institutes of Health (NIH) regulation of early research on recombinant DNA).

4 For example, in the case of Dr. Eric Poehlman, who pled guilty to lying on a federal grant application and to fabricating data, over more than a decade, on obesity, menopause, and aging. See Jeneen Interlandi, "An Unwelcome Discovery," *New York Times*, October 22, 2006, § 6 (Magazine), 98 (reporting on the Poehlman case). Plea Agreement, United States v. Poehlman, No. 2:05-Cr-38–1 (D. Vt. Mar. 16, 2005); Judgment in Criminal Case, United States v. Poehlman, No. 2:05-Cr-38–1 (D. Vt. June 29, 2005) (Sentencing Agreement).

5 Bonnichsen v. United States Dep't of Army, 367 F.3d 864 (9th Cir. 2004). See also Jeff Benedict, *No Bone Unturned: The Adventures of a Top Smithsonian Forensic Scientist and the Legal Battle for American's Oldest Skeletons* (New York: HarperCollins Publishers, 2003).

6 See, e.g., Selman v. Cobb Cnty Sch. Dist., 390 F. Supp. 2d 1286 (N.D. Ga. 2005) (vacated and remanded by 11th Circuit for additional evidentiary inquiry by the district court); Kitzmiller v. Dover Area Sch. Dist., 400 F. Supp. 2d 707 (M.D. Pa. 2005). Humes, *Monkey Girl* (note 2 above) tells the background story of *Kitzmiller*, and summarizes the trial proceedings. For a summary history of Establishment Clause cases over the teaching of evolution in public high schools, see Susan Haack, "Cracks in the Wall, A Bulge Under the Carpet: The Singular Story of Religion, Evolution, and the U.S. Constitution," *Wayne Law Review*, 57, no. 4 (2011): 1303–32.

7 Unless otherwise indicated, in this article the phrase "the culture of the law" will refer specifically to the US legal culture.

rules and procedures; and the aspirations of the sciences are essentially theoretical, while the law is inevitably oriented to policy.

The first step will be to sketch how the legal system began to use scientific experts, and how it has tried to accommodate their testimony to its own purposes (§1); the next, to understand what it is about the nature of science and the culture of law that makes the scientific expert, as Dr. Himes says, "a sort of intractable, incompatible, inharmonious factor, disturbing the smooth current of legal procedure" (§2); then to illustrate how the tensions between science and the law reveal themselves in practice (§3); and finally to comment, very briefly, on some efforts to alleviate the tensions (§4).

2 THE SCIENTIFIC WITNESS

Of course, there haven't always been scientific witnesses; in fact, there haven't always been witnesses. In England, even after jury trials had taken hold, for a long time no witnesses were called. Instead, jurors might go around town investigating for themselves, or might be specially chosen for their expertise—a jury of vintners in a case where a defendant was accused of selling bad wine, for example, or a jury of butchers when the charge was selling putrid meat.[8]

And even when witnesses first began to be called, the system was still pre-adversarial, with witnesses serving, not a party to the case, but the court.[9] Gradually, however, the present adversarial practice developed, with witnesses prepared and presented by one party and cross-examined by the other, and formal rules restricting what evidence is admissible for the jury to hear. There had long been expert witnesses: courts had called on Latin scholars, for example, to help them construe unclear documents, and on physicians to give their opinion on the medicinal value of wolf-flesh in healing wounds;[10] but now experts, like other witnesses, served the parties.

Learned Hand takes the essential characteristic of an expert witness, in the modern sense, to be that he or she is not bound by the "opinion rule," according to which a witness's conclusions are inadmissible;[11] and dates the first appearance of such witnesses to 1619, when in *Alsop v. Bowtrell*[12] physicians

8 Learned Hand, "Historical and Practical Considerations Regarding Expert Testimony," *Harvard Law Review* 15 (1901): 40–58, 41.

9 See generally Stephan Landsman, "Of Witches, Madmen and Product Liability: An Historical Survey of the Use of Expert Testimony," *Behavioral Science and Law*, 13, no. 2 (1995): 131–57.

10 *Id*, 135–38.

11 Learned Hand, "Historical and Practical Considerations Regarding Expert Testimony" (note 8 above), 45.

12 Alsop v. Bowtrell, (1619) 79 Eng. Rep. 464 (K.B.); (1619) Cro. Jac. 541.

testified that it was possible for a woman to bear a legitimate child "forty weeks and nine days" after the death of her husband.[13] Stephan Landsman, following James Thayer, takes the more important point to be that expert witnesses are called by the parties and subject to cross-examination;[14] and suggests a later date, 1782, when in *Folkes v. Chadd*[15] engineers appeared for each side in an action in which the plaintiff sought damages because a harbor had silted up, allegedly as a result of the construction of a bank to prevent flooding in a nearby meadow.[16] Tal Golan argues, however, that experts presented by each party and subject to cross-examination by the other had been seen long before, as early as 1678,[17] and that what was novel in *Folkes v. Chadd* was, rather, that in this case the scientists involved relied on general, hypothetical scientific principles.[18]

As soon as the US legal system came to rely significantly on scientific experts, complaints arose from all sides: expert witnesses, physicians especially, complained about the way they were treated under cross-examination; and both legal and scientific commentators expressed concern about the rise of what they perceived as a new class of partisan and untrustworthy professional expert witnesses. And as the use of scientific experts grew, so did the complaints. As early as 1858 the Supreme Court was observing wryly that "experience has shown that opposite opinions of persons professing to be experts can be obtained to any amount";[19] in 1874 John Ordronaux was complaining in the *Journal of Insanity* that "[f]atal exhibitions of scientific inaccuracy and self-contradiction … can not but weaken public confidence in the value of all such evidence";[20] in 1884 the court in *Ferguson v. Hubbell*[21] advised that expert testimony "should not be much encouraged and should

[13] Hand, "Historical and Practical Considerations Regarding Expert Testimony" (note 8 above), 45 (explaining that the expert witness, as an exception to the opinion rule, is a kind of relic left over from the older system, before the opinion rule limited lay witnesses' testimony).

[14] Stephan Landsman, "Of Witches, Madmen and Product Liability" (note 9 above), 141.

[15] Folkes v. Chadd, (1782) 99 Eng. Rep. 589 (K.B.); 3 Doug. 157, 157–58. James Thayer, *Select Cases on Evidence at the Common Law* (Boston, MA: C. W. Sever, 1892), 666.

[16] Landsman, "Of Witches, Madmen, and Product Liability" (note 9 above), 141.

[17] Tal Golan, *Laws of Men and Laws of Nature: The History of Scientific Expert Testimony in England and America* (Cambridge, MA: Harvard University Press, 2004), 41 (citing The Trial of the Earl of Pembroke (1678), 6 Cobb. St. Tr. 1310. (K.B.) (Eng.), in Thomas J. Howell, ed., *Cobbett's Complete Collection of State Trials and Proceedings for High Treason and Other Crimes and Misdemeanors from the Earliest Period to the Present Time* (London: R. Bagshaw, 1810), vol. 7, 185–86).

[18] Golan, *Laws of Men and Laws of Nature* (note 17 above), 43–44.

[19] Winans v. N.Y. & Erie R.R. Co., 62 U.S. 88, 101 (1858).

[20] John Ordronaux ("State Commissioner in Lunacy"), "On Expert Testimony in Judicial Proceedings," *Journal of Insanity* 30, no. 3 (1874): 312–22, 317.

[21] Ferguson v. Hubbell, 97 N.Y. 507, 514 (1884).

be received only in cases of necessity," because experts' opinions "cannot fail generally to be warped by a desire to promote the cause in which they are enlisted";[22] in 1893, Dr. Himes observed that scientific witnesses "are selected on account of their ability to express a favorable opinion, which, there is great reason to believe, is in many instances alone the result of employment [in the case] and the bias growing out of it";[23] in 1910, a contributor to the *Yale Law Journal* wrote that "[t]here is constant complaining and mistrust on the part of the judges, juries and lawyers of the expert witness."[24]

In 1925, John Scopes was convicted of teaching evolution to a high-school biology class, in contravention of Tennessee's Anti-Evolution Act.[25] Clarence Darrow had recruited a whole team of scientific experts to testify in Scopes's defense; but Judge John T. Raulston excluded all but one of them. Historian Edward Larson comments that at the time "nationally accepted court rules discouraged expert testimony."[26] In fact, what is now seen as a key step towards domesticating scientific testimony had been taken just a couple of years before, when in *Frye v. United States*[27] the DC court had given a test to determine, not just whether a scientific witness is qualified to testify, but whether novel scientific testimony is good enough for the jury to hear: the "scientific principle or discovery" on which it is based must be "sufficiently established to have gained general acceptance in the field to which it belongs."[28] It would be decades before the "*Frye* Rule" began to spread; but by the early 1980s *Frye* had become the accepted standard in many states.[29]

[22] *Ibid.*

[23] Himes, "The Scientific Expert in Forensic Procedure" (note 1 above), 409.

[24] Lee M. Friedman, "Expert Testimony, Its Abuse and Reformation," *Yale Law Journal* 19 (1910): 247–57, 247.

[25] See Scopes v. State, 278 S.W. 57, 57 (Tenn. 1925) ("The plaintiff has been convicted of a violation of chapter 27 of the Public Acts of 1925, known as the Anti-Evolution Act, and has appealed on error to this court.").

[26] Edward J. Larson, *Trial and Error: The American Controversy Over Creation and Evolution* (New York: Oxford University Press, 3rd ed., 2003), 68 (citing Thomas Stewart and Arthur Hayes, *The World's Most Famous Court Trial: State of Tennessee v. John Thomas Scopes* (1925), ed. Leonard W. Levy (New York: Da Capo Press, 1971), 137, 150–53; David W. Louisell and Christopher B. Mueller, *Federal Evidence* (Rochester, NY: Lawyers Cooperative Publishing Co., 1979), vol. 3, 629–30, 633, 649–56, 687–88 (1979)). By contrast, in *Kitzmiller* (note 6 above), a whole parade of expert witnesses, on both sides, dominated the proceedings.

[27] Frye v. United States, 293 F. 1013 (D.C. Cir. 1923).

[28] *Id.*, 1014.

[29] Alice B. Lustre, Annotation, "Post-*Daubert* Standards for Admissibility of Scientific and Other Expert Evidence in State Courts," *ALR* (*American Law Reports*) 5th, 90 (2001): 453–545. Michigan stuck with *Frye* until 2004, when it shifted to *Daubert*. Mich Rule Evidence (MRE) 702; see also People v. Wright, No. 261380, 2006 WL 2271264, *5 (Mich. Ct. App. Aug. 8, 2006) ("MRE 702 was specifically amended, effective January 1, 2004, to incorporate the *Daubert* standards"). See note 102 below on the recent change in Florida evidence law.

But in 1975 the Federal Rules of Evidence (FRE) were adopted; and Rule 702, on scientific, technical or other expert testimony, said nothing explicit about "general acceptance," only that a qualified expert may testify provided that his or her evidence is relevant to facts at issue, and not otherwise legally excluded.[30] Had *Frye* been superseded, or not? This wasn't clear until 1993, when the Supreme Court's ruling in *Daubert*[31] established that in federal jurisdictions the new Rule 702 had indeed superseded *Frye*; but also that federal courts' "gatekeeping" role nevertheless requires them to screen proffered expert testimony for reliability as well as relevance.[32] In 1997 the *Joiner* Court confirmed that the standard of review for such evidentiary rulings is abuse of discretion;[33] and in 1999, in *Kumho Tire*, the Court confirmed that *Daubert* applies to all expert testimony, not just the scientific.[34] In 2000 FRE 702 was revised to require that expert testimony be based on "sufficient facts or data," arrived at by "reliable principles and methods," "reliably" applied to the facts of the case.

As we will see in the papers that follow, the *Daubert* ruling is quite flawed: its philosophical underpinnings are far from sound,[35] for example, and its articulation of the idea of evidentiary reliability far from transparent.[36] Moreover, though Justice Blackmun's rhetoric suggested that the intent in *Daubert* was to relax the standards of admissibility,[37] at least in civil cases the upshot may well have been to tighten them.[38] The *Joiner* ruling distances itself somewhat from the *Daubert* Court's muddled philosophy of science—but creates further

30 "If scientific, technical, or other specialized knowledge will assist the trier of fact to understand the evidence or to determine a fact at issue, a witness qualified as an expert by knowledge, skill, experience, training, or education, may testify in the form of an opinion or otherwise." FRE 702 (1975).

31 Daubert v. Merrell Dow Pharm., Inc., 509 U.S. 579 (1993) ("*Daubert* III").

32 *Id.*, 589 ("[The *Frye* Rule is an] austere standard, absent from, and incompatible with, the Federal Rules of Evidence, [and] should not be applied in federal trials.").

33 Gen. Elec. Co. v. Joiner, 522 U.S. 136, 139 (1997) ("*Joiner* III") ("We hold that abuse of discretion is the appropriate standard.").

34 Kumho Tire Co. v. Carmichael, 526 U.S. 137, 141 (1999) ("We conclude that Daubert's general holding—setting forth the trial judge's general 'gatekeeping' obligation—applies not only to testimony based on 'scientific' knowledge, but also to testimony based on 'technical' and 'other specialized' knowledge.").

35 "Trial and Error: Two Confusions in *Daubert*," pp. 104–21 in this volume, 106–16; "Federal Philosophy of Science: A Deconstruction—And a Reconstruction," pp. 122–55 in this volume, 125–40.

36 "What's Wrong with Litigation-Driven Science?" pp. 180–207 in this volume, 200–201.

37 *Daubert* III (note 31 above), 589.

38 See, e.g., Lisa Heinzerling, "Doubting *Daubert*," *Journal of Law and Policy* 14 (2006): 65–83, 68 ("[T]he [*Daubert*] Court's casually offered guidelines on admitting expert scientific evidence have served as the vehicle for transforming *Daubert* from an evidence-liberalizing decision into an evidence-narrowing one.").

concerns about the blurring of questions of admissibility with questions of the weight or sufficiency of evidence. The ruling in *Kumho Tire* finally acknowledges that what really matters isn't whether expert testimony is science, but whether it is reliable—but seems to leave the tricky stuff to courts' discretion. And the revised FRE 702, with its emphatic repetition of "reliable," "reliably," "sufficient,"[39] is apt to leave you wondering how *any* verbal formula, by itself, could make it possible to determine whether the data on which a scientific witness bases his opinion are sufficient, or whether his methods are reliable.

So it comes as no surprise that the old complaints about tainted, partial experts and ignorant, credulous attorneys, jurors, and judges are still heard—and now, also, a new complaint, as would-be scientific witnesses whose testimony has been ruled inadmissible by a court protest the professional insult of being "dauberted out" when a judge deems their proffered testimony unreliable, even "unscientific."[40]

No doubt there *are* biased and incompetent experts, attorneys who encourage such experts into the legal system, gullible jurors over-impressed by the supposed authority of a witness merely on account of his scientific credentials, *and* scientifically illiterate judges too ready to dismiss an expert witness's unwelcome proffered testimony as not really science at all. But underlying these familiar complaints is the threat of those "irreconcilable differences" to which my title alludes: the deep tensions between the goals, the processes, the values, and the timetable of scientific inquiry, and legal goals, processes, values, and schedules.

3 THE NATURE OF SCIENCE AND THE CULTURE OF LAW

It is sometimes said that science is a search for truth; and this is right, if rightly understood. The core business of the sciences is inquiry; the object of the enterprise is to figure out answers to questions about the world and how it works; and it goes almost without saying that, whenever you want the answer to a question, you want the true answer. This is not to say that scientists seek THE TRUTH, in some quasi-religious sense; nor is it to suggest that scientific truths are the only truths there are, or that scientific truths are ever known with

39 FRE 702 (effective December 1, 2000).

40 George Lakoff, "A Cognitive Scientist Looks at *Daubert*," *American Journal of Public Health* 95 (2005): S114–S120, S117 ("When a scientist is 'Dauberted out' of a trial, the repercussions for the scientist are serious."); "De-*Daubertizing* Economic Damages Evidence," LostCompensation.com (January 2006), http://wwwlostcompensation.com/newsletters/v3_i1_2006.html ("A 'dauberted out' economic expert in injury and wrongful death cases can be particularly disastrous").

absolute certainty.[41] It is only to say that when, for example, James Watson and Francis Crick worked to "solve the structure of DNA," what they wanted was to reach the answer that DNA is a double-helical, backbone-out macromolecule with like-with-unlike base pairs if DNA *is* a double-helical, backbone-out macromolecule with like-with-unlike base pairs, to reach the answer that DNA is a triple-helical backbone-in macromolecule with like-with-like base pairs if it *is* a triple-helical, etc., macromolecule, and so on.

As the example suggests, once scientists have figured out the answer to one question, almost invariably new questions arise—sometimes a whole cascade of them: as, once they had worked out the structure of DNA, molecular biologists next had to tackle the "Coding Problem," which it would take more than a decade to solve.[42] And as this in turn suggests, even though there is no guarantee that every step will be in the right direction, it is in the nature of the scientific enterprise to push forward, to tackle new questions with the help of answers to older ones.

Of course, scientists seek not just true answers, but substantive, explanatory, fruitful, illuminating answers ("either DNA is a double-helical, etc., macromolecule, or it isn't," though undeniably true, won't do). While scientific investigation sometimes focuses on particular things or events—a particular planet, earthquake, eclipse, epidemic, or whatever—even when it does, there is always a concern with laws, explanation, prediction; in short, with the general. Medical scientists, for example, might investigate why this individual seems unusually resistant to HIV infection; but the goal would be to figure out *what it is about him* that makes him less susceptible.

Like historians, investigative journalists, detectives, or anyone seriously trying to figure something out,[43] scientists make informed guesses at the answers to their questions, work out the consequences of these informed guesses, seek out evidence to check how well those consequences hold up, and use their judgment about how to proceed from there. There is no algorithmic "scientific

[41] It is, however, to reject both the instrumentalist view that theoretical "statements" in science are not really genuine statements at all, and so are neither true nor false, but only tools or instruments for making observational predictions; and the constructive-empiricist view that, although theoretical statements are statements, and do have truth-values, the goal of science is empirical (i.e., observational) adequacy, not truth. I shan't argue either point here, but refer readers to *Defending Science* (note 3 above), 137–41.

[42] Horace Freeland Judson, *The Eighth Day of Creation: Makers of the Revolution in Biology* (New York: Simon and Schuster, 1979), 488.

[43] Nowadays, of course, detectives and crime-scene investigators (though themselves neither scientists nor lawyers) use scientific techniques, and also have to be concerned with certain legal constraints, especially to avoid obtaining evidence in such a way that it will not be admissible in court.

method"; i.e., no formal, or formalizable, procedure available to all scientists and only to scientists, and which, faithfully followed, guarantees success, or even progress. But over centuries of work scientists have gradually developed a vast array of special tools and techniques: ever more powerful instruments of observation, ever more cunning (and sometimes very formally precise) experimental designs, ever more sophisticated mathematical and statistical techniques, ever fancier computer programs, and so on. These scientific "helps" to inquiry usually develop in an *ad hoc* way, in response to some problem at hand; and almost always they rely on some earlier scientific innovation, theoretical or practical.[44] The evolution of these "technical" helps to inquiry has been an untidy, pragmatic, fallible, bootstrap process—but an untidy, pragmatic, fallible, bootstrap process that has gradually made it possible to get more and better-focused evidence, and to assess more accurately where evidence leads; in short, to extend and amplify unaided human cognitive powers.

Because the core business of science is inquiry, the core values of science are epistemological: among them, honesty, with yourself and others, about what the evidence is and what it shows, and willingness to make your evidence available to others in the field—essentially, the values Robert Merton articulated long ago under the labels "disinterestedness" and "communism."[45] Instilling and sustaining commitment to these values isn't easy; scientists are fallible human beings, with the usual mixed and sometimes dubious motives, hopes, and fears. Still, besides those technical helps, the sciences have developed informal social mechanisms to enable the pooling of evidence and to provide incentives and disincentives of reputation, etc.—social mechanisms that, up to a point, harness such potentially pernicious motives as vanity or the desire for prestige to serious scientific work.[46] However, while the technical

44 See, e.g., Bettyann Holtzmann Kevles, *Naked to the Bone: Medical Imaging in the Twentieth Century* (New Brunswick, NJ: Rutgers University Press, 1997), on the history of medical-imaging techniques.

45 Robert Merton, "Science and Democratic Social Structure," in Merton, *Social Theory and Social Structure* (Chicago: Free Press of Glencoe, 1949), 307–16. (Merton's understanding of science is nowadays regarded in some circles as hopelessly passé; but my view of the matter is, on the contrary, that some insights of Merton's are now in danger of being lost.) See also Haack, *Defending Science* (note 3 above), 299–328 (on the values of science); "The Integrity of Science: What It Means, Why It Matters" (2006), reprinted in Haack, *Putting Philosophy to Work: Inquiry and Iits Place in Culture* (Amherst, NY: Prometheus Books, 2008); expanded ed. 2013, 121–40, 124 (where I adopt and adapt some of Merton's ideas about the norms of science).

46 Some professional scientific organizations now have formal codes of ethical conduct. See, e.g., American Society for Microbiology, http://www.asm.org/index.php/governance/code-of-ethics; Gerontological Society of America, http://www.geron.org/Membership/code-of-ethics; International Union of Biochemistry and Molecular Biology,

helps enabling scientists to acquire and assess evidence keep getting better and better, these "social" helps do not; in fact, they are coming under increasing strain both from the ever-growing scale of the scientific enterprise and from the alien values of the governments and large industrial concerns on the financial support of which science increasingly depends—especially in the most commercialized areas of science, the medical sciences in particular.[47]

Where all but the very simplest scientific claims and theories are concerned, the evidence will ramify in many directions; it is usually mediated by sophisticated instruments; more often than not it is the shared resource of many people, who may be working together or may be rivals, and may be working in the same laboratory or thousands of miles or many decades or even centuries apart; it is almost invariably incomplete; and it is quite often ambiguous or misleading. At any time, some scientific claims and theories are so well-established that it would be astounding if they turned out to be wrong, some reasonably well-grounded but not quite *so* well-established . . ., some rather speculative, some very speculative, some highly speculative, and some downright wild and wacky. The proportion of the well-warranted to the highly speculative varies, obviously, from field to field; at any time, some areas of science are more speculative than others, and some are mostly speculative—for some fields of science are more advanced, more "mature" as we say, others relatively new and thus-far undeveloped, and some so undeveloped, so entirely speculative, that you might understandably hesitate to call them "sciences" at all. The boundaries of the enormously complex and uneven enterprise to which we refer by the commodious word "science" are fuzzy, indeterminate, and frequently contested.

When the available evidence on some question is seriously incomplete, those who work in the relevant scientific community—some of them probably more radical in temperament, others more conservative—may reasonably disagree about the likelihood that this or that answer is correct. As new evidence comes in, a consensus may eventually form that this once-merely-speculative theory is probably right, or that once-promising-seeming approach probably wrong. But there are no rules determining when a scientific claim is well enough warranted by the evidence to be accepted, or badly enough undermined by the evidence to be rejected; and neither, of course, do scientists reach their

http://www.iumb.org/index.php?id=155; American Medical Association, http://www.ama-assn.org/ama/pub/physician-resources/medical-ethics/code-medical-ethics.page. Courses in ethics for science students are not uncommon, though more formal arrangements like these cannot compensate for an erosion of the ethos of science.

[47] See again Haack, "The Integrity of Science: What It Means, Why It Matters" (note 45 above), 129–38.

"verdict" by taking a vote.[48] Instead, consensus arises as a by-product when enough members of the relevant scientific sub-community come to see the evidence as strong enough to warrant this claim or that theory.

Ideally, such consensus would form when, and only when, the evidence is sufficient; in practice, acceptance and warrant sometimes come apart.[49] This may be because significant evidence gets lost or neglected;[50] it may be because some widely-held but unwarranted assumption skews scientists' judgment;[51] or it may be the result of the influence or the persuasiveness of some individual, or group, in the field.[52] But what counts in the end is not *what person* is most powerful or most persuasive, but *which approach* proves most fruitful, i.e., results in theories that stand up best as evidence comes in. Watson really, really wanted to beat out Linus Pauling and win a Nobel prize;

48 In 2006, an international congress of astronomers, prompted by developments in the field that made it necessary to get a clearer agreement on what counts as a planet, voted to adopt the verbal convention that to count as a planet, a heavenly body should have these and those characteristics—and in consequence, demoted Pluto from "planet" to "dwarf planet." Dennis Overbye, "Astronomers in Quandary Over Pluto's Planet Status," *New York Times*, August 23, 2006, A20; Kenneth Chang, "Dwarf Planet, Cause of Strife, Gains 'The Perfect Name,'" *New York Times*, September 15, 2006, A20. But this certainly wasn't a vote to determine *whether Pluto has or lacks those characteristics*—that just isn't the kind of thing that *could* be so decided.

49 Perhaps the first phrase of the *Frye* Rule, that the underlying scientific principle must be "*sufficiently established to be* generally accepted in the field" (my italics), was an implicit acknowledgment of this possibility. If so, it is an insight that is lost when the Rule is abbreviated, as it usually is, to "general acceptance." This prompts the speculation that the Florida Supreme Court's ruling in *Ramirez III*—where it seems on its face as if the court conducted a *Daubert* inquiry to determine whether the kind of knife-mark identification on which Mr. Ramirez's conviction turned is generally accepted in the field—might more plausibly be read as implicitly recognizing the significance of this initial phase of the test proposed in *Frye*. Ramirez v. State, 810 So. 2d 836, 845 (Fla. 2001) ("*Ramirez* III").

50 I am thinking, for example, of the decades in which Gregor Mendel's paper, effectively establishing the particulate theory of inheritance, lay neglected and unread in the journal of the Natural History Society of Brno (Brünn), Moravia. Frank Maloney, Gregor Johann Mendel O.S.A., http://astro4.ast.vill.edu/mendel/gregor.htm.

51 I am thinking, for example, of the tetranucleotide hypothesis (attributed to Phoebus Levene), according to which DNA is a "monotonous" molecule, with regularly repeating base pairs; which, though merely a conjecture, was so widely accepted as to hold back recognition that DNA is the genetic material. Judson, *The Eighth Day of Creation* (note 42 above), 30.

52 I am thinking, for example, of the long period in Soviet genetics when Trofim Lysenko's (badly mistaken) ideas became an orthodoxy. See, e.g., William Broad and Nicholas Wade, *Betrayers of the Truth* (New York: Simon and Schuster, Touchstone Books, 1982), 186–92; George S. Counts and Nucia Lodge, *The Country of the Blind: The Soviet System of Mind Control* (Boston: Houghton Mifflin, 1949); Nils Roll-Hansen, *The Lysenko Effect: The Politics of Science* (Amherst, NY: Humanity Books, 2005); Valerii N. Soifer, *The Tragedy of Soviet Science*, trans. Leo Gruliow and Rebecca Gruliow (New Brunswick, NJ: Rutgers University Press, 1994).

but it would not have satisfied him to win simply by being more persuasive than Pauling was—the point was *to solve the structure of* DNA first. Had he aimed only to win the debate, only to persuade others to his point of view, he would have been engaged in sham inquiry, i.e., in advocacy disguised as investigation, not the real thing.[53] Indeed, as Michael Polanyi once put it, "[o]nly if scientists remain loyal to scientific ideals rather than try to achieve success with their fellow scientists can they form a community which will uphold those ideals."[54]

Though some science is certainly policy-relevant, scientific investigation as such is, in an important sense, policy-neutral.[55] Scientists may, for example, explore the risks and benefits of making this or that drug or pesticide available, or the long-run effects of damming that river or of relying on this rather than that energy source; but whether the risks of the drug outweigh the benefits, whether the river should be dammed, or whether we would be wise to switch to an alternative energy source, are not themselves scientific questions—though, admittedly, when scientific work bears closely on policy questions, the line between scientific inquiry and policy-advocacy can only too easily get blurred.

Quite often, a scientist or scientific team will need to come up with some kind of answer on a specific timetable: when they are working under pressure in an epidemic or in wartime,[56] for example, or simply because they need to report *some* result at the end of the grant period to the outfit that funded

53 See Susan Haack, "As for That Phrase 'Studying in a Literary Spirit,'" (1997), reprinted in Haack, *Manifesto of a Passionate Moderate: Unfashionable Essays* (Chicago: University of Chicago Press, 1998), 48–68 (developing Peirce's idea of sham inquiry). Now I can suggest a splendid illustration: the "Wedge Document" produced by the Center for Science and Culture at the Discovery Institute (and made public, apparently without the Center's authorization, in 1999). Resembling nothing so much as a marketing plan for Intelligent Design Theory, this document gives the lie to the pretense that IDT is a scientific conjecture giving rise to a *bona fide* research program. Center for the Renewal of Science and Culture, The Wedge Strategy, www.kcfs.org/Fliers_articles/Wedge.html. On Intelligent Design Theory generally, and the Discovery Institute's Wedge Document specifically see Barbara Forrest and Paul R. Gross, *Creationism's Trojan Horse: The Wedge of Intelligent Design* (New York: Oxford University Press, 2004).

54 Michael Polanyi, *Science, Faith and Society* (Cambridge: Cambridge University Press, 1946), 40.

55 See Susan Haack, "Six Signs of Scientism" (2010), in *Putting Philosophy to Work* (note 45 above), 105–20. (Some might argue that political science is an exception; but this is not an issue that can be pursued here.)

56 See, e.g., John M. Barry, *The Great Influenza: The Epic Story of the Deadliest Plague in History* (New York: Penguin Books, 2004) (a history of the hurried work to figure out the cause of the 1918 flu epidemic); William Cooper [H. S. Hoff], *The Struggles of Albert Woods* (1952; Harmonsdsworth, Middlesex, UK: Penguin Books, 1966) (a fictional account of hurried poison-gas research during World War II).

them. But in such circumstances the work is very apt to be skimped; for the unavoidable fact is that *scientific inquiry takes the time it takes*, and its progress is ragged and unpredictable. To be sure, it may be possible to say ahead of time how long it will take to run this series of experiments, or how long that epidemiological study will continue; but even the best-informed specialist can make only very, very tentative and fallible estimates of how long it might be before this problem is solved, that phenomenon understood. Moreover, at any time there are many scientific questions to which there is as yet no warranted answer, and about which an honest scientist in the field could only say, "at the moment, we just don't know; we're working on it, but we can't tell you when we'll have it figured out."

I have stressed that the core business of science is inquiry; but of course not all those who describe themselves as scientists are engaged in this core business (and most of those who are will likely be engaged in fairly routine kinds of investigation, not in the profound intellectual work of the heroes of the history of science). Some scientists are mostly occupied with developing new instruments, new techniques of purification, new computer programs, and so forth and so on; another large class of people who might be described as engaged in "scientific work" in an ample sense of that phrase are simply applying well-established scientific techniques in relatively routine kinds of testing; and some have borrowed the honorific description "science" for no better reason than that they rely on scientific equipment of one kind or another—or just because it makes their work seem more respectable.[57]

Nevertheless, the core business of science *is* inquiry. And scientific inquiry, and in particular inquiry in the natural sciences, is by nature tentative and thoroughly fallibilist; it focuses on the general law or principle rather than the particular instance; its core values are intellectual honesty and willingness to share evidence; its procedures are problem-oriented, pragmatic, and usually quite informal; it is open-ended and forward-looking; and, though it is quite often relevant to policy, it is, ideally anyway, strictly disinterested on questions of policy. So it is hardly surprising that the legal system has had trouble handling scientific testimony, for the legal culture could hardly be more different: adversarial, focused on the specific case, formally-procedurally-anchored, valuing promptness and finality, relying on precedent, and not only relevant, but also highly sensitive, to policy.

~

Justice Blackmun writes in *Daubert* that there are "important differences between the quest for truth in the courtroom and the quest for truth in the

[57] Or, as in the case of "creation science," in hopes of circumventing legal problems.

laboratory."[58] That's putting it mildly. The core business of a legal system is to resolve disputes; and a trial aims, not to *find out whether* the defendant is guilty, etc., but (as we say) to *arrive at a determination* of the defendant's guilt or liability—"determine," here, probably being closer to "deem" than to "discover." This is not to deny that inquiry plays a role in the legal process—of course it does;[59] nor is it to deny that, while some cases are focused on legal technicalities, others are centrally concerned with factual issues. But it *is* to deny that inquiry is quite as central to the law as it is to science.

Moreover, as Justice Blackmun intimates, the way our legal system goes about making its determinations of the truth is really quite *un*like the processes of scientific investigation: the law relies on an adversarial procedure, subject to the relevant standard of proof, under the constraint of rules some of which mandate the exclusion of relevant evidence for reasons that aren't even obliquely truth-related. And the advocacy that is at the core of the adversarial process is a very different matter from inquiry: for inquiry starts with a question and, aiming to arrive at an answer, seeks out evidence; while advocacy, aiming to persuade, starts with a proposition to be defended and marshals the best evidence it can in its favor.

Some, apparently taking for granted that, in respect of seeking truth, the legal system is in the relevant respects in the same business as the sciences, object that it goes about that business in a peculiar and ineffective way. As we saw in "Epistemology Legalized,"[60] C. S. Peirce didn't mince his words when he wrote that "[l]ogic puts it heel" on the idea "that hot and partisan debate is the way to investigate;"[61] and neither did Judge Frankel when he

58 *Daubert* III (note 31 above), 596–97.

59 Failure to investigate is one criterion of "ineffective assistance of counsel" in death-penalty cases. See Rompilla v. Beard, 545 U.S. 374, 383 (2005) (reversing on the grounds that "the lawyers were deficient in failing to examine the court file on Rompilla's prior conviction"); Wiggins v. Smith, 539 U.S. 510, 524 (2003) (reversing based on the counsel's decision not to expand the investigation beyond the presentence investigation (PSI) and Department of Social Service (DSS) records, which "fell short of the professional standards that prevailed in Maryland in 1989"); Williams v. Taylor, 529 U.S. 362, 373 (2000) (reversing the death penalty and remanding on the grounds that counsel for the petitioner had failed to seek Williams's juvenile and social service records, "erroneously believ[ing] that 'state law didn't permit it'"). See also American Bar Association, *Guidelines for the Appointment and Performance of Defense Counsel in Death Penalty Cases*, Guideline 10.7, 76 (revised ed., Feb. 2003), available at http://www.fjc.gov/public/pdf.nsf/lookup/DPen0709.pdf/$file/DPen0709.pdf ("counsel at every stage have an obligation to conduct thorough and independent investigations relating to the issues of both guilt and penalty").

60 "Epistemology Legalized: Or, Truth, Justice, and the American Way," pp. 27–46 in this volume.

61 Charles Sanders Peirce, *Collected Papers*, eds. Charles Hartshorne, Paul Weiss and (vols. 7 and 8) Arthur Burks (Cambridge, MA: Harvard University Press, 1931–58), 2.635 (1878). Also

wrote that, though lawyers, judges, and legal scholars profess to believe that "the clash of adversaries is a powerful means for hammering out the truth," everyone knows that *real* inquirers—historians, scientists, etc.—go about their investigations very differently.[62] If the legal system were in the same business as history, geography, physics, etc., I agree, its way of conducting that business would be strange to say the least. But the law really *isn't* in exactly the same business. This is not at all to deny that it's desirable that legal determinations of guilt or liability be, so far as possible, factually correct; on the contrary, it is *highly* desirable. But that "so far as possible" includes "consistent with satisfying such non-truth-related desiderata as reaching a resolution within a reasonable period of time, proceeding in accordance with constitutional constraints, and taking certain policy-related considerations into account."[63]

Implicit in the previous paragraphs, but needing to be made explicit, are the crucial differences between the legal and the scientific timetables. In the wake of a major discovery, scientific investigation sometimes advances at an impressive pace, rather as filling in a long, central crossword entry sometimes enables you to solve a whole slew of others; often, though, scientific work is halting and fumbling, slowed sometimes by lack of funds or by political resistance to potentially unwelcome results, and often enough by the sheer intellectual difficulty of the question(s) concerned. And there is always, at least in principle, the possibility of having to go back and start over on what had been thought to be settled questions. By contrast, not without reason, we want the legal system to reach its determinations within a reasonable period of time; and, again not without reason, we want those determinations, once the appeals process is exhausted, to stand.

Also implicit in the preceding paragraphs, and also needing to be made explicit, is that the legal process is highly regimented, conducted under formal rules of procedure and of evidence, etc. Paul Feyerabend, self-styled "court jester" of the philosophy of science, wrote of the "methodological anarchism" of the sciences;[64] and despite his tendency to wild exaggeration, there

in *Writings: A Chronological Edition*, eds. Peirce Edition Project (Indianapolis, IN: Indiana University Press, 1982–present), 3.331.

62 Marvin F. Frankel, "The Search for Truth: An Umpireal View," *University of Pennsylvania Law Review* 123, no. 5 (1975): 1031–59, 1036.

63 As Robert Heilbrun's fictional public defender Arch Gold comments, "[t]his [the capital-sentencing hearing in which he is participating] wasn't the real world.... It was a twisted kind of theater, a 'reality-based' drama that had nothing to do with what really went on down there on Twentieth Street." Robert Heilbrun, *Offer of Proof* (New York: Harper Torchbooks, 2003), 208.

64 Paul K. Feyerabend, *Against Method: Outlines of an Anarchistic Theory of Knowledge* (London: New Left Press, 1975), 10 (claiming that "[s]cience is an essentially anarchistic enterprise"); but see also the criticisms in Haack, *Defending Science* (note 3 above), 49–50.

is a grain of truth in this idea. It's not exactly that absolutely *anything* goes; still, scientific inquiry *does* have a kind of free-ranging, "just do it," improvising character. By contrast, the regimented procedures of the law look more like a formal dance—a minuet, perhaps.

Also implicit, and also needing to be made explicit, is that some of the questions answers to which are to be determined at trial will be case-specific: did his mother's taking Bendectin cause *Jeffrey Blum*'s birth defects?[65] Did his occupational exposure to PCBs (polychlorinated biphenyls) promote *Mr. Joiner*'s cancer?[66] What is the probability that the match between this DNA sample from the crime scene and *this defendant* is a matter of chance?

4 THOSE "IRRECONCILABLE DIFFERENCES" AT WORK

Against this background we can readily see why, as Mr. Humes so bluntly puts it, "courts don't do science very well"; or, as I might say, why the law has such difficulty in handling scientific testimony, and so often gets less than the best out of science.[67] But it's a very complicated, very tangled tale; for there are many tensions between science and the law, tensions that interact and reinforce each other. I had hoped to be able to shoehorn the difficulties into simple categories like "finality vs. fallibilism," "advocacy vs. inquiry," "inertia vs. innovation," and so on; but now this seems impossibly neat and tidy. Here, instead, is a not-so-tidy list:

- *Because it is called on to resolve disputed issues about the cause of plaintiffs' injury, especially in toxic tort cases the law often calls on those fields of science where the pressure of commercial interests is most severe.*

In toxic tort litigation, much of the scientific work bearing on issues of causation is likely to have been conducted by a drug company or a chemical manufacturer, for marketing purposes or, quite often, with an eye to protecting itself

65 Blum v. Merrell Dow Pharm., Inc., 1 Pa. D. & C.4th 634 (Phila. Cnty. Ct. 1988) ("*Blum* I"), *rev'd*, 560 A.2d 212 (Pa. Super. Ct. 1989) ("*Blum* II"), *aff'd*, 626 A.2d 537 (Pa. 1993) ("*Blum* III"), *remanded to* 33 Phila. Cnty. Rep. 193 (1996) ("*Blum* IV"), *rev'd*, 705 A.2d 1314 (Pa. Super. 1997) ("*Blum* V"), *aff'd*, 764 A.2d 1 (Pa. 2000) ("*Blum* VI"). This case is discussed in some detail in "What's Wrong with Litigation-Driven Science?" (note 36 above), 188–94.

66 Joiner v. Gen. Elec. Co., 864 F. Supp. 1310 (N.D. Ga. 1994) ("*Joiner* I"), *rev'd*, 78 F.3d 524 (11th Cir. 1996) ("*Joiner* II"), *rev'd*, 522 U.S. 136 (1997) ("*Joiner* III"), *remanded to* 134 F.3d 1457 (11th Cir. 1998) ("*Joiner* IV").

67 Its interactions with the law can also have deleterious effects on science: for example, scientists whose work potentially bears on litigation are quite likely to find themselves interrupted and overburdened by subpoenas and depositions. "Legal Demands Take Time from Scientists' Real Work," *Wall Street Journal*, January 27, 2007, A5. But I can't pursue those issues here.

against litigation—exactly the kind of scientific work where commercial interests most severely strain the informal scientific mechanisms that encourage honesty and discourage the withholding of evidence.[68] I think in this context of the wave of litigation by plaintiffs alleging that their cardiovascular problems were aggravated by Merck's arthritis drug, Vioxx; for by now we know that Merck's first large clinical trial, the VIGOR study, on the basis of which the FDA approved the drug, was designed in such a way as to be more likely to identify favorable than unfavorable trends;[69] and that the APPROVe study, which prompted the withdrawal of the drug, didn't use the statistical method the published report of the study said it used, and would have been even less favorable to Vioxx if it had.[70]

- *Because the legal aspires to resolve disputes promptly,*[71] *the scientific questions on which it seeks answers will often be those where all the evidence is not yet in.*

The cases that come to trial will normally be those where the evidence is thus far incomplete and ambiguous. For one thing, plaintiffs must sue before the possibility of redress is legally foreclosed; for another, when the evidence that a drug or chemical is dangerous is overwhelming, plaintiffs' claims are likely to be settled out of court.

- *Because of its case-specificity, the law often demands answers of a kind that science is not well-equipped to supply.*

68 See again "What's Wrong with Litigation-Driven Science?" (note 36 above), 200.

69 The VIGOR study was designed to track gastrointestinal effects (anticipated to be favorable to the drug) longer than cardiovascular effects (more likely to be unfavorable). Claire Bombadier et al., "Comparison of Upper Gastrointestinal Toxicity of Rofecoxib and Naproxen in Patients with Rheumatoid Arthritis," *New England Journal of Medicine* 433, no. 21 (2000): 1520–28; David Armstrong, "How the New England Journal Missed Warning Signs on Vioxx: Medical Weekly Waited Years to Report Flaws in Article That Praised Pain Drug—Merck Seen as 'Punching Bag,'" *Wall Street Journal*, May 15, 2006, A1, A10. For more details, see "Peer-Review and Publication: Lessons for Lawyers," pp. 156–79 in this volume, 169–71.

70 Scott D. Solomon et al., "Cardiovascular Events Associated with Rofecoxib in a Colorectal Adenoma Prevention Trial," *New England Journal of Medicine* 352 (2005): 1071–80; "Correction," 355–2 *New England Journal of Medicine* 355–2 (2006), 221; Heather Won Tesoriero, "Vioxx Study Correction May Add Pressure to Merck's Defense," *Wall Street Journal*, June 27, 2006, A2. In November 2007, Merck made a $4.85 billion settlement deal with (a large class of) Vioxx plaintiffs. Heather Won Tesoriero et al., "Vioxx Settlement for $4.85 Billion Largely Vindicates Merck's Tactics," *Wall Street Journal*, November 11, 2007, A1, A5.

71 I say "aspires" because in practice litigation is sometimes alarmingly protracted; for example, the Blums first brought suit against Merrell Dow in 1982, but the case was not finally resolved until 18 years later, in 2000. See note 65 above, giving the history of *Blum*.

This is well illustrated in *Joiner*: by the time of Mr. Joiner's suit, the toxicity of PCBs was well-established; but how much, if at all, Mr. Joiner's occupational PCB exposure contributed to his developing small-cell lung cancer—given that he had been a smoker, and that there was a family history of this disease—was an almost impossibly difficult question.[72] It is in response to this kind of problem that some courts have proposed to treat epidemiological evidence that exposure to a substance more than doubles the risk of a certain disorder as necessary and/or sufficient to prove "by a preponderance of the evidence" that his exposure to the substance caused *the plaintiff's* developing the disorder—a badly confused idea, as we shall see in "Risky Business."[73]

- *The legal system constitutes virtually the entire market for certain fields of forensic science (or quasi-science), and for certain psychiatric specialties.*

The clearest illustrations come from such forensic-identification fields as hair- or knife-mark analysis,[74] and such psychiatric specialties as the recovery of supposedly suppressed memories or assessments of future dangerousness[75]—surely among the weakest of what we sometimes call the "soft," or social sciences.

- *Because of its adversarial character, the legal system tends to draw in as witnesses scientists who are in a sense marginal, i.e., more willing than most of their colleagues to give an opinion on the basis of less-than-overwhelming evidence; moreover, the more often he serves as an expert witness, the more unbudgeably confident a scientist may become in his opinion.*

[72] *Joiner* III (note 33 above), 139–40.

[73] "Risky Business: Statistical Proof of Specific Causation," pp. 264–93 in this volume.

[74] See, e.g., Adina Schwartz, "A Systemic Challenge to the Reliability and Admissibility of Firearms and Toolmark Identification," *The Columbia Science & Technology Law Review* VI (2005): 1–42, 1 (arguing that "all firearms and toolmark identifications should be excluded until adequate statistical empirical foundations and proficiency testing are developed for the field").

[75] See, e.g., Thomas Regnier, "*Barefoot* in Quicksand: The Future of Future Dangerousness Predictions in Death Penalty Sentencing in the World of *Daubert* and *Kumho*," 37.3 *Akron Law Review* 37, no. 3 (2004): 467–507. (Besides such psychiatric predictions of future dangerousness, there are now actuarial instruments for making such assessments based on information about a person's upbringing, childhood, criminal history, and so on; which seem to be, though very far from perfect, somewhat better than psychiatrists' assessment. There is some evidence, however, that jurors put more stock in (less reliable) clinical predictions than in (more reliable) actuarial predictions. See generally Daniel A. Krause, John G. McCabe, and Joel D. Lieberman, "Dangerously Misunderstood: Representative Jurors' Reaction to Expert Testimony on Future Dangerousness in a Sexually Violent Predator Trial," *Psychology, Public Policy, and Law* 198, no. 1 (2012): 18–49).

An attorney obligated to make the best possible case for his client will have an incentive to call on those scientists in an area who are ready to accept an answer to some scientific question as warranted while others in the field still remain agnostic; and sometimes on scientists whose involvement in litigation has hardened their initially more-cautious attitudes into unwarranted certainty. I think, in this context, of Merrell Dow's Dr. Robert Brent, always ready to testify that Bendectin does not cause birth defects, or plaintiffs' expert Dr. Alan Done, always ready to testify that it could;[76] or of psychiatrist Dr. James Grigson, testifying over and over in Texas death-penalty hearings that the defendant would, to a medical certainty, be dangerous in future.[77]

The adversarial process may distort even relatively strong science from relatively strong fields, sometimes to such a degree that it creates a kind of artificial scientific doubt,[78] or artificial scientific certainty; and can generate a public perception that this product is well-known to be dangerous, or that product well-known to be harmless, when really the evidence is weak, ambiguous, or lacking—as, for a time, public fear that silicone breast-implants may cause systemic connective-tissue disorders was in part generated by the legal system.[79]

76 In *Blum* (note 65 above), Merrell Dow's experts included Dr. Brent, who had not only testified over and over that Bendectin was not teratogenic, but had even published an article in which he analyzed seventeen Bendectin cases, and concluded that every one of the plaintiffs had lied; and the Blums' experts included Dr. Alan Done, who had served as plaintiffs' expert in a number of Bendectin cases, and—troubled by some flaws in the clinical trials and animal studies on which the defendants relied—was willing to conclude that his mother's taking Bendectin while pregnant could have caused Jeffrey Blum to be born with clubbed feet. *Blum* IV (note 65 above), 203–06.

77 See again Regnier, "*Barefoot* in Quicksand" (note 75 above), 480–82.

78 For example, in "Manufacturing Uncertainty: Contested Science and the Protection of the Public's Health and Environment," *American Journal of Public Health* 95 (2005): S39–S48. David Michaels and Celeste Monforton argue that "opponents of public health and environmental regulation often try to 'manufacture uncertainty' by questioning the validity of scientific evidence on which the regulations are based."

79 One study found a statistically significant correlation between silicone breast-implants and connective-tissue disorders: Charles H. Hennekens et al., "Self-Reported Breast Implants and Connective-Tissue Diseases in Female Health Professionals," *Journal of the American Medical Association* 275, no. 8 (1996): 616–21. However, this study was seriously flawed, depending on *subjects' own reports* of their medical problems. In 1998 the National Science Panel set up by Judge Samuel Pointer in *In re* Silicone Gel Breast Implant Prods. Liab. Litig. (MDL 926), No. CV 92-P-10000-S (N.D. Ala. 1998) concluded that there was no evidence that the implants cause such disorders. National Science Panel, *Silicone Breast Implants in Relation to Connective Tissue Diseases and Immunologic Dysfunction* (November 30, 1998), available at http://www.fjc.gov/BREIMLIT/SCIENCE/report.htm. Not long afterwards, an independent National Institute of Medicine Panel reached the same conclusion. Stuart Bondurant, Virginia Ernster, and Roger Herdman, eds., *Safety of Silicone Breast Implants* (Washington, DC: National Academies Press, 2000), 211–232, 231 ("[t]he committee finds no

Adversarialism can also cause distortions in the forensic sciences; not only by encouraging the startling dogmatism with which knife-mark examiners, for example, routinely assert that they can make a match with 100% certainty, and that they never make mistaken identifications,[80] but also by fostering the kinds of mistake that can occur in the application even of scientifically very solid forensic identification techniques, such as DNA analysis, when technicians are too anxious to be "helpful," to get the results law-enforcement needs.[81]

- *Legal rules can make it impossible to bring potentially useful scientific information to light.*

Courts' obligation to screen out unreliable scientific evidence has amplified the epistemological atomism of the rules of evidence, as judges rule not only on which proffered expert witnesses may testify, but also on whether they may testify to this or that question specifically.[82] This can be a problem: for interlocking pieces of evidence (e.g., toxicological information, animal studies, and epidemiological data), none of which is sufficient by itself, may jointly constitute adequate warrant for a claim that this exposure likely caused a plaintiff's injury;[83] but precisely because no individual piece of it is sufficient, a

convincing evidence for atypical connective tissue ... disease in women with silicone breast implants").

80 See *Ramirez* III (note 49 above), 840–41 (2001) (reporting that expert witness Robert Hart's "specific knife mark identification evidence played a crucial role in the trial: The trial court allowed the expert to state, 'The result of my examination made from the microscopic similarity, which I observed from both the cut cartilage and the standard mark, was the stab wound in the victim was caused by this particular knife *to the exclusion of all others.*'").

81 In 2006, for example, there was a scandal over the many weaknesses of the Houston DNA lab, a story extensively reported in the *Houston Chronicle*. See, e.g., Alan Bernstein, "Crime Lab Scandal Leaves Prosecutor Feeling Betrayed: Owmby Says Sutton Case Tests Faith in Justice System," *Houston Chronicle*, May 16, 2003, 23; Roma Khanna and Steve McVicker, "Police Chief Shakes Up Crime Lab; 2 Officials Quit, Others Disciplined," *Houston Chronicle*, June 13, 2003, A1; Roma Khanna and Steve McVicker, "HPD Ignored Warnings, Ex-Lab Man Says: Retired Official Says He Cited 'Train Wreck,'" *Houston Chronicle*, June 23, 2003, A1; Steve McVicker and Roma Khanna, "3 Say Chief Knew of Lab Woes; Bradford Says Some Disgruntled Employees Trying to Discredit Him," *Houston Chronicle*, June 22, 2003, A1; Steve McVicker and Roma Khanna, "93 HPD Lab Cases Under Scrutiny: Investigator's New Report Raises Figure from 27," *Houston Chronicle*, May 11, 2006, B1.

82 See, e.g., United States v. Llera Plaza, Nos. CR 98–362–10, 98–362–11, 98–362–12, 2002 WL 27305, *19 (E.D. Pa. Jan. 7, 2002) ("*Llera Plaza* I") (allowing FBI fingerprint examiners to testify about how they raised latent prints, about the characteristics of these latents from the crime scene, etc., but not to testify as to whether there was a match with the defendant). But see also note 101 below.

83 The point is argued in detail in "Proving Causation: The Weight of Combined Evidence," pp. 208–38 in this volume, 235–38.

jury may never hear such evidence. The issue of "weight of evidence methodology" was explicit both in the court of appeals' reversal of the district court's exclusion of Mr. Joiner's expert testimony, and in Justice Steven's dissent in *Joiner*;[84] but it was already implicit in *Daubert*, coming to the surface when, on remand, arguing with respect to each of the Dauberts' experts that he would have to be excluded under *Daubert* as he had been under *Frye*, Judge Kozinski affirmed the district court's summary judgment in favor of Merrell Dow.[85]

- *The legal penchant for rules, "indicia," etc., sometimes transmutes scientific subtleties into formulaic legal shibboleths.*

The brief verbal formulae on which the law sometimes relies to encapsulate key concepts or principles, to provide guidelines, or to give "indicia" of this or that, can "rigidify" ideas that scientists themselves treat much more flexibly. For example: though peer-reviewed publication is now standard practice at scientific and medical journals, I don't suppose many working scientists imagine that the fact that work has been accepted for publication after peer review is any guarantee that it is good stuff, or that its not having been published necessarily undermines its value.[86] The legal system, however, has come to invest considerable epistemic confidence in peer-reviewed publication[87]—perhaps for no

[84] In *Joiner* I (note 66 above), 1324–26, noting that none of the animal studies or the epidemiological studies on which Joiner's experts relied was sufficient by itself to establish that PCB exposure promoted his small-cell lung cancer, the District Court ruled that Joiner's expert testimony was inadmissible. In *Joiner* II (note 66 above), 532, the Court of Appeals reversed this decision, finding that "[o]pinions of any kind are derived from individual pieces of evidence, each of which by itself might not be conclusive, but when viewed in their entirety are the building blocks of a perfectly reasonable conclusion...." At the Supreme Court, Justice Stevens endorsed this idea. *Joiner* III (note 66 above), 152 (Stevens, J., dissenting in part). I am being deliberately noncommittal about whether the evidence Mr. Joiner's attorneys presented really did interlock in such a way as sufficiently to warrant his claim, in part because only part of that evidence is described in the ruling in *Joiner* III. In any case, the point here is only that, as I argue in "Proving Causation" (note 83 above), evidence *may* interlock in this way, and that evidence law may prevent this from becoming apparent.

[85] Daubert v. Merrell Dow Pharm., Inc., F.3d 1311, 1312 (9th Cir. 1995) ("*Daubert* IV").

[86] For example, the scientists on Judge Pointer's National Science Panel (set up to sift through the evidence about silicone breast-implants and connective-tissue disorders) included unpublished dissertations and letters, as well as published material, as providing evidence relevant to their task. National Science Panel, National Science Panel, *Silicone Breast Implants in Relation to Connective Tissue Diseases and Immunologic Dysfunction* (note 79 above), 8. I also note that book chapters in scientific textbooks are not peer-reviewed but invited.

[87] The legal preoccupation now extends beyond issues of scientific testimony; for example, in *Kitzmiller* (note 6 above), 735, the fact that there are no publications on Intelligent Design Theory (IDT) in peer-reviewed scientific journals was taken as an indication that IDT is not science, but religion.

better reason than that the law reviews are *not* peer-reviewed! Again, though requiring that epidemiological studies be statistically significant is now also routine scientific practice, I assume that most scientists are aware of the element of arbitrariness in the usual standards;[88] but legal actors sometimes seem to invest statistical significance with—well, with undue significance. And the law sometimes tinges scientific concepts with policy considerations—which partly explains why, for example, legal and scientific conceptions of causation don't quite mesh: the legal conception is informed by considerations about incentives and disincentives, about who should bear the costs of potentially risky enterprises, and sometimes about whose fault it is that evidence is lacking, considerations quite alien to science.

And the brief verbal formulae on which the law often relies can be ambiguous. For example, as we will see in "Peer Review and Publication,"[89] Justice Blackmun's observations could be taken as requiring that scientific testimony be based on work that has survived the pre-publication peer review process of scientific journals—which is relatively easy for a court to determine, but a poor indication of reliability; or they could be taken as requiring that such testimony be based on work that has survived and will continue to survive the long-run scrutiny of scientists in the field—which is a better (if still imperfect) indication of reliability, but impossible for a court to determine. And, as we will see in "What's Wrong with Litigation-Driven Science?"[90] there is a similar ambiguity in Judge Kozinski's new "*Daubert* factor," whether the work on which scientific testimony is based is "litigation-driven":[91] it is reasonably easy for a court to determine whether the work on which testimony is based was undertaken after litigation began—but this is a very weak indicator of unreliability; whether the design or the interpretation of the work on which testimony is based was significantly affected by litigation-related considerations is a better indicator of unreliability—but much harder for a court to determine.

- *Because of its concern for precedent, and the value it places on finality, the legal system has a tendency to inertia, and sometimes lags behind science.*

88 I noticed with interest that reviewers for the *Journal of the American Medical Association* imposed a higher than usual standard of statistical significance in assessing the worth of a re-analysis of the Women's Health Initiative data on hormone replacement therapy. Tara Parker Pope, "New Study Reassures Most Users of Hormones," *Wall Street Journal*, April 4, 2007, A1, A12.

89 "Peer Review and Publication" (note 69 above), 173.

90 "What's Wrong with Litigation-Driven Science?" (note 36 above), 204–205.

91 *Daubert* IV (note 85 above), 1317.

The novel scientific testimony excluded by the *Frye* court was proffered by the defense: Mr. Frye had passed a then-new blood-pressure deception test—"monograph" evidence, as you might say; but by the time Florida first endorsed the *Frye* test in *Kaminski* (1952) what was at stake was the admissibility of *polygraph* evidence.[92] The introduction of DNA "fingerprinting" in the late 1980s met with significant resistance in the ensuing "DNA Wars"; and even after the reliability of DNA analysis and its power to enable justice was acknowledged, prosecutors pushed back against requests for post-conviction testing.[93] You might conjecture that *Daubert* and, especially, *Joiner*, would have lessened the tendency for courts to follow other courts' rulings about the reliability of this or that kind of scientific evidence; but some commentators believe that *Joiner* has led judges uneasy about the possibility that the very same evidence might be ruled reliable by one court and unreliable by another in the same jurisdiction to treat such evidentiary rulings as precedential.[94]

5 CAN THIS MARRIAGE BE SAVED?

Obviously, divorce is out of the question; the law can't do without scientific testimony.

Both partners have tried to adapt. For example, there have been small but significant legal changes, including extensions of the statute of limitations to

[92] Kaminski v. State, 63 So.2d 399, 340 (Fla. 1953) (ruling lie-detector evidence inadmissible, and citing *Frye*). The court doesn't specify the nature of the lie-detector technology at issue. But according to Don Grubin and Lars Madsen, "Lie Detection and the Polygraph: A Historical Review," *Journal of Forensic Psychiatry & Psychology* 16 (2005): 357–69, 359–60, the systolic blood pressure deception test at issue in *Frye* was devised by William Marston in 1915; in 1921 John Larson developed the first modern polygraph machine (measuring blood pressure, pulse rate, and respiration rate); and in 1939 Leonarde Keeler added the galvanic skin response channel to the polygraph.

[93] See, e.g., David Lazer, "Introduction," in David Lazer, ed., *DNA and the Criminal Justice System: The Technology of Justice* (Cambridge, MA: MIT Press, 2004), 3–12, 5 (writing of the "lack of receptivity of the system to postconviction application of DNA analysis"); Margaret Berger, "Lessons from DNA: Restriking the Balance Between Finality and Justice," in the same volume, 109–31, 120 (writing that "[p]rosecutors have been reluctant to report possible failings in the laboratory...."). But see also Joseph L. Peterson and Anna S. Leggett, "The Evolution of Forensic Science: Progress amid the Pitfalls," *Stetson Law Review* 36, no. 3 (2007): 621–60, 630 (reporting that "[s]oon after DNA evidence's initial introduction to courts in the mid-1980s, defense attorneys mounted a more vigorous challenge to prosecution test results....").

[94] See, e.g., Heinzerling, "Doubting *Daubert*" (note 38 above), 81 (arguing that "[o]ne consequence of this lax [abuse of discretion] standard of review is that district judges may come to different conclusions on the same evidence.... One can imagine, therefore, the (perhaps unconscious) desire of judges to tidy up this mess by applying *stare decisis* principles to evidentiary rulings").

enable the prosecution of long-ago crimes when the perpetrator can now be identified by DNA analysis, or to enable testing of samples that might exonerate those already convicted—small compromises of the law's concern for promptness and finality; and there has been a modest increase in courts' use of their power to appoint their own experts—a small compromise of adversarialism. And on the scientific side, besides efforts to provide legally-relevant scientific education for judges, the American Association for the Advancement of Science (AAAS) set up the Court Appointed Scientific Experts (CASE) project to compile a register of "neutral" experts on whom courts might call.[95]

Not surprisingly, however, such adaptations don't always work out quite as planned. The AAAS soon learned that, quite often, when a judge announced that he would seek their advice in identifying independent experts, the upshot wasn't that CASE experts were appointed, but that the case was promptly settled.[96] And judges have learned that there is no guarantee that court-appointed experts will agree among themselves; in *Soldo v. Sandoz Pharmaceuticals, Inc.*, for example, while two of three court-appointed experts[97] concluded that the methodology that plaintiff's expert witnesses Drs. Kuilg and Pietro had used in arriving at the opinion that Ms. Soldo's stroke had been caused by the anti-lactation drug Parlodel was not reliable, the third concluded that it was.[98] (The court granted summary judgment to the defendant.)[99]

~

Just as I began writing this paper, when I had little more than the title, a local radio station began playing Beatles music all day long; and I toyed with the idea of entitling the last section "We Can Work It Out." A nice idea: but it would have promised more than I can deliver. Still, let me try, at least, to suggest what might be fruitful ways to think about the problems I have diagnosed. In *Defending Science* I wrote that, rather than expending all our ingenuity and energy on trying to refine legal rules on expert testimony, we might do better to consider other ways of mitigating the tensions;[100] now I will add that

[95] Doug Bandow, "Keeping Junk Science Out of the Courtroom," *Wall Street Journal*, July 26, 1999, A23.

[96] As I learned from Dr. Mark Frankel (Director of the CASE Project) at a workshop at Albany Law School in December 2006. By 2013, however, the CASE Project was apparently defunct; for details, see "Trial and Error" (note 35 above), note 47 and accompanying text.

[97] The court ordered the three court-appointed experts (David Flockhart, William J. Powers, and David Savitz) to file their reports as part of the record. Soldo v. Sandoz Pharm. Corp., No. 98–1712, 2003 WL 22005007 (W.D. Pa. Jan. 16, 2002).

[98] Soldo v. Sandoz Pharm. Corp., 244 F. Supp. 2d 434, 503–04 (W.D. Pa. 2003).

[99] *Id.*, 577.

[100] Haack, *Defending Science* (note 3 above), 256.

it seems desirable—given that no complete or perfect solution is likely to be forthcoming—to think about what the most significant concerns are, and what could be done about these.

One major concern is that, whatever the effect of *Daubert* in civil cases, it has had startlingly little effect on issues about forensic testimony in criminal cases[101]—though we have ample reason to believe that such testimony is at best variable in quality. When Florida was a *Frye* state,[102] criminal defense attorneys sometimes speculated wistfully about how much better things would be in a *Daubert* jurisdiction; but it isn't easy to share their optimism. "The only way to guard against the misapplication of forensic science is to impose controls and reforms long before the cases come to court," writes Peter Neufeld;[103] and, whether or not this is the *only* way, it is hard to deny that it might well be a *better* way. In the case of DNA identification, where there is solid underlying science, the most important thing is to ensure that these techniques aren't misapplied through haste, sloppiness, mismanagement, or dishonesty, conscious or unconscious. In the case of latent-fingerprint or knife-mark identifications and the like, however, where the underlying science is weak or non-existent, the first thing is to find out just how reliable such identifications are.[104]

Another major concern is highlighted by Justice Breyer's observation about trying to ensure that the "powerful engine" of tort litigation is directed, not at harmless and useful products but at harmful stuff[105]—of all places, in his concurring opinion in *Joiner*, where the substance in question was PCBs, so toxic they had already been banned for decades! What we want, I take it, is so far as possible to prevent dangerous stuff from coming on the market, and to do this without discouraging the production of useful and harmless stuff; and to ensure that, if dangerous drugs or chemicals *are* marketed and people are damaged, the victims are taken care of, and the danger of future injury

101 For example, by the time of *Llera Plaza* I (note 82 above), there had been more than forty *Daubert* challenges to latent-fingerprint identification testimony, but none had succeeded. (And eight weeks later, in *United States v. Llera Plaza*, 188 F. Supp. 2d 549 (E.D. Pa. Mar. 13, 2002) ("*Llera Plaza* II"), Judge Pollak reversed his restriction of such testimony.)

102 Very recently (2013), Florida Rule of Evidence 702 was revised to conform to FRE 702 as interpreted by the Supreme Court in *Daubert, Joiner,* and *Kumho Tire*. Act of June 4, 2013, Chapter 2013–07, Laws of Florida, to be codified at Fla Stat §§ 90.702, 90.704, available at http://laws.flrules.org/2013/107.

103 Peter J. Neufeld, "The (Near) Irrelevance of *Daubert* to Criminal Justice and Some Suggestions for Reform," *American Journal of Public Health* 95 (2005): S107–113, S107.

104 As would be urged—the very year this paper was first published—by the National Research Council of the National Academies of Science. National Research Council, *Strengthening Forensic Science in the United States: The Path Forward* (Washington, DC: The National Academies Press, 2009).

105 *Joiner* III (note 33 above), 148–49 (Breyer, J., concurring).

promptly averted. I suspect that we rely too much on the tort system—which too often seems, in practice, to be something of a lottery, and which in any case ought to be the *last* resort—when it might be better to think about other ways of achieving those highly desirable ends. Maybe we could learn something from the experience of other countries which are equally technologically advanced, but which have different regulatory and legal arrangements; certainly, I think, we would do well to approach these problems in a more empirical, experimental—a more scientific—spirit.

—5—

Trial and Error: Two Confusions in *Daubert*

> [U]nder the [Federal Rules of Evidence] the trial judge must ensure that any and all scientific testimony or evidence admitted is not only relevant, but reliable.... The subject of an expert's testimony must be "scientific ... knowledge." The adjective "scientific" implies a grounding in the methods or procedures of science.... [I]n order to qualify as "scientific knowledge," an inference or assertion must be derived by the scientific method.... "Scientific methodology today is based on generating hypotheses and testing them to see if they can be falsified; indeed, this methodology is what distinguishes science from other fields of inquiry."
>
> —*Daubert v. Merrell Dow Pharmaceuticals, Inc.* (1993)[1]

After Mrs. Daubert had taken Bendectin for morning-sickness in pregnancy, her son Jason was born with severe birth defects. Believing that Bendectin was the cause, in 1989 the Dauberts brought suit against the manufacturers of the drug, Merrell Dow Pharmaceuticals. At trial, however, the court excluded the expert witnesses the Dauberts had proffered to testify on the question of causation, on the grounds that the consensus in the relevant scientific community was that Bendectin does not cause birth defects. With the plaintiffs' causation experts excluded, there was no case to answer, and the trial court granted summary judgment in favor of Merrell Dow; the appeals court affirmed.[2]

1 Daubert v. Merrell Dow Pharm., Inc., 509 U.S. 579, 589–90, 593 (1993) ("*Daubert* III)"). The internal quotation is from Michael D. Green, "Expert Witnesses and Sufficiency of Evidence in Toxic Substances Litigation: The Legacy of Agent Orange and Bendectin Litigation," *Northwestern University Law Review* 86, no. 3 (1991–92), 643–99, 645; his (mis)-understanding of "scientific methodology" is discussed in "Federal Philosophy of Science: A Deconstruction—And a Reconstruction," pp. 122–55 in this volume, 138–39.

2 See *Daubert* III (note 1 above), 583–84.

This was a very rare instance in which the old *Frye* Rule,[3] requiring that novel scientific testimony be generally accepted in the relevant field—a rule which arose in a criminal case, and had until then been cited in criminal cases almost exclusively—had been used in a civil trial.[4] Moreover, the status of the *Frye* Rule was in question, since the relevant provision of the Federal Rules of Evidence enacted in 1975 made no reference to *Frye* or to general acceptance. And so *Daubert v. Merrell Dow Pharmaceuticals* ended up at the Supreme Court, which granted *certiorari* to determine whether the Federal Rules had or hadn't superseded *Frye*. Justice Blackmun's ruling in this landmark 1993 case, however, did much more than settle whether *Frye* had survived the Federal Rules; it was also a remarkable judicial foray into philosophy of science.

Yes, Justice Blackmun wrote for the majority, the FRE *had* superseded *Frye*; but the Rules themselves require judges to screen proffered expert testimony not only for relevance, *but also for reliability*.[5] The legal or "evidentiary" reliability of scientific testimony, he continued, is a matter of its scientific "validity"; and in assessing whether proffered scientific testimony is legally reliable courts must look, not at the conclusions an expert draws, but at the "methodology" by which he reached them, to determine whether the proffered evidence is really "scientific ... knowledge," and hence reliable.[6] As to what the methodology is that marks out the genuinely scientific, Justice Blackmun cited law professor Michael Green citing philosopher of science Karl Popper; added an observation of Carl Hempel's for good measure; and suggested a flexible list of four factors that courts might use in assessing reliability: "falsifiability," i.e., whether proffered evidence "can be and has been tested"; the known or potential error rate; peer review and publication; and (in a nod to *Frye*), acceptance in the relevant community.[7]

In partial dissent, however, Justice Rehnquist noted that the word "reliable" nowhere occurs in the text of Rule 702; warned that there would be

3 Frye v. United States, 293 F. 1013 (D.C. Cir. 1923).

4 The relevant legal history is told in detail in "Proving Causation: The Weight of Combined Evidence," pp. 208–38 in this volume, n. 21.

5 *Daubert* III (note 1 above), 588–89.

6 *Id.*, 590.

7 *Id.*, 593–95. The *Daubert* Court did not itself scrutinize the disputed testimony; on remand, Judge Kozinski again granted summary judgment for the defendants, arguing that the plaintiffs' proffered expert testimony would be no more admissible under *Daubert* than it was under *Frye*. Daubert v. Merrell Dow Pharm., Inc., 43 F.3d 1131 (9th Cir. 1995) ("*Daubert* IV"). For a more detailed discussion of Judge Kozinski's ruling, see "What's Wrong with Litigation-Driven Science?" pp. 180–207 in this volume, 185–88 and 202–205, and "Risky Business: Statistical Proof of Specific Causation," pp. 264–93 on this volume, 275–75.

difficulties down the road about whether, and if so how, *Daubert* should be applied when courts have to determine whether expert testimony that *isn't* scientific is admissible; worried aloud that federal judges, few of whom have any scientific training, were in effect now required to decide substantive scientific issues on which even experts in the field disagree; and argued that it would have been better for the Court simply to have settled the narrow question of the standing of *Frye*, rather than engaging in an ambitious argument about the nature of scientific knowledge.[8] Justice Rehnquist was right to suspect that something was seriously amiss; indeed, this paper might be read as an exploration, amplification, and partial defense of his reservations about his colleagues' philosophical excursus.

1 *DAUBERT'S* CONFUSIONS: POPPER AND HEMPEL

Apparently equating the question "is this expert testimony reliable?" with the question "Is this expert testimony genuinely scientific?", taking for granted that there is some scientific "methodology" which, faithfully followed, guarantees reliable results, and casting about for a philosophy of science to fit this demanding bill, the *Daubert* Court settled on an unstable amalgam of Popper's and Hempel's very different approaches—neither of which, however, is suitable to the task at hand.

Popper describes his philosophy of science as "Falsificationist" (by contrast with the "Verificationism" of the Logical Positivists),[9] because he holds that scientific statements can *never* be shown to be true, or even probable. Hence his criterion of demarcation: to be genuinely scientific, a statement must be "testable"—meaning, in Popper's mouth, "refutable" or "falsifiable," i.e., susceptible to evidence that could potentially show it to be false, if it *is* false.[10] Curiously, Popper acknowledged from the beginning that his criterion of demarcation is a "convention"; and in 1959, in his Introduction to the English edition of *The Logic of Scientific Discovery*, even affirmed that scientific knowledge is continuous with commonsense knowledge.[11] Nevertheless,

8 *Id.*, 598–601 (Rehnquist, C.J., dissenting in part).

9 Verificationism, however, was proposed as a criterion of the empirically meaningful; it is not, like Popper's Falsificationism, a criterion of the scientific. (I write about this difference in Susan Haack, *Defending Science—Within Reason: Between Scientism and Cynicism* (Amherst, NY: Prometheus Books, 2003), 34 ff., but won't pursue it here.)

10 Here I will sketch the Popperian ideas needed for present purposes in a deliberately minimal way; much more detail will be found in "Federal Philosophy of Science" (note 1 above), 125–34.

11 Karl R. Popper, *The Logic of Scientific Discovery* (first published in German in 1934; English edition, London: Hutchinson, 1959), 18.

his falsificationist criterion of demarcation is a very important element of his philosophy of science. Falsifiability is supposed to discriminate real empirical science (such as Einstein's theory of relativity) from pre-scientific myths, from non-empirical disciplines like pure mathematics or metaphysics, from non-scientific disciplines like history, and from what Popper takes to be pseudo-sciences, such as Freud's and Adler's psychoanalytic theories and Marx's "scientific socialism."[12] Falsifiability is also vital to Popper's account of the scientific method as "conjecture and refutation": making a bold, highly falsifiable guess, testing it as severely as possible, and, if it is falsified, giving it up and starting over rather than protecting it by *ad hoc* or "conventionalist" modifications. (Readiness to accept falsification, and repudiation of *ad hoc* stratagems protecting a theory from contrary evidence, is Popper's "methodological criterion" of the genuinely scientific.)

Popper also describes his philosophy of science as "Deductivist," by contrast with "Inductivism," whether in the strong, Baconian form that posits an inductive logic for arriving at hypotheses or in the weaker, Logical Positivist form that posits an inductive logic of confirmation. According to Popper, David Hume showed long ago that induction is unjustifiable. But science doesn't need induction; the method of conjecture and refutation requires only deductive logic—specifically, *modus tollens*,[13] the rule invoked when an observational result predicted by a theory fails, and we conclude that the theory is false.

Theories which have been tested but not yet falsified, Popper says, are "corroborated," degree of corroboration at a time depending on the number and severity of the tests passed. However, he tells us, the fact that a theory has been corroborated, to however high a degree, doesn't show that it is true, or even that it is probable; indeed, the degree of testability of a hypothesis is *inversely* related to its degree of logical probability.[14] Corroboration is not a measure of verisimilitude or "truth-likeness,"[15] but at best an indicator of how

12 Karl R. Popper, "Philosophy of Science: A Personal Report," in C. A. Mace, ed., *British Philosophy in Mid-Century* (London: George Allen and Unwin, 1957), 155–91; reprinted under the title, "Science: Conjectures and Refutations" in Popper, *Conjectures and Refutations: The Growth of Scientific Knowledge* (London: Routledge and Kegan Paul, 1962), 33–65.

13 *Modus tollendo tollens* (usually called, for short, "*modus tollens*") is the rule licensing inferences from premises of the form "if A then B," and "not-B" to a conclusion of the form "not A."

14 Popper, *The Logic of Scientific Discovery* (note 11 above), § 83. Notice that Popper speaks here of *degrees* of testability, while Justice Blackmun treats testability as categorical.

15 "Verisimilitude" is a technical term of Popper's meaning "nearness to the truth." See Karl R. Popper, "Truth, Rationality and the Growth of Scientific Knowledge" in Popper, *Conjectures and Refutations* (note 12 above), 215–250; Karl R. Popper, "Two Faces of Common Sense: An Argument for Commonsense Realism and against the Commonsense Theory of Knowledge," in Popper, *Objective Knowledge: An Evolutionary Approach* (Oxford: Clarendon Press, 1972), 32–105.

the verisimilitude of a theory *appears*, relative to other theories, at a time;[16] and the fact that a theory is corroborated doesn't mean that it is rational to believe it.

One problem with the *Daubert* Court's reliance on Popper is that applying his criterion of demarcation is no trivial matter. Indeed, Popper himself doesn't seem quite sure how to apply it. Sometimes, for example, he says that the theory of evolution is not falsifiable, and so is not science; at one point he suggests that "survival of the fittest" is a tautology, or "near-tautology," and elsewhere that evolution is really a historical theory, or perhaps metaphysics. Then he changes his mind: evolution *is* science, after all.[17] It's ironic; for Popper's criterion of demarcation had already found its way into the US legal system, a decade before *Daubert*, in a 1982 first-amendment case: *McLean v. Arkansas Board of Education*, where Michael Ruse's testimony that creation science isn't falsifiable, and so isn't science, but the theory of evolution is, apparently persuaded Judge Overton.[18]

But there is an even more serious problem with the *Daubert* Court's reliance on Popper, of which Justice Rehnquist doesn't seem aware: Popper's philosophy of science is signally inappropriate to the Court's concern with reliability. Popper's account is unremittingly negative; he explicitly denies that a scientific theory can ever be verified, or even confirmed—*or* shown to be reliable. When Popper describes his approach as "Critical Rationalism," it is to emphasize that the rationality of the scientific enterprise lies in the susceptibility of scientific theories to criticism, i.e., to testing, and potentially to falsification, and emphatically *not* in their verifiability or confirmability.[19]

[16] Popper, "Two Faces of Common Sense," *Objective Knowledge* (note 15 above), 102.

[17] Karl. R. Popper, "Natural Selection and Its Scientific Status" (1977), in David Miller, ed., *The Pocket Popper* (London: Fontana, 1983), 239–46.

[18] McLean v. Ark. Bd. of Educ., 529 F. Supp. 1255 (E.D. Ark. 1982). Prof. Ruse did not, by the way, say explicitly that it was Popper's criterion of demarcation he was applying—presumably because he was well aware of Popper's reservations and vacillations over whether the theory of evolution is scientific. See Michel Ruse, "Expert Witness Testimony Sheet" (1982), in Ruse, ed. *But Is It Science? The Philosophical Question in the Creation/Evolution Controversy* (Amherst, NY: Prometheus Books, 1996), 281–306; and Ruse, *Darwinism Defended; A Guide to the Creation/Evolution Controversies* (London: Addison-Wesley Publishing Company, 1982), 132–33. Larry Laudan's scathing critique of Ruse's testimony, "Science at the Bar—Causes for Concern" (1982), is also reprinted in Ruse, ed., *But Is It Science?* 351–55. See also Susan Haack, "Cracks in the Wall, A Bulge under the Carpet: The Singular Story of Religion, Evolution, and the US Constitution," *Wayne Law Review* 57, no. 4 (2011):1303–32.

[19] But see "Federal Philosophy of Science" (note 1 above), 133–34 for discussion of the one consequential occasion when Popper, who was not a native English speaker, himself used "confirm" where he meant "corroborate."

The degree of corroboration of a theory represents its past performance only, and "*says nothing whatever about future performance, or about the 'reliability' of a theory*"; even the best-tested theory "is not 'reliable'"[20]—so scornful is Popper of the concept of reliability that he refuses even to use the word without putting it in precautionary scare quotes! Reiterating that he puts the emphasis "on *negative arguments*, such as negative instances or counter-examples, refutations, and attempted refutations—in short, criticism—while the inductivist lays stress on '*positive instances*', from which he draws 'non-demonstrative *inferences*', and which he hopes will guarantee the '*reliability*' of the conclusions of these inferences," Popper specifically identifies Hempel as representative of those inductivists with whom he disagrees.[21]

Hempel is not, perhaps, the prototypical inductivist: he describes the method of science as "hypothetico-deductive"; he affirms that scientific claims should be subject to empirical check or testing; and unlike Hans Reichenbach or Rudolf Carnap, he doesn't explain confirmation by appeal to the mathematical calculus of probabilities. Nevertheless, Popper is surely right to see Hempel's approach as very significantly at odds with his own: Hempel is not centrally concerned with demarcating science; he questions the supposed asymmetry between verification and falsification, and argues that Popper's criterion "involves a very severe restriction of the possible forms of scientific hypotheses," e.g., in ruling out purely existential statements;[22] when he speaks of "testing" he envisages not only disconfirmation but also *confirmation* of a hypothesis; and one of his chief projects was to articulate the "logic of confirmation," i.e., of the support of general hypotheses by positive instances.

Apparently the Supreme Court hoped, by combining Hempel's account of confirmation with Popper's criterion of demarcation, to craft a crisp test to identify genuine, and hence reliable, science. But, though Hempel's philosophy of science *is* more positive than Popper's, it isn't much more help with the question of reliability. For one thing, the confirmation of generalizations by positive instances that preoccupies Hempel is far too simplified to apply to the complex congeries of epidemiological, toxicological, etc., etc., evidence at stake in a case like *Daubert*. For another, what Hempel offered was an account

[20] Popper, "Conjectural Knowledge" (1971) in Popper, *Objective Knowledge* (note 15 above), 1–33, 18, 22.

[21] *Id.*, 20. The reference to Hempel is in Popper's footnote 29.

[22] Carl G. Hempel, "Studies in the Logic of Confirmation" (1945); reprinted in Hempel, *Aspects of Scientific Explanation and Other Essays in the Philosophy of Science* (New York: Free Press, 1965), 3–46. See also Carl G. Hempel, "Empiricist Criteria of Cognitive Significance: Problems and Changes" (1950–51), reprinted in *Aspects of Scientific Explanation* 99–119; and Carl G. Hempel, "Postscript (1964) on Cognitive Significance," *Aspects of Scientific Explanation*, 120–22.

of supportiveness of evidence, or as he said, of "relative confirmation," i.e., of the *relation between* observational evidence and hypothesis, expressible as "E confirms H [to degree n]," or "H is confirmed [to degree n] by evidence E." This, as Hempel acknowledged, falls short of an account of "absolute confirmation," the warrant of a scientific claim, which would be expressed in non-relative terms, as "H is confirmed [to degree n], period." To discriminate reliable testimony from unreliable, however, it looks as if we would need an account of the absolute concept—which Hempel doesn't supply. Moreover, Hempel himself seems eventually to have concluded that confirmation isn't a purely syntactic or logical notion after all,[23] and late in life began to think that maybe Thomas Kuhn had been on the right track in focusing on historico-politico-sociological, rather than logical, aspects of science.[24]

2 *DAUBERT'S* CONFUSIONS: "SCIENTIFIC" AND "RELIABLE"

So, the *Daubert* Court mixes up its Hoppers and its Pempels; but isn't this just a slip, of merely scholarly interest? No: it is symptomatic of a serious misunderstanding of the place of the sciences within inquiry generally, a serious misunderstanding revealed by the Court's equation of "scientific" and "reliable."

The word "science" and its cognates have (besides a descriptive use in which they simply refer to such disciplines as physics, chemistry, biology, etc.) what one might call an "honorific" use, serving, in effect, as vague terms of all-purpose epistemic praise—as in those old television advertisements where actors in white coats assured us that a new, "scientific" detergent would get our clothes even cleaner. This honorific use of "science," "scientific," etc., is unmistakably at work in the *Daubert* ruling; indeed, it seems to be implicit even in the way Justice Blackmun writes of "scientific … knowledge," strategically excising three significant words from the reference in FRE 702 to "scientific or other technical knowledge," and apparently signaling an expectation that

23 What changed Hempel's mind was Nelson Goodman's "grue" paradox. "X is grue" is defined as: "either x is examined before time t, and is green, or x is not examined before time t, and is blue." Setting t as, say, 2020, it follows that, e.g., "All emeralds are grue" is exactly as well confirmed by or present evidence as "All emeralds are green." See Nelson Goodman, "The New Riddle of Induction," in Goodman, *Fact, Fiction, and Forecast* (1954; 2nd ed., Indianapolis, IN: Bobbs-Merrill, 1965), 59–83; Hempel, "Postscript (1964) on Confirmation" (note 22 above).

24 Carl G. Hempel, "The Irrelevance of the Concept of Truth for the Critical Appraisal of Scientific Theories" (1990), in Richard Jeffrey, ed., *Selected Philosophical Essays [by] Carl G. Hempel* (Cambridge: Cambridge University Press, 2000), 75–84; Thomas S. Kuhn, *The Structure of Scientific Revolutions* (Chicago: University of Chicago Press, 1962).

a criterion of the genuinely scientific will also discriminate reliable testimony from unreliable.

If "scientific" is used honorifically, it is a tautology that genuinely scientific evidence is reliable; but a trivial verbal truth is of no help to a judge trying to screen proffered scientific testimony for reliability. If "scientific" is used descriptively, however, "scientific" and "reliable" come apart: for, obviously enough, physicists, chemists, biologists, medical scientists, etc., are sometimes incompetent, confused, self-deceived, dishonest, or simply mistaken, while historians, detectives, investigative journalists, legal and literary scholars, plumbers, auto-mechanics, etc., are sometimes good investigators. In short, not all, and not only, scientists are reliable inquirers; and not all, and not only, scientific evidence is reliable. Nor is there a "scientific method" in the sense the Court assumed: no uniquely rational mode of inference or procedure of inquiry used by all scientists and only by scientists. Rather, scientific inquiry must respect the desiderata, constraints, and inferences of all serious empirical inquiry; but has developed, in addition, a vast array of constantly evolving, and often local, ways and means of stretching the imagination, amplifying reasoning power, extending evidential reach, and stiffening respect for evidence.

Every kind of empirical inquiry, from the simplest everyday puzzling over the causes of delayed buses or spoiled food to the most complex investigations of detectives, of historians, of legal and literary scholars, and of scientists, involves making an informed guess about the explanation of some event or phenomenon, figuring out the consequences of its being true, and checking how well those consequences stand up to evidence. This is the procedure of all scientists; but it is not the procedure only of scientists. Something like the "hypothetico-deductive method" really *is* the core of all inquiry, scientific inquiry included. But it is not distinctive of scientific inquiry, not used exclusively by scientists; and the fact that scientists, like inquirers of every kind, proceed in this way tells us nothing substantive about whether or when their testimony is reliable.

The sciences have extended the senses with specialized instruments; stretched the imagination with metaphors, analogies, and models; amplified reasoning power with numerals, the calculus, statistics, computers, etc.; and evolved a social organization that enables cooperation, competition, and evidence-sharing, allowing each scientist to take up his investigation where others left off. Astronomers devise ever more sophisticated telescopes, chemists ever more sophisticated techniques of analysis, medical scientists ever more sophisticated methods of imaging bodily states and processes, and so on; scientists work out what controls are needed to block a potential source of experimental error, what statistical techniques to rule out a merely coincidental correlation, and so forth. But these scientific "helps" to inquiry are local and evolving, and are not used by all scientists.

You may object that, since I have acknowledged that scientific inquiry is continuous with everyday empirical inquiry, I have in effect agreed with Popper that science is an extension of common sense. Indeed, I think science *is* well-described, in Gustav Bergmann's wonderfully evocative phrase, as the Long Arm of Common Sense.[25] But the continuity is not between the content of scientific and of commonsense knowledge, but between the basic ways and means of everyday and of scientific inquiry; and it is precisely because of this that the Popperian preoccupation with the "problem of demarcation" is a distraction.

Or you may object that the *Daubert* Court's Popperian advice that courts ask whether proffered scientific testimony "can be and has been tested" surely is potentially helpful. This is true; but it is no real objection to my argument. "Ask whether proffered testimony has been tested" *is* very good advice when a purported expert hasn't made even the most elementary effort to check how well his claims stand up to evidence: such as the knife-mark examiner in *Ramirez*,[26] who testified that he could infallibly identify this knife, to the exclusion of all other knives in the world, as having made the wound in the victim's neck—though no study had established the assumed uniqueness of individual knives, and his purported ability to make such specific identifications had never been tested. This is not, however, because falsifiability is the criterion of the scientific, but because *any* serious inquirer is required to seek out all the potentially available evidence and to go where it leads, even if he would prefer to avoid, ignore, or play down information that pulls against what he hopes is true.

Yes, this is a requirement on scientists; as Darwin recognized when he wrote in his autobiography that he always made a point of recording recalcitrant examples and contrary arguments in a special notebook, to safeguard against his tendency to forget inconveniently negative evidence.[27] But it is no less a requirement on other inquirers, too; as we all realized some years ago when a historian announced that he had evidence that Marilyn Monroe had

[25] Gustav Bergmann, *Philosophy of Science* (Madison, WI: University of Wisconsin Press, 1957), 20. It is from Bergmann, of course, that I adopted "The Long Arm of Common Sense" as the title of chapter 4 of *Defending Science* (note 9 above).

[26] Ramirez v. State, 542 So. 2d 352 (Fla. 1989) ("*Ramirez* I"), *appeal after remand* 651 So. 2d 1164 (Fla. 1995) ("*Ramirez* II"), *appeal after new trial* 810 So. 2d 836 (Fla. 2001) ("*Ramirez* III").

[27] Charles Darwin, *Selected Letters on Evolution and Origin of Species: With an Autobiographical Chapter*, ed. Francis Darwin (New York: D. Appleton and Company, 1893; reprinted New York: Dover, 1958), 45.

blackmailed President Kennedy; but then turned out to have ignored the fact that the supposedly incriminating letters were typed with correction ribbon, and that the address included a zip code—when neither existed at the time the letters were purportedly written![28]

"Non-science" is an ample and diverse category, including the many human activities other than inquiry, the various forms of pseudo-inquiry, inquiry of a non-empirical character, and empirical inquiry of other kinds than the scientific; and of course there are plenty of mixed and borderline cases. The honorific use of "science" and its cognates tempts us—like the *Daubert* Court—to criticize poorly-conducted science as not really science at all. But rather than sneering unhelpfully that this or that work is "pseudo-scientific," it is always better to specify what, exactly, is wrong with it: that it is not honestly or seriously conducted; that it rests on flimsy or vague assumptions—assumptions for which there is no good evidence, or which aren't even susceptible to evidential check; that it seeks to impress with decorative or distracting mathematical symbolism or elaborate-looking apparatus; that it fails to take essential precautions against experimental error; or whatever.

3 *DAUBERT*'S LEGAL PROGENY

So, the *Daubert* Court's philosophy of science was muddled; but haven't subsequent Supreme Court rulings cleared things up? Not exactly: it would be more accurate to say that in *Joiner* (1997) and *Kumho Tire* (1999) the Supreme Court quietly backed away from *Daubert*'s confused philosophy of science.[29] At any rate, those references to Hepper, Pompel, falsifiability, etc., so prominent in *Daubert*, are conspicuous by their absence from *Joiner* and *Kumho*. But there are points of epistemological interest.

In *Joiner* there is a kerfuffle over "methodology" worthy of our attention: Mr. Joiner's attorneys had argued that the lower court erred in excluding their proffered expert testimony because, instead of focusing exclusively on their experts' methodology—which, they maintain, was the very same "weight of evidence" methodology used by the other party's (G.E.'s) experts—improperly concerned itself with the experts' conclusions. Apparently anxious to sidestep this argument, the *Joiner* Court (with the exception of Justice Stevens) denies the legitimacy of the distinction between methodology and conclusions. Opining that this is No Real Distinction, the Court sounds like nothing so

28 Evan Thomas et al., "The JFK-Marilyn Hoax," *Newsweek*, June 6, 1997, 36.

29 Gen. Elec. Co. v. Joiner, 522 U.S. 136 (1997) ("*Joiner* III"); Kumho Tire Co. v. Carmichael, 526 U.S. 137 (1999).

much as a conclave of medieval logicians; but given their citation to *Turpin*[30] it seems likely that they didn't really intend to make a profound metaphysical pronouncement, only to acknowledge that if an expert's conclusions are problematic enough, this alerts us to the possibility of some methodological defect—as Judge Becker had suggested in *Paoli*,[31] the case on which the court of appeals had relied in reversing the trial court's exclusion of Joiner's experts.[32]

This focus on "methodology"—an accordion concept expanded and contracted as the argument demands[33]—obscured a much deeper epistemological question. Mr. Joiner's attorneys proffered a collage of bits of information, none sufficient by itself to warrant the conclusion that exposure to PCBs promoted Mr. Joiner's cancer, but which, they argued, *taken together* gave strong support to that conclusion; G.E.'s attorneys replied, in effect, that piling up weak evidence can't magically transform it into strong evidence. In response, Mr. Joiner's attorneys refer to the EPA guidelines for assessing the combined weight of epidemiological, toxicological, etc., evidence. But no one addresses the key question: is there a difference between a congeries of evidence so interrelated that the whole really is greater than the sum of its parts, and a collection of unrelated and insignificant bits of information, between true consilience and the "faggot fallacy"[34]—and if so, what is it?

There *is* a difference. Evidence of means, motive, and opportunity may interlock to give much stronger support to the claim that the defendant did it than any of these pieces of evidence alone could do. Similarly, evidence of increased incidence of a disease among people exposed to a suspected substance may interlock with evidence that animals biologically similar to humans are harmed by exposure to that substance and evidence indicating what chemical mechanism may be responsible to give much stronger support to the claim that this substance causes, promotes, or contributes to the disease than any of

30 Turpin v. Merrell Dow Pharm., Inc., 959 F.2d 1349 (6th Cir. 1992).

31 *In re* Paoli R.R. Yard PCB Litig., 35 F.3d 717 (3d Cir. 1994).

32 Joiner v. Gen. Elec. Co., 78 F.3d 524 (11th Cir. 1996) ("*Joiner* II").

33 The term "accordion concept' was introduced by Wilfrid Sellars in "Scientific Realism or Irenic Instrumentalism?", in Robert Cohen and Marx Wartofsky, eds., *Boston Studies in Philosophy of Science* (New York: Humanities Press, 1965), 171–204, 172.

34 The word "consilience," meaning etymologically "jumping together," was coined by the nineteenth-century philosopher of science William Whewell, and recently made famous as the title of a best-selling book, E. O. Wilson, *Consilience: The Unity of Knowledge* (New York: Knopf, 1998). The phrase "faggot fallacy" was introduced in Petr Skrabanek and J. McCormick, *Follies & Fallacies in Medicine* (1989; Amherst, NY: Prometheus Books, 1990), 35, and adopted by General Electric's attorneys in *Joiner*. Brief for Petioners, *Joiner* III (note 29 above) (No. 96–118), 1997 WL 304727, *49.

these pieces of evidence alone could do. However, the interlocking will be less robust if, e.g., the animals are unlike humans in some relevant way, or if the mechanism postulated to cause damage is also present in other chemicals not found to be associated with an increased risk of disease, or, etc.[35]

"Interlocking" is exactly the right word, given the ramifying, crossword-like structure of evidence. And because of the ramification of reasons, the desirable kind of interlocking of evidence gestured at in *Joiner* is subtle and complex, not easily captured by any mechanical weighting of epidemiological data relative to animal studies or toxicological evidence. Nor, moreover—as Justice Rehnquist already saw in the context of *Daubert*—can its quality readily be judged by someone who lacks the necessary background knowledge.

In *Kumho Tire* the Supreme Court made a real epistemological step forward. In this products-liability case, which turned on the proffered testimony of an expert on tire failure, the Court tried to sort out the problems about the admissibility of non-scientific expert testimony which, as Justice Rehnquist had anticipated, soon arose in the wake of *Daubert*. Judges can't evade their gatekeeping duty on the grounds that proffered expert testimony is not science, the Court ruled: the key word in FRE 702, after all, is not "scientific," but "knowledge."[36] No longer fussing over demarcation, recognizing the gap between "scientific" and "reliable," in *Kumho Tire* the Supreme Court acknowledges that *what matters is whether proffered testimony is reliable, not whether it is scientific*. Quite so.

Far from backing away from federal courts' gatekeeping responsibilities, however, the *Joiner* Court had affirmed that a judge's decision to allow or exclude scientific testimony, even though it may be outcome-determinative, is subject only to review for abuse of discretion, not to any more stringent standard; and the *Kumho* Court, pointing out that (depending on the nature of the expertise in question) the *Daubert* factors may or may not be appropriate, held that it is within judges' discretion to use any, all, or none of them. A year later, a revised FRE 702 made explicit what according to *Daubert* had been implicit in Rule 702 all along: admissible expert testimony must be based on "sufficient" data, the product of "reliable" testimony "reliably" applied to the facts of the case. As a result, federal judges now have large responsibilities and broad discretion in screening not only scientific testimony but expert testimony generally; but they have very little specific guidance about how to perform this difficult task.

35 For a much more detailed discussion of these issues, see "Proving Causation: The Weight of Combined Evidence," pp. 208–38 in this volume.

36 *Kumho Tire* (note 29 above), 147.

Post-*Daubert* courts seem to have been significantly tougher than before on expert testimony proffered by plaintiffs in civil cases. This isn't the place for a full-scale discussion of the frequently-heard criticism that *Daubert* and its progeny tend to favor defendant corporations over plaintiffs; but I think things are a good deal more complicated than this criticism suggests. No doubt there are heartless and unscrupulous companies more concerned with profit than with the dangers their products may present to the public; and it is certainly easier to sympathize with poor Jason Daubert or poor Mr. Joiner than with a vast, impersonal outfit like Merrell Dow or General Electric. But no doubt there are also greedy and opportunistic plaintiffs and plaintiffs' attorneys; and the people thrown out of work when meritless litigation forces a company to downsize or close surely also deserve our sympathy.[37] Moreover, while we certainly hope the tort system will discourage the manufacture of dangerous substances and products, we also want it *not* to discourage the manufacture of safe and useful ones. And I will add that, while it seems that since *Daubert* courts have not, at least not yet, been as tough on expert testimony proffered by prosecutors in criminal cases as they have on plaintiffs' experts in civil cases, we surely also want to avoid convicting innocent criminal defendants on flimsy forensic testimony—and leaving the real offenders at liberty. That said, I will leave it to others to pursue *Daubert*'s policy ramifications, and pick up the epistemological thread once more.

4 WHERE DO WE GO FROM HERE?

So, since *Kumho Tire*'s epistemological step forward, the other problem Justice Rehnquist worried about—that judges generally lack the background knowledge that may be essential to a serious appraisal of the worth of scientific (or other technical) testimony—looms larger than ever. But hasn't the legal system by now found ways to help judges handle their quite burdensome responsibilities for keeping the gate against unreliable expert testimony? Up to a point, yes; but *only* up to a point. Ways have been explored to give judges some of the background knowledge they may need, and to enable them to call on the scientific community for help; but these have been relatively small steps, and sometimes (understandably) fumbling.

Daubert prompted various efforts to educate judges scientifically. In May 1999, for example, about two dozen Massachusetts Superior Court judges attended a two-day seminar on DNA at the Whitehead Institute for Biomedical Research. A report in the *New York Times* quoted the Director of the Institute

[37] As one character says to another in a cartoon for which I have a particular fondness, "Politically, I suppose you could say I'm a member of the lunatic middle."

assuring readers that, while in the O. J. Simpson case lawyers had "befuddled everyone" over the DNA evidence, after a program such as this judges will "understand what is black and white … what to allow in the courtroom."[38] To be candid, this report left me a little worried about the danger of giving judges the false impression that they *are* qualified to make subtle scientific determinations; when it is hardly realistic to expect that a few hours in a science seminar will transform judges into scientists competent to make subtle and sophisticated scientific judgments—any more than a few hours in a legal seminar could transform scientists into judges competent to make subtle and sophisticated legal determinations.

It really isn't feasible to bring—let alone keep—judges up to speed with cutting-edge genetics, epidemiology, toxicology, or whatever. (I mean, not to denigrate judges' abilities, but to draw the analogy with expecting a few lessons to turn a professional football player into a ballet-dancer, or me into a concert pianist.) It *should* be feasible, however, to educate judges in the elements of probability theory, to give them a sense of how samples may be mishandled or this or that kind of mistake made at the laboratory, to explain how information about the probability that the lab made a mistake is such-and-such affects the significance of a random-match probability, and so forth. More generally, it seems both feasible and useful to try to ensure that judges understand the more commonly-employed scientific ideas they are likely to encounter most frequently: the role of suggestion, for example, and its significance for how DNA samples or suspect knives or etc., should be presented, or how photo-arrays or line-ups should be conducted. Of course, when the issues are subtle, the subtleties need to be conveyed: one would hope, for example, that judges understand the concept of statistical significance—but also grasp the element of arbitrariness it involves.

Courts have the power to appoint experts of their own selection.[39] Used in a number of asbestos cases in 1987 and 1990,[40] the practice came to public

38 Cary Goldberg, "Judges' Unanimous Verdict on DNA Lessons: Wow!" *New York Times*, April 24, 1999, A10.

39 Various legal authorities are cited for such appointments: courts' "inherent power" (as in *In re* Peterson, 253 U.S. 300 (1920); rules of evidence (FRE 706, providing for court-appointed expert witnesses); and rules of procedure (FRCP 53, providing for the appointment of "Special Masters"). But see note 42 below, on *Hall*, where the court relied in part on FRE 104, on "preliminary questions"). There is a useful summary in Laura E. Ellsworth, "Court-Appointed Experts in State and Federal Courts: From Hens-Teeth to High Priests," *Pennsylvania Bar Association Quarterly* 71 (October 2000): 172–79; and a useful discussion in Reilly v. United States, 682 F. Supp. 150, 152–55 (D.R.I.), *aff'd in part, rev'd in part*, 863 F.2d 149 (1st Cir. 1988) (affirming District Court's appointment and use of technical advisor).

40 Carl R. Rubin and Laura Ringenbach, "The Use of Court Experts in Asbestos Litigation," *Federal Rules Decisions* 137 (1999): 35–52, 35.

attention in the late 1990s. In his concurrence in *Joiner*, Justice Breyer had urged the potential usefulness of court-appointed experts, citing an amicus brief from the *New England Journal of Medicine* suggesting that "[j]udges should be strongly encouraged to make greater use of their … authority… to appoint experts"[41] and the practice became prominent in the context of a wave of lawsuits against the manufacturers of silicone breast-implants then under way. It was adopted, for example, by Judge Jones in *Hall*,[42] and most notably by Judge Samuel Pointer, who in 1996 appointed a National Science Panel to help him sift through the scientific evidence in the several thousand federal silicone breast-implant cases that had been consolidated to his court.[43] And it seems that, as their gatekeeping responsibilities have grown, more judges have been willing, as Justice Breyer had urged, to call directly on the scientific community for help:[44] court-appointed experts have advised judges on, for example, the potential dangers of seat-belt buckles, the diet drug fen-phen, the anti-lactation drug Parlodel—and, in the Court of Appeals in Michigan, on Bendectin.[45]

For a while, the Court-Appointed Scientific Experts (CASE) Project at the American Association for the Advancement of Science (AAAS) offered to make available "independent scientists … [to] educate the court, testify at trial, assess the litigants' cases, and otherwise aid in the process of determining the truth";[46] and Duke University's Registry of Independent Scientific and Technical Advisors also provided the names of independent experts.[47] Neither

[41] *Joiner* III (note 29 above), 149–51 (Breyer, J., concurring) (citing Brief of Amici Curiae The New England Journal of Medicine and Marcia Angell, M.D., in Support of Neither Petitioners nor Respondents, *Joiner* III (note 29 above) (No. 96–188), 1997 WL 304759, *18).

[42] Hall v. Baxter Healthcare Corp., 947 F. Supp. 1387 (D. Or. 1996). Referring to federal courts' "inherent authority" to appoint expert advisors, and citing *Daubert* III (note 1 above), at 592–93 ("the court must determine at the outset, pursuant to Rule 104(a), 'whether the expert is proposing to testify to (1) scientific knowledge that (2) will assist the trier of fact to understand or determine a fact in issue'"), Judge Jones also relied on his authority under FRE 104 ("[t]o keep the advisors independent of any ongoing proceedings, I appointed them under FRE 104, not FRE 706…"). *Hall*, 1392 & n.8, 1396.

[43] *In re* Silicone Gel Breast Implant Prods. Liab. Litig. (MDL 926) (Alabama), No. CV 92-P-10000-S, 1996 WL 34401813 (N.D. Ala. May 31, 1996). Judge Pointer relied on his authority under FRE 706. *Id.*, *1.

[44] See Howard M. Erichson, "Mass Tort Litigation and Inquisitorial Justice," *Georgetown Law Journal*, 87 (1999): 1983–2004.

[45] DePyper v. Navarro, No. 191949, 1998 WL 1988927 (Mich. Ct. App. Nov. 6, 1998); *DES Litigation Report*, "Denial of Expert Witness Testimony Violates *Daubert*, Appeal States" (December 1998).

[46] Doug Bandow, "Keeping Junk Science Out of the Courtroom," *Wall Street Journal*, July 26, 1999, A23. The CASE Project website is available at http://www.aaas.org.spp/case/case.htm.

[47] This list of names was available at http://www.law.duke.edu/pacregistry/index.html; but this site is no longer available.

registry, however, has survived: the Duke Registry was closed in 2003, in part for lack of funds;[48] and by 2008 the CASE Project, though still nominally in existence, was "no longer being marketed, [and] ha[d] not received any requests for experts recently."[49]

Sometimes it is thought that there can be no neutral experts of any kind. The concept of neutrality, however, requires closer attention. Of course, everyone has some beliefs even at the outset of an investigation; they couldn't investigate unless they did. What matters for present purposes, though, is that there is a kind of trade-off between an expert's being neutral in the sense of having no preconceptions relevant to the task at hand, and his or her being competent to that task. If neutrality is taken to mean freedom from all relevant preconceptions, it is true that there are few if any neutral experts: anyone competent to the task of a court-appointed scientist is virtually certain to have some view at the outset. And if neutrality is taken, rather, in a more sociological way, to mean freedom from all contact, direct or indirect, with either party, again there probably won't be many neutral scientists: given, for example, the dependence of much medical research on drug-company funding,[50] most scientists competent to the task will probably know people, or know people who know people, involved with one party or the other. But it doesn't follow, and it isn't true, that some experts aren't, in the essential sense, more honest and upright, less biased, than others: i.e., more willing to go where the evidence leads, even if it pulls against what they were initially inclined to believe.

Bias, in the sense at issue here, isn't the same thing as conflict of interest; nevertheless, we certainly want to avoid conflicts of interest—both because they may lead to bias in the relevant sense, and because, even if they don't, we want to avoid the appearance of such bias. But we should be conscious that there is a broad continuum from a court-appointed scientist's being financially supported in some way by a defendant company or plaintiffs' attorneys, to his discussing his court-appointed work with an acquaintance who is supported in some way by a defendant company or plaintiffs' attorneys, to his simply having such acquaintances, to his being completely out of any professional loop in the field in question.

48 Ryan M. Seidemann et al., "Closing the Gate on Questionable Expertwitness Testimony: A Proposal to Institute Expert Review Panels," *Southern University Law Review* 33, no. 1 (2005): 29–91, 62.

49 Andrew Jurs, "Balancing Legal Process with Scientific Expertise: Expert Witness Methodology in Five Nations and Suggestions for Reform of Post-Daubert U.S. Reliability Determinations," *Marquette Law Review* 95, no 4 (2012): 1329–415, 1413.

50 See Susan Haack, "The Integrity of Science: What It Means, Why It Matters" (2006), reprinted in Haack, *Putting Philosophy to Work: Inquiry and Its Place in Culture* (Amherst, NY: Prometheus Books, 2008), 121–40.

Yes, it is disturbing that, while serving on Judge Pointer's panel, one scientist signed a letter asking for financial support for another project from one of the defendant companies;[51] and it is worrying that just four scientists were, in effect, responsible for the disposition of several thousand cases. Moreover, given that even competent and honest scientists will sometimes legitimately disagree, we need to think about what will happen when court-appointed scientists are not of one mind. Both legal issues and practical questions need to be addressed:[52] should court-appointed experts help judges with their *Daubert* screening duties, or should they testify before juries, along with the parties' experts? How could court-appointed experts best be selected? Who should pay for their services? How should they be instructed about conflicts of interest? We could learn a lot from Judge Pointer's experience, and (if we are careful to avoid the pitfalls of facile cross-cultural comparisons) from the experience of other legal systems, about how and when court-appointed experts might be most helpful.

Such experts are potentially very useful in some kinds of case; but of course they are no panacea—in fact, I don't suppose for a moment that there *is* a panacea. Rather, there is a range of possibilities worth pursuing: thinking about the unhappy interaction of the FDA (Food and Drug Administration) and the tort system in the silicone breast-implants affair, for example, you might wonder how the FDA could have acted to prevent the panic in the first place;[53] thinking about the AAAS's willingness to help, you might wonder about other ways of making the scientific community more responsive when legal disputes turn on scientific issues irresoluble by the presently available evidence; thinking of the weaknesses of other techniques of forensic identification, and the mistakes made by crime labs, etc., revealed in the wake of those dramatic DNA exonerations, you might wonder how we could make the forensic-science business more rigorous (the temptation to say "more scientific" is strong; but I shall resist it!).

~

Shortly before *Daubert*, writing of expert testimony in pharmaceutical product liability actions—and echoing Learned Hand's diagnosis of the problem,

[51] "Pointer Rules Federal Science Panel Not Tainted by Payments to Panelist," *Medical-Legal Aspects of Breast Implants* 7, no. 5 (April 1999): 1, 4 & 5, 1.

[52] See, e.g., Joe S. Cecil et al., "Assessing Causation in Breast Implant Litigation: The Role of Science Panels," *Law & Contemporary Problems* 64 (2001): 139–90; Laurens Walker and John Monahan, "Scientific Authority: The Breast Implant Litigation and Beyond," *University of Virginia Law Review* 86 (2000): 801–33.

[53] The wave of litigation began after the FDA banned silicone breast-implants, formerly "grandfathered in"; they were not known to be unsafe, but the manufacturers had failed to submit evidence of their safety, as they had been required to do.

that we "set the jury to decide, where doctors disagree," when "it is just because they are incompetent for such a task that the expert is necessary at all"[54]—Marc Klein had written that:

> Expert testimony is an absurd enterprise. We require expert testimony in pharmaceutical product liability actions because the medical and scientific details are well beyond the comprehension of laymen. Yet, we then ask those same laymen to choose between the competing sets of experts and resolve the very issues that are, by definition, beyond their comprehension.[55]

Daubert shifted more of the burden to judges; but the fundamental problem remains. Almost a century after Hand posed the essential question—how can the legal system make the best use of expert testimony?—we are still fumbling towards an answer.

[54] Learned Hand, "Historical and Practical Considerations Regarding Expert Testimony," *Harvard Law Review* 15 (1901): 40–58, 54.

[55] Marc S. Klein, "Expert Testimony in Pharmaceutical Product Liability Actions," 45 *Food, Drug, and Cosmetics Law Journal* 45, no. 4 (1990): 393–442, 441–42.

—6—

Federal Philosophy of Science: A Deconstruction—and a Reconstruction

> It seems to me that there is a good deal of ballyhoo about scientific method. I venture to think that the people who talk most about it are the people who do least about it.... No working scientist, when he plans an experiment in the laboratory, asks himself whether he is being properly scientific.... When the scientist ventures to criticize the work of his fellow scientist, he does not base his criticism on such glittering generalities as failure to follow the "scientific method," but his criticism is specific.... The working scientist is always too much concerned with getting down to brass tacks to be willing to spend his time on generalities.
>
> —Percy Bridgman[1]

1 A TANGLED TALE

With *Daubert,* Ronald Allen observed in an article published the following year, the Supreme Court had "replaced a judicial anachronism [*Frye*] by a philosophical one [Popper]."[2] It's a nice one-liner; and there's an element of

[1] Percy W. Bridgman, "On 'Scientific Method'" (1949), in Bridgman, *Reflections of a Physicist* (New York: Philosophical Library, 2nd ed., 1955), 81–83, 81

[2] Ronald J. Allen, "Expertise and the *Daubert* Decision," *Journal of Criminal Law & Criminology* 84, no. 4 (1994): 1157–75, 1164. This observation, Prof. Allen tells us, is drawn from a paper by his student Christopher Kamper. *Id.*, n.14. I note that *Frye* is not quite the legal anachronism Prof. Allen's observation suggests; it remains the law in a number of states (Alabama, Arizona, California, Illinois, Kansas, Maryland, Minnesota, New Jersey, New York, Nevada, North Carolina, Pennsylvania, South Carolina, Washington, and Wisconsin). Terence W. Campbell and Demosthenes Lorandos, *Cross Examining Experts in the Behavioral Sciences* ([Eagan, MN?]: West/Thomson Reuters, September 2012), §1:16.1, n.7. (In 2013 Pennsylvania Rule of Evidence 702 was modified, but not substantively.) I have, however, omitted Florida from Campbell and Lorandos's list because in 2013 it shifted, in effect, from *Frye* to *Daubert*. See "Irreconcilable Differences: The Troubled Marriage of Science and Law," pp. 78–103 in this volume, n. 102 for details.

truth in it. For decades, Karl Popper was enormously influential in philosophy of science (though, interestingly, less so in the US than elsewhere), and much admired by some important scientists. But by the time *Daubert* came down the year before his death at the age of 93, he was no longer the major player he had once been. The English edition of his *Logic of Scientific Discovery* first appeared in 1959;[3] and since that time numerous rivals to his falsificationist approach had found supporters: Thomas Kuhn's picture of routine, "normal" science conducted under a ruling paradigm, and the overturning and replacement of an old paradigm by a new in periods of "revolutionary" science (1962);[4] Imre Lakatos's attempt to distinguish progressive from degenerating research programs (1970);[5] Paul Feyerabend's methodological anarchism (1978);[6] and, more recently, the many and various styles of "science studies," Bayesian and decision-theoretical currents in mainstream philosophy of science, etc., etc. Popper still has his devotedly loyal followers, though they are fewer than they once were. But by now there are those who describe him as a philosophical "sloganeer,"[7] or as trafficking in superficially appealing but ultimately disappointing philosophical "soundbites";[8] and the reviewer of a biography of Popper goes so far as to write that, because of his notorious unwillingness to listen to anyone who dared to criticize his views, Popper "condemned himself to a lifetime in the service of a bad idea."[9]

3 Karl R. Popper, *The Logic of Scientific Discovery* (first published in German in 1934; English ed., London: Hutchinson, 1959).

4 Thomas S. Kuhn, *The Structure of Scientific Revolutions* (Chicago: University of Chicago Press, 1962).

5 Imre Lakatos, "Falsification and the Methodology of Scientific Research Programmes," in Imre Lakatos and Alan Musgrave, eds., *Criticism and the Growth of Knowledge* (Cambridge: Cambridge University Press, 1970), 91–195.

6 Paul K. Feyerabend, *Against Method: Outlines of an Anarchistic Theory of Knowledge* (London: New Left Books, 1978).

7 Noretta Koertge, "Popper and the Science Wars" (lecture for the Summer School of Theory of Knowledge, Madralin, Warsaw [August 16–31, 1997], available at http://www.indiana.edu/~koertge/PopLectI.html].) This Summer School was supported by the financier George Soros, a long-time admirer of Popper, especially of his political philosophy. *Id.* See also William Shawcross, "Turning Dollars into Change," *Time* 150, no. 9, September 1, 1997, 48–57, 51 (telling us that "[a]fter leaving Soviet-controlled Hungary for London in 1947, Soros fell under the spell of ... Karl Popper," whose philosophy informed his banking practice, prompted his founding of the Open Society Institute, and influenced "his whole life."

8 Rebecca Goldstein, "The Popperian Soundbite," in John Brockman, ed., *What Have You Changed Your Mind About? Today's Leading Minds Rethink Everything* (New York: Harper Perennial, 2009), 8–10.

9 David Papineau, "The Proof Is in the Disproof," review of Malachi Haim Hacohen, *Karl Popper: The Formative Years*, *New York Times Book Review*, November 12, 2000, available at http://www.nytimes.com/book/00/11/12/reviews/001112.12papinet.html. Another reviewer of the same biography, also commenting on Popper's notoriously difficult personality,

However, Prof. Allen's comment may suggest that Justice Blackmun was knowingly endorsing Popper's philosophy "whole cloth," as it were—which would be a serious over-simplification. For, as I noted in "Trial and Error,"[10] in the same sentence in which he cites Popper, Justice Blackmun hedged his bets by also referring to another, quite different, philosopher of science, Carl Hempel; and, as this suggests, he seems not to have been fully aware how radical Popper's philosophy of science really is.

In any case, "out of date" just doesn't cut it in philosophy. The real difficulty with *Daubert*'s appeal to Popper isn't, as Professor Allen's word "anachronism" suggests, that by 1993 Popper's ideas were going out of style, overshadowed by the success of Thomas Kuhn's *Structure of Scientific Revolutions*.[11] No: the most glaring problem, as anyone familiar with Popper's philosophy of science would realize right away, is much more serious: it was downright bizarre to call on Popper—Popper, of all people!—to help determine whether expert scientific testimony is sufficiently reliable to be admissible. For a key thesis of Popper's is that *scientific claims can never be shown to be true, probable, or reliable*. A second problem follows hard on the heels of the first: if Popper's account were true, *there would be no way to recognize reliable scientific testimony*, and the Court's preoccupation with the reliability of such testimony would rest on a serious misconception.

I will begin by presenting Popper's philosophy of science in enough detail to show that it can't possibly provide the criterion of reliability of scientific testimony the Court was seeking (§2). The next step will be to spell out how Justice Blackmun misconstrues Popper's ideas, and to identify some sources of this misunderstanding—in the amicus briefs in *Daubert* and in the then-recent legal literature, as well as in Popper himself (§3). Then it will be time to look at what federal courts have made of the Supreme Court's allusions to Popper, falsifiability, etc., as *Daubert* has played out in subsequent rulings on the admissibility of scientific testimony—which will reveal that courts (and legal scholars) have continued to misunderstand how radical Popper's ideas really are and, more importantly, how unsuitable for their purposes (§4). This will conclude the "deconstruction" of which my title speaks.

But, as my title also signals, my ultimate purpose is reconstruction: I hope, that is, to make some positive headway on legal issues about scientific

conjectures that he adopted the manner and speech-patterns of a much bigger man to compensate for being so short in stature. Ivor Grattan-Guinness, "Truths and Contradictions about Karl Popper," *Annals of Science* 59 (2002): 89–96, 93.

10 On the differences between Popper's philosophy of science and Hempel's, see "Trial and Error: Two Confusions in *Daubert*," pp. 104–21 in this volume, 106–10.

11 In any case, by 1993 Kuhn was no longer so dominant a figure as *he* had once been, either.

testimony. So my concluding argument will be, first, that the justice system's concern with reliability is both legally essential and philosophically legitimate; and second that, ironically enough—though the philosophy of science to which *Daubert* appeals is less than no help in determining reliability—the misinterpretation many federal courts have given the first, quasi-Popperian *Daubert* factor is closer to the truth than the Popperian philosophy of science from which it ostensibly derives (§5).

2 WILL THE REAL KARL POPPER PLEASE STAND UP?

Popper's work poses considerable difficulties for an expositor, not least because—to adapt a turn of phrase from J. L. Austin—there are the parts where Popper says it, and then there are the parts where he takes it back.[12] Besides (what I take to be) the authentic, tough-minded, falsificationist Popper, there is also a kind of shadow Popper: a more moderate and more plausible Popper, perhaps, but a more moderate and more plausible Popper who offers not so much a fully articulated philosophy of science as a congeries of sound fallibilist aperçus and a couple of very appealing metaphors—which, however, are neither easily reconciled with the main thrust of his arguments, nor easily put together to form a better alternative picture. I'll get to this shadow Popper later; but let me begin with what I take to be the core themes of Popper's official account.

His Big Idea came to him, Popper tells us, around 1919 (when, I note, he would have been seventeen years old). Many years later, he explained that it was disenchantment with the Marxist "scientific socialism" of which he had been enamored at sixteen that first made him aware how crucial the difference is between dogmatic thinking (bad) and a critical attitude (good). This awareness, he continues, was reinforced by his encounters with Freud's and Adler's psycho-analytic theories, and emphatically underscored when Einstein's eclipse predictions were "successfully tested."[13]

[12] J. L. Austin, "Performative Utterances," (1956), in Urmson and Warnock, eds., *Philosophical Papers of J. L. Austin*, 1961), 220–39, 228 (asking, now we "feel the firm ground of prejudice glide away beneath our feet, ... what next?", and replying, "[y]ou will be waiting for ... the bit where we take it all back"); and J. L. Austin, *Sense and Sensibilia* (Oxford: Clarendon Press, 1962), 2 (noting that philosophers who profess to believe that the objects of perception are not physical objects but sense data sometimes say that really this is just what we believed all along: "[t]here's the bit where you say it and the bit where you take it back").

[13] Karl R. Popper, *Unended Quest* (La Salle, IL: Open Court, 1979), 34–38 (first published in Schilpp, ed., *The Philosophy of Karl Popper* (La Salle, IL: Open Court, 1974), vol. 1, 3–181); the quotation comes from 37. The ambiguity of the phrase "successfully tested" is worthy of note. Popper is not entitled to any meaning stronger than "the tests were conducted according to

As I noted in "Trial and Error," the specific shape that Popper's Big Idea took is best understood in terms of his reaction to the approach taken by the Logical Positivists of the Vienna Circle,[14] the main thrust of which was to draw the line between good, clean scientific work and meaningless metaphysical speculation. The Logical Positivists proposed *verifiability* as the criterion of demarcation of *meaningful* from *meaningless* statements; and envisaged scientific theories' being confirmed *inductively*: i.e., as being warranted by evidence which, though not absolutely conclusive, makes it likely that the theory is true. But Popper came to see the asymmetry between verification and falsification as crucial: positive instances, no matter how many, cannot show that an unrestricted universal claim is true, but a single counter-instance is enough to show that it is false. Moreover, he argued, induction is neither necessary nor justifiable: scientists don't arrive at hypotheses by inductive reasoning from particular instances, and hypotheses are never inductively supported by positive instances, either.

So Popper turned Logical Positivism on its head.[15] In *The Logic of Scientific Discovery* (first published, in German, in 1934) he proposed *falsifiability* as a criterion of demarcation of *science* from *non-science*, and a purely *deductive* account of science and its method. The core ideas of this, as one might call it, Logical Negativist[16] position, are in brief:

- Falsifiability is a criterion for demarcating science, the real thing, both from pseudo-sciences such as "scientific socialism" and psychoanalysis, and from history, metaphysics, mythology, religion, "pre-science," etc.[17]

plan and Einstein's account was not falsified"; but what the phrase inevitably suggests is that the tests were conducted, Einstein's predictions were confirmed, and Einstein's theory was shown to be successful.

14 Popper was not a member of the Circle, but presented papers at what Prof. Singer describes as "epicycles" of the group. Peter Singer, "Discovering Karl Popper," *New York Review of Books* 21, no. 7, May 1, 1974, 22–28, 22.

15 David Stove—probably Popper's severest critic, and certainly the funniest—observes that "the idea of reversal … is the key to Popper's philosophy of science," and that "[a] Freudian might see, or imagine he sees, something more than adolescent revolt, something actually obsessive, in Popper's compulsion to *reverse* things." David Stove, "Cole Porter and Karl Popper: The Jazz Age in the Philosophy of Science" (1991), in Roger Kimball, ed., *Against the Idols of the Age* (New Brunswick, NJ: Transaction Press, 1999), 3–32, 5, 7.

16 If I recall correctly, I learned the phrase "Logical Negativism" from my former colleague David Miller. This label, though very apt, is not very common; the more usual labels for Popper's position are those I used in "Trial and Error": "Critical Rationalism," "falsificationism," or "deductivism."

17 Popper, *The Logic of Scientific Discovery* (note 3 above) ("the falsifiability of a system is to be taken as a criterion of demarcation"), 40. In *Unended Quest* (note 13 above), 41, Popper tells us that the criterion of demarcation was originally intended to exclude Marxism and psychoanalysis, and only later extended to exclude metaphysics.

- A statement is falsifiable, and hence scientific, if and only if it is incompatible with some basic statement;[18] i.e., a statement reporting the occurrence of an observable event at a specified place and time.[19]
- A statement is falsified when a basic statement with which it is incompatible is accepted.[20]
- The acceptance of basic statements is a matter for decision on the part of the relevant scientific community, and is *purely conventional*. What a scientist observes may *motivate* a scientist to accept a basic statement; but no observation can ever constitute evidence *justifying* or *warranting* the acceptance of such a statement.[21]
- The only logical relations are deductive; there is no inductive logic, nor does science use induction.[22]
- Science proceeds by "conjecture and refutation": a scientist makes an informed guess about the explanation of some puzzling phenomenon; deduces the consequences of this guess; and—this is the distinctively Popperian methodological point—*tries to refute it* by subjecting those consequences to the severest possible tests.[23]

18 Popper, *The Logic of Scientific Discovery* (note 3 above), 86 (explaining that a theory is falsifiable if "it divides the class of all possible basic statements into those with which it is inconsistent … [and] the class of all possible basic statements which it does not contradict." In other words, as Popper also puts it, "the class of its potential falsifiers is not empty").

19 *Id.*, 103 ("Basic statements are … statements asserting that an observable event is occurring in a certain individual region of space and time").

20 *Id.*, 86 ("We say that a theory is falsified only if we have accepted basic statements which contradict it"). Popper goes on to add that "[w]e shall take [a claim] as falsified only if we discover *a reproducible* effect which refutes the theory"; but note that this addendum runs together *basic statements* and *the events they describe*.

21 *Id.*, 105 ("Experiences can *motivate a decision*, and hence an acceptance or rejection of a statement, but a basic statement cannot be justified by them—no more than by thumping the table"). The argument seems to be twofold. (i) justification is a logical relation, and logical relations can hold only among statements; so, since observations are not statements but events, they cannot stand in any kind of logical relation to a statement. (ii) even a basic statement like "here is a glass of water" is imbued with theory. So the content of basic statements goes beyond what can be determined by observation; and if observations *could* stand in logical relations to basic statement, the relation would have to be an inductive (or, better, an ampliative) one—but there are no such relations. (This involves some rational reconstruction of Popper's text, disentangling two strands of argument that he runs together; for details, see Susan Haack, *Evidence and Inquiry* (1993; 2nd ed., Amherst, NY: Prometheus Books, 2009), 144–49.)

22 Popper, *The Logic of Scientific Discovery* (note 3 above), 30 (arguing that "the various difficulties of inductive logic … are insurmountable.… The theory to be developed in the following pages stands directly opposed to all attempts to operate with the idea of inductive logic").

23 *Id.*, 32–33; see also Karl R. Popper, "Science: Conjectures and Refutations" (1957), reprinted in Popper, *Conjectures and Refutations: The Growth of Scientific Knowledge* (London: Routledge and Kegan Paul, 1963), 33–65, 51 (arguing that "*there is no more rational procedure than the method of trial and error—of conjecture and refutation*: of boldly proposing

- This method uses only deductive logic—most importantly, the deductive rule of *modus tollens*, which licenses the inference from "if *p* then *q*" and "not-*q*" to "not-*p*," used in the refutation phase.[24]
- Scientists should make bold, highly falsifiable conjectures; test them as severely as possible; and, should they be falsified when they are tested, drop them and start again rather than making *ad hoc* adjustments to save them.[25] This willingness to accept falsification is another criterion of the genuinely scientific.[26]
- The probability of a claim is inversely related to its content; i.e., the more a statement says—and hence, the more falsifiable it is—the more *im*probable it is.[27]
- Theories which have been tested but not yet falsified have been (in a technical sense explained below) "corroborated," to a degree depending on the number and severity of the tests passed.[28]
- To say that a theory is corroborated is to say that it has been subjected to such-and-such tests, and has not, so far, been falsified. This is strictly a report on the past. That a theory has been corroborated, to however high a degree, doesn't show that it is true, that it is probable, that there is reason to believe it—*or* that it is reliable.

On this last point—which in the present context is obviously crucial—Popper is unambiguously clear:

> Corroboration (or degree of corroboration) is ... an evaluating *report of past performance.... [I]t says nothing whatever about future performance, or about the 'reliability' of a theory.*[29]

theories; of trying our best to show that these are erroneous; and of accepting them tentatively if our critical efforts are unsuccessful").

24 Popper, *The Logic of Scientific Discovery* (note 3 above), 76 (explaining that "[t]he falsifying mode of inference—is the *modus tollens* of classical logic").

25 *Id.*, 82 (urging that "we decide that, in the case of a threat to our system, we will not save it by any kind of *conventionalist stratagem*").

26 *Id.*, 82 (explaining that "my criterion of demarcation cannot be applied immediately to a *system of statements*," but that "*[o]nly with reference to the method applied* is it possible to ask whether we are dealing with a conventionalist or an empirical theory").

27 *Id.*, 269. See also Karl R. Popper, "Conjectural Knowledge: My Solution of the Problem of Induction" (1971), in Popper, *Objective Knowledge: An Evolutionary Approach* (Oxford: Clarendon Press, 1972), 1–33, 18 (arguing that the degree of testability of a theory is inversely related to its probability).

28 Popper, *The Logic of Scientific Discovery* (note 3 above), 265–69. The English translation of the heading of this section of the book speaks of "How a Hypothesis May 'Prove Its Mettle'"; but in footnote *1, p.53, added in the English edition, Popper acknowledges that this phrase is potentially misleading.

29 Popper, "Conjectural Knowledge" (note 27 above), 18.

Again:

> I lay stress on *negative* arguments, such as negative instances or counter-examples, refutations, and attempted refutations—in short, criticism—while the inductivist lays stress on '*positive instances*' from which he draws 'non-demonstrative *inferences*' and which he hopes will guarantee the '*reliability*' of those inferences.[30]

In short, the core Popperian philosophy—eschewing verifiability, inductive logic, confirmation, supportive evidence, *and* reliability, and urging scientists to make bold, highly falsifiable, and hence improbable, conjectures and then test them to destruction—is thoroughly negative. In fact, it's far *more* negative even than Popper acknowledges. Presenting himself as a champion of science, Popper purports to provide a thoroughly fallibilist, but still fully cognitivist, picture; but what he actually gives us is a kind of covert skepticism.[31] For if, as Popper maintains, induction is wholly unjustifiable, there can be no reason to believe that a theory that passed a certain test today would pass the same test tomorrow. Moreover, if, as he also maintains, the acceptance of basic statements is not justified by scientists' observations, but is purely a matter of decision on the part of the scientific community, there is no guarantee that a scientific statement that has been "falsified," in Popper's sense, is actually false; and this implies that scientific claims can no more be shown to be false than they can be shown to be true.

~

But as Søren Kierkegaard observes, "[i]n relation to their systems most systematizers are like a man who builds an enormous castle and lives in a shack nearby."[32] Popper is no exception; when he finds his forbidding Logical Negativist castle uninhabitable, he takes refuge in humbler but more comfortable fallibilist quarters. And this shadow Popper qualifies, amends, amplifies, and restates his Logical Negativism in ways that obfuscate matters considerably. Numerous qualifications obscure both the character and the motivation of the Logical Negativist criterion of demarcation. Appealing analogies purportedly illustrating Logical Negativism actually suggest, instead, a much more modest fallibilism. New ideas are added that seem, superficially, to moderate Logical Negativism, but on closer inspection turn out to leave it untouched.

30 *Id.*, 20.

31 "Skepticism" is used here in the philosophical sense in which it refers to the thesis that we can know nothing, not in the ordinary-language usage in which it means "taking a critical, questioning attitude."

32 Søren Kierkegaard, *Journals* (1846), in Alexander Dru, ed., *A Selection from the Journals of Søren Kierkegaard* (New York: Oxford University Press, 1938), 156.

And, all along, Popper continues to use familiar, reassuring words—while, all along, stripping them of essential meaning.

Despite his stress on the importance of distinguishing genuine science from impostors (and his claim to have discovered what is wrong with Marxism, Freudian psychoanalytic theory, etc.),[33] in the introduction to the English edition of *The Logic of Scientific Discovery* Popper tells us that scientific knowledge is continuous with everyday empirical knowledge;[34] and in the body of the book he describes his criterion of demarcation as a convention[35]—leaving one wondering what, exactly, the motivation is for wanting a criterion of demarcation in the first place. Then in section 9 he acknowledges that the deduction of basic statements from a scientific theory will require auxiliary assumptions, and that modifying these could shield a theory from falsification by contrary evidence. So his criterion of demarcation is not, after all, purely logical, but partly methodological; and his methodological advice is not, after all, categorical ("drop a theory when it is falsified"), but conditional ("drop a theory if you can't find a way of accounting for contrary evidence that isn't *ad hoc*").[36] By now one is left wondering what, exactly, the criterion amounts to; what, exactly, it excludes; and what, exactly, it is intended to demarcate from what. Does it apply to theories? And if so, is it intended to demarcate scientific theories from non-scientific theories, or empirical theories from non-empirical ones? Or is it intended, rather, to demarcate scientific from non-scientific procedures, or scientific attitudes to evidence from non-scientific attitudes—or what?

In *The Open Society and Its Enemies* (1945) Popper tells us that the problem with Marxist scientific socialism was not, after all, that it was unfalsifiable, but that after it was falsified by the events of the Russian revolution, Marxists

33 See e.g., Popper, "Science: Conjectures and Refutations," (note 23 above), 34 (recalling that his initial question, when it all began in 1919, was "[w]hat is wrong with Marxism, psychoanalysis, and individual psychology?"); *Unended Quest* (note 13 above), 38 (recalling. that by the end of that year he had arrived at the conclusion that "the scientific attitude … did not look for verifications but for critical tests: tests which could refute the theory tested, though they could never establish it").

34 Karl R. Popper, "Preface to the English edition, 1958," *The Logic of Scientific Discovery* (note 3 above), 15–23, 18 (telling us that "scientific knowledge can only be an extension of common-sense knowledge").

35 Popper, *The Logic of Scientific Discovery* (note 3 above), 37 (explaining that "[m]y criterion of demarcation will … have to be regarded as a convention").

36 *Id.*, 82 (suggesting that it is willingness to accept falsification, not simple falsifiability, that being scientific requires). But in "Conjectural Knowledge" (note 27 above), Popper returns in a footnote to the old, logical understanding: "The 'problem of demarcation' is what I call the problem of finding a criterion by which we can distinguish the *statements* of empirical science from non-empirical *statements*." *Id.*,12, n.19.

reinterpreted their theory to avoid having to admit that it had been falsified.[37] But by the time of "Conjectural Knowledge" (1971), recognizing that modifying a theory in the face of contrary evidence isn't *always* bad practice, Popper acknowledges "the value of a *dogmatic* attitude," writing that "somebody [has] to defend a theory against criticism or it would succumb too easily."[38] One is left unsure whether Popper is really offering a stringent methodological regimen, or only the tritest of methodological bromides.

In *The Logic of Scientific Discovery*,[39] and again in *Conjectures and Refutations*,[40] Popper describes the "empirical basis" of science as like piles driven into a swamp—a nice analogy[41] which, however, suggests a plausible fallibilist picture of basic statements as partially but not fully justified by scientists' observations. But this picture can't possibly be squared with Popper's insistence that observation is *irrelevant* to justification. And in an article published in 1968 Popper describes scientific work as like building a cathedral[42]—a really splendid analogy which, however, suggests a more or less cumulative picture of scientific progress. But this picture can't possibly be squared with his falsificationist theory, which suggests that science is more like a Kafkaesque building site where, each day, workers try to demolish the previous day's work and, when they succeed, begin building anew—until the next day.[43] One is

37 Karl R. Popper, *The Open Society and Its Enemies* (1945; revised ed., Princteton, NJ: Princeton University Press, 1950), 374 (arguing that "[e]xperience shows that Marx's prophecies were false. But experience can always be explained away. And, indeed, Marx himself, and Engels, began the elaboration of auxiliary hypotheses to [evade falsification]"). See also *Unended Quest* (note 13 above), 43.

38 Karl R. Popper, "Conjectural Knowledge" (note 27 above), 30.

39 Popper, *The Logic of Scientific Discovery* (note 3 above), 111.

40 Popper, "Addenda: Some Technical Notes," *Conjectures and Refutations* (note 23 above), 377–413, 385–88; the analogy is on 387. See also A. J. Ayer, "Truth, Verification and Verisimilitude," in Schilpp, ed., *The Philosophy of Karl Popper* (note 13 above), vol. 2, 684–92, and Popper's reply, "Ayer on Empiricism and Against Verisimilitude," *id.*, vol. 2, 1100–04; and A. M. Quinton, "The Foundations of Knowledge," in Bernard Williams and Alan Montefiore, eds., *British Analytical Philosophy* (London: Routledge and Kegan Paul, 1966), 55–86.

41 A nice analogy anticipated more than fifty years earlier by C. S. Peirce. Peirce, *Collected Papers*, eds. Charles Hartshorne, Paul Weiss, and (vols. 7 and 8), Arthur Burks (Cambridge, MA: Harvard University Press, 1931–58), 5.589 (1898) (observing that our knowledge "is not standing on the bedrock of fact. It is walking on a bog, and can only say, this ground seems to the hold for the present").

42 Karl R. Popper, "On the Theory of the Objective Mind" (1968), in Popper, *Objective Knowledge* (note 27 above), 153–90, 185 (arguing that "[s]cience is ... a branch of literature; and working on science is a human activity like building a cathedral").

43 Popper adds that "the method of problem solving, the method of conjecture and refutation, is practised by both [science and the humanities]," and goes on to compare constructing a theory of radioactivity and reconstructing a damaged text. *Ibid.* But once the method

left with the distinct impression that Popper wants to have it both ways: he is anxious to claim credit for a big, radical idea, but is unwilling to swallow its big, radically unpalatable consequences.

In a note appended to the English edition of *The Logic of Scientific Discovery* Popper tells us that after he encountered Alfred Tarski's theory of truth[44] (which he, unlike Tarski himself, saw as a version of the correspondence theory),[45] he overcame his earlier reluctance to speak of the truth of scientific theories.[46] In due course he developed his account of "verisimilitude" or, as he also says, "truth-likeness," or "nearness to the truth."[47] But it turns out that degree of corroboration is not, as one might have hoped, a measure of degree of verisimilitude, but only of what the verisimilitude of a theory *appears* to be, relative to other theories, at a given time.[48] Again, in *Unended Quest* Popper tells us that it is rational to act on the basis of a well-corroborated theory; but—since he insists that the fact that a theory is corroborated, to however high a degree, is absolutely *no* reason to believe that it is it true, that it is probable, or that it is reliable—the only rationale he can offer is that "actions ... are 'rational' ... if they are carried out in accordance with the state ... of the critical scientific discussion." This isn't as reassuring as it might sound; for the next

of conjecture and refutation has been elided into generic "problem-solving," and applied to the humanities and even to literature, it is not clear why "demarcation" should be a priority.

44 Alfred Tarski, "The Concept of Truth in Formalised Languages" (originally published in Polish in 1933), trans. J. H. Woodger in Tarski, *Logic, Semantics, Metamathematics* (Oxford: Clarendon Press, 1956), 152–278; "The Semantic Conception of Truth" (1944), reprinted in Herbert Feigl and Wilfrid Sellars, eds., *Readings in Philosophical Analysis* (New York: Appleton-Century-Crofts, 1949), 52–84.

45 Alfred Tarski, "The Semantic Conception of Truth" (note 44 above), 54 (claiming that several accounts of truth, among them the correspondence theory, "can lead to various misunderstandings," and that "none of them can be considered a satisfactory definition"). Compare Popper, *Unended Quest* (note 13 above), 98 (reporting that in 1935, after Tarski explained his theory of truth to him, he realized that "[Tarski] had finally rehabilitated the much maligned correspondence theory of truth").

46 Popper, *The Logic of Scientific Discovery* (note 3 above), 274 (arguing that "[w]e need not say that the theory is 'false', but may say instead that it is contradicted by a certain set of basic statements. Nor need we say of basic statements that they are 'true' or 'false', for we may interpret them as the result of a conventional decision ..."); & n.*1 (added in the English edition) (explaining that "[o]wing to Tarski's teaching, I am no longer hesitant in speaking of 'truth' and 'falsity'").

47 Karl R. Popper, "Truth, Rationality and the Growth of Scientific Knowledge" (1963), in Popper, *Conjectures and Refutations* (note 23 above), 215–50, 223.

48 Popper, "Conjectural Knowledge" (note 27 above), 22. (As Popper defines it, the "verisimilitude" of a theory is the proportion of its truth-content to its falsity-content; so his gloss "nearness to the truth" seems to be somewhat misleading.)

sentence reveals that, by Popper's lights, it is a trivial verbal truth: "[t]here is no better synonym for 'rational' than 'critical.'"[49] So, after all, Popper has given no substantive reason for thinking that it is more rational to act on the basis of well-tested theories than on sheer speculation or wishful thinking.

And, as we saw, in *The Logic of Scientific Discovery* Popper uses words like "knowledge" and "discovery" without their usual connotation of truth,[50] and (though less openly) "falsified" without its usual connotation of falsity.[51] He also tells us that what he calls "objective scientific knowledge" is all "conjectural,"[52] meaning that none of it is believed, any or all of it may turn out to be false, and none of it is ever warranted by good evidence—in fact, it is nothing but "a woven web of guesses."[53] Again, his repeated references to "objective scientific knowledge" may sound reassuring; but the fact is that none of this does anything to alleviate the covert skepticism.

And, most consequentially for present purposes, before Popper realized how misleading this was, and adopted the word "corroboration" instead, he went along with Rudolf Carnap's translation of his word "*Bewährung*" as "confirmation,"[54] and for a while even used the word "confirmation" himself. But in a

49 Popper, *Unended Quest* (note 13 above), 87. See also Popper, "Conjectural Knowledge" (note 27 above), 22 (acknowledging that "choosing the best-tested theory as the basis of action ... is not 'rational' in the sense that it is based upon *good reasons* for expecting that it will in practice be a successful choice; *there can be no good reasons* in this sense").

50 *See* David Stove, *Popper and After: Four Modern Irrationalists* (1982), reprinted under the title *Anything Goes: Origins of the Cult of Scientific Irrationalism* (Paddington, Australia: Macleay Press, 1999) (criticizing Popper's *penchant* for "neutralising success-words"). Stove does not, however, note that Popper also neutralizes failure-words like "falsified."

51 Later, Popper tells us that the "objective knowledge" to which he refers consists of "theories published in books and journals...; discussions of such theories; difficulties or problems ... with such theories," and even "the logical content of our genetic code"; and that it belongs not to "world 1" (the realm of physical objects) or "world 2" (the realm of mental states), but to "world 3" (the realm of abstract objects such as numbers). Karl R. Popper, "Two Faces of Common Sense: An Argument for Commonsense Realism and Against the Commonsense Theory of Knowledge" (from a talk given in 1970), in Popper, *Objective Knowledge* (note 27 above), 32–105, 73.

52 *See e.g.* Popper, "Conjectural Knowledge" (note 27 above), 31.

53 Karl R. Popper, "Toleration and Intellectual Responsibility" (lecture delivered at the University of Tübingen, 1981), in Popper, *In Search of a Better World: Lectures and Essays from Thirty Years*, trans. Laura J. Bennett (London: Routledge, 1992), 188–203, 195. (The phrase comes from Xenophanes, but Popper is here using it on his own behalf.) Popper adds: 'scientific knowledge ... consists of ... *conjectures* only.... The *content* of these ... conjectures may be called *knowledge in the objective sense*." *Id.*, 197, 198.

54 It is not entirely clear that Carnap's translation of the German word Popper had used was mistaken. It *is* clear, however, that given the state of play in philosophy of science at the time, the effect of translating "*Bewährung*" as "confirmed" was extremely misleading. See *Pons' Global Wörterbuch Deutsch-Englisch* (Stuttgart: Klett, and London: Collins, 1983).

footnote added to the English translation of *The Logic of Scientific Discovery* he writes:

> Carnap translated my term 'degree of corroboration' … as 'degree of confirmation.'… I fell in with his usage, thinking that words do not matter.… I myself used the word 'confirmation' for a time.… Yet it turned out that I was mistaken: the association of the word 'confirmation' did matter.… '[D] egree of confirmation' was soon used as a synonym … of 'probability'. I have therefore now abandoned it.…[55]

Small wonder, then, that—while Popper's official story, the Big Idea, is about as ill-suited as it could be to discriminate reliable from unreliable scientific testimony, the parts where he takes it back have made it all too easy to misconstrue what the Popperian story really is. So it should come as no surprise to find that the idea that Popper's philosophy of science will be helpful to courts needing to determine whether scientific testimony is reliable enough to be admitted turns out to rest on mistakenly taking him to hold that *a claim that has been tested but not falsified is thereby confirmed, i.e., shown to be probable, warranted, valid, or reliable*—which, however, he repeatedly and emphatically denied.

3 HOW DID *DAUBERT* GET POPPER SO WRONG?

Popper's ideas entered judicial thinking on the admissibility of expert scientific testimony, as we saw earlier, with Justice Blackmun's observations about how federal courts might go about determining whether such testimony is reliable enough to be admitted. Since FRE 702 refers to "scientific … knowledge," Justice Blackmun argued, courts must determine whether proffered scientific evidence really *is* scientific knowledge. "The word 'knowledge' connotes more than subjective belief or ungrounded speculation," he explained, citing Webster's dictionary; and "[t]he adjective 'scientific' implies a grounding in the methods and procedures of science."[56]

But what is the mark of genuine science, and what are the methods and procedures followed in genuinely scientific work? The unmistakably Popperian flavor of Justice Blackmun's answer is clear from the first consideration on his "flexible list" of indicia of reliability:

> [A] key question … in determining whether a theory or technique is scientific knowledge … is whether it can be (and has been) tested. "Scientific

[55] Popper, *The Logic of Scientific Discovery* (note 3 above), 251–52, n.*1.

[56] Daubert v. Merrell Dow Pharm., Inc., 509 U.S. 579, 590 (1993) ("*Daubert* III"), 590.

knowledge today is based on generating hypotheses and testing them to see if they can be falsified; indeed, this methodology is what distinguishes science from other fields of human inquiry."[57]

The internal quotation here is from a law review article by Michael Green; but in the next sentence Justice Blackmun cites Popper himself: "the criterion of the scientific status of a theory is its falsifiability, or refutability, or testability."[58]

Unfortunately, the article of Popper's from which this quotation is taken, first published in 1957, is one of the places where he used Carnap's word, "confirmation"—which, only two years later, he would repudiate. Perhaps this begins to explain why, in the very same sentence, Justice Blackmun *also* quotes Carl Hempel ("the statements constituting a scientific explanation must be capable of empirical test")[59]—apparently quite unaware that Popper's understanding of "testable" ("potentially falsifiable") and Hempel's ("potentially *confirmable or* falsifiable") are quite different; that Popper specifically identifies Hempel as a proponent of the inductivist philosophy of science he repudiates;[60] and that by 1959 Popper had realized the danger of confusing his negativist, deductivist concept of corroboration with the positivist, inductivist idea of confirmation. And neither, obviously, does Justice Blackmun realize that Popper expressly disavows any interest in the reliability of scientific theories, and indeed avoids even using the word "reliable" without precautionary scare quotes.

As I argued in "Trial and Error," it looks as if—perhaps unduly influenced by that honorific use of "science," "scientific," etc., as generic terms of epistemological praise, and perhaps forgetting that not all scientific expert testimony is reliable, nor all reliable expert testimony scientific[61]—Justice Blackmun ran

57 *Id.*, 593 (citations omitted).

58 *Id.* The citation is to Popper, *Conjectures and Refutations* (note 23 above), 37. Justice Blackmun cites the 5th ed. (1989), as if this were a then-recent work. But this book of Popper's was first published in 1963, and is an anthology of previously-published papers. The article Justice Blackmun cites, "Science: Conjectures and Refutations," was first published, under the title, "Philosophy of Science: A Personal Report," in C. A. Mace, ed., *British Philosophy in Mid-Century*, ed. C. A. Mace (London: George Allen and Unwin, 1957), 155–91. Unfortunately, when this paper was reprinted in *Conjectures and Refutations*, Popper neither noted nor corrected the misunderstanding over "confirmed" and "corroborated." Notice also that in this article Popper writes of falsifiability as "*the*" not "*a*" criterion of demarcation.

59 Carl G. Hempel, *Philosophy of Natural Science* (Englewood Cliffs, NJ: Prentice-Hall, 1966), 49.

60 Popper, "Conjectural Knowledge" (note 27 above), 20, n. 29. For more details, see "Trial and Error" (note 10 above), 109–10.

61 FRE 702 speaks of "scientific, *technical, or other specialized* knowledge" (emphasis added); so the ellipses in Justice Blackmun's reference to "scientific ... knowledge" are significant.

"reliable" and "scientific" together. Then, looking for some criterion to distinguish the genuinely scientific from pretenders, he fastened on Popper's criterion of falsifiability but—not realizing that this was part of a thoroughly negative philosophical package that is no help at all on the question of reliability—ran Popper's and Hempel's quite different understandings of "testable" together.[62]

But *Daubert*'s pseudo-Popper was probably not entirely Justice Blackmun's own creation; the same misinterpretation of Popper was to be found in several amicus briefs filed in the case, as well as in the law-review article cited in the relevant part of the ruling. Three of the four "*Daubert* factors" were already prefigured in an amicus brief submitted by the United States Department of Justice: arguing that expert testimony must reach a certain level of reliability if it is to be, as FRE 702 required, helpful to the trier of fact, these amici suggested error rates, peer review, and acceptance in the field as indicia of reliability.[63] The first, quasi-Popperian *Daubert* factor isn't found in this amicus brief; but it is prefigured in several of the others.

For example, an amicus brief submitted by the American Medical Association, which avers that "[a]n opinion is only based upon scientific knowledge if it is developed in accordance with the scientific method," goes on to say—citing Popper—that "[i]f a hypothesis is repeatedly corroborated by empirical testing, it is ... *generally accepted as valid*." In principle, these amici admit, "no scientific theory is ever definitively confirmed"; however, they continue, "[a]s a practical matter ..., some theories are *so thoroughly tested that they become virtually incontrovertible*."[64] Given how close being incontrovertible is to being unfalsifiable, this is about as un-Popperian as it could be.

Another amicus brief, this one from the Product Liability Advisory Council, describes the scientific method like this:

> (1) first set forth a hypothesis, (2) design an experiment, or ... experiments, to test the hypothesis, (3) conduct the experiment, collect the data, and then analyze those data, (4) publish the results so that they may ... be subject to external scrutiny, and (5) ensure that those results are replicable *and verifiable*.[65]

[62] It may also be relevant that what is usually meant in legal context by saying that testimony is "corroborated" is something like "other witnesses tell the same story."

[63] Brief for the United States as Amicus Curiae Supporting Respondent, *Daubert* III (note 56 above) (No. 92–102), 1993 WL 13006291, *11–*12. However, these amici suggest that acceptance by at least a significant minority in the field would suffice, whereas *Daubert* says that "widespread acceptance can be an important factor in ruling particular evidence admissible...." *Daubert* III (note 56 above), 594.

[64] Brief of the American Medical Ass'n et al. as Amici Curiae in Support of Respondent, *Daubert* III (note 56 above) (No. 92–102), 1993 WL 13006385, *11 (my italics).

[65] Brief of Product Liability Advisory Council, Inc. et al. as Amici Curiae in Support of Respondent, *Daubert* III (note 56 above) (No. 92–102) 1993 WL 13006388, *23 & n.20 (my italics) (other footnotes omitted).

Each of these clauses has its own citation (omitted here); the last—appended to the part about the results being "replicable *and verifiable*"—is to *The Logic of Scientific Discovery*. Given Popper's repudiation of verificationism (and his conventionalism about basic statements), this too is an exegetical travesty.

An amicus brief from the Carnegie Commission on Science, Technology and Government argues that "opinions based on claims that are not capable of being tested should not be admitted into evidence," and cites Popper;[66] and immediately adds, citing a report from a Panel of the National Academy of Sciences,[67] that results that cannot be replicated should also be excluded, and that "scientists have the responsibility to replicate *and reconfirm* their results."[68] Fair enough; except that the failure of these amici to note that Popper expressly eschews the notion of confirmation conveys the false impression that claims that have been subjected to repeated tests but not falsified have been "reconfirmed." But of course results can't be *re*confirmed unless they have first been *confirmed.*

And an amicus brief from the American Association for the Advancement of Science, though it doesn't mention Popper by name, makes free use of his term "corroborated," and comments that:

> [S]cience ... proceed[s] through a series of interrelated steps centered on the generation and testing of hypotheses. Hypotheses are educated guesses about a particular phenomenon or event.... Scientists conduct rigorous experimental testing in an attempt to falsify hypotheses.[69]

This all sounds entirely Popperian—until the next sentence:

> An hypothesis is *accepted as generally valid to the extent that it has survived repeated attempts at falsification.*[70]

—which, of course, is the by now familiar pseudo-Popperian line.[71]

66 Brief of the Carnegie Commission on Science, Technology, and Government as Amicus Curiae in Support of Neither Party, *Daubert* III (note 56 above) (No. 92–102), 1992 WL 12006530, *13 & n.12 ("Brief of the Carnegie Commission") (other footnote omitted).

67 Panel on Scientific Responsibility and the Integrity of the Research Process, National Academy of Sciences, *Responsible Science: Ensuring the Integrity of the Research Process* (Washington, DC: National Academy Press, 1992), vol. I.

68 Brief of the Carnegie Commission (note 66 above), *13 n.13. (The passage from the Panel's report concludes by speaking of "an ongoing process of revision and refinement that corrects errors and strengthens the fabric of research." *Responsible Science* [note 67 above], 59.)

69 Brief for the American Ass'n for the Advancement of Science et al. as Amici Curiae in Support of Respondent, *Daubert* III (note 56 above) (No. 92–102), 1993 WL 13006281, *8–*9.

70 *Id.*, *9 (my italics).

71 In a paper published the same year, one of the signatories, Bert Black, had published an article (written jointly with Francisco Ayala) which calls explicitly on Popper—and perpetrates

The crucial misreading of Popper was also, apparently, circulating in the law reviews, and is found specifically in the article by Michael Green[72] that Justice Blackmun quotes in *Daubert*. The key passage of Green's paper (a very small part of a long article most of which is taken up with a complex discussion of issues about epidemiological evidence in toxic tort litigation) reads as follows:

> Hume criticized the inductive, rather than the deductive, methodology. From that criticism emerged the idea that while induction could never conclusively prove a proposition, it could falsify one. Thus, based on the framework provided by Karl Popper, knowledge is gained by attempting to falsify a hypothesis based on empirical investigation. Scientific methodology today is based on generating hypotheses and testing them to see if they can be falsified; indeed, this methodology is what distinguishes science from other fields of human inquiry. Of course, *if a hypothesis repeatedly withstands falsification, we may tend to accept it, even if conditionally, as true.*[73]

Setting aside the first sentence, and skating over the second (where, I suspect, Green said "induction" when he meant to say "deduction"), I turn to the sentence Justice Blackmun quotes, the one beginning "Scientific methodology today...."

This sentence vaguely suggests that Popper's ideas were by then the consensus position in contemporary philosophy of science, or among scientists themselves—perhaps, even, that working scientists *en masse* had by then come to recognize the virtues of the methodology Popper recommended. This suggestion is misleading, to say the least. As I said earlier, at one time Popper's ideas were not only very influential among philosophers of science, but also endorsed by a number of distinguished scientists (among them Sir Herman Bondi, Sir Peter Medawar, and Sir John Eccles—known in England as the "Popperian knights").[74] And as I also said, there are still enthusiastic

the same misunderstanding. Francisco J. Ayala and Bert Black, "Science and the Courts," *American Scientist* 81 (June 1, 1993): 230–39, 237 (arguing that "[b]ecause scientific hypotheses can be falsified but not absolutely established, they can only be accepted contingently," and citing Popper; and then going on to give "[a]n example of how a critical test can crystallize understanding *and certainty*") (my italics).

[72] Michael D. Green, "Expert Witnesses and Sufficiency of Evidence in Toxic Substances Litigation: The Legacy of Agent Orange and Bendectin Litigation," *Northwestern University Law Review* 86, no. 3 (1991–92): 643–99.

[73] *Id.*, 645–46 (my italics).

[74] I suspect that what scientists found attractive about Popper's ideas may have been his picture of the scientist as making bold conjectures and fearlessly testing them, and his stress on the rational, critical, character of science and the objectivity of scientific knowledge. But John Eccles, who seems to have had the clearest understanding of the views he was endorsing,

Popperians about. But Popper's philosophy of science was *never* "generally accepted in the field to which it belongs";[75] and by the time of Green's article only a relatively few Popperian philosophers of science remained. It is the last clause of the last sentence of this passage, however, that is most to the present purpose: "if a hypothesis repeatedly withstands falsification, we may tend to accept it, even if conditionally, as true." This is a real rhetorical humdinger, managing to suggest, without ever actually saying, that a claim that has been tested but not falsified is thereby shown to be ("conditionally") true—a completely un-Popperian suggestion.

In a footnote to the passage I quoted, Green cites *The Logic of Scientific Discovery*—the whole thing, giving no page numbers—and a law review article by David Faigman, published shortly before his own. It seems possible that Green hadn't actually read Popper, but was relying on Faigman's account.[76] If so, it wasn't an entirely happy choice of source. Here is Faigman on Popper's philosophy of science:

> Falsifiability or testability represents the line of demarcation between science and pseudo-science, and *the strength of particular scientific statements depends on the extent to which they have been tested appropriately....* [77]

makes it very plain that their real appeal, for him, was the idea that it was not shameful, but a good thing, if your hypothesis was refuted—which, he reports, helped him out of a severe depression. John C. Eccles, "The World of Objective Knowledge," in Schilppp, ed., *The Philosophy of Karl Popper* (note 13 above), vol. 1, 349–70, 350. Peter Medawar writes that "[s]cientific methodology has to do with ... *validation and justification*," and though later in the same paper he sounds somewhat more Popperian, he adds that the critical part of scientific reasoning aims to find out whether scientists' imaginative stories "are stories about real life." Peter Medawar, "Science and Literature," *Encounter* XXXII, no. 1 (1969), 15–23, 17, 20. And I can testify from personal experience that Herman Bondi did not fully understand what he was endorsing. In the course of a 1998 lecture at the University of Miami, which he opened by explaining that he was "a strong Popperian," Bondi told us that cosmology became a science in 1826, when Wilhelm Olbers made the first falsifiable cosmological conjecture; and that this conjecture was in due course falsified, and a new conjecture devised—a new conjecture which, he continued, was by now "well-confirmed by observation."

75 D. H. Mellor's critical notice of the two large volumes of *The Philosophy of Karl Popper* (note 13 above) conveys something of the state of play in the late 1970s. He writes, for example: "Take Popper's attitude to induction, a central point of Popperian method and mythology. Popperians find us obtuse who do not see that Popper has solved the problem of induction. The feeling is mutual.... [A. J.] Ayer here repeats some long-standing objections to Popper's solution, of which Popper once again fails to see the point." D. H. Mellor, "The Popper Phenomenon," *Philosophy* 52 (1977): 195–202, 196.

76 In July 2009 I asked Prof. Green whether, when he wrote this paper, he had read Popper, or had relied on Faigman's article; he replied that it was too long ago to remember! E-mail from SH to Michael D. Green (July 8, 2009) date, and from Green to SH (July10, 2009), on file with author.

77 David Faigman, "To Have and Have Not: Assessing the Value of Social Science to Law as Science and Policy," *Emory Law Journal* 38 (1989): 1005–95, 1014–15 (my italics).

> Popper devoted much of his philosophical efforts to articulating a criterion by which scientific statements could be distinguished from nonscientific statements, especially pseudo-scientific, prescientific, and metaphysical statements. . . .[78] *Empirical research might corroborate [a] hypothesis by finding evidence supporting it. . . .*[79]

Faigman apparently *did* read (some) Popper; but didn't understand him very well. For one thing, the word "strength" in his first sentence is a fudge.[80] For another, there is slippage between this first sentence, which talks about science vs. pseudo-science, and the next, which also includes pre-science, etc., under non-science; but there is no indication that Faigman realizes that the fact that Popper's criterion is intended to do several different jobs itself presents problems. But most importantly, the last sentence here, according to which corroboration is a matter of finding supportive evidence, encapsulates the key misunderstanding of Popper, the misunderstanding that will be passed down, via Prof. Green, to Justice Blackmun—and to the federal courts.

4 FALSIFIABILITY IN THE FEDERAL COURTS

Only two of Justice Blackmun's colleagues on the *Daubert* Court—then-Chief Justice Rehnquist, and Justice Stevens, who joined in Justice Rehnquist's partial dissent—seem to have been even half-aware of how muddled the philosophy of science built into the majority ruling was. Yes, *Frye* had been superseded, Justice Rehnquist wrote; and yes, nevertheless courts' responsibility for screening expert testimony remained. But, he continued, Justice Blackmun's observations about "scientific . . . knowledge" were too vague and too general to be helpful. And he was baffled—as well he might be—by Justice Blackmun's allusions to falsifiability:

> I defer to no one in my confidence in federal judges; but I am at a loss to know what is meant when it is said that the scientific status of a theory depends on its "falsifiability," and I suspect some of them will be, too.[81]

Subsequent rulings in which federal judges refer to Popper, falsifiability, or testability suggest that Justice Rehnquist was right to suspect that they would be somewhat at a loss. Sometimes, after quoting the passage in *Daubert*

78 *Id.*, 1016.
79 *Id.*, 1018 (my italics).
80 Popper would indeed say that the strength of a claim depends on its content, i.e., that more falsifiable hypotheses are "stronger," in one sense; but Faigman's words vaguely suggest, without actually saying, that well-tested hypotheses are "strong" in the sense of "well-confirmed."
81 *Daubert* III (note 56 above), 600 (Rehnquist, C.J., dissenting in part).

presenting the Court's "flexible list" of indicia of reliability, courts quietly set the Popperian rhetoric aside,[82] and focus instead on some other aspect of the proffered testimony. But some courts take the first, Popperian *Daubert* factor to be primary;[83] and when judges actually try to *use* this factor, the results generally have been—well, quite strange.

A particularly egregious example—almost amusing, if what was at stake were not so serious—is *U.S. v. Bonds*, which came down very shortly after *Daubert*. Faced with a defense challenge to the FBI laboratory's DNA analyses, the court read its new gatekeeping obligations strictly *au pied de la lettre*. The defendants proffered evidence that DNA identifications conducted by the FBI laboratory had been found to be unreliable, but the court reasoned that, nonetheless, the FBI identifications were admissible under *Daubert*; arguing that, in proffering evidence about the deficiencies of the FBI lab, "the defendants have conceded that the theory and methods can be tested. The dispute ... is over *how* the results have been tested, not over *whether* the results can be or have been tested."[84] In other words, the fact that the FBI lab's DNA work had been tested and shown to be unreliable showed that the FBI's testimony could be and had been tested; and hence was grounds for admitting it—as reliable! Good grief.

Sometimes courts engage in a little light philosophy of science on their own behalf. In *U.S. v. Hines* (1999) the court relates in a footnote that the *Daubert* ruling had been accused of "simply tak[ing] the definition of science from Karl Popper, a definition that others have criticized as *deriving from a culturally defined, time-bound paradigm*."[85] Perhaps this vaguely Kuhnian talk

82 See e.g., Nat'l Bank of Commerce v. Associated Milk Producers, Inc., 22 F. Supp. 2d 942, 947 (E.D. Ark. 1998) (citing the four *Daubert* factors, but relying on Bernard D. Goldstein and Mary Sue Henifin, "Reference Guide on Toxicology," Federal Judicial Center, *Reference Manual on Scientific Evidence* [Washington, DC: Federal Judicial Center 1994], 181–220); Savage v. Union Pac. R.R. Co., 67 F. Supp. 2d 1021 (E.D. Ark. 1999) (citing the four *Daubert* factors, but relying primarily on the fact that the plaintiff did not prove his level of exposure to creosote).

83 Chikovsky v. Ortho Pharm. Corp., 832 F. Supp. 341, 345 (S.D. Fla. 1993) (arguing that, since *Daubert*, "[a]n issue of primary importance in the determination of whether a theory or technique is 'scientific knowledge' that will assist the trier of fact is 'whether it can be (and has been) tested'"). Bradley v. Brown, 42 F.3d 434, 438 (7th Cir. 1994) (arguing that "[t]he first and most significant *Daubert* factor is whether the scientific theory has been subjected to the scientific method"). See also Haggerty v. Upjohn Co., 950 F. Supp. 1160, 1163 (S.D. Fla. 1996) (arguing that testimony's having been arrived at by the scientific method is "the most significant of the *Daubert* factors," and citing *Chikovsky v. Ortho* and *Bradley v. Brown*).

84 United States v. Bonds, 12 F.3d 540, 559 (6th Cir. 1993).

85 United States v. Hines, 55 F. Supp. 2d 62, 65 n.7 (D. Mass. 1999) (my italics), citing, *inter alia*, Alexander Morgan Capron, "*Daubert* and the Quest for Value-Free 'Scientific Knowledge' in the Courtroom," *University of Richmond Law Review* 30 (1996): 85–108. The court does *not*

signals that Green's reference to "scientific methodology today" had not gone unnoticed. Also worthy of note is *Bitler v. A. O. Smith Corp.* (2005) where—instead of alluding, like Justice Blackmun, to the incongruous philosophical firm of Popper, Hempel & Associates—the court actually manages to distinguish the falsificationist Popper from the verificationist Hempel;[86] but unfortunately it fails to note that Popper's and Hempel's views are not only different, but flat-out incompatible.

Legally more significant, probably, are two fingerprint cases that misinterpret *Daubert*'s reference to "testability" as referring not to scientific, empirical testing, but to legal, dialectical testing in court. In *U.S. v. Havvard*, the court reasons that "[the] claim of uniqueness and permanence [of fingerprints] is a scientific claim in the sense that it can be falsified.... In the roughly 100 years since fingerprints have been used for identification purposes, no one has managed to falsify the claim of uniqueness...."[87] Of course, the crucial issue isn't really whether fingerprints are unique, but whether accurate identifications can be made on the basis of latent prints representing, on average, 20% of a full fingerprint; but set that aside. The most interesting point for present purposes is the way the court goes on to construe "testing": in terms, not of empirical testing in a laboratory or in the field, but of in-court "testing" through cross-examination:

> [T]he methods of latent print identification can be and have been tested. They have been tested for roughly 100 years. They have been tested in adversarial proceedings with the highest possible stakes—liberty and sometimes life.[88]

Whatever, exactly, Popper understood by "testing," we can be quite sure it wasn't argument and counter-argument in adversarial legal proceedings.[89]

note, however, that Prof. Capron had quoted a passage in which Popper expressly repudiates any interest in whether a theory is true or acceptable. *Id.*, 92 n.23, citing Popper, *Conjectures and Refutations* (note 23 above), 33. Capron's is, in fact, the *only* law review article I have found that gets Popper right on this.

86 Bitler v. A.O. Smith Corp., 400 F.3d 1227, 1235 (10th Cir. 2004) (referring to the Supreme Court's citation to "Popper's method of falsification" and, a few lines later, to "the logical positivist Carl Hempel").

87 United States v. Havvard, 117 F. Supp. 2d 848, 852 (S.D. Ind. 2000).

88 *Id.*, 854.

89 Nor, I believe—recalling his angry dissent in *Barefoot v. Estelle*—was it what Justice Blackmun had in mind. Barefoot v. Estelle, 463 U.S. 880 (1983). Justice White, writing for the majority, had argued that psychiatrists' predictions that the defendant would be dangerous in future had correctly been admitted, despite the fact that an amicus brief filed by the American Psychiatric Association acknowledged that such predictions were wrong two times out of three. Reliability, he reasoned, was a matter to be determined through cross-examination and the presentation of contrary witnesses. *Id.*, 898–9. Justice Blackmun, however, argued that in this case the adversarial process had failed to expose unreliable testimony. *Id.*, 929–30

And in *U.S. v. Mitchell*, ruling that the lower court did not abuse its discretion in admitting latent-fingerprint identification testimony, the court first looks to Webster's dictionary for a definition of "falsifiable": "capable of being proved false, defeasible"; then glosses this in a way that starts out sounding entirely Popperian: "for instance, the hypothesis 'all crows are black' is falsifiable (because an albino crow could be found tomorrow)";[90] but then wanders into more comfortable legal territory: "a clairvoyant's statement that he receives messages from dead relatives is not [falsifiable] (because there is no way *for the departed to deny this*)."[91] Then, after conflating "falsify" and "deny," the court argues that:

> In this case, the relevant premises were posed as explicit questions to many of the government experts: (1) Are human friction ridge arrangements unique and permanent? and (2) Can a positive identification be made from fingerprints containing sufficient quantity and quality of detail? *The government's experts responded in the affirmative.*[92]

But then, apparently realizing that relying the FBI's experts' *ipse dixit* won't quite do, the court reverts to the same strictly-literal interpretation of the first *Daubert* factor we encountered in *Bonds*: "We must consider not whether we agree as a factual matter ... but rather whether these hypotheses are testable (or tested). We conclude that they are."[93]

By far the commonest pattern, however, is for courts using the first *Daubert* factor simply to take for granted that theories that have withstood testing without being falsified are thereby shown to be reliable. In *Bradley v. Brown* (1994), Judge Moody observes that "the court must weed out the speculative hypothesis from the tested theory";[94] evidently he is unaware that according to Popper *all* scientific theories are in effect "speculative hypotheses." Similarly, in *U.S. v. Starzecpyzel* (1995)—after holding a *Daubert* hearing on forensic-document identification testimony the conclusion of which was that such testimony isn't scientific, and therefore falls outside the scope of *Daubert*![95]—the court explained that "[t]he *Daubert* test is grounded in the

(Blackmun, J., dissenting) (arguing that "[t]here is every reason to believe that ... jurors will be still less capable [than judges] of 'separating the wheat from the chaff,' despite the Court's blithe assumption to the contrary").

90 United States v. Mitchell, 365 F.3d 215, 235 (3d Cir. 2004) (my italics).

91 *Id.*, 235.

92 *Ibid.*

93 *Id.*, 235–36.

94 Bradley v. Brown, 852 F. Supp. 690, 700 (N.D. Ind. 1994).

95 Confirming Justice Rehnquist's concern that the ruling in *Daubert* would lead to confusion over the standards of admissibility of non-scientific expert testimony. *Daubert* III (note 56 above), 600 (Rehnquist, C.J., dissenting in part).

scientific process and directs the judge to evaluate the quality of *the testing supporting the scientific conclusion*."[96] We see the same assumption in *Haggerty v. Upjohn Co.* (1996), where the court excluded plaintiff's expert Dr. Mash on the grounds that he offered nothing but "a hypothesis which he had yet to attempt *to verify or disprove* by subjecting it to ... testing;"[97] and in *In re TMI Litigation* (1996), where Judge Rambo excluded Dr. Gunckel's testimony on the grounds that, though he had "advanced a hypothesis capable of falsification," he had made "no effort ... *to verify either methodology or the conclusions reached*."[98] We see it again in *Moore v. Ashland Chemical* (1997), where the court relies on that fatal sentence from Green's article, that while "[t]heoretically ... hypotheses are not affirmatively proved, only falsified of course, if a hypothesis repeatedly withstands falsification, one may tend to accept it ... [as] true."[99]

And we see it again in *Downs v. Perstorp. Components, Inc.* (1999), where the court reasons that "the scientific method must be an objective one. This is the essence of what the Supreme Court referred to as *scientific validity, also known as 'falsifiability*.'"[100] Here the court equates scientific validity (which *Daubert* had identified with evidentiary reliability, and defined in a footnote as the testimony's being trustworthy, i.e., showing what it purports to show)[101] with falsifiability (which, however, is entirely consistent with the testimony's being plain false). The same year, in *Rogers v. Secretary of Health and Human Services*, the court reasons that "[f]or scientists, a new idea or explanation *is not valid unless there is a possibility that empirical testing can prove it false and until it has withstood thoughtful efforts at falsification*."[102]

[96] United States v. Starzecpyzel, 880 F. Supp. 1027, 1040 (S.D.N.Y. 1995) (my italics) (footnotes omitted).

[97] *Haggerty* (note 83 above), 1163–64 (my italics).

[98] *In re* TMI (Three Mile Island) Litig. Cases Consol. II, 911 F. Supp. 775, 805 (M.D. Pa. 1996) (my italics).

[99] Moore v. Ashland Chem., Inc., 126 F.3d 679, 685 (5th Cir. 1997).

[100] Downs v. Perstorp Components, Inc., 126 F. Supp. 2d 1090, 1127 (E.D. Tenn. 1999) (my italics).

[101] *Daubert* III (note 56 above), 590, n.9.

[102] Rogers v. Sec'y of Health & Human Servs., No. 94–0089 V, 1999 WL 809824, *12 (Fed. Cl. Sept. 17, 1999) (my italics), citing Bert Black, Francisco J. Ayala, and Carol Saffran-Brinks, "Science and the Law in the Wake of *Daubert*: A New Search for Scientific Knowledge," *Texas Law Review* 72, no. 4, 1994: 715–802. Black et al. write that "[t]esting either establishes or fails to establish falsehood; it never establishes *absolute* truth." *Id* at 762 (my itallics). Their word "absolute" hints that corroboration *might* establish provisional truth; and indeed, they continue, "[b]ecause the truth of scientific hypotheses can never be established conclusively, they can only be accepted contingently," and "scientists do not have the same degree of confidence in all hypotheses that have survived falsification."

In *Tobin v. Smithkline Beecham Pharms* (2001), the court denied the defendant's motion to exclude plaintiff's expert testimony, holding that it had been "*tested to an extent sufficient to demonstrate ... reliability....*"[103] The same year, in *Cloud v. Pfizer*, the court excluded plaintiff's expert Dr. Johnstone, arguing that, while the proposition that Zoloft causes suicide is testable, the fact that he "[could] not point to one scientific study that *supports his conclusion*" showed that his testimony is unreliable.[104] Then there's the gloss on the first *Daubert* factor given in *Caraker v. Sandoz Pharmaceuticals* (2001): "The hallmark of [*Daubert's*] reliability prong is the scientific method, *i.e.*, the generation of testable hypotheses that are then subjected to the real world crucible of experimentation, *falsification/validation*, and replication."[105] This passage, and especially that fused phrase "falsification/validation," encapsulates the crucial misunderstanding in a nutshell; and it is cited verbatim in several subsequent cases.[106]

In one of those cases, *Soldo v. Sandoz Pharmaceuticals* (2003), the court first runs through the epidemiological evidence presented: the "ERI study" (where the relative risk was "not statistically significant");[107] the "Witlin-Sibai study" (which showed a *decreased* risk of postpartum stroke in women taking the drug);[108] the "HCIA study" (where there were "huge amounts of uncertainty in the data");[109] the "Kittner study" (where there was "no evidence whatsoever" in support of the plaintiff's claim);[110] and the "Herings and Stricker study" (which "does not support" the plaintiff's hypothesis).[111] Then, to conform to the language of *Daubert*, the court puts all this in terms of the plaintiff's failure to falsify the null hypothesis—here, the hypothesis that any difference, in the sample studied, between the rate of postpartum

103 Estates of Tobin *ex rel.* Tobin v. Smithkline Beecham Pharm., Civil No. 00-CV-0025-Bea, 2001 WL 36102161, *9 (D. Wyo. May 8, 2001) (my italics).

104 Cloud v. Pfizer Inc., 198 F. Supp. 2d 1118, 1135 (D. Ariz. 2001) (my italics).

105 Caraker v. Sandoz Pharm. Corp., 188 F. Supp. 2d 1026, 1030 (S.D. Ill. 2001) (my italics).

106 See Krutsinger v. Pharmacia Corp., No. 03-CV-0111-MJR, 2004 WL 5508617, *4 (S.D. Ill. May 20, 2004) (using precisely these words from *Caraker*, but citing to *Daubert*); Bickel v. Pfizer, Inc., 431 F. Supp. 2d 918, 922 (N.D. Ind. 2006); Hardiman v. Davita Inc., No. 2:05-CV-262-JM, 2007 WL 1395568, *2 (N.D. Ind. May 10, 2007); Bauer v. Bayer A.G., 564 F. Supp. 2d 365, 380 (M.D. Pa. 2008); Perry v. Novartis Pharm.Corp., 564 F. Supp. 2d 452, 459 (E.D. Pa. 2008).

107 Soldo v. Sandoz Pharm. Corp., 244 F. Supp. 2d 434, 455 (W.D. Pa. 2003) ("*Soldo*—falsifiability").

108 *Id.*, 455.

109 *Id.*, 456.

110 *Id.*, 457.

111 *Ibid.*

stroke among women who take Parlodel and those who do not is the result of chance—and reasons that:

> To "falsify" a hypothesis in this context means to prove that the "null hypothesis"—that Parlodel® has no effect on the risk of postpartum stroke—is false, i.e, that Parlodel® in fact significantly increases the risk of postpartum stroke. The failure of plaintiff's experts to show any study proving that the null hypothesis has been falsified demonstrates that their causal hypothesis has not been *tested or verified* by the means of science.[112]

But as the phrase "tested or verified" suggests, what this really says is that the *plaintiff's experts have produced no statistically significant evidence supporting the claim that Parlodel increases the risk of postpartum stroke.*

And—my personal favorite—in *Fuesting v. Zimmer, Inc.* (2005), supposedly applying *Daubert*'s Popperian clause, the court writes that:

> Pugh did not *conduct any scientific tests or experiments to bolster his theory* relating polyethylene delamination to gamma irradiation in air, nor did he produce or *rely upon any studies to verify his conclusions.*[113]

~

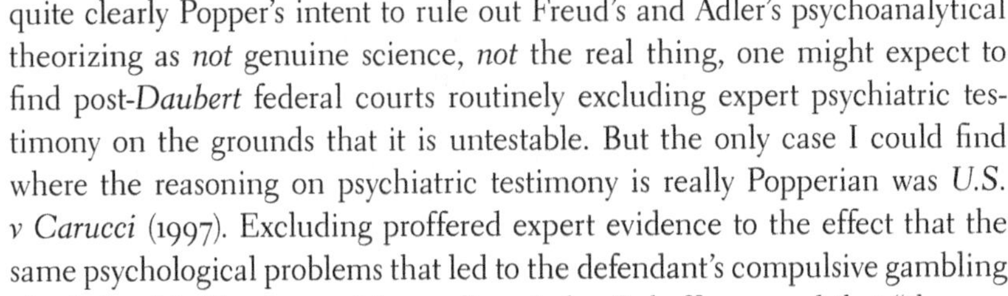

Probably I should also mention the dog that *didn't* bark. Given that it was quite clearly Popper's intent to rule out Freud's and Adler's psychoanalytical theorizing as *not* genuine science, *not* the real thing, one might expect to find post-*Daubert* federal courts routinely excluding expert psychiatric testimony on the grounds that it is untestable. But the only case I could find where the reasoning on psychiatric testimony is really Popperian was *U.S. v Carucci* (1997). Excluding proffered expert evidence to the effect that the same psychological problems that led to the defendant's compulsive gambling also led to his illegal securities trading, Judge Rakoff reasoned that "the psychological construct proffered by the defense is sufficiently flexible to accommodate even … calculated misconduct." And in a footnote, citing Popper's *Conjectures and Refutations*, he continued, "[p]ut differently, the construct

[112] *Ibid* (my italics).

[113] Fuesting v. Zimmer, Inc., 421 F.3d 528, 536 (7th Cir. 2005) (my italics), *vacated in part on reh'g by* 448 F.3d 936 (7th Cir. 2006) (vacating part of its earlier ruling and ordering a new trial instead of a directed verdict). See also Robinson v. Garlock Equip. Co., No. 05-CV-6553-CJS, 2009 WL 104197, *2, *4 (W.D.N.Y. Jan. 14, 2009) (denying motion to exclude expert testimony regarding an allegedly defective spigot on the grounds that "Daubert does not require that the hypothesis be tested by its proponent, only that it can be tested," and that the fact that Dr. Quisnel "*could have bolstered his conclusions through conducting experiments*" goes to weight rather than admissibility) (my italics). Note that what *Daubert* III requires is not just that evidence *can be* tested, but also that it *has been* tested.

suffers from being *unfalsifiable, and therefore, unverifiable*."[114] The cited passage is exactly on point; Judge Rakoff, it appears, had actually read Popper, or at least the page of Popper that Justice Blackmun cites.

As in *U.S. v. Hines*, in *Kokoraleis v. Illinois Dept. of Corrections* (1997) we encounter a little judicial foray into philosophy of science. Ruling that there was no real basis for psychiatric evidence that the appellant had borderline personality disorder, Judge Zagel notes that Prof. Allen disapproves of *Daubert* in part because he "prefers" Kuhn's philosophy of science to Popper's; and comments that "[i]f I had to choose between Popper and Kuhn, I would pick Popper despite his flaws and so would nearly all scientists." But, he admits, the point may not be of much practical consequence, since what is seen in the courtroom is usually normal, not revolutionary, science.[115]

As in *U.S. v. Havvard*, in Judge Garza's concurring opinion in *Flores v. Johnson* (2000) we find "testing" interpreted as referring to adversarial, rather than empirical, trials. Judge Garza argues that psychiatric predictions of future dangerousness flunk all the *Daubert* factors; and, regarding the first factor, reasons that the accuracy of such predictions has never really been tested—because such predictions "*are not susceptible to cross-examination and rebuttal*."[116]

But most cases involving psychiatric testimony follow the now-familiar pattern: courts take for granted that a theory's successfully withstanding testing indicates that it is reliable. For example, in *Isely v. Capuchin Province* (1995) the court explains that:

> [T]he witness should testify as to whether [his] theory can be, or has been, tested or corroborated and, if so, by whom and under what circumstances; *whether the theory has been proven out or not proven out* under clinical tests or some other accepted procedure *for bearing it out*.... [T]he witness must be able to show, through the use of reliable, viable extrinsic evidence, whether repressed memory or post-traumatic stress disorder is ... accepted in the field of psychology....[117]

[114] United States v. Carucci, 33 F. Supp. 2d 302, 303 & n.3 (S.D.N.Y. 1999) (my italics), citing Popper, *Conjectures and Refutations* (note 23 above), 37 (arguing that, because nothing could possibly falsify Freud's or Adler's theories, supposed "confirming" instances are really nothing of the kind). This observation is from the very bottom of the page; the sentence Justice Blackmun had quoted in *Daubert* is near the top.

[115] United States *ex rel.* Kokoraleis v. Dir. of Ill. Dep't. of Corr., 963 F. Supp. 1473, 1489 n.9 (N.D. Ill. 1997). The same note tells us that Judge Zagel took a logic class with Dudley Shapere.

[116] Flores v. Johnson, 210 F.3d 456, 465 (5th Cir. 2000) (Garza, J., concurring) (my italics).

[117] Isely v. Capuchin Province, 877 F. Supp. 1055, 1064 (E.D. Mich. 1995) (my italics) (admitting expert testimony on post-traumatic stress syndrome, with limitations).

The next year, *Isely* is cited in *Shahzade v. Gregory*, where the court also finds recovered memory testimony admissible: "[though] repressed memory, as is true with ordinary memories, 'cannot be tested empirically,' and may not always be accurate, however, the *theory* itself *has been established to be valid*...."[118]

In *U.S. v. Hall* (1997), the court finds that "testimony which is simply not amenable to the scientific method should not be subject to the strictures of *Daubert*" but treated as "specialized knowledge"; but qualifies this by noting that if testimony "posits an explanatory theory to draw a conclusion or determine causation ... this would normally require experimental *verification*...."[119] And in *Discepolo v. Gorgone* (2005), denying a *Daubert* motion to exclude plaintiff's expert Dr. Pratt from testifying that the plaintiff suffered from PTSD (post-traumatic stress disorder), on the grounds that the psychiatric evaluation of alleged victims of child sexual abuse is "an inexact science at best,"[120] the court determined that Dr. Pratt's diagnosis had been found to be "*substantially accurate*."[121]

The next year, in *U.S. v. Thomas* (2006), both sides presented evidence as to the level of risk that would be posed if the defendant were released from pre-trial detention. The court found SSA (Supervisory Special Agent) Clemente's testimony for the prosecution inadmissible, on the grounds that he was "unable to demonstrate that his risk assessment methodology had been (or could be) tested";[122] and argued that, though it is difficult to collect empirical data in this context, "this difficulty cannot, by itself, render a risk assessment methodology reliable or exempt it from any sort of *testing or validation*."[123] However, Dr. Blumberg's testimony for the defendant was found admissible, on the grounds that "there is *substantial support* from a variety of sources, based in part on empirical data" establishing the reliability of his approach.[124]

~

"Enough already!" you may be thinking. "So federal judges aren't right on top of all the vagaries of twentieth-century philosophy of science. It would be more remarkable, surely, if they *were* fully conversant with the work of Popper, Hempel, Kuhn, Lakatos, Feyerabend, et al." Indeed. What is much more

118 Shahzade v. Gregory, 923 F. Supp. 286, 290 (D. Mass. 1996) (second italics mine) (ruling testimony on PTSD admissible, and citing *Isely* (note 117 above), 1065).

119 United States v. Hall, 974 F. Supp. 1198, 1200, 1201 (C.D. Ill. 1997) (my italics).

120 Discepolo v. Gorgone, 399 F. Supp. 2d 123, 126 (D. Conn. 2005).

121 *Id.*, 127.

122 United States v. Thomas, No. CRIM CCB-03–0150, 2006 WL 140558, *19 (D. Md. Jan. 13, 2006).

123 *Ibid.* (my italics).

124 *Id.*, *16 (my italics).

interesting, as I will argue in conclusion, is that the conception of science we find implicit in many of these rulings, albeit in an inarticulate and half-baked form, is a much more plausible understanding of the scientific enterprise than Popper's official Logical Negativist account.

5 THE STING IN THE TALE

To be sure, it *is* a mistake to conflate "scientific" and "reliable," as Justice Blackmun apparently did; and it is at least arguable that, in requiring courts to assess the reliability of expert testimony, *Daubert* fudged the legal line between questions of the admissibility of evidence (a matter for courts to determine) and questions of its weight (a matter for juries to decide). Moreover, other critics have suggested numerous flaws in, and unintended consequences of, the *Daubert* ruling.[125] Nevertheless, all these issues aside, in any case involving scientific testimony the question of reliability is bound to arise, and must be determined *somehow*. If Popper's account were true, however, the legal system's interest in the question of the reliability of scientific testimony would be completely misconceived.[126]

I don't believe that this concern *is* misconceived; and I don't believe you do, either.[127] I think again of Kerry Kotler, freed from prison in 1993 after DNA analysis revealed that he was innocent of the rape for which he had served eleven years of a twenty-five to fifty-year sentence; and three years later convicted of another rape—of which DNA evidence showed he was guilty.[128] If you believe, as I do, that there is such a thing as objectively more and less reliable evidence, it will seem to you that in this instance justice was (probably)[129]

[125] See, e.g., Lisa Heinzerling, "Doubting *Daubert*," *Journal of Law & Policy* 14 (2006): 65–83, 65 (arguing that "*Daubert* … is dubious, for many reasons").

[126] Indeed, if I am right that Popper's account is really a kind of closet skepticism, it would imply that the legal system's interest in the reliability of testimony generally would be misconceived. Like Richard Rorty's repudiation of epistemology, Popper's covertly skeptical epistemology ideas would make a mockery of the legal system (as I argued, with respect to Rorty, in "Epistemology and the Law of Evidence: Problems and Projects," pp. 1–26 in this volume, 3–4).

[127] Nor do I believe that even Popperians *really* believe we never have rational grounds for our expectations. See Mellor, "The Popper Phenomenon" (note 75 above), 196 (asking, "Why will Popperians not admit to such beliefs, which they reveal every time they turn on the light or use the telephone?" and commenting: "[a]s Carnap would say, none are so blind as those who pretend they cannot see … ").

[128] See John T. McQuiston, "Prosecutor Says DNA Evidence May Free Man," *New York Times*, December 1, 1992, B7; John T. McQuiston, "Man Freed After a DNA Test Is Sentenced in a Second Rape," *New York Times*, October 24, 1997, B4.

[129] "Probably" because, without knowing a lot more than I do, I can't say with full confidence that the DNA analyses in question were well-conducted, the chain of evidence impeccable,

well-served by science; but if you believe, as Popper professes to, that *there is no such thing as good reasons for believing anything*, you will be obliged to conclude that in this—and in *every* legal case turning on scientific evidence—the hope that science could contribute to justice is vain. This doesn't show that Popper is wrong; but it does show how radical the consequences of Popper's Logical Negativist epistemology would be for our—or any[130]—legal system.

So perhaps it is no wonder that federal courts' misinterpretation of Popper implicitly relies on inarticulate assumptions that are more plausible than Popper's official story. As we saw, the predominant pattern of federal rulings calling on the first *Daubert* factor is that courts realize that they need to know, not only whether the basis of proffered expert testimony is empirically testable, but more importantly whether it has actually been tested, and if it has, how well it has performed on those tests; and if a theory has succeeded when tested, they take this to be evidence, albeit less than absolutely conclusive evidence, that it is reliable—as just about everybody, except for Popper and his most loyal followers,[131] would do. I agree.

It should be clear by now, however, that it is impossible just to take Popper's official story and add to it that the fact that a claim that has been tested but

etc. It appears that both cases were messy, to say the least. See Peter J. Boyer, "Annals of Justice: DNA on Trial," *New Yorker*, January 17, 2000, 42–53.

130 In this context it is worth noting that *Daubert* (or something much like it) has been adopted by a majority of states (Alaska, Arkansas, Colorado, Connecticut, Delaware, Georgia, Hawaii, Idaho, Iowa, Kentucky, Louisiana, Maine, Massachusetts, Michigan, Mississippi, Montana, Nebraska, New Hampshire, New Mexico, Ohio, Oklahoma, Oregon, Rhode Island, South Dakota, Tennessee, Texas, Utah, Vermont, Virginia, West Virginia, and Wyoming) and by the Military Courts. Terence Campbell and Demosthenes Lorandos, *Cross Examining Experts in the Behavioral Sciences* ([Eagan, MN?: West/Thomson Reuters, September 2012)) § 1:16, n.6. The list now includes Florida (see note 2 above). According to a report published in 1999, only 3% of judges in *Daubert* states understood the concept of falsification; some, reportedly, explained it as "*If there is white-out on the page, then the document has been falsified.*" State Justice Institute, *A Judge's Deskbook on the Basic Philosophies and Methods of Science: Model Curriculum* (March 1999), 31. Unfortunately, the authors of the *Deskbook* don't fully understand Popper either; for they write that according to Popper "predictions are … compared with observations *to see whether the theory is supported.*" *Id.*, 28 (my italics). *Daubert* has also influenced other, non-US jurisdictions. For details, see "Epistemology and the Law of Evidence" (note 126 above), 24–25 and notes 109–113.

131 The only other people known to me who doubt this (or profess to) are, ironically enough, the wildest of the irrationalists against whom Popper set himself. See Stove, *Popper and After* (note 50 above) (presenting Popper as the father of late twentieth-century scientific irrationalism); Koertge, "Popper and the Science Wars" (note 7 above) (suggesting that constructivist postmodernists might find solace in Popper's philosophy of science); Alan Olding, "Popper for Afters," *Quadrant* 143, no. 12 (December 1999): 19–22, 21 (arguing that a historicist brand of relativism was "already a bit more than latent in Popper"). In the now-famous words of Louis-Sébastien Mercier (the title of chapter 48, vol. 4, of his *Tableau de Paris* (revised ed., Amsterdam, the Netherlands, 1782–88), "les extrèmes se touchent."

not falsified shows the claim to be to some degree reliable. This would transform Logical Negativism into something utterly different from what Popper actually proposed.[132] So I should at least sketch what a reconstruction of the philosophy of science implicit in courts' rulings might look like. This reconstructed account will, of course, be thoroughly *un*like hard-line Popperism (though it will accommodate some elements from the shadow Popper): in particular, it will be, not skeptical, but fallibilist; it will focus less on demarcation than on continuities between scientific and other kinds of empirical inquiry; and it will be, not purely logical, but worldly—i.e., not confined exclusively to statements and their logical relations, but also giving a role to the world and to scientists' interactions with the world. In short, it will be much like the Critical Common-sensist account I developed in *Defending Science—Within Reason*.[133]

The first thing to do is to *get over the Popperian preoccupation with demarcation*:

- Although (no doubt because of the remarkable successes of the natural sciences) the words "science," "scientific," and their cognates are often used as generic terms of epistemic praise, this honorific usage is misleading. There is bad scientific work as well as good. Moreover, rather than dismissing bad scientific work with the generic accusation "pseudo-science," it is always better to say what, specifically, is wrong with the work.
- That a purported explanation rules out some possible upshots is, not a sign that it is scientific, but a sign that it actually is explanatory.
- Willingness to take negative evidence seriously is a mark, not of the scientist, but of the honest inquirer generally, be he a scientist, a historian, a legal or a literary scholar, or whatever.
- The word "science" (or, better, the phrase "the sciences") is best construed as referring to a loose federation of kinds of inquiry into natural and social phenomena; and as distinguished from such other, legitimate kinds of inquiry as legal or literary scholarship, history, metaphysics, mathematics, etc., by their subject-matter.

[132] Nor would it be possible to rely instead on Hempel's inductivist philosophy of science. For—though it *is* less grossly unsuitable for legal purposes than Popper's account—even if Hempel's "logic of confirmation" were viable (which he himself came to doubt late in life) it world be hopelessly inadequate to cope with the enormously complex congeries of scientific evidence now routinely proffered in toxic-tort and other cases. The argument is made in more detail in "Trial and Error" (note 10 above), 109–10.

[133] Susan Haack, *Defending Science—Within Reason: Between Scientism and Cynicism* (Amherst, NY: Prometheus Books, 2003).

The next step is to *re-think the whole idea of "Scientific Method,"* starting by distinguishing (i) the procedures followed by all serious empirical inquirers, and (ii) the specialized instruments, techniques, etc., gradually developed by the various sciences.

- Any serious empirical inquirer will proceed by making an educated guess as to the explanation of a puzzling phenomenon or event, figuring out the consequences of the conjecture's being true, checking how well those consequences stand up to the evidence he has and any further evidence he can obtain, and then using his judgment whether to keep the conjecture, modify it, drop it and start again, or wait for more evidence.
- Over time, the various sciences have gradually developed instruments of observation, techniques of extraction, purification, titration, etc., mathematical tools like the calculus, statistical techniques, computer programs, incentives to honesty and evidence-sharing, etc., etc., to amplify and refine the ways of all serious empirical inquiry.

Obviously, the procedures of all serious empirical inquiry are not used *only* by scientists, and the gradually evolving specialized scientific tools, techniques, etc., often local to a specific field of science, are not used by *all* scientists. So neither can be identified with "the Scientific Method"; and yet, together, they help explain how the sciences have been as successful as they have.

Next, we must *set aside Popper's conventionalism about the empirical basis of science.* What we need is to distinguish observations from statements reporting what is observed, replace a sharp distinction of observational vs. theoretical statements by a continuum of more and less observational, and recognize that observation can give a scientist grounds, albeit fallible grounds, for believing that (say) the needle on the dial points to 7, or there is a black swan on the pond, and so can contribute to the solidity of the evidence for a scientific theory, i.e., to how warranted the theory is.

- It is in part scientists' observations that justify them in accepting claims like "Here is a glass of water"; even though, because even so simple a statement as this carries some theoretical baggage, only in part.
- Because all empirical inquiry ultimately depends on people's sensory interactions with the world, the degree to which a claim is warranted by the evidence possessed by a person at a time is primary. The degree to which a claim is warranted by the evidence shared by a group of people at a time, and the degree to which a claim is warranted by the

evidence available at a time, must be understood as (legitimate but) derivative.[134]

So we will have to *get a grip on the complexities of evidence and the determinants of evidential quality.*[135]

- The evidence with respect to any serious scientific claim ramifies in all directions, rather as the entries in a crossword puzzle do.
- How well evidence warrants a claim depends on how well it supports it, how secure it is, independent of the claim itself, and how much of the relevant evidence it includes.

Because the determinants of evidential quality are multi-dimensional, they will not necessarily yield a linear ordering; moreover, if there is insufficient evidence either way, neither *p* nor not-*p* may be warranted to any degree. So the next step is to *distinguish epistemic likelihoods from probabilities.*[136]

- The better the evidence is with respect to a theory, the likelier that it is true. But these are *epistemic* likelihoods, and cannot be construed in terms of the mathematical calculus of probabilities.

As this reveals, it is possible to repudiate probabilism without, as Popper supposes, *also* rejecting the idea of supportive evidence or well-warranted theory.

Next, we need *an understanding of what makes evidence supportive with respect to a claim.*

- How well evidence supports a claim depends on how tightly evidence and claim fit together to form an explanatory account.

Explanation is vocabulary-dependent, since a genuinely explanatory account requires general terms identifying real kinds of thing; so supportiveness is not a purely formal, logical relation, but depends in part on the fit of scientific vocabulary to the world.

So the final step is to *stop thinking of scientific rationality in purely logical terms,* and acknowledge that successful scientific inquiry, like successful

[134] This contrasts, once again, with Popper's approach, which takes the impersonal conception of warrant as primitive, and doesn't so much as acknowledge the legitimacy of the personal conception.

[135] All this is spelled out in detail in "Epistemology and the Law of Evidence" (note 126 above).

[136] All this is spelled out in detail in "Legal Probabilism: An Epistemological Dissent," pp. 47–77 in this volume, 56–64.

empirical inquiry of any kind, is a matter in part of our interactions with the world, and so is possible only because we, and the world, are a certain way.

- Our senses give us information about particular things and events in the world, and these things and events are of kinds, kinds the behavior of members of which falls into patterns—the patterns of natural laws.
- And so it is possible, by making guesses as to the possible explanation of puzzling phenomena or events, devising ways to check them, and seeing how well they stand up to evidence—even though there will be many more false starts than successful guesses, and even though every step forward will be fallible and imperfect—to make contributions to the still only very partially-completed cathedral of scientific knowledge.[137]

~

Unlike Popper's, this account acknowledges the legitimacy of questions about the reliability of expert testimony. Moreover, it enables us to distinguish "reliable" from "scientific," and to acknowledge that not all reliable expert testimony is scientific, nor all scientific testimony reliable; and it suggests (precisely in line with the Supreme Court's ruling in *Kumho Tire*)[138] that what matters legally should be whether expert testimony is reliable, whether or not it is scientific.

It will not, of course, provide a simple formula that judges could apply to assess the worth of proffered scientific testimony; there can be no such formula, no easy substitute for getting into the nitty-gritty of the specific scientific work concerned. Rather, my account reveals that any simple verbal formula supposedly encapsulating the Scientific Method is likely to be a distraction from the real complexities of evidence and from the multiple, interconnected questions relevant in assessing reliability. It tells us that the fact that a theory or technique has not been tested is a warning sign, suggesting that investigation is as yet incomplete, or that it has not been as thorough or as honest as it should; but also that the fact that a theory or technique has performed successfully under rigorous testing is an indication of its reliability. And it tells us (also

[137] Compare this, from the same paragraph in which Peirce anticipates Popper's "swamp" analogy: "[t]he translations of the cuneiform inscriptions … began as mere guesses, in which their authors could have no real confidence. Yet by piling new conjecture upon former conjecture apparently verified, this science has gone on to produce under our very eyes a result so bound together by the agreement of the readings with one another, with other history, and with the known facts of linguistics, that we are unwilling any longer to apply the word theory to it." Peirce, *Collected Papers* (note 41 above), 5.589 (1898).

[138] Kumho Tire Co. v. Carmichael, 526 U.S. 137, 147 (1999) (arguing that it is the word "knowledge" in FRE 702, and not the word "scientific," that establishes the standard of evidentiary reliability).

in line with *Kumho Tire*) that the kinds of test that are appropriate will vary depending on the nature of the evidence in question,[139] and may—for example in the case of rival tests of statistical significance, or of the conclusions to be drawn from a DNA analysis—itself depend on other scientific knowledge. This is both philosophically more plausible, and legally more helpful, than the Popperian theory on which post-*Daubert* courts ostensibly rely.

[139] *Id.*, 150 (arguing that "we can neither rule in nor rule out, for all cases and for all times, the applicability of the factors mentioned in *Daubert*. . . . Too much depends upon the particular circumstances of the particular case at issue").

—7—

Peer Review and Publication: Lessons for Lawyers

> [A] pertinent consideration [in determining whether a theory or technique is scientific knowledge that will assist the trier of fact] is whether the theory or technique has been subjected to peer review and publication.
>
> —*Daubert v. Merrell Dow Pharmaceuticals, Inc.* (1993)[1]

The phrase "peer review" connotes the evaluation ("review") of scientific or other scholarly work by others presumed to have expertise in the relevant field ("peers"). Specifically, and most to the present purpose, it refers to the evaluation of submitted manuscripts to determine what work is published in professional journals and what books are published by academic presses (in which context it is also called "refereeing," "editorial peer review," or "pre-publication peer review").[2] Occasionally, however, the phrase is used in a much broader sense, to cover the whole long-run history of the scrutiny of a scientist's work within the scientific community, and of others' efforts to build on it,[3] a long-run process of which peer review in the narrower sense is only a small part.

These two conceptions of peer review, the narrow and the broad, both came into play in the arguments over the admissibility of the plaintiffs' expert testimony in *Daubert*.[4] In 1989, granting Merrell Dow's motion for summary

1 Daubert v. Merrell Dow Pharm., Inc., 509 U.S. 579, 593 (1993) ("*Daubert* III").

2 The phrase also sometimes refers to the evaluation of clinical performance by senior practitioners in a field (in which context it is called "clinical peer review"); to the evaluation of grant proposals to decide what projects are funded (in which context it is called "grant peer review" or "merit review"); and to the evaluation of abstracts, or sometimes submitted papers, to determine what is presented at conferences.

3 "In the broadest sense of the term, *peer review* can be said to have existed ever since people began to identify and communicate what they thought was new knowledge." David A. Kronick, "Peer Review in 18th-Century Scientific Journalism," *Journal of the American Medical Association* 263 (1990): 1321–22, 1321.

4 Effie J. Chan, Note, "The 'Brave New World' of *Daubert*: True Peer Review, Editorial Peer Review, and Scientific Validity," *NYU Law Review* 70 (1995): 100–134, 113.

judgment on the grounds that the Dauberts' proffered causation evidence was inadmissible, the district court had stressed that "none of the *published* studies show a statistically significant association between the use of Bendectin and birth defects";[5] and affirming this decision in 1991, observing that "no published epidemiological study had demonstrated a statistically significant association between Bendectin and birth defects," and that "the normal peer[-]review process … is one of the hallmarks of reliable scientific investigation," Judge Kozinski also took peer-reviewed publication to be a key factor.[6]

But in 1993, when the case came to the Supreme Court, an amicus brief from Chubin et al. criticized the lower courts' reliance on peer-reviewed publication, arguing that "the peer review system is designed to provide a common and convenient starting point for scientific debate, not the final summation of existing scientific knowledge," and that "contrary to the 'generally accepted' myth, publication of an article in a peer review journal is no assurance that the research, data, methodologies, [or] analyses … are true, accurate, … reliable, or certain or that they represent 'good science.'"[7] And while Justice Blackmun's ruling included "peer review and publication" as one factor to which courts might look to determine whether expert scientific testimony is "reliable" in the sense required to make it admissible, it did so in a very hedged and cautious way—acknowledging that pre-publication peer review doesn't guarantee "evidentiary reliability," and may hold back well-grounded but innovative work; and that a much better indicator is survival of the long-run scrutiny of the scientific community, i.e., peer review in the broad sense.

Finally, in 1995, ruling on the case on remand from the Supreme Court, and now acknowledging, as Justice Blackmun had, that peer-reviewed publication is no guarantee that testimony is trustworthy, Judge Kozinski argued that nevertheless, the fact "[t]hat the research is accepted for publication in a reputable scientific journal … is a significant indication that … it meets at least the minimal criteria of good science"; and noted that "[n]one of the plaintiffs' experts has published his work on Bendectin in a scientific journal." The lower court's summary judgment was affirmed yet again.[8]

5 Daubert v. Merrell Dow Pharm., Inc., 727 F. Supp. 570, 575 (S.D. Cal. 1989) ("*Daubert* I").

6 Daubert v. Merrell Dow Pharm., Inc., 951 F.2d 1128, 1129, 1131 n.3 (9th Cir. 1991) ("*Daubert* II").

7 Brief of Amici Curiae Daryl E. Chubin et al. in Support of Petitioners, *Daubert* III (note 1 above) (No. 92–102), 1992 WL 12006443, *8, *13 ("Brief of Daryl Chubin et al.") (italics and footnote omitted).

8 Daubert v. Merrell Dow Pharm., Inc., 43 F.3d 1311, 1318 (9th Cir. 1995) ("*Daubert* IV"). For a closer analysis of Judge Kozinski's ruling in this case, see "What's Wrong with Litigation-Driven Science?" pp. 180–207 in this volume, 185–88 and 202–206.

The aim here is to understand how the peer-review process works, how good an indicator it is that scientific testimony is reliable in the legally-relevant sense, and how courts might best use this *Daubert* factor. So for most of what follows, the focus will be on peer review in the narrow sense—pre-publication peer review. The starting point will be a sketch of the origins of this practice, the ragged process by which it gradually became standard at scientific and medical journals, and the many roles it now plays (§1); the next step will be to articulate the rationale for pre-publication peer review, and the inherent limitations of the system as a quality-control mechanism (§2); and the next an exploration of the changes in science, in scientific publication, and in the academy that have put the peer-review system under severe strain, and of some recent instances in which flawed or even fraudulent work has passed peer review (§3).

But at the next step, an examination of Justice Blackmun's observations about "peer review and publication" in *Daubert*, the broad sense of "peer review" will play a part alongside the narrow. The argument here will be, in brief, that *neither* Justice Blackmun's observation that peer-reviewed publication is not necessary and not sufficient for evidentiary reliability, and that surviving the long-term process of review by the scientific community is a much better indicator of scientific validity, *nor* his advice to courts—that peer-reviewed publication is a relevant, but not a dispositive, consideration in determining admissibility—is of much practical help (§4).

Subsequently, whether they have excluded scientific testimony in part because it wasn't based on peer-reviewed publication, or admitted it even though it wasn't so based, courts seem by and large not to have asked the questions that might throw light on what peer-reviewed publication, or its absence, means in a particular instance. But a Pennsylvania court's uncommonly commonsense scrutiny of the peer-reviewed Bendectin literature reveals how weak a reed "peer review and publication" can be—and leaves one wondering rather uncomfortably about the way this "*Daubert* factor" got on the legal radar screen in the first place (§5).

1 PRE-PUBLICATION PEER REVIEW: ITS HISTORICAL ROOTS, ITS PRESENT ROLES

Scientists have always been concerned that their work be acknowledged as theirs, and worried about what Robert Boyle charmingly described as "philosophicall robbery," a.k.a. plagiarism. Even before the *Philosophical Transactions* of the Royal Society of London were inaugurated in 1655, the Society would give its official stamp to a scientist's priority in discovery by recording the date on which it received a letter announcing an experiment or observation. As Henry Oldenburg, the first editor of the *Transactions*, told Boyle, the Society would be "very carefull of registring as well the person and the time of any new matter, imparted to ym, as the matter itselfe; whereby the honor of ye invention will be inviolably preserved to all posterity."[9] Gradually the *Transactions* began to indicate which work had and which had not been evaluated before publication by representatives of the Society; and by 1702 the *Journal de Scavans*, founded just before the *Transactions*, had assigned responsibility for screening submissions in a given area to various members of the editorial board.[10]

In the course of the eighteenth century several other important medical and scientific publications adopted what we would now call "peer review": in 1731, the Preface to the first volume of the *Medical Essays and Observations* published by the Royal Society of Edinburgh announced that "[m]emoirs sent by correspondence are distributed according to the subject matter to those members who are most versed in these matters";[11] in 1752, the Royal Society set up a committee authorized to call on "any other members of the Society who are knowing and well skilled in that particular branch of Science that shall happen to be the subject matter" of an article submitted to the *Transactions*;[12] in 1782, the regulations of the Académie Royale de Médicine stated that "[n]othing will be printed in the *Histoire*, or in the *Receuil des memoires* of the Society ... which assemblies especially called for this purpose have not decided by a majority vote to publish";[13] and in 1785 the Literary and Philosophical Society of Manchester set up a reviewing committee to select papers "with as much impartiality, and as strict attention to their comparative merits" as possible.[14]

According to historian John Burnham, the spread and evolution of the practice of pre-publication peer review through the nineteenth century

9 Harriet Zuckerman and Robert K. Merton, "Patterns of Evaluation in Science: Institutionalism, Structure, and Functions of the Referee System," *Minerva* 9 (1971): 66–100, 70 (citing *The Correspondence of Henry Oldenburg*, translated and edited by A. Rupert Hall and Marie Boas Hall [Madison, WI: University of Wisconsin Press, 1966] vol. 1, 319).

10 Stephen Lock, *A Difficult Balance: Editorial Peer Review in Medicine* (London: Nuffield Provincial Hospitals Trust, 1985), 2.

11 Kronick, "Peer Review in 18th-Century Journalism" (note 3 above), 1321 (citing *Essais et observations de médecine de la Société d'Edinbourg* [1740] vol. 1, preface).

12 *Id.*, 1321 (citing John M. Ziman, "Information, Communication, Knowledge," *Nature* 224 [1969]: 318–24, 318).

13 *Id.*, 1321–22 (citing *Histoire de l'Académie Royale de Medécine* 13 [1782]: 19–21).

14 *Id.*, 1322 (citing *Memoirs of the Literary and Philosophical Society of Manchester* 1 (1785): preface.

and the early decades of the twentieth was neither systematic nor orderly.[15] Some of the earliest medical journals of the 19th century were, as Burnham puts it, "personal vehicle[s]" for editors like Thomas Wakely, founder of *The Lancet*, or Henry Maunsell, a founder of the *Dublin Medical Press*, who subsequently also became owner of the *Dublin Evening Mail*. Somewhat closer to present-day scientific and medical journals were the official publications of European (especially, of German) research institutes; these more specialized fora relied on the expert judgment of the editor or the colleagues who made up his editorial staff, but were essentially outlets for the work of members of the institute.[16]

But in the early days of both scientific and medical publishing an editor's problem was more likely to be finding enough material to fill his pages than deciding which of too many articles to publish. In 1876 a commentator observed that "the demand for brief papers and reports of single cases, exceeds the supply. The weekly and monthly periodicals are omnivorous and insatiable in their requests for contributions";[17] and as late as 1921 the editor of the *Journal of Neurology and Psychopathology* was complaining to a correspondent about the difficulty of getting enough material to fill his journal.[18] It was only after World War II that peer review as we now know it became common practice in medical and scientific journals;[19] for by this time a significant shift in the number of papers offered meant that editors were looking, not for material to fill their pages, but for a way to select which of the too-many papers submitted they would publish.[20]

By now, pre-publication peer review is routine at medical and scientific journals;[21] and standard procedure, too, in scholarly publication in other

15 John C. Burnham, "The Evolution of Editorial Peer Review," *Journal of the American Medical Association* 263 (1990): 1323–29, 1327–28.

16 *Id.*, 1324, 1326.

17 *Id.*, 1324–25 (citing John Shaw Billings, "Literature and Institutions," *American Journal of Medical Science* 72 [1876]: 439–480, 460).

18 *Id.*, 1325 (citing a letter from C. Stanford Read to Smith Ely Jelliffe (February 3, 1921), in *Papers of Smith Ely Jelliffe*, 1866–1940 [on file with Library of Congress, Washington, D.C., Box 16]).

19 Marjorie Sun, "Peer Review Comes under Peer Review," *Science* 224 (1989): 910–12, 910. James McKeen Cattell, who edited *Science* from 1894 until his death in 1945, reportedly relied heavily on his son (who had a degree in physiology from Harvard) to help screen submissions; but when the American Association for the Advancement of Science took over the journal in 1945, a system of peer reviewing was instituted.

20 Burnham, "The Evolution of Editorial Peer Review" (note 15 above), 1236–37.

21 Lock, *A Difficult Balance* (note 10 above), 3. By 1985 at least three-quarters of major scientific journals in the West relied on peer review. On the following page, Lock reports that in 1980 the 100 Soviet scientific journals also used peer review. *Id.*, 4 (citing Arthur Relman, "Moscow in January," *New England Journal of Medicine* 302 [1980]: 523).

areas, including the humanities (though not the law reviews).[22] It has, in consequence, also become a very important factor in the economics of medical, scientific, and other academic publishing; for the prestige of the big scientific and medical publishing houses and of the academic presses, and hence the high prices they can command for their publications,[23] derive in part from these publications' being perceived as somehow "certified" by peer review.

Moreover, peer review is now deeply entrenched in the tenure and promotion systems of universities, which may require peer-reviewed publications, or look less favorably on publications which are not peer-reviewed; and may count a faculty member's acting as referee for scholarly journals or presses as part of his or her "service." In fact, universities often use pre-publication peer review as a proxy—I'm tempted to say, as a lazy substitute—for substantive assessment of the quality of a person's work. As an unusually candid editorial in *Nature* complained, "universities ... have slipped into the sloppy habit of substituting for their own judgement of their own achievements the judgement of external assessors as delivered by the appropriate sub-net of the peer-review system."[24]

As Percy Bridgman once observed, while "[a] dog is content to turn around three times before lying down," a human being would have to think up some reason why this is the *best* way to lie down; "[t]here is not a single human institution which has not originated in hit or miss fashion, but, nevertheless, every one of these institutions is justified by some rationalizing argument as the best possible."[25] So it is no surprise that, as pre-publication peer review has spread and become entrenched in academic publishing and in the academy itself, some are tempted to exaggerate its virtues—to think of the system, not just as a rough-and-ready preliminary filter, but as a strong indication of

22 At law reviews it is usually student editors, not faculty, who decide what papers are accepted. See Richard A. Posner, "Against the Law Reviews," *Legal Affairs* (November/December 2004): 57–58, 57 (pointing out that student editors ultimately decide which articles to publish, and arguing that law-review publication is, for this reason, less rigorously controlled than publication in other academic fields). But see also Brief of Daryl Chubin et al. (note 7 above), *8 n.8 (pointing out that law reviews are in some respects *more* rigorous, since student editors, who check every citation and footnote, spend far more time on papers than peer reviewers for scientific journals can do).

23 In October 2003 scientists at the University of California, San Francisco, staged a protest over Elsevier's $91,000 bill for 6 biology journals; eventually the university negotiated "a 25% price reduction to $7.7 million a year for 1,200 Elsevier periodicals." Bernard Wysocki, Jr., "Scholarly Journals' Premier Status Is Diluted by Web," *Wall Street Journal*, May 23, 2005, A1, A8.

24 Editorial, "Is Science Really a Pack of Lies?" *Nature* 303 (1983): 361.

25 Percy Bridgman, "The Struggle for Intellectual Integrity" (1933), in Bridgman, *Reflections of a Physicist* (New York: Philosophical Library, 2nd ed., 1955), 361–79, 368.

quality. In 1968, John Ziman described the referee as "the lynchpin [*sic*] about which the whole business of science is pivoted"; more recently, life scientist Paul Gross writes that he sees "peer-reviewed" as—speaking "loosely but not incorrectly"—a "kind of antonym" for "biased."[26]

But even if the pre-publication peer-review system worked perfectly, it would be inherently limited in what it could do to ensure quality—of which, in any case, "reliability" in the legally-relevant sense is only one dimension; what's more, there's good reason to fear that, because of changes in the scale and culture of the sciences since the system became standard, the system now works very imperfectly indeed.

2 PRE-PUBLICATION PEER REVIEW: ITS RATIONALE, ITS INHERENT LIMITATIONS

In 1946, just as the practice was becoming standard procedure at scientific journals, Michael Polanyi gave the classic statement of an epistemological rationale for pre-publication peer review. Some system for rationing limited publication opportunities is essential, he argued; for the scientific enterprise depends on effective evidence-sharing and mutual scrutiny, and without such a system scientists will be obliged to waste their time sifting through the work of cranks and incompetents to find the worthwhile stuff:

> Suppose … that no limitations of value were imposed on the publication of scientific contributions in journals. The selection—which is indispensable in view of the limited space—would have to be done by some neutral method—say drawing lots. Immediately the journals would be flooded with rubbish and valuable work would be crowded out. Cranks are always abounding who will send in spates of nonsense. Immature, confused, fantastic, or else plodding, pedestrian, irrelevant material would be pouring in. Swindlers and bunglers combining all variants of deception and self-deception would seek publicity. Buried among so much that is specious or slipshod, the few remaining valuable publications could hardly have a chance of being recognized.[27]

Rationing by pre-publication peer review, Polanyi continues, is a way to ensure that what is published at least meets minimal standards of professional competence:

[26] E-mail from Paul R. Gross, Professor of Life Sciences Emeritus, University of Virginia, to Susan Haack, July 11, 2005 (copy on file with author). See also John M. Ziman, *Public Knowledge* (Cambridge: Cambridge University Press, 1968), 111.

[27] Michael Polanyi, *Science, Faith, and Society* (Cambridge: Cambridge University Press, 1946), 35–36.

> No proposed contribution to science has a chance of becoming generally known unless it is published in print; and its chances of recognition are very poor unless it is published in one of the leading scientific journals. The referees and editors of these journals are responsible for excluding all matter which they consider unsound or irrelevant. They are charged with guarding a minimum standard for all published scientific literature.[28]

The key phrases for our purposes are "unsound or irrelevant" and "guarding a minimum standard."

"Unsound" and "minimum standard" make the point that pre-publication peer review cannot be expected to guarantee truth, sound methodology, rigorous statistics, etc. From the very beginning, scientific editors have stressed that they and their reviewers have no choice but to rely on the integrity of authors. In 1665, Denis de Sallo, the first editor of the *Journal des Scavans*, wrote in the first issue that "we aim to report the ideas of others without guaranteeing them"[29]; the Edinburgh Society's 1731 statement of its refereeing policy concludes with the observation that "[r]esponsibility concerning the truth of facts, the soundness of the reasoning, in the accuracy of calculations is wholly disclaimed; and must rest alone, on the knowledge, judgement, or ability of the authors who have respectfully furnished such communications."[30]

And Polanyi's "irrelevant" reminds us that editors and peer reviewers are not concerned *only* with truth, methodological soundness, and such; they also care, reasonably enough, about the interest of the work, the readability of the article, and its suitability for this particular journal. As the former editor of the *Journal of the National Cancer Institute* puts it, writing of "[r]eliability … and other inappropriate goals in peer review," "editorial decisions can, do, and should make use of other criteria … [such as] originality, the suitability of the topic for a given journal, … the need for a balance of topics in journals with broad coverage, the importance of findings to readers…."[31]

Polanyi is clear that what gives scientific results some authority is not peer-reviewed publication as such, but what happens *after* work is published:

> On its publication a paper is laid open to scrutiny by all scientists who will proceed to form, and possibly also to express, an opinion on its value. They may doubt or altogether reject its claims, while its author will probably

28 *Id.*, 33.

29 Drummond Rennie, "Editorial Peer Review: Its Development and Rationale," in *Peer Review in Health Sciences*, eds. Fiona Godlee and Tom Jefferson (London: BMJ Publishing Group, 2nd ed., 2003), 1, 2.

30 Kronick, "Peer Review in 18th-Century Journalism" (note 3 above), 1322.

31 John C. Bailar, "Reliability, Fairness, Objectivity, and Other Inappropriate Goals in Peer Review," *Behavioral and Brain Sciences* 14 (1991): 137–38, 138.

> defend them. After a time a more or less settled opinion will prevail. The third stage of public scrutiny through which a contribution to science must pass in order to become generally known and established is its incorporation in text-books or at least standard books of reference.[32]

Moreover, he acknowledges that the peer-review system will succeed even in the modest task of "guarding a minimum standard" only given certain assumptions:

> If each scientist set to work each morning with the intention of doing the best bit of safe charlatanry which would just help him into a good post, there would soon exist no effective standards by which such deception could be detected.... Only if scientists remain loyal to scientific ideals rather than try to achieve success with their fellow scientists can they form a community which will uphold those ideals.[33]

Obviously (though Polanyi doesn't say so explicitly) the effectiveness of the system depends not only on the integrity of authors, but also on the integrity of reviewers, editors, and publishers. And the problem isn't only that the system will fail if every scientist sets to work to do "the best bit of safe charlatanry" he can get away with; it is also that it will function less effectively the heavier the burdens on referees and editors, the greater the pressures on journals, and the greater the temptations for scientists to cut corners, or to fudge, trim, or even fake results.

3 PRE-PUBLICATION PEER REVIEW: RECENT STRESSES AND STRAINS, FLAWS AND FAILURES

Even in ideal circumstances reviewers are better placed to judge the readability of a paper or the interest of its topic or results than its truth or accuracy, and may in good faith reject important work that is too innovative to seem plausible; so perhaps it's not surprising that by 1994 historian of science Horace Freeland Judson, describing the "structural transformations" taking place in the sciences, should have included "declining standards and the growing, built-in tendency towards corruption of the peer-review and refereeing processes" on his list.[34] For today there are many pressures putting the peer review system under severe strain: the explosion of scientific and medical

32 Polanyi, *Science, Faith and Society* (note 27 above), 33–34.

33 *Id.*, 40.

34 Horace Freeland Judson, "Structural Transformations of the Sciences and the End of Peer Review," *Journal of the American Medical Association* 272 (1994): 92–94, 92.

publications; the increasing financial influence of large drug companies on the medical journals; the pressures on young scientists to get grants and to publish; the temptations to celebrity-seeking; the burgeoning expert-witness business; and so on.[35]

There are variations among the scientific and medical journals, but the refereeing process usually works roughly like this: An editor carries out what Lock describes as "triage": "classifying articles into self-evident masterpieces, obvious rubbish, and the remainder needing careful consideration";[36] for these—the large majority—the editor then chooses one or two (seldom more) referees to look at each paper chosen to review, generally informing referees of authors' names, but not vice versa;[37] referees are usually given a list against which to check for various aspects of style and presentation and certain kinds of obvious error; the reviewers are given a time limit, often of no more than two weeks,[38] to respond with their assessment and recommendation; and they spend an average of around 2.4 hours evaluating a manuscript—which usually involves, not simply giving a "yes or no" verdict, but making suggestions as to how the paper might be improved.[39] Many journals don't check the statistical calculations in accepted papers;[40] and reviewers are in no position to repeat

35 See, e.g., Susan Haack, *Defending Science—Within Reason: Between Scientism and Cynicism* (Amherst, NY: Prometheus Books, 2003), 27–29, 107–09.

36 Lock, *A Difficult Balance* (note 10 above), 6.

37 Some journals are moving towards "open" review, in which authors also know reviewers' names. See Richard Smith, "Peer Review: Reform or Revolution?" *British Medical Journal* 315 (1997): 759–60, 760 (arguing that open review is the most ethical form because it places authors and reviewers in equal positions and allows for increased accountability). By contrast, in philosophy journals, and as far as I know in humanities journals generally, both reviewers' and authors' names are normally "blinded."

38 In philosophy journals, and so far as I know in humanities journals generally, the time allowed is much longer.

39 See, e.g., Stephen Lock and Jane Smith, "What Do Peer Reviewers Do?" *Journal of the American Medical Association* 263 (1990): 1341–43, 1342 (reporting that study results show that reviewers spend less than two hours reviewing a manuscript); Alfred Yankauer, "Who Are the Peer Reviewers and How Much Do They Review?" *Journal of the American Medical Association* 263 (1990): 1338–40, 1339 (reporting that for twelve issues of the *American Journal of Public Health*, the average review time was 2.4 hours per reviewer per paper—amounting in all to 3,360 hours of uncompensated time).

40 See Martin J. Gardner and Jane Bond, "An Exploratory Study of Statistical Assessment of Papers Published in the *British Medical Journal*," *Journal of the American Medical Association* 263 (1990): 1355–57, 1355 (quoting statistics from a study on accuracy of papers submitted to *The British Medical Journal*; only 11% of submitted papers were found to be statistically accurate, and only 84% of published papers were accurate); Ann C. Weller, "Editorial Peer Review in U.S. Medical Journals," *Journal of the American Medical Association* 263 (1990): 1344–47, 1345 (reporting that most journals don't make any independent check of authors' statistical calculations); see also Dianne Bryant et al., "How Many Patients? How Many Limbs? Analysis of Patients or Limbs in the Orthopedic Literature: A Systematic Review," *Journal of Bone and*

authors' experiments or studies, which will ordinarily have taken a good deal of time and/or money. Acceptance rates vary widely from field to field; where the rate is low, most of the papers initially submitted to, but rejected by, one or more of the most desirable journals eventually appear in some lower-ranked publication, and a paper "may have been rejected at ten or twenty journals before it is finally accepted." Textbook chapters are usually invited, not peer-reviewed. Nor are all the articles in "peer-review" journals peer-reviewed; some are invited, and some appear by editorial privilege; and sometimes the authors have been asked—as I have been asked myself—to nominate their own referees.[41]

As the scale of the operation increases, with more and more papers submitted to more and more journals, the quality of referees and the time and attention they can give to their task are likely to decline. As the career pressures on scientists intensify, the temptation grows for referees to recommend acceptance of work they perceive as likely to advance their careers, to recommend rejection of work they perceive as a professional threat, and to plagiarize ideas from work they are asked to review.[42] And as pressures on the journals and their staff increase, the hope of prestige and profit causes further distortions: some journals suspend the peer-review process when they publish symposia sponsored by pharmaceutical companies (for which the journal may charge the company a significant fee); some reap large sums from the sale of

Joint Surgery 88 (2006): 41–45, 41 (concluding that 42% of clinical studies in highly-rated orthopedic journals are biased by the inclusion of multiple observations of different limbs of single individuals); Emili García-Berthou and Carles Alcaraz, "Incongruence between Test Statistics and P Values in Medical Papers," *BMC Medical Research Methodology* 4, no. 13 (2004): 1–5, 1, "Results and Discussion" (finding that "11.6% [21 of 181] and 11.1% [7 of 63] of the statistical results published in *Nature* and the *British Medical Journal* respectively during 2001 were incongruent" and noting that "[a]t least one such error appeared in 38% [12 of 32] and 25% [3 of 12] of the papers of *Nature* and the *British Medical Journal* respectively, indicating that they are widespread and not concentrated in a few papers"); Julie A. Neville et al., "Errors in the *Archives of Dermatology* and the *Journal of the American Academy of Dermatology* from January through December 2003," *Archives of Dermatology* 142 (2006): 737–40, 738 (reporting that from January through December 2003, the *Archives of Dermatology* and the *Journal of the American Academy of Dermatology* published 364 studies where "59 [38.1%] of 155 [that used statistical analysis] contained errors or omissions in statistical methods or the presentation of the results"); Andy Vail and Elizabeth Gardener, "Common Statistical Errors in the Design and Analysis of Subfertility Trials," *Human Reproduction* 18, no. 5 (2003): 1000–04, 1000 (reporting that of thirty-nine trials studied, "[s]ix trials were fatally flawed by design" and "[o]nly five trials reported live birth rates sufficiently to allow valid meta-analysis").

41 Brief of Daryl Chubin et al. (note 7 above), 11–19.

42 In this context, it is worth noting the title of a deservedly well-known paper criticizing the system of grant peer review: Daniel H. Osmond, "Malice's Wonderland: Research Funding and Peer Review," *Journal of Neurobiology* 14, no. 2 (1983): 95–112.

large numbers of reprints to the companies concerned;[43] some put pressure on authors to cite other papers in the same journal, thus raising its "impact factor" and boosting library orders;[44] and so on.

Editors themselves have begun to express concern. Richard Smith, editor of *The Lancet*, writes that peer review is "expensive, slow, prone to bias, open to abuse, possibly anti-innovatory, and unable to detect fraud."[45] Drummond Rennie, associate editor of the *Journal of the American Medical Association* (*JAMA*), is even more outspoken: "[t]here seems to be no study too fragmented, no hypothesis too trivial, no literature citation too biased or too egotistical, no design too warped, no methodology too bungled, no argument too circular, no conclusion too trifling or too unjustified, and no grammar or syntax too offensive for a paper to end up in print."[46]

~

According to a study reported in *JAMA* in 2004, a survey of 122 published articles found that 50% of efficacy and 65% of harm outcomes were incompletely reported.[47] According to a study reported in *Nature* in 2005, more than 10% of 3,247 scientists polled admitted withholding details of methodology or results from papers or proposals; more than 15% admitted dropping observations or data points; and more than 27% admitted keeping inadequate records of research projects.[48] According to a study reported in *JAMA* the same year, of 45 highly-cited studies published in prestigious journals and claiming effective medical interventions, 15 were later contradicted in whole or in part by other studies.[49] And according to an article published in the Rockefeller University magazine *Scientist* in the spring of 2006, over the four years in which the *Journal of Cell Biology* had been examining every image in every paper accepted, checking for alterations made in

43 "Two editors reported that their journals charged $400 to $2,500 per page to publish symposiums, and another reported charging a flat fee of $100,000. The journals charged an average of $15 per reprint, and reprint requests for symposiums [averaged] 25,000." Lisa A. Bero et al., "The Publication of Sponsored Symposiums in Medical Journals," *New England Journal of Medicine* 327 (1992): 1135–40, 1136–37.

44 Sharon Begley, "Science Journals Artfully Try to Boost Their Rankings," *Wall Street Journal*, June 5, 2006, B1, B8.

45 Smith, "Peer Review: Reform or Revolution?" (note 37 above), 759.

46 Drummond Rennie, "Guarding the Guardians: A Conference on Editorial Peer Review," *Journal of the American Medical Association* 256 (1986): 2391–92, 2391.

47 An Wen Chan et al., "Empirical Evidence for Selective Reporting of Outcomes in Randomized Trials," *Journal of the American Medical Association* 291 (2004): 2457–65, 2457.

48 Brian C. Martinson et al., "Scientists Behaving Badly," *Nature* 435 (2005): 737–38, 737.

49 John P. A. Ionnadis, "Contradicted and Initially Stronger Effects in Highly Cited Clinical Research," *Journal of the American Medical Association* 294 (2005): 218–28, 220.

Adobe Photoshop, 14 of 1,400 articles were rejected after fraudulent image alteration was detected.[50]

Moreover, other studies suggest that even after serious scientific misconduct or outright fraud has been discovered, the process of cleaning up the scientific literature so that such work is retracted, and others' innocent citations to it corrected, is at best patchy and uneven.[51] For example, a year after the Office of Research Integrity informed ten journals that papers they had published co-authored by Dr. Eric Poehlman were fraudulent, only eight had retracted; and even after the *Annals of Internal Medicine* had retracted one of these papers, other authors continued to cite it.[52]

In fact, there are so many recent reports of failures of the peer-review system that the difficulty is to select the most instructive. Should it be the notorious case of Dr. Hwang Woo Suk, the Korean researcher whose apparently stunning work on cloning, published in *Science* and *Nature*, turned out to rest on fabricated data?[53] Or should it be that extraordinary article in the *Journal of Reproductive Medicine*, claiming to have shown that intercessory prayer by strangers of another faith in another country doubled the success-rate of attempted in vitro fertilizations—the supposed lead author of which later admitted that he learned of the study only 6 to 12 months after it was completed, and another author of which, an attorney with no scientific training, subsequently pled guilty to (unrelated) charges of business fraud?[54] Or

50 Lauren Gravitz, "Biology's Image Problem," *Rockefeller University Scientist* 1 (Spring 2006): 1, 10–12.

51 Paul J. Friedman, "Correcting the Literature Following Fraudulent Publication," *Journal of the American Medical Association* 263 (1990): 1416–19, 1417; Mark P. Pfeiffer and Gwendolyn L. Snodgrass, "The Continued Use of Retracted, Invalid Scientific Literature," *Journal of the American Medical Association* 263 (1990): 1420–23, Abstract.

52 Jennifer Couzin and Katherine Unger, "Cleaning up the Paper Trail," *Science* 312 (2006): 38–43, 39; Harold C. Sox and Drummond Rennie, "Research Misconduct, Retraction, and Cleansing Medical Literature: Lessons from the Poehlman Case," *Annals of Internal Medicine* 144 (2006): 609–13, 609 (noting that in 1989, in order to evaluate allegations of scientific fraud, Congress created the Office of Scientific Integrity, later renamed the Office of Research Integrity). The article that was retracted was Eric T. Poehlman et al., "Changes in Energy Balance and Body Composition at Menopause: A Controlled Longitudinal Study," *Annals of Internal Medicine* 123 (1995): 673–76. Sox and Rennie (above), 609.

53 Nicholas Wade and Choe Sang-Hun, "Human Cloning Was All Faked, Koreans Report," *New York Times*, January 10, 2006, A1 (quoting Dr. Benjamin Lewin, former editor of *Cell*, commenting that *Science* should have been more careful and certainly shouldn't have published a paper with "several identical photos").

54 Benedict Carey, "Researcher Pulls His Name from Paper on Prayer and Fertility," *New York Times*, December 4, 2006, A15; Bruce Flamm, "The Columbia University 'Miracle' Study: Flawed and Fraud," *Skeptical Inquirer* 28 (September/October 2004): 25–31, 27–8. The article concerned was Kwang Y. Cha et al., "Does Prayer Influence the Success of In

maybe the papers by Jon Sudbø in *The Lancet* and the *New England Journal of Medicine* (*NEJM*), claiming to have shown that non-steroidal anti-inflammatory drugs reduced the risk of oral cancer, all of which turned out to have been based on fabricated data?[55] Or should it be something lower-key, such as the article in the *New England Journal of Medicine*, cited in litigation against Metabolife, in which the information in a table of 11 patients listing adverse effects and pre-existing conditions is contradicted by the text on the very same page?[56]

But no: the extraordinary saga of the report of Merck's large-scale clinical trial of Vioxx, the VIGOR study, stands out as an object-lesson in what can go wrong. After FDA approval, the report of the study—concluding that Vioxx carried a lower risk of adverse gastrointestinal effects than older pain-relievers, and that for most patients its risk of adverse cardiovascular effects was not significant—was submitted to the *NEJM*, where it appeared in November 2000.[57] In 2002, however, Merck was obliged to add a warning about cardiovascular risks to the package insert. And in September 2004—after the data safety monitoring board halted another major clinical trial, the APPROVe study (designed to show that Vioxx lowered the risk of colon polyps), when it emerged that patients given 25 mg. of Vioxx for more than 18 months had a fourfold greater

Vitro Fertilization-Embryo Transfer? Report of a Masked, Randomized Trial," *Journal of Reproductive Medicine* 46 (2001): 781–87, 782. Flamm (above), 27–28.

55 John Sudbø et al., "Non-Steroidal Anti-Inflammatory Drugs and the Risk of Oral Cancer: A Nested Case-Control Study," *Lancet* 366 (2005): 1359–66. The database of 908 participants in this study, reportedly, was simply invented; 250 of the fictional persons involved supposedly had the same birth date! *Forbes*, "Many Researchers Break the Rules: Study," http://www.forbes.com/forbeslife/health/feeds/hscout/2006/04/13/hscout532110.html (April 13, 2006). See also Richard Horton, "Expression of Concern: Non-Steroidal Anti-Inflammatory Drugs and the Risk of Oral Cancer," *Lancet* 367 (2006): 196 (expressing concern over verbal admission by Sudbø that he fabricated data for the study previously published in the *Lancet* and acknowledging possible misconduct in two of his research papers published in the *New England Journal of Medicine*); Richard Horton, "Retraction—Non-Steroidal Anti-Inflammatory Drugs and the Risk of Oral Cancer: A Nested Case-Control Study," *Lancet* 367 (2006): 382 (retracting the Sudbø article based on confirmation that data was fabricated).

56 Christine Haller and Neal L. Benowitz, "Adverse Cardiovascular and Central Nervous System Events Associated with Dietary Supplements Containing Ephedra Alkaloids," *New England Journal of Medicine* 343 (2000): 1833–38, 1836. Table 4 on page 1836 lists patient number seven as having no pre-existing conditions or concurrent risks, yet the text on the same page indicates that an autopsy of this patient "showed mild cardiomegaly with four-chamber dilatation and coronary artery disease, with narrowing of 50 to 75 percent in four vessels."

57 Claire Bombadier et al., "Comparison of Upper Gastrointestinal Toxicity of Rofecoxib and Naproxen in Patients with Rheumatoid Arthritis," *New England Journal of Medicine* 343, no. 2 (2000): 1520–28.

incidence of serious thromboembolic events—Merck withdrew the drug from the market.[58]

In December 2005, in the midst of a gathering storm of litigation by patients claiming they had been injured by the drug, the *NEJM* issued an "Expression of Concern" acknowledging that three heart attacks among patients taking Vioxx had been omitted from the report of the VIGOR study it had published in 2000. These adverse events had been included in the data on the FDA website since February 2001; and two of the three authors had known of them well in advance of the publication of the paper. Including these adverse events would have raised the rate of heart attacks among those taking Vioxx from the 0.4% claimed in the paper to 0.5% (compared to 0.1% among patients taking naproxen), and moreover contradicted the claim in the paper that only those already at risk showed an increase in heart attacks after taking Vioxx. Merck claimed that the additional heart attacks occurred after the cut-off date for the study; but the editor-in-chief of the journal, Dr. Jeffrey Drazen, told reporters that the design of the study, which continued to track gastrointestinal effects after it stopped tracking cardiovascular effects, had been misleading.

But the problem here wasn't only with the authors; nor was it only that the journal's reviewers didn't have the raw data, or that they failed to notice the suspicious oddity in the study design. We now know that in June 2001 the editors of the *NEJM* had received a letter from pharmacist Jennifer Hrachovec asking that the article be corrected in light of the information on the FDA website, but had declined to publish it on the grounds that the journal "can't be in the business of policing every bit of data we put out"; that when deposed by the parties in federal litigation in Texas in November 2005, executive editor Dr. Gregory Curfman acknowledged that neither the reviewers nor the editors had questioned Merck's theory that the higher rate of cardiovascular events among Vioxx patients was attributable to a cardio-protective effect of naproxen, even though an FDA official had noted that it "is not supported by any … controlled trials"; that the journal had sold 929,000 copies of reprints of the article, most of them to Merck, for revenue estimated to be between $697,000 and $836,000; and that the "Expression of Concern" about the study had been published on the urgent last-minute advice of public-relations specialist Edward Cafasso that testimony to be presented the next day in the Vioxx case in which Dr. Curfman had been deposed made it essential for the journal to post something right away, to "drive the media away from the

[58] Simon R. J. Maxwell, and David J. Webb, "Cox-2 Selective Inhibitors—Important Lessons Learned," *Lancet* 365 (2005): 449–51, 449.

NEJM and toward the authors, Merck, and plaintiff attorneys."[59] As Richard Smith, former editor of the *British Medical Journal*, observed, the conduct of the *New England Journal* in the dispute over the VIGOR trial "raised doubts about the journal's integrity"; "the journal failed its readers [and] damaged its reputation."[60]

And just as you thought it could hardly get worse, in July 2006 the *NEJM* published a correction to the report it had earlier published of the APPROVe study: key results claimed in the article had not been arrived at by the statistical method the authors said they used; moreover, using the method the authors had said they were using, but had not in fact used, the results undermined the claim in the article that cardiovascular risks increased only after 18 months.[61]

Not long before, Lawrence Altman had written in the *New York Times* that "recent disclosures of fraudulent or flawed studies in medical and scientific journals have called [the peer-review system] into question as never before … ";[62] it's hard to disagree.

~

For obvious reasons they are harder to track, and for obvious reasons they are often not known until long after the event; but it's pretty clear that there are also many instances in which important and innovative work has been rejected by peer reviewers. Lock tells the story of Edward Jenner's report of his smallpox vaccination, which was rejected by the *Transactions of the Royal Society* in 1796, after Sir Joseph Banks had looked it over and reported that he "wanted faith" in its conclusion.[63] Charles McCutcheon, lamenting the way "reviewing weeds out good manuscripts as well as poor ones," lists

59 David Armstrong, "Bitter Pill: How the *New England Journal of Medicine* Missed Warning Signs in Vioxx—Medical Weekly Waited Years to Report Flaws in Article That Praised Pain Drug—Merck Seen as 'Punching Bag,'" *Wall Street Journal*, May 15, 2006, A1, A10.

60 Medical News Today, "*New England Journal of Medicine* Damaged by Its Conduct over Vioxx, Says Former Editor of *British Medical Journal*," www.medicalnewstoday.com/medicalnews.php?newsid=46831 (July 9, 2006).

61 Heather Won Tesoriero, "Vioxx Study Correction May Add Pressure to Merck's Defense," *Wall Street Journal*, June 27, 2007, A2. The original article was Robert S. Bresalier, et al., "Cardiovascular Events Associated with Rofecoxib in a Colorectal Adenoma Chemoprevention Trial," *New England Journal of Medicine* 352 (2005): 1092–1102. Ironically enough, the same issue of the journal includes a short paper by Jeffrey M. Drazen entitled "COX-2 Inhibitors—A Lesson in Unexpected Problems," *New England Journal of Medicine* 352 (2005): 1131–2. The following year, Bresalier et al. published a correction: "Correction," *New England Journal of Medicine* 355 (2006): 221.

62 Lawrence K. Altman, "For Science's Gatekeepers, a Credibility Gap," *New York Times*, May 2, 2006, F1.

63 Lock, *A Difficult Balance* (note 10 above), 2.

"Frederick Lanchester's 1894 circulation theory of how wings lift, Chandra Bose's photon statistics in 1924, Enrico Fermi's theory of beta decay in 1933, Herman Almquist's discovery of vitamin K_2 in 1935, Hans Krebs's nitric acid cycle in 1937, and Raymond Lindeman's trophic-dynamic concept in ecology in 1941"; all were "turned down at least once."[64] David Horrobin adds that Krebs's paper, "possibly the most important article in modern biochemistry, … eventually led to a Nobel prize";[65] and lists many other examples, including a "seminal paper[] in immunology" by Glick et al. on the identification of B lymphocytes, which was "rejected by leading general and specialist journals and eventually appeared in *Poultry Science* because of the species on which the work was done";[66] and a paper by New Zealand farmer Gladys Reid suggesting that facial eczema in sheep might be caused by a marginal zinc deficiency, which was rejected by the journals in the field until Horrobin published it in *Medical Hypotheses*—after which her work was confirmed, the disease was eliminated, and Ms. Reid was awarded a decoration for services to New Zealand agriculture.[67]

By now it should hardly need saying: *the fact that work has passed prepublication peer review is no guarantee that it is not flawed or even fraudulent; and the fact that work has been rejected by reviewers is no guarantee that it is not an important advance.*

4 LESSONS FOR LAWYERS

"Enough already!" you may be thinking. To be sure, Judge Kozinski's confidence that "the normal peer review process … is one of the hallmarks of reliable scientific investigation" was over-optimistic;[68] but didn't Justice Blackmun clear all this up in his ruling for the Supreme Court in *Daubert* III?

Well, evidently Justice Blackmun paid attention to the brief from amici Chubin et al., for he acknowledges that:

> [p]ublication (which is but one element of peer review) is not a sine qua non of admissibility; it does not necessarily correlate with reliability … and in some instances well-grounded but innovative theories will not have been

64 Charles W. McCutchen, "Peer Review: Treacherous Servant, Disastrous Master," *Technology Review* 94 (1991): 28–51, 33.

65 David F. Horrobin, "The Philosophical Basis of Peer Review and the Suppression of Innovation," *Journal of the American Medical Association* 263 (1990): 1438–41, 1440 (cited in *Daubert* III [note 1 above], 593).

66 Horrobin, "The Philosophical Basis of Peer Review" (note 65 above), 1440.

67 *Id.*

68 *Daubert* IV (note 8 above) 1131 n.3.

> published.... But submission to the scrutiny of the scientific community ... increases the likelihood that substantive flaws in methodology will be detected.[69]

It would have been desirable to have made the distinction between the broad and the narrow senses of "peer review" more explicit; nevertheless, what Justice Blackmun has in mind seems reasonably clear; moreover, it seems true: poor scientific work may pass pre-publication peer review, and good work may not, but when scientific work is published and made available for the scrutiny of other scientists, the likelihood increases that, eventually, any serious methodological flaws will be spotted. And Justice Blackmun's advice about the weight courts should give this "*Daubert* factor"—in effect, that it's a relevant consideration, but not necessarily a decisive one—seems at first blush quite unexceptionable:

> The fact of publication ... in a peer reviewed journal thus will be a relevant, though not dispositive, consideration in assessing the scientific validity of a particular technique or methodology on which an opinion is premised.[70]

"At first blush": but at second blush you find yourself beset by worries, both theoretical and practical: the meaning of "reliable" threatens to unravel into indeterminacy; and the Court's advice about the bearing of peer review on the determination of reliability sounds less and less helpful. Ambiguities strike one almost immediately: are courts to ask whether the work on which proffered testimony is based was published after surviving peer review, or is it enough that it be published in a "peer-review journal"? Should *the witness's* work have been subject to peer review and publication, or is it enough that the witness rely on *others*' peer-reviewed and published work? And so on.

Justice Blackmun's sense that survival of the long-run scrutiny of the scientific community is about the best indicator of scientific validity a layperson can have, albeit a fallible one, is perfectly correct; but it is of no real practical help. For obvious reasons the scientific issues at stake in legal cases are not likely to turn on the most firmly-established science, but on the still-controversial stuff; and it would be hopelessly unrealistic to imagine that courts could somehow figure out which still-controversial scientific claims *will*, eventually, survive such "peer review," when scientists themselves cannot.

And rather than clarifying the concept of "evidentiary reliability" (which the *Daubert* Court equates with "scientific validity"),[71] Justice Blackmun's

69 *Daubert* III (note 1 above), 594.
70 *Id.*, 594.
71 *Id.*, 590–91.

observations contribute to its obscurity. In ordinary speech, "reliable" has a whole tangle of uses: but whether we are describing inanimate objects, like clocks or cars, or persons ("informants," or "sources," as we say), or information, databases, etc., reliability—fitness to be relied upon—is ordinarily conceived as a matter of degree. But the *Daubert* ruling is about admissibility, which is *not* a matter of degree; and so obliges us to adopt a categorical conception.

If evidence must be reliable *enough* to be admissible, *how* reliable does it have to be, and how is a court to determine whether evidence meets the standard? (Is the same degree of reliability to be imposed on "soft" scientific evidence as on "hard," or on non-scientific expert testimony as on the scientific?) It makes sense, as Judge Becker argued in *Paoli*, that "[t]he evidentiary requirement of reliability [should be] lower than the merits standard of correctness";[72] for if the threshold for admissibility were as high as the standard of proof, a party seeking to introduce expert testimony would be required, in effect, to prove his case twice—and the court would be trespassing on the jury's turf. But now you start to wonder: is peer-reviewed publication enough, after all, to guarantee that proffered evidence meets a minimal threshold standard of reliability? If not, is it at least enough to guarantee that, even if the conclusions drawn are unreliable, the methodology followed meets minimal standards? Isn't that what Judge Kozinski had in mind when he wrote in 1995 that peer-reviewed publication "is a significant indication that it … meets *at least the minimal criteria* of good science"?[73]

Justice Blackmun's ruling leaves all this open. Justice Rehnquist's opinion for the *Joiner* Court, casting doubt on the robustness of the distinction between methodology and conclusions on which *Daubert* had relied, doesn't help.[74] And Justice Breyer's opinion for the *Kumho* Court—holding that *Daubert* gatekeeping extends to non-scientific as well as scientific testimony, but that courts may use any, all, or none of the *Daubert* factors, and/or other factors more appropriate to the task at hand—confirms that the tricky stuff is to be left to courts' discretion.[75]

72 *In re* Paoli R.R. Yard PCB Litig., 35 F.3d 717, 744 (3d Cir. 1994).

73 *Daubert* IV (note 8 above), 1318 (my italics).

74 Gen. Elec. Co. v. Joiner, 522 U.S. 136, 146 (1997) ("*Joiner* III") ("conclusions and methodology are not entirely distinct from one another").

75 Kumho Tire Co. v. Carmichael, 526 U.S. 137, 141 (1999). The Court held that: Daubert's general holding—setting forth the trial judge's general "gatekeeping" obligation—applies not only to testimony based on "scientific" knowledge, but also to testimony based on "technical" and "other specialized" knowledge.… [A] trial court *may* consider one or more of the more specific factors that Daubert mentioned when doing so will help.… But … Daubert's list of specific factors neither necessarily nor exclusively applies to all experts or in every case."

Of course, it's no surprise that the *Daubert* Court didn't come up with a precise formula for deciding questions of evidentiary reliability; and even if such a thing were feasible, it would probably be, not desirable precision, but the kind of "delusive exactness" Oliver Wendell Holmes once decried as "a source of fallacy throughout the law."[76] And, especially given that "peer review and publication" is only one factor on *Daubert*'s flexible list, perhaps it is no surprise, either, to find no clear correlation of decisions to admit, or to exclude, expert testimony, with whether it satisfies this factor or not. Instead:

(i) some courts (citing Justice Blackmun's concession that peer-reviewed publication is not a *sine qua non* of admissibility) have admitted expert testimony not based on work that has been peer-reviewed and published;[77]
(ii) some courts (citing Justice Blackmun's concession that peer-reviewed publication does not necessarily correlate with reliability) have excluded expert testimony based on work which has been peer-reviewed and published.[78]

[76] Truax v. Corrignan, 257 U.S. 312, 342 (1921) (Holmes, J., dissenting).

[77] See, e.g., Ruiz Troche v. Pepsi Cola of P. R. Bottling Co., 161 F.3d 77, 84 (1st Cir. 1998) (reversing the district court's exclusion of Dr. O'Donnell's testimony regarding the effects of cocaine on a driver's behavior, on the grounds that, although the secondary sources he cited were not peer-reviewed or published, other peer-reviewed, published studies made the same point); Kannankeril v. Terminix Int'l, Inc., 128 F.3d 802, 809 (3d Cir. 1997) (vacating and remanding the lower court's decision, which had (i) excluded Dr. Gerson's testimony, arguing that "although Dr. Gerson did not write on the topic, his opinion is supported by widely accepted scientific knowledge of the harmful nature of organophosphates"; and (ii) noted that McCullock v. H.B. Fuller Co., 61 F.3d 1038, 1042 (2d Cir. 1995) held that peer review, publication, and general acceptance go to the weight, not the admissibility, of evidence); Metabolife Int'l, Inc. v. Wornick, 264 F.3d 832, 843 (9th Cir. 2001) (citing *Daubert* IV [note 8 above], 1317 for the proposition that "when research is begun pre-litigation, it may be reliable without peer review"); United States v. Hankey, 203 F.3d 1160, 1168 (9th Cir. 2000) (holding that the district court did not abuse its discretion in admitting the testimony of a police expert on gang codes and citing *Kumho Tire*, 526 U.S., 152, saying a court must have latitude not only in deciding whether to admit expert testimony, but also in deciding "how to test an expert's reliability").

[78] See, e.g., Allison v. McGhan Med. Corp., 184 F.3d 1300, 1313, 1316, 1319, n.24 (11th Cir. 1999) (upholding lower court's exclusion of experts' testimony on role of silicone breast implants in causing the plaintiff's injuries, in part on the grounds that the fact that a study was peer-reviewed and published "does not mean it constituted an adequate basis" for experts' opinion, that "scrutiny by one's peers does not insure admissibility," and that the fact that a witness had published many articles in peer-reviewed journals "does not substantiate the scientific validity of his premise"); United States v. Cordoba, 194 F.3d 1053, 1059 (9th Cir. 1999) (upholding the district court's exclusion of polygraph evidence, even though hundreds of articles have been published on polygraphs, including many in peer-reviewed journals).

(iii) some courts (citing Justice Blackmun's acknowledgment that peer-reviewed publication is a pertinent consideration) have admitted testimony in part because it was based on peer-reviewed and published work;[79]

and:

(iv) some courts (also citing Justice Blackmun's acknowledgment that peer-reviewed publication is a relevant factor) have excluded testimony in part because it was not so based.[80]

Nor, given Justice Blackmun's shifts from broader to narrower senses of "peer review," is it altogether surprising that some courts have interpreted "peer review" to cover kinds of exposure to other people in a field other than pre-publication peer review.[81] Nor is it any surprise that "peer review and publication" has found its way into courts in states that have not adopted *Daubert*,[82]

79 See, e.g., *In re* Silicone Gel Breast Implants Prods. Liab. Litig. (California), 318 F. Supp. 2d 879, 896 (C.D. Cal. 2004) (finding that Dr. Neugebauer's analysis and criticism of the existing epidemiological evidence is admissible, in part because "[t]he statistical underpinnings of epidemiology … have been subjected to peer review and publication").

80 See, e.g., Berry v. City of Detroit, 25 F.3d 1342, 1350–51 (6th Cir. 1994) (excluding testimony regarding police training of the plaintiffs' witness Leonard Postill, in part on the grounds that "[t]here certainly is no testimony as to any peer review of Postill's theory"); Nat'l Bank of Commerce v. Associated Milk Producers, Inc., 191 F.3d 858, 864–65 (8th Cir. 1999) (affirming the lower court's exclusion of expert's testimony as to connection between aflatoxin M-1 (AFM) and the plaintiff's cancer, in part on the grounds that "[t]here are no scientific studies or medical literature that show any correlation between AFM and laryngeal cancer"); Nelson v. Tenn. Gas Pipeline Co., No. 95–1112, 1998 WL 1297690, *8–*9, *13 (W.D. Tenn. Aug. 31, 1998) (excluding the testimony of Nelson's experts Drs. Kilburn and Hirsch that the plaintiffs' injuries were caused by PCB exposure from the gas pipeline, in part on the grounds that their work had not been published or peer-reviewed).

81 See, e.g., United States v. Bonds, 12 F.3d 540, 559–60 & n.16, 568 (6th Cir. 1993) (affirming the lower court's decision to admit FBI's expert testimony on DNA, even though "many of the articles introduced as … exhibits did not appear in a 'peer-reviewed journal' in the strict sense of that term," since "all of the articles gave the FBI's procedures exposure within the scientific community"); United States v. Havvard, 117 F. Supp. 2d 848, 854 (S.D. Ind. 2000) (admitting the FBI's fingerprint-identification testimony, arguing and concluding that it satisfies *Daubert*; in particular, a fingerprint examiner's methods are subject to peer review because "any other qualified examiner can compare the objective information upon which the opinion is based and may render a different opinion if warranted"). *Havvard*, I believe, stretches the meaning of "peer review" well beyond all reasonable limits.

82 See, e.g., Berry v. CSX Transp., Inc., 709 So. 2d 552, 569–70 (Fla. Dist. Ct. App. 1998) (arguing that, even under *Frye*, "[w]hile the existence of numerous peer-reviewed, published … studies does not guarantee that the studies are without flaws, such publication … alleviates the necessity of thorough judicial scrutiny … at the admissibility stage").

and even into cases involving quite different issues from questions of admissibility of expert testimony.[83]

But it is disappointing to find that courts' analyses of "peer review and publication" seem to have been, mostly, quite shallow. For this investigation of the virtues and vices of the pre-publication peer review system has suggested a whole raft of questions that might throw light on the significance of the fact that the expert testimony proffered in a given case is, or is not, based on work published in a peer-reviewed journal. How epistemologically respectable is the field in question,[84] and are there serious ongoing methodological disagreements? Is this a highly-regarded journal in the field, or a second- or third-tier publication—or a last resort of the desperate-to-publish? Was work published in a "peer-review journal" in fact peer-reviewed, or was it published by editorial privilege, or invited? If it was peer-reviewed, were the reviewers suggested by the author(s)? If it was invited, was this because of the author's good reputation, or because of his or her personal relationship with the editor? Is the author (or an author) associated with the journal, e.g., by serving on the editorial board? Does the journal in which the work was published receive support, direct or indirect, from one of the parties to the case or to closely related litigation? Was the work rejected by other journals before being accepted by this one, and if so, by how many, and which, and on what grounds? If testimony is based on work which has not been published, is that because it is too recent, or because, though not recent, it was never submitted for publication, or because it was submitted, but was rejected? Have there been subsequent expressions of concern or retractions,[85] or have other papers criticized the work?

These are not easy questions to answer, and it is not remarkable that courts have not routinely asked them. But when some of them *were* explored by a court—as it happens, in another Bendectin case, less well-known than *Daubert*—the results were instructive, to say the least; and quite disturbing.

[83] See, e.g., Kitzmiller v. Dover Area Sch. Dist., 400 F. Supp. 2d 707, 743–45 (M.D. Pa. 2005) (finding that, while the plaintiffs' experts' testimony is based on peer-reviewed literature, defendants' experts' testimony is not based on material that has been subject to peer review, which is "exquisitely important" in the scientific process, helping to ensure "that research papers are scientifically accurate[], meet the standards of the scientific method, and are relevant to other scientists in the field").

[84] See *Kumho Tire* (note 75 above), 151 (1999) ("[n]or ... does the presence of Daubert's general acceptance factor help show that an expert's testimony is reliable where the discipline itself lacks reliability").

[85] To find retractions in medical journals, visit PubMed (*available at* http://www.ncbi.nlm.nih.gov/entrez/query.fcgi?db=PubMed&itool=toolbar) and search for "retracted publication" in the MeSH (Medical Subject Heading) database, then click on Links and select PubMed.

5 FULL CIRCLE? "PEER REVIEW AND PUBLICATION" IN THE BENDECTIN LITERATURE

Blum v. Merrell Dow Pharmaceuticals was a long-drawn-out Bendectin case in the Pennsylvania courts which began several years before *Daubert*, in 1982, but wasn't finally concluded until 2000.[86]

In *Blum* as in *Daubert*, Merrell Dow's attorneys argued that the plaintiffs' expert testimony should be excluded on the grounds that it wasn't generally accepted in the relevant scientific community. The Blums' attorneys argued, however, that *Merrell Dow*'s expert testimony should be excluded, on the grounds that the supposed "scientific consensus" on the matter was completely artificial; that it had been created by the Merrell Dow's support of favorable research and—the key point for present purposes—its support of questionably peer-reviewed journals that would publish results helpful to the company in defending itself against Bendectin litigation. Judge Bernstein's 1996 ruling (*Blum* IV) doesn't mince words: the testimony in this case, he observes, demonstrated "how 'scientific consensus' can be created through purchased research and the manipulation of a 'scientific' literature, funded as part of a litigation defense, and choreographed by counsel."[87] It clearly demonstrated "that not all 'peer review' journals are created equal," that "not all the articles contained in 'peer review' journals were even reviewed...," and that "[a]rticles were intentionally inserted in peer review journals for use in court."[88]

The testimony to which Judge Bernstein is referring here will be discussed at length in the next paper, so for now I will mention just a couple of examples: Dr. Robert Brent, the editor of *Teratology*,[89] who had been retained as an expert by Merrell Dow for 18 years, testified that an article he published in his own journal, "Litigation-Produced Pain, Disease, and Suffering: An

[86] Blum v. Merrell Dow Pharm., Inc., 1 Pa. D. & C.4th 634 (Phila. Cnty. Ct. 1988) ("*Blum* I"), *rev'd*, 560 A.2d 212 (Pa. Super. Ct. 1989) ("*Blum* II"), *aff'd*, 626 A.2d 537 (Pa. 1993) ("*Blum* III"), *remanded to* 33 Phila. Cnty. Rep. 193 (1996) ("*Blum* IV"), *rev'd*, 705 A.2d 1314 (Pa. Super. 1997) ("*Blum* V"), *aff'd*, 764 A.2d 1 (Pa. 2000) ("*Blum* VI"). See "What's Wrong with Litigation-Driven Science?" pp. 180–207 in this volume, 188–94, for more details of this fascinating, but disturbing, case. Pennsylvania, by the way, hasn't adopted *Daubert*, but remains a *Frye* state. A revised Pennsylvania Rule of Evidence 702 came into effect March 2013; but its key test remains whether "the expert's methodology is generally accepted in the field." Pa Rule Evid 702.

[87] *Blum* IV (note 86 above), 230.

[88] *Id.*, 246–47.

[89] In Wells v. Ortho Pharm. Corp., 615 F. Supp. 262, 291 (N.D. Ga. 1985) (cited in *Blum* VI (note 86 above), 10 (Castille, J., dissenting)), Dr. Brent's testimony was found to be incredible because "[his] testimony and manner suggested a degree of conviction in his own conclusions unwarranted in a discipline in which ... explanations are only more or less probable."

Experience with Congenital Malformation Lawsuits,"[90] hadn't been peer-reviewed; and that he had sent another article of his, "Bendectin: The Most Comprehensively Studied Human Non-Teratogen, and the Foremost Tortogen-Litigen," to Merrell Dow's attorneys for editing before it was submitted for publication.[91] And another of Merrell Dow's experts, Dr. Bracken, acknowledged under cross-examination that his peer-reviewed and published epidemiological study was, well, "less than good."[92]

In Appendix B to his opinion, entitled "Science and Justice," Judge Bernstein adds:

> The testimony demonstrated medical-scientific peer review journal literature created and manipulated for use in the courts.... The testimony demonstrated that articles were inserted in "peer review" journals, without review by independent authorities, but edited by lawyers ... [and] revealed factual editing of supposedly scientific research literature by the very lawyers defending in litigation.[93]

This reinforces Justice Blackmun's acknowledgment that peer-reviewed publication is no guarantee of "scientific validity" but at best a very fallible indicator; and also suggests that, if courts were to pursue the questions suggested here, this *Daubert* factor could, and should, be handled with more caution, and more subtlety, than it has usually been up till now.

But Judge Bernstein's ruling is also quite disturbing: for it suggests that the scientific literature in the litigation by way of which "peer review and publication" entered the official legal vocabulary of admissibility may have been tainted by litigation interests. Ironically, it seems that the same commercialization of medical research that has contributed to the creeping corruption of peer review and publication may also have been partly responsible for the legal system's coming to rely on that process as a factor in determining evidentiary reliability. This leads us rather directly to the topic of litigation-driven science, the subject of the next paper—where, once again, we will meet the Blums.

[90] Robert L. Brent, "Litigation-Produced Pain, Disease, and Suffering: An Experience with Congenital Malformation Lawsuits," *Teratology* 16, no. 1 (1997): 1–13, 5, table1.

[91] *Blum* IV (note 86 above), 223–28. Dr. Brent had hoped to publish this paper, he said, in the *NEJM*, the *Lancet*, or *JAMA*. By 1996 (though Judge Bernstein's ruling doesn't tell us this) the article in question had already been published, in a less prestigious forum. Robert L. Brent, "Bendectin: Review of the Medical Literature of a Comprehensively Studied Human Nonteratogen and the Most Prevalent Tortogen-Litigen," *Reproductive Toxicology* 9, no. 4 (1995): 337–49.

[92] *Blum* IV (note 86 above), 207–08.

[93] *Id.*, 248–49.

—8—

What's Wrong with Litigation-Driven Science?

> If Science, for a consideration, can be induced to prove anything which a party litigant needs in order to sustain his side of the issue, then Science is fairly open to the charge of venality and perjury, rendered the more base by the disguise of natural truth in which she robes herself.
>
> —John Ordronaux (1874)[1]

Because the factual truths at issue in a case often go beyond what the average juror can be expected to know, courts have come increasingly to rely on expert witnesses, among them scientists from just about every specialty you can think of: experts on blood, bullets, bite-marks, battered wives; on PCBs, paternity, poisons, post-traumatic stress; on radon, recovered memories, rape trauma syndrome, random DNA-match probabilities; on psychosis, asbestosis, silicosis (and for all I know, on psittacosis!). But as long as courts have relied significantly on scientific witnesses, there have been complaints: about the scientific ignorance and gullibility of attorneys, judges, and jurors; about "witness-shopping"; and—as my opening quotation illustrates—about the irresponsibility and venality of professional scientific experts willing to say whatever is needed to advance the cause of the party that hires them.[2] And as reliance on expert witnesses has grown, so has the felt need for courts to ensure that the expert testimony admitted is not just flimsy or interested speculation, but reliable enough to be more helpful than misleading.

One factor that courts have sometimes taken as indicating that proffered scientific testimony may *not* be reliable is that it is based on "litigation-driven"

[1] John Ordronaux, "On Expert Testimony in Judicial Proceedings," *Journal of Insanity* 30, no. 3 (1874): 312–22, 312.

[2] See also "Irreconcilable Differences? The Troubled Marriage of Science and Law," pp. 78–103 in this volume, 81–82.

science. As it happens, the context in which I first encountered criticisms of proffered scientific testimony as "litigation-driven" was Judge Kozinski's 1995 ruling in *Daubert*,[3] on remand from the Supreme Court. As I subsequently discovered, however, the fact that expert testimony is based on litigation-driven research has been construed not only as bearing on its admissibility, but also as lowering its weight;[4] and has been construed as bearing on the admissibility of scientific testimony under *Frye*[5] as well as under *Daubert*.[6]

This prompts a host of questions, legal and epistemological, theoretical and practical: What role has this factor played in courts' handling of scientific testimony? What exactly does it mean to describe research as "litigation-driven"? What reasons have courts given for regarding litigation-driven science with suspicion? Are these reasons sound? And if they are, does this suffice to show that Judge Kozinski's new "*Daubert* factor"—whether the science on which testimony is based is litigation-driven—is a useful indicator of the (un)reliability of proffered expert testimony?

3 Daubert v. Merrell Dow Pharm., Inc., 43 F.3d 1311, 1317 (9th Cir. 1995) ("*Daubert* IV").

4 See, e.g., Perry v. United States, 755 F.2d 888, 892 (11th Cir. 1985) ("[Plaintiff's expert witness] Dr. Goldfield had reached a conclusion as to the connection between encephalitis and the [swine flu] vaccine before commencing his research"); other courts cited similar criticism of Dr. Goldfield's testimony in O'Gara v. United States, 560 F. Supp. 786, 790 (E.D. Pa. 1983), and in Robinson v. United States, 533 F. Supp. 320, 328 (E.D. Mich. 1982).

5 Frye v. United States, 293 F. 1013 (D.C. Cir. 1923). See, e.g., Lofgren v. Motorola, Inc., No. CV-93-05521, 1998 WL 299925 (Ariz. Super. Ct. June 1, 1998), *32 (excluding the testimony of plaintiff's expert witness Dr. Kilburn that the injuries were caused by a single exposure to Rubiflex, in part on the grounds that "the conclusion appeared to be more litigation-driven than science oriented").

6 Daubert v. Merrell Dow Pharm., Inc., 509 U.S. 579, 594 (1993) ("*Daubert* III"); see, e.g., Burleson v. Tex. Dep't of Criminal Justice, 393 F.3d 577, 584 (5th Cir. 2004) ("Dr. Carson's 'radiation hot spot theory' is nothing more than litigation-driven speculation, not science"); Prohaska v. Sofamor, S.N.C., 138 F. Supp. 2d 422, 437 (W.D.N.Y. 2001) (Dr. Austin's testimony that pedicle screws manufactured by the defendant were defective excluded because "[l] itigation-driven expertise has been found to be a negative factor in admissibility"); Downs v. Perstorp Components, Inc., 126 F. Supp. 2d 1090, 1094, 1129 (E.D. Tenn. 1999) (excluding Dr. Kilburn's testimony because it "appeared to be more litigation-driven than science oriented," and is "based upon nothing more than conjecture, speculation, and litigation animus") (internal citations omitted); Mancuso v. Consol. Edison Co. of N.Y., Inc., 967 F. Supp. 1437, 1445 (S.D.N.Y. 1997) (Dr. Schwartz's testimony that PCB exposure caused Mr. Mancuso's ailments inadmissible because he "rel[ied] upon plaintiffs' attorney to provide him with the scientific literature"); Celotex Corp. v. AIU Ins. Co. (*In re* Celotex Corp.), 196 B.R. 973, 984–85 (Bankr. M.D. Fla. 1996) ("[T]he 'scientific' evidence regarding asbestos ... in buildings ... [seems] more litigation driven than science driven."); Nelson v. Tenn. Gas Pipeline Co., No 95-1112, 1998 WL 1297690, *8, *13 (W.D. Tenn. Aug. 31, 1998) (excluding Dr. Kilburn's testimony partly on the grounds that his study "was performed in connection with litigation and funded by plaintiffs' counsel," and Dr. Hirsch's partly on the grounds of his "failure to have ... conducted prelitigation research").

In §1, I will look in some detail at two Bendectin cases: *Daubert* itself, and *Blum*—the Pennsylvania case mentioned briefly in "Peer Review and Publication"[7]—which was initiated years before *Daubert*, in 1982, but didn't come to a final resolution until 2000.[8] In both cases we find expert opinion criticized as based on "litigation-driven science"—though in *Daubert* this criticism was directed at the reliability of the *plaintiff's* experts' testimony, while in *Blum* it was directed at the legitimacy of the "scientific consensus" to which the *defendants'* experts appealed; and both Judge Kozinski (in *Daubert*) and Judge Bernstein (in *Blum*) try to articulate why litigation-driven science is apt to be less dependable than independently-conducted research. In §2, I will explore the differences between investigation, plain and simple, and "advocacy research"; and then clear up an ambiguity in "litigation-driven" and some unclarities in "reliable." This will reveal that research that is litigation-driven in the stronger of the two senses distinguished is inherently in danger of bias, and in consequence is inherently less likely to be—at least in one understanding of that somewhat elusive concept—reliable in the legal sense. This in turn will suggest some conclusions, articulated in §3. There is some truth, as both Judge Kozinski and Judge Bernstein argue, in the idea that litigation-driven science is likely to be unreliable. But there is something not quite right about Judge Kozinski's arguments for this conclusion; and the flaws in his arguments reveal that his new *Daubert* factor is not, after all, as helpful as he hopes, or as it might initially seem. This diagnosis leads to some disturbing thoughts about how scientific work can be distorted and impeded when it gets entangled with litigation, and some hard questions about these interactions of science with the law.

1 A LEGAL THICKET: THE TORTUOUS TALE OF *DAUBERT* AND *BLUM*

Merrell Dow Pharmaceuticals had taken Bendectin off the market in 1983, shortly after the first reports appeared of children with limb defects being born to women who had taken the drug[9]—though the company maintained that the withdrawal was prompted, not by the alleged dangers, but by the potential costs of litigation.[10] Bendectin litigation continued, of course, for many years

7 "Peer Review and Publication: Lessons for Lawyers," pp. 156–79 in this volume.

8 Blum v. Merrell Dow Pharm., Inc., 1 Pa. D. & C.4th 634 (Phila. Cnty. Ct. 1988) ("*Blum* I"), *rev'd*, 560 A.2d 212 (Pa. Super. Ct. 1989) ("*Blum* II"), *aff'd*, 626 A.2d 537 (Pa. 1993) ("*Blum* III"), *remanded to* 33 Phila. Cnty. Rep. 193 (1996) ("*Blum* IV"), *rev'd*, 705 A.2d 1314 (Pa. Super. 1997) ("*Blum* V"), *aff'd*, 764 A.2d 1 (Pa. 2000) ("*Blum* VI").

9 *See* Michael H. Gottesman, "From *Barefoot* to *Daubert* to *Joiner*: Triple Play or Double Error?" *Arizona Law Review* 40 (1998): 753–80, 767.

10 Astara March, "Drug Revived to Fight Morning Sickness," *Nurse Week* (October 11, 2000), available at http://www.nurseweek.com/news/00-10/1011morn.asp. Duchesnay Inc. sells

after the drug was withdrawn. The first trial in *Daubert*—an apparently routine Bendectin case, that would, however, in due course become the Supreme Court's leading case on scientific testimony—was held in 1989.[11]

The Dauberts proffered experts to testify that their re-analyses of the existing data showed a statistical link between Bendectin and limb-reduction birth defects; that Bendectin causes birth defects in laboratory animals, and so probably causes them in humans too; and that Bendectin is chemically similar to other drugs suspected of causing such defects.[12] Merrell Dow's attorneys presented evidence that no clinical trial had ever been published that showed Bendectin to be teratogenic;[13] that despite a wave of Bendectin litigation the FDA had continued to approve the drug for use by pregnant women, because "available data do not demonstrate an association between birth defects and Bendectin";[14] and that the consensus among medical scientists was that the drug was safe.[15]

the chemically identical drug under the name "Diclectin," in Canada; and at that time was seeking FDA approval to sell it in the US. Declectin, http://www.diclectin.com/index.html. At an FDA/NIH conference held on December 4, 2000, Dr. Gideon Koren of the University of Toronto asked "How safe is safe?" and answered that while in the first meta-analysis, conducted in Toronto, there were 130,000 case controls, and an odds ratio of 1.0, "there was a confidence interval going to 155, which means we cannot say for sure that there isn't a 55 percent increased risk." "Interface of Clinical Pharmacology and Drug Safety" at FDA/NIH Conference (December 4, 2000), available at http://www.fda.gov/cder/present/clinpharm2000/1204preg.txt.

In 2013, the FDA approved a version of Duchesnay's drug, now under the name Diclegis, for use in the US. "FDA approves Diclegis for pregnant women experiencing nausea and vomiting," *FDA News Release* (April 8, 2013), available at http://www.fda.gov.NewsEvents/Newsroon/PressAnnouncments/ucm347087.htm. (The FDA's announcement tells us that "Diclegis was tested in 261 women experiencing nausea and vomiting due to pregnancy," assigned randomly to the control group or to the group—presumably 130 or 131 subjects—who were given the drug for two weeks between the seventh and the fourteenth week of pregnancy (the others were given a placebo); and that the drug was found to be effective. All it says abut safety is that epidemiological studies "have shown that the combination of active ingredients in Diclegis does not pose an increased risk to the fetus." *Id.*

11 Daubert v. Merrell Dow Pharm., Inc., 727 F. Supp. 570 (S.D. Cal. 1989) ("*Daubert* I").

12 *Daubert* IV (note 3 above), 1314.

13 A teratogen (the word comes from the Greek, *teras*, meaning "monster") is a substance that causes birth defects.

14 *United States Department of Health and Human Services News*, No. P80–45 (October 7, 1980). The ruling in *Daubert* IV ends the quotation here; however, it continues "[Bendectin] should be used only when conservative treatment fails." Joseph Sanders, "From Science to Evidence: The Testimony on Causation in the Bendectin Cases," *Stanford Law Review* 46, no. 1 (1993): 1–86, 7. According to the FDA *Orange Book Detail Record*, "[Bendectin] was not discontinued or withdrawn for safety or efficacy reasons." Bendectin: FDA Approved Drugs, http://www.fdaapproveddrugs.us/bendectin.html.

15 *Daubert* IV (note 3 above), 1314.

Before *Daubert*, the *Frye* Rule had been used almost exclusively in criminal cases.[16] Unusually, however, in *Daubert* the trial court (citing *United States v. Kilgus* (1978) and *Barrel of Fun v. State Farm Fire and Casualty Co.* (1984))[17] had implicitly relied on *Frye* in ruling the plaintiffs' expert evidence inadmissible.[18] The Dauberts' proffered scientific testimony had not, as *Frye* requires, gained general acceptance in the field to which it belongs; for, the court continues, this would require that there be statistically significant epidemiological evidence of causation,[19] but "none of the *published* studies show a statistically significant association between the use of Bendectin and birth defects."[20] So the trial court granted Merrell Dow summary judgment; and in 1991 (citing *United States v. Solomon* (1985)),[21] the US Court of Appeals for the Ninth Circuit affirmed.

The same year, Peter Huber's influential book *Galileo's Revenge* appeared,[22] fueling fears that flimsy, biased, and wildly speculative science was flooding the courts; and some judges on the Federal Rules Advisory Committee were seeking to change Federal Rule of Evidence 702 to include a reliability requirement.[23] But these proposed changes were preempted when the Supreme Court

16 So when Peter Huber argued that *Frye* had helped keep junk science out of tort cases before the FRE relaxed the standards of admissibility, he misrepresented the relevant legal history. See Peter Huber, "Junk Science in the Courtroom," *Valparaiso Law Review* 26 (1992): 723–55; Peter Huber, *Galileo's Revenge: Junk Science in the Courtroom* (New York: Basic Books, 1993), 14–17, 41, 150, 176–77, 199–201, 204. See also Kenneth J. Cheseboro, "Galileo's Retort: Peter Huber's Junk Scholarship," *American University Law Review* 42 (1993): 1637–1726, 1687–96.

17 United States v. Kilgus, 571 F.2d 508, 510 (9th Cir. 1978) (quoting United States v. Brown (Michigan), 557 F.2d 541, 546 (6th Cir. 1977) ("A necessary predicate to the admission of scientific evidence is that the principle upon which it is based 'must be sufficiently established to have gained general acceptance in the particular field to which it belongs'"). This was a criminal case in which testimony identifying the defendant's aircraft using a "forward looking infrared system" had been excluded under *Frye*. *Barrel of Fun* was a fire-insurance fraud case in which polygraph testimony had been excluded under *Frye*. Barrel of Fun, Inc. v. State Farm Fire & Cas. Co., 739 F.2d 1028 (5th Cir. 1984). For more details, see "Proving Causation: The Weight of Combined Evidence," pp. 208–38 in this volume, note 21.

18 Note 11 above.

19 *Daubert* I (note 11 above), 573.

20 *Id.*, 575.

21 Daubert v. Merrell Dow Pharm., Inc., 951 F.2d 1128, 1129–30 (9th Cir. 1991) ("*Daubert* II") (citing United States v. Solomon, 753 F.2d 1522, 1526 (9th Cir. 1985), a murder case in which the higher court affirmed the trial court's exclusion, under *Frye*, of evidence concerning narcoanalysis).

22 Huber, *Galileo's Revenge* (note 16 above).

23 See Gottesman, "From *Barefoot* to *Daubert* to *Joiner*" (note 9 above), 757–59 (citing Preliminary Draft of Proposed Amendments to the Federal Rules of Civil Procedure and the Federal Rules of Evidence, 137 F.R.D. 53, 73, 156 (September 1991) (proposal of the Civil Rules Advisory Committee)); Dan Quayle, "Agenda for Civil Justice Reform in America," *University of Cincinnati Law Review* 60 (1992): 997–1007, 999 (proposal of the President's Competitiveness Committee).

granted *certiorari* in *Daubert*, to determine whether the Federal Rules had or hadn't superseded the older rule. Holding that they had, the Supreme Court reversed and remanded.[24]

Rehearing the case on remand, in a memorable passage that would soon be much cited by judges and legal commentators,[25] Judge Kozinski wrote of the formidable task the Supreme Court had set for him and his colleagues on the federal bench when it interpreted FRE 702 as requiring them to screen scientific testimony for reliability as well as relevance:

> Federal judges ruling on the admissibility of expert scientific testimony face a far more complex and daunting task in a post-*Daubert* world than before.... [T]hough we are largely untrained in science and certainly no match for any of the witnesses whose testimony we are reviewing, it is our responsibility to determine whether those experts' proposed testimony amounts to "scientific knowledge," constitutes "good science," and was "derived by the scientific method." ... [W]e take a deep breath and proceed with this heady task.[26]

The Supreme Court, he noted, didn't supply a "definitive checklist" of indicia of reliability, only an illustrative list of the factors to which courts might look;[27] but this list raised some tricky questions:

> [H]ow do we determine whether the rate of error is acceptable, and by what standard? ... [W]hat should we infer from the fact that the methodology has been tested, but only by the party's own ... experts? Do we ask whether the methodology they employ to test their methodology is itself methodologically

[24] *Daubert* III (note 6 above), 593–94.

[25] See, e.g., Sofia Adrogue, "The Post-*Daubert* Court: 'Amateur Scientist' Gatekeeper or Executioner?" *Houston Lawyer* 35 (1998): 10–16, 10; Mark S. Brodin, "Behavioral Science Evidence in the Age of *Daubert*: Reflections of a Skeptic," *University of Cincinnati Law Review* 73 (2005): 862–943, 867 (2005); Judge Harvey Brown, "Eight Gates for Expert Witnesses," *Houston Law Review* 36 (1999): 743–882, 784; Lee Epstein and Gary King, "Empirical Research and the Goals of Legal Scholarship: The Rules of Inference," *University of Chicago Law Review* 69 (2002): 1–133, 133; David L. Faigman, "The Law's Scientific Revolution: Reflections and Ruminations on the Law's Use of Experts in Year Seven of the Revolution," *Washington and Lee Law Review* 57 (2000): 661–84, 684; G. Michael Fenner, The *Daubert* Handbook: The Case, Its Essential Dilemma, and Its Progeny," *Creighton Law Review* 29 (1996): 939–1089, 1066–67; Robert J. Goodwin, "The Hidden Significance of *Kumho Tire v. Carmichael*: A Compass for Problems of Definition and Procedure Created by *Daubert v. Merrell Dow Pharmaceuticals, Inc.*,' *Baylor Law Review* 52 (2000): 603–46, 646 n.60.

[26] *Daubert* IV (note 3 above), 1315–16.

[27] As the Court confirmed in *Kumho Tire Co. v. Carmichael*, 526 U.S. 137, 138 (1999) (quoting *Daubert* III (note 6 above), 594): "A trial judge determining the admissibility of an engineering expert's testimony *may* consider one or more of the specific *Daubert* factors. The emphasis on the word 'may' reflects *Daubert*'s description of the Rule 702 inquiry as 'a flexible one.'"

> sound? ... [T]he basic problem ... is that we must devise standards for acceptability where respected scientists disagree on what's acceptable.[28]

Reviewing the Supreme Court's flexible list of indicia of reliability, Judge Kozinski proposes a new "*Daubert* factor" of his own: whether the proffered expert testimony is based on work undertaken in the normal course of scientific business, or on work conducted specifically for the purposes of litigation. He stresses the likely flaws and failings of litigation-driven science:

> One very significant fact to be considered is whether the experts are proposing to testify about matters growing naturally and directly out of research they have conducted independent of the litigation, or whether they have developed their opinion expressly for purposes of testifying. That an expert testifies for money does not necessarily cast doubt on the reliability of his testimony, as few experts appear in court merely as an eleemosynary gesture. But in determining whether proposed expert testimony amounts to good science, we may not ignore the fact that a scientist's normal workplace is the lab or the field, not the courtroom or the lawyer's office.[29]

Referring to Huber's book, Judge Kozinski suggests that the fact that an expert testifies on the basis of work he has conducted independent of litigation "provides important, objective proof that the research comports with the dictates of good science";[30] and that the fact that research is litigation-driven is an indication that it may *not* comport with those dictates. In this context he cites Judge Johnson's ruling in *Perry* (1985): "the examination of a scientific study by a cadre of lawyers is not the same as its examination by others trained in the field of science or medicine."[31]

Judge Kozinski gives two main reasons why science conducted independently of the needs of litigation is more likely to be reliable than litigation-driven science:

(a) "[E]xperts whose findings flow from existing research are less likely to have been biased toward a particular conclusion by the promise of remuneration."

[28] *Daubert* IV (note 3 above), 1316–17 n.3.

[29] *Id.*, 1317 (footnote omitted).

[30] *Ibid.*

[31] *Id.*, 1318 n.8 (citing *Perry* (note 4 above), 892). Now, of course, this stress on the important differences between in-court "testing" by cross-examination and testing in the sciences will bring to mind Judge Pollak's comments about fingerprint identification. United States v. Llera Plaza, Nos. CR 98–362–10, 98–362–11, 98–362–12, 2002 WL 27305, *10 (E.D. Pa. Jan. 7, 2002) ("Llera Plaza I").

(b) "[I]ndependent research carries its own indicia of reliability, as it is conducted ... in the usual course of business and must normally satisfy a variety of standards to attract funding and institutional support."[32]

Referring again to Huber's book, Judge Kozinski suggests that proffered scientific testimony that is not based on research conducted independently of litigation requires some other indication of reliability;[33] specifically, he suggests, had their work been subjected to peer review and publication, this would provide some assurance that the plaintiffs' experts' research was in accordance with the scientific method, as understood by at least a minority of the relevant scientific community. But not only had the plaintiffs' proffered experts conducted their work for the purposes of litigation; not one of them had published his Bendectin research in peer-reviewed journals, as they had their other scientific work. Given that their findings would surely be of interest to the scientific community, Judge Kozinski continues, the fact that they had been unable or unwilling to publish them undermines the idea that these results are, as the *Daubert* standards required, "grounded in the methods and procedures of science."[34]

In a startling but tantalizingly brief footnote to which we shall have to return in due course, he adds that "there are, of course, exceptions"—kinds of litigation-driven science of which, he believes, there is no reason to be skeptical. Some forensic sciences, such as fingerprinting or DNA identification techniques, "have the courtroom as a principal theatre of operations"; but here the fact that an expert has developed an expertise primarily for purposes of litigation "will obviously not be a substantial consideration."[35]

Early in his ruling, Judge Kozinski had observed that "apart from the small but determined group of scientists testifying on behalf of the Bendectin plaintiffs in this and many other cases, there doesn't appear to be a single scientist who has concluded that Bendectin causes limb reduction defects";[36] under *Frye*, which had been the law of the circuit at the time the Dauberts' experts submitted their affidavits, their testimony would certainly have to be excluded. However, given that the law had changed in the meantime, they might have been given an opportunity to submit additional proof that their proffered evidence was, as required by *Daubert*, "derived by the scientific method"—but for the fact, Judge Kozinski argues, that it was already clear this wouldn't change

32 *Id.*, 1317.
33 *Id.*, 1316–17.
34 *Id.*, 1318 & n.9 (citing *Daubert* III (note 6 above), 589–90).
35 *Id.*, 1317 n.5.
36 *Id.*, 1314.

the outcome: the Dauberts' proffered expert testimony would clearly have to be excluded under the new standards, as it was under the old.[37]

Surprisingly, however, Judge Kozinski's reasoning to this conclusion makes little use of the idea that litigation-driven science is especially suspect. In fact—despite his mock-modest announcement at the outset that he will "take a deep breath and proceed with [the] heady task" of assessing the reliability of the proffered science—it leaves scientific issues essentially untouched. Moreover, it calls on the reliability prong of *Daubert* with respect to only one of the plaintiffs' experts, Dr. Palmer—the only proffered expert who would testify that Bendectin actually *did* cause Jason Daubert's birth defects, rather than that it *could possibly* have caused them; and the fact that Dr. Palmer's research was litigation-driven plays no specific role in Judge Kozinski's argument why it would have to be excluded, which is simply that "Dr. Palmer offers no tested or testable theory to explain how … he was able to eliminate all other potential causes of birth defects."[38] The other proffered experts, who would speak in terms of probabilities, would have to be excluded under the relevance prong; for none of them even claimed to show—as, Judge Kozinski wrote, California law required[39]—that Bendectin more than doubles the risk of such defects.[40]

~

Like Mrs. Daubert, Mrs. Blum took Bendectin for morning-sickness; like Jason Daubert, Jeffrey Blum was born with severe defects—in his case, clubbed feet; like the Dauberts, the Blums believed Bendectin was the cause of their child's birth defects. In 1982, seven years before the Dauberts, Jeffrey Blum's parents brought suit against Merrell Dow; and the case slowly wound its way through the Pennsylvania courts for eighteen years before being finally resolved, five years after *Daubert*, in 2000.

The first trial ended in 1987 with a jury verdict for the plaintiffs.[41] Merrell Dow appealed, on the grounds that the verdict had been reached by only

37 *Id.*, 1319–20.

38 *Id.*, 1319.

39 This claim was at best misleading; but I won't pursue that here, since it is discussed at length in "Risky Business: Statistical Proof of Specific Causation," pp. 264–93 in this volume, 275–81, 291.

40 *Id.*, 1320–21 ("California tort law requires … that plaintiffs must establish not just that their mothers' ingestion of Bendectin increased somewhat the likelihood of birth defects, but that it more than doubled [the risk]…. None of plaintiffs' epidemiological experts claims that ingestion of Bendectin during pregnancy more than doubles the risk of birth defects."); see also Sanders, "From Science to Evidence" (note 14 above), 16 n.63, on this standard for proof of specific causation. The more-than-doubled-risk criterion is discussed at length in "Risky Business" (note 39 above).

41 *Blum* I (note 8 above), 635.

11 jurors (the twelfth had fallen ill part-way through the trial); and in 1993 was granted a new trial.[42] On remand, in 1996 the Court of Common Pleas again entered judgment on jury verdict for the plaintiffs (this time with the full complement of jurors).[43] Merrell Dow appealed again, this time on the grounds that the plaintiffs' scientific testimony should have been excluded by the court; the jury—on the vital importance of which they had earlier insisted!—should never have been allowed to hear it. In 1997, the Superior Court held that plaintiffs' expert testimony regarding the causal link between Bendectin and birth defects was not admissible under *Frye*, and remanded the case with instructions to the trial court to enter judgment *n.o.v.* in favor of Merrell Dow.[44] In 1999, the Supreme Court of Pennsylvania granted *allocatur*[45] to consider whether the *Frye* Rule still governed the admissibility of expert scientific testimony in Pennsylvania, or had been superseded by *Daubert*. In 2000, declining to replace *Frye* by (what it took to be)[46] the more relaxed standards of *Daubert*, but arguing that the Blums' expert testimony was inadmissible under either standard, the Pennsylvania Supreme Court affirmed the decision of the Superior Court in favor of the defendant manufacturers.[47]

While Merrell Dow had maintained that the plaintiffs' proffered expert scientific testimony should have been excluded because it wasn't generally accepted in the scientific community, the Blums' attorneys had maintained that Merrell Dow's expert testimony should have been excluded because the supposed "scientific consensus" on this matter was largely Merrell Dow's doing: the agreement in the field was an artifact of the company's support of favorable research and of dubious journals that would publish results helpful to the company in defending itself against Bendectin litigation. Dissenting in

42 *Blum* III (note 8 above), 549.

43 *Blum* IV (note 8 above), 243.

44 *Blum* V (note 8 above), 1325. (The term "*n.o.v*" is short for "*non obstante veredicto*," "notwithstanding the verdict").

45 "*Allocatur*" (pronounced with the accent on the first syllable, as in "allocate") is the Pennsylvania equivalent of "*certiorari*." Timothy P. Wile and Marc A. Werlinsky, *West's Pennsylvania Practice Driving Under the Influence* (St. Paul, MN: Thomson/West, 2006–07 ed.) §30:53 (explaining that "[a]nother name for allowance of appeal is *allocatur*".)

46 The Supreme Court's rhetoric had described the *Frye* Rule as an "austere standard" which the Federal Rules had relaxed. *Daubert* III (note 6 above), 589. Other states besides Pennsylvania—Florida, for one—also took this rhetoric at face value. Brim v. State, 695 So. 2d 268, 271–72 (Fla. 1997) ("[d]espite the federal adoption of a more lenient standard … we [Florida] have maintained the higher standard of reliability as dictated by *Frye*").In 2013 Florida adapted its Rule of Evidence 702, becoming in effect a *Daubert* state. For details, see "Irreconcilable Differences" (note 2 above), note 102.

47 *Blum* VI (note 8 above), 4–5.

part from the Pennsylvania Supreme Court's final disposition of the case in favor of Merrell Dow, Justice Castille summed up the issue like this:

> [I]n the litigation-driven Bendectin "scientific community" described to the court in this case, the notion of "general acceptance" or scientific "orthodoxy"... on the question of causation was a questionable proposition to begin with ... because the trial court had heard extensive evidence concerning Merrell Dow's active and deliberate role, motivated by its litigation interests, ... in actually creating and influencing the scientific orthodoxy that would then operate to suppress any contrary opinion that might harm its Bendectin litigation.[48]

Justice Castille refers us to Judge Bernstein's ruling at the second trial.

As we saw in "Peer Review and Publication," the tone of Judge Bernstein's ruling is unusually impassioned. It opens with a remarkable excerpt from the testimony of James Newberne, Merrell Dow's Vice-President for Drug Safety:

> Q: Sir, it has been the pattern and practice and custom of the Merrell Company, in reporting to the FDA, to pick and choose selective information over the past thirty years, relating to the drug Bendectin; correct?
>
> A: Yes; that's correct.[49]

Judge Bernstein first summarizes the testimony of the Blums' expert witnesses (including some who had been unsuccessfully proffered by the Dauberts),[50] and then subjects the testimony given by Merrell Dow's experts to devastating scrutiny.

Plaintiffs' expert Dr. Gross testified that a review of Merrell Dow's animal testing revealed that there were significant numbers of abnormalities, including club limbs, that weren't reported to the FDA.[51] Dr. Done testified to the chemical similarity of doxylamine succinate, one of the active ingredients in Bendectin, to other known teratogens; to *in vitro* studies showing its detrimental effect on limb bud cells; and to his re-analyses of two epidemiological studies which, in his opinion, showed an increased risk of clubfeet in the infants of women who took Bendectin in the first four months of pregnancy.[52] Dr. Newman testified that doxylamine succinate can pass through the

[48] *Id.*, 7–8 (Castille, J., dissenting). Justice Castille later returns to the issue, citing his own dissenting opinion in *Blum* in his concurring opinion in Grady v. Frito-Lay, Inc., 839 A.2d 1038, 1048 (Pa. 2003) (Castille, J., concurring).

[49] *Blum* IV (note 8 above), 194 (footnote omitted).

[50] Among the Dauberts' proffered experts were Dr. Gross, Dr. Newman, and Dr. Done. *Daubert* IV (note 3 above), 1321 & n.14.

[51] *Blum* IV (note 8 above), 202.

[52] *Id.*, 203–06.

placental barrier and affect the embryo.[53] The testimony given by Dr. Stolley at the previous trial, that there was three times the risk of malformations in babies whose mothers had filled more than one prescription for Bendectin, was read into evidence.[54]

Most important here, however, is Judge Bernstein's summary of, and scathing commentary on, Merrell Dow's experts' testimony:

- Defense expert Dr. Bracken, a professor of epidemiology at Yale, testified that his study (based on interviews with 1,427 mothers, of whom only 122 had taken Bendectin) concluded that Bendectin carried no significant risk of birth defects except for pyloric stenosis; however, he acknowledged that it showed there was a more than two-and-a half times greater risk of birth defects in infants born to women who took Bendectin and also smoked. On cross-examination, he agreed not only that articles that are "less than good" can pass peer review, but also that his own published study of Bendectin and birth defects was less than good.[55]
- Defense expert Dr. Klebanoff, who began his work on Bendectin long after the drug was taken off the market, testified that Bendectin does not cause birth defects; but acknowledged that his own article showed a statistically significant association with congenital cataracts, underdevelopment of the lungs, and microcephaly. Under cross-examination, he agreed that Bendectin is positively associated with clubbed feet.[56]
- Defense expert Dr. Tyl, a developmental toxicologist, was hired by the federal government, also long after Bendectin had been withdrawn, to perform animal studies on the drug. She testified that "Bendectin is not a teratogen, but it is a 'developmental toxicant,'" and that as a result of her work the drug had been placed on the "List of Developmental Toxicants" maintained by the US Government. A developmental toxicant, she explained, is defined as an indicator of such defects as reduced body weight, reduced survival, increased number of variations, reduced ossification, and certain morphological changes.[57]
- Defense expert Dr. Shapiro (whose formal training in epidemiology amounted only to 11 credits towards a Master's degree) was head of the Slone Center for Epidemiology at Boston University in a period when the unit received over one-and-a-half million dollars in research-

53 *Id.*, 206.
54 *Ibid.*
55 *Id.*, 207–08.
56 *Id.*, 208–09.
57 *Id.*, 209–14.

support funds from Merrell Dow. He testified that Bendectin could not cause birth defects. However, the data on which he based his opinion lumped together women who took Bendectin during the period when limbs were forming, and those who took the drug only after the baby's limbs had formed. He agreed that this resulted in an underestimate of the incidence of clubfeet in the group exposed to Bendectin, but refused to attribute any significance to this. If Bendectin did cause birth defects, he explained, his study might have underestimated the risk; but since Bendectin doesn't cause birth defects, his study could not have done so.[58]

- Defense expert Dr. Newberne admitted that Merrell Dow had engaged in a consistent pattern of under-reporting of adverse effects of Bendectin to the FDA. He acknowledged that in the period when a study by Dr. Smithells supposedly showing the safety of Bendectin had been rejected by the *British Medical Journal*, the *Lancet*, and the *New England Journal of Medicine*, and eventually was accepted by the much less prestigious journal *Teratology*, the author was actively seeking funds from the company, writing that "much clearly depends upon the value of this publication to Merrell Dow.... If it may save the company large sums of money ... in the California court (which is rather what I thought when we undertook this study), they may feel magnanimous." Dr. Newberne also testified that Merrell Dow had supported Dr. Shapiro's research at Boston University and Dr. Hendrickx's in California out of its legal defense funds.[59]
- Defense expert Dr. Brent, the editor of *Teratology*, who had been retained as an expert by Merrell Dow for 18 years, testified that his only formal education in epidemiology was one course in statistics; but considered himself the world authority in "secular trend data"—a scientific field in which, Judge Bernstein adds, there was apparently only one practitioner, Dr. Brent himself. Using his editorial prerogative to sidestep peer review, he had published in his own journal an article entitled "Litigation-Produced Pain, Disease, and Suffering: An Experience with Congenital Malformation Lawsuits" which concluded, based on his review of deposition and trial transcripts, that seventeen out of seventeen

[58] *Id.*, 214–17. (The record says that Dr. Shapiro was head of the Department of Epidemiology at Boston University, but Dr. Richard Clapp of the Boston University School of Public Health tells me this is incorrect.)

[59] *Id.*, 218–22.

> plaintiffs lied.[60] He also testified that he had submitted a draft article entitled "Bendectin: The Most Comprehensively Studied Human Non-Teratogen, and the Foremost Teratogen[*sic*]-Litigen" to Merrell Dow's attorneys for editing, hoping to publish it in the *New England Journal of Medicine*, the *Journal of the American Medical Association*, or *Obstetrics and Gynecology*.[61]

Dr. Newberne's testimony, Judge Bernstein comments, revealed "[t]he interaction of 'scientific studies' and litigation defense";[62] and Dr. Brent's testimony "clearly revealed a sycophantic relationship between Dr. Brent and the attorneys representing Merrell Dow."[63] But most immediately to the present purpose is Judge Bernstein's exasperated commentary on Dr. Shapiro's testimony: When asked by the court whether his study underestimated the risks of Bendectin, Dr. Shapiro replied, "yes"; but immediately went on to add that what he meant was only that, if there *were* a causal relationship, it *would have been* underestimated, but "[i]f there were no causal relationship, which is what I believe, ... there could not have been any underestimates." "The circularity

60 Robert L. Brent, "Litigation-Produced Pain, Disease, and Suffering: An Experience with Congenital Malformation Lawsuits," *Teratology* 16, no.1 (1977):1–13.

61 *Blum* IV (note 8 above), 223–28. The article in question appears to be Robert L. Brent, "Bendectin: Review of the Medical Literature of a Comprehensively Studied Human Nonteratogen and the Most Prevalent Tortogen-Litigen," *Reproductive Toxicology* 9, no.4 (1995): 337–49 (the ruling has the subtitle wrong). This paper prompted a lawsuit for defamation by Dr. Stuart A. Newman (one of the Blums' experts), whom Dr. Brent had misquoted, against Dr. Brent and the editor of *Reproductive Toxicology*. Newman v. Brent, Civ. No. 97–1647 (TFH), 1998 U.S. Dist. LEXIS 10476 (D.D.C. July 8, 1998). At the suggestion of the presiding judge, the parties were invited to air their differences in a scientific forum. See Stuart A. Newman, "Dr. Brent and Scientific Debate," *Reproductive Toxicology* 13, no.4 (1999): 241–44, 242 (complaining of the "partisan" nature of Dr. Brent's work, which "should have raised questions about the objectivity of the peer review and editorial process," and noting his association with the law firm of Dinsmore & Shohl, which represented Merrell Dow in many of its Bendectin cases); Robert L. Brent, "Response to Dr. Stuart Newman's Commentary on an Article Entitled "Bendectin: Review of the Medical Literature of a Comprehensively Studied Human Nonteratogen and the Most Prevalent Tortogen-Litigen," *Reproductive Toxicology* 13, no.4 (1999): 245–53 (pointing out that Dr. Newman's testimony had been excluded in several Bendectin cases); Stuart A. Newman, "A Response to Dr. Brent's Commentary on 'Dr. Brent and Scientific Debate,'" *Reproductive Toxicology* 13, no. 4 (1999): 255–60, 256 (noting that much of Dr. Brent's response relies on judges' opinions regarding scientific issues). See also Robert L. Brent, "Bendectin and Birth Defects: Hopefully, the Final Chapter," *Birth Defects Research* Part A, 67 (2003): 79–87 (urging the reintroduction of Bendectin as effective and harmless).

62 *Blum* IV (note 8 above), 222. See also "Peer Review and Publication," (note 7 above).

63 *Id.*, 225 (responding to Dr Brent's claim that there was "a sycophantic alliance between the expert witness and the plaintiff's attorney").

of this reasoning," Judge Bernstein comments, makes it unmistakably clear that Dr. Shapiro was engaged in "justification science not inquisitive science"; and, he continues, "Clearly revealed in this testimony is the unalterable preconception from which Dr. Shapiro's 'scientific conclusion' was derived."[64] Dr. Shapiro's conviction that Bendectin is not teratogenic was so firm from the outset that he was virtually impervious to any evidence that might suggest otherwise.

~

Is Bendectin teratogenic? After reading only *Daubert*, an intelligent, fair-minded layperson would have to say: "very likely not." After reading *Blum*, however, he would have to say, as I would: "I'm not quite so sure as before; it all seems very confusing, and I'd need a lot of time and work, not to mention intelligent and fair-minded help, to form an opinion." Maybe Merrell Dow overstepped ethical boundaries in protecting its interests, in that self-defeating way to which defendant manufacturers seem prone;[65] maybe they really had something to hide. For someone outside the relevant fields, it's very hard to know.[66] My purpose here isn't to settle that question, but to explore some of the epistemological issues raised by the intertwining stories of *Daubert* and *Blum*.

64 *Id.*, 217.

65 I am thinking here, for example, of the instructions to salespeople uncovered by Dan Bolton, attorney for Maria Stern in her 1984 case against Dow Corning alleging injuries caused by her silicone breast-implants. The incriminating memo reads, in part: "[I]t has been observed that the new mammaries with responsive gel have a tendency to appear oily after being manipulated. This could prove to be a problem with your detailing activity. ... You should make plans to change samples often. Also, be sure that samples are clean and dry before customer detailing." Marcia Angell, *Science on Trial: The Clash of Medical Evidence and the Law in the Breast Implant Case* (New York: W. W. Norton, 1996), 59.

66 Professor Sanders provides a pretty thorough survey of the relevant science as presented in Bendectin cases prior to 1993. Sanders (note 14 above). His conclusion is that the weight of the scientific work indicated that Bendectin is probably not teratogenic, but that the evidence presented to juries in Bendectin cases did not accurately represent the true state of the science. *Id.*, 3. He acknowledges, however, that some *in vivo* studies had shown a teratogenic effects; that six epidemiological studies had found a statistically significant correlation between Bendectin and certain types of defect; that many studies failed to pinpoint the time in pregnancy during which mothers took Bendectin; and that the presence of the suspect ingredient, doxylamine succinate, in two over-the-counter drugs (Unisom and Nyquil) that some subjects may have taken could have skewed study results. *Id.*, 25–6. Professor Sanders's description of some of the supposedly reassuring animal-testing work undertaken by Merrell Dow in 1966–67, in the wake of the Thalidomide disaster, also leaves one a little uneasy: "Although their test animals suffered several defects, Newberne and Gibson did not attribute the defects to Bendectin." *Id.*, 21.

2 AN EPISTEMOLOGICAL SWAMP: THE SINKING SANDS OF "LITIGATION-DRIVEN" AND "EVIDENTIARY RELIABILITY"

In the present context we need to understand, at a minimum: the difference between inquiry and advocacy; the nature of advocacy research; the contrast between disinterestedness and bias; and the relation of all these to issues about truth and reliability.

Inquiry, investigation—the professional business of scientists, historians, legal and literary scholars, investigative journalists, and so forth—is a matter of trying to discover the answer to some question: who committed the crime, what caused the cancer or made it advance so quickly, where the money went, etc. Advocacy, by contrast—the professional business of lobbyists, attorneys, and so on—is a matter of trying to persuade an audience of the truth of some proposition: that my client didn't do it, that it was work-related PCB exposure that promoted the tumor, that the stolen money has been hidden in a numbered account in a Swiss bank, etc.

Magistrate Judge Breen observes in *Nelson* that we want expert opinions to be "about science, not advocacy."[67] That distinction is clear enough; but the most relevant distinction here is between inquiry, investigation, or (as we might say) "real research," i.e., really trying to find the true answer to some question, whatever that truth may be, and advocacy research, i.e., trying to find the strongest possible evidence for the truth of some proposition determined in advance. This, I take it, was the distinction Judge Bernstein had in mind when he contrasted Dr. Shapiro's "justification science" (i.e., advocacy research) with "inquisitive science" (i.e., real research, or as I shall also say, inquiry plain and simple).

Distinguishing genuine inquiry, the real thing, from pseudo-inquiry or "sham reasoning," C. S. Peirce—a working scientist as well as the greatest of American philosophers—wrote that "[t]he spirit ... is the most essential thing—the motive"; that genuine inquiry consists in "actually drawing the bow upon truth with intentness in the eye, with energy in the arm."[68] For the same reason, I am tempted to write of "real research" but of "advocacy [scare quotes] 'research'"; for it is something of a stretch to call advocacy research "research" at all. Advocacy research is like inquiry insofar as it involves seeking out evidence. But it is part of an advocacy project insofar as it involves seeking out evidence favoring a predetermined conclusion; and it is undertaken

[67] Nelson (note 6 above), *9.

[68] Charles Sanders Peirce, *Collected Papers*, eds. Charles Hartshorne, Paul Weiss, and (vols. 7 and 8) Arthur Burks (Cambridge, MA: Harvard University Press, 1931–58), 1.34 (1903) and 1.235 (1902).

in the spirit, from the motive, of an advocate. In short, it is a kind of pseudo-inquiry.

There's nothing wrong with advocacy, as such. There's nothing wrong, even, with a scientist taking on the role of advocate—even on matters related to his own field; indeed, it might be argued that if a medical or environmental scientist, for example, discovers a hitherto unsuspected health risk or benefit, he has a moral obligation to bring it to the public's attention as effectively as possible. But there *is* something epistemologically wrong with advocacy research. Investigating the risks and benefits of taking this dietary supplement or damming that river is a quite different enterprise from advocating that the supplement be banned or that the dam be built; and while it is highly desirable that advocacy be based on the results of well-conducted investigation, it is highly *un*desirable that advocacy be allowed to slant investigation.

Obviously enough, someone straightforwardly investigating a question and someone engaged in advocacy research on behalf of a particular answer take different attitudes to the evidence. The plain-and-simple inquirer wants to find the answer (though the upshot may be a realization that his question was in some way misconceived; and when he does find an answer, he will often find himself faced with a slew of new questions). He is motivated to seek out all the evidence he can lay hands on, to weigh it as judiciously as possible, to assess where it leads as carefully as he can, and to suspend judgment unless and until his evidence warrants drawing a conclusion. An advocacy researcher, by contrast, is motivated to seek out all the evidence that favors his predetermined conclusion, but to ignore, play down, or explain away any evidence contrary to that conclusion.

So, (other things being equal), because he is motivated to seek out all the evidence, the plain-and-simple inquirer will be *more thorough* than the advocacy researcher looking only for favorable evidence; because he is concerned to find the answer whatever the answer may be, he will be *less partial* than the advocacy researcher trying to minimize the importance of unfavorable evidence he can neither ignore nor explain away; and, because he is ready to acknowledge evidence either way, he will be *more honest* than the advocacy researcher trying to disguise what doesn't suit his purpose. This is why he is likelier than an advocacy researcher—again, other things (his ability, energy, resources, etc.) being equal—to discover the truth; the more so, the longer he inquires.

Connections with the concepts of interestedness and bias now begin to come into focus. In one sense, to describe an inquirer as "interested" means that he takes an interest in the question he is investigating (he isn't bored by it or uninterested in it, nor is he just dutifully but unenthusiastically doing what is required by his job or demanded by his Ph.D. supervisor). In another and potentially more problematic sense, it means that he has an interest in the answer to the question coming out this way rather than that, i.e., he stands to gain in some way from reaching this conclusion rather than a different one. And in a third sense, the most problematic, an interested investigator is really only an "investigator"; for the way he proceeds is distorted by his desire that the answer come out in the way by which he stands to gain. Often, but not always or inevitably, someone who is interested in the second sense is also interested in the third.

It is the third sense that chiefly concerns us here; for an "inquirer" who is interested in this sense is bound to be biased: that is, to lean in one direction, to play up the evidence on one side of his question and play down anything negative. (This reveals the connection between the two senses of "partial": an investigator who is partial, in the sense of "biased towards one side of an issue," will concentrate selectively on evidence that is partial, in the sense of "incomplete.")

Peirce's prime example of sham reasoning was the "seminary philosophy" dominant in his day. Theologians, he argued, being professionally committed to the truth of certain propositions, are professionally obliged to adjust their philosophical arguments so as to preserve and support those propositions.[69] So perhaps it's no wonder that a prime contemporary example that comes to my mind is the "research" offered by its proponents in favor of Intelligent Design Theory. So far as I can see, this amounts only to efforts, often botched, and sometimes apparently outright dishonest,[70] to identify "gaps and problems" in the theory of evolution, and to cover up the much more formidable gaps and problems in Intelligent Design Theory.[71] Judge Jones's analysis in

69 *Id.*, 1.620 (1898).

70 For example, the Intelligent Design biology text, Percival Davis and Dean Kenyon, *Of Pandas and People* (Dallas, TX: Haughton Publishing Co., 3rd ed., 1993), 104, stresses the absence of transitional fossils of creatures between fishes and amphibians, and the large differences between the two. But when in 2006 it was announced that scientists had discovered the fossil remains of the 375 million-year-old crocodile-headed giant fish, the tiktaalik, which appears to have been precisely such a transitional creature, a spokesperson for the Discovery Institute, which has been aggressively promoting Intelligent Design Theory, professed unconcern: "few leading [Intelligent Design] researchers have argued against the existence of transitional forms." John Noble Wilford, "Fossil Called Missing Link from Sea to Land Animals," *New York Times*, April 6, 2006, A1; "If It Walks Like a Fish…," *Newsweek*, April 27, 2007, 8.

71 See also Susan Haack, *Defending Science—Within Reason: Between Scientism and Cynicism* (Amherst, NY: Prometheus Books 2003, paperback ed. 2007), X–XIII, 272–82; "Fallibilism and Faith, Naturalism and the Supernatural, Science and Religion" (2005), reprinted in Haack, *Putting Philosophy to Work: Inquiry and Its Place in Culture* (Amherst, NY: Prometheus Books, 2008; expanded ed. 2013), 199–208.

Kitzmiller (2005)—noting that even some of the expert witnesses for the defendant school district acknowledge that there is no real scientific research supporting Intelligent Design Theory—does a pretty good job of unmasking this sham reasoning.[72]

Of course, the real world is always much messier than philosophers would like. Rather than a simple division into genuine and pseudo-inquiry, honest and dishonest inquirers, we find just about every degree and shade of intellectual honesty and dishonesty.[73] The categorical distinction between genuine inquiry and advocacy research with which I have been working thus far, while agreeably neat and tidy conceptually, isn't adequate to the complexities of real life; it needs to be reconstrued as identifying the two extremes of a continuum. No investigator can approach his question free of any preconceptions whatever; most investigators have some preconception of the expected upshot from the beginning—though those who really want the truth will change their minds should the evidence demand it; and even the most honest and single-minded investigator is vulnerable to that very natural tendency to duck or resist or conveniently forget evidence that pulls against the view he has previously defended in print, or against his fond hope that this, finally, will be the key to finding a vaccine …, and so on.[74] Figuring things out can be really hard; and the temptation to cut corners is ever-present.

So Intelligent Design "research" is only one example among many, for the sad fact is that inquiry that is not quite plain-and-simple, something less than

72 Kitzmiller v. Dover Area Sch. Dist., 400 F. Supp. 2d 707 (M.D. Pa. 2005). See also Edward Humes, *Monkey Girl: Evolution, Education, and the Battle for America's Soul* (New York: Ecco, 2007) (telling the story of the *Kitzmiller* trial, including Eric Rothschild's devastating cross-examination of Michael Behe, expert witness for the defendant school district); Susan Haack, "Cracks in the Wall, A Bulge Under the Carpet: The Singular Story of Religion, Evolution, and the US Constitution," *Wayne Law Review* 57, no.4, 2011: 1303–32 (telling the history of Establishment Clause cases over the teaching of evolution in public high schools).

73 In Arthur Hailey's novel, *Strong Medicine* (London: Pan Books, 1984)—clearly based on the Bendectin saga, but telling the story of a fictional drug company, Felding-Roth, and its fictional morning-sickness drug, Montayne—one fictional scientist, Martin Peat-Smith, is a paradigm of the honest inquirer, and another, Vincent Lord, of the self-deceived advocacy researcher. See also Susan Haack, "The Ideal of Intellectual Integrity, in Life and Literature" (2005), in Haack, *Putting Philosophy to Work: Inquiry and Its Place in Culture* (Amherst, NY: Prometheus Books, 2008, expanded ed. 2013), 209–20.

74 Sinclair Lewis's novel, *Arrowsmith* (1925; New York: Signet Classics, 1998), conveys the point: Martin Arrowsmith destroys the integrity of his test of a vaccine by giving it, out of sympathy with their suffering and hope of saving them, to all those who have been exposed. John M. Berry's historical study, *The Great Influenza* (New York: Penguin Books, 2004), illustrates it: scientists desperate to find a vaccine ignored evidence that influenza is not bacterial; only Oswald Avery patiently held out. Dr. Brent, whom we encountered in *Blum*, seems to have been motivated in part by the fear that, with Bendectin off the market, physicians would have no effective treatment for a potentially serious condition.

perfectly honest, and tainted, if not by outright dishonesty, by convenient self-deception, is ubiquitous. We are all only too familiar with the phenomenon of the "Public Inquiry" the purpose of which is to reassure the public that there is no real danger, or that the corruption is all the fault of one junior official; with the "Customer Survey" the purpose of which is to fish for favorable material the publicity department can use; with the "departmental review" the purpose of which is to get friends from outside to endorse the faculty's grandiose hopes for expansion. We are all aware, also, that in many disciplines—economics, public health, the environmental sciences, to mention just a few—the pressures to nudge inquiry in the direction of advocacy are subtle, and the boundary easily transgressed. And we all know that, even in the disciplines furthest removed from policy or practice, academics often succumb to the temptation to divert energy from finding out what they can, or seriously thinking things through, into efforts to promote their area or their line or their clique.[75]

There are many kinds of advocacy research, and many sources of bias: some advocacy researchers are too concerned to arrive at a result favorable to a sponsor; some are over-anxious to find a cure quickly; some are too protective of a pet approach or theory, or too deferential to an idea endorsed by a hero of their profession; some get careless out of concern over global warming or pollution, or etc.; some want to reach politically-correct conclusions potentially beneficial to their careers, or to avoid reaching politically-incorrect conclusions potentially damaging to their careers; and many are simply too certain they are right—and so feel entirely justified in suppressing apparently unfavorable evidence which, as they see it, can only be misleading.[76]

~

To describe research as "litigation-driven" may mean either (a) that the need for this work *arises out of* litigation, or (b) that the work is undertaken *for the*

[75] Issues explored in Susan Haack, "Out of Step: Academic Ethics in a Preposterous Environment," in Haack, *Putting Philosophy to Work* (note 73 above), 251–68.

[76] William McBride, the Australian physician who first drew attention to the teratogenic effects of Thalidomide, was apparently so distressed at the delay before his warnings about Thalidomide were heeded that when, subsequently, he began to suspect Bendectin (sold in Australia under the name "Debendox") of causing birth defects, he resorted to fraud in his study of pregnant rabbits given the related anti-cholinergic scopolamine. Before the fraud was revealed, Dr. McBride had testified for the plaintiffs in 17 Bendectin cases. Sanders, "From Science to Evidence" (note 14 above), 36. See Andrew Skolnik, "Key Witness Against Morning Sickness Drug Faces Scientific Fraud Charges," *Journal of the American Medical Association* 263 (1990): 1468–1473; George F. Humphrey, "Scientific Fraud: The McBride Case," *Medicine, Science, and the Law* 32 (1992): 199–203; George F. Humphrey, "Scientific Fraud: The McBride Case—Judgment," *Science Law* 34 (1994): 299–306. Scopolamine is now marketed in the form of a patch as an anti-nausea drug, under the name "Transderm Scop." See RXList.com, Clinical Pharmacology, http://www.rxlist.com/cgi/generic2/transscop_cp.htm.

purpose of finding evidence favoring one side in litigation, and explaining away or otherwise playing down evidence favoring the other side. Research which is litigation-driven in sense (a) may, but need not, also be litigation-driven in sense (b). Research which is litigation-driven in the first sense is not peculiarly susceptible to bias merely in virtue of being, in this sense, litigation-driven. But research which is litigation-driven in the second sense is (one kind of) advocacy research; and so, if my analysis is correct, *is* inherently in danger of bias.

This danger is mitigated somewhat if advocacy research rests on science which has non-judicial as well as judicial uses; but it is not completely averted. Think of DNA identifications: the underlying theoretical principles are deeply interconnected with a whole range of other areas of well-established science; and these techniques are used, for example, to identify disaster victims as well as to identify the perpetrators of crimes. The theory is about as solid as scientific theory gets. But it's not the underlying principles that are disputed at trial; courts are not (by now, anyway) trying to determine whether these principles are sound, but whether they have been reliably applied in the case at hand. And there's plenty of room for bias to creep into the application even of the soundest science.

Research may be prompted by the needs of a particular case, or class of cases; or it may be prompted, not by cases already ongoing, but by the fear that there will, or may, be litigation. Moreover, there is very often more than one motive for conducting research; which may, for example, be intended to make the case for FDA approval, to be useful for marketing purposes, and to provide protection against possible litigation. Obviously enough, not only the hope of prevailing in litigation, but also some of these other motives—the marketing-oriented, for example—are also likely to introduce bias.

We also need to give some thought to what it means to describe scientific testimony as "reliable," since this concept plays a starring role in *Daubert*. *Merriam Webster's* definition is: "suitable or fit to be relied on, giving the same results in successive trials"; the *Oxford English Dictionary's* (*OED*)'s is: "may be relied on, of sound & consistent character or quality." Unless it is intended to be read disjunctively, *Webster's* definition seems a little odd; for the second clause seems to allow that a procedure or technique may be reliable even though it usually gives false results, provided it does so consistently—which hardly seems compatible with fitness to be relied on. (A weighing machine that consistently takes fifty pounds off a person's real weight, or a clock that runs perfectly but was set to the wrong time to begin with, is not, in the ordinary sense of the term, reliable; though I suppose you might describe them as, though "off," at least reliably off.) The *OED's* definition, in virtue of its reference to the "soundness" of the results, is closer to my understanding of the word.

Not unexpectedly, however, the legal concept of reliability articulated in *Daubert* diverges somewhat from the ordinary sense; as Justice Blackmun's phrase "evidentiary reliability" signals, it is a specialized legal concept. It is also far from transparent. Justice Blackmun writes:

> We note that scientists typically distinguish between "validity" (does the principle support what it purports to show?) and "reliability" (does application of the principle produce consistent results?). Although "the difference between accuracy, validity, and reliability may be such that each is distinct from the other by no more than a hen's kick" ... our reference here is to *evidentiary* reliability—that is, trustworthiness.... In a case involving scientific evidence, *evidentiary reliability* will be based upon *scientific validity*.[77]

This tells us that the legal or "evidentiary" concept of reliability is to be tied to scientific "validity," not to scientific "reliability"; which seems to mean, in part, that yielding consistent results (which is Justice Blackmun's understanding of "scientific reliability") is not enough. The reference to "trustworthiness" points in the same direction: "evidentiary reliability" requires scientific testimony to be based on methods and processes that yield "sound," and not merely consistent, results. But Justice Blackmun's understanding of "sound" is apparently quite modest; it does not require that the principle on which expert testimony is based yield true or even probably true results, but only that "the principle support[s] what it purports to show."

The fact that research is litigation-driven in the stronger sense, I have argued, makes it likely to be biased. Biased research doesn't necessarily produce false results; nor does it necessarily produce false results more often than true. After all, the proposition(s) towards which it is slanted may be true; indeed, when there is biased research on both sides of a legal case, if the propositions on each side genuinely contradict each other, the proposition(s) towards which one side's research is slanted *must* be true. But biased research *tends towards the predetermined conclusion irrespective of where the evidence points*; the results it produces don't depend on where the evidence really leads. So if this is a reasonable interpretation of the *Daubert* Court's "evidentiary reliability," then, indeed, biased research is unreliable in the relevant sense.

[77] *Daubert* III (note 6 above), 590 n.9 (citations omitted). The internal quotation is from James Starrs, "*Frye v. United States* Restructured and Revitalized: A Proposal to Amend Federal Rule of Evidence 702," *Jurimetrics Journal* 26 (1986): 249–59, 256.

3 THROUGH THE THICKET, OUT OF THE SWAMP, AND ONTO THE HIGH ROAD? NOT YET!

So there is some foundation for Judge Bernstein's strictures against "justification science"; indeed, his observation that Dr. Shapiro's work seems to have been based on an "unalterable preconception" that Bendectin was harmless closely parallels the argument I have given here, that science that is litigation-driven in the stronger sense fails to meet Justice Blackmun's standard of evidentiary reliability because the conclusions drawn are not sensitive to the evidence in the way they ought to be. And, again provided that "litigation-driven" is understood in the stronger sense, there is some foundation, also, for Judge Kozinski's conclusion that the fact that testimony is based on litigation-driven research speaks negatively to its (evidentiary) reliability.

However, there is something amiss with Judge Kozinski's arguments for that conclusion. His first argument, remember, is that science flowing from existing, independent research is less likely to be biased towards a particular conclusion by the promise of remuneration; this is true, but it proves much more than he intends. Many studies confirm that company-sponsored research into drugs or medical devices is significantly more likely than independent research to be favorable to the sponsor's product;[78] but this suggests, not just that litigation-driven science may be below par, but that marketing-oriented science should also be regarded with suspicion.

Moreover, this first argument also undermines the exception Judge Kozinski makes with regard to evidence from the forensic sciences. It is true, as he says, that the fact that forensic scientists acquire their expertise for the purposes of the justice system is not in itself grounds for doubting the reliability of their testimony; but this is not enough to establish his point. Perhaps the thought implicit here is that forensic science is litigation-driven only in the weaker, less troubling sense: that while it is needed only because there are crimes to be solved and prosecuted, it is not inherently motivated by the desire to make one side of a case. But this is Pollyannish to say the least. After all, such work is undertaken almost exclusively for the police or prosecution;[79] and it seems

[78] See, e.g., Richard A. Davidson, "Source of Funding and Outcome of Clinical Trials," *Journal of General Internal Medicine* 1 (1986): 155–58; Paula Rochon et al., "A Study of Manufacturer-Supported Trials of Non-Steroidal Anti-Inflammatory Drugs in the Treatment of Arthritis," *Archives of Internal Medicine* 154, no.2 (January 24, 1994): 157–63; Lee S. Friedman and Elihu D. Richter, "Relationship Between Conflict of Interest and Research Results," *Journal of General Internal Medicine* 19, no.1 (January 2004): 51–6.

[79] See, e.g., William C. Thompson, "A Sociological Perspective on the Science of Forensic DNA Testing," *University of California Davis Law Review* 30 (1997): 1113–36, 1114 ("The primary clients of the vast majority of forensic scientists are law enforcement agencies. Most

likely that forensic scientists' and technicians' understandable but inappropriate desire to be helpful, to find something to make a case against a suspect, sometimes biases their judgment. Or perhaps the thought is that forensic experts will curb their biases because they know they will be called on to testify on numerous other occasions;[80] but this seems no less doubtful. After all, the fact that expert witnesses in tort cases are "repeat testifiers" or "professional expert witnesses," as we say pejoratively, is often seen, not without reason, precisely as grounds for distrusting them.[81] Judge Bernstein's worry that "general acceptance in the field to which it belongs" is a poor indicator of reliability if the consensus is an artificial one is also relevant here; for in some areas of forensic science there is a real danger that a supposed "scientific consensus" has been generated by a kind of guild or trade union of mutually supportive practitioners with an interest in protecting their livelihoods.[82]

Judge Kozinski's second argument, that litigation-driven science is not, like university science, kept up to the mark by the need to attract funding and institutional support, rests on a dubious premiss. For by now a significant proportion of the medical research in universities is not truly independent, but

forensic scientists are employed directly by law enforcement agencies. Their role in litigation is typically, and often exclusively, to provide evidence in support of criminal prosecutions. Forensic scientists who work in private laboratories may occasionally be employed by criminal defense lawyers. However, the bulk of their work is for law enforcement as well. The major market for commercial laboratories that develop new technologies for forensic testing also consists of law enforcement personnel.")

80 Dr. Thompson (the author of the article cited in note 79 above) tells me that this is the reason Judge Kozinski gave him.

81 In the first *Blum* trial, the court prevented the plaintiffs' attorneys from referring to the fact that Merrell Dow's experts had testified in other Bendectin trials. Appendix 6, Order and Opinion of Philadelphia Court of Common Pleas, May 12, 1988, 28 (D'Alessandro, J.) (on file with author). Judge Kozinski himself suggests that the fact that the Dauberts' proffered experts have been testifying in Bendectin cases all over the country is reason to be suspicious of them. *Daubert* IV (note 3 above), 1314. In fact, there were numerous repeat testifiers on both sides throughout the Bendectin litigation. Sanders, "From Science to Evidence" (note 14 above), at 36. Compare Chaulk by Murphy v. Volkswagen of Am., Inc., 808 F.2d 639, 644 (7th Cir. 1986) (Posner, J., dissenting) (writing that an expert's testimony was either the work of "a crank or, what is more likely, of a man who is making a career out of testifying for plaintiffs in automobile accident cases in which a door may have opened; at the time of trial he was involved in 10 such cases. His testimony illustrates the age-old problem of expert witnesses who are 'often the mere paid advocates or partisans of those who employ or pay them'" (quoting Keegan v. Minneapolis & St. Louis R.R. Co., 78 N.W. 965, 966 (Minn. 1899)).

82 See, e.g., D. Michael Risinger, Mark P. Denbeaux and Michael J. Saks, "Brave New 'Post-*Daubert* World'—A Reply to Professor Moenssens," *Seton Hall Law Review* 29 (1998): 405–90. The knife-mark examiners in Ramirez v. State, 542 So. 2d 352 (Fla. 1989) ("*Ramirez* I"), Ramirez v. State, 651 So. 2d 1164 (Fla. 1995) ("*Ramirez* II"), and Ramirez v. State, 810 So. 2d 836 (Fla. 2001) ("*Ramirez* III") illustrate the problem.

is sponsored by drug companies and such[83] (and a significant proportion of research in the social sciences is in one way or another politically motivated). And in combination with the first argument, this suggests that there may be reason to doubt the reliability of such university science, as well as science specifically undertaken to support one side or another in litigation, or to provide data that can be used in marketing.

Moreover, as I argue in "Peer Review and Publication,"[84] the peer-review process for funding and publication, on which Judge Kozinski puts quite a lot of weight, is a frail safeguard at best. Even if all the work published in peer-review journals were peer-reviewed—which it isn't—this would be only very weak assurance of its reliability. As the *Daubert* Court's comments on "peer-review and publication" obliquely acknowledge, it is not peer-reviewed publication as such that indicates reliability, but the long-run survival of published results on which other scientists find they can build successfully.[85]

Still, given that, as I have argued, there is merit in the idea that the fact that science is litigation-driven in the stronger sense indicates that it is likely to be unreliable, in something like the sense Justice Blackmun explained in *Daubert*, might this not be a helpful factor to be added to his list of indicia of (un)reliability? Unfortunately, matters are not so simple; for the sad fact—obvious once you think about it—is that there *can be no* simple, mechanically applicable test that would accurately discriminate strong science from weak. The *Daubert* Court observes that its list of indicia of reliability is "flexible," and can't simply be applied mechanically. And a mechanical application of Judge Kozinski's new *Daubert* factor would certainly be quite as ill-advised as a mechanical application of a requirement that testimony be based on research that has been published in peer-reviewed journals—and for structurally similar reasons: "peer-reviewed" and "litigation-driven" both have (a) a readily-applicable sense that has little to do with reliability, and (b) a subtler sense which bears more closely on reliability, but isn't readily applicable. "Published after peer review" is easily applied, but is a frail indicator of reliability; "has been out there long enough, has been read by enough others knowledgeable enough in the field, links up in an explanatory way with enough other bits of scientific theorizing, and has proven robust enough when new experiments or theoretical work assume its reliability" is a much better indicator of reliability,

83 See, e.g., Sheldon Krimsky, *Science in the Private Interest* (Lanham, MD: Rowman and Littlefield, 2003); Marcia Angell, "Is Scientific Medicine for Sale?" *New England Journal of Medicine* 342 (2000): 1516–18.

84 "Peer Review and Publication" (note 7 above), 172–73.

85 Brief of Amici Curiae Daryl E. Chubin et al. in Support of Petitioners, *Daubert* III (note 6 above) (No. 92-102), 1992 WL 12006443.

but is much more difficult to apply. Similarly, "undertaken in the course of or in anticipation of litigation" is easily applied, but a frail indicator of reliability; "skewed by the desire to advance one side in litigation" indicates unreliability, all right, but is much more difficult to apply.

~

I haven't forgotten that the epistemological rationale for the adversarial system is that having rival advocates each present the evidence favoring their side of a case is a good way to ensure, so far as possible, that the truth comes out. As I argued in "Epistemology Legalized," the best argument that could be made for the epistemological efficacy of such a system would run something like this:

> Since for good reason the legal process, unlike the process of scientific inquiry, has to be concluded within a relatively short time frame, we need a way of ensuring that the search for and scrutiny of evidence is as thorough as that time frame allows. An adversarial system is one way to do this. If everyone involved knows that eventually, at the trial stage, the determination will be made by an impartial jury weighing the evidence developed and presented by the parties, and subject to cross-examination by the other, this should encourage precisely the kind of thoroughness we are aiming to achieve. For an advocate's goal is to win; so counsel for each party is motivated to seek out evidence favoring his side of the case, and to bring out flaws in evidence pointing the other way. To be sure, the process isn't perfect; but it is a reasonable substitute for the ideal. . . .[86]

This is a good argument—in principle; but, as I also said in "Epistemology Legalized," it is a serious question how well it applies to our adversarial system, as it functions in practice.

A quite general problem is that there is often a vast asymmetry between the resources available to one side in litigation and those available to the other. And where scientific testimony is concerned there are further problems as well. In 1901, Judge Learned Hand complained that the expert-witness system "set[s] juries to decide, where doctors disagree";[87] more than a century later, Justice Rehnquist and Judge Kozinski complain, in effect, that now it sets judges to decide, where doctors disagree.[88] The fact is that judges, jurors, or

86 Haack, "Epistemology Legalized: Or, Truth, Justice, and the American Way," pp. 27–46 in this volume, 35.

87 Learned Hand, "Historical and Practical Considerations Regarding Expert Testimony," *Harvard Law Review* 15 (1901): 40–58, 54.

88 "I do not doubt that Rule 702 confides to the judge some gatekeeping responsibility in deciding questions of the admissibility of proffered expert testimony. But I do not think it imposes on them either the obligation or the authority to become amateur scientists in order

attorneys, however conscientious and thorough, probably don't fully understand scientific testimony; and to make matters worse, the more an area of science gets entangled with litigation, the more scientists in that area seem (like Dr. Brent and Dr. Newman) to fall into advocacy mode. And this makes the difficult business of getting at the truth of the questions at issue even harder than it would otherwise be—which is presumably what Justice Castille had in mind when he expressed concern about "the litigation-driven Bendectin 'scientific community' described to the court" in *Blum*.[89]

In the criminal justice system, besides a troubling asymmetry between the scientific resources ordinarily available to the defense and those available to the prosecution, there seem to be grounds for concern both that, in some areas of forensic science, a self-serving guild mentality may predominate over the scientific attitude; and that courts are reluctant to reconsider their long-standing reliance on identification techniques such as fingerprinting (about the reliability of which much is claimed, but little seems to be known)[90] or psychiatric techniques such as predictions of future dangerousness.[91] And in the civil arena, toxic tort and product liability litigation too often seems like a kind of lottery, where it is hard to feel confident either that all and only those plaintiffs who really were injured by defendants' products are compensated, or that the system provides good incentives to manufacturers to investigate their products as thoroughly as possible.

In any case, while compensating the victims of dangerous products after the damage has been done, insofar as such compensation is possible, is better than nothing, it is hardly the ideal. It would be better, surely, to ensure so far as humanly possible that safe and beneficial drugs, devices, chemicals,

to perform that role." *Daubert* III (note 6 above) 600–01 (1993) (Rehnquist, J., dissenting in part). "[W]e are largely untrained in science and certainly no match for any of the witnesses whose testimony we are reviewing." *Daubert* IV (note 3 above) 1316.

89 *Blum* VI (note 8 above), 13–14 (Castille, J., dissenting).

90 See, e.g., Simon Cole, "What Counts for Identity? The Historical Origins of the Methodology of Latent Fingerprint Identification," *Science in Context* 12 (1999): 139–72; Robert Epstein, "Fingerprints Meet *Daubert*: The Myth of Fingerprint 'Science' is Revealed," *Southern California Law Review* 75 (2002): 605–58, 605; Jennifer Mnookin, "Fingerprints: Not a Gold Standard," *Issues in Science and Technology* 20 (fall 2003): 47–54; Simon Cole, "Grandfathering Evidence: Fingerprint Admissibility from *Jennings* to *Llera Plaza* and Back Again," *American Criminal Law Review* 41 (2004): 1189–1276; Sharon Begley, "Despite Its Reputation, Fingerprint Evidence Isn't Really Infallible," *Wall Street Journal*, June 4, 2004, B1.

91 See, e.g., Erica Beecher-Monas and Edgar Garcia-Rill, "Genetic Predictions of Future Dangerousness: Is There a Blueprint for Violence?" *Law & Contemporary Problems* 69 (2006): 301–41; Thomas Regnier, "*Barefoot* in Quicksand: The Future of 'Future Dangerousness' Predictions in Death Penalty Sentencing in the World of *Daubert* and *Kumho*," *University of Akron Law Review* 37 (2004): 467–507.

etc., are available, but dangerous or damaging drugs, etc., are kept off the market, or taken off the market as soon as the dangers are known; and that manufacturers are discouraged from hiding or disguising risks posed by their products. The story of *Daubert* and *Blum* prompts some tough questions: Do we rely too much on what Justice Breyer describes as "the powerful engine of tort litigation,"[92] ideally the last resort? Are other technologically advanced countries where the engine of tort litigation is less powerful invariably less successful, also, in keeping beneficial products on, and dangerous products off the market? Are other countries' regulatory agencies more effective, and if so, why? Might some of the energy now devoted to discussions of how best to fine-tune the rules of admissibility of expert testimony be more profitably diverted to thinking about other and possibly better ways to approximate the ideal more closely? And (perhaps you will think this a naive question, but I'll ask it anyway): what if the time, energy, intelligence, and resources spent on cases like *Daubert* and *Blum* had been spent instead on independent, honest, solid scientific investigation of the factual issues? ...

92 Recall Justice Breyer's comment that courts' gatekeeping can help ensure that "the powerful engine of tort liability, which can generate strong financial incentives to reduce, or eliminate, production, points toward the right substances and does not destroy the wrong ones." Gen. Elec. Co. v. Joiner, 522 U.S. 136, 148–49 (1997) ("*Joiner* III") (Breyer, J., concurring).

—9—

Proving Causation: The Weight of Combined Evidence

> *The Consilience of Inductions* takes place when an Induction, obtained from one class of facts, coincides with an Induction, obtained from a different class. This Consilience is a test of the truth of the Theory in which it occurs.
>
> —William Whewell[1]

This paper focuses on causation evidence in toxic-tort litigation, and makes two main arguments, the first epistemological and the second legal. The epistemological argument is that, under certain conditions, a congeries of evidence warrants a conclusion to a higher degree than any of its components alone would do; the legal argument, interlocking with this, is that our evidence law encourages a kind of atomism that can actually impede the process of arriving at the conclusion most warranted by the evidence—an atomism the effects of which have been especially salient to causation evidence in toxic-tort cases.

§1 will set the stage by looking at two cases where the epistemological issue to be tackled here came explicitly to courts' attention; §2 will develop the epistemological argument, first in a general form, and then as it applies to the kinds of causation evidence typically encountered in toxic-tort litigation; §3 will rely on this account to answer some of the epistemological questions about causation evidence that have been at issue in such cases; and §4 will develop the legal argument, showing that, ironically enough, *Daubert*'s requirement that proffered expert testimony is admissible only if it is reliable may sometimes stand in the way of an adequate assessment of the reliability of causation evidence.

1 William Whewell, *Philosophy of the Inductive Sciences* (1840), in *Selected Writings of William Whewell*, ed., Yehuda Elkana (Chicago: University of Chicago Press, 1984), 121–259, 257. (The word "consilience," which I believe Whewell introduced, derives from the Latin "*con*" and "*siliere*," "jumping together.")

1 SETTING THE STAGE

Mary Virginia Oxendine was born in 1971. Her right forearm was foreshortened, and she had only three fingers, fused together, on her right hand. Believing that their daughter's birth defects had been caused by her mother's taking Bendectin for morning-sickness while pregnant with Mary, the Oxendines sued the manufacturers, Merrell Dow Pharmaceuticals.[2]

At the first, jury trial, Dr. Alan Done testified for the Oxendines that certain antihistamines are known to have teratogenic effects on animals, and that one ingredient of Bendectin is the antihistamine doxylamine succinate; that animal studies conducted by Merrell Dow found small limb alterations in the fetuses of pregnant rabbits given Bendectin—alterations that the company's scientists disregarded as insignificant—as well as miscarriages, which, Dr. Done believed, may have occurred because the fetuses were malformed; that *in vitro* studies conducted by the National Institutes of Health found that Bendectin interfered with the development of limb-bud cells; and that the data from an epidemiological study conducted for Merrell Dow by Drs. Bunde and Bowles, when adjusted to exclude Canadian subjects (who could have bought the drug without a prescription), revealed that mothers who took Bendectin had a 30% greater risk of having a deformed baby than those who didn't.[3] Dr. Done explained that his opinion—that Mary Oxendine's birth defects had been caused by the Bendectin her mother had taken during the period of pregnancy in which fetal limbs were forming—was based, not on any one of these studies or any one of these lines of evidence by itself, but on *all* of the various pieces of evidence to which he testified, *taken together*.[4]

In 1983, at the first trial, a jury awarded the Oxendines $750,000 in compensatory damages. But, overriding this decision, writing that "[i]t is clear …

[2] Oxendine v. Merrell Dow Pharm., Inc., 506 A.2d 1100 (D.C. 1986) ("*Oxendine* I"), *on subsequent appeal* 563 A.2d 330 (D.C. 1989) ("*Oxendine* II"), *cert. denied*, 493 U.S. 1074 (1990), *appeal after remand* 593 A.2d 1023 (D.C. 1991) ("*Oxendine* III"), *appeal after remand* 649 A.2d 825 (D.C. 1994) ("*Oxendine* IV"), *remanded to* Civ. No. 82–1245, 1996 WL 680992 (D.C. Super. Ct. Oct. 24, 1996) ("*Oxendine* V"). The description of Ms. Oxendine's birth defects comes from *Oxendine* I, 1103.

[3] *Oxendine* I (note 2 above), 1104–08 (reporting part of Dr. Done's testimony). What I have given in the text is obviously only a very sketchy summary of Dr. Done's testimony; he was on the witness stand for three and a half days, and the transcript of his testimony runs to almost 600 pages. *Id.*, 1108. (I have, however, tried to find out whether the Canadian equivalent of Bendectin was ever, as Dr. Done claimed, available in Canada without a prescription. So far as I have been able to determine, it was not.)

[4] *Id.*, 1108 (reiterating that "[Dr. Done] conceded his inability to conclude that Bendectin was a teratogen on the basis of any of the individual studies which he discussed, but he also made clear that all of these studies must be viewed together, and that, so viewed, they supported his conclusion").

that *no conclusion one way or the other can be drawn from any of the above relied upon bases*, respecting whether Bendectin is a human teratogen,"[5] the trial court granted the defendant's motion for judgment notwithstanding the verdict. The Oxendines appealed; and the Court of Appeals reversed and remanded with instructions to reinstate the jury verdict, finding that the trial court had erred in emphasizing Dr. Done's acknowledgment that none of the individual studies to which he testified was sufficient by itself to establish causation, and "failing to consider [his] testimony that all of the studies, *taken in combination*, did support such a finding." Associate Judge Terry continued:

> Like the pieces of a mosaic, the individual studies showed little or nothing when viewed separately from one another, but *they combined to produce a whole that was greater than the sum of its parts*: a foundation for Dr. Done's opinion that Bendectin caused appellant's birth defects.[6]

Of course, this wasn't the end of the *Oxendine* story: in fact, the case went to the DC Court of Appeals three more times before it was finally resolved in 1996. On remand, Merrell Dow moved for a new trial, claiming that Dr. Done had misrepresented his credentials;[7] and in 1988 this motion was granted. The Oxendines appealed again and in 1989, finding that the trial judge had erred in granting a new trial, the Court of Appeals reversed again, once more ordering the trial court to reinstate the original verdict.[8] Back at the trial court, the Oxendines asked the court to enter a judgment affirming the verdict, but Merrell Dow appealed once more; and in 1991 the Court of Appeals ruled that the trial court could not enter a final, appealable judgment on compensatory damages until the punitive-damages stage of the trial was completed.[9] In 1993 the Oxendines withdrew their claim for punitive damages, and moved for the verdict on compensatory damages to be affirmed; and Merrell Dow asked the trial court to reconsider the original verdict, this time on the grounds that new studies published since the first trial exonerated Bendectin. The trial court,

5 *Id.*, 1103 (my italics).

6 *Id.*, 1110 (my italics in block quote) (determining that trial court's judgment notwithstanding the verdict was in error, because when the evidence was viewed as a whole, it was not appropriate to conclude that no reasonable juror would find for the appellant).

7 *Oxendine* II (note 2 above), 332 (reporting that on May 3 and May 11, 1983, Dr. Done had testified that he was a member of the Wayne State Medical School Faculty, when in fact he had submitted a letter of resignation on April 24th, which was accepted by the Dean on April 29th; and listing four other respects, in addition to his position at Wayne State University, in which Dr. Done falsely represented his credentials at trial).

8 *Id.*, 331 (finding that the motions judge did not abuse his discretion in finding that the motion to vacate was timely, but that he did err in vacating the judgment and granting a new trial). *Id.*, 338 (reversing and ordering the trial court to reinstate the jury verdict).

9 *Oxendine* III (note 2 above), 1023 (reversing award for compensatory damages before punitive damages stage of trial was completed).

declining to consider these new studies, entered a judgment reaffirming the original jury verdict. Merrell Dow appealed again; and in 1994, acknowledging that "reopen[ing] the trial's determination of scientific truth" was at odds with the legal concern for finality,[10] and therefore setting a high standard for Merrell to prevail, the Court of Appeals remanded yet again—as the court says, reluctantly, and evidently expecting that the case would be quickly resolved in favor of the Oxendines.[11]

But in 1996—now taking into account the new studies Merrell Dow presented,[12] the decisions in numerous other Bendectin cases concluded since the original trial,[13] and actions of the FDA[14] and the Canadian

[10] *Oxendine* IV (note 2 above), 831–32 (stressing the importance of finality in the legal system). See also "Irreconcilable Differences? The Troubled Marriage of Science and Law," pp. 78–103 in this volume, 92.

[11] *Id.*, 827 (finding that "we are reluctantly compelled to remand for further limited consideration"); see also *id.*, 834–35 (Associate Judge Schwelb, concurring, commenting that "[t]he delays to date ... have *already* done intolerable damage ... [T]his is not 1982 or 1984 or even 1990. Given where we are today, considerations of finality have become so compelling that ... nothing short of an extraordinarily persuasive proffer by Merrell Dow would warrant ... further delaying Ms. Oxendine's recovery").

[12] *Oxendine* V (note 2 above), 14–21 (reporting that Merrell had presented two post-1983 meta-analyses of epidemiological data on Bendectin (Einarson et al., 1988; McKeigue et al., 1994), and 14 epidemiological studies ((1) Mitchell, 1983; (2) Aselton and Jick, 1984; (3) Hearey, 1984; (4) McCredie, 1984; (5) Winship, 1984; (6) Asleton-Jick, 1985; (7) Elbourne, 1985; (8) Zieler, 1985; (9) Jedd, 1988; (10) Adams, 1989; (11) Shiono, 1989; (12) Erickson, 1991; (13) Khoury, 1994; (14) McDonald, 1994). Plaintiffs' counsel argued that these studies, where they were relevant, were flawed, e.g., that the 1991 Erickson study omitted crucial safeguards such as "critical times" (presumably, the period of pregnancy in which subjects took Bendectin); but the court downplayed these criticisms as "counsel's critique of a scientific study, rather than a contrary scientific study or an expert's evaluation." *Id.*,15 (citing and dismissing plaintiffs' counsel's arguments).

[13] *Id.*, 4–7 (listing eight federal cases concluded in favor of Merrell: Lynch v. Merrell-Nat'l Labs., 646 F. Supp. 856 (D. Mass. 1986), *aff'd*, 830 F.2d 1190 (1st Cir., 1987); Richardson v. Richardson-Merrell, Inc., 857 F.2d 823 (D.C. Cir. 1988); Brock v. Merrell Dow Pharm., Inc., 874 F.2d 307 (5th Cir. 1989); DeLuca v. Merrell Dow Pharm., Inc., 911 F.2d 941 (3d Cir. 1990); Ealy v. Richardson-Merrell, Inc., 897 F.2d 1159 (D.C. Cir. 1990); Wilson v. Merrell Dow Pharm., Inc., 893 F.2d 1149 (10th Cir., 1990); Turpin v. Merrell Dow Pharm., Inc., 959 F.2d 1349 (6th Cir. 1992); Daubert v. Merrell Dow Pharm., Inc., 43 F.3d 1311 (9th Cir. 1995) ("*Daubert* IV"). The court also mentions *Blum* and *Havner*, but observes that both are on appeal. Both were eventually resolved in favor of the defendants. See Blum v. Merrell Dow Pharm., Inc., 764 A.2d, 1 (Pa. 2000) (affirming Superior Court's decision in favor of Merrell); Merrell Dow Pharm., Inc. v. Havner, 953 S.W.2d 706 (Tex. 1997) (reversing the court of appeals and finding in favor of Merrell). The two names of the defendant company—Richardson-Merrell, Merrell-Dow—reflect changes in ownership over the relevant period. See Joseph Sanders, *Bendectin on Trial: A Study of Mass Tort Litigation* (Ann Arbor, MI: University of Michigan Press, 1998), 213–14 (describing the history of the company); Michael D. Green, *Bendectin and Birth Defects: The Challenges of Mass Toxic Substances Litigation* (Philadelphia: University of Pennsylvania Press, 1996) (describing the history of Bendectin litigation).

[14] *Oxendine* V (note 2 above), 23 (referring to a monograph issued by the FDA in 1994 on over-the-counter antihistamine drugs, which concluded that doxylamine succinate is safe to include as an ingredient of such antihistamines).

government[15]—the trial court found that this high standard was met, and found in favor of Merrell Dow.[16]

The best known of the other Bendectin cases cited was, of course, *Daubert*, which had been finally resolved a year before *Oxendine*, when Judge Kozinski affirmed the trial court's summary judgment for Merrell Dow.[17] Jason Daubert's birth defects were similar to Mary Oxendine's,[18] and his parents, like hers, believed these defects had been caused by Bendectin; but legally *Daubert* followed a different path from *Oxendine*. In 1989 the District Court had granted Merrell Dow's motion for summary judgment after excluding the Dauberts' proffered expert witnesses on the grounds that scientific evidence is admissible only if it is "sufficiently established to have [gained] general acceptance in the field to which it belongs."[19] Finding that, since none of the numerous published epidemiological studies had found a statistically significant association between Bendectin and birth defects, the Dauberts' experts' opinions were *not* generally accepted in the field to which they belonged, and hence not admissible. The Court of Appeals for the Ninth Circuit affirmed, now specifically citing *Frye*.[20] And it was because of this reliance on *Frye*—almost unprecedented in a civil case[21]—that the Supreme Court granted *certiorari*, to

15 *Ibid.* (reporting that in 1989 the consultants for the Special Advisory Committee on Reproductive Physiology to the Health Protection Branch of the Canadian government concluded that Bendectin should not be withdrawn from the Canadian market, and that the warning label should be modified in light of the lack of evidence of an association with birth defects). But see also *id.*, 23, n.45 (noting that plaintiffs' counsel pointed out that the members of the Canadian panel "were tied to Merrell—a fact of which the Canadian government was not aware"). In 2013 the FDA approved the same drug (now called "Diclegis," and manufactured by a Canadian Company, Duchesnay) for sale in the US. For more details, see "What's Wrong with Litigation-Driven Science? pp. 180–207 in this volume, n. 10.

16 *Oxendine* V (note 2 above), 34. (In telling the story of this long-running legal saga I have relied in part on the history recounted in Joseph Sanders, "Science, Law, and the Expert Witness," *Law & Contemporary Problems*, 72, no. 1 [2009]: 63–90.) Elsewhere Prof. Sanders speculates, very plausibly, that Merrell Dow expended so much time and money on its defense in *Oxendine* "in order to maintain an unblemished record in the Bendectin litigation. Even one final plaintiff verdict might make it more difficult to argue for a summary judgment in other cases." Sanders, *Bendectin on Trial* (note 13 above), 30.

17 *Daubert* IV (note 13 above) (affirming summary judgment in favor of Merrell).

18 Natalie Angier, "High Court to Consider Rules on Use of Scientific Evidence," *New York Times*, January 2, 1993, 1, available at ProQuest Historical Newspapers The New York Times (1851–2003) (reporting that "Jason Daubert, of San Diego, was born 19 years ago with only two fingers on his right hand and without a lower bone on his right arm").

19 Daubert v. Merrell Dow Pharm., Inc., 727 F. Supp. 570, 572 (S.D. Cal. 1989) ("*Daubert* I") (citing United States v. Kilgus, 571 F.2d 508, 510 (9th Cir. 1978), which cited United States v. Brown (Michigan), 557 F.2d 541, 556 (6th Cir. 1977), which in turn cited Frye v. United States, 293 F. 1013 (D.C. Cir. 1923).

20 Daubert v. Merrell Dow Pharm., Inc., 951 F.2d 1128, 1129–1130 (9th Cir. 1991) ("*Daubert* II").

21 Kenneth J. Cheseboro, "Galileo's Retort: Peter Huber's Junk Scholarship," *American University Law Review* 42: 1993: 1637–1726, 1695 (reporting that "there was not a single case

determine whether or not *Frye* had been superseded when the Federal Rules of Evidence (FRE) were adopted in 1975.

An amicus brief from Kenneth Rothman and other epidemiologists raised several important epistemological issues; the lower courts' analyses in *Daubert*, these amici argued, put too much weight on whether studies were statistically significant, over-estimated the importance of peer-reviewed publication[22]—and, most to the present purpose, that they "*foreclose[d] the use of valid inferences that may be drawn from the combination of many studies, even when none of the studies standing alone would justify such inferences.*"[23] But the Supreme Court's ruling—that *Frye had* been superseded, but that FRE 702 still required that courts screen proffered expert testimony for reliability as well as relevance—doesn't pick up this theme.

Justice Blackmun's ruling for the Supreme Court in *Daubert* had stressed that in screening for reliability courts should look, not to an expert's conclusions, but to his "methodology."[24] And so, when *General Electric Co. v. Joiner*[25] came to the Supreme Court in 1997, the dispute over the question of the joint weight of combined causation evidence was couched in terms of the parties' rival experts' "methodologies." Robert Joiner, who had worked for many years as an electrician for a municipality in Georgia, was diagnosed with small-cell lung cancer in 1991; he was only 37. Believing that his cancer had been

decided by the federal appellate courts prior to 1975 that applied the *Frye* rule in a civil case of any kind. As of April 7, 1993, only three such decisions had been reported, two of which were decided in 1991"). These three decisions were Barrel of Fun, Inc. v. State Farm Fire & Cas. Co. 739 F.2d 1028, 1031 (5th Cir. 1984); Christophersen v. Allied-Signal Corp., 939 F.2d 1106, 1115–16 (5th Cir.1991), and *Daubert* II (note 20 above), 1129–30. Whether *Christophersen* really "relies" on *Frye* might be questioned, since the court lists four considerations, of which *Frye* is only one. *Christopherson*, 1110. However, when the Supreme Court denied *certiorari* in 1992, Justice White, with Justice Blackmun, dissented, arguing that the question, whether *Frye* had been superseded by the FRE, "is an important and recurring issue." Christophersen v. Allied-Signal Corp., 503 U.S. 912, 912 (1992) (White, J., dissenting) (contending *certiorari* should be granted). *Barrel of Fun*, which more unambiguously relies on *Frye*, was a fire-insurance fraud case in which the excluded evidence involved a "psychological stress evaluation" of proffered testimony, which the court held to be essentially similar to polygraph evidence, which was the kind of evidence at issue in *Frye*.

22 See also Brief of Amici Curiae Daryl E. Chubin et al. in Support of Petitioners, Daubert v. Merrell Dow Pharm., Inc., 509 U.S. 579 (1993) (No. 92–102), 1992 WL 12006443; "Peer Review and Publication: Lessons for Lawyers," pp. 156–179 in this volume.

23 Brief Amici Curiae of Professors Kenneth Rothman et al. in Support of Petitioners, Daubert v. Merrell Dow Pharm., Inc., 509 U.S. 579 (1993) (No. 92–102), 1992 WL 12006438, *10 ("Brief of Kenneth Rothman et al.") (my italics).

24 Daubert v. Merrell Dow Pharm., Inc., 509 U.S. 579, 592–93 (1993) ("*Daubert* III") (applying Rule 702 requires "a preliminary assessment of whether the reasoning or methodology underlying the testimony is scientifically valid and of whether that reasoning or methodology properly can be applied to the facts at issue").

25 Gen. Elec. Co. v. Joiner, 522 U.S. 136 (1997) ("*Joiner* III").

promoted by his exposure to polychlorinated biphenyls (PCBs) contaminating the insulating oil in the transformers his job required him to disassemble and repair, he sued the manufacturer, General Electric (G.E.). Mr. Joiner's attorneys had proffered a number of expert witnesses, who proposed to testify to a variety of toxicological, *in vitro, in vivo*, and epidemiological studies; arguing that, *taken together*, this congeries of evidence would be sufficient to establish causation.

The district court, focusing one-by-one on (some of) the individual studies to which Joiner's experts appealed, excluded Joiner's expert testimony as inadmissible, and granted G.E.'s motion for summary judgment. But the Court of Appeals reversed, holding that where, as in this case, exclusion of expert testimony is outcome-determinative, appellate review should be especially stringent; and, moreover, found Joiner's experts' methodology scientifically acceptable:

> Opinions of any kind are derived from individual pieces of evidence, each of which by itself might not be conclusive, but *when viewed in their entirety are the building blocks of a perfectly reasonable conclusion*, one reliable enough to be submitted to a jury....[26]

The Supreme Court granted *certiorari*, to determine the standard of review for such evidentiary rulings.

In their brief to the Supreme Court, Joiner's attorneys explained that their experts used "weight of evidence methodology"—the same methodology the Environmental Protection Agency used in assessing carcinogenic risk and, they argued, the same methodology G.E.'s own experts used in this very case;[27] and they quoted Laurence Tribe's "Trial by Mathematics":

> Few categories of evidence ... could ever be ruled admissible if each category had to stand on its own, unaided by the process of cumulating information that characterizes the way any rational person uses evidence to reach conclusions.[28]

[26] Joiner v. Gen. Elec. Co., 78 F.3d 524, 532 (11th Cir. 1996) ("*Joiner* II") (my italics). Subsequently, in their brief to the Supreme Court, General Electric's attorneys will claim that "[a]lmost those very words have been cited by scientists and scholars as violating the methodology of science." Brief for Petitioners, Joiner III (note 25 above) (No. 96–188), 1997 WL 304727, *49 ("Brief for Petitioners") (citing Petr Skrabanek and James McCormick, *Follies & Fallacies in Medicine* [Glasgow, Scotland: Tarragon Press, 1989; reprinted Amherst, NY: Prometheus Books 1990], 35.)

[27] Brief for Respondents, *Joiner* III (note 25 above) (No. 96–188), 1997 WL 436250, *41 ("Brief for Respondents").

[28] *Id.*, *43 n.59, quoting Laurence Tribe, "Trial by Mathematics: Precision and Ritual in the Legal Process," *Harvard Law Review* 84 (1971): 1329–93, 1350.

G.E., however, argued that what Joiner's attorneys presented as reputable scientific methodology was nothing more than the "faggot fallacy": the fallacy of supposing that a pile of weak evidence, if it is large enough, is magically transmuted into strong evidence.[29]

Ruling unanimously that the proper standard of review remained abuse of discretion, the *Joiner* Court sidestepped Joiner's argument about "weight of evidence methodology" with the brisk observation that methodology and conclusions "are not entirely distinct from one another," and that a court may reasonably conclude that there is "simply too great an analytical gap between the data and the opinion proffered."[30] And then, briefly reviewing (some of) the testimony that Joiner's experts would have given had they been admitted, the court found, almost unanimously, that the district court had not abused its discretion in excluding Joiner's experts.[31]

But on this last point there was one dissenter, Justice Stevens, who argued that it would have been better to have remanded the case to the appeals court for reconsideration under the appropriate standard of review. Joiner's experts had referred to numerous studies, he points out, only one of which was in the record, and only six of which were ever considered by the District Court; moreover, he continues, the majority view on the question of reliability, which required it to play down the distinction of methodology and conclusions, "arguably is not faithful to … *Daubert*."[32] (Indeed: after all, the distinction of methodology vs. conclusions, which the majority rather casually sets aside in *Joiner*, was front-and-center in *Daubert*.)[33] And, like the Court of Appeals, Justice Stevens believed there was merit in Joiner's experts' epistemological argument:

> It is not intrinsically "unscientific" for experienced professionals *to arrive at a conclusion by weighing all available scientific evidence*—this is not the sort of "junk science" with which Daubert was concerned. After all, as Joiner points out, the Environmental Protection Agency (EPA) uses the same methodology to assess risks, albeit using a somewhat different threshold. …[34]

Of course, whether, and if so how, a compilation of pieces of evidence none of which is sufficient by itself to warrant a causal conclusion to the required

29 Brief for Petitioners (note 26 above), *49.

30 *Joiner* III (note 25 above), 146.

31 *Id.*, 146–47 (holding that abuse of discretion is the applicable standard, and that the district court did not abuse its discretion in excluding Joiner's experts).

32 *Id.*, 152 (Stevens, J., dissenting in part).

33 *Daubert* III (note 24 above), 595 ("The focus, of course, must be solely on principles and methodology, not on the conclusions that they generate").

34 *Joiner* III (note 25 above), 153 (Stevens, J., dissenting in part) (my italics) (footnote omitted).

degree of proof might do so jointly is a question that arises over and over in toxic-tort cases, though not always as explicitly as in *Oxendine* and *Joiner*—and, more recently, in *Milward v. Acuity Specialty Products*.[35] The epistemological puzzle comes out particularly vividly in the first case described here, in Dr. Done's testimony in *Oxendine*: the structure-activity toxicological evidence is not sufficient to make the case for causation, he acknowledges; nor is the evidence from *in vitro* studies, nor the evidence from animal studies, nor his statistical re-analyses. But put them all together, he continues, and somehow—presto!—they amount to proof of causation.[36] But *how*, exactly? He doesn't say; and neither, but for that nice metaphor of a mosaic, does Judge Terry. The purpose of the next section is to fill this "analytical gap."[37]

2 MAKING THE EPISTEMOLOGICAL ARGUMENT

The first thing to notice is that, while up to now we have been approaching it from the perspective of causation evidence in toxic-tort cases, where legally it has been especially salient, the epistemological question at issue is really quite general, arising in virtually every area of inquiry.[38]

Think, for example, of that meteorite discovered in Antarctica in 1984 and believed, on the basis of the gases it gives off when heated, to have come from Mars about 4 billion years ago. A chemist at Stanford discovered that the meteorite contained molecules of polycyclic aromatic hydrocarbons (PAHs), which are found not only in diesel exhaust and soot, but also in decomposed organic matter; and other scientists discovered that the crystals of carbonate in the meteorite were shaped like cubes and teardrops, like those formed by bacteria on earth. By 1997, Dr. David Mackay of the Johnson Space Center was ready to say, in an interview for *Newsweek*, that "*[w]e have these lines of*

35 Milward v Acuity Specialty Prods. Grp., Inc., 639 F.3d 11 (1st Cir. 2011). See also Castillo v. E.I. du Pont de Nemours & Co., 854 So. 2d 1264, 1272 (Fla. 2003) (reporting that Dr. Van Velzen "repeatedly asserted that he used the in-vitro testing as one source of data, in conjunction with other reliable data, to reach the conclusion. He testified that *the consideration of all the data together is a commonly accepted scientific practice*") (my italics).

36 See *Oxendine* I (note 2 above), 1108 (reporting that "[t]hroughout his testimony [Dr. Done] repeatedly stated that this opinion was based not on any single study or type of evidence, but on four different types of scientific data viewed in combination").

37 These examples will recur throughout the paper; so perhaps it is necessary for me to say right away that my argument is *not* that Bendectin causes birth defects, or that PCBs cause small-cell lung cancer—or, of course, that they don't. Even if I had all the evidence—which, obviously, I don't—I would not be competent to make such judgments.

38 Perhaps Prof. Rothman and his colleagues had noticed this. See Brief Kenneth Rothman et al. (note 23 above), *10 (commenting that "[t]his commonsense observation is not novel or controversial").

evidence. None of them in itself is definitive, but taken together the simplest explanation is early Martian life";[39] and as more evidence came in over more than a decade of further research, this conclusion has become more firmly warranted.[40] Nor is this an isolated example; on the contrary, with respect to virtually any well-warranted scientific claim of any importance—that DNA is the genetic material,[41] for example, or that species evolve through a process of natural selection[42]—the evidence is a complex mesh of interwoven elements.

Nor, for that matter, is this reliance on many intersecting lines of evidence confined to the sciences. Think, for example, of a historian relying on archaeological and on documentary evidence (and perhaps also on the scientific theory underlying techniques for dating remains, or for identifying the paper on which or the ink with which a document is written), or on a combination of

39 Sharon Begley and Adam Rogers, "War of the Worlds: There Are No Little Green Men on Mars. But There Are Some Very Hostile Fellows on Earth Debating Whether There Was Life on the Red Planet," *Newsweek*, February 10, 1997, 56–58 (my italics).

40 See Thomas H. Maugh III, "Probe Enters Mars Orbit," *Los Angeles Times*, March 11, 2006, A12 (reporting that it is now known that there was once water on Mars, and that a second Martian meteorite also contains what may be Martian fossils). See also Michael Hanlon, "Is This Proof of Life on Mars? The Meteorite That May Finally Have Resolved the Great Mystery," *Daily Mail* (London, UK), February 10, 2006, 40. In 2013 NASA sent up a new rover, Curiosity, five times the size of its predecessors (Spirit and Opportunity, which landed on Mars in 2004). This new rover includes a small, mobile laboratory that can drill for and analyze samples. See Konstantin Kakaes, review of Roger Weins, "*Red Rover*: Inside the Story of Robotic Space Exploration, from Genesis to the Mars Rover Curiosity," *Washington Post*, May 10, 2013, available at http://articles.washington post.com/opinions/red-rover-inside-the-story-of-robotic-space-exploration-from-genesis-to-the-mars-rover-curiosity-by-roger-weins/2013/05/10/9afeb994-b0e-11e2-baf7–5bc2a9dc6f44_story.html; Planetsave, "Mars Rover Curiosity—NASA's Rover Gearing Up For Second Ever Rock Drilling and Sampling On Mars," May 12, 2013, available at http://planetsave.com/2013/05/12/mars-rover-curiosity-nasas-gearing-up-for-second-ever-rock-drilling-and-sampling-on-mars#GCFgQ8G1BAQAQ0XH.03.

41 In 1944, when Oswald Avery published the report of the experiments that are now recognized as having established that DNA, not protein, is the genetic material, he was unwilling to draw the conclusion in print, and it was not generally accepted until after Hershey and Chase's experiments, published in 1952. See Oswald T. Avery, Colin M. MacCleod, and Maclyn McCarty, "Studies of the Chemical Nature of the Substance Inducing Transformation in Pneumococcal Types," *Journal of Experimental Medicine* 79 (1944):137–58; A. D. Hershey and Martha Chase, "Independent Functions of Viral Protein and Nucleic Acid in Growth of Bacteriophage," *Journal of General Physiology* 36 (1952): 39–56. By 1953, when Watson and Crick published their paper on the structure of DNA, the role of DNA in heredity was only very imperfectly understood, and according to Crick only in the 1980s was the conclusion firmly established. See James D. Watson and Francis Crick, "Molecular Structure of Nucleic Acids: A Structure for Deoxyribonucleic Acid," *Nature* 171, no. 3 (April 25, 1953): 737–38; see also Francis Crick, *What Mad Pursuit: A Personal View of Scientific Discovery* (New York: Basic Books, 1988), 7.

42 For a helpful summary of this extraordinarily extensive and varied evidence, see *Understanding Evolution: Your One-Stop Source for Information about Evolution*, available at http://evolution.berkeley.edu/evolibrary/articles/0_0_0?lines_01.

written records and the testimony of still-living witnesses. In fact, this kind of reliance on a whole mesh of evidence is ubiquitous—the rule, not the exception. It is commonplace in everyday life: when, for example, after reading a startling story in a newspaper, I buy a different paper,[43] or turn on the television news, to check whether other sources confirm it. And this reliance on a combination of lines of evidence is familiar in many legal contexts too: when, for example, we ask a jury to arrive at a conclusion based on the testimony of eyewitnesses, plus the testimony of a psychologist testifying to the circumstances in which eyewitnesses are more, or less, reliable, plus forensic evidence, plus testimony about the error-rate of this laboratory, plus, … etc.

The epistemological question at issue is quite general, so we need a general answer. And since warrant is clearly a matter of degree (as I took for granted in describing the hypothesis that there was early Martian bacterial life as weakly warranted fifteen years ago, and significantly more strongly warranted by now), this general answer should tell us under what conditions the factors that determine degree of warrant work in such a way as to enhance degree of warrant when diverse pieces of evidence are combined. My answer—based on the account of the determinants of degree of warrant presented in "Epistemology and the Law of Evidence"[44]—is that a combination of pieces of evidence will warrant a conclusion to a higher degree than any of its components alone would do *when, but only when*, combining the various elements:

(i) enhances *supportiveness*; and/or

(ii) enhances the *independent security* of evidence favorable to the conclusion, or diminishes the *independent security* of evidence unfavorable to the conclusion; and/or

(iii) enhances *comprehensiveness* by introducing further evidence no less favorable than the rest.

The reference to "favorable" evidence in (ii) and (iii) reflects the fact that the three determinants of evidential quality are not quite symmetrical. Supportiveness is directly correlated with degree of warrant; i.e., the more supportive the evidence is of a conclusion, the better warranted the conclusion (as a crossword entry is more reasonable the better it fits with the clue and other completed entries). But the connection between independent security

43 During a 2008 visit to Spain, intrigued by their names, I bought copies of both of the two newspapers published in Murcia: *La Verdad* ("*Truth*") and *La Opinión*. (Friends told me that *La Verdad* is a very conservative publication, *La Opinión* more liberal.) Both carried the same front-page story, of a woman strangled in the center of the town.

44 "Epistemology and the Law of Evidence: Problems and Projects," pp. 1–26 in this volume, 12–16.

and warrant is a bit more complicated. The more independently secure evidence *for* a conclusion is, the more warranted the conclusion; but the more independently secure the evidence *against* a conclusion is, the less warranted the conclusion (as, in a crossword, the fact that our answer to 4 down fits with our answer to 2 across is the more reassuring the more confident we are that 2 across is right; but if our answer to 4 down *doesn't* fit with 2 across, this is less troubling the *less* confident we are that 2 across is right). Similarly, the more comprehensive evidence *for* a conclusion is, the better warranted the conclusion; but if making the evidence more comprehensive also makes it less positive, the increase in comprehensiveness lowers the degree of warrant of the conclusion (as completing more of the crossword makes us more confident in the correctness of the completed entries if they all fit together, but undermines our confidence if it introduces inconsistencies.)

If we apply this rather abstract analysis to a schematic example based on the kinds of congeries of evidence typically encountered in toxic-tort cases, and look at the effect of combining evidence on supportiveness, independent security, and comprehensiveness, we will see how—as Justice Stevens and Judge Terry believed—combining evidence really can enhance the degree of warrant of a causal conclusion.

Suppose the claim at issue is that exposure to substance S causes, or promotes, disorder D: e.g., that a pregnant woman's taking Bendectin causes birth defects in her baby, or that exposure to PCBs promotes the development of lung cancer. The evidence, E, relevant to the conclusion, C, might include, in the foreground, most directly relevant, any or all of the following elements:

- epidemiological studies (from clinical trials or medical surveys) of the incidence of D among those exposed to S, as compared with its incidence among those not exposed to S;
- meta-analyses of such epidemiological studies, indicating what, if any, elevated risk of D is suggested by their combined data;
- information about whether the incidence of D in the population falls when S is withdrawn from the market (or cleared out of buildings, or whatever);
- information about what the components of S are (say a, b, and c), and of whether exposure to any other substance(s) containing one or more of these, or to chemicals of the same general type, is associated with elevated risk of D;
- results of *in vivo* studies indicating whether animals deliberately exposed to S develop D or precursors of D;

- results of *in vitro* studies indicating whether cells or embryos deliberately exposed to S develop D or precursors of D;
- ideas about whether there is (are) any biological mechanism(s) by which exposure to S (or to a, b, and/or c) might cause D, or reasons for believing that S (or a, b, or c) could not cause D.

But the evidence with respect to a causal conclusion may also include a good deal of background information of other kinds, bearing on it a bit less directly:

- meta-evidence with respect to all the types of evidence listed above: for example, about what is required of a well-designed and well-executed epidemiological, toxicological, *in vitro*, or *in vivo* study (e.g., what variables need to be controlled for, etc.), and what constitutes a well-designed and well-conducted meta-analysis (e.g., what determines which studies are good enough to be included in a meta-analysis and which are best disregarded);
- background information about what other factors (such as genetic susceptibilities) might contribute to the development of D;
- background information (or conjecture) about what proportion of cases of D derive from what kinds of known (or suspected) cause;
- relevant chemical, biological, physiological, genetic, etc., theory potentially bearing on S or on D;[45]
- ideas about what, in what is not yet known, is reasonably believed to be potentially relevant to the etiology of D.

And there may, additionally, be obliquely relevant evidence (meta-meta-evidence?) about the sources of all these kinds of evidence,[46] bearing indirectly on its credibility, and hence, at one remove, on the credibility of C:

- the fact that relevant studies were published after peer review in well-respected journals, or were published by editorial privilege in low-status journals, or were not published at all;

45 For example, as late as the early 1950s it was widely believed that nothing harmful could cross the placenta from mother to fetus. Since 1955, however, it was known that substances with a molecular weight of less than 1,000 *could* cross the placenta into fetal blood. Rock Brynner and Trent Stephen, *Dark Remedy: The Impact of Thalidomide and Its Revival as a Vital Medicine* (Cambridge, MA: Perseus Publishing, 2001), 12.

46 Because legal players are not experts in epidemiology, toxicology, etc., and don't have the kind of extensive background knowledge required to make judicious judgments of plausibility, this kind of (indirect, external) evidence probably plays a more significant role in legal contexts than, ideally, it might.

- facts about who conducted the relevant research: perhaps the manufacturer, or scientists funded by the manufacturer (and whether the research was paid for out of the manufacturer's research budget, or out of its litigation fund), or university scientists receiving some perks from the manufacturer, or independent scientists with no connections to either party in a suit;
- the fact that this witness is (or is not) a repeat testifier in such cases as this, that his resumé shows that he is (or is not) a professional expert witness rather than an active scientist; etc.
- facts (meta-meta-meta-evidence?) about whether studies funded by manufacturers tend to be more favorable to their products than studies conducted independently,[47] how often peer reviewed papers are retracted,[48] whether papers in lower-ranked journals are retracted more often than those published in more prestigious fora, etc., etc.

E may include evidence of all the kinds listed, or only some; and it may be all positive (i.e., supportive of C over not-C), or all negative, or mixed. For obvious reasons, though, in the cases that come to court the evidence is usually incomplete, mixed, or, most often, both; for if it were entirely unambiguous one way or the other, either the claim would never have been brought, or it would have been settled out of court.

[47] In fact, many studies-of-studies confirm that company-funded research on drugs or medical devices is significantly more likely than independent research to be favorable to the company's products. See e.g., Richard A. Davidson, "Sources of Funding and Outcomes of Clinical Trials," *Journal of General. Internal Medicine* 1 (1986): 155–58; Paula Rochon et al., "A Study of Manufacturer-Supported Trials of Non-Steroidal Anti-Inflammatory Drugs in the Treatment of Arthritis," *Archives of Internal Medicine* 154, no. 2 (January 24, 1994): 157–63; Lee S. Friedman and Elihu D. Richter, "Relationship Between Conflict of Interest and Research Results," *Journal of Internal Medicine* 19, no. 1 (January 2004): 51–56. While legal commentators tend to be preoccupied with litigation-driven science, we should not forget that marketing-driven science may also be tendentious. See e.g., Kevin P. Hill at al., "The ADVANTAGE Seeding Trial: A Review of Internal Documents," *Annals of Internal Medicine* 149, no. 4 (August 19, 2008): 251–58, 251 (arguing that internal documents show that Merck's 1999 ADVANTAGE trial of Vioxx was "a seeding trial developed by Merck's marketing division to promote prescription of Vioxx (rofecoxib) when it became available … in 1999").

[48] The medical indexing service PubMed assigns a number or "PMID" (PubMed Identifier) to each article, and it is possible to search for e.g., "Retraction of Publication." On retractions of fraudulent work, see e.g., Laura Bonetta, "The Aftermath of Scientific Fraud," *Cell* 124, no. 5 (March 10, 2006): 873–75; Harold C. Sox and Drummond Rennie, "Research Misconduct, Retraction, and Cleansing the Medical Literature: Lessons from the Poehlman Case," *Annals of Internal Medicine* 144 (2006): 609–613; Jennifer Couzin and Katherine Unger, "Cleaning Up the Paper Trail," *Science* 312 (2006): 38–43.

No single element of a congeries of evidence such as E will be sufficient by itself to establish a causal conclusion. The effects of S on animals may be different from its effects on humans. The effects of b when combined with a and c may be different from the effects of b alone, or when combined with x and/or y. If our toxicological knowledge is incomplete, we may have failed to take into account, e.g., that different optical isomers of the suspect substance have different physiological effects.[49] Even an epidemiological study showing a strong association between exposure to S and elevated risk of D would be insufficient by itself: it might be poorly-designed, for example, and/or poorly-executed. Moreover, what constitutes a well-designed study—e.g., what controls are needed—itself depends on further information about the kinds of factor that might be relevant. And even an excellent epidemiological study may pick up, not a causal connection between S and D, but a common underlying cause of both exposure to S and D; or possibly reflect the fact that people in the very early stages of D develop a craving for S. Nor is evidence that the incidence of D fell after S was withdrawn sufficient by itself to establish causation—perhaps vigilance in reporting D was relaxed after S was withdrawn, or perhaps exposure to X, Y, Z was also reduced, and one or all of these cause D, or, etc.[50]

But combining evidence, as in my schematic example, *can* help exclude explanations other than S's causing D, and thus warrant the conclusion more firmly. To understand under what conditions E would warrant C to a higher degree than any of $e_1, e_2, \ldots, e_n$ individually, we need to look at the effect of combining these on the overall supportiveness of E, on the independent security of each element of E, and on the comprehensiveness of E.

(i) *The effect of combining evidence on supportiveness*: How supportive evidence is of a conclusion depends on how well the evidence and the

49 As, apparently, was the case with Thalidomide; see note 86 below.

50 Dr. Robert Brent, the editor of *Teratology*, who testified repeatedly for Merrell Dow in the Bendectin cases as an expert on "secular trend data," emphasized that though Bendectin had been off the US market since 1983, the rate of reported birth defects had remained steady. But, by a parallel argument to the one in the text, this is insufficient by itself to rule out a casual conclusion. And indeed, we know that after the withdrawal of Bendectin, some doctors began prescribing vitamin B6 and half a Unisom tablet for morning-sickness; and that doxylamine succinate, the suspect ingredient in Bendectin, is also an ingredient of Unisom (and of Nyquil). See Janelle Yates, "Nausea and Vomiting of Pregnancy: Q&A with T. Murphy Goodwin," *OBG Management* 16, no. 8 (August 2004): 54–67, 55 (recommending vitamin B6 and, if vomiting continues, adding 12.5 mg doxylamine by halving the over-the-counter Unisom tablet). On Nyquil (as well as Unisom), see also Joseph Sanders, "From Science to Evidence: The Testimony on Causation in the Bendectin Cases," *Stanford Law Review* 46, no. 1 (1993): 1–86, 10.

conclusion fit together to form an explanatory account. So combined evidence will support a conclusion better than its component parts individually if the conjunction of E and C makes a better explanatory account than the conjunction of e_1 and C, a better explanatory account than the conjunction of e_2 and C, . . ., and so on. What makes the degree of support given to C by E greater than the degree of support given to C by e_1, the degree of support given to C by e_2, etc., is *how tightly its components interlock* to form an explanatory account. For example, evidence of a biological mechanism by which S might bring about D interlocks with epidemiological evidence of increased risk of D among those exposed to S, to explain a formerly-unexplained aspect of the story; evidence that S contains b, and that it is b that is associated with increased risk of D, interlocks with epidemiological evidence of an increased risk of D among those exposed to S to make a formerly superficial explanation deeper; and background biological, physiological, chemical, etc., theory interlocks with evidence of the risks to humans of exposure to S to increase the scope of a formerly narrow explanatory account.

For the elements of E to interlock at all, the same terms ("S," "b," "D," etc) must occur throughout, as they do in my schematic list; and the elements will interlock more tightly the more narrowly these terms are characterized, i.e., the more specific they are. For example, joint support will be enhanced more if "D" is "small-cell lung cancer" than if it is simply "lung cancer" or "cancer," or if it is "limb-reduction birth defects" rather than "birth defects"; if "b" is "doxylamine succinate" rather than "antihistamine," or "Benlate"[51] rather than "fungicide"; and so on.

The elements of E will also interlock more tightly the more physiologically similar the animals used in any *in vivo* studies are to human beings. The results of tests on hummingbirds or frogs would barely engage at all with epidemiological evidence of risk to humans, while the results of tests on mice, rats, guinea-pigs, or rabbits would interlock more tightly with such evidence, and the results of tests on primates more tightly yet. Of course, "similar" has to be understood as elliptical for "similar in the relevant respects"; and *which* respects are relevant may depend on, among other things, the mode of exposure: if humans are exposed to S by inhalation, for example, it matters whether the laboratory animals used have a similar rate of respiration. Again, the results of animal tests will interlock more tightly with evidence of risk to humans the

[51] In *Castillo* (note 35 above), Benlate was the fungicide to which Ms Castillo claimed she had been exposed, and which she believed had caused her baby's birth defect, severely underdeveloped eyes (microophthalmia).

more similar the dose of S involved. (One weakness of Joiner's expert testimony was that the animal studies relied on involved injecting massive doses of PCBs into a baby mouse's peritoneum, whereas Mr. Joiner had been exposed to much smaller doses when the contaminated insulating oil splashed onto his skin and into his eyes.)[52] The timing of the exposure may also matter, e.g., when the claim at issue is that a pregnant woman's being exposed to S causes this or that specific type of damage to the fetus.

Again, the elements of E will interlock more tightly the more closely *in vitro* studies match the conditions of human exposure. For example, the plaintiffs in *Castillo v. du Pont* go to great pains to show that exposure of cells to Benlate in the *in vitro* studies to which they appealed was as nearly as possible the same as the exposure Ms. Castillo's unborn baby had allegedly undergone when his mother was accidentally sprayed with Benlate being used on neighboring fields.[53]

(ii) *The effect of combining evidence on independent security*: Combining evidence may also enhance independent security—just as the fact that this crossword entry interlocks with others which in turn interlock with others, ..., and so on, makes you more confident that it is correct. To be sure, adding evidence from animal studies won't make a flawed epidemiological study any less flawed, adding evidence of a physiological mechanism won't make a sloppily-conducted *in vitro* study any more rigorous, nor ..., etc.; which seems to be the point Skrabanek and McCormick are making when they explain that the "faggot fallacy" is a fallacy because "a bundle of insecure evidence remains insecure."[54] However, if we add, to only modestly secure epidemiological evidence of an elevated risk of D among those exposed to S, the further evidence that there is a biological mechanism by which S leads to D, this additional evidence enhances the security of the conclusion of the epidemiological study. (Similarly, if I add a column of numbers and reach the answer *n*, but am not sure my answer is right because I was interrupted in the middle of my calculation, asking someone else to check the arithmetic and

52 *Joiner* III (note 25 above), 144.

53 See e.g., *Castillo* (note 35 above), 1274 (reporting that "Dr. Howard considered what clothes Donna Castillo was wearing when she was exposed, and her height and weight to determine the amount of skin exposed, and used DuPont's data to calculate the amount of benomyl [the suspect ingredient in Benlate] that would have been absorbed and passed though [*sic*] her system")

54 Skrabanek and McCormick, *Follies & Fallacies in Medicine* (note 26 above), 35. See also Alvan R. Feinstein, "Scientific Standards in Epidemiologic Studies of the Menace of Everyday Life," *Science* 242, no. 4883 (December 2, 1988): 1257–63.

finding that they get the same answer properly increases my confidence in the answer I got the first time—even though, obviously, it doesn't change the fact that I was interrupted, nor the fact that, without this evidence, I should be less confident of the answer.)

(iii) *The effect of combining evidence on comprehensiveness*: E is of course more comprehensive than any of its components alone; and this may enhance the degree of warrant of C (as completing a new entry in a crossword puzzle in a way compatible with the existing entries gives you reason to be more confident in them all). If, for example, we add to epidemiological evidence indicating an elevated risk of D among those exposed to S [e_1], evidence about the chemical composition of S and the damaging physiological effects of its components [e_2], and evidence of the biological mechanism by which exposure to S causes D [e_3], this combined evidence will warrant the causal conclusion to a higher degree than any component part of this evidence standing alone. Evidence of a statistical association of smoking and lung cancer,[55] for example, warrants a causal conclusion to a higher degree if it is combined with evidence of a causal mechanism; statistical evidence that women are more susceptible than men would warrant a causal conclusion to a higher degree if it is combined with evidence of the role of female hormones in speeding things up.[56] However, the degree of warrant will go down, rather than up, if

55 Five studies published in 1950 are now seen as ground-breaking: Richard Doll and Austin Bradford Hill, "Smoking and Carcinoma of the Lung: Preliminary Report," *British Medical Journal* 2 (4682) (September 30, 1950): 739–48; Morton L. Levin, Hyman Goldstein, and Paul R. Gerhardt, "Cancer and Tobacco Smoking: A Preliminary Report," *Journal of the American Medical Association* 143, no. 4 (1950): 336–38; Clarence A. Mills and Marjorie Mills Porter, "Tobacco Smoking Habits and Cancer of the Mouth and Respiratory System," *Cancer Research* 10, no. 9 (1950): 539–42; Robert Schrek, Lyle A. Baker, George P. Ballard, and Sidney Dolgoff, "Tobacco Smoking as an Etiologic Factor in Disease. Part I: Cancer," *Cancer Research* 10, no. 1 (1950): 49–58; Ernest L. Wynder and Evarts A. Graham, "Tobacco Smoking as a Possible Etiologic Factor in Bronchiogenic Carcinoma: A Study of 684 Proved Cases," *Journal of the American Medical Association* 143, no. 4 (May 27, 1950): 329–36. (By 1953, 13 more such studies had appeared.)

56 Michaela Kreuzer et al., "Hormonal Factors and Risk of Lung Cancer in Women?" *International Journal of Epidemiology* 32, no. 1 (2003): 263–71 (suggesting exactly this). But see also Leno Thomas, L. Austin Doyle, and Martin J. Edelman, "Lung Cancer in Women: Emerging Differences in Epidemiology, Biology, and Therapy," *Chest* 128, no. 1 (2005): 370–81, 370 ("[e]merging evidence suggests there are differences in the pathogenesis and possibly increased susceptibility to lung cancer in women"); International Early Lung Cancer Action Program Investigators, "Women's Susceptibility to Tobacco Carcinogens and Survival After Diagnosis of Lung Cancer," *Journal of the American Medical Association* 296, no. 2 (2006): 180–84, 180 ("[w]omen appear to have increased susceptibility to tobacco carcinogens but have a lower rate of fatal outcome of lung cancer compared to men"); Geoffrey C. Kabat, Anthony B. Miller, and Thomas E. Rohan, "Reproductive and Hormonal Factors and Risk

the additional evidence is negative, or even less positive, than the rest. If, for example, we add to evidence from animal studies indicating an elevated risk of D in those exposed to S [e_1], evidence that an epidemiological study finds *no* elevated risk in humans [e_2], the degree of warrant given C by this combined evidence will be lower, not higher.

~

What I have offered is a theoretical analysis, an abstract characterization of the determinants of evidential quality—an analysis powerful enough, as we have seen, to show that combined evidence may indeed warrant a causal conclusion better than any of its components. It does not, however, purport to be a decision-procedure for arriving at a conclusion about the reliability or otherwise of causation (or other) evidence. Nevertheless, it sheds some light on the kerfuffle over "weight of evidence methodology" in *Joiner.* It should already be apparent that G. E.'s accusation that Joiner's experts committed a fallacy[57] in supposing that combined evidence warrants their causal conclusion better than its individual elements rests on a mistake. But it should also be clear—though it is, perhaps, not quite so obvious—that Joiner's appeal to "weight of evidence methodology" is itself somewhat misleading, at least if it is intended to suggest that there is something like an algorithm or protocol, i.e., a mechanical procedure for calculating the combined worth of evidence.

This is also apparent if one looks closely at the 1986 EPA Guidelines for Carcinogen Risk Assessment,[58] to which Joiner's attorneys refer.[59] These guidelines advise that ""[t]he question of how likely an agent is to be a human carcinogen should be answered in the framework of a weight-of-evidence

of Lung Cancer in Women: A Prospective Cohort Study," *International Journal of Cancer* 120, no. 10 (2007): 2214–20, 2214 ("[s]everal lines of evidence suggest that endocrine factors may play a role in the development of lung cancer in women, but the evidence is limited and inconsistent"); Diana C. Marquéz-Garbán et al., "Estrogen Receptor Signaling Pathways in Human Non-Small Cell Lung Cancer," *Steroids* 72, no. 2 (February 2007): 135–43, 136 ("[e]strogen status appears to be a significant factor in lung cancer in women ..."); Patricia O'Keefe and Jyoti Patel, "Women and Lung Cancer," *Seminars in Oncology Nursing*, 24, no. 1 (February 2008): 3–8, 4 ("[w]omen may be more susceptible to the carcinogenic effects of lung carcinogens than men.... Research in this area is ongoing and is highly debated"); Neal D. Freedman, et al., "Cigarette Smoking and Subsequent Risk of Lung Cancer in Men and Women: Analysis of a Prospective Cohort Study," *Lancet Oncology* 9, no. 7 (July 2008): 649–56, available at http://oncology.thelancet.com (suggesting that the claim that women are more susceptible than men is questionable).

57 See note 26 and accompanying text above.

58 Environmental Protection Agency (EPA), Guidelines for Carcinogen Risk Assessment, 51 Fed Reg 33992 (1986).

59 *Joiner* III (note 25 above), 153–54 (Stevens, J., dissenting in part) (citing Brief for Respondents (note 27 above), *40–*41).

judgment";[60] however, they don't use the phrase "weight of evidence methodology," or offer anything like an algorithm for determining the joint weight of evidence. The section headed "Categorization of Overall Weight of Evidence for Human Carcinogenicity" simply describes how categories are assigned: "(1) The weight of evidence in human studies or animal studies is summarized; (2) these lines of information are combined to yield a tentative assignment to a category (see Table 1); and (3) all relevant supportive information is evaluated to see if the designation of the overall weight of evidence needs to be modified"—which amounts to little more than a fancy way of saying, "we look at all the available evidence and use our judgment to assess what it shows." Table 1—described as "for illustrative purposes" only—is a little more specific: for example, it indicates that a substance is categorized as a human carcinogen only when there is "sufficient" epidemiological evidence, and as a probable human carcinogen if there is "limited" epidemiological evidence but "sufficient" evidence from animal studies.[61] But this amounts to little more than requiring epidemiological evidence before putting a substance in the highest-risk category—provided that this epidemiological evidence is "sufficient."

The more recent, 2005, EPA Guidelines include a section with the curious but revealing heading "Weight of Evidence Narrative," which explains that the EPA still "emphasize the importance of weighing all of the evidence in reaching conclusions about the human carcinogenic potential of agents" but, moving away from the "step-wise approach" of the 1986 guidelines, now takes "a single integrative step." Data from epidemiological studies are generally preferred, but "all of the [epidemiological, *in vivo, in vitro*, toxicological, etc.] information … could provide valuable insights."[62] So far, perhaps, not much more helpful than the 1986 guidelines; but as one reads on, there are several observations worth noting.

First, these guidelines use the same metaphor of "fitting together" that I have used here:

> [t]he narrative explains the kinds of evidence available and *how they fit together* in drawing conclusions, and … points out significant issues/strengths/limitations of the data and conclusions.[63]

60 EPA, Guidelines for Carcinogen Risk Assessment (1986) (note 58 above), 33996.

61 *Id.*, 34000.

62 Environmental Protection Agency (EPA), *Guidelines for Carcinogen Risk Assessment* (Mar. 2005), § 1.3.3, 1–11, available at http://www.epa.gov/ttnatw01/cancer_guidelines_final_3-25-05.pdf.

63 *Id.*, 1–12 (my italics).

Second, they take for granted—just as I have here, in articulating *to what degree* evidence warrants a conclusion, and when a congeries of evidence warrants a conclusion *to a higher degree* than its components—that warrant is a matter of degree:

> descriptors ["human carcinogen," "probable human carcinogen," etc.] represent points along *a continuum of evidence*; … there are gradations and borderline cases….[64]

And third, they acknowledge the distinction I have stressed[65] between mathematical, frequency or propensity, probabilities (as in "the probability that a Swede is a Protestant is *n%*," or "the probability that a 60-year old American male will live to be 75 is *m%*") and epistemic likelihoods (as in "it is overwhelmingly likely that PCBs are carcinogenic"):

> [a]lthough the term "likely" can have a probabilistic connotation in other contexts, its use as a weight of evidence descriptor *does not correspond to a quantifiable probability* of whether the chemical is carcinogenic.[66]

But when it comes to the core question, "what determines the weight of combined evidence?" these guidelines fall back on the so-called "Bradford Hill criteria," drawn from Sir Austin Bradford Hill's now-classic 1965 lecture, "The Environment and Disease."[67] The next essay, "Correlation and Causation,"[68] will explore these in detail. So for now I will just point out, first, that what Hill offers aren't really "criteria," but only factors to be considered in determining whether a correlation is causal; second, that Hill's focus is much narrower than mine, concerned only with assessing the weight of combined evidence of causation, not the weight of combined evidence generally; and, third, that Hill's factors only apply where there is already epidemiological evidence of a positive correlation.

64 *Id.*, § 2.5, 2–51 (my italics).

65 See "Legal Probabilism: An Epistemological Dissent," pp. 47–77 in this volume, 56–64.

66 Environmental Protection Agency, *Guidelines for Carcinogen Risk Assessment* (2005) (note 62 above), § 2.5, 2–53 (my italics).

67 Austin Bradford Hill, "The Environment and Disease: Association or Causation?" *Proceedings of the Royal Society of Medicine* 58 (1965): 295–300. According to Michael D. Green, D. Michal Freedman, and Leon Gordis, "Reference Guide on Epidemiology," in Federal Judicial Center, *Reference Manual on Scientific Evidence*, 2nd ed., 333–400, 376, Bradford Hill was amplifying criteria proposed by the US Surgeon General in assessing the relationship between smoking and lung cancer. United States Department of Health, Education, and Welfare, *Smoking and Health Report of the Advisory Committee of the Surgeon General*, Public Health Service Publications No. 1103 (Washington, DC, 1964).

68 "Correlation and Causation: The 'Bradford Hill Criteria' in Epidemiological, Legal, and Epistemological Context," pp. 239–63 in this volume.

3 ANSWERING SOME CONTESTED QUESTIONS

The theoretical apparatus now in place suggests (at least the beginnings of) answers to a range of questions often hotly disputed in court—questions about proof of general causation (the main topic here), and even some questions about proof of specific causation.

(i) *Is epidemiological evidence of an elevated risk of D among those exposed to S essential to proof of general causation?*[69] No. "Epidemiologic studies," the 1986 EPA guidelines observe, "provide unique information about the response of humans who have been exposed to suspect carcinogens."[70] "[D]escriptive" epidemiological studies, they continue, "are useful in generating hypotheses and providing supportive data, but can rarely be used to make a causal inference"; however, "analytical" case-control or cohort studies "are especially useful in assessing risks to exposed humans."[71] Obviously, well-designed and well-conducted epidemiological studies showing an elevated risk would significantly increase the degree of warrant of a causal conclusion; and, of course, unlike animal studies, where there is always a question whether the animals used are enough like human beings in the relevant respects, epidemiological studies involve human subjects (which, no doubt, is why Table 1 in the 1986 EPA guidelines in effect allows epidemiological studies to trump animal studies). Nevertheless, if there is sufficient positive evidence of other kinds, a

[69] *Daubert* I (note 19 above), 575 (holding that, given that there was a vast body of epidemiological evidence regarding Bendectin, expert opinion not based on epidemiological evidence was not admissible). See also, e.g., Grimes v. Hoffmann-LaRoche, Inc., 907 F. Supp. 33, 35 (D.N.H. 1995) (excluding Dr. Lerman's testimony that Acutane played a role in Mr. Grimes's developing cataracts in part on the grounds that "[r]ather than relying on epidemiological data, Dr. Lerman bases his general causation opinion primarily on scientific theory, an in vitro experiment, and what he considers certain 'generally accepted' scientific facts"). Sutera v. Perrier Grp. of Am., 986 F. Supp. 655, 662 (D. Mass. 1997) (excluding plaintiffs' expert testimony because they have "produced no scientific peer-reviewed epidemiological studies which would associate APL [acute promyelocytic leukemia] ... and benzene exposure" at the relevant levels). *In re* Rezulin Prods. Liab. Litig., 369 F. Supp. 2d 398, 411 (S.D.N.Y. 2005) (excluding plaintiffs' expert testimony that the diabetes drug Rezulin caused "silent" liver damage, in part on the grounds that "[t]here are no clinical trials and no observational epidemiological studies supporting the plaintiffs' position"). *In re* Bextra & Celebrex Mktg. Sales Practices & Prod. Liab. Litig., 524 F. Supp. 2d 1166, 1175 (N.D. Cal. 2007) (excluding plaintiffs' expert testimony that Celebrex could cause cardiovascular effects at a dose of 200 mg. daily in part on the grounds that "there are no randomized controlled trials or meta-analyses of such trials or meta-analyses of observational studies that find an association between Celebrex 200 mg/d and a risk of heart attack or stroke").

[70] EPA, Guidelines for Carcinogen Risk Assessment (1986) (note 58 above), 33995.

[71] *Ibid.*

causal conclusion might be warranted to a non-negligible degree even in the absence of epidemiological evidence.

This is particularly significant when, for one reason or another, no relevant epidemiological studies are available, or possible.[72] Michael Gottesman argues that "it is quite rare" that "conclusive human epidemiological evidence is available"; for when it is suspected that a drug or chemical may be harmful, manufacturers are likely either to institute "protective procedures for future use of the product" or else to withdraw it from the market, which makes such epidemiological work much more difficult.[73] For example, he continues, PCBs had been routinely used in electrical transformers until reports began to link them to certain cancers, after which, in 1977, they were banned;[74] and after that, they were no longer used in transformers, and there was no longer any realistic possibility of conducting epidemiological studies of a possible link between PCBs and the kind of cancer Mr. Joiner developed.[75]

In any case, "there is no epidemiological evidence of an elevated risk of D in those exposed to S" is not equivalent to "there is epidemiological evidence that there is no elevated risk of D among those exposed to S." (Unlike the so-called "faggot fallacy," confusing these two very different propositions really *is* a fallacy.) For example, at one time there was no evidence one way or the other about whether patients who took Vioxx for less than 18 months had elevated cardiovascular risk—and early on in the Vioxx litigation, Merck argued as if this were evidence that there was no elevated cardiovascular risk among patients who took the drug only for a short time.[76] But when later

72 See, again, *Castillo* (note 35 above), 1269–70 (reporting that the plaintiff's expert argued that "clinical epidemiological studies are not available because Benlate is a toxic chemical and thus not suitable for human experiment," and that "in situations where exposure is very rare to begin with, there are inherent problems with epidemiological studies because a scientist cannot [ethically] expose a human to a known teratogen in order to study the effects").

73 Michael H. Gottesman, From *Barefoot* to *Daubert* to *Joiner*: Triple Play or Double Error?" 48 *Arizona Law Review* 40 (1998): 753–80, 767. (Mr. Gottesman argued for Mr. Joiner at the Supreme Court.)

74 Toxic Substances Control Act, Pub L No. 94–469, 90 Stat 2003, 2025 (1976), codified at 15 USC § 2605(e).

75 Gottesman, "From *Barefoot* to *Daubert* to *Joiner*" (note 73 above), 767.

76 "In an admission that could undermine one of its core defenses in Vioxx-related lawsuits, Merck said yesterday that it had erred when it reported in early 2005 that a crucial statistical test showed that Vioxx caused heart problems only after 18 months of use." Alex Berenson, "Merck Admits a Data Error on Vioxx," *New York Times*, May 3, 2006, C1, available at 2006 WLNR 9291555. In Plunkett v. Merck & Co. ("*Vioxx*—Plunkett/Experts"), 401 F. Supp. 2d 565, 596–99 (E.D. La. 2005) the plaintiffs moved to exclude Merck's testimony that Vioxx only causes prothombotic effects if taken for 18 months or more; but was denied on the grounds that both parties relied on the same study (the APPROVe study), while the court should be concerned only with methodology, not with the conclusions drawn.

studies looked at short-term Vioxx use, they found evidence suggesting that such risk went up as early as the first dose.[77] This brings home the lesson: that the absence of evidence that *p* is just that—an absence of evidence; it is not evidence that not-*p*.

(ii) *If there are relevant epidemiological studies, and they find no elevated risk of D among those exposed to S, is this always and inevitably fatal to a claim of general causation?* No, not always or necessarily. If they are good studies, yes; but if they are significantly flawed in ways that make it likely that they underestimated the risk, their negative results are not fatal to such a claim. In *Blum v. Merrell Dow*, for example, defendant's expert Dr. Shapiro acknowledged under cross-examination that his epidemiological study had lumped together women who took Bendectin during the period of pregnancy in which fetal limbs were forming, and women who took the drug only after the limbs had formed; so that it may have underestimated any elevated risk of limb-reduction defects.[78] Or, to take a more recent example, we now know that the VIGOR study, Merck's first large clinical trial of Vioxx, kept track of the gastrointestinal effects of Vioxx for longer than it kept track of the cardiovascular effects; and as a result, failed to find a statistically significant elevated risk of heart attack and stroke.[79]

(iii) *Is it acceptable to disregard, or on principle to exclude, epidemiological studies the results of which are not statistically significant?*[80] No. To be sure, the less statistically robust a study, the less it contributes to the warrant of

77 Patricia McGettigan and David Henry, "Cardiovascular Risk and Inhibition of Cyclooxygenase: A Systematic Review of the Observational Studies of Selective and Non-Selective Inhibitors on Cyclooxygenase," *Journal of the American Medical Association* 296, no. 2 (October 4, 2006), 1633–44, citing studies finding elevated risk with early Vioxx use; Wayne A. Ray et al., "COX-2 Selective Non-Steroidal Anti-Inflammatory Drugs and Risk of Serious Coronary Heart Disease," *Lancet* 360 (October 5, 2002): 1071–73; Daniel H. Solomon et al., "Relationship Between Selective Cyclooxygenase-2 Inhibitors and Acute Myocardial Infarction in Older Adults," *Circulation* 109 (2004): 2068–73; Linda Lévesque, James M. Brophy, and Bin Zhang, "Time Variations in the Risk of Myocardial Infarction Among Elderly Users of Cox-2 Inhibitors," published electronically at www.cmj.ca (May 2, 2006) and, abridged, in *Canadian Medical Association Journal* 174, no. 11 (May 23, 2006): 1563–69.

78 Blum v. Merrell Dow Pharm., Inc., 33 Phila. Cnty. Rep. 193, 215–17 (1996) ("*Blum* IV"). On the defendant's expert testimony in this case, see also "What's Wrong with Litigation-Driven Science?" pp. 180–207 in this volume, 188–94.

79 *See* David Armstrong, "Bitter Pill: How the *New England Journal of Medicine* Missed Warning Signs on Vioxx—Medical Weekly Waited Years to Report Flaws in Article that Praised Pain Drug—Merck Seen as 'Punching Bag,'" *Wall Street Journal*, May 15, 2006, A1, A10 (exploring problems with Merck's reporting of the VIGOR study). See also "Peer Review and Publication" (note 22 above), 169–71.

80 See again *In re* Bextra (note 69 above), 1166 (excluding plaintiffs' testimony on the risk of adverse events in those taking 200 mg. of Celebrex a day in part on the grounds that the

a causal conclusion. But the crucial point is that statistical significance is a matter of degree, and that the cut-off degree conventionally accepted is just that, a convention—a cut-off point adopted by the relevant scientific community, and set high to ensure that the risk of false positives is minimized.[81] Hill was right when he wrote, almost half a century ago, that the then fast-growing emphasis on statistical significance meant that "too often … we grasp the shadow and lose the substance" as we "deduce 'no significance' from 'no statistical significance.'"[82] But the trend he deplored is now firmly-entrenched practice.[83] And unfortunately, as Rothman et al. observe in their amicus brief in *Daubert*, "a factfinder who is told that a body of data is not 'statistically significant' is made to believe that the data has no value"; and, as they continue, the "talismanic" phrase "statistically significant" can create the completely misleading impression that statistically significant data are infallible.[84]

(iv) *Is it appropriate to disregard (or in principle to exclude) evidence from animal studies?*[85] Of course not. Obviously such studies can contribute to the warrant of a causal conclusion—the more so, the better-designed and better-conducted they are, using appropriate animals, doses, modes of delivery, times

epidemiological studies found no statistically significant association). See also *Daubert* I (note 19 above), 575 (giving this as part of the reason for excluding the Dauberts' expert testimony).

81 Moreover, there are different ways of calculating statistical significance, which sometimes give different results, and the choice of which is sometimes itself a matter of controversy. Keith J. Winstein, "Boston Scientific Stent Study Flawed," *Wall Street Journal*, August 14, 2008, B1, B6.

82 Hill, "The Environment and Disease" (note 67 above), 299–300.

83 Winstein, "Boston Scientific Stent Study Flawed" (note 81 above), B6 (noting that "medical journals typically won't publish" studies the results of which are not statistically significant).

84 Brief of Kenneth Rothman et al. (note 23 above), *4.

85 See e.g., Metabolife Int'l. Inc. v. Wornick, 72 F. Supp. 2d 1160, 1169 (S.D. Cal. 1999) (excluding Metabolife's scientific evidence, in part on the grounds that as a matter of law animal studies are inadmissible, "due to the uncertainties in extrapolating from effects on mice and rats to humans"). In 2001 the US Court of Appeals for the Ninth Circuit reversed this exclusion as an abuse of discretion by the trial court. Metabolife Int'l. Inc. v. Wornick, 264 F.3d 832 (9th Cir. 2001). See also *In re* Silicone Gel Breast Implants Prods. Liab. Litig. (California), 318 F. Supp. 2d 879, 891 (C.D. Cal. 2004) (excluding plaintiffs' evidence from animal studies on the grounds that "[e]xtrapolations of animal studies to human beings are generally not considered reliable in the absence of a scientific explanation of why such extrapolation is warranted") (quoting Hall v. Baxter Healthcare Corp., 947 F. Supp. 1387, 1410 (D. Or. 1996)). In *Joiner*, the District Court had agreed with G.E. that the animal studies on which his experts relied were inadequate to establish that Joiner's exposure to PCBs had promoted his cancer; at appeal, Joiner's attorneys (unwisely) argued as if the issue was whether animal studies, as such, can ever be a proper foundation for an expert's opinion. See *Joiner* III (note 25 above), 144.

of delivery, etc.[86] Of course, and no less obviously, there is always the possibility that animals are adversely affected by S, but humans are not, or vice-versa;[87] and if well-designed and well-conducted tests on animals show an elevated risk of D with exposure to S, but well-designed and well-conducted epidemiological studies show no elevated risk of D in humans exposed to S, we would rightly suspect that there might be relevant physiological differences of which we are not yet aware.

(v) *Is epidemiological evidence of at least a doubling of risk either necessary or sufficient to establish specific causation*? As we shall see in "Risky Business," the answer to both these questions is categorically "no." Evidence of relative risk greater than 2 isn't sufficient: if the study showing a more-then-doubled risk is poorly designed or poorly conducted, we would have only a low epistemic

86 I should stress, however, that what is involved in ensuring that animal studies are well-designed, use appropriate animals, doses, etc., can be enormously complex. The story of Thalidomide—initially sold as a sleeping pill, and now, decades later, used in the treatment of several disorders, notably multiple myeloma—illustrates the point. The manufacturers, Grünenthal, had tested Thalidomide on rats; and had found no bad effects. The scientists should have known that something was wrong, however, because *the rats didn't fall asleep*; but instead they responded by devising a non-standard test supposedly showing that the rats *were* sedated after all. Only after it was known that the drug caused terrible birth defects in human babies did chemists at St. Mary's Hospital, London, check the optical isomers of Thalidomide (which is asymmetrical, having two non-superimposable structures, or "mirror-images," the "left-handed" [–] and "right-handed" [+] forms). While the (+/–) form had no observable effect on mice, they found, the (–) form was highly toxic. Sergio Fabro, Robert L. Smith, and Richard T. William, "Toxicity and Teratogenicity of Optical Isomers of Thalidomide," *Nature* 215 (July 15, 1967): 296; see also Phillip Knightley, Harold Evans, Elaine Potter, and Marjorie Wallace, *Suffer the Children: The Story of Thalidomide* (New York: Viking, 1979), chapter 3. A recent article indicates that the left-handed (–) form works as a teratogen, and the right-handed (+) form as a sedative. Takumi Ito, Hideki Ando, and Horoshi Handa, "Teratogenic Effects of Thalidomide: Molecular Mechanisms," *Cell and Molecular Life Sciences*, available at http://link.springer.com/article/10.1007/s00018–010–0619–9 (2011). (Apparently, it is more expensive to separate the two isomers, so Grünenthal had used the (+/–) form.) The mechanism leading to limb-reduction birth defects was identified by Trent Stephens in 2000. Rock Brynner and Trent Stephens, *Dark Remedy: The Impact of Thalidomide and its Revival as a Vital Medicine* (Cambridge, MA: Perseus Publishing, 2001), chapter 11. I have, however, as yet been unable to find an explanation of why Thalidomide doesn't cause birth defects in rats and mice, as it does in humans.

87 "[O]ne can usually rely on the fact that a compound causing an effect in one mammalian species will cause it in another species. This is a basic principle of toxicology. . . ." Bernard D. Goldstein and Mary Sue Henifin, "Reference Guide on Toxicology," in Federal Judicial Center, *Reference Manual on Scientific Testimony* (Washington, DC: Federal Judicial Center, 2nd ed., 2000), 401–38, 410. However, animal studies have two disadvantages: the difficulty in extrapolating to humans because "differences in absorption, metabolism, and other factors may result in interspecies variation in responses"; and because "the high doses customarily used in animal studies" leave open questions about dose-response relation in humans. *Id*, 409.

likelihood of a more-than-doubled statistical probability. And evidence that relative risk is greater than 2 isn't necessary, either: there may be good reason to believe that some sub-group of the population is especially susceptible.

There is a related problem with another argument sometimes encountered, that if it is believed on reliable evidence that 10% of cases of D are genetic, and 20% caused by environmental factors, while the causes of the remaining 70% are unknown, the odds are that this plaintiff's D was not caused, as alleged, by exposure to S. Here the confusion of statistical and epistemic probabilities is overlaid by confusions of two other kinds: a false presumption that the cause of D must be *either* genetic *or* environmental (when there may be interaction between the two); and: treating "unknown" as if it referred to another type of cause, like "genetic" or "environmental"—when really, obviously, it is an expression of ignorance. If a plaintiff argues that it was exposure to S that caused him to develop D, and the defendant replies that this is unlikely, since we know that 70% of cases of D stem from unknown causes, the defendant's response is defective—because if the plaintiff's claim is true, what we *think* we know about what proportion of cases of D are caused by known factors, and what by unknown factors, may not, after all, be genuine knowledge.

When Donald Rumsfeld made that notorious remark about "unknown unknowns,"[88] the topic, of course, was US intelligence in Iraq. Perhaps I was the only person in the country who didn't laugh derisively; at any rate, from a strictly epistemological perspective, at least, Secretary Rumsfeld had a genuinely important point: not only may we not have all the evidence we know would be relevant (the "known unknowns" in Rumsfeldese); there may be evidence we don't have that we don't even realize is relevant. This—the Rumsfeld Problem of unknown unknowns—also bears on the next question on my list.

(vi) *Can we infer from the fact that the causes of D are as yet unknown, and that a plaintiff developed D after being exposed to S, that it was this exposure that caused* Ms. X's *or* Mr. Y's *D?*[89] No. Such evidence would certainly give

[88] Donald H. Rumsfeld, US Secretary of Defense, Department of Defense, News Briefing (February 12, 2002), transcript available at http://www.defenselink.mil.transcripts/transcript.aspx?transcriptid=2636: "Reports that say that something hasn't happened are always interesting to me. Because as we know, there are known knowns, there are things that we know we know. We also know that there are known unknowns, that is to say we know there are some things we do not know. But there are also unknown unknowns—the ones we don't know we don't know."

[89] See e.g., Rosen v. Ciba-Geigy Corp., 78 F.3d 316, 318 (7th Cir. 1996) (holding that the district court had not abused its discretion in excluding Dr. Fozzard's testimony that Mr. Rosen's heart attack was caused by his having worn a nicotine patch for three days before it occurred: "[w]hen an unusual event follows closely on the heels of another unusual event, the ordinary

us reason to look into the possibility that S is the, or a, cause of D. But loose talk of "inference to the best explanation" disguises the fact that what presently seems like the most plausible explanation may not really be so—indeed, may not really be an explanation at all. We may not know all the potential causes of D, or even which other candidate-explanations we would be wise to investigate.

4 EXPLORING THE PROBLEM OF EVIDENTIARY ATOMISM

Under *Daubert* courts must screen proffered expert testimony[90] for relevance and ("evidentiary") reliability. The focus here is on the reliability prong.

Reliability, I take it, is a matter of degree; admissibility, by contrast, is (normally) categorical: a witness is either allowed to testify, or to testify to this or that question,[91] or not.[92] So a court determining whether or not testimony is admissible is imposing a sharp, yes-or-no dichotomy on a continuum of degrees of reliability.[93] And the fact that parties facing a *Daubert* challenge

person infers a causal relation.... But lay speculations on medical causality, however plausible, are a perilous basis for inferring causality....").

[90] Some might prefer to put this a little differently: that *Daubert* clearly imposed this requirement with respect to scientific testimony, but only when the Supreme Court clarified the scope of *Daubert* in *Kumho Tire* was it clear that the requirement also applies to expert testimony other than the scientific. Kumho Tire Co. v. Carmichael, 526 U.S. 137 (1999).

[91] See e.g. United States v. Llera Plaza, Nos. CR 98–362–10, 98–362–11, 98–362–12, 2002 WL 27305 (E.D. Pa. Jan. 7, 2002) ("*Llera Plaza* I"). Judge Pollak ruled that fingerprint examiners' testimony was admissible on certain matters: "the parties will not be permitted to present testimony expressing an opinion of an expert witness that a particular latent print matches, or does not match, the rolled prints of a particular person and hence is, or is not, the fingerprint of that person." *Id.*, **19. (On reconsideration, Judge Pollak vacated his prior opinion and held that fingerprint experts may be allowed to testify in accordance with *Daubert* and Federal Rule of Evidence 702. United States v. Llera Plaza, 188 F. Supp. 2d (E.D. Pa. 2002) ("*Llera Plaza* II").)

[92] But see United States v. Brown (New York), 05 Cr. 00538 (JBR) (S.D.N.Y. June 18, 2008), 1468, 1484 (transcript of bench ruling from Southern District Reporters), *aff'd*, 374 F. App'x 208 (2d Cir. 2010) (reasoning that admissibility under *Daubert* need not be construed as categorical, and permitting ballistics examiners to testify only that their conclusions were more likely than not; and observing that the court "had a discussion about a year ago with Prof. Dan Capra [of Columbia and Fordham Law Schools]" and asked him "was Rule 702 supposed to be an absolute rule, in the sense of either it is in or it is out" and he said, no, not at all.... Of course, it is just his opinion.... But there are many situations where you may find that the methodology and the testimony is reliable to a degree not to a greater degree—not to the degree suggested by a witness and that Rule 702 then says don't throw the whole thing out but cabin it within certain limits"). See also United States v. Glynn, 578 F. Supp. 2d 567, 568–69 (S.D.N.Y. 2008) (referring to court's ruling in *Brown* (New York)).

[93] *See* Dale Nance, "Two Concepts of Reliability," American Philosophical Association, *Newsletter on Philosophy and Law* (Fall 2003): 123–27, 123.

to their proffered expert testimony must show "by a preponderance of the evidence" that this testimony meets the legal standard of reliability compounds the complexities. What they must show, apparently, is that *it is more likely than not* that this testimony is *likely enough* to satisfy the reliability prong of *Daubert.*

But the problem most immediately relevant to present purposes is that *Daubert* can encourage a kind of evidentiary atomism[94] that pulls against the quasi-holistic character of most causation evidence. Judge Kozinski's ruling in *Daubert* in remand from the Supreme Court is notably atomistic in tendency: Because the law had changed since the trial court granted summary judgment for Merrell Dow in 1989, Judge Kozinski argues, there might be a case for allowing the plaintiffs the opportunity to make a showing that their proffered expert testimony met the new standard;[95] however, he continues, this is unnecessary if it was already clear that their experts would have to be excluded under *Daubert,* as they had been under *Frye.* And in fact, he continues, this *is* already clear. Looking at each of the Dauberts' experts' proffered testimony one by one, Judge Kozinski observes, first, that all but one of them proposed to testify only that there was a possibility that Bendectin causes birth defects, and didn't even claim, let alone show, that a mother's taking the drug more than doubled the risk, and so would have to be excluded under the relevance prong;[96] and then that Dr. Palmer, the only expert who claimed more, that Bendectin caused Jason Daubert's birth defects, simply had no methodology to speak of, and so would have to be excluded under the reliability prong.[97] And, given its skepticism about Joiner's experts' "weight of evidence methodology," and its readiness to look one by one at (some of) the studies Joiner's experts would have cited had they been admitted, *Joiner* III can also encourage evidentiary atomism.[98]

94 Also sometimes called "corpuscularism." See Thomas O. McGarity, "Our Science Is Sound Science and Their Science Is Junk Science: Science-Based Strategies for Avoiding Accountability and Responsibility for Risk-Producing Products and Activities," *Kansas Law Review* 52, no. 4 (2004): 897–937, 921.

95 See *Daubert* IV (note 13 above), 1315. Indeed, the rhetoric of *Daubert* III was that the new standard was *more* hospitable to the admission of expert testimony than the old, "austere" *Frye* Rule. *Daubert* III (note 24 above), 589: "[t]hat austere standard, absent from, and incompatible with, the Federal Rules of Evidence, should not be applied in federal trials."

96 *Daubert* IV (note 13 above), 1321.

97 *Id.*, 1321 n.18.

98 True, as Professors Sanders and Green have pointed out, the talk in *Joiner* III (note 25 above) of "analytical gaps" between evidence and conclusion has encouraged some courts to look at plaintiffs' proffered expert testimony as a whole and, if they deem the "analytical gap" too large, to grant summary judgment for the defendants. Joseph Sanders and Michael D. Green, "Admissibility versus Sufficiency: Controlling the Quality of Expert Witness Testimony in

An atomistic approach requires that *each item* of expert evidence is to be screened for (relevance and) reliability. To be admissible, e_1 must be (relevant and) reliable, e_2 must be (relevant and) reliable, e_3 must be (relevant and) reliable, …, and so on.[99] But if my epistemological argument is correct, the combination of $e_1, e_2, \ldots, e_n$ may warrant a causal conclusion better than any of its components alone—may be, in *Daubert*'s terminology, more reliable than any of its components.

It might be thought—for a while I thought myself—that this difficulty could be avoided if *Daubert* were interpreted as requiring, not that each item of expert testimony reliably enough indicate the ultimate conclusion that exposure to S causes or promotes D, but that each item reliably enough indicates the conclusion of the study referred to: e.g., that the data from an epidemiological study reliably enough indicates the conclusion "there is an elevated risk of *n%*, among those exposed to S, of developing D," that the data from an animal study reliably enough indicate the conclusion "when animals of this kind are exposed to this dose of S, delivered in this manner, *m%* of them develop D," …, and so on. Arguably, there is some justification for this interpretation of the ruling in Justice Blackmun's footnote about the intended meaning of evidentiary reliability.[100] But it doesn't solve the problem.

"[D]elusive exactness," Oliver Wendell Holmes once shrewdly observed, "is a source of fallacy throughout the law."[101] And indeed, it's not clear that giving a precise meaning to "preponderance of the evidence" would be desirable, even if it were possible. But for the purposes of my argument it doesn't matter what, exactly, the "preponderance of the evidence" standard—a phrase which, interestingly enough, has the "weighing" metaphor built in[102]—amounts to. For the essential point is that, *however* one sets that standard, there could be instances in which the evidence is equally balanced, i.e., in which the evidence warrants C and not-C to the same degree; and in such circumstances even a minimal increment of warrant one way or the other would give a "preponderance" in favor of C, or against it. And while it is true that evidence

the United States," in Diego Papayannis, ed., *Uncertain Causation in Tort Law* (Cambridge: Cambridge University Press, forthcoming) (citing *Joiner* III (note 25 above), 146).

99 See McGarity, "Our Science Is Sound Science and Their Science Is Junk Science" (note 94 above), 924: "[u]nder the corpuscular approach, a study is either valid or it is invalid, and it is either relevant or irrelevant. A conclusion based on invalid or irrelevant studies cannot be relevant or reliable and must therefore be rejected."

100 *Daubert* III (note 24 above), 590 n.9 (characterizing "evidentiary reliability").

101 Truax v. Corrigan, 257 U.S. 312, 342 (1921) (Holmes, J., dissenting).

102 Merriam-Webster, *Webster's Ninth New Collegiate Dictionary* (Springfield, MA: Merriam-Webster Publishing, 1991), 929, defines "preponderance" as "superiority in weight, power, importance, or strength." (Compare "ponderous.")

e_j, favorable to C, will improve the warrant of C less if it is itself less than solid (and evidence e_k, unfavorable to C, will decrease the warrant of C less if it is itself less than solid), even such less-than-solid evidence might tip the scales, i.e., might make the difference between "evenly balanced" and "marginally favors C over not-C," or vice versa. And so, if some element of evidence that might have tipped the scale is excluded under the reliability prong of *Daubert*, this may actually impede assessment of the reliability of the scientific testimony in its entirety—because the jury will never hear any element that the court excludes on the grounds that it is insufficient by itself to meet the standard.[103]

Courts excluding scientific testimony under the reliability prong of *Daubert* may (at least sometimes) be motivated by concern that a jury presented with a lot of weak evidence may draw an unwarranted conclusion. A jury may, indeed, be misled in this way: for it doesn't follow from the fact that a combination of bits of evidence each of which, individually, is insufficient may jointly warrant a conclusion to a higher degree than any component element, that *any and every* combination of such evidence warrants the conclusion to the required standard of proof. But of course a jury may also be misled in the opposite direction; for it doesn't follow from the fact that a combination of pieces of evidence each individually insufficient may also be jointly insufficient, that *any and every* combination of such evidence fails to warrant the conclusion to the required degree. Whether this particular combination of evidence, in this particular case, does or doesn't fit together in such a way as to warrant the conclusion more than any of its components is a subtle and complex matter, challenging for a jury *or* for a judge—and even for highly-qualified and competent experts

[103] Of course, some rules of evidence—spousal privilege, for example, or FRE 407(b), under which "evidence of subsequent repair" is inadmissible—deliberately allow considerations of policy to preclude the presentation of evidence that may be highly relevant to the truth of claims at issue. Whether and when such rules are justifiable is a whole other issue, touched on in "Epistemology Legalized: Or Truth, Justice, and the American Way," pp. 27–46 in this volume, 41–42. But for present purposes I set this tangle of issues aside, since FRE 702 is clearly not such a policy-oriented rule.

—10—

Correlation and Causation: The "Bradford Hill Criteria" in Epidemiological, Legal, and Epistemological Perspective

> "So the litigation is used to shock the market?"
>
> "Yes, and, of course, to compensate the victims. I don't want tumors in my bladder, benign or malignant. Most jurors would feel the same way. Here's the scenario: You put together a group of fifty or so plaintiffs, and file a big lawsuit on behalf of all Dyloft patients. At precisely the same time you launch a series of television ads soliciting more cases. You hit fast and hard, and you'll get thousands of cases. The ads run coast to coast—quickie ads that'll scare folks and make them dial your toll-free number right here in D.C., where you have a warehouse full of paralegals answering the phones and doing the grunt work. It's gonna cost you some money, but if you get, say, five thousand cases, and you settle them for twenty thousand bucks each, that's one hundred million dollars. Your cut is one third."
>
> "That's outrageous!"
>
> "No, . . . that's mass tort litigation at its finest. . . ."
>
> —John Grisham[1]

1 THE BETTER PART OF VALOR

Of course, this cynical conversation (from John Grisham's novel *The King of Torts*) is fiction, not fact; still, it comes close enough to reality to bring an old proverb to mind. "Discretion is the better part of valor," I reminded myself when, shortly after cheerfully accepting an invitation to speak at a workshop on "proof of causation in mass torts," I realized I'd bitten off more than I could chew. For the fact is that mass torts—where large numbers of plaintiffs allege the same or closely similar injuries caused by the same defendant or group of

[1] John Grisham, *The King of Torts* (New York: Doubleday/Dell, 2003), 152.

defendants—raise far too many issues, legal, historical, and philosophical, for me to handle in one short paper (or even, I suspect, in one short lifetime!).

Very briefly, then: mass tort claims may involve allegations of injuries sustained when many people are involved in a large-scale accident, or are exposed to the same environmental or occupational toxin, or suffer the side effects of the same drug; or they may involve allegations of quite different kinds of injury, e.g. when many customers of car retailers or mortgage lenders, etc., or many employees of a large firm, are subject to discriminatory treatment. In the US, such claims have prompted a variety of legal responses. As the title of a 1991 article, "From 'Cases' to 'Litigation,'" suggests, aggregation of civil cases, with many plaintiffs coming together in preparation for trial or other types of adjudication, or for settlement, is a relatively recent phenomenon, arising only in the 1960s.[2] The procedures for handling such aggregated litigation include consolidation,[3] multi-district litigation,[4] bellwether trials,[5] and (the target of Grisham's cynicism) class-action lawsuits.

Each of these has its own history and its own complexities. For example, as Justice Souter explained in *Ortiz v. Fibreboard Corporation* (1999), "[a]lthough

2 Judith Resnick, "From 'Cases' to 'Litigation,'" *Law & Contemporary Problems*, 5 (1991): 6–68, 25. As Resnick observes, now-familiar phrases like "asbestos litigation,' "the Dupont fire litigation," and "Agent Orange Litigation" indicate the shift that took place in these decades. *Ibid.* (So too, of course, do the many citations in this paper of the form "*In re* ___ Litig.")

3 Federal Rule of Civil Procedure 42 provides that a court may consolidate actions before it that involve common questions of law or fact. See e.g., *In re* Paoli R.R. Yard PCB Litig., 35 F.3d 717 (3d Cir. 1994). The origin of Rule 42 (which came into effect in 1938) can be traced back to an Act of 1813. Suits and Costs in the Courts of the United States Act of 1813, 3 Stat 19, 21.

4 Multi-District Litigation (MDL), as provided in 28 USC § 1407 (2006), is "[f]ederal-court litigation in which civil actions pending in different districts and involving common fact questions are transferred to a single district for coordinated pretrial proceedings, after which [they] are returned to their original districts for trial." Bryan A Garner, ed., *Black's Law Dictionary* (St. Paul, MN: Thomson Reuters, 9th ed., 2009), 1112. This provides a way of establishing a centralized forum in which related cases are treated jointly for the purposes of coordinating pre-trial discovery. See e.g., *In re* Propulsid Prods. Liab. Litig., No. 1355, 2000 WL 35621417 (J.P.M.L. Aug. 7, 2000); *In re* Vioxx Prods. Liab. Litig., 360 F. Supp. 2d 1352 (J.P.M.L. 2005) ("*Vioxx*—§ 1407 Centralization"). Eldon E. Fallon, Jeremy T. Grabill, and Robert Pitard Wynne, "Bellwether Trials in Multi-District Litigation," *Tulane Law Review* 82 (2008): 2323–67. Such "transferee courts" have also functioned to establish a mechanism for conducting bellwether trials (note 5 below). *Id.*, 2332.

5 A "bellwether" refers, literally, to the male sheep that was "belled" (i.e., had a bell put around his neck) to lead his flock. In the legal context, it is a metaphor for a "test" or "representative" case. Fallon, Grabill, and Wynne, "Bellwether Trials in Multi-District Litigation" (note 4 above), 2324. For example, the transferee court in the Vioxx MDL (note 4 above) conducted six bellwether trials, five of which resulted in verdicts for the defendants, and one in a verdict for the plaintiff. *Id.*, 2335. See also Federal Judicial Center, *Manual for Complex Litigation, Fourth* (St. Paul, MN: Thomson West, 2004), 224 (on transferee courts' role in establishing bellwether trials), 360 ff. (on test cases).

representative suits have been recognized in various forms since the earliest days of English law, … class actions as we recognize them today developed as an exception to the formal rigidity of the necessary parties rule in equity."[6] Such suits turn in part on satisfaction of the requirements for class certification under Federal Rule of Civil Procedure (FRCP) 23[7]—a rule drafted before the rise of mass tort litigation on the present scale, and designed for different purposes, but then gradually adapted to the new legal needs—now including certification of a *settlement* class as well as certification of a *litigation* class.[8] And, on top of the legal complexities, there are hard policy questions about the appropriate role of the tort system vis à vis regulatory agencies such as the Food and Drug Administration (FDA) and the Environmental Protection Agency (EPA)—and a juicy philosophical question issue about how well individual justice can be served by multi-party litigation. Perhaps, one day, I shall feel able to tackle some of these; but not today.

So, as the saying goes, I have good news and I have bad news. The bad news is that I will have little to say here specifically about the "mass" in "mass torts," and nothing to say about tort litigation involving other kinds of injuries than those allegedly caused by drugs or toxic substances. The good news is that (though my illustrations will be drawn from US cases over the last couple of decades, and I won't be able to resist commenting on some epistemological weaknesses of the *Daubert* régime under which scientific evidence is now handled federally and in many states) the arguments developed here will

6 Ortiz v. Fibreboard Corp., 527 U.S. 815, 832 (1999). In this context Justice Souter cites Raymond B. Marcin, "Searching for the Origin of Class Action," *Catholic University Law Review* 23, no. 3 (1974): 515–24, Steven C. Yeazell, *From Medieval Group Litigation to the Modern Class Action* (New Haven, CT: Yale University Press, 1987), and Geoffrey C. Hazard, Jr., John L. Gedid, and Stefan Sowle, "An Historical Analysis of the Binding Effect of Class Suits," *University of Pennsylvania Law Review* 146 (1998): 1849–1948. The necessary parties rule, Justice Souter continues, citing West v. Randall, 29 F. Cas. 718, 721 (C.C.D.R.I, 1820) (No. 17,424), required "that all persons materially interested, either as plaintiffs or defendants in the subject matter … ought to be made parties to the suit, however numerous they may be."

7 "1. The class is so numerous that joinder of all members is impracticable. 2. There are questions of law or fact common to the class. 3. The claims or defenses of the representative classes are typical of the claims or defenses of the class. 4. The representative parties will fairly and adequately protect the interests of the class." FRCP 23. On the history of the Rule, and how it was gradually adapted to serve purposes that the drafters didn't intend, see generally Resnick, "From 'Cases' to 'Litigation'" (note 2 above).

8 See e.g. William W. Schwarzer, "Settlement of Mass Tort Actions: Order out of Chaos," *Cornell Law Review* 80 (1995): 837–44, 838–39; Jack B. Weinstein, *Individual Justice in Mass Tort Litigation: The Effect of Class Actions, Consolidations, and Other Multiparty Devices* (Evanston, IL: Northwestern University Press, 1995), 26, 128ff. Examples would be *In re* Vioxx Prods. Liab. Litig., 239 F.R.D. 450 (E.D. La. 2006) ("*Vioxx*—Rule 23 Certification") (a class-action suit alleging injuries from a drug); Wal-Mart Stores, Inc. v. Dukes, 131 S. Ct. 2541 (2011) (a class-action suit alleging injuries from systematic sex discrimination by an employer).

apply to questions about proof of general causation in toxic torts quite generally, not just to questions about a specific legal system at a specific time.

My topic will be the so-called "Bradford Hill criteria"—"criteria" frequently used by causation experts, featured in more than one edition of the federal *Reference Manual on Scientific Evidence*,[9] and cited in numerous toxic-tort cases in both federal and state courts—for determining when epidemiological evidence of a positive association likely indicates a causal connection. As the word "criteria" suggests, Hill is often taken to have offered a checklist of conditions satisfaction of which is necessary and/or sufficient to conclude that evidence of a causal claim is probative or, more commonly, that it is reliable enough to be admissible. But Hill himself never suggested that the factors he listed were anything more than fallible indicia of causation; and an analysis of how these factors map onto the determinants of evidential quality reveals that, indeed—though all are relevant, and all favorable, to a claim of general causation—Hill's factors are not sufficient or even, with one exception, necessary to establish such a claim, nor appropriate as a mechanical test of evidentiary reliability.

My first step will be to look closely at Hill's now-classic lecture, "The Environment and Disease," spelling out the nine factors he proposes and his comments about how they should be used (§2). Next, I will trace the ways in which these "Bradford Hill criteria" have been invoked in a range of toxic-tort cases (§3), showing that they have sometimes been badly misunderstood, and have often been applied in ways Hill didn't envisage, and probably wouldn't have endorsed. Then it will be time to put Hill's ideas in epistemological context. What Hill offers, I will argue, is best conceived as a rough sketch-map of one part of a much larger territory: evidence potentially relevant to causal claims; a rough sketch-map, moreover, focused—not surprisingly, given Hill's professional interests—on epidemiological findings, and on when intervention, especially intervention to lower the level of suspected occupational toxins, is justified. Like the sketch-map that gets you to the post office starting from the gas station with which you're familiar, Hill's list is helpful; but when it is superimposed on a more detailed map of the whole county, it is seen to be partial and incomplete (§4).

9 Michael D. Green, D. Michal Freedman, and Leon Gordis, "Reference Guide on Epidemiology," Federal Judicial Center, *Reference Manual on Scientific Evidence* (Washington, DC: Federal Judicial Center, 2nd ed., 2000), 333–400, 375. Michael D. Green, D. Michal Freedman, and Leon Gordis, "Reference Guide on Epidemiology," Federal Judicial Center/National Research Council, *Reference Manual on Scientific Evidence* (Washington, DC: Federal Judicial Center, 3rd ed., 2011), 549–632, 600.

And this reveals, finally, some underlying reasons why Hill's ideas have so often been misinterpreted and misapplied in legal contexts: though he himself was very clear that there can be no hard-and-fast rules for determining when epidemiological evidence indicates causation, the legal *penchant* for convenient checklists has led many to construe his list of (as he says) "viewpoints" as criteria for the reliability of causation testimony; and though he himself seems to have grasped the quasi-holistic character of the determinants of evidential quality, against the backdrop of the atomistic tendencies of US evidence law, his partial sketch-map has led many astray (§5).

2 THE "BRADFORD HILL CRITERIA" IN EPIDEMIOLOGICAL CONTEXT

Sir Austin Bradford Hill (1897–1991), a respected British medical statistician, was a leading proponent of the now-standard practice of randomized clinical trials. He is well-known for his very successful textbook, *Principles of Medical Statistics*,[10] and for his work on smoking and lung cancer;[11] and best-known—at least in US legal circles—for his presidential address to the Section of Occupational Medicine at the Royal Society of Medicine in 1965, "The Environment and Disease."[12]

Of course, correlation doesn't always or necessarily indicate causation;[13] and in this lecture Hill suggests nine factors to be considered in determining whether a statistical association in a population between exposure to some substance and incidence of some disease or disorder is indicative of causation—these being the (so-called) "Bradford Hill criteria." Five of the nine factors Hill mentions were already to be found in the US Surgeon General's

[10] Austin Bradford Hill, *Principles of Medical Statistics* (London: Lancet, Ltd., 1937; 9th ed., 1971).

[11] For a brief biographical sketch see Peter Armitage, "Austin Bradford Hill" (version 3), *StatProb: The Encyclopedia Sponsored by Statistics and Probability Societies* (n.d.), available at http://statprob.com/encyclopedia/AustinBradfordHILL.html; for an account of Hill's pioneering work on randomized clinical trials, see Peter Armitage, "Bradford Hill and the Randomized Controlled Trial," *Pharmaceutical Medicine* 6 (1992): 23–37; for Hill's work on smoking and lung cancer, see Richard Doll and Austin Bradford Hill, "Smoking and Carcinoma of the Lung: Preliminary Report," *British Medical Journal* (September 30, 1950): 739–48.

[12] Austin Bradford Hill, "The Environment and Disease: Association or Causation?" *Proceedings of the Royal Society of Medicine* 58 (1965): 295–300.

[13] A recent press report illustrates the point amusingly: after the mayor of a city in California introduced recordings of birdsong to be played along a main street, the rate of minor crimes fell about 15%, and the rate of major crimes about 6%. The mayor believed this was the soothing effect of the birdsong; but skeptics point out that over the same period crime rates also fell in other cities (*without* the birdsong!). John Letzing, "A California City Is Tweeting—Chirping, Actually—in a Big Way," *Wall Street Journal*, January 17, 2012, A1, A12.

report on smoking and lung cancer, published the previous year,[14] and cited in Hill's lecture;[15] but Hill's list is articulated in much more detail—and, of course, in much more general terms, since it is not limited to only one kind of exposure or to only one disease.[16]

Hill "liked to tell people that he was trained in neither medicine nor statistics" (his degree was in economics); and the mathematical techniques he used were generally quite simple.[17] His *forte*, besides a keen eye for study design, was a robust, critical, and articulate common sense—a robust, critical, and articulate common sense much in evidence in the famous lecture on which I shall focus here.

Hill sets the stage like this:

> [W]e see that event B is associated with environmental feature A, [e.g.] that some form of respiratory illness is associated with dust in the environment. In what circumstances can we pass from this observed *association* to a verdict of *causation*? On what basis should we do so?
>
> I have no wish, nor the skill, to embark upon a philosophical discussion of the meaning of 'causation'. . .
>
> Disregarding any such problem in semantics, we have this situation. Our observations reveal an association between two variables . . . beyond what we would care to attribute to the play of chance. What aspects of that association should we especially consider before deciding that the most likely interpretation of it is causation?[18]

14 US Department of Health, Education, and Welfare, *Smoking and Health*, Public Health Service Publications No. 1103 (Washington, DC, 1964), chapter 3. (And well before that, there were the "Koch-Henle Postulates"; see note 45 below.)

15 Hill, "The Environment and Disease" (note 12 above), 300.

16 Subsequently there have been various other indications of causality proposed, besides Hill's: e.g., for determining when viruses cause cancers (Harald Zur Hausen, "Viruses in Human Cancers," *Current Science* 81, no. 5 [2001], 523–27; Brooke T. Mossman, George Klein, and Harald zur Hausen, "Modern Criteria to Determine the Etiology of Human Carcinogens," *Seminars in Cancer Biology* 14 [2004]: 449–52; Harald Zur Hausen, "Papilloma Viruses in the Causation of Human Cancers—A Brief Historical Account," *Virology*, 384 [2008]: 260–65); for determining whether there is a causal relationship polio vaccines containing SV40 and cancer (Kathleen Stratton, Donna A. Almario, and Marie C. McCormick, eds., *Immunization Safety Review* [Washington, DC: National Academies Press, 2003]); and for determining what causes cancer more generally (International Agency for Research on Cancer, "Preamble" to "A Review of Human Carcinogens," *IARC Monographs on the Evaluation of Carcinogenic Risks to Humans* [Lyon, France: World Health Organization, vol. 100, 2008]). All these, as well as the Hill "criteria," are cited in Gannon v. United States, 571 F. Supp. 2d 615, 623–24 (E.D. Pa. 2007). See also the "Shepard Criteria" for determining teratogenicity (Thomas H. Shepard, "'Proof' of Human Teratogenicity," *Teratology* 50 [1994]: 97–98 [letters section]).

17 Armitage, "Austin Bradford Hill" (note 11 above), 2.

18 Hill, "The Environment and Disease" (note 12 above), 295–6.

Of course, I don't share Hill's dismissive attitude to philosophical questions as merely problems of "semantics"; indeed, I hope to convince you that a good philosophical account of the determinants of evidential quality can help us understand the real significance of his ideas about when, and to what degree, it is reasonable to infer that a statistical correlation indicates causality. But let me begin by describing Hill's proposed indicia of causation, and the very significant caveats and qualifications he introduces as he presents them:

(1) **Strength of the association**. *A strong association, i.e., a large increase in the incidence of D among those exposed to S compared to the incidence of D in those not so exposed, is one indication that the association is causal. In this context Hill mentions the enormously increased risk of scrotal cancer in chimney sweeps—200 times that of workers not exposed to tar or mineral oils;*[19] *and the very significantly increased risk of lung cancer among smokers—9–10 times the rate in non-smokers.*[20]

However, Hill adds, even when there is a strong association between S and D, the possibility should be considered that the explanation is not that exposure to S causes D, but that some other factor causes both the exposure and the disorder—e.g., that stress causes both smoking and lung cancer;[21] and even when the increased risk is very slight, the relationship may nevertheless be causal—after all, he points out, relatively few people exposed to rat urine develop Weil's disease,[22] but the connection is causal nonetheless.

(2) **Consistency**. *That different studies, conducted by different investigators and in different places and circumstances and at different times, yield the same or closely similar results, is a second indication that the connection may be causal. In this context Hill mentions that, by 1964, 29 retrospective and 7 prospective studies had found cigarette smoking to be associated with cancer of the lung.*[23]

19 *Id.*, 295, citing Richard Doll, "Cancer," in Leslie John Witts, ed., *Medical Surveys and Clinical Trials: Some Methods and Applications of Group Research in Medicine* (London: Oxford University Press, 2nd ed., 1964), 333–49 (the original discovery was made by Percival Pott in the 18th century).

20 Hill, "The Environment and Disease" (note 12 above), 296.

21 Hill himself didn't draw this conclusion at first, but only after more evidence came in. See Armitage, "Austin Bradford Hill" (note 11 above), 3.

22 Weil's disease (leptospirosis) is a bacterial disease spread by the urine of infected animals; the symptoms are fever, headache, chills, vomiting, jaundice, anemia, and rash. Some people, apparently, are much more susceptible to the disease than others. See http://www.health.ny.gov/diseases/communicable/leptospirosis/fact_sheet.htm; http://www.btninternet.com/~ringwood.canoe/Weils.htm.

23 Hill, "The Environment and Disease" (note 12 above), 297, citing US Department of Health, Education, and Welfare, *Smoking and Health* (note 14 above).

However, Hill adds, the fact that a different inquiry yields different results doesn't necessarily undermine the original evidence;[24] and the fact that repeated studies are unavailable, or are impossible, doesn't show that the connection *isn't* causal. After all, there was only one study of the incidence of cancers of the nose and lung in nickel refiners in Wales—a study that couldn't be repeated, because the refining process was changed shortly after it was conducted.[25]

(3) **Specificity**. *That the association is restricted to specific workers, specific sites, and a specific type of disease, is a third indication that the connection may be causal.*[26]

However, Hill adds, this factor shouldn't be over-emphasized. Those nickel refiners, he points out, had an increased risk of not one but two types of cancer; and, he adds, milk can carry a whole range of infections, including scarlet fever, diphtheria, undulant fever, dysentery, and typhoid. Indeed, Hill continues, "multi-causation" is more common than single causation; so lack of specificity doesn't necessarily mean that there is no casual connection.[27]

(4) **Temporal precedence**. *For exposure to S to be a cause of D, the exposure must precede the disease.*[28]

Hill presents this factor more categorically than the others; but he immediately adds a significant qualification: that it is not always a trivial matter to determine temporal order—to tell, for example, whether such and such a diet leads to a disease, or the early stages of the disease lead to these food preferences.[29]

(5) **Biological gradient** *(dose-response curve). That the rate of D varies as the degree of exposure to S varies is a fifth indication that the connection may be casual. In this context Hill mentions that death rates from lung cancer rise linearly with the number of cigarettes smoked daily; and such a clear dose-response curve, he continues, "admits of a simple [causal] explanation."*[30]

[24] Hill, "The Environment and Disease" (note 12 above), 297.

[25] *Ibid*, citing Austin Bradford Hill, "The Statistician in Medicine" (Alfred Watson Memorial Lecture), *Journal of the Society of Actuaries* 88, no. II (1962): 178–91. (Presumably, though Hill doesn't say this, a new study under the changed circumstances *would* have been relevant to the eighth of his factors, "experiment," explained below.)

[26] Hill, "The Environment and Disease" (note 12 above), 279.

[27] *Ibid*.

[28] *Id*., 297–98.

[29] *Ibid*.

[30] *Id*., 298.

However, he adds, even if the rate of death from lung cancer was higher among *lighter* smokers, this wouldn't necessarily mean that the relation is *not* causal; moreover, biological gradient may be hard to establish, because evidence of the degree of exposure to S may be hard to come by.

(6) **Biological plausibility**. *If the purported causal connection is biologically plausible, i.e., fits in with our current knowledge of biological mechanisms, this is another indication that the connection really is causal.*[31]

However, Hill continues, "we cannot demand" that this factor be satisfied, since what is biologically plausible at a time depends on the biological knowledge then available. For a long time, he continues, there was no biological knowledge to support the statistical evidence that a woman's contracting rubella (German measles) during pregnancy could cause birth defects in her baby; but the causal inference was reasonable nonetheless. Again, John Snow's study of the opening weeks of the 1854 London cholera epidemic was strong evidence that the disease was waterborne,[32] even though it would be another 30 years before Robert Koch discovered the role of bacteria in causing disease.[33] "In short," Hill writes, "the association we observe may be one new to science or medicine and we must not dismiss it too light-heartedly as just too odd."[34]

(7) **Coherence**. *On the other hand, Hill continues, a causal interpretation of statistical data shouldn't seriously conflict with known facts about the biology of the disease in question. It is important, for example, that a causal connection between smoking and lung cancer coheres with histopathological evidence from smokers' bronchial epithelium and with the fact that we find substances known to cause skin cancer in laboratory animals in cigarette smoke.*[35]

However, Hill adds (repeating what he had already said under the heading "plausibility"), that we don't know the biological mechanism involved doesn't mean that the connection *isn't* causal.

[31] *Ibid.*

[32] *Id.*, 296, citing John Snow, *On the Mode of Communication of Cholera* (London: John Churchill, 1855) (reprinted, with other material, in *Snow on Cholera* [Cambridge, MA: Harvard Medical Library, 1936]).

[33] For a summary account of Koch's work, see Christoph Gradmann, "Heinrich Hermann Robert Koch," *Encyclopedia of Life Sciences*, available at http://www.els.net (Wiley, 2001).

[34] Hill, "The Environment and Disease" (note 12 above) 298, 299, citing Snow, *On the Mode of Communication of Cholera* (note 32 above), and Hill, "The Statistician in Medicine" (note 25 above).

[35] Hill, "The Environment and Disease" (note 12 above), 298.

(8) **Experiment**. *Evidence that, when a suspected substance is eliminated from, or reduced in, an environment, the rate of the disease or disorder goes down, Hill says, may be "the strongest support" for the causal hypothesis.*[36]

(9) **Analogy**. *Evidence that another disease or drug causes a certain kind of disorder is some reason to think that the suspect drug or chemical causes the similar disorder with which it is statistically associated. In this context, Hill mentions that the fact that rubella and Thalidomide are known to cause birth defects makes it reasonable to accept "similar but weaker evidence" with respect to exposure to another drug, or to another viral infection, during pregnancy.*[37]

Two points Hill makes here—one quite explicitly, the other initially implicitly, but stated explicitly a few pages later—will prove significant further on: that we must allow for the possibility of two kinds of *multiple causation* (more than one cause of the same disease, and more than one disease resulting from the same cause); and that the likelihood that a correlation is causal depends in some way on whether S's causing D constitutes a good *explanation* of the observed correlation.

More immediately relevant to the persistent misunderstandings of Hill's work, nowhere in this celebrated lecture does he use the word "criterion" or "criteria"; and there is every indication that his intention was quite modest. Temporal priority seems to be the only factor Hill thinks is absolutely required; and—but for the suggestion that "experimental" evidence is the strongest—he says nothing about the relative importance of these factors, suggesting rather that weighing them is a matter of judgment. In fact, as I said earlier, he expressly *denies* that any cut-and-dried rules can be given for inferring causation:

> ... I do not believe ... that we can usefully lay down some hard-and-fast rules of evidence that *must* be obeyed before we accept cause and effect. None of my nine [factors] can bring indisputable evidence for or against the cause-and-effect hypothesis, and none can be required as a *sine qua non*. What they can do, with greater or less strength, is to help us make up our minds on the fundamental question—is there any other way of explaining the facts before us, is there any other answer equally, or more, likely than cause and effect?[38]

36 *Id.*, 299.
37 *Ibid.*
38 *Ibid.*

Nor should I omit to mention that Hill also emphatically denies that tests of statistical significance can answer this question:

> No formal tests of significance can answer these questions. Such tests can, and should, remind us of the effects that the play of chance can create, and they will instruct us in the likely magnitude of those effects. But beyond that they contribute nothing to the 'proof' of our hypothesis. . . . [I]n the USA, . . . I am told, some editors of journals will return an article because tests of significance have not been applied. Yet there are innumerable situations in which they are totally unnecessary. . . . [T]he glitter of the *t* table diverts attention from the inadequacy of the fare.[39]

In short, Hill is best understood as offering rough-and-ready guidelines—indicia, if you like, *not* "criteria"—of causality. As I said, he prefers the word "viewpoints"; and he acknowledges:

- that the factors he lists are to be applied *only* where there is already epidemiological evidence of a positive association between S and D;
- that they are not "criteria" for inferring causation—not, at any rate, on the common understanding of "criteria" as necessary and sufficient conditions;[40]
- that mathematical tests of statistical significance, though often described as ruling out the possibility that the association is due to chance, cannot determine whether an association is causal.

Several other caveats, not mentioned specifically in Hill's lecture, are also needed. First: the nine factors are not very clearly individuated: e.g., whether the incidence of D increases as the dose of or exposure to S increases (biological gradient) and whether the incidence of D falls if S is removed from or reduced in the environment (experiment) seem to be two sides of the same coin. Biological plausibility and coherence seem to be similarly interrelated: plausibility requires the causal claim to fit in with current biological knowledge, while coherence requires that it not conflict with such knowledge; and what Hill calls "analogy" is arguably just one aspect of biological plausibility. Second, with the exception of temporality, Hill's factors all come in degrees; so that we could infer, not that an association *is* causal, but only that it is *more likely to be* causal, the more this or that factor is satisfied. And third, except

[39] *Ibid.*

[40] True—despite his claim that none of the factors is a *sine qua non*—Hill suggests that temporality *is* a necessary condition; but he makes clear that no one factor, nor any combination of some or all of the nine, is sufficient.

for the apparently categorical requirement of temporal precedence and for Hill's comment that experimental evidence is especially convincing, there is no suggestion of any simple way to determine the weight to be given to one factor vis à vis the others.

3 THE "BRADFORD HILL CRITERIA" IN LEGAL CONTEXT

No doubt because he offers an apparently simple list of factors apparently easily comprehensible not only to specialists but also to attorneys, judges, and jurors, Hill's ideas about how to assess the likelihood that a statistical association indicates a causal connection have proved very attractive not only to medical scientists, but also to attorneys needing to establish causation or to impugn the other side's causation evidence, and to judges obliged to rule on the evidentiary reliability, and hence admissibility, of causation testimony.

A standard epidemiology text, Kenneth Rothman's *Modern Epidemiology*—though marred, unfortunately, by a broad streak of Popperism[41]—presents Hill's factors quite accurately, including most of his many caveats and qualifications. Rothman quotes Hill's comment that none of his nine factors "can bring indisputable evidence for or against the causal hypothesis";[42] and observes, correctly, that actually this isn't quite right: temporal precedence really *is* necessary for causation. And he refers approvingly to Hill's comment that "[a]ll scientific work is incomplete, … liable to be upset or modified by advancing knowledge."[43] Indeed.

I find no reference to Hill in the 1994 edition of the *Reference Manual on Scientific Evidence*;[44] though the chapter on epidemiology provides a list, attributed to Koch and Henle, of seven factors, all but one of which ("alternative explanations") is also found in Hill.[45] In the 2000 and 2011 editions,

[41] Kenneth Rothman, *Modern Epidemiology* (Boston: Little, Brown, 1986), 9 ff. For a detailed critique of Popper's philosophy of science, which I believe to be completely broken-backed, see "Federal Philosophy of Science: A Deconstruction—and a Reconstruction," pp. 122–55 in this volume, 125–34, and "Just Say 'No' to Logical Negativism," in Haack, *Putting Philosophy to Work: Inquiry and Its Place in Culture* (Amherst, NY: Prometheus Books, 2008; expanded ed., 2013), 179–94.

[42] Rothman, *Modern Epidemiology* (note 41 above), 19.

[43] *Id.*, 20.

[44] Linda A. Bailey, Leon Gordis, and Michael D. Green, "Reference Guide on Epidemiology," Federal Judicial Center, *Reference Manual on Scientific Evidence* (Washington, DC: Federal Judicial Center, 1st ed., 1994), 101–80, 161. (I say that "I find" no such reference because the index to this volume is quite inadequate, and of course I haven't been able to read every word of this substantial brick of a book.)

[45] The authors give no citation. But see Alfred S. Evans, "Causation and Disease: The Koch-Henle Postulates Revisited," *Yale Journal of Biology and Medicine* 49 (1976): 175–95 for a

however, Hill is mentioned specifically, and so is at least his most important caveat. In the 2000 edition we read:

> There is no formula or algorithm that can be used to assess whether a causal inference is appropriate based on these guidelines. One or more of these [Hill] factors may be absent even when a true causal relationship exists. Similarly, the existence of some factors does not ensure that a causal relationship exists.[46]

And in the 2011 edition:

> There is no formula or algorithm that can be used to assess whether a causal inference is appropriate based on these [Hill's] guidelines.... Although the drawing of causal inferences is informed by scientific expertise, it is not a determination that is made using an objective or algorithmic methodology.[47]

Nonetheless, when Hill's ideas are cited in court, these careful formulations seem to be ignored, and we are soon entangled in a great thicket of oversimplifications, misunderstandings, and misapplications.

Some of the confusions are relatively trivial. For example, apparently Hill was known to his friends as "Tony," and he only added the "Bradford" to his name late in life;[48] so perhaps it's not altogether surprising that we find him referred to by such a variety of names: not only as "Hill,"[49] "Bradford Hill,"[50]

history of the "Koch-Henle Postulates" from Jakob Henle's book on causation, published in 1840, and developments by his student, Robert Koch, in lectures of 1884 and 1890; and K. Codell Carter, "Koch's Postulates in Relation to the Work of Jakob Henle and Edwin Krebs," *Medical History* 29 (1985): 353–74 for an argument that Krebs was a more important source than Henle.

46 Green, Freedman, and Gordis, "Reference Guide on Epidemiology," *Reference Manual on Scientific Evidence*, 2nd ed. (note 9 above), 375.

47 Green, Freedman, and Gordis, "Reference Guide on Epidemiology," *Reference Manual on Scientific Evidence*, 3rd ed. (note 9 above), 600. Very oddly, the authors cite as authority for this claim, not Hill himself, but a much more recent article, Douglas Weed, "Epidemiologic Evidence and Causal Inferences," *Hematology/Oncology Clinics of North America* 124, no. 4 (2000): 797–807.

48 Armitage, "Austin Bradford Hill" (note 11 above), 1.

49 See e.g., LeBlanc v. Chevron USA, Inc., 513 F. Supp. 2d 641, 647 (E.D. La. 2007); *In re* Trasylol Prods. Liab. Litig., No. 08-MD-01928, 2010 WL 1489734, *5, *8, *10 (S.D. Fla. Mar. 8, 2010) ("*Trasylol*—Parikh"); *In re* Trasylol Prods. Liab. Litig., No. 08-MD-01928, 2010 WL 1489730, *4, *8 & n.24 (S.D. Fla. Mar. 19, 2010) ("*Trasylol*—Derschwitz"); DePyper v. Navarro, No. 83–303467-NM, 1995 WL 788828, *24 (Mich. Cir. Ct. Nov. 27, 1995); Lofgren v. Motorola, Inc., No. CV-93–05521, 1998 WL 299925, *25, *28, *29 (Ariz. Super. Ct. 1998).

50 See e.g., *In re* Breast Implant Litig., 11 F. Supp. 2d 1217, 1243 (D. Colo. 1998); Ferguson v. Riverside Sch. Dist. No. 416, No. CS-00–0097-FVS, 2002 WL 34355958, *6 (E.D. Wash. Feb. 6, 2002); Dunn v. Sandoz Pharm. Corp., 275 F. Supp. 2d 672, 67–80 (M.D.N.C. 2003); *In re* Phenylpropanolamine (PPA), 2003 WL 22417238, *16, *20, *29 (N.J. Super. Law Div. July 21, 2003); *In re* Viagra Prods. Liab. Litig., 572 F. Supp. 2d 1071, 1080 (D. Minn. 2008)

"Bradford-Hill,"[51] "A. Bradford Hill,"[52] "Dr. Bradford Hill" and "Dr. Austin Bradford Hill,"[53] "Sir Austin Bradford Hill,"[54] "Sir Bradford Hill,"[55] and (oops) "Arthur Bradford Hill,"[56] but even—this one really takes the biscuit!—"Brad Hill."[57]

And as we saw earlier, the nine factors Hill lists aren't easily individuated; so perhaps it's not altogether surprising that in one case we find an expert described as adding a tenth factor (sensitivity) to the original nine,[58] in another case an expert who "seemed unclear whether there were 8, 9, or 10 factors,"[59] and in another again, an expert who mentions seven of the factors and comments that "[t]here were two others that Hill added later."[60]

A less trivial misunderstanding is that one of Hill's nine factors, "experiment," is sometimes misinterpreted as referring not, as he quite clearly intended, to information about the result of removing the suspect substance from, or reducing it in, the workplace or the environment, but to *in vivo* experimentation, i.e., testing of drugs or suspected toxins on animals: in In re *Joint Eastern & Southern District Asbestos Litigation*,[61] for example, where the district court seems to have made this mistake; and in In re *Asbestos Litigation*,[62] where Dr. Lemen's testimony seems to reveal the same misunderstanding.

("In re *Viagra* I"); *In re* Viagra Prods. Liab. Litig., 658 F. Supp. 2d 936, 942 (D. Minn. 2009) ("In re *Viagra* II"); *In re* Stand 'N Seal Prods. Liab. Litig., 623 F. Supp. 2d1355, 1372 & n.2, 1373 (N.D. Ga. 2009); *In re* Fosamax Prods. Liab. Litig., 645 F. Supp. 2d 164, 175, 187–88 (S.D.N.Y. 2009); *In re* Asbestos Litig. (Delaware), C.A. No. 05C-11–257 ASB, 2009 WL 1034487, *7 (Del. Super. Ct. Apr. 8, 2009); *In re* Neurontin Mktg., Sales Practices, & Prods. Liab. Litig., 612 F. Supp. 2d 116, 132, 137, 153, 158 (D. Mass. 2009); Arabie v. Citgo Petroleum Corp., 49 So. 3d 529, 540 (La. Ct. App. 2010); Lewis v. Airco, Inc., No. A-3509–08T3, 2011 WL 2731880, *24 (N.J. Super. Ct. App. Div. July 15, 2011).

51 See e.g., *In re* Breast Implant Litigation (note 50 above), 1233 n.5; Soldo v. Sandoz Pharm. Corp., No. 98–1712, 2003 WL 22005007, *10 (W.D. Pa. Jan. 16, 2002) ("*Soldo*—Bradford Hill"); Matt Dietz Co. v. Torres, 198 S.W.3d 798, 803 (Tex. Ct. App. 2006). (It seems likely that some may believe there were *two* epidemiologists concerned, Bradford and Hill.)

52 See e.g., *In re* Joint E. & S. Dist. Asbestos Litig., 52 F.3d 1124, 1128 & n.2 (2d Cir. 1995).

53 See e.g., *Arabie* (note 50 above), 540.

54 See e.g., Rains v. PPG Indus., Inc., 361 F. Supp. 2d 829, 835 n.4 (S.D. Ill. 2004); *Gannon* (note 16 above), 624); Nonnon v. City of New York, 932 N.Y.S.2d 428, 433 (App. Div. 2011). (And in *Arabie* (note 50 above), 539, we find "Sir Austin Bradford-Hill.")

55 See e.g., Chapin v. A & L Parts, Inc., 732 N.W.2d 578, 584–85 (Mich. Ct. App. 2007). See also *id*, 588 & n.1 (Meter, J., concurring).

56 Milward v. Acuity Specialty Prods. Grp., Inc., 639 F.3d 11, 17 (1st Cir. 2011). (However, n.6, on the same page, citing Hill's lecture, refers to "Austin Bradford Hill.")

57 In re *Fosamax* (note 50 above), 188 n.14 (reporting testimony of Dr. Etminan).

58 In re *Phenylpropanolamine* (note 50 above), *20 (reporting testimony of Dr. Levine).

59 In re *Fosamax* (note 50 above), 188 (reporting testimony of Dr. Etminan).

60 *Arabie* (note 50 above), 540 (reporting testimony of Dr. Levy).

61 In re *Joint E. & S. Dist. Asbestos Litig.* (note 52 above), 1129.

62 In re *Asbestos Litig.* (Delaware) (note 50 above), *7 (reporting testimony of Dr. Lemen).

We also find some experts claiming to have used the Hill "criteria" *in the absence of any epidemiological evidence showing a positive association* between the suspected toxin and the alleged injury. The testimony of Dr. Kulig, a plaintiff's expert in more than one case against the manufacturer of the anti-lactation drug Parlodel, suspected of causing post-partum stroke, is a striking example:

> Dr. Kulig states that he has identified an association between Parlodel and stroke based on the pharmacological properties of bromocriptine, epidemiology, clinical studies, case reports, and animal studies.... [He testified]: "I believe causation exists because I've applied the Bradford-Hill criteria and here's what my analysis shows.... *I've taken the extra step and applied a published, generally accepted criteria* [sic] *to the analysis.*[63]

However (as Sandoz did not fail to point out), though Dr. Kulig specifically mentions epidemiology, there were in fact *no* epidemiological studies finding a positive association--and the Hill "criteria" kick in only where there *is* such evidence.[64]

No less striking is the testimony of Dr. Etminan in In re *Fosamax*. Fosamax was prescribed to prevent the advance of osteoporosis; but—after it was given to hundreds of thousands of patients, and not just the few thousand in the manufacturers' clinical trials—was alleged to have caused severe jaw problems in some patients. Dr. Etminan, like Dr. Kulig, had applied the Hill factors, in the absence of epidemiological evidence, to "case reports, case series, prevalence studies, and animal studies"; and even testified that they are applicable in "situations where basically, you are only left with case reports." But the court points out that Rothman's *Modern Epidemiology*—which Dr. Etminan himself had described as the "Holy Grail" of epidemiology textbooks—notes that these factors apply only when we already have evidence of a positive association.[65] The manufacturer, Merck, also comes in for criticism from the court: not, however, because they argue that the Hill factors kick in only when there is *controlled* epidemiological evidence of a *statistically significant* association[66]

[63] *Dunn* (note 50 above), 677 (reporting testimony of Dr. Kulig). See also *Soldo*—Bradford Hill (note 51 above), *9–10, where Dr Kulig testified to the same effect.

[64] *Dunn* (note 50 above), 678. I will add (though Sandoz's attorneys apparently didn't) that temporal precedence seems to be once again an exception, necessary whether or not we have epidemiological evidence of an association.

[65] In re *Fosamax* (note 50 above), 187–88.

[66] *Id.*, 175–t6. Thinking that Merck might have been misled by additions made by other authors to later editions of Hill's textbook on medical statistics, I checked the latest I could find, Austin Bradford Hill and I. D. Hill, *Bradford Hill's Principles of Medical Statistics* (London: Edward Arnold, 1991); but found, on the contrary, that it includes an entire section on

(embellishments the court allows to pass without comment),[67] but because they ignore findings by, among others, the American Dental Association that oral bisphosphonates can cause ONJ (osteonecrosis of the jaw).[68]

Most important, though, are the persistent misunderstandings of the status of the so-called "Hill criteria"[69]—which in one case are even described as "Sufficiency Criteria,"[70] and are also variously characterized as "considerations,"[71] "Principles,"[72] as an "evaluation scheme,"[73] *and* as a "methodology."[74] As this last term suggests, Hill's work typically figures in toxic-tort cases in the context of the Supreme Court's ruling in *Daubert* III.[75] In screening proffered scientific testimony for reliability, the *Daubert* Court observed, courts should look, not to an expert's conclusions, but to the methodology by which he arrived at those conclusions: "[t]he focus," Justice Blackmun wrote, "must be solely on principles and methodology, not on the conclusions they generate."[76] Four years later, the *Joiner* Court would back

"statistical significance and clinical importance," arguing that the common idea that a statistically significant result is invariably clinically important, and a statistically insignificant result clinically unimportant, is thoroughly confused.

67 For what it's worth, I found no case where Hill's animadversions against over-emphasis on tests of statistical significance were taken seriously; though in In re *Viagra* I (note 50 above), 1081, the court finds that the lack of statistical significance in data underlying Dr. McGwin's testimony did not make that testimony inadmissible. However, an amicus brief urging the Supreme Court to grant *certiorari* in *Daubert*, under the lead authorship of Prof. Rothman, cites Hill's lecture in support of the claim that "the talismanic phrase 'statistically significant' creates a misleading aura of infallibility totally out relation to its actual value." Brief Amici Curiae of Professors Kenneth Rothman et al. in Support of Petitioners, Daubert v. Merrell Dow Pharm., Inc., 509 U.S. 579 (1993) (No. 92–102), 1992 WL 12006438, *4, *6.

68 In re *Fosamax* (note 50 above), 186 (citing report by the American Dental Association, itself appealing to Hill's work).

69 See, e.g., the following federal cases: In re *Breast Implant Litig.* (note 50 above), 1233 n.5; *Ferguson v. Riverside* (note 50 above), *6; *Soldo*—Bradford Hill (note 51 above), *10; *Dunn* (note 50 above), 677, 678; In re *Viagra Prods. Liab. Litig.* II (note 50 above), 946; In re *Stand 'N Seal* (note 50 above), 1372 & n.2, 1373; *In re* Fosamax (note 50 above); In re *Trasylol*—Parikh (note 49 above), *8 & n.24, *10; In re *Trasylol*—Derschwitz (note 49 above), *4. See also the following state cases: *DePyper* (note 49 above), *24; *Lofgren* (note 49 above), *25; In re *Phenylpropolamine* (note 50 above), *16; *Matt Dietz* (note 51 above), 804.

70 In re *Joint E. & S. Dist. Asbestos Litig.* (note 52 above), 1128, 1130.

71 In re *Asbestos Litig.*(Delaware) (note 50 above), *7 (reporting testimony of Dr. Lemen).

72 See e.g., *Arabie* (note 50 above), 540 (reporting testimony of Dr. Levy).

73 See e.g., *Nonnon* (note 54 above), *4 (reporting testimony of Dr. Bernard).

74 See e.g., *Gannon* (note 16 above), 623 (listing various "methodologies," including Bradford Hill's, for evaluating whether an association is causal); In re *Neurontin* (note 50 above), 132 (endorsing defendant's criticism of plaintiffs' causation testimony); *DePyper* (note 49 above), *24 (reporting testimony of Dr. Preus); *Chapin* (note 55 above), 588 & n.1 (Meter, J., concurring, reporting testimony of Dr. Lemen).

75 Daubert v. Merrell Dow Pharm., Inc., 509 U.S. 579 (1993) ("*Daubert* III").

76 *Id.*, 595.

away from the distinction of methodology vs. conclusions, observing that "methodology and conclusions are not entirely distinct from one another."[77] But expert witnesses', and courts', preoccupation with "methodology" continued; indeed, even Dennis Carlson, the Carmichaels' proffered expert on tire failure analysis in *Kumho Tire*, had a methodology: "the visual inspection method"(!).[78] No wonder, then, that the "Bradford Hill criteria" are sometimes presented as a "methodology"—or, better yet, as a "generally accepted methodology"—for determining causation; nor that satisfaction of the Hill "criteria" is sometimes taken as a touchstone for the evidentiary reliability, and hence the admissibility, of causation testimony.

So, notwithstanding Hill's quite explicit insistence that there *can be no* hard-and-fast rules for inferring causation, and despite some sober epidemiologists' acknowledgments that Hill never intended to offer such a checklist, his factors are apparently often presented to students in epidemiology as "causal criteria";[79] and are certainly often presented in court, and taken by attorneys and judges, as a decision-procedure for determining whether general causation evidence is probative, or is reliable. This kind of misunderstanding seems to take two equal and opposite forms. Expert witnesses sometimes talk as if all that's needed to establish causation is to run their evidence quickly by the list—"strength": check; "consistency": check; …, etc.—as if applying the Hill factors were a simple, mechanical task; and a few courts seem to treat Hill's factors the same way.[80] By contrast, other courts talk as if the "Bradford Hill methodology" were an arcane algorithm, comparable to a complex, technical mathematical procedure for assessing statistical significance, in which epidemiologists require specialized training: e.g., in In re *Fosamax*, where the court complains that Dr. Etminan "has not received any formal training in the application of the Bradford Hill factors."[81]

Other courts seem to assimilate the "Bradford Hill criteria" to *legal* tests for the admissibility of expert testimony. Perhaps, when the court in In re *Stand 'N Seal* observes that Dr. Spiller's testimony satisfies FRE 702 and is consistent with the Hill "criteria," it means only to suggest that consistency with the Hill factors suffices for evidentiary reliability;[82] but when, in *Matt Dietz Co.*

[77] Gen. Elec. Co. v. Joiner, 522 U.S. 136, 146 (1997) ("*Joiner* III").

[78] Kumho Tire Co. v. Carmichael, 526 U.S. 137, 146 (1999).

[79] Carl V. Phillips and Karen J. Goodman, "The Missed Lessons of Sir Austin Bradford Hill," *Epidemiologic Perspectives & Innovations*, 1, no. 3 (October 4, 2004), available at http:/www.epi-perspectives.com/content/1/1/3, 1.

[80] See e.g., *Rains* (note 54 above), 836 ff. (running Dr. Poser's [!] testimony by Hill's factors, and concluding that it meets none of them).

[81] In re *Fosamax* (note 50 above), 188 (criticizing Dr. Etminan's testimony).

[82] In re *Stand 'N Seal* (note 50 above), 1372 (admitting Dr. Spiller's testimony).

v. Torres, the court observes that "Torres does not explain how either under the Bradford-Hill criteria or the *Robinson* factors Dr. Brautbar's testimony is reliable"[83]—*Robinson* being the case in which Texas adopted *Daubert*[84]—it seems to be treating Hill's factors and the legal test for admissibility as on a par. In one case, a more-than-usually confused expert witness even suggests that the Hill "criteria" establish causation "beyond a reasonable doubt" (!).[85] And, most important for present purposes, some courts take satisfaction of the Hill "criteria" to be *sufficient*, and others take satisfaction of these factors to be *necessary*, for general causation testimony to be reliable, and hence admissible, under *Daubert*.[86]

Sufficiency: In In re *Trasylol*, for example, Dr. Parikh's testimony is ruled admissible because he gives a Hill analysis;[87] in In re *Stand 'N Seal* Dr. Spiller's testimony is ruled admissible because it is "consistent with" Hill's factors (even though he doesn't himself apply them explicitly);[88] and in In re *Neurontin* the plaintiff's causation testimony is ruled admissible because some of Hill's factors are met.[89] We see the same thing in some state court rulings: e.g., the concurrence in a Michigan case (*Chapin*) argues that it was acceptable to admit Dr. Lemen's causation testimony because it was based on a Hill analysis;[90] and in In re *Asbestos Litigation* a Delaware appeals court rules that the lower court was correct to deny a motion to exclude Dr. Lemen's causation testimony under *Daubert*, again because that testimony was based on the reliable Hill methodology.[91] Again, in *Lewis v. Airco*, arguing that Dr. Kipen correctly applied the Hill factors, a New Jersey appeals court reverses the trial court's ruling that his causation testimony is inadmissible.[92]

Necessity: In In re *Fosamax*, for example, the court excludes Dr. Etminan's general causation testimony on the grounds that he didn't apply the Hill "criteria" correctly;[93] in In re *Breast Implant Litigation* the court excludes the

83 *Matt Dietz* (note 51 above), 804 (describing deficiencies in Torres's causation evidence).
84 E.I du Pont de Nemours & Co. v. Robinson, 923 S.W.2d 549 (Tex. 1995).
85 Dr. Parikh in In re *Trasylol*—Parikh (note 49 above), *8–9.
86 But see *Nonnon* (note 54 above), *4ff for discussion of the Hill factors in the context of a *Frye* jurisdiction.
87 In re *Trasylol*—Parikh (note 49 above), *10.
88 In re *Stand 'N Seal* (note 50 above), 1372, 1378.
89 In re *Neurontin* (note 50 above), 158.
90 *Chapin* (note 55 above), 588.
91 In re *Asbestos Litig.* (Delaware) (note 50 above), *8.
92 *Lewis* (note 50 above), *24.
93 In re *Fosamax* (note 50 above), 188.

testimony of plaintiff's experts Drs. Kassan, Klapper, and Blais in part because it doesn't satisfy the Hill "criteria";[94] and in *Rains* the testimony of Drs. Poser and Sultan,[95] and in *LeBlanc* the testimony of Dr. Gardner,[96] is excluded in part for the same reason. We see the same thing in some state court rulings: e.g., in *Lofgren v. Motorola*, where an Arizona court excludes the testimony of Dr. Olshan, who, it is said, is "incapable of applying the Hill criteria,"[97] and of Dr. Miller, who "could not articulate the Hill criteria and admitted that he didn't know what the criteria were or how to apply them";[98] and in *Matt Dietz Co. v. Torres*, where, as we saw earlier, a Texas court excludes Torres's proffered expert testimony on the ground that it meets neither the Hill nor the *Robinson* standard.[99]

On this matter, though, some courts disagree—holding, in effect, that satisfaction of the Hill factors is *not* necessary for admissibility: in *Ferguson v. Riverside*, for example, the court rules that there is no reason to exclude Dr. Jennings's testimony just because the dose-response relationship Hill mentions isn't present;[100] and in In re *Viagra* I Dr. McGwin's testimony is ruled admissible even though it doesn't satisfy all the Hill factors[101]—but the next year, in In re *Viagra* II, his testimony is excluded, though the court grants that "failure to satisfy the Bradford Hill criteria does not necessarily compel exclusion of an opinion as unreliable."[102]

In short, when Hill's ideas are used in court what we encounter is not the robust, critical common sense that characterizes his own writings, but a confused, and confusing, farrago of misunderstandings and misapplications. We can better understand why, I believe, when we see how the Hill factors fit into a larger epistemological picture.

94 In re *Breast Implant Litig.* (note 50 above), 1233 n.5 (Dr. Kassan); 1236 (Dr. Klapper); 1243 (Dr. Blais).

95 *Rains* (note 54 above), 835–38.

96 *LeBlanc* (note 49 above), 646–51, 663. (This case was subsequently vacated and remanded to the district court, to reconsider its ruling on the admissibility of Dr. Gardner's testimony in light of the ATSDR Benzene Toxicology Report, which at the time of its earlier decision was in draft form only. Hill's factors are not mentioned specifically.) 275 F. App'x (5th Cir. 2008). On remand, the court denied the oil company's motion to exclude Dr. Gardner's testimony, but again doesn't mention Hill. Civil Action No. 05–5485, 2009 WL 482160 (E.D. La. 2009).

97 *Lofgren* (note 49 above), *25.

98 *Id.*, *28 (excluding Dr. Olshan's testimony), *31 (excluding Dr. Miller's testimony).

99 *Matt Dietz* (note 51 above), 804.

100 *Ferguson* (note 50 above), *6, *8.

101 In re *Viagra* I (note 50 above), 1080, 1081.

102 In re *Viagra* II (note 50 above), 946.

4 THE "BRADFORD HILL CRITERIA" IN EPISTEMOLOGICAL CONTEXT

Up to now I have been speaking, with deliberate vagueness, of "causal claims" or claims of a "causal connection" between a suspect substance and some disease or disorder. Now it's time to be a little more specific, and explain that I intended such vague forms of words to refer to propositions to the effect that, at least in some instances, exposure to S contributes to bringing about the occurrence of D. This doesn't, of course, go very far towards explaining "causal."[103] It does, however, acknowledge both the possibility that a disease might have multiple causes, and the possibility that multiple diseases might be causally related to the same substance; and it allows me to distinguish general causation ("in some instances") from specific causation ("in the present instance").

I take for granted here, as I have argued elsewhere,[104] that legal degrees of proof are to be construed, not as mathematical probabilities, but as epistemic likelihoods, i.e., as degrees of warrant of the proposition at issue by the evidence presented[105] (in common-law jurisdictions, by the admissible evidence presented). And I shall of course rely on the account of warrant I have developed elsewhere[106]—an account which, to repeat, is neither simply atomistic nor fully holistic, but might best be described as a kind of articulated holism; and which is neither formal nor "wordy," but emphatically *worldly*.[107] In particular, I take for granted that the degree to which evidence warrants a proposition depends on how supportive the evidence is with respect to the proposition in question, how secure the reasons favorable to the proposition are, independent of the proposition in question, and how comprehensive the evidence is;

103 For a brief discussion of the relation of legal to other concepts of causation, see "Risky Business: Statistical Proof of Specific Causation," pp. 264–93 in this volume, 264–66.

104 See especially "Legal Probabilism: An Epistemological Dissent," pp. 47–77 in this volume, 56–64.

105 It is worth noting that, in certain cases, plaintiffs may be making a claim weaker than "S causes D"—e.g., that S accelerates or "promotes" D. See e.g. *Joiner* III (note 77 above), 139 (noting that Joiner's attorney argued that exposure to PCBs promoted his early development of small-cell lung cancer). The weaker the causal claim, the less strong the evidence needed to warrant it to a given degree.

106 See Susan Haack, *Evidence and Inquiry* (1993; 2nd ed., Amherst, NY: Prometheus Books, 2009), chapter 4; and *Defending Science—Within Reason: Between Scientism and Cynicism* (Amherst, NY: Prometheus Books, 2003), chapter 3. The theory is summarized in "Epistemology and the Law of Evidence: Problems and Projects," pp. 1–26 in this volume, 11–16.

107 Susan Haack, *Defending Science* (note 106 above), 52. (The word "wordy," in its present use, was suggested to me by Philip Dawid.)

and that evidence may be positive, negative, or neutral with respect to a conclusion, which will be better warranted the *more* secure the *positive* reasons are, but the *less* secure the *negative* reasons are.

Relevance is a matter of degree, which is why we describe information as "highly," "somewhat," or only "marginally" relevant to some proposition at issue. Moreover, whether and if so to what degree some piece of evidence, e, is relevant to a conclusion—e.g., whether the way a drug affects ants, or geckos, or chickens, or chimps, is relevant to whether how it would affect humans—is not a simple formal relation, but can be a matter of material fact.[108] In my example, it depends on whether, and if so in what respects and to what degree, which of these creatures are physiologically like human beings—and, of course, on how similar to the drug being tested the substance they are given is.[109]

How well (combined) evidence E supports conclusion C depends on the degree of explanatory integration of the conjunction [E & C]; and how much a specific item of evidence, E_n, contributes to supporting C depends on how much better explanatorily integrated [E & E_n & C] is than [E & C] alone would be, *without* the addition of e_n. Degree of explanatory integration, in turn, is a matter of how well evidence and conclusion fit together in an explanatory account. It is enhanced to the degree that different elements of evidence interlock with each other; which in turn depends in part on their having overlapping content (e.g., referring to the same substance and the same disease)—the more so the more narrowly specific that content is (e.g. referring to small-cell lung cancer rather than, more broadly, to lung cancer, or to doxylamine rather than, more broadly, to antihistamines).[110] Supportiveness is also enhanced if the evidence interlocks with a broader explanatory story (e.g., about the type of genetic damage caused by a class of substances).

The evidence with respect to causal claims in toxic-tort cases may be drawn from any or all of a whole range of disciplines: toxicological studies analyzing the components of a suspected substance and the known effects of these or similar kinds of stuff; *in vivo* studies of the effects of the suspected substances

[108] *Id.*, 77 (where I argue that Kuhn's claim that standards of evidential quality are paradigm-relative is a kind of epistemological illusion: specifically, a misconstrual of the fact that judgments of relevance are perspectival, i.e., depend on one's factual beliefs).

[109] See "Proving Causation: The Weight of Combined Evidence," pp. 208–38 in this volume, n.86, on the problems with Grünenthal's animal studies of Thalidomide.

[110] Doxylamine succinate was the antihistamine in Bendectin (the drug at issue in *Daubert*), which was suspected of being teratogenic, as some other antihistamines are. International Agency for Research on Cancer, "Some Thyrotropic Agents," in *IARC Monographs on the Evaluation of Carcinogenic Risks to Humans* (Lyon, France: World Health Organization, vol. 79, 2001), 145–59, available at http://www.drugs.com/mongraph/doxylamine-succinate.html.

on animals; *in vitro* studies of the effects of the suspect substance on cells; epidemiological studies of the occurrence and distribution of the disease in question in a population; and meta-analyses drawing conclusions from multiple epidemiological studies. Ideally, it would include evidence of some biological mechanism by which S causes D. It may also include physicians' case-studies and differential diagnoses; background information about human biology, about various diseases, and about what might make some subjects especially susceptible to a disease; and—at least in the context of litigation—it will often also include information about by whom studies were funded, about whether and if so how sources of funding tend to affect the results reached, about whether and, if so, where studies have been published, and about the effectiveness of pre-publication peer review as a quality-control device.[111]

The epidemiological evidence on which Hill focuses is an important part of such a congeries of evidence; but it is obviously *only* a part. And the question he is trying to answer is also, in a sense, partial, namely: suppose that we have an epidemiological study showing an increased incidence of D among those exposed to S than among those not so exposed; then what factors bear on whether, or to what degree, it is reasonable to infer a causal connection? And with the broader epistemological understanding now in place we can begin to see how Hill's factors map—somewhat roughly and unsystematically, to be sure—onto the more complex territory of the determinants of degree of warrant.

As I noted earlier in passing, Hill's fourth factor, temporal precedence, is a horse of an entirely different color from the rest: it really is a necessary condition of causality, for one thing, and it is relevant not only in the context of epidemiological evidence, but quite generally.[112] So I will focus here on the other eight Hill factors.

Suppose that e_1 represents the results of an epidemiological study showing a positive association between S and D. How do the remaining eight Hill factors bear on how well e_1 warrants the conclusion that exposure to S causes D?

- The strength of the association (factor 1) found in the study, and its specificity (factor 3), matter because, the more the incidence of D increases

[111] For more detailed discussion of the kinds of causation evidence routinely produced in toxic-tort cases, see "Proving Causation" (note 109 above) 219–21; and on issues about peer review specifically, "Peer Review and Publication: Lessons for Lawyers," pp. 156–79 in this volume, 164–72.

[112] Though, as we now know, some effects occur much longer after their cause than we might previously have imagined; e.g., that diethystilbestrol (DES), given to pregnant women to prevent miscarriage, can cause reproductive cancers in the daughters, and sterility in the sons, born to these women—decades after they took the drug. See Sarina Schrager and Beth E. Potter, "Diethylstilbestrol Exposure," *American Family Physician* 69, no. 10 (May 15, 2004), available at http://www.aafp.org/afp2004/0515/p2393.html.

with exposure to S, and the more tightly S and D are characterized, the more alternative explanations of D—other than that exposure to S causes it—are ruled out.

- If, in addition to e_1, we also have evidence from *other* studies also finding a positive association (factor 2, consistency), we have combined evidence [e_1 & e_2 & e_3] that, for the same reason, is more supportive of C than e_1 alone would be—the more so, as Hill mentions, if the studies are from different times and places.
- If, in addition to e_1, we also have evidence of a strong dose-response relationship (factor 5), then we have combined evidence [e_1 & e_4] that, for the same reason, is more supportive of C than e_1 alone would be.
- And so, similarly, if we have additional "experimental" evidence (factor 8, the other face of the dose-response relationship), evidence of biological plausibility (factor 6), of coherence (factor 7, the other face of plausibility), or of biological analogy (factor 9).

Of course, Hill was an epidemiologist, not an epistemologist. Still, he refers explicitly to explanatoriness; and a gradational understanding of warrant is implicit in his approach. He also acknowledges that it is relevant how well an epidemiological study fits into a larger explanatory account; and when he alludes to biological knowledge we don't yet have, he even half-acknowledges the role of comprehensiveness. True, in his 1965 lecture he hasn't much to say about what makes an epidemiological study better or worse—i.e., in my terminology, about its independent security—but questions about study design and execution are key themes in his famous text on medical statistics. And, even though another study with similar results can't turn a poorly-designed or poorly-conducted study into a well-designed and well-conducted one, adding the results of other studies pointing in the same direction as the one we started with itself raises the independent security of the results of the first study.

In any case, I believe Hill was right to insist that there can't be hard-and-fast rules for inferring causation. Only one of his factors (temporal precedence) is necessary, and none is sufficient, to establish a causal claim. The most one could say is that, *if* all of Hill's factors are satisfied in some degree, *and* the epidemiological and other evidence is itself reasonably secure, *and* no important relevant evidence is missing, *then* (depending in part on the degree to which his factors are satisfied), a causal conclusion is warranted to some degree.

5 ENVOI: THE PROBLEM OF EVIDENTIARY ATOMISM

So why have Hill's ideas been—by and large and on the whole, of course—so poorly handled in the US legal system?

A significant part of the explanation seems to be simply that very few attorneys and judges, and not many expert witnesses, have so much as *glanced* at Hill's (quite modestly-sized) paper, or even at the qualifications acknowledged in Rothman's textbook and in later editions of the *Reference Manual on Scientific Evidence*. Instead, it seems, they have picked up various garbled versions of Hill's ideas third-hand, so that he appears as a kind of mythological figure.

But another part of the explanation is that Hill's focus was, of course, not on issues about legal standards of admissibility or of proof, but on whether and when intervention is justified—when we should withdraw a drug from the market or, especially, clean up a workplace to remove or reduce the level of some suspected toxin. Many of the distortions of his ideas seem to be due to judges', attorneys', and expert witnesses' efforts to adapt the Hill factors to their quite different legal purposes. In fact, as we have seen, Hill's work stands in stark contrast with the legal *penchant* for simple decision-procedures; it aligns very poorly with legal threshold requirements; and—the point I want to emphasize here—it is markedly at odds with the atomistic tendencies of US evidence law generally, and of the Supreme Court's ruling in *Daubert* specifically.

This ruling encourages courts to screen each expert witness, and sometimes each item of testimony such a witness proposes to offer, for (relevance and) reliability. To be sure, the ruling doesn't explicitly require this; but the way it speaks of courts' responsibility to screen the proffered testimony of "an expert" or "the expert"[113] suggests it. And subsequent rulings in important cases like *Paoli*,[114] and Judge Kozinski's ruling when *Daubert* came back to the Ninth Circuit on remand,[115] do precisely this. Such atomistic screening means, in effect, that any item of evidence deemed not to be sufficiently warranted to satisfy the requirement of (relevance or) evidentiary reliability will be excluded. But, as I have argued, the determinants of the quality of evidence are quasi-holistic:[116] they depend, that is, in part on how well various elements interlock (contributing to explanatory integration and hence

[113] *Daubert* III (note 75 above), 589–90 ("the subject of an expert's testimony must be 'scientific … knowledge'") (footnote omitted); 592 ("the trial judge must determine … whether the expert is proposing to testify to (1) scientific knowledge that (2) will assist the trier of fact …").

[114] Note 3 above.

[115] *Daubert v. Merrell Dow Pharm.*, Inc., 43 F.3d 1311, 1320 (9th Cir. 1995) ("*Daubert* IV") (only Dr. Palmer's testimony would meet the relevance requirement, and it flunks the reliability prong of the Supreme Court's ruling in *Daubert* 1993).

[116] See "Epistemology and the Law of Evidence" (note 106 above), 15.

supportiveness), and in part on how much of the relevant evidence is included (the comprehensiveness dimension).

So how strong a plaintiff's evidence is that S sometimes causes D, or how strong a defendant's evidence is that it does not, depends in part on how tightly the components of the whole body of their expert testimony interlock, and in part on how much of the relevant information it includes.[117] Focusing exclusively on the independent security of each piece of evidence, and not on the quality of whole congeries of evidence, stands in the way of an adequate assessment of the strength of conjoined information—exactly the kind of assessment one would *want* the law to make; and can prevent parties to a suit from making what may be a legitimate claim, positive or negative, about causation.

Ironically enough, the essential epistemological point was already made in one of the amicus briefs submitted to the Supreme Court in *Daubert*, when Prof. Rothman and his epidemiologist colleagues argued that:

> ... by focusing on ... what conclusions, if any, can be reached from any one study, the trial court forecloses testimony about inferences that can be drawn from the combination of results reported by many such studies, even when those studies, standing alone, might not justify such inferences.[118]

All the more reason, then—after twenty years (and at a time when the influence of *Daubert* extends well beyond the US)[119]—to emphasize how much, and to what ill effect, evidentiary atomism pulls against the quasi-holistic character of warrant implicit in Hill's work, and articulated quite explicitly in my own.

[117] See also *Milward* (note 56 above), 26 (arguing that "the sum of Dr. Smith's testimony was that a weighing of the Hill factors, including biological plausibility, supported the inference that the association between benzene exposure and APL is genuinely causal").

[118] Brief for Kenneth Rothman et al. (note 67 above), *3.

[119] See "Epistemology and the Law of Evidence" (note 106 above), n. 109–113 and accompanying text.

—11—

Risky Business: Statistical Proof of Specific Causation

> The law embodies the story of a nation's development through many centuries.… In order to know what it is, we must know what it has been, and what it tends to become. We must alternately consult history and existing theories of legislation. But the most difficult labor will be to understand the combination of the two into new products at every stage. The substance of the law at any given time pretty nearly corresponds, so far as it goes, to what is then understood to be convenient; but its form and machinery, and the degree to which it is able to work out desired results, depend very much upon its past.
>
> —Oliver Wendell Holmes.[1]

1 A PRAGMATIST PREAMBLE: HOW LEGAL CONCEPTS EVOLVE

This paper may not be what you were expecting; at least, if you were anticipating that I would come up with a new analysis of the concept of causation that I could apply in legal contexts, or even with a new critique of Hart and Honoré's ideas, or a new defense of them, I shall have to disappoint you. Why so?—not because I have tried, but failed, to contribute something to this analytic genre of legal philosophy; rather, because I'm inclined to think it's more productive to tackle questions about causation, risk, and responsibility in the law in a somewhat different way, better suited to highlighting two facts that seem, at least where the common law is concerned, undeniable: first, that legal concepts generally diverge, in greater or lesser degree, from the everyday concepts in which they have their roots; and second, as Holmes emphasized, that legal concepts aren't fixed and static, but gradually shift and evolve as

[1] Oliver Wendell Holmes, *The Common Law* (1881), in Sheldon M. Novick, ed., *Collected Works of Justice Holmes* (Chicago: University of Chicago Press, 1995), vol. 3, 109–324, 115.

social values and priorities change, as new discoveries are made, and as new technology is introduced.[2]

The first point is apparent, for example, in the difference between our ordinary understanding of what it means to say that someone is drunk, and the precise legal definition of "intoxicated";[3] in the difference between our ordinary understanding of what it means to describe someone as crazy or out of his mind, and legal conceptions of a defendant's being not guilty by reason of insanity, or (to mention just a few of the whole raft of related conceptions that various US jurisdictions now employ) guilty but mentally ill, guilty except insane, suffering from diminished capacity, unfit to stand trial, or, etc.;[4] or in the difference between our ordinary understanding of what it means to say that a witness, or his evidence, is reliable, and the technical legal concept of "evidentiary reliability"—a matter for judges, and not for jurors, or for scientists, or other experts, to determine—introduced by the US Supreme Court in *Daubert*,[5] and embodied in the revised Federal Rule of Evidence (FRE) 702 since 2000.[6]

[2] On this point see also Susan Haack, "The Pluralistic Universe of Law: Towards a Neo-Classical Legal Pragmatism," *Ratio Juris* 21, no. 4 (2008): 453–480; "The Growth of Meaning and the Limits of Formalism, in Science and Law," *Análisis Filosófico* XXIX, no. 1 (2009): 5–29.

[3] For example, Florida law defines "driving under the influence" (of alcohol) as being in control of a vehicle while under the influence of alcohol, with normal capacities impaired, and a blood alcohol level of 0.08 gram or more per 100 milliliters of blood or 0.08 grams of alcohol or more per 210 liters of breath. Fla Stat § 316.193.

[4] "Guilty but mentally ill" is a verdict permitted in Michigan law, "guilty except insane" a verdict permitted in Arizona law. My source is Henry F. Fradella, "From Insanity to Beyond: Diminished Capacity, Mental Illness, and Criminal Excuse in the Post-*Clark* Era," *University of Florida Journal of Law and Public Policy* 18, no. 1 (2007): 7–91 (giving a fascinating history of the evolution of insanity defenses from the thirteenth-century "Wild Beast Defense" through the *M'Naughten* Rule to present-day psychiatric defenses such as Post-Traumatic Stress Syndrome, Battered Woman Syndrome, etc.) See also Barbara A. Weiner, "The Insanity Defense: Historical Development and Present Status," *Behavioral Sciences and the Law* 3, no.1 (1985): 3–35; Michael L. Perlin, *The Jurisprudence of the Insanity Defense* (Durham, NC: Carolina Academic Press, 1994). On the history of intoxication as a defense against criminal charges, see Mitchell Keiter, "Just Say No Excuse: The Rise and Fall of the Intoxication Defense," *Journal of Criminal Law & Criminology* 87, no.2 (1997): 482–520, 484: "[t]he doctrines of *actus reus, mens rea,* insanity, mistake, justification, and duress have historically provided the tools for a constantly shifting adjustment of the tension between the evolving aims of the criminal law and changing religious, moral, philosophical, and medical views of the nature of man" (citing Powell v. Texas, 392 U.S. 514, 536 (1968)).

[5] Daubert v. Merrell Dow Pharm., Inc., 509 U.S. 579, 590 n.9 (1993) ("*Daubert* III"): "We note that scientists typically distinguish between 'validity' (does the principle support what it purports to show?) and 'reliability' (does application of the principle produce consistent results?).... In a case involving scientific evidence, *evidentiary reliability* will be based upon *scientific validity*" (citations omitted).

[6] "If scientific, technical, or other specialized knowledge will assist the trier of fact to understand the evidence or to determine a fact in issue, a witness qualified as an expert by

Legal concepts of causation, my focus here, are certainly no exception to this pattern: the flexibility and context-dependence of our ordinary talk of the causes of this or that event or condition contrasts with a thicket of legal distinctions between cause-in-fact versus proximate (or "legal") cause, general vs. specific causation, dependent vs. independent intervening causes, . . ., liability based on intent or on negligence vs. strict liability, and so on and on. And the ideas about causation, proof of causation, negligence, and liability that US law now deploys also illustrate my second point very vividly: they have evolved over centuries in response to new forms of manufacturing, distribution, and sale of goods, new methods of mining, of construction, of transportation, and so forth—not to mention newly-emerging scientific understandings of and criteria for assessing cause and effect and, in modern times, a more or less self-conscious effort on the part of the legal system to assign responsibility for the risks that industrial, medical, and other advances have inevitably brought with them.

"The modern [US] law of torts," Prof. Friedman writes, "must be laid at the door of the industrial revolution, whose machines had a marvelous capacity for smashing the human body."[7] From around 1850, he continues, tort law grew apace—in large part because of the enormous growth of the railroads: in the late 1840s there had been under 3,000 miles of track across the country; by 1870, there were close to 52,000 miles. And in the wake of this great expansion there were many injuries, most the result of railway-crossing accidents.[8] The body of tort law that evolved to handle this new situation was built on the concepts of breach of duty to the public—failure to take precautions a reasonable man would take—and of proximate cause,[9] contributory negligence,[10] the doctrine of assumption of risk,[11] and the fellow servant rule:[12] a body of law in

knowledge, skill, experience, training, or education, may testify thereto in the form of an opinion or otherwise, if (1) the testimony is based upon sufficient facts or data, (2) the testimony is the product of reliable principles and methods, and (3) the witness has applied the principles and methods reliably to the facts of the case." FRE 702 (2000) (effective Dec. 1, 2000).

7 Lawrence M. Friedman, *A History of American Law* (New York: Simon and Schuster, 1973), 409.

8 *Id.*, 412.

9 The defendant's actions should have caused the plaintiff's injury "with no other man or event intervening." *Id.*, 411.

10 "If the plaintiff was negligent himself, ever so slightly, he could not recover from defendant." *Id.* See also Fleming James, Jr., "Contributory Negligence," *Yale Law Journal* 62, no.1 (1953): 691–735.

11 "A plaintiff could not recover if he put himself willingly in a position of danger." Friedman, *A History of American Law* (note 7 above), 413.

12 "[A] servant (employee) could not sue his master (employer) for injuries caused by the negligence of another employee." *Id.*

which, Friedman observes, "[e]nterprise was favored over workers, slightly less so over passengers and members of the public."[13] As time passed, however, the balance shifted somewhat: the new doctrines of "last clear chance"[14] and *res ipsa loquitur*[15] made it a little easier to prove a defendant's negligence; and a whole raft of new statutes raised the standard of care required of railroads and other industries.[16] By the late nineteenth century, numerous statutes regulated safety conditions in mines, in factories, on trains, on steamships, etc., and statutory negligence became an important concept; and as the rate of industrial accidents rose, the fellow servant rule was eroded by courts trying to ensure that an employer bore "a due and just share of the responsibility for the lives and limbs of the persons in [his] employ."[17]

In 1916, Judge Cardozo held in *MacPherson v. Buick Motor Co.*[18] that a buyer injured by a defective car could sue the manufacturer, even though he hadn't bought it directly from them, but through a dealer. In two famous cases from the 1940s, *Ybarra v. Spangard* (1944)[19] and *Summers v. Tice* (1948)[20]—where it was certain that one of a limited number of people had caused an injury, but impossible to determine which—both (*Summers*) or all (*Ybarra*) defendants were held liable. In several cases, most famously perhaps *Haft v. Lone Palm Hotel*[21]—where the hotel was held liable when Mr. Haft and his son drowned in the hotel pool, because no lifeguard was provided, and guests weren't warned of this—liability was based on the theory that a defendant's failure to warn a plaintiff of, or safeguard him against, some hazard could be deemed to constitute the factual connection needed to establish causation.

By the latter part of the twentieth century, with the rise of huge pharmaceutical and chemical companies, the tort system was adapting to handle cases where the alleged injury occurred long after someone was exposed to a

13 *Id.*, 412–17; the quotation is from 417.

14 A defendant's failing to take his "last clear chance" to avoid an accident "canceled out the consequences of plaintiff's earlier act of fault." *Id.*, 418.

15 "The thing speaks for itself": a plaintiff did not need to prove negligence if the accident obviously could not have happened but for some fault on the defendant's part. *Id.*: 418–9. The expression was introduced by Baron Pollock in a famous English case (Byrne v. Boadle, (1863) 159 Eng. Rep. 299 (Ex.); 2 H.& C. 722), where the fact that a barrel fell out of the defendant's warehouse onto the plaintiff's head was held to be sufficient by itself to permit the jury to find the defendant negligent. Louis L. Jaffe, "*Res Ipsa Loquitur* Vindicated," *Buffalo Law Review* 1, no. 1 (1951):1–15, 1.

16 Friedman, *A History of American Law* (note 7 above), 417–18.

17 *Id.*, 422, quoting from Gilmore v. N. Pac. Ry. Co., 18 F. 866, 870 (C.C.D. Or. 1884).

18 MacPherson v. Buick Motor Co., 111 N.E. 1050 (N.Y. 1916).

19 Ybarra v. Spangard, 154 P.2d 687 (Cal. 1944).

20 Summers v. Tice, 199 P.2d 1 (Cal. 1948).

21 Haft v. Lone Palm Hotel, 478 P.2d 465 (Cal. 1970).

chemical or a drug; and where there were questions as to which of a large class of potential plaintiffs were actually harmed by it, or which company made the drug or chemical that caused the harm. By the 1980s, manufacturers of DES (diethylstilbestrol)—a drug given to prevent miscarriage which, however, turned out to cause reproductive cancers, twenty-odd years later, in some of the daughters, and sterility in some of the sons, who were born to the women who took it—were held partly liable, in accordance with their market share, if they were selling the drug at the time, even if the plaintiff could not show that it was their brand of the drug that her mother took;[22] and in *Hymowitz v. Eli Lilly*[23] a manufacturer was held partly liable even though it could show it had *not* sold the DES taken by the plaintiff's mother (the idea being that, this way, even if a company sometimes had to pay compensation for injuries it hadn't caused, over the long haul each manufacturer would have to pay compensation for roughly its share of the damage).

This gradual evolution of specifically juridical conceptions of causation, responsibility, negligence, etc., continues to this day. Here I will focus on a recent development in toxic-tort litigation: the rise of the idea that evidence that exposure to a defendant's product more than doubles the risk of some disease or disorder in a population is key to establishing that a particular plaintiff's injury was caused by this product.

The first, and necessarily the longest, part of this paper (§2) will be historical and interpretive, tracking the rise of this idea and the many ways it has been construed, and exploring the reasons some courts have given for adopting it, and others for rejecting it. The next part (§3) will be philosophical—more precisely, it will be epistemological, showing that evidence of more than doubled risk, though certainly relevant, is neither necessary nor sufficient for proof of specific causation, and proposing a more defensible account of the role such evidence *can* play. And the last part (§4) will be policy-oriented: arguing, first, that treating evidence of more than doubled risk as sufficient for proof of specific causation, as courts have sometimes done, will likely allow undeserving plaintiffs to recover, while treating evidence of more than doubled risk as

[22] Sindell v. Abbot Labs., 607 P.2d 924, 937 (Cal. 1980) ("holding that "[e]ach defendant will be held liable for the proportion of the judgment represented by its share of that market unless it demonstrates that it could not have made the product which caused plaintiff's injuries"). Bichler v. Eli Lilly & Co., 436 N.Y.S.2d 625, 632 (App. Div. 1981) (holding that "[i]t does not strain one's sense of fairness to allow a limited expansion of the doctrine of concerted action to cover the type of circumstance faced in a DES case where the traditional evidentiary requirements of tort law may be insurmountable").

[23] Hymowitz v. Eli Lilly & Co., 539 N.E.2d 1069, 1078 (N.Y. 1989) (holding that "there should be no exculpation of a defendant who, although a member of the market producing DES for pregnancy use, appears not to have caused a particular plaintiff's injury").

necessary for proof of specific causation, as courts have sometimes done, will likely preclude deserving plaintiffs from recovering; second, that to require, as some courts have done, that a plaintiff must produce evidence of more than doubled risk for his expert testimony on specific causation to be even admissible imposes an unreasonable burden; and finally, that the more adequate understanding of the role of evidence of increased relative risk developed here would be more conducive to the "desired ends" of which Holmes writes than a crude "more than doubled risk" test.

2 A LEGAL HISTORY: HOW EVIDENCE OF MORE THAN DOUBLED RISK BECAME A TEST FOR SPECIFIC CAUSATION

In a toxic-tort case the plaintiff has the burden of proving that he took a drug or was exposed to a chemical made by the defendant; that this drug or chemical *can* cause the kind of injury that he suffered ("general causation"); and that it was his exposure to this substance that caused *his* injury ("specific causation").[24]

Perhaps needless to say, it's not easy to show that the disease or disorder you now have was caused by a drug you took or a substance to which you were exposed perhaps years or even decades ago. After all, not all the women who took the morning-sickness drug Bendectin subsequently gave birth to babies with limb-reduction defects; not all the women who took the anti-lactation drug Parlodel subsequently suffered a stroke; not all the arthritis patients who took Vioxx subsequently suffered heart attacks; and so on. Moreover, women who didn't take Bendectin sometimes give birth to babies with limb-reduction defects; women who didn't take Parlodel sometimes have strokes after childbirth; people who didn't take Vioxx sometimes have heart attacks, and so forth. So—given that not *all* and not *only* people exposed to substance S develop disease or disorder D—how can the plaintiff in a toxic-tort case prove that S caused *his* D?

The evidence in such cases typically includes—besides, quite often, clinical testimony based on differential diagnosis—toxicological studies of the chemical composition of the suspect substance and the known effects of its

[24] See Michael D. Green, D. Michal Freedman, and Leon Gordis, "Reference Guide on Epidemiology," *Reference Guide on Scientific Evidence* (Washington, DC: Federal Judicial Center, 2nd ed., 2000), 333–400, 382; Stuart M. Speiser, Charles F. Krause, and Alfred W. Gars, *The American Law of Torts* (Rochester, NY: The Lawyers' Cooperative Publishing Co., and San Francisco, CA: Bancroft-Whitney Co., 1983–), vol. 6 (1989), §18:379; W. Page Keeton et al., *Prosser and Keeton on the Law of Torts* (St. Paul, MN: West Publishing Co.,1984), chapter 17, §103.

components; *in vivo* studies of the effects of exposing laboratory animals to the suspect substance; *in vitro* studies of the effects of the suspect substance on cells; and epidemiological studies of the incidence of the disorder in a population and its association, if any, with exposure to the suspect substance. With drugs, manufacturers will have conducted randomized controlled clinical trials as part of the process of applying for FDA (Food and Drug Administration) approval to market the drug; plaintiffs—who are rarely, if ever, in a position to conduct such clinical trials themselves—may be able to rely on other, independent studies, not conducted by the manufacturers, or may have to introduce re-analyses of manufacturers' studies to make a case that the risks are greater than the manufacturer concluded. But epidemiological evidence won't always be available: in the case of environmental toxins, such as the PCBs (polychlorinated biphenyls) that Robert Joiner claimed had contributed to his developing lung cancer at the age of 37, there certainly won't be clinical trials, and may be no directly relevant epidemiological studies of any kind.[25]

Like the more familiar word "epidemic," "epidemiology" derives from the Greek, *epi*, "upon," and *demos*, "people" (as in "democracy"). Epidemiological evidence is by definition evidence *about a population*. Not every positive association of S and D will be causal, so such evidence is not sufficient by itself to establish even general causation;[26] and its bearing on the question of specific causation is even trickier. Suppose we know, e.g., that Vioxx causes cardiovascular problems in some patients; how can Mr. X, who had a heart attack shortly after he began taking Vioxx, show that the drug was the cause? It is far from obvious whether, or how, epidemiological evidence could bear on this issue. But some courts have come up with a simple answer: implicitly or explicitly equating the statistical probability that this particular plaintiff's D was caused by his exposure to S with the legal degree of probability or proof required, they have looked to what has come to be known as a "doubling of risk" criterion, according to which epidemiological evidence that exposure to S more than doubles the risk of developing D is crucial in establishing specific causation to the required degree of proof.

Where did this idea come from, and how did it spread?[27] The story begins in the aftermath of a 1976 outbreak of swine flu, in response to which the US

[25] Gen. Elec. Co. v Joiner, 522 U.S. 136 (1997) ("*Joiner* III"). See also Michael Gottesman, "From *Barefoot* to *Daubert* to *Joiner*: Triple Play or Double Error?" *Arizona Law Review* 40 (1998): 753–99.

[26] See "Proving Causation: The Weight of Combined Evidence," and "Correlation and Causation: The 'Bradford Hill Criteria' in Epidemiological, Legal, and Epistemological Context," respectively pp. 208–38 and pp. 239–63 in this volume.

[27] My discussion of relevant cases will be illustrative, not exhaustive. Russellyn S. Carruth and Bernard D. Goldstein, "Relative Risk Greater than Two in Proof of Causation in Toxic

government introduced a massive immunization program. The Centers for Disease Control (CDC) soon began receiving reports of a disturbing number of cases of Guillain-Barré Syndrome (GBS), a rare neurological disorder,[28] among those recently vaccinated; and the government discontinued the vaccination program only eleven weeks after it began. This epidemic was legally consequential in more ways than one. First, in its wake Congress passed a law requiring that suits for injuries allegedly caused by vaccines be brought against the federal government rather than against vaccine manufacturers or against the clinics, health departments, etc., that administered the vaccination program.[29] And this was a first step in a direction that would eventually lead—after another scare, this time over pertussis (whooping-cough) vaccinations, in the 1980s—to special vaccine laws and a special Vaccine Court set up to handle questions of compensation.[30] This system has of late been in the public eye: first, because of the rulings issued by the Vaccine Court in 2009, to the effect that the evidence does not indicate that MMR (Mumps, Measles, and Rubella) vaccination, as some had feared, causes autism;[31] and

Tort Litigation," *Jurimetrics* 45 (2001): 195–209 is a good source on cases up to the time of its publication; Andrew Jurs, "Judicial Analysis of Complex and Cutting-Edge Science in the *Daubert* Era: Epidemiological Risk Assessment as a Test Case for Reform Strategies," *Connecticut Law Review* 42, no.1 (2009): 49–100 is a useful source on more recent cases.

28 GBS is a disorder (normally affecting around one in a hundred thousand people) in which the immune system attacks the peripheral nervous system, leading to weakness and tingling, increasing in severity and in severe cases leading to complete paralysis. It is recognized that occasionally surgery or vaccinations can trigger the syndrome. See "Guillain-Barré Syndrome Fact Sheet," available at http://www.ninds.nih.gov/disorders/gbs/detail_gbs.htm.

29 Harold M. Schmeck, Jr., "Swine Flu Program Brings $10.7 Million in Claims," *New York Times*, Global Edition, February 5, 1977, 8. The National Swine Flu Immunization Program of 1976, Pub L No 94–380, 90 Stat 1113, codified at 42 USC § 247b (j)–(1), repealed by § 928, Pub L No 97–35, 95 Stat 357, 569 (1981) was passed in August 1976.

30 National Childhood Vaccine Injury Act of 1986, Pub L No 99–660, 100 Stat 3743, 3755–84, codified at 42 USC §§ 300aa-1–300aa-34. The Act protects manufacturers from being sued in state or federal court for "unavoidable" injuries caused by their vaccines. The Office of Special Masters of the US Court of Federal Claims, or "Vaccine Court," compensates families whose children have been injured by vaccines, out of a compensation fund provided by the manufacturers. Wendy Davis, "The Immune Response," *ABA (American Bar Association) Journal* (October 2010): 48–54. See also Arthur Allen, *Vaccine: The Controversial Story of Medicine's Greatest Lifesaver* (New York: W. W. Norton, 2007); but note that the suggestion (261) that these arrangements were set up immediately after the swine flu debacle is mistaken.

31 Snyder v. Sec'y of Health & Human Servs., No. 01–162V, 2009 WL 332044 (Fed. Cl. Feb. 12, 2009); Cedillo v. Sec'y of Health & Human Servs., No. 98–916V, 2009 WL 331968 (Fed. Cl. Feb. 12, 2009); Hazlehurst v. Sec'y of Health & Human Servs., No. 03–654V, 2009 WL 332306 (Fed. Cl. Feb. 12, 2009). For details of Yates Hazlehurst's condition, see Theodore H. Davis, Jr., and Catherine B. Bowman, "No-Fault Compensation for Unavoidable Injuries: Evaluating the National Childhood Vaccine Injury Compensation Program," *University of Dayton Law Review* 16, no.2 (2010): 48–54.

then because of a 2011 Supreme Court case that raised questions about exactly what is covered by vaccine makers' immunity from lawsuits under the 1986 Act—specifically, about exactly when the side effects from which injury results really *are* "unavoidable."[32]

With these developments, we see the US legal system gradually adapting to a new environment in which massive vaccination programs bring not only important public-health benefits, but also an unavoidable risk of serious injury to a few. More to the present purpose, though, the 1976 swine flu epidemic also gave rise to the earliest case I found where evidence of more than doubled risk was used as a test for proof of specific causation: *Cook v. United States*, decided in 1982.[33]

Mr. Cook and two other plaintiffs alleged that vaccination against swine flu had caused them to develop GBS between twelve-and-a-half and thirteen-and-a-half weeks later. Finding for the defendant, the court observed that "[t]he dispute between the parties ... is how soon the attack rate in the vaccinated population drops below the point where the relative risk is not sufficiently large to assure the Court that a given GBS case was more likely than not caused by swine flu vaccination rather than by some other event."[34] Dr. Schonberger, the lead author of a study based on data collected by the CDC,[35] argued for the defendant that, while there was a greatly increased risk of GBS immediately after vaccination, the increased risk fell off rapidly after three weeks, and "drop[ped] below twice that of non-vaccinees shortly before the tenth week";[36] the plaintiff's experts disputed this.[37] But neither party disputed the key principle articulated by the court: the plaintiff's case could be proven by a preponderance of the evidence only if the relative risk was shown to be greater than 2.

32 *Bruesewitz v. Wyeth*: the question at issue was whether the Third Circuit erred in holding that the National Childhood Vaccine Injury Act provides blanket immunity from tort actions in state or federal court by plaintiffs claiming injury from defectively designed vaccines. See *Legal Information Bulletin*, Bruesewitz v. Wyeth, Inc. (09–152), available at http://topics.law.cornell.edu/supct/cert/09–152; *Vaccine News Daily*, "Supreme Court to decide if vaccine makers can be sued," available at http://vaccinenewsdaily.com/news/212259; editorial, "A Real Vaccine Scare," *Wall Street Journal*, October 16–17, 2010, A16. In 2011, the Supreme Court ruled on the issue: "the National Childhood Vaccine Injury Act preempts all design-defect claims against vaccine manufacturers ... who seek compensation for injury or death caused by vaccine side effects." Bruesewitz v. Wyeth, Inc., 131 S. Ct. 1068, 1082 (2011).

33 Cook v. United States, 545 F. Supp. 306 (N.D. Cal. 1982).

34 *Id.*, 308.

35 Lawrence B. Schonberger et al., "Guillain-Barre [*sic*] Syndrome Following Vaccination in the National Influenza Vaccination Program, United States 1976–1977," *American Journal of Epidemiology* 110, no.2 (1979): 105–23.

36 *Cook* (note 33 above), 308.

37 *Id.*, 309–11.

A footnote reveals that the court takes evidence of more than doubled risk to be not only necessary, i.e., required for proof of specific causation, but also sufficient, i.e., enough by itself to constitute such proof:

> Suppose the relative risk for vaccin[e]es … is two—i.e., … they are twice as likely to experience onset of GBS after that interval as are persons in the unvaccinated population during [that] calendar week. If fifty GBS cases occur among a million unvaccinated persons that week, then a hundred cases would be expected among a million nine-week vaccinees. Of that hundred, fifty would have been expected without vaccination, while the other fifty are explained only by the … vaccination. Thus, the likelihood that a given nine-week vaccinated case of GBS is attributable to vaccination is 50%.… *Once the relative risk rises above two, it becomes more probable than not that a given case was caused by the vaccine.*[38]

A couple of years later, in In re *"Agent Orange,"*[39] while denying that evidence of more than doubled risk should be sufficient to prove specific causation—which, he argued, would allow *all* plaintiffs to recover when *ex hypothesi* many had not been injured by the product in question, Judge Weinstein held that "at least a two-fold increase in incidence of the disease attributable to Agent Orange exposure is required to permit recovery."[40] He immediately added a crucial caveat: "*if* epidemiological studies alone are relied upon";[41] but, as we shall see, when his ruling is subsequently cited, it is sometimes read as favoring the "more than doubled risk" idea more than it really does.[42]

Two years after this, in *Manko v. United States*,[43] where again the plaintiff alleged that swine flu vaccination had caused his GBS, the court took doubling of relative risk as a sufficient condition for proof of specific causation (though not, as in *Cook*, as also necessary). Given that—though he claimed to have developed symptoms within three weeks—Mr. Manko wasn't admitted to hospital until thirteen weeks after vaccination, there was dispute about how soon after his flu shot he developed GBS. Entering a judgment for the plaintiff, Judge Bartlett argued that "a relative risk of '2' means that, on the average, there is a fifty percent likelihood that a particular case of the disease was caused by the event under investigation and a fifty percent likelihood

[38] *Id.*, 308 n.1 (my italics). The court eventually found for the defendant. *Id.*, 316.

[39] *In re* "Agent Orange" Prod. Liab. Litig., 597 F. Supp. 740 (E.D.N.Y. 1984).

[40] *Id.*, 785 (my italics).

[41] *Ibid.*

[42] E.g., in *Havner* (note 73 below).

[43] Manko v. United States, 636 F. Supp. 1419 (W.D. Mo. 1986). See also David A. Freedman and Philip B. Stark, "The Swine Flu Vaccine and Guillain-Barré Syndrome: A Case Study in Relative Risk and Specific Causation," *Law & Contemporary Problems* 64 (2001): 49–62.

that the disease was caused by chance alone." A relative risk greater than 2, he continued, "means that the disease more likely than not was caused by the event."[44] And so, accepting the plaintiff's expert testimony that the relative risk of contracting GBS 11–16 weeks after vaccination was 3.89—or 3.396 if, as the defendant suggested, Mr. Manko had contracted a viral disease very shortly after being vaccinated—the court concludes that "it is more likely than not that plaintiff's swine flu vaccination caused his GBS."[45]

So even in the early days, as what I have called, with deliberate vagueness, "the 'more than doubled risk' idea" gained influence in the courts, its role shifted and changed: in *Cook*, a showing of relative risk greater than 2 was taken to be both necessary and sufficient to establish specific causation to the "more probably than not" standard; in "*Agent Orange*," it was taken to be necessary, but only if epidemiological evidence was the sole evidence offered, and definitely not sufficient; in *Manko*, it was taken to be sufficient, but the question of its necessity was not addressed.

~

By the 1990s the "more than doubled risk" had become—well, epidemic. In 1990, it appeared in the Bendectin litigation—the line of cases that includes *Daubert*. This part of the story begins with *DeLuca v. Merrell Dow Pharmaceuticals* (1990).[46] Amy Deluca's parents alleged that Merrell Dow's morning-sickness drug, Bendectin, had caused their daughter's limb-reduction birth defects. The district court, excluding the testimony of plaintiff's expert witness Dr. Done on the grounds that it was not based on the kind of data reasonably relied on by experts in the field, had granted summary judgment for the defendant. The US Court of Appeals for the Third Circuit reversed the exclusion of Dr. Done's testimony, and remanded the case for further proceedings.[47] In doing so, however, the court observed, citing *Manko*, that if, on remand, the DeLucas were again to rely solely on Dr. Done's testimony, "to avoid summary judgment, the relative risk of limb reduction defects arising from the epidemiological data Done relies upon will, at a minimum, have to exceed '2.'"[48] This is the first sign of a whole new legal twist—that more than doubled risk might be required for epidemiological testimony to be even admissible.

The same year, in In re *Joint Eastern and Southern District Asbestos Litigation*, the court cited *Manko* for the proposition that a relative risk greater

44 *Manko* (note 43 above), 1434.

45 *Id.*, 1437.

46 DeLuca v. Merrell Dow Pharm., Inc., 911 F.2d 941 (3d Cir. 1990).

47 *Id.*, 959.

48 *Id.*, 958–59.

than 2 is sufficient to show that the plaintiff's injury was more likely than not caused by the exposure in question, and In re "*Agent Orange*" for the proposition that, if epidemiological studies alone are relied on, it is necessary.[49] And the "more than doubled risk" idea was given a significant boost when the authors of the chapter on epidemiology in the *Reference Manual on Scientific Evidence* put out by the FJC (Federal Judicial Center) endorsed it in their section on individual causation:

> [C]ourts have confronted the role that epidemiology plays with regard to the sufficiency of evidence. The civil burden of proof is described ... as requiring the fact finder to "believe that what is sought to be proved ... is more likely than not true." The relative risk from an epidemiological study can be adapted to this 50% plus standard to yield a probability or likelihood that an agent caused an individual's disease. The threshold for concluding that an agent was more likely than not the cause of a disease than not is a relative risk greater than 2.0.[50]

In this context, they cited *DeLuca*.

In *Daubert*, as in *DeLuca*, the district court had granted summary judgment to the defendant, and the court of appeals had affirmed. What was different about *Daubert* was that, in affirming the district court's exclusion of the Dauberts' expert testimony, the court of appeals had relied on the *Frye* Rule; prompting the Supreme Court to grant *certiorari* to determine whether or not the *Frye* Rule had been superseded by the Federal Rules of Evidence. Ruling that the *Frye* Rule *had* been superseded, but that federal courts nevertheless still had a responsibility to screen expert testimony both for relevance or "fit" with the case, and for reliability,[51] the Supreme Court remanded the case to the Ninth Circuit.[52] On remand, rather than sending the case back to the district court, Judge Kozinski affirmed the district court's summary judgment in favor of the defendants,[53] arguing that the Dauberts' expert testimony was clearly no more admissible under the new *Daubert* standard than under the old *Frye* Rule.[54]

49 *In re* Joint E. & S. Dist. Asbestos Litig., 827 F. Supp. 1014, 1027 (S.D.N.Y. 1993), *rev'd* 52 F.3d 1124 (2d Cir. 1995); In re "*Agent Orange*" (note 39 above).

50 Linda A. Bailey, Leon Gordis, and Michael D. Green, "Reference Guide on Epidemiology," in *Reference Manual on Scientific Evidence* (Washington, DC: Federal Judicial Center, 1st ed., 1994), 123–80, 168 (internal citations omitted).

51 *Daubert* III (note 5 above), 589.

52 *Id.*, 597.

53 Daubert v. Merrell Dow Pharm., Inc., 43 F.3d 1311, 1322 (9th Cir. 1995) ("*Daubert* IV").

54 *Id.*, 1315.

Only one of the Dauberts' experts, Judge Kozinski reasoned—Dr. Palmer—could meet the relevancy requirement; and since he didn't seem even to *have* a methodology, let alone a reliable one, he would obviously fail the reliability prong of *Daubert*.[55] And the testimony of all the Dauberts' other proffered experts, he continued, would have to be excluded on grounds of irrelevance: for none of them even claimed, let alone showed, that taking Bendectin more than doubled the risk of limb-reduction birth defects.[56] "California tort law requires plaintiffs to show not merely that Bendectin increased the likelihood of injury, but that it more likely than not caused *their* injuries,"[57] Judge Kozinski writes, and:

> [i]n terms of statistical proof, this means that plaintiffs must establish not just that their mothers' ingestion of Bendectin increased somewhat the likelihood of birth defects, but that it more than doubled it—only then can it be said that Bendectin is more likely than not the source of their injury.[58]

So, he continues, citing *DeLuca*, to be admissible a study "must show that children whose mothers took Bendectin are more than twice as likely to develop limb reduction birth defects as children whose mothers did not."[59]

The new requirement on admissibility imposed in Judge Kozinski's 1995 ruling in *Daubert* was soon being cited in other cases. The same year (1995), in *Ambrosini v. Upjohn*, the court granted summary judgment for the defendant after—citing Judge Kozinski's ruling—excluding the testimony of plaintiff's expert Dr. Strom because he wasn't prepared to say that a mother's having taken Depo-Provera to avert miscarriage more than doubled the risk of birth defects in her baby.[60] The following year (1996) the new requirement turns

55 *Id.*, 1319.

56 *Id.*, 1320–21.

57 *Id.*, 1320. It should not escape notice that—though, as we shall see, this has sometimes been taken as saying that California tort law requires a showing of more than doubled risk—what it actually says is that California tort law requires proof to the "more probable than not" standard, on which the "more than doubled risk" idea is Judge Kozinski's gloss.

58 *Ibid.* In a footnote that has attracted much less attention than the text of his ruling, Judge Kozinski adds that a showing of more than doubled risk would not be necessary for evidence of specific causation to be admissible if there were other evidence that this plaintiff was especially susceptible. But he immediately dismisses this consideration with the brisk observation that the Dauberts had proffered no such evidence. *Id.*, 1321 n.16.

59 *Id.*, 1321. See also Judge Kozinski's discussion of his ruling and its ramifications. Alex Kozinski, "Brave New World," *University of California Davis Law Review* 10 (1996–97): 997–1101.

60 Ambrosini v. Upjohn Co., Civ. A. No. 84-3483 (NJH), 1995 WL 637650, *4 (D.D.C. Oct. 18, 1995). (On appeal, the court held that Dr. Strom's testimony didn't warrant exclusion simply because it failed to establish causation to the required degree of probability, and in fact "comfortably cleared the hurdle of admissibility established by *Daubert*." 101 F.3d 129, 135, 140 (D.C. Cir. 1996)).

up in another Bendectin case, *Oxendine v. Merrell Dow Pharmaceuticals.*[61] Quoting defendant's expert Dr. Bracken, who had argued that, if it was true that taking Bendectin doubled the risk that a mother would give birth to a baby with a specific birth defect, when the drug was withdrawn from the market the incidence of that defect should have fallen 23%—which it didn't[62]—and noting that that Judge Kozinski had deemed Dr. Newman's proffered affidavit inadmissible because it didn't claim, let alone show, that Bendectin doubled the risk of limb reduction birth defects, the court found that there was overwhelming evidence that Bendectin was not teratogenic, and entered a judgment for the defendant.[63] The same year, also citing Judge Kozinski's ruling[64] and noting that none of Ms. Sanderson's experts would go so far as to say that exposure to the defendant's products more than doubled the risk of the chemical sensitivities she had suffered,[65] the court in *Sanderson v. International Flavors and Fragrances* ruled the plaintiff's expert testimony inadmissible[66] and granted the defendant's motion for summary judgment.[67] And in *Hall v. Baxter Healthcare*, also in 1996, Judge Jones cited Judge Kozinski's ruling several times;[68] referred to the article by Bailey et al. in the *Reference Manual*;[69] observed that Oregon law required plaintiffs to show a relative risk greater than 2,[70] and that none of the epidemiological studies of silicone breast implants *did* find a more than doubled relative risk of connective tissue disorders;[71] and concluded that the plaintiff's expert testimony didn't meet the *Daubert* standard.[72]

The next year (1997) the idea turns up in yet another Bendectin case, this time in state court. In *Merrell Dow Pharmaceuticals v. Havner*[73] the Supreme

61 Oxendine v. Merrell Dow Pharm., Inc., Civ. No. 82–1245, 1996 WL 680992 (D.C. Super. Ct. Oct. 24, 1996) ("*Oxendine* V").
62 *Id.*, *22.
63 *Id.*, *26.
64 Sanderson v. Int'l Flavors & Fragrances, Inc., 950 F. Supp. 981, 988 (C.D. Cal. 1996).
65 *Id.*, 999–1000.
66 *Id.*, 1004.
67 *Id.*,1005.
68 Hall v. Baxter Healthcare Corp., 947 F. Supp. 1387, 1397, 1403, 1404 (D. Or. 1996).
69 *Id.*,1403.
70 *Ibid.* So, in effect, Judge Jones is adopting Judge Kozinski's gloss on California's "more probable than not" standard (*Daubert* IV (note 53 above), 1320) as his own gloss on Oregon's "more probable than not" standard.
71 *Hall* (note 68 above), 1406.
72 *Id.*, 1415. However, Judge Jones deferred the effective date of his decision pending a report from the National Science Panel set up by Judge Pointer in the major consolidated breast-implant case.
73 Merrell Dow Pharm., Inc. v. Havner, 953 S.W.2d 706 (Tex. 1997).

Court of Texas—citing *Cook*,[74] *DeLuca*,[75] the 1995 ruling in *Daubert*,[76] and In re *"Agent Orange"*[77]—concludes that, though "there is not a precise fit between science and legal burdens of proof," well-conducted epidemiological studies may properly be part of the causation evidence in a toxic tort case, and that "there is a rational basis for relating the requirement that there be more than a 'doubling of the risk' to our ... evidence standard of review and to the more likely than not burden [*sic*] of proof."[78] The same year, the US Court of Appeals in the Ninth Circuit argued in *Schudel* that—since Washington tort law was virtually identical to California tort law—the more-than-doubled risk standard Judge Kozinski had invoked applied: the plaintiff's evidence must show that more probably than not defendant's drug caused the injuries, "*i.e.*, that use of the drug more than doubled the likelihood the injuries would occur."[79]

The year after that (1998), the federal court in *Bartley* wrote that "[a]ssuming, without deciding, that *Havner*'s rule controls, the evidence ... more than satisfies the relative risk of 2.0 standard";[80] and Judge deMoss, dissenting, gave the *Havner* standard a much stronger endorsement, writing that a scientific study is probative of "legal causation" only if it establishes that the alleged cause is more likely than not the actual cause of the injury, and went on, "[i] n other words" it is not probative "if it fails to demonstrate that the suspected cause doubles the risk of injury...."[81] The same year, the district court in In re *Hanford Nuclear Reservation* wrote, citing Judge Kozinski's ruling in *Daubert* IV, that "'[d]oubling of the risk' is the legal standard for evaluating the sufficiency of the plaintiffs' evidence and for determining which claims should be heard by the jury";[82] and in another consolidated breast-implant case, In

74 *Id.*, 716–17.
75 *Ibid.*
76 *Id.*, 719.
77 *Id.*, 715.
78 *Id.*, 717.
79 Schudel v. Gen. Elec. Co., 120 F.3d 991, 996 (9th Cir. 1997), *abrogated on other grounds by* Weisgram v. Marley Co., 528 U.S. 440 (2000) (my italics). Here, as Judge Jones had done in *Hall* (note 68 above), the court is adopting Judge Kozinski's gloss on the "more probable than not" standard (*Daubert* IV (note 53 above), 1320).
80 Bartley v. Euclid, Inc., 158 F.3d 261, 273 (5th Cir. 1998) ("*Bartley* I") (footnote omitted), *vacated by* 169 F.3d 215 (5th Cir.) ("*Bartley* II"), *on reh'g* 180 F.3d 175 (5th Cir. 1999) ("*Bartley* III"). Unlike the other cases discussed in this paper, this was not a toxic-tort case, but a personal-injury suit; unlike the 1998 opinion, the 1999 opinions do not mention *Havner* at all.
81 *Bartley* I (note 80 above), 285 (DeMoss, J., dissenting); in *Bartley* II (note 80 above), dissenting again, Judge DeMoss incorporates his arguments as given in *Bartley* I.
82 *In re* Hanford Nuclear Reservation Litig. (part of "*Hanford* Group A"), No. CY-91–3015-AAM, 1998 WL 775340, *8 (E.D. Wash. Aug. 21, 1998) (but see also text accompanying note 115 below).

re *Breast Implant Litigation*,[83] also citing this ruling,[84] the court argued that "[u]nder Colorado law, testimony about medical causation is only relevant if it allows a jury to find that it is more likely than not" that the defendant's product caused the injury; and that "[t]his means that Plaintiffs must present expert testimony demonstrating that exposure to breast implants more than doubled the risk of their alleged injuries."[85] So what is significant is that "the substantial body of epidemiological evidence demonstrates that silicone breast implants do not double the risk of any known diseases."[86]

The following year (1999), in another silicone breast-implant case, *Allison v. McGhan Medical Corporation*,[87] the court affirmed the district court's *Daubert* ruling excluding the plaintiff's experts and affirming summary judgment to McGhan,[88] arguing—citing the article by Bailey et al.—that:

> The threshold for concluding that an agent more likely than not caused a disease is 2.0.... A relative risk of 2.0 ... implies a 50% likelihood that the agent caused the disease. Risks greater than 2.0 permit an inference that the plaintiff's disease was more likely than not caused by the agent.[89]

The second edition of the *Federal Reference Manual* appeared in 2000. The new chapter on epidemiological evidence (now under lead author Michael Green) included a paragraph on the "more than doubled risk" idea much like the one in the previous edition—except that now it concluded: "A substantial number of courts in a variety of toxic substances cases have accepted this reasoning," and cited a whole list of cases including *Cook, Manko, DeLuca, Sanderson*, and *Havner*.[90] This paragraph, as we shall see, seems to have attracted much more attention than the passage earlier in the chapter in which the authors say that the question of specific causation "is not addressed by epidemiology," and that what follows should be understood as "an explanation of judicial opinions."[91]

In the new century, federal courts continued to cite Judge Kozinski's 1995 *Daubert* ruling as grounds for requiring that, to be admissible, epidemiological

83 *In re* Breast Implant Litig., 11 F. Supp. 2d 1217 (D. Colo. 1998).
84 *Id.*, 1225.
85 *Id.*, 1226. (Here again we see the court adopting Judge Kozinski's gloss on "more probable than not" (*Daubert* IV (note 53 above), 1320), now as an interpretation of Colorado's "more probable than not" standard.)
86 In re *Breast Implant Litig.* (note 83 above),1228.
87 Allison v. McGhan Med. Corp., 184 F.3d 1300 (11th Cir. 1999).
88 *Id.*, 1322.
89 *Id.*, 1315, n.16 (the first sentence is a direct quotation from Bailey, Gordis, and Green, "Reference Guide on Epidemiology" [note 50 above]).
90 Green, Freedman, and Gordis, "Reference Guide on Epidemiology" (note 24 above), 384.
91 *Id.*, 382.

evidence must show a more than doubled risk. In 2004, for example, in yet another consolidated breast-implant case, In re *Silicone Gel Breast Implants*, the court writes, citing *Daubert* IV, that "under California law [statistical] analyses must show a relative risk greater than 2.0 to be 'useful' to the jury."[92] This, the court continues, quoting the key passage from the 2000 *Reference Manual*, is because "a relative risk greater than 2.0 is needed to extrapolate from generic population-based studies to conclusions about what caused a specific person's disease."[93] In *Henricksen v. ConocoPhillips Co.* (2009), the court excludes the plaintiff's expert testimony on the grounds that in the Ninth Circuit an epidemiological study can be probative of specific causation "only if [it] shows the relative risk is greater than 2.0"; and observes that "a relative risk that is greater than 2.0 permits the conclusion that the agent was more likely than not responsible for a particular individual's disease."[94] And in early 2010, the Supreme Court of Vermont ruled in *Estate of George v. Vermont League of Cities and Towns* that the trial court had not abused its discretion in taking a showing of a relative risk greater than 2 as a benchmark for the admissibility of plaintiffs' epidemiological evidence, finding that this "easily tied into Vermont's 'more likely than not' civil standard...."[95]

And Texas courts continued to cite *Havner* as authority for requiring that plaintiffs show that exposure to the substance in question more than doubles the risk of the disorder it allegedly caused—but now transmute this into a requirement on admissibility. In 2003, for example, in *Daniels v. Lyondell Citgo Refining Co., Ltd*,[96] the court affirms the exclusion of the plaintiff's expert testimony on the grounds that none of the studies relied on meets the "relative risk greater than 2" standard, and cites *Havner*.[97] We see the same thing in 2006 in *Mobil Oil Corp. v. Bailey*;[98] and the following year in the ruling from a federal court in Texas in *Burton v. Wyeth-Ayerst Laboratories*.[99]

So in the cases from *DeLuca* to *Henricksen* a new line of judicial argument emerges, now focused on admissibility. In *DeLuca*, the question of sufficiency

[92] *In re* Silicone Gel Breast Implants Prods. Liab. Litig. (California), 318 F. Supp. 2d 879, 893 (C.D. Cal. 2004). Once again, as in *Hall* (note 68 above), *Schudel* (note 79 above), and In re *Breast Implant Litig.* (note 83 above), the court is adopting Judge Kozinski's gloss on "more probable than not" in *Daubert* IV (note 53 above), 1320.

[93] In re *Silicone Gel Breast Implants* (California) (note 92 above), 893.

[94] Henricksen v. ConocoPhillips Co., 605 F. Supp. 2d 1142, 1158 (E.D. Wash. 2009).

[95] Estate of George v. Vt. League of Cities & Towns Prop. & Cas. Intermunicipal Fund, Inc., 993 A.2d 367, 375 (Vt. 2010).

[96] Daniels v. Lyondell-Citgo Ref. Co., 99 S.W.3d 722 (Tex. App. 2003).

[97] *Id.*, 727.

[98] Mobil Oil Corp. v. Bailey, 187 S.W.3d 265, 268 (Tex. App. 2006).

[99] Burton v. Wyeth-Ayerst Labs., 513 F. Supp. 2d 719 (N.D. Tex. 2007).

was not addressed, but a showing of more than doubled risk was apparently taken to be necessary and, it was at least implied, required for admissibility. In 1995 this was made explicit in *Daubert* IV; and was soon adopted by many courts.

~

However, courts have by no means been unanimous in their endorsement of the "more than doubled risk" idea; on the contrary, some have expressed important reservations. Only a couple of years after *Cook*, the court in *Allen* (1984) rejected the argument that more than doubled risk is necessary for proof of specific causation with the comment that "such [an] argument assumes the absence of other factual connections tying the increased risk to plaintiff's particular injuries"; and objected to the "mechanical application of a 'greater-than-100%-increase' test."[100] The same year, the court in *Johnston v. United States* rejected the argument that it was sufficient: "[a] statistical method which shows a greater than 50% probability does not rise to the required level of proof";[101] and in In re"*Agent Orange*," as we saw earlier,[102] Judge Weinstein had rejected the idea that a relative risk greater than 2 was sufficient, and argued that it was necessary only if there was no evidence other than epidemiological studies.

More recently, in *Grassis* (1991) a New Jersey court rejected the defendant's argument that, before an expert is allowed to rely on epidemiological evidence, he must meet the threshold requirement that he show at least doubling of relative risk. This "proves too much," the court argued: it would exclude a plaintiff's evidence of a relative risk of 1.99 even if there were significant evidence eliminating other known causes in the case of this particular plaintiff; while at the same time, if a new study found a relative risk of 2, *all* plaintiffs could use the epidemiological evidence even though *ex hypothesi* this risk factor *wasn't* the cause in almost half of them.[103] The following year (1992), in *Landrigan*, the Supreme Court of New Jersey noted defense counsel's argument on appeal that "a relative risk of 2.0 is not so much a password to a finding of causation

[100] Allen v. United States, 588 F. Supp. 247, 418 (D. Utah 1984) (referring specifically to the argument as articulated in Richard Delgado, "Beyond *Sindell*: Relaxation of Cause-in-Fact Rules for Indeterminate Plaintiffs," *California Law Review* 70 (1982): 881–908); this case was subsequently reversed on other grounds, 816 F.2d 1417 (10th Cir. 1987) (holding the government immune from suit).

[101] Johnston v. United States, 597 F. Supp. 374, 412 (D. Kan. 1984).

[102] Note 39 above.

[103] Grassis v. Johns-Manville Corp., 591 A.2d 671, 676 (N.J. Super. Ct. App. Civ. 1991) (The policy argument against treating RR > 2 as sufficient for proof of specific causation used here parallels Judge Weinstein's in In re "*Agent Orange*" [note 39 above].)

as one piece of evidence, among others"[104] and, in line with this, argued that on remand the trial court should consider the validity of the studies on which Dr. Sokolowski relied, and of his assumptions about the decedent's asbestos exposure, about the absence of other risk factors, etc. A few years later, in In re *Joint Eastern & Southern District Asbestos Litigation* (1995), the Second Circuit argued that it would be best to allow a jury to decide "whether many studies over the 1.0 mark have any significance in combination."[105] The year after that, in *Jones v. Owens-Corning* (1996) a New Jersey appellate court cited *Grassis* and *Landrigan* as it rejected the doubled-risk threshold.[106]

In *Pick v. American Medical Systems* (1997)[107]—this one a case involving disorders allegedly caused by a silicone penile implant—after pointing out that *any* increase of risk associated with a product suggests that it may play some causal role,[108] and that FRE 401 defines relevant evidence as evidence having "'any tendency' to prove or disprove a fact of consequence in the case," the court concluded that a showing of more than doubled risk is *not* required for evidence to be admissible.[109] The same year, the Supreme Court of Tennessee ruled in *McDaniel v. CSX Transportation* that a showing of more than doubled risk "is certainly relevant," but "reject[ed] the contention that it should be adopted as matter of law."[110]

Even in *Havner*—frequently cited as authority for the more-than-doubled-risk standard—the Texas Supreme Court had expressed some significant reservations:

> We do not hold ... that a relative risk of more than 2.0 is a litmus test or that a single epidemiological test is legally sufficient evidence of causation. There may in fact be no causal relationship even if the relative risk is high.... [Moreover] there are a number of reasons why reliance on a relative risk of 2.0 as a bright-line boundary would not be in accordance with sound scientific methodology in some cases.[111]

The following year (1998), in *Minnesota Mining and Manufacturing v. Atterbury*,[112] another Texas court picked up on this caveat, and pointed out that the *Havner* court "refused to set any strict rules," and that "[t]here is no

104 Landrigan v. Celotex Corp., 605 A.2d 1079, 1087 (N.J. 1992).
105 In re *Joint E. & S. Dist. Asbestos Litig.* (note 49 above), 1134.
106 Jones v. Owens-Corning Fiberglas Corp., 672 A.2d 230, 234–35 (N.J. Super. Ct. App. Div. 1996).
107 Pick v. Am. Med. Sys., Inc., 958 F. Supp. 1151 (E.D. La. 1997).
108 *Id.*, 1160 (citing Turpin v. Merrell Dow Pharm., Inc., 959 F.2d 1349, 1353, n.1 (6th Cir. 1992)).
109 *Ibid.*
110 McDaniel v. CSX Transp., Inc., 955 S.W.2d 257, 264 (Tenn. 1997).
111 *Havner* (note 73 above), 718–19.
112 Minn. Mining & Mfg. Co. v. Atterbury, 978 S.W.2d 183 (Tex. App.1998). In this context, the court also cites *Pick* (note 106 above).

requirement in a toxic tort case that a party must have reliable epidemiological evidence of a relative risk of 2.0 or greater."[113] The same year, noting that Judge Kozinski's 1995 *Daubert* ruling seemed to require a showing of more than doubled of risk for the testimony to be even admissible, an Arizona court dismissed this idea with the laconic observation that "other courts have not followed such an arbitrary requirement";[114] and a court of appeals in Florida—which at that time had not adopted *Daubert*, but remained a *Frye* state—cited *McDaniel* as it overruled the trial court's exclusion of the plaintiff's epidemiological testimony.[115]

In 2002, reversing the ruling in In re *Hanford Nuclear Reservation*,[116] and arguing that this case was *not* like *Daubert*, where "there was no definitive evidence that Bendectin is ... capable of causing birth defects," the court of appeals argued that the lower court had erred in applying the "more than doubled risk" test.[117] In 2005, a California court of appeals held that the lower court's exclusion of plaintiff's expert testimony on the grounds that an epidemiological study can provide a reasonable basis for an opinion on causation only if it shows a relative risk greater than 2 was in error.[118] And in his 2010 dissent in *Estate of George*—though apparently accepting that a study that meets the "2.0 standard" thereby satisfies the more-likely-than-not standard of proof—Vermont Chief Justice Reiber pointed out that to impose this as a requirement on admissibility "sets a threshold that requires each study to *prove* that claimant[s] should win on the merits." And this, he continued, is incompatible with the accepted principle that "admitted evidence does not alone have to meet the proponent's burden of proof on a particular issue."[119]

113 *Id.*, 198.

114 Lofgren v. Motorola, Inc., No. CV-93–05521, 1998 WL 299925, *14 (Ariz. Super. Ct. June 1, 1998).

115 Berry v. CSX Transp., Inc., 709 So. 2d 552, 569, n.14 (Fla. Dist. Ct. App. 1998). (On Florida's subsequent shift to *Daubert*, see "Irreconcilable Differences? The Troubled Marriage of Science and Law," pp. 78–103 in this volume, n.102.)

116 *Hanford* (note 82 above).

117 *In re* Hanford Nuclear Reservation Litig., 292 F.3d 1124, 1136, 1137 (9th Cir. 2002) (referred to collectively, together with In re *Hanford*, 1998 WL 775340 (note 82 above), as "*Hanford* Group A"). In 2005, a bellwether trial ensued, and numerous issues unrelated to doubling of risk were appealed. *In re* Hanford Nuclear Reservation Litig., 497 F.3d 1005 (9th Cir. 2007), *amended and superseded by* 521 F.3d 1028 (9th Cir.), *amended and superseded by* 534 F.3d 986 (9th Cir. 2008) (collectively referred to as "*Hanford* Group B"). As of February 2014, the case was pending in the District Court for the Eastern District of Washington.

118 *In re* Lockheed Litig. Cases, 23 Cal. Rptr. 3d 762, 765 (Cal. Ct. App.), *review granted and superseded by* 110 P.3d 289 (Cal. 2005), *review dismissed*, 192 P.3d 403 (Cal. 2007) (this case was dismissed because a majority of the judges had a financial interest in the matter).

119 *Estate of George* (note 95 above), 387 (Reiber, J., dissenting) (citing US Gen New England, Inc., v. Town of Rockingham, 862 A.2d 269 (Vt. 2004), and *In re* Paoli R.R. Yard PCB Litig., 35 F.3d 717 (3d Cir. 1994)).

So opinions expressing reservations about the "more than doubled risk" idea are as manifold as those that endorse it: some (e.g., *Pick*, Justice Reiber's dissent in *Estate of George*) reject it as a requirement on admissibility, while others deny that it is necessary for proof of specific causation (e.g., *Allen*), or sufficient (e.g., *Johnston*), or either (e.g., *Grassis*).

Scientists too have expressed reservations about the appropriateness of the "more than doubled risk" idea. Indeed, Dr. Greenlick, one of the experts whom Judge Jones had himself appointed to help him sift through the evidence in *Hall*, had tried to articulate what was wrong with the idea that a relative risk greater than 2 is necessary for proof of specific causation:

> From a scientific point of view it is not appropriate to disregard relative risks of less than 2.0. First of all, relative risk is a term that applies to a population, not to an individual.... It is ... appropriate to believe that the average increased risk is made up by averaging across individuals with a range of blood pressures.[120]

Epidemiologist Sander Greenland wrote in the *American Journal of Public Health* that he was:

> ... aware of no real example in which enough is known of cancer biology to justify a claim that the rate fraction [relative risk] approximates the probability of causation. Nonetheless, many experts claim in court ... that PC [probability of causation] = RF without supplying any evidence to support this claim.[121]

And David Egilman et al. urged in the *Food and Drug Law Journal* that:

> [i]n treating each piece of medical and scientific evidence that does not meet the arbitrary standard of a rate ratio of two as irrelevant or unreliable, judges deprive juries of the opportunity to aggregate evidence in making causation determinations.[122]

[120] *Hall* (note 68 above), 1450–51 (Appendix B., report of court-appointed expert Merwyn R. Greenlick, Ph.D.).

[121] Sander Greenland, "Relation of Probability of Causation to Relative Risk and Doubling Dose: A Methodologic Error That Has Become a Social Problem," *American Journal of Public Health* 89, no. 8 (1998): 1166–69, 1167. See also Greenland, "The Need for Critical Appraisal of Expert Witnesses in Epidemiology and Statistics," *Wake Forest Law Review* 39 (2004): 291–310.

[122] David Egilman, Joyce Kim, and Molly Biklen, "Proving Causation: The Use and Abuse of Medical and Scientific Information inside the Courtroom—An Epidemiologist's Critique of the Judicial Interpretation of the *Daubert* Ruling," *Food and Drug Law Journal* 56 (2003): 223–50, 225. See also Joseph V. Rodricks and Susan H. Reith, "Toxicological Assessment in the Courtroom: Are Available Methodologies Suitable for Evaluating Toxic Tort and Product Liability Claims?" *Regulatory Toxicology and Pharmacology* 27 (1998): 21–31, 28–29.

Legal scholars, not surprisingly, have been especially exercised by the requirement of a showing of more than doubled risk as a requirement on admissibility; an idea which, as Lucinda Finley suggests, soon became sufficiently entrenched as a principle of causation law to lead Judge Jones to ignore the sound scientific advice of his own expert, Dr. Greenlick.[123] Daniel Berger (with scientist Jan Beyea) criticized *Daubert* IV for equating the legal "more likely than not" standard with a statistical probability, arguing that "the doubling-of-risk methodology for assigning individual causation is based on false science."[124] More recently, Andrew Jurs writes that "use of the doubling-of-risk methodology provides a false sense of pure objective analysis," and that this is "a textbook example" of bright-line legal rules trumping sound scientific principles.[125]

And in 2011, the new version of the chapter on epidemiology in the new edition of the *Federal Reference Manual*, after acknowledging that some courts have taken evidence of more than doubled risk to meet the preponderance standard with respect to specific causation, *also* acknowledges that "[w]hile this reasoning has a certain logic as far as it goes, there are a number of significant caveats and assumptions that require explication."[126]

To the best of my knowledge, however, these issues have been ignored by epistemologists; so, as you can imagine, my fingers are itching.

3 AN EPISTEMOLOGICAL ANALYSIS: WHY EVIDENCE OF MORE THAN DOUBLED RISK IS NEITHER NECESSARY NOR SUFFICIENT TO PROVE SPECIFIC CAUSATION

So now I want to focus on two straightforward epistemological questions: is evidence that exposure to substance S more than doubles the relative risk

[123] Lucinda M. Finley, "Guarding the Gate to the Courthouse: How Trial Judges Are Using Their Evidentiary Screening Role to Remake Tort Causation Rules," *DePaul Law Review* 49 (1999–2000): 335–76, 348–50, 352–3.

[124] Jan Beyea and Daniel Berger, "Scientific Misconceptions among *Daubert* Gatekeepers: The Need for Reform of Expert Review Procedures," *Law & Contemporary Problems* 64 (2001): 327–72, 349.

[125] Andrew Jurs, "Judicial Analysis of Complex and Cutting-Edge Science in the *Daubert* Era: Epidemiological Risk Assessment as a Test Case for Reform Strategies" (note 27 above), 58 (false impression of objectivity) and 75 (bright line rules trumping scientific validity).

[126] Michael D. Green, D. Michal Freedman, and Leon Gordis, "Reference Guide on Epidemiology," *Reference Manual on Scientific Evidence* (Washington, DC: Federal Judicial Center, 3rd ed., 2011), 549–632, 612. Moreover (though they have no explicit epistemological framework in which to set them), these authors go on to list, among those caveats, some of the factors I raise in the next section. Since this new version of the *Federal Reference Manual* appeared while the present article, completed in November 2010, had been circulated but was still in press, I hardly know whether to laugh or to cry!

of a person's contracting disease or disorder D *necessary* to establish that, more probably than not, it was his exposure to S that caused this individual to develop D? And: is such evidence *sufficient* to establish that, more probably than not, it was his exposure to S that caused this individual to develop D? The answers, in my opinion, are as straightforward as the questions: no, and no. Such evidence, though relevant, is neither necessary nor sufficient to warrant the conclusion to the required ("more probable than not") degree of proof.

Let me begin by explaining what goes wrong with a key argument for sufficiency—first encountered in *Cook*, also heard in a number of subsequent cases, and offered again in that much-cited article by Bailey et al. in the first edition of the *Federal Reference Manual*: evidence that the probability is more than 50% that a randomly chosen individual with disorder D contracted it through exposure to S implies that it is more probable than not that *this* plaintiff, who was exposed to S and then developed D, contracted D as a result of his exposure to S. As Bailey's et al.'s comment about "adapting" the relative risk found by an epidemiological study to the preponderance standard of proof reveals, this argument clearly relies on equating a *statistical probability* with a *degree of proof*:[127] if *n*/*m* of cases of D are associated with exposure to S, then it is proven to degree *n*/*m* that it was his exposure to S that caused Mr. X's D.

But, as I argued in "Legal Probabilism,"[128] although we often speak of degrees of proof in terms of how probable, or how likely, the evidence makes a conclusion, this is a completely different conception of probability from the statistical; so the key argument for sufficiency is a fallacy of equivocation. Relative risk is a matter of the relative frequency of occurrence of D in two populations, those exposed to S, and those not so exposed; degree of proof is a matter of the degree to which the evidence warrants the claim that the plaintiff's D was caused by his exposure to S. These are entirely different things—as the legal system recognizes in other contexts: the argument from "The [statistical] probability of a random match between this DNA sample from the crime scene and the defendant is *n*/*m*" to "the [epistemic] probability that the defendant is guilty is *n*/*m*" is now generally recognized as a *non sequitur*, "the prosecutor's fallacy."[129] Indeed—as I have argued

[127] Ironically enough, a footnote in Bailey, Gordis, and Green, "Reference Guide on Epidemiology" (note 50 above), 168, n. 127, recognizes the problem; but instead of giving a satisfactory answer, simply relies on suggesting, without argument, that both statistical probabilities and degrees of warrant can be understood as degrees of belief.

[128] "Legal Probabilism: An Epistemological Dissent," pp. 47–77 in this volume, 56–64.

[129] A phrase—I believe first introduced in William C. Thompson and E. L. Schumann, "Interpretation of Statistical Evidence in Criminal Trials: The Prosecutor's Fallacy and the Defense Attorney's Fallacy," *Law and Human Behavior* II, no.3 (1987): 67–87—that now turns

elsewhere,[130] and as others had argued before me[131]—unlike statistical probabilities, degrees of warrant don't even satisfy the axioms of the standard probability calculus. But now I'm getting ahead of myself.

How well evidence warrants a conclusion depends on three factors: how supportive it is of that conclusion; how secure it is, independently of the conclusion itself; and how much of the relevant evidence it includes.[132] Degrees of warrant are not probabilities in the sense of the standard mathematical calculus: first because, since there are multiple determinants of evidential quality, there is no guarantee even of a linear order of degrees of warrant; second because, while the probability of *p* and the probability of not-*p* must add up to 1, when there is insufficient evidence either way, neither *p* nor not-*p* may be warranted to any degree; and third because, while (assuming logical independence) the probability of *p* & *q* is the product of their individual probabilities, and thus always less than the probability of either, when several component pieces of evidence interlock appropriately they may jointly warrant a conclusion to a higher degree than any element alone would do.[133]

This is enough to show that the key argument for sufficiency fails, but not, by itself, enough to show that its conclusion is false; so more argument is needed. With the false equation of statistical probabilities and epistemic likelihoods set aside, it is clear that a relative risk greater than 2 has no special significance; *any* increase in relative risk, however small, is supportive of the conclusion to some degree. Why so? Because how supportive evidence is with respect to some conclusion depends on how well that evidence and that conclusion fit together in an explanatory story. And if D is commoner among people exposed to S than among people not exposed to S, it is possible that

up in legal rulings. See e.g., State v. Spann, 617 A.2d 247, 258 (N.J. 1993); People v. Pizarro, 12 Cal. Rptr. 2d 436, 461 n.26 (Ct. App. 1992) (since 1992, *Pizarro* has had three reversals and a vacated opinion; but there is no further mention of the "prosecutor's fallacy.").

130 In Susan Haack, *Defending Science—Within Reason: Between Scientism and Cynicism* (Amherst, NY: Prometheus Books, 2003), 75–7; "Formal Philosophy: A Plea for Pluralism" (2005), in Haack, *Putting Philosophy to Work: Inquiry and Its Place in Culture* (Amherst, NY: Prometheus Books, 2008), 223–242, 232; and of course in "Legal Probabilism" (note 128 above).

131 John Maynard Keynes, *A Treatise on Probability* (London: MacMillan, 1921); Richard von Mises, *Probability, Statistics, and Truth* (London: Allen and Unwin, 2nd revised English ed., 1928); Bertrand Russell, *Human Knowledge, Its Scope and Limits* (New York: Simon and Schuster, 1948), Part 5; L. Jonathan Cohen, *The Provable and the Probable* (Oxford: Clarendon Press, 1977).

132 I rely on the theory I developed in *Evidence and Inquiry* (1993; 2nd ed., Amherst, NY: Prometheus Books, 2009), chapter 4, and in *Defending Science* (note 130 above), chapter 3; and explained in "Epistemology and the Law of Evidence: Problems and Projects," pp. 1–26 in this volume.

133 See "Legal Probabilism" (note 128 above); "Proving Causation" (note 26 above), 216–26.

Mr. X is one of those who would not have developed D but for his exposure to S; and since his exposure to S might explain Mr. X's developing D, it supports the conclusion to some degree (a higher degree, the higher the relative risk), as in the following evidentiary scenario:

E1: Mr. X was exposed to S, and subsequently developed D.
E2: There is a small/a modest/a large/a very large increased relative risk of developing D among those exposed to S.
CC: Mr. X's D was caused by his exposure to S.[134]

Unless the relative risk is *very* high,[135] however, the degree of support such evidence gives the conclusion is very modest; for—since we lack any specific, detailed, explanatory story—the explanatory integration of evidence and conclusion is quite loose.

A combination of evidence of increased risk with additional evidence could, of course, support the causal conclusion to a higher degree—or a lower. To see this, compare the congeries of evidence described above with other possible combinations of pieces of evidence:

E1: Mr. X was exposed to S, and subsequently developed D.
E2: There is a small/a modest/a large/a very large increased risk of developing D among those exposed to S.
E3: S causes such-and-such physiological damage, which leads to D.
E4: Mr. X shows signs of this type of physiological damage.
CC: Mr. X's D was caused by his previous exposure to S.

This combined evidence is significantly *more* supportive of the conclusion than evidence of increased risk alone would be, because the additional physiological evidence interlocks with the rest to indicate a mechanism by which exposure to S causes D, enhancing explanatory integration.

But other kinds of additional evidence may *lower* the degree of support, as in the following scenario:

E1: Mr. X was exposed to S, and subsequently developed D.
E2: There is a small/a modest/a large/a very large increased relative risk of developing D among those exposed to S.

134 Here and in what follows, "E" refers to evidence, "CC" to the conclusion of specific causation.

135 Since the examples discussed here have involved quite modest relative risks, I will mention that the relative risk of lung cancer in smokers is roughly 10:1, of pancreatic cancer in smokers 2:1—and the relative risk of scrotal cancer in chimney sweeps is 200:1. *Landrigan* (note 104 above), 1085 (smoking and lung cancer, smoking and pancreatic cancer); Austin Bradford Hill, "The Environment and Disease: Association or Causation?" *Proceedings of the Royal Society of Medicine* 58 (1965): 295–300, 295 (chimney sweeps and scrotal cancer).

E3: A small percentage/a modest percentage/a large percentage/a very large percentage of the cases of D are hereditary.
E4: There is a history of D in Mr. X's family.
CC: Mr. X's D was caused by his previous exposure to S.

This combined evidence is significantly *less* supportive of the conclusion than evidence of increased risk alone would be—how much less depending in part on the percentage of cases of D that are hereditary. For if the proportion of case of D that are hereditary is high, the explanatory integration of the evidence with the conclusion is very flimsy, since there is an alternative explanation (heredity) of what caused X's D that is as well, or better, integrated with the evidence than an explanation in terms of X's having been exposed to S.

In any case, it doesn't follow from the fact that evidence of more than doubled risk *supports* the conclusion that it was exposure to S that caused this plaintiff's D that such evidence is sufficient to *warrant* that conclusion to the desired degree of proof; and it isn't true. If the evidence of increased risk is not independently secure—if, e.g., it is based on a poorly-conducted study[136]—we will have a low epistemic likelihood of a high statistical probability; and the conclusion that the plaintiff developed D as a result of exposure to S will be poorly warranted. This is the relevance of the court's shrewd observation in *Johnston* that "when one probes how Dr. Morgan got to his final conclusion, one realizes that it is statistical speculation based upon speculative dose estimates and speculative risk assumptions. In other words, it is speculation based upon other speculation."[137] And even if the evidence of a significantly increased relative risk *is* independently secure, if some significant evidence is missing—e.g., evidence that subjects in a certain sub-class are much less vulnerable, much less likely than others to develop D after exposure to S, and that the plaintiff has the characteristics of this sub-class—once again the conclusion that the plaintiff developed D as a result of exposure to S will be poorly warranted.

The next task is to show that evidence of more than doubled risk is no more necessary to prove specific causation to the "more probably than not" standard than it is sufficient. Suppose, first, that we have evidence of an increased risk,

[136] An example would be Charles H. Henneckens, et al., "Self-Reported Breast Implants and Connective Tissue Diseases in Female Health Professionals: A Retrospective Cohort Study," *Journal of the American Medical Association* 275, no.8 (1996): 616–21—the only study that showed an increased risk of connective-tissue disorders associated with silicone breast-implants—which relied on *the subjects' own reports* of their supposed disorders.

[137] *Johnston* (note 101 above), 394.

but an increased risk less than 2—say, of 1.99; but suppose that we *also* have evidence that some people (older people, pregnant women, people with blond hair, people who drink more than two cups of tea a day, or whatever) are much more vulnerable to the effects of exposure to S than others, *and* that the plaintiff in this case falls into this much more vulnerable class. Assuming that this evidence is itself secure, and that there is no significant evidence missing, this may be sufficient to warrant the conclusion that this plaintiff's D was caused by his exposure to S to the required degree; from which it follows that evidence of more than doubled risk is not necessary.

Does this mean that evidence of *some* increased risk *is* necessary? Again, my answer is "no." Suppose there is no directly relevant epidemiological evidence of any kind, and so *a fortiori* no epidemiological evidence of increased risk; but that we *do* have evidence of a biological mechanism by which S causes certain physiological damage that leads to D, *and* evidence that this plaintiff didn't manifest these physiological changes before, but did after, he was exposed to S, *and* evidence excluding other known causes of D in this instance. Again, assuming that this evidence is itself reasonably secure and reasonably comprehensive, this may be sufficient to warrant the conclusion that this plaintiff's D was caused by his exposure to S to the required degree of proof.

I have presented these arguments in a deliberately simplified way, in terms of S's causing the plaintiff to develop D. Had I also taken account of the possibility that exposure to S might be, not *the* cause of, but *a contributory factor in* the development of, D, or that it might, not *cause*, but *accelerate* the development of D, or, etc., the arguments would have been more complex.[138] But the conclusion would obviously have been the same: evidence of a relative risk greater than 2 is nothing like an epistemological master-key, but only "one piece of [causation] evidence, among others."[139] Or, as Prof. Jaffe had put it decades before:

> [A]bstract [statistical] probability may play a role in finding a fact, but what is referred to in the traditional formula ["balance of probabilities"] is the greater probability in the case at hand.... The conditions for a finding are not satisfied merely by showing a greater statistical probability.... There must be a *rational*, i.e., evidentiary basis on which the jury can choose the competing [epistemic] probabilities.[140]

[138] See *Joiner* III (note 25 above); Greenland, "Relation of Probability of Causation to Relative Risk and Doubling Dose" (note 120 above).

[139] *Landrigan* (note 104 above), 1087 (reporting defense counsel's argument on appeal).

[140] Jaffe, "*Res Ipsa Loquitur* Vindicated," *Buffalo Law Review* 1, no. 1 (1951): 1–15, 4.

4 A PRACTICAL POSTSCRIPT: WHY BETTER EPISTEMOLOGY WOULD ALSO BE BETTER POLICY

If a showing of relative risk > 2 is taken to be *sufficient* for proof of specific causation, whenever evidence of more than doubled risk is available any plaintiff who can show that he was exposed to the suspect substance and subsequently developed the disorder in question will be able to recover; so that defendants will be obliged to compensate plaintiffs to whom their products did no harm. And if a showing of relative risk > 2 is taken to be *necessary* for proof of specific causation, whenever evidence of more than doubled risk is not available some plaintiffs whose disorder was in fact caused by the defendant's product will be unable to recover.

And, I believe, making a showing of more than doubled risk a requirement on *admissibility*, as Judge Kozinski does in his 1995 ruling in *Daubert*, imposes an unreasonable burden on plaintiffs. The concern here is *admissibility* versus *weight* of evidence. The US legal system makes admissibility a matter for the court to determine, and weight a matter for the finder of fact (normally, the jury) to decide. The Supreme Court's ruling in *Daubert* fudged the line a bit; but the judicial screening of expert testimony required by FRE 702, even as interpreted in *Daubert*, is clearly not meant to preempt juries' fact-finding task. The intention, rather—as Justice Reiber said in *George*, and as Judge Becker had earlier insisted in *Paoli*[141]—is that, to be admissible, expert testimony has to be good enough to justify putting it before the jury for consideration along with other evidence in the case, *not* that it be *so* good that it is sufficient by itself to satisfy the standard of proof. Moreover, as the court in *Pick* points out, the Federal Rules define "relevant" evidence as any evidence that tends either to raise or to lower the probability of some fact at issue, without specifying any threshold *degree* of relevance—and *a fortiori* without requiring that this degree be sufficient to meet the "more probable than not" standard.

No, of course I haven't forgotten that observation of the Texas Supreme Court in *Havner*, that "there is not a precise fit between science and legal burdens of proof."[142] And of course I don't mean to deny that courts must often make do with less-than-perfect proxies for epistemologically-impeccable assessments. But I am not persuaded that, while evidence of more than doubled risk

[141] In re *Paoli* (note 119 above), 744 ("[plaintiffs] do not have to demonstrate … by a preponderance of the evidence that the assessments of their experts are *correct*, they only have to demonstrate by a preponderance of evidence that their opinions are reliable"), and ("[t]he evidentiary requirement of reliability is lower than the merits standard of correctness").

[142] *Havner* (note 73 above), 717 (I conjecture that what the court meant to say was that there was no precise fit with legal *standards* of proof).

may be, strictly speaking, neither necessary nor sufficient for proof of specific causation, it is nonetheless good enough as a rule of thumb. In fact, I believe, the RR>2 idea doesn't serve the purposes of tort law as well as the epistemological account I have offered.

Judge Weinstein emphasizes the fundamental distinction between the "avoidance of risk through regulation and compensation for injuries after the fact."[143] The central goal of the regulatory system is to *prevent* dangerous substances from causing injury; the central goal of the tort system to *compensate* those who, despite the preventative efforts of the regulatory system, suffer injury through the fault of a manufacturer. But, as different as these goals are in principle, they are tightly interconnected. Most to the present purpose, as Justice Breyer writes in his concurring opinion in *Joiner*, "the powerful engine of tort liability ... can generate strong financial incentives to reduce, or to eliminate, production," and we need to ensure that this "powerful engine" "points towards the right substances and does not destroy the wrong ones."[144] A more careful statement might have noted that the case at issue involved PCBs, which were so well known to be dangerous that they had been banned for decades before *Joiner* reached the Supreme Court; but set that aside. Justice Breyer is certainly right thus far: large verdicts against a manufacturer can be a strong incentive to withdraw the product concerned; and it is of course desirable that, so far as possible, these incentives target dangerous products rather then safe and useful ones.

So two "desired ends" might be put like this: that (rather than being in effect a legal lottery in which who recovers damages from a manufacturer bears little relation to who was actually injured by a product made by that firm), so far as possible the tort system compensate those, but only those, who were actually injured by a product; and that so far as possible the incentives and disincentives to produce drugs and chemicals that tort verdicts bring in their wake encourage production of the good stuff and discourage production of the bad.

However, there is no perfectly clean distinction between safe products, on the one hand, and dangerous ones, on the other: some drugs, for example, while effective for many people, are safe for only some of those many. Ideally, then, the tort system would compensate those people—including those

143 In re "*Agent Orange*" (note 39 above), 781. Judge Weinstein also stresses the different standards appropriate to each: "[a] government agency may regulate or prohibit the use of toxic substances ... despite a very low probability of any causal relationship. A court, in contrast, must observe the tort law requirement that a plaintiff establish a probability of more than fifty percent that the defendant's action injured him." *Id.*, 785.

144 *Joiner* III (note 25 above), 148–49 (Breyer, J., concurring).

especially susceptible to the side effects of a drug that is safe and beneficial for others—who really are injured when they take it; and encourage making such drugs available to people whom they would benefit without bad side effects, while discouraging their use by people who are especially susceptible to those ill effects.

Obviously enough, the crude more-than-doubled-risk criterion, so far from helping the tort system achieve this ideal, stands in its way. But if courts recognized that a showing of a relative risk greater than 2 is neither necessary nor sufficient to prove specific causation to the preponderance standard, but one piece of relevant evidence among many, this would, first, give both plaintiffs and defendants an incentive to look for evidence about the specific vulnerabilities of sub-classes of the population, and of specific plaintiffs; and hence enable deserving plaintiffs to recover even when the increased risk to the population at large is minimal. And at one remove, this might be expected to have the desirable effect of enhancing manufacturers' awareness that drugs may be good for some, but not all, patients, and of encouraging them to label drugs and advise prescribing physicians accordingly; and perhaps also, at another remove, of encouraging the FDA to require manufacturers to do this. Better epistemology, in short, would also be better policy.

—12—

Nothing Fancy: Some Simple Truths about Truth in the Law

The truth is too simple; one must always get there by a complicated route.

—George Sand.[1]

The truth is rarely pure and never simple. Modern life would be very tedious if it were either.

—Oscar Wilde.[2]

Truth is, at its core, quite a simple concept. At the same time, however, it is a concept mired in philosophical confusions. Moreover, on many questions the truth is complicated and subtle—hard to articulate, and difficult to discriminate from plausible falsehoods. And all this, as we shall see, is especially true of truth in the law.

The first step will be to clarify the distinction between truth (the property or phenomenon of being true) and truths (particular true claims), and to then to argue for my first thesis: *that, though some propositions are true only at a given place or time, or are vague, or are only partially true, or, etc., truth itself isn't relative, doesn't come in degrees, and doesn't decompose into parts*, etc. (§1). The next will be to develop an approach to the understanding of truth along the lines of F. P. Ramsey's, which will lead to my second thesis: that *whatever the subject-matter of the proposition concerned, what it means to say that a proposition is true is the same*—that it is the proposition that *p*, and *p* (§2). After that, I will explore the (deceptively simple-seeming) distinction between

[1] George Sand, letter to Armand Barbes, 1867, in John Gross, ed., *The Oxford Book of Aphorisms* (New York: Oxford University Press, 1983), 228.

[2] Actually, the words are Algernon's, from *The Importance of Being Earnest* ("and modern literature [would be] a complete impossibility," Algernon continues). Oscar Wilde, *The Importance of Being Earnest* (1895) in *The Plays of Oscar Wilde* (New York: H. S. Nichols, 1914) 105–228, 206.

factual and legal truths, and argue for my third thesis: that *legal truths, specifically truths about legal provisions, are a special sub-class of truths about social institutions, and make sense only relative to a jurisdiction and a time* (§3). Then it will be time to say something about what it is that makes legal truths true, and to develop my fourth thesis: *that legal truths are socially constructed, i.e., made true by things people do—primarily, by legislators' decisions, but in some measure by judges' interpretations of statutes and precedents* (§4). And finally, addressing the normative character of legal provisions, I will argue that *though legal systems, legal provisions, and legal decisions may be morally better or worse, and though the law* can *be an engine of moral progress, legal norms should not be assimilated to moral norms, nor conceived as true or false representations of moral principles* (§5).

1 TRUTH AND TRUTHS

Abstract nouns like "beauty," or "life"—or "truth"—have two uses, referring *both* to a property or a phenomenon, *and* to particular instances of that property or phenomenon. Sayings like "life is real, life is earnest," or "life is hard, and then you die," are about the phenomenon, living; but talk of a wasted life is about a particular instance, and a description of the lives of slaves on the cotton plantations as short and brutal is about particular instances, of life. Similarly, the saying "beauty is in the eye of the beholder" is about the phenomenon, being beautiful; but a description of the gardenia in bloom in my front garden as "a real beauty" is about a particular instance, and talk of "the beauties of the undersea world" is about particular instances, of beauty.

Most to the present purpose, of course, are the two uses of the abstract noun "truth," in one of which it refers to the property of being true, and in the other of which it refers to particular true claims, propositions, statements, beliefs, theories, etc. And with "truth," just as with "life" and "beauty," the distinction is marked grammatically. In the second use, but not the first, "truth" takes the definite article, "*a* truth"—as in the famous opening line of Jane Austen's *Pride and Prejudice*: "[i]t is *a* truth universally acknowledged that a single man in possession of a good fortune must be in want of a wife";[3] and the plural form, "truths"—as in the second sentence of the American Declaration of Independence: "[w]e hold these truths to be self-evident, that all Men are created equal...."[4]

3 Jane Austen, *Pride and Prejudice* (1813), in *The Works of Jane Austen* (London: Spring Books, 1966), 171–343, 172.

4 American Declaration of Independence (1776).

The same double usage appears in other languages, too. In Spanish, Jane Austen's famous line would be: "*[e]s* una *verdad universalmente reconocida* ...," and that ringing statement in the Declaration of Independence: "*[s]ostemos como evidentes estas verdades,*. . . ." Miguel de Unamuno writes in "*Verdad y vida*" that "*[h]ay muchas, muchísimas más verdades por decir que tiempo y ocasiones para decirlas.*"[5] In an interview in *El País*, Joaquín Sabina observes that "*[l]as verdades científicas son como el amor: eternas mientras duran.*"[6] And, of course, everyone knows "*esa es una verdad de perogrullo.*"[7]

But this double usage, though clear enough in ordinary contexts, has caused much confusion.[8] Some philosophers have treated "truth," the abstract noun, as if it referred to some very special, supposedly all-important, true proposition; and spoken reverently of this as "the Truth" with a capital "T," as in "the Truth shall set you free." But this is as big a muddle as, say, identifying Beauty itself with my gorgeous gardenia. Others—perhaps reacting against the kind of exaggerated reverence for the Truth that the first confusion is apt to generate—overshoot the mark in the opposite direction, and conclude that it is a mistake to place any value on truth, that truth is of no importance. Others go so far as to deny that truth is a legitimate concept at all. Supposed truths, these philosophers remind us, only too often turn out to be simplifications, half-truths, or outright falsehoods; and so, they argue, truth itself must be a kind of illusion. The premise is true, but the argument is fallacious; indeed, not only does the conclusion not follow from the premise, it actually undermines it—for if truth *were* an illusion, half-truth and falsehood would be illusions too.[9]

5 "There are many, many more truths to be said than there is time or occasion to say them." Miguel de Unamuno, "Verdad y vida," in *Mi religión y otros ensayos breves* (1910; Madrid: Espasa-Calpe, S. A., 4th ed., 1964), 16–22, 27.

6 "Scientific truths are like love: eternal as long as they last." Cited in Jordi Ferrer Beltrán, *La valoración racional de la preuba* (Barcelona: Marcial Pons, 2007), 9.

7 "That is a truth everyone knows." We see the same distinction between truth and truths in, e.g., German. Heidegger writes that "[d]ie Aussage ist also der Ort und Sitz der Whahrheit. Deshalb sagen wir auch einfach: Diese und jene Aussage ist eine Wahrheit. Wahrheiten und Unwahrheiten—das sind Aussagen." ["The assertion is also the locus and bearer of truth. Therefore we simply say: this or that assertion is a truth. Truths and untruths—these are assertions."] Martin Heidegger, *Frage nach dem Ding* (1935–36), in Heidegger, *Gesamtausabe* (Frankfurt am Main: Vittorio Klostermann, 1984), vol. 41, ed. Petra Jaeger, 1–254, 35.

8 As, I recently discovered, Ramsey had noted long ago. Frank Plumpton Ramsey, *On Truth: Original Manuscripts (1927–29) from the Ramsey Collection at the University of Pittsburgh*, eds. Nicholas Rescher and Ulrich Majer (Pittsburgh, PA: University of Pittsburgh Press, 1991), 18.

9 I call this plausible-sounding but invalid argument the "Passes-for fallacy," since it argues from the true premise that what passes for truth is often no such thing to the false conclusion that truth is an illusion. I introduced the term in Susan Haack, "Knowledge and

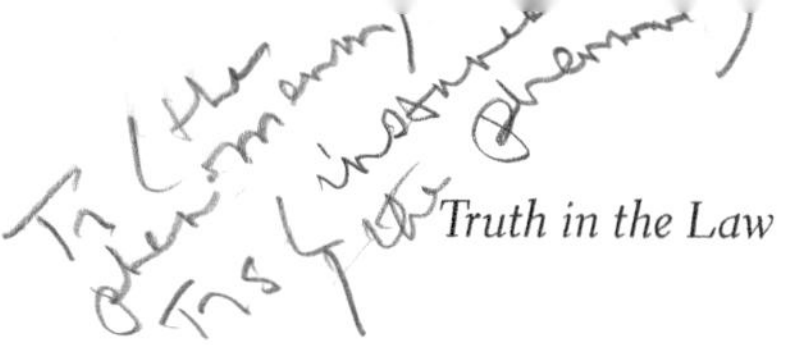

For present purposes, however, it is a different kind of confusion, also encouraged by the dual usage of "truth," that looms largest: attributing to truth, the phenomenon, what are really properties of some, but not all, truths. Some claims are true only in part, or are only part of the truth, or are true only at a particular time and in a particular place, a particular society, etc.; and this has tempted some to conclude that truth decomposes into parts, or is relative to place, time, society, etc. But this too is a fallacy—like supposing that, because some lives are wasted, life is worthless or, because some beautiful things are red, beauty is red. If we keep the distinction between truth (the phenomenon) and truths (instances of the phenomenon) clearly in mind, we can readily see that:

- There are many and various true propositions; but only one truth.
- Some true propositions are vague; but truth is not a matter of degree.
- Some propositions are only partly true; but truth doesn't decompose into parts.
- Some true propositions are made true by things people do; but truth is objective.
- Some true propositions make sense only understood as relative to a place, a time, a legal system, etc.; but truth is not relative.

My arguments about "the unity of truth and the plurality of truths," vagueness, and partial truth can be found elsewhere.[10] But here it is the last two points—both of which have particular relevance to issues about truth in the law—that will be crucial.

Propaganda: Reflections of an Old Feminist"(1993), in Haack, *Manifesto of a Passionate Moderate: Unfashionable Essays* (Chicago: University of Chicago Press, 1998), 123–36. The idea also plays a role in Haack, "Multiculturalism and Objectivity" (1995), in *Manifesto of a Passionate Moderate*, 137–48; in Haack, "Confessions of an Old-Fashioned Prig," *Manifesto of a Passionate Moderate*, 7–30; in Haack, "Staying for an Answer: The Untidy Process of Groping for Truth" (1999), in Haack, *Putting Philosophy to Work: Inquiry and Its Place in Culture* (Amherst, NY: Prometheus Books, 2008, expanded ed., 2013), 35–46; and in Haack, "The Unity of Truth and the Plurality of Truths" (2005), in *Putting Philosophy to Work*, 53–68.

[10] On the thesis that there is one truth, but many truths, see Susan Haack, "The Unity of Truth and the Plurality of Truths" (note 9 above). On vagueness, see Susan Haack, *Deviant Logic* (Cambridge: Cambridge University Press, 1974); 2nd expanded ed., under the title *Deviant Logic, Fuzzy Logic: Beyond the Formalism* (Chicago, IL: University of Chicago Press, 1996), 109–25; Haack, "Do We Need 'Fuzzy Logic?'"(1979), in *Deviant Logic, Fuzzy Logic*, 232–42; and Haack, "Is Truth Flat or Bumpy?" (1980), in *Deviant Logic, Fuzzy Logic*, 243–58. On partial truth, see Haack, "The Whole Truth and Nothing but the Truth," *Midwest Studies in Philosophy* XXXIII (2008): 20–35.

2 THE MEANING OF TRUTH

The points just listed all concern truth as it applies to propositions—which is what is at issue when we talk about truth in the law. But it is worth noting that, besides propositional truth, the English word "true" also expresses a whole range of related, but different, ideas.

Like virtually all philosophically interesting concepts, the concept of truth has a history. The English word "true" derives from the old verb "*treowe*," meaning to promise, to give one's word;[11] and a trace of this old verb still remains in the old-fashioned phrase "betrothed," meaning "engaged to be married" (and in the near-obsolete phrase "plighting one's troth," meaning getting engaged). And, besides the use on which philosophers focus, in which "true" indicates that things are as a proposition says, the word still has many other uses—all deriving from the same root idea of promising or giving one's word. When we speak of "true friends," "true believers," or "true likenesses," for example, "true" means "faithful"; when we speak of "true love," or describe the frog as "not a true reptile," "true" means "genuine, real"; when we describe a method or procedure as "tried and true," "true" means "reliable"; and when we describe a beam or a door or a shelf as "out of true," or speak of "truing the wheels" on a bicycle, "true" means "straight."

Even if we focus—as I shall do from here on—exclusively on propositional truth, i.e., truth as it applies to claims, theories, beliefs, etc., the sheer variety of apparently competing philosophical theories is daunting; we find:

- a large, unruly family of correspondence theories, explaining truth as consisting in beliefs' or propositions' mirroring, or copying, reality, or in a relation of correspondence between propositions and facts, or between statements and states of affairs;[12]
- a large, unruly family of coherence theories, explaining truth in terms of a relation of coherence (understood significantly differently by different

[11] *Oxford English Dictionary* Online. However, other English words for related concepts, like "verdict," "verify," "verisimilitude," the old-fashioned word "verities," and the near-obsolete "verily," derive—like the Spanish "*verdad*," the Portuguese "*verdade*," the Italian "*verità*," and the German "*Wahrheit*"—from the Latin, "*veritas*."

[12] See, e.g., Bertrand Russell, "The Philosophy of Logical Atomism" (1918), in Russell, *Logic and Knowledge: Essays 1901–1950*, ed. Robert C. Marsh (New York: Capricorn Books, 1956), 177–281, and "On Propositions: What They Are and How They Mean" (1919), in *Logic and Knowledge*, 283–320; Ludwig Wittgenstein, *Tractatus Logico-Philosophicus* (London: Routledge and Kegan Paul, 1922); J. L. Austin, "On Truth" (1950), in J. O. Urmson and Geoffrey Warnock, *Philosophical Papers of J. L. Austin* (Oxford: Oxford University Press, 1961), 85–101.

proponents, but usually taking consistency to be necessary but not sufficient) among our beliefs;[13]

- a tangled skein of pragmatist and neo-pragmatist theories: C. S. Peirce's account of truth as the opinion "fated to be believed by all who investigate";[14] William James's idea of truth as verifiability, as the expedient or the satisfactory in the way of belief, as successful leading, and of truths as becoming true as we verify them;[15] and John Dewey's attempt to combine elements of coherence and correspondence in an understanding of truth as the upshot of successful testing, the "tried and true"[16]—not to mention F. C. S. Schiller's radical-pragmatist conception of "human" truth as whatever forwards our ends,[17] or Richard Rorty's wearily dismissive vulgar-pragmatist equation of truth with "what you can defend against all comers."[18]
- another tangled skein of so-called "redundancy, " "minimalist," "deflationist," "disquotationalist," "prosententialist," etc., theories,[19] all deriving

[13] See, e.g., F. H. Bradley, *Appearance and Reality: A Metaphysical Essay* (Oxford: Clarendon Press, 1895), and *Essays on Truth and Reality* (Oxford: Clarendon Press, 1914), 202 ff.; Nicholas Rescher, *The Coherence Theory of Truth* (Oxford: Clarendon Press, 1973); Ralph Charles Sutherland Walker, *The Coherence Theory of Truth: Realism, Anti-Realism, Idealism* (New York: Routledge, 1989).

[14] Charles Sanders Peirce, *Collected Papers*, eds. Charles Hartshorne, Paul Weiss, and (vols.7 and 8) Arthur Burks (Cambridge, MA: Harvard University Press 1931–58), 5.407; also in Peirce, *Writings: A Chronological Edition*, eds. Peirce Edition Project (Indianapolis, IN: Indiana University Press, 1982–), 3:273 (1878). Later, Peirce would propose instead a more realist, subjunctive formulation of the Pragmatic Maxim of Meaning, which would lead to a conception of truth as the opinion that *would* be believed *were* inquiry to continue indefinitely. *Collected Papers*, 5.457 (1905).

[15] See e.g., William James, *Pragmatism* (1907), eds. Frederick Burkhardt and Fredson Bowers (Cambridge, MA: Harvard University Press, 1975), 97, 105 (truth as verifiability); 106 (truth as the expedient or satisfactory in the way of belief); 103 (truth as successful leading).

[16] John Dewey, "The Problem of Truth" (1911), in Larry M. Hickman and Thomas M. Alexander, eds., *The Essential Dewey* (Indianapolis, IN: Indiana University Press, 1998), vol. 2, 101–30 (developing a pragmatist theory intermediate between correspondence and coherence accounts). But see also John Dewey, *Logic: The Theory of Inquiry* (New York: Henry Holt, 1938), 345n. (describing Peirce's as "the best definition of truth").

[17] Ferdinand Canning Scott Schiller, "The Making of Truth," in Schiller, *Studies in Humanism* (New York: MacMillan, 1907), 179–203.

[18] Richard Rorty, *Philosophy and the Mirror of Nature* (Princeton, NJ: Princeton University Press, 1979), 308. See also Richard Rorty, *Objectivity, Relativism and Truth* (Cambridge: Cambridge University Press, 1991), 32 ("Truth [is] entirely a matter of solidarity"), and "Trotsky and the Wild Orchids," *Common Knowledge* 1, no. 3 (1992): 140–53, 141 ("I do not have much use for notions like … 'objective truth'").

[19] See, e.g., C. J. F. Williams, *Being, Identity and Truth* (Oxford: Oxford University Press, 1992); Dorothy Grover, *A Prosententialist Theory of Truth* (Princeton, NJ: Princeton University Press, 1992); Paul Horwich, *Truth* (Cambridge, MA: Blackwell, 1990); Marian Alexander

more or less directly from Frank Ramsey's account, according to which "it is true that *p*" means, simply, "*p*."[20]

And, besides all these philosophical theories, we have a quasi-mathematical contender:

- Alfred Tarski's semantic theory of the concept of truth in formalized languages, culminating in his definition of truth as satisfaction of a closed wff (well-formed formula) by all infinite sequences of objects.[21]

Not surprisingly perhaps, given this plethora of theories, confusion abounds—especially, it seems, about Tarski's contribution. Karl Popper claims that Tarski "rehabilitated" correspondence;[22] but Tarski himself criticizes correspondence accounts.[23] W. V. Quine sometimes seems to assimilate Tarski's theory to disquotationalism;[24] but Tarski's understanding of quotation marks clearly precludes this.[25] Rorty suggests that his "conversationalist"

David, *Correspondence and Disquotation: An Essay on the Nature of Truth* (New York: Oxford University Press, 1994); María-José Frápolli, "The Logical Enquiry into Truth," *History and Philosophy of Logic* 17 (1996): 197–97; Paul Horwich, *From a Deflationary Point of View* (Oxford: Clarendon Press, 2004); C. J. F. Williams, *What Is Truth?* (Cambridge: Cambridge University Press, 2009).

20 Frank Plumpton Ramsey, "Facts and Propositions" (1927), in Ramsey, *The Foundations of Mathematics and Other Logical Essays*, ed. Richard B. Braithwaite (London: Routledge and Kegan Paul, 1931), 138–55; Ramsey, *On Truth* (note 8 above).

21 The semantic theory is given in full detail in Alfred Tarski, "The Concept of Truth in Formalised Languages" (1933), trans. J. H. Woodger in Tarski, *Logic, Semantics, Metamathematics* (Oxford: Clarendon Press, 1956), 152–278; a more popular treatment is given in Alfred Tarski, "The Semantic Conception of Truth" (1944), reprinted in Herbert Feigl and Wilfrid Sellars, eds., *Readings in Philosophical Analysis* (New York: Appleton-Century-Crofts, 1949), 52–84. For a relatively simple explanation of how the theory works, see Susan Haack, *Philosophy of Logics* (Cambridge: Cambridge University Press, 1978), 99–127.

22 "Tarski's theory ... is a *rehabilitation* and an elaboration of the classical theory that truth is correspondence to the facts." Karl R. Popper, "Comments on Tarski's Theory of Truth," in Popper, *Objective Knowledge: An Evolutionary Approach* (Oxford: Clarendon Press, 1972), 319–40, 323.

23 A formulation involving correspondence "can lead to various misunderstandings," and "cannot be considered a satisfactory definition of truth." Tarski, "The Semantic Conception of Truth" (note 21 above), 54.

24 "Truth is disquotation." W. V. Quine, *Quiddities* (Cambridge, MA: Harvard University Press, 1987), 213. "Ascription of truth just cancels the quotation marks.... Moreover, disquotation is a full account [of truth]." W. V. Quine, *Pursuit of Truth* (Cambridge, MA: Harvard University Press, 1992), 80, 93. "I have been guided by Tarksi's *Wahrheitsbegriff* ever since it first came out. There is nothing to add to Tarski's analysis ... so far as the concept of truth is concerned." W. V. Quine, "Reactions," in Paulo Leonardo and Marco Santambrogio, eds., *On Quine* (Cambridge: Cambridge University Press, 1995), 347–61, 353.

25 "Every quotation-mark name is ... a constant individual name of a definite expression (the expression enclosed by the quotation marks).... For example, the name '*p*' denotes one of the letters of the alphabet." Tarski, "The Concept of Truth in Formalised Languages" (note 21

understanding of truth is the conception that "Tarski [... is] attending to";[26] but there is no hint of any such easy-going conversationalism in Tarski's work. The editors of Ramsey's papers on truth suggest that his account anticipates Tarski's;[27] but the innocent simplicity of Ramsey's approach stands in stark contrast to the elaborate mathematical complexities of the semantic theory. And so on.

More importantly, there are tricky questions about the interrelations among these various projects and theories. The older pragmatists, for example, all acknowledge that the correspondence idea is correct, so far as it goes—but they all also think this is a merely verbal or "nominal" definition, yielding no real understanding of the concept of truth.[28] It is a real question, even, which of these theories of truth really are mutually incompatible rivals, and which better conceived as offering mutually compatible answers to different questions about the truth-concept:[29] for example, while Tarski and Ramsey, like correspondence theorists, focus on the meaning of "true" and its cognates, coherentists like Bradley focus, rather, on the criteria of truth; and Peirce, James, and Dewey would probably have said that this is a distinction without a difference—that a real, pragmatic understanding of truth must tell us what difference it makes whether a proposition is true. (One of James's statements of the Pragmatic Maxim of meaning, after all, is that "there can *be* no difference anywhere that doesn't *make* a difference elsewhere.")[30]

above), 159–60, explaining why "for all *p*, '*p*' is a true sentence if and only if *p*" can *not* serve as a general definition of truth.

26 Rorty, *Philosophy and the Mirror of Nature* (note 18 above), 308.

27 Rescher and Majer, "Editors' Introduction" to Ramsey, *On Truth* (note 8 above), xiv–xv. (Indeed, these editors assert not only "how close Ramsey came to anticipating Tarski's theory of truth" (xiv), but also that "[w]here Tarski rests content with marking the equivalence of the sentence-predication '*p* is true' with the objective assertability of *p* itself, Ramsey ... pressed on into an inquiry to clarify the very idea of assertability...." This is seriously misleading.) See also Tarski, "The Semantic Conception of Truth" (note 21 above), 68–69 (arguing against an unspecified possible objector that "true" is not redundant because there is no way to eliminate it from, e.g., "the first sentence written by Plato is true").

28 "Truth is the conformity of a representation to its object," says Kant.... [This] is nearly correct, so far as it is intelligible.... [But] how futile was to imagine that we were to clear up the idea of *truth* by the more occult idea of *reality*!" Peirce, *Collected Papers* (note 14 above), 1.578 (1902–03). The notion of an independent reality "lies at the base of the pragmatist definition of truth. With some such reality any statement, in order to be counted true, must agree." But "Pragmatism defines 'agreeing' to mean certain ways of 'working.'" William James, *The Meaning of Truth* (1909), eds. Frederick Burkhardt and Fredson Bowers (Cambridge, MA: Harvard University Press, 1975), 117. "To be sure, a statement is true if it states things as they 'really are,' but how are they 'really'?" Dewey, "The Problem of Truth" (note 16 above), 112.

29 As Frápolli points out in "The Logical Enquiry into Truth" (note 19 above).

30 James, *Pragmatism* (note 15 above), 30.

Still, if what we want to know is the core linguistic meaning of "true" (and its equivalents in other languages) as it applies to propositions, beliefs, theories, etc., a good place to start is with the Aristotelian insight that "to say of what is that it is, or of what is not that it is not, is true."[31] Correspondence theorists, semantic theorists, and others tried to articulate this insight more fully. But the Logical Atomist correspondence theories developed by Wittgenstein and Russell required a formidable ontological apparatus of propositions and facts (perhaps including negative as well as positive, and logical as well as empirical, facts), and a relation of correspondence that proved very challenging to articulate;[32] while the less ontologically-burdened version of the correspondence theory developed by J. L. Austin, in terms of a coincidence of statements and states of affairs determined by the "demonstrative" and "descriptive" conventions of language, apparently applied only to indexical statements.[33] And while Tarski's semantic theory—explicitly intended as an articulation of the Aristotelian insight[34]—achieved admirable precision, Tarski himself acknowledged that this came at the price of restricted applicability; his definition works only for formal, strictly regimented logical and mathematical languages, not for natural languages like English or Polish.[35]

Of all the efforts to articulate the Aristotelian Insight, the simplest and most direct is Ramsey's, which I shall follow here. "[My] definition that a belief is true if it is a belief that '*p*' and *p*, but false if it is 'a belief that *p*' and –*p*," Ramsey writes, "is … substantially that of Aristotle.… [A] belief that Smith is either a liar or a fool is true, is true if Smith is either a liar or a fool, and not otherwise."[36] Again: "the most certain thing about truth is that '*p* is true' and

31 Aristotle, *Metaphysics*, Book Gamma (IV), 7, 1011b25, trans. W. D. Ross, in Richard McKeon, ed., *The Basic Works of Aristotle* (New York: Random House, 1941), 689–935, 749.

32 See especially Russell, "On Propositions" (note 12 above).

33 Austin, "On Truth" (note 12 above).

34 "I do not have any doubt that [my] formulation does conform to the intuitive content of that of Aristotle." Tarski, "The Semantic Conception of Truth" (note 21 above), 69.

35 Tarski, "The Concept of Truth in Formalised Languages" (note 21 above), 153 ("With respect to [natural, colloquial] language, not only does the definition of truth seem impossible, but even the consistent use of this concept in conformity with the laws of logic"); see also Tarski, "The Semantic Conception of Truth" (note 21 above), 57–58. Later, Donald Davidson would try to apply Tarski's methods as the basis of a theory of meaning for natural languages; but eventually even he concluded that this couldn't be done. See Donald Davidson, "Truth and Meaning" (1967), in Davidson, *Inquiries into Truth and Interpretation* (Oxford: Clarendon Press, 1984, 2nd ed., 2001), 17–36; Davidson, "What Metaphors Mean," (1978), in *Inquiries into Truth and Interpretation*, 245–64; Davidson, "A Nice Derangement of Epitaphs," Ernest Lepore, ed., in *Truth and Interpretation* (Oxford: Blackwell, 1986), 433–46. See also the discussions in Haack, "The Unity of Truth and the Plurality of Truths" (note 9 above), and Haack, "The Growth of Meaning and the Limits of Formalism, in Science and Law," *Análisis Filosófico* XXIX, no. 1 (2009): 5–29.

36 Ramsey, *On Truth* (note 8 above), 11.

'*p*,' if not identical, are equivalent"; truth is "when a man believes that A is B, and A *is* B." This is "merely a truism," Ramsey observes; but a truism that needs to be stressed, because "there is no platitude so obvious that eminent philosophers have not denied it."[37]

However, the usual label for Ramsey's approach, "redundancy theory," is potentially misleading[38]—"laconicism" would be a better term.[39] For Ramsey was well aware that, far from being redundant, the word "true" plays an important role. We can eliminate "it is true that" without loss from, e.g., "it is true that Caesar crossed the Rubicon"; but we *can't* eliminate "true" from, e.g., "everything Plato said was true," or from "all logical consequences of true propositions are true." These—as Ramsey evidently realized, since he observes that "ordinary language treats what should really be called *pro-sentences* as if they were *pronouns*"[40]—would have to be understood as (respectively): "for all *p*, if Plato said that *p*, then *p*"; and "for all *p* and for all *q*, if *p*, and if *p* then *q*, then *q*."

As this reveals, to spell out Ramsey's account more fully would require an adequate understanding of propositional quantifiers; and this, on pain of vicious circularity, would have to be an understanding that doesn't itself call on the concept of truth.[41] Moreover, as Ramsey recognizes, his account has nothing to say about criteria of truth;[42] and it gives no answer to what he calls the question of "propositional reference," i.e., what makes a belief the belief *that p*.

37 *Id.*,12. (By modern standards, Ramsey is a bit sloppy about the distinction between use and mention; so the somewhat random internal quotation marks here are probably best ignored.)

38 I used the label "redundancy theory" myself in *Philosophy of Logics* (Cambridge: Cambridge University Press, 1978), 127; but since 1991, when Ramsey's 1927–29 papers on truth were published, it has been clear that it is best dropped.

39 The word is not mine, but was coined by Dr. Kiriake Xerohemona. It is exactly the *mot juste*: the English word "laconic" means "terse, short"; and "Laconia" was the ancient Greek name for Sparta.

40 Ramsey, *On Truth* (note 8 above), 10.

41 This is no trivial matter, since both the usual interpretations of the quantifiers *do* rely, implicitly or explicitly, on the concept of truth. This is explicit in a substitutional interpretation pf propositional quantifiers, according to which, e.g., "For all *p*, if Plato asserts that p, then p" means "every substitution-instance of 'if Plato asserts that *p*, then *p*' *is true*." And it is implicit in an objectual interpretation, for on this interpretation "*p*" is not a sentence but the name of a proposition, and "for all propositions *p*, if Plato asserts that *p*, then the proposition that *p*" is grammatically incomplete without the addition of "is true." The problem is spelled out, and a possible solution articulated (based on ideas from Arthur Prior and C. J. F. Williams, and interpreting propositional quantifiers as "inference-tickets") in Frápolli, "The Logical Enquiry into Truth" (note 19 above).

42 Ramsey, *On Truth* (note 8 above), 13 (agreeing with Kant that no general criterion of truth is possible).

Still, if—as I believe—Ramsey's approach is on the right lines, it is enough to show us that, whatever the subject-matter of the proposition concerned, what it means to say that it is true is the same.[43] One might say it means that things are as the proposition says; but even this vague reference to "things" is perhaps too metaphysical. The essential point is that there aren't different senses of "true" for different kinds of proposition; whatever the proposition concerned, to say that it is true is just to say that it is the proposition that *p*, and *p*. It is true that Socrates was sentenced to death for corrupting the young just in case Socrates *was* sentenced to death for corrupting the young; it is true that 7 + 5 is 12 just in case 7 + 5 *is* 12; it is true that DNA is a double-helical, backbone-out macromolecule with like-with-unlike base pairs just in case DNA *is* a double-helical, backbone-out macromolecule with like-with-unlike base pairs; it is true that current Florida law imposes the death penalty for murder in special circumstances just in case current Florida law *does* impose the death penalty for murder in special circumstances; and so on.

Of course, there is disagreement about whether certain kinds of (supposed) claim even *have* truth-values. Specifically, emotivists deny that what look like statements about what is good or bad, right or wrong, are really statements at all; rather, they maintain, these are just expressions of emotion—like "mm-hmm" or "yay," and "yuck" or "eee-uuw"—and hence, not capable of being true *or* false.[44] Nothing in my argument thus far has any bearing on this issue, the question of moral cognitivism.[45] My argument does imply, however, that, *if* moral claims have truth-values, then it is true, for example, that it is a morally bad thing to torture small babies for fun iff it *is* a morally bad thing to torture small babies for fun, that it is true that the death penalty is morally indefensible iff the death penalty *is* morally indefensible, etc.

Anyway—whether or not moral claims are included—there are certainly many very different kinds of truths, i.e., many very different kinds of true proposition: conceptual, logical, mathematical, natural-scientific, social-scientific, historical, literary, etc., etc., …, and legal. What differentiates logical from historical truths, or natural from social-scientific truths, isn't that they are true in different senses of "true"—for, as I just said, whatever the subject-matter of a proposition, what it means to say that it is true is the same. Instead, what distinguishes logical from historical truth, for example, is just what distinguishes

43 As this formulation reveals, I shall adapt Ramsey's account in one respect, bypassing the problem of propositional reference by focusing on "true" as a predicate of propositions.

44 See e.g., A. J. Ayer, *Language, Truth and Logic* (London: Victor Gollancz Ltd., 1936), chapter VI; Charles Stevenson, "The Emotive Meaning of Ethical Terms" (1947), in Morris Weitz, ed., *20th-Century Philosophy: The Analytic Tradition* (New York: Free Press, 1966), 237–53.

45 But see §5, pp. 317–22 below.

logic from history: namely, *what the propositions are about*—and so, what *makes* them true.

3 LEGAL TRUTHS AND FACTUAL TRUTHS

It's easy enough to distinguish, in a rough and ready way, between factual truths like "there was a clearly visible stop sign at the intersection at the time of the accident," and legal truths like "one whose conduct [brings] about an unintended death in the commission or attempted commission of a felony [is] guilty of murder."[46] Indeed, in the US legal system—where legal questions are the province of the judge, and factual questions the province of the "finder of fact," normally the jury—the distinction is crucial.

It is sometimes suggested, as then-Attorney-General Janet Reno wrote in her introduction to a 1996 survey of DNA exonerations, that a "system of criminal justice is … [a] search for [factual] truth."[47] But while there is some truth in this, it can easily mislead. Yes, factual truth is crucial to substantive justice; it really matters, that is, whether the person found guilty of a crime is actually the perpetrator (and whether the person or outfit held liable for an injury actually caused it). And, yes, in many trials, though by no means all, the key issue is, in this narrow sense, a factual one: Was it the defendant, or someone else, who killed the victim? Was the substance found hidden in the defendant's home cocaine, or something else? Was the plaintiff's illness caused by the drug he took or the pollutant to which he was exposed, or would he have fallen sick even if he hadn't taken the drug or been exposed to the pollutant? Did the plaintiff's car crash because the tires were badly designed, or because he was driving recklessly? And so on.

Nonetheless, even when the crucial issues *are* narrowly factual, the task of the "fact-finder" is *not* to discover whether the crucial factual claims are true, but to give a verdict as to whether or not they have been established by the evidence presented (to whatever degree of proof is required, and under whatever procedural rules apply). Perhaps this is what the Supreme Court meant when it said in *Tehan*—somewhat more circumspectly than Ms. Reno—that "[t]he

46 Henry Campbell Black, *Black's Law Dictionary* (St. Paul, MN: West Publishing Co., 6th ed., 1990), 617. In the same entry we read that, while some states still follow this old common-law rule, today the law of felony murder differs from state to state, mainly as a result of efforts to limit its scope.

47 Janet Reno, "Message from the Attorney General," in Edward Connors, Thomas Lundgren, Neal Miller, and Tom McEwen, eds., *Convicted by Juries, Exonerated by Science: Case Studies in the Use of DNA Evidence to Establish Innocence after Trial* (Alexandria, VA: Institute for Law and Justice, June 1996), available at http://www.ncjrs.gov/pdffiles/dnaevid.pdg, iii–iv, iii.

basic purpose of a trial is the *determination* of truth"[48] ("determine" being closer to "deem" than to "discover").

Moreover, the crucial issues in many trials are not factual, but legal. Think, for example, of the evidentiary questions that, in a common-law system, may be vital to the final resolution of the kinds of factual issue I mentioned earlier. Did the trial court abuse its discretion in excluding lie-detector evidence indicating that Mr. Frye was telling the truth when he denied committing the murder of which he was accused?[49] Was it proper to allow a lay witness to give her opinion that the substance found hidden in Mr. Paiva's shoe was cocaine?[50] Did the Federal Rules of Evidence adopted in 1975, providing *inter alia* that the testimony of a qualified expert is admissible provided it is relevant and not otherwise excluded by law, supersede the old rule derived from the *Frye* case, under which novel scientific testimony is admissible only if it is generally accepted in the field to which it belongs?[51] Was the expert testimony proffered by the plaintiffs in *Paoli*, that contamination by PCBs (polychlorinated biphenyls) in the vicinity of the Paoli railroad yard had caused their illnesses, admissible under the new federal standard spelled out by the Supreme Court's interpretation of FRE 702 in *Daubert*, requiring courts to screen expert scientific testimony for reliability as well as relevance?[52] Was a non-scientific expert, such as the specialist on the design and wear of motor tires proffered by the manufacturers in *Kumho Tire*, subject to the same *Daubert* requirements as a scientific expert?[53]

Or, to turn to the vast variety of other kinds of legal question on which cases sometimes turn: Were Mr. Barefoot's constitutional rights violated when he was sentenced to death after two experts testified "to a psychological certainty" that he would be dangerous in future?[54] Did Pennsylvania law require that a jury verdict be overturned because one juror was taken ill at the last minute, and only eleven jurors voted?[55] Did the one-minute evolution-disclaimer

[48] Tehan v. United States *ex rel.* Shott, 382 U.S. 406, 416 (1966) (my italics).

[49] Frye v. United States, 293 F. 1013 (D.C. Cir. 1923).

[50] United States v. Paiva, 892 F.2d 148 (1st Cir. 1989).

[51] Daubert v. Merrell Dow Pharm., Inc., 509 U.S. 579 (1993) ("*Daubert* III") (ruling that FRE 702 superseded the *Frye* Rule, but that federal courts were required to screen proffered expert testimony for relevance and reliability; and providing a list of factors they might look to in determining the latter).

[52] *In re* Paoli R.R. Yard PCB Litig., 35 F.3d 717 (3d Cir. 1994).

[53] Kumho Tire Co. v. Carmichael, 526 U.S.137 (1999).

[54] Barefoot v. Estelle, 463 U.S. 880 (1983). This case is discussed in more detail in "Epistemology Legalized: Or, Truth, Justice, and the American Way," pp. 27–46 in this volume, 36–37.

[55] Blum v. Merrell Dow Pharm., Inc., 626 A.2d 537 (Pa. 1993) ("*Blum* III"). This case is discussed in more detail in "What's Wrong with Litigation-Driven Science," pp. 180–207 in this volume, 188–94.

statement read before ninth-grade biology class in Dover, Pennsylvania, violate the Establishment Clause of the First Amendment?[56] Did the City of New London's compulsory purchase of Ms. Kelo's house violate the "public use" restriction in the "Takings" Clause of the Fifth Amendment?[57] Do the principles of comment k of the Second Restatement of Torts apply to negligence claims against a vaccine maker?[58] Are the plaintiffs in a libel case "public figures" in the legal sense?[59] Etc., etc.

Up to now, I have written as if the distinction between legal and factual truths were unproblematically robust; but it doesn't take much thought to realize that this isn't so. One complication, resulting from relatively recent developments in US evidence law, is that, since the US Supreme Court's 1993 ruling in *Daubert*,[60] the line between the *admissibility* and the *weight* of evidence has been blurred, and the illusion created that judges' rulings can determine what scientific claims are, and what are not, true. A judicial ruling can indeed determine that a scientific claim is legally-reliable; but what makes scientific claims true is something entirely different: whether the things, events, and phenomena in the world that that they describe are as they describe them.[61]

But it is two other complications—neither of which is specific to the US (or any other) legal system—that most require attention here. First: The abstract noun "law," has the same double usage as "life," "beauty," "truth," etc. In one use, it refers to the phenomenon, law—as in "law is distinct from morality," or "the rule of law is essential to a civilized society"; in the other, it refers to particular legal systems and provisions—as in "since 1986 the US has had laws relating specifically to injuries allegedly caused by vaccines."[62] So legal truths come in two kinds: truths about law (the phenomenon), and truths about laws (the legal provisions of this or that jurisdiction). In what follows I shall focus primarily on the latter; but this leads us directly to a second, more pervasive complication.

[56] Kitzmiller v. Dover Area Sch. Dist., 400 F. Supp. 2d 707 (M.D. Pa. 2005).

[57] Kelo v. City of New London, 545 U.S. 469 (2005). The Fifth Amendment provides in part that no private property be taken for public use without just compensation. US Const Amend V (takings clause).

[58] Toner v. Lederle Labs., 732 P.2d 297 (Idaho 1987). Restatement (Second) of Torts § 402A (1965).

[59] Underwager v. Salter, 22 F.3d 730 (7th Cir. 1994).

[60] *Daubert* III (note 51 above).

[61] The argument is made in detail in Susan Haack, "Of Truth, in Science and in Law," *Brooklyn Law Review* 73, no. 3 (2007): 985–1008.

[62] National Childhood Vaccine Injury Act of 1986, Pub L No 99–660, 100 Stat 3743, 3755–84, codified at 42 USC §§ 300aa-1–300aa-34. The relevant history is briefly presented in "Risky Business: Statistical Proof of Individual Causation," pp. 264–93 in this volume, 270–72.

The distinction between factual truths and legal truths, in the sense of truths about legal provisions, is a somewhat artificial one. Legal truths like "Florida adopted the *Frye* Rule in 1953,"[63] "Michigan abandoned the *Frye* Rule in 2004,"[64] or "Illinois abolished the death penalty in 2011"[65] *are* factual truths—they are truths about social institutions, albeit of a distinctive kind. Legal systems (like systems of class or caste, of marriage, banking, education, etc.) are a special sub-class of social institutions; and so legal truths are a special sub-class of truths about social institutions generally. Or rather, more strictly speaking, legal truths are a *sub*-sub-class of these truths: a sub-class of that sub-class of truths that concern the *norms* of this or that society: which includes truths about its rules of etiquette, its aesthetic sensibilities, its moral principles, etc.—and its legal norms. I shall begin, however, with the ways in which legal truths are like social truths generally.

Unlike natural-scientific truths, which are normally unrestricted in scope, many social truths are local to a place and a time: e.g., truths about the sexual mores of the people of Papua New Guinea when Margaret Mead studied them; truths about the system of serfdom in Tsarist Russia; truths about the US mortgage-finance system in the years leading up to the 2008 financial crisis; etc., etc. Moreover, unlike natural-scientific truths, which are normally made true by the phenomena and events in the world that they describe, social truths are made true, in whole or in part, by what people do. Some are even made true, in whole or in part, by what people believe, hope, or fear: the hyper-inflation that Germany suffered between the two World Wars, for example, or that Zimbabwe is suffering now, came about in part because people lost confidence in the currency.

This doesn't mean that social institutions aren't real; they are. Social class, for example, is constituted by what human beings do, believe, etc.; nevertheless, though a person may change his social class by what he does in the course of his life, the social class into which he was *born* isn't something he can alter. Social institutions aren't completely independent of us, and may not even be completely independent of what most people in a society believe about them. But they *are* independent of what you or I or any individual believes about

63 Kaminski v. State, 63 So. 2d 339, 340 (Fla. 1953).

64 Michigan Supreme Court, "Rule 702. Testimony by Experts" and "Staff Comment to 2004 Amendment," in *Michigan Rules of Court—State* ([Eagan, MN?]: Thomson/West, 2008), 587.

65 Steve Mills, "What Killed Illinois' Death Penalty?" *Chicago Tribune*, March 10, 2011, available at http://articles.chicagotribune.com/2011-03-10/news/ct-met-illinois-death-penalty-history/20110309_1_death-penalty-death-row-death-sentence.

them; and this is enough to make them real—and to make the truth of propositions about social institutions objective.[66]

Many truths about social institutions—a system of marriage customs, say, or of banking practices—make sense only relative to a place and a time. Similarly, truths about legal provisions make sense only when a jurisdiction and a time are specified. The Establishment Clause of the First Amendment to the US Constitution was ratified in 1791,[67] and first applied to the actions of the states as well as of the federal government in 1947.[68] Florida adopted the *Frye* Rule in 1953;[69] reaffirmed its commitment to *Frye* in 1993;[70] moved significantly closer to *Daubert* in 2001;[71] and effectively adopted *Daubert* when it revised its Rule of Evidence 702 in 2013.[72] In 2004, Michigan abandoned *Frye* in favor of *Daubert*.[73] In 2007, the Supreme Court of Mexico proposed indicia of scientific reliability strongly resembling those offered by the US Supreme Court in *Daubert*.[74] In 2011, the Law Commission's report on expert evidence in criminal proceedings in England and Wales proposed a *Daubert*-like screening process for such testimony.[75] And so on.

Moreover, like other social-scientific truths, legal truths are made true by things people do. I choose this vague phrase deliberately, needing a form of words that will accommodate the actions of a whole variety of people and bodies. "Things people do" is intended to include, e.g., the actions of bodies like

66 On the social sciences generally, see Susan Haack, *Defending Science—Within Reason: Between Scientism and Cynicism* (Amherst, NY: Prometheus Books, 2003), chapter 6. On the reality of social institutions, etc., see Susan Haack, "Realisms and Their Rivals: Recovering Our Innocence," *Facta Philosophica* 4, no. 1 (2002): 67–88, *Defending Science*, chapter 5; and Susan Haack, "Die Welt des Unschuldigen Realismus," in Markus Gabriel, ed., *Der Neue Realismus* (Berlin: Suhrkamp, forthcoming).

67 US Const Amend I (establishment clause).

68 Everson v. Bd. of Educ. of Ewing Twp., 330 U.S. 1 (1947).

69 *Kaminski* (note 63 above).

70 Flanagan v. State, 625 So. 2d 827, 829 n.2 (Fla. 1993).

71 Ramirez v. State, 810 So. 2d 836, 844 (Fla. 2001) ("*Ramirez* III").

72 Act of June 4, 2013, Chapter 2013–107, Laws of Florida, to be codified at Fla Stat §§ 90.702, 90.704, available at http://laws.flrules.org/2013/107.

73 Note 64 above.

74 Conocimientos Científicos. Características que deben tener para que pueden ser tomados en cuenta por el juzgador al momento de emitir su fallo, Suprema Corte de Justicia [SCJN] [Supreme Court], Semanario Judicial de la Federación y Su Gaceta, Novena Época, tomo XXV, Marzo de 2007, Tesis Aislada 1a. CLXXXVII/2006, Página 258 (Mex.).

75 Law Commission, Report No. 325, *Expert Evidence in Criminal Proceedings in England and Wales* (March 21, 2011) (London: The Stationery Office, 2011), also available at http://www.official-documents.gv.uk/.

the Convention that met in Philadelphia in 1787 "to render the constitution of government adequate to the exigencies of the Union," and drafted a constitution which, after much controversy, was eventually ratified in 1789;[76] and the actions of the analogues of such bodies and processes in founding other legal systems. It is also intended to include the actions of parties to treaties that make international law; and of course the actions of the legislatures that pass laws within an already-established legal system. We might also want to allow it to include the work of the formal advisory bodies, and even the less-formal political groups, that influence legislation: for example, the work of the concerned parents and others who have successfully advocated in many states for the enactment of laws setting up sex-offender registers, or restricting where sex-offenders may live after they have served their time, or, etc.[77]—laws usually known by the name of a child victim, such as "Megan's Law"[78] or the "Jimmy Ryce Law."[79] (Such advocacy groups can't themselves *make* laws; but

they may persuade the bodies that can make laws to do so.)

The First Amendment to the US Constitution became law when it was ratified by the state of Virginia;[80] the Eighteenth Amendment (prohibiting "the manufacture, sale, or transportation of intoxicating liquors") became law in 1919 when it was passed by the required majority in Congress and ratified by the required number of states, and was repealed in 1933, when the

76 Richard B. Bernstein, "Introduction," in Bernstein, ed., *The Constitution of the United States with the Declaration of Independence and the Articles of Confederation* (New York: Barnes and Noble, 2002), 5–26, 15–22. The Constitution was finally ratified only after a compromise proposed by the Massachusetts ratifying convention, that a list of recommended amendments to be sent to the first Congress to meet under the new Constitution, was accepted.

77 For a summary of current policies relating to the management and supervision of sex offenders, see Karen J. Terry and Alissa R. Ackerman, "A Brief History of Major Sex Offender Laws," in Richard G. Wright, ed., *Sex-Offender Laws: Failed Policies, New Directions* (New York: Springer, 2009), 65–98, 76–78. "Megan's Law" refers to a subsection of a federal act of 1996, initiated in New Jersey, requiring notification about sex offenders in the community (repealed in 2006 when new federal law was enacted). *Id.*, 76; 90.

78 Megan's Law, 42 USC §§ 13701 (note), 14071(d) (1994 & Supp 1996), was repealed by the Adam Walsh Child Protection and Safety Act of 2006 § 129, Pub L No 109–248, 120 Stat 587, 600. Megan's Law, NJ Stat Ann §§ 2C:7–1 to -19 (West 2005) (the 1994 statutes (§§ 2C:7–1 to -11) and the 2001 statutes (§§ 2C:7–12 to -19) were designated as "Megan's Law" by 2001 NJ Sess Law Serv 167 § 8 (West)).

79 The "Jimmy Ryce Law" is a Florida law allowing for long-term civil commitment of sex offenders deemed "high risk." Terry and Ackerman, "A Brief History of Major Sex Offender Laws" (note 77 above), 77. Jimmy Ryce Involuntary Civil Commitment for Sexually Violent Predators' Treatment and Care Act (Jimmy Ryce Law), 1998 Fla Laws 98–64, as amended, codified at Fla Stat § 394.910 et seq.

80 Bernstein, "Introduction" to Bernstein, ed., *The U.S. Constitution with the Declaration of Independence and Articles of Confederation* (note 76 above), 18.

Twenty-First Amendment was adopted.[81] Illinois abolished the death penalty when the governor signed the bill to this effect passed by the state legislature.[82] Michigan shifted from *Frye* to *Daubert* when the Michigan Supreme Court promulgated a formal amendment to the Rules of Court.[83]

But it is not only what we might call legislative, quasi-legislative, and pre-legislative actions that create law; so, too, do (some) judicial interpretations of statutes and precedents. Florida's adoption of the *Frye* Rule, for example, was brought about by judicial rulings: first by the Florida Supreme Court in *Kaminski*, when it cited *Frye* for the proposition that "every court of last resort that has been called on to decide the question has ruled that results obtained from the so-called lie detector test are not admissible as evidence";[84] then by the same court in *Flanagan* when, after noting the change in federal standards brought about by *Daubert*, it affirmed that "Florida continues to adhere to the *Frye* test for the admissibility of scientific evidence";[85] and again by the same court in *Ramirez*, when it reinterpreted *Frye* as requiring that "[i]n gauging acceptance, the court must look to properties that traditionally inhere in scientific acceptance for the type of methodology or procedure under review—i.e., 'indicia' or 'hallmarks' of acceptability,"[86] bringing Florida law on scientific testimony much closer to the federal, *Daubert* standard.

Here is another, higher-level, example of legal shifts brought about by judicial interpretation. The First Amendment reads in part: "Congress shall make no law respecting an establishment of religion"[87] (the "Establishment

81 To become part of the Constitution, a proposed amendment must win a two-thirds vote in both houses of Congress, and then be ratified by three-fourths of the states (38 of 50). *Id.*, 23. For a more detailed account of the process by which Prohibition was passed, and later repealed, see Bill Severn, *The Roaring Twenties: Prohibition and Repeal* (New York: Julian Messner, 1969).

82 Ray Long and Monique Garcia, "Quinn Expected to Sign Death Penalty Ban," *Chicago Tribune*, March 8, 2011, available at http://articles.chicagotribune.com/2011–03–08/news/ct-met-quinn-death-penalty-0309–20110308_1_death-penatlty-error-and-incompetence-capital-punishment; Mills, "What Killed Illinois' Death Penalty?" (note 65 above).

83 Michigan Supreme Court, Rule 702, "Testimony by Experts" and "Staff Comment" (note 64 above). On the procedure for making such amendments, see Pamela Lysaght, *Michigan Legal Research* (Durham, NC: Carolina Academic Press, 2006), 50–52. The first case applying the new rule was Gilbert v. DaimlerChrysler Corp., 685 N.W.2d 391, 407, 408 (Mich. 2004).

84 *Kaminski* (note 63 above), 340.

85 *Flanagan* (note 70 above), 829 n.2. (Florida courts had long before moved from taking the *Frye* Rule to be about lie-detector evidence to construing it as a rule about novel scientific testimony generally.)

86 *Ramirez* III (note 71 above), 844. (But see also note 72 above and accompanying text on current Florida evidence law.)

87 US Const Amend I (note 67 above).

Clause"). For many years this clause was understood simply as precluding the establishment of a national church.[88] In 1947, however, when it was applied to the states for the first time, under the "Due Process" Clause of the Fourteenth Amendment, Justice Black wrote for the majority of the Supreme Court that it required government *neutrality* with regard to religion: meaning that no level of government, federal or state, may set up a church; pass laws favoring one religion over other religions, or favoring religion over non-religion (or, presumably, vice versa); force anyone to attend, or not to attend, church; or levy any tax to support religious activities.[89] In 1963 the concept of neutrality was amplified in Justice Clark's ruling in *Schempp*, which construed it as requiring that no government action have either the *purpose* or the *effect* either of advancing or of inhibiting religion.[90] In 1970 Justice Burger added, in his ruling in *Walz*, that the Establishment Clause precludes *excessive entanglement* of the state with religion.[91] By 1971 these ideas had coalesced into the *Lemon* test: to be constitutional under the Establishment Clause, (i) a statute must have *a secular purpose*; (ii) its primary effect must be *neither to advance nor to encourage religion*; and (iii) it must not foster *excessive entanglement with religion*.[92] By now, though courts still rely on the *Lemon* test, the "entanglement" clause seems to be fading into the background, and Justice O'Connor's proposed clarification of the "purpose" and "effect" clauses—that state action may neither *subjectively express* (purpose) nor *objectively convey to a reasonable observer* (effect) *either government approval or government disapproval of religion*[93]—seems to be increasingly influential.

Of course, these examples are only a couple from a vast range I might have used to illustrate how the courts that interpret statutes and precedents—and, more indirectly, the attorneys whose arguments persuade courts in the direction of this or that interpretation and, more indirectly yet, the wider social currents that influence these arguments—help bring legal truths into being. This

88 "[T]he ... object of the [F]irst [A]mendment was not to countenance, much less to advance, Mahometanism, or Judaism, or infidelity, but to exclude any rivalry among Christian sects, and to prevent any national ecclesiastical establishment which should give to an hierarchy the exclusive patronage of the national government." Joseph Story, *Commentaries on the Constitution of the United States* (Boston, MA: Hilliard, Gray & Co., and Cambridge, MA: Shattuck & Co., 1883), vol. II, 630–32.

89 *Everson* (note 68 above), 15–16.

90 Sch. Dist. of Abington Twp. v. Schempp, 374 U.S. 203 (1963).

91 Walz v. Tax Comm'n, 397 U.S. 664, 670 (1970).

92 Lemon v. Kurtzman, 403 U.S. 602, 612–13 (1971).

93 Lynch v. Donnelly, 465 U.S. 668, 690 (1984) (O'Connor, J., concurring). Subsequently, Justice Blackmun incorporated Justice O'Connor's clarification into the majority ruling in Cnty. of Allegheny v. ACLU, 492 U.S. 573, 595–602 (1989).

is "construction" in the sense explained in *Black's Law Dictionary*: "interpretation of statute, regulation, court decision or other legal authority." The processes of judicial interpretation are so complex and intricate, however, that they deserve (at least) their own section.

4 THE JUDICIAL CONSTRUCTION OF LEGAL TRUTHS

As Black's dictionary acknowledges, judicial interpretation is no simple matter: it is "the process, or the art, of determining the sense, real meaning, or proper explanation of obscure, complex, or ambiguous terms or provisions in a statute, written instrument, or oral agreement, or the application of such subject to the case in question"; a process that will require "reasoning in the light derived from extraneous circumstances or laws or writings bearing upon the same or a connected matter," or "seeking and applying the probable aim and purpose of the provision."[94] The varieties of construction-as-interpretation ramify alarmingly as the entry under "construction" continues: "*See also:* "Broad interpretation; Comparative interpretation; Contemporaneous construction; Construe; Four corners rule; Interpretation; Last antecedent rule; Literal construction *or* interpretation; Statutory construction; Strict construction."[95]

"Statutory construction," for example, is characterized as "[a] judicial function required when a statute is invoked and different interpretations are in contention." "Where [a] legislature attempts to do several things one of which is invalid," this entry continues, "it may be discarded if [the] remainder of the act is workable and in no way depends upon [the] invalid portion."[96] Recent challenges to the constitutionality of President Obama's new healthcare legislation,[97] passed in 2010, illustrate the point. As of May 2011 (when I finished the original version of this paper), three federal district courts had found the legislation constitutional;[98] two, however, had disagreed. One court found that the provision requiring every citizen to maintain a minimum level of health insurance coverage or pay a penalty on his or her tax return

94 Black, *Black's Law Dictionary* (note 46 above), 312.

95 *Ibid.* (capitalization exactly as in the original text). The delightfully-named "Four corners rule" is so-called because of the legal use of the expression "four corners" to refer to the entirety of a written document. In line with this, the rule is that "intentions of parties, especially that of grantor, is to be gathered from the instrument as a whole and not from isolated parts thereof." *Id.*, 657.

96 *Id.*, 1412.

97 Patient Protection and Affordable Care Act, Pub L No 111–148, 124 Stat 119 (2010).

98 Thomas More Law Ctr. v. Obama, 720 F. Supp. 2d 882 (E.D. Mich. 2010); Liberty Univ., Inc. v. Geithner, 753 F. Supp. 2d 611 (W.D. Va. 2010); Mead v. Holder, 766 F. Supp. 2d 16 (D.D.C. 2011).

(the "individual mandate") imposed a fine rather than a tax, and hence was unconstitutional;[99] but that this provision was severable from the remainder of the act.[100] In a more radical ruling, another court found that "[t]he individual mandate is outside Congress's Commerce Clause power, and it cannot be otherwise authorized by an assertion of power under the Necessary and Proper Clause.[101] It is not Constitutional";[102] and furthermore that this individual mandate is *not* severable from the rest of the Act, which is therefore itself unconstitutional.[103] In 2012, however, the Supreme Court determined that the individual mandate *is* constitutional.[104]

"Strict (or literal) construction," by contrast with "liberal" construction, "is construction of a statute or other instrument according to its letter, which recognizes nothing that is not expressed, takes the language used in its exact and technical meaning, and admits no equitable considerations."[105] Some of the time, perhaps most of the time, courts are just applying (or of course *mis*applying) extant law, trying to figure out its implications for the case before them.

But while some legal scholars—notably, Christopher Columbus Langdell, first Dean of Harvard Law School—have conceived of a legal system as something like a set of axioms from which the correct legal conclusions may be

99 Virginia *ex rel.* Cuccinelli v. Sebelius, 728 F. Supp. 2d 768, 788 (E.D. Va. 2010) (finding that "Section 1501 of the Patient Protection and Affordable Care Act—specifically the Minimum Essential Coverage Provision—exceeds the constitutional boundaries of congressional power").

100 *Id.*, 790 ("Accordingly, the Court will sever only Section 1051 and directly-dependent provisions"). This decision was vacated in 2011 when the 4th Circuit determined that Virginia lacked standing. 656 F.3d 253 (4th Cir. 2011).

101 Section 8 of the Constitution reads in part: "The Congress shall have Power To … regulate Commerce with foreign Nations, and among the several States, and with the Indian Tribes …" US Const Art I, § 8, cl 3 (Commerce Clause); and "To make all Laws which shall be necessary and proper for carrying into Execution the foregoing Powers…." US Const Art I, § 8, cl 18 (Necessary and Proper Clause).

102 Florida *ex rel.* Bondi v. U.S. Dep't of Health & Human Servs., 780 F. Supp. 2d 1256, 1298–1299 (N.D. Fla. 2011).

103 *Id.*, 1304 ("[this Act] has approximately 450 separate pieces, but one essential piece (the individual mandate) is defective and must be removed. It cannot function as originally designed"); and 1306 ("I must reluctantly conclude that Congress exceeded the bounds of its authority in passing the Act"). See also Judge Vinson's subsequent Clarification of his ruling, 780 F. Supp. 2d 1307 (N.D. Fla. 2011). On appeal, however, the 11th Circuit found that the individual mandate could be severed. 648 F.3d 1235, 1328 (11th Cir. 2011).

104 Nat'l Fed'n of Indep. Bus. v. Sebelius, 132 S. Ct. 2566 (2012). The same year, the Supreme Court vacated the 4th Circuit's judgment and remanded the case for further consideration in light of its *National Federation* decision in Liberty Univ., Inc. v. Geithner, 133 S. Ct. 679 (2012). In 2013, the Fourth Circuit affirmed the district court's ruling (note 98 above) against the plaintiffs. Liberty Univ., Inc., v. Lew, No. 10–2347, 2013 WL 3470532 (4th Cir. July 11, 2013).

105 Black, *Black's Law Dictionary* (note 46 above), 313.

logically derived, I believe this seriously overstates the role of logic in the law.[106] As Oliver Wendell Holmes put it long ago, "the life of the law has not been logic; it has been experience"; "experience" including "[t]he felt necessities of the time, the prevalent moral and political theories, intuitions of public policy avowed or unconscious, even the prejudices which judges share with their fellow-men."[107] Indeed. Manifestly, when statutes and precedents must be interpreted so as to apply to new situations, formal-logical reasoning won't suffice.[108] Judicial interpretation requires judgment, discretion; and may call on legal history, on explicit or imputed legislative intent, on considerations of equity, and on a whole range of forward-looking policy considerations.

As Edward Levi writes, "new situations arise [and] and people's wants change. The categories used in the legal process must be left ambiguous … to allow the infusion of new ideas."[109] As I would say, if it is to be flexible enough to cope with inevitable social, technological, etc., changes, the law needs concepts and rules open-textured enough to allow, and indeed enable, a certain "play in the joints."[110] Levi illustrates the point with a fine history of the evolution of the legal concept of an "inherently dangerous object."[111] I think of the late nineteenth-century evolution of US tort law as it gradually adapted to cope with the risks posed by new forms of mining, construction, manufacture, and especially, with the rapid growth of the railroads across the country, transportation;[112] and of its late twentieth-century adaptations to cope with the new risks, and new legal problems, posed by the rise of huge pharmaceutical and chemical companies—such as how to handle cases where an alleged injury occurred long after someone was exposed to a drug or a chemical, so that there were hard questions about which of a large class of potential

[106] See Christopher Columbus Langdell, *A Selection of Cases on the Law of Contracts, with a Summary of the Topics Covered by the Cases* (Boston: Little, Brown, 2nd ed., 1879); Oliver Wendell Holmes, Review of Langdell, *A Selection of Cases on the Law of Contracts*, 2nd ed. (1880; in Sheldon Novick, ed., *Collected Works of Oliver Wendell Holmes* (Chicago: University of Chicago Press, 1995)), vol. 3, 102–104; and, for a detailed discussion of this debate between Langdell and Holmes, Susan Haack, "On Logic in the Law: 'Something, but Not All,'" *Ratio Juris* 20, no. 1 (2007): 1–31.

[107] Holmes, Review of Langdell, *A Selection of Cases on the Law of Contracts* (note 105 above), 115.

[108] On the place of logic in the law generally, see also Edward Levi, *Introduction to Legal Reasoning* (Chicago: University of Chicago Press, 1949); Haack, "On Logic in the Law" (note 105 above); and Haack, "The Growth of Meaning and the Limits of Formalism, in Science and Law" (note 35 above).

[109] Levi, *Introduction to Legal Reasoning* (note 108 above), 4.

[110] This phrase is from Justice Burger's ruling in *Walz* (note 91 above), 669.

[111] Levi, *Introduction to Legal Reasoning* (note 109 above), 9–27.

[112] Lawrence M. Friedman, *A History of American Law* (New York: Simon and Schuster, 1973), 409 ff.

plaintiffs had actually been harmed by the drug or chemical, and which of several companies in the market made the stuff that allegedly caused a particular plaintiff's injury.[113]

A different kind of example would be courts' adaptation to the Supreme Court's ruling in *Melendez-Diaz*, that criminal defendants have a right under the Confrontation Clause of the Sixth Amendment to have the scientists responsible for forensic evidence against them present testimony at trial and be available for cross-examination.[114] As the dissenters at the Supreme Court pointed out, this decision imposed new obligations on the forensic-science community, new obligations that they feared might overwhelm the system.[115] After *Melendez-Diaz* came down, one could see courts trying to ensure that this doesn't happen. Because military personnel are subject to routine random drug testing, and those who fail a drug test are liable to find themselves facing a court-martial, the problem was particularly acute for military courts, where one can see judges working to distinguish the class of cases where *Melendez-Diaz* must be applied from those where it need not be.[116] In 2011 the US Supreme Court returned to the issue in *Williams v. Illinois*.[117]

The law, to quote Holmes again, "is not a brooding omnipresence in the sky."[118] To put it more prosaically, legal systems and legal provisions are human creations; and legal truths come into being only when they are made true by the actions of a legislature, a court, etc. Perhaps this sounds radical; properly

[113] See "Risky Business: Statistical Proof of Specific Causation," pp. 264–93 in this volume, 268 and notes 22 and 23, on courts' handling of this problem in cases against the manufacturers of diethylstilbestrol (DES).

[114] Melendez-Diaz v. Massachusetts, 557 U.S. 305 (2009). The Sixth Amendment (ratified in 1791) reads in part: "In all criminal prosecutions, the accused shall enjoy the right … to be confronted with the witnesses against him." US Const Amend VI (confrontation clause).

[115] *Melendez-Diaz* (note 113 above), 340–343 (Kennedy, J., with Roberts, C.J., Alito, J., and Breyer, J., dissenting).

[116] For example, Judge Gregory's ruling in United States v. Skrede, No. 2009–09, 2009 WL 4250031 (A.F. Ct. Crim. App. Nov. 23, 2009), in effect points out that there is a continuum of laboratory reports ranging from detailed reports of raw data generated by machines (clearly not testimonial and not requiring the technician to appear in court) to summary affidavits prepared by technicians expressly at the direction of law-enforcement personnel for use in criminal prosecutions (clearly testimonial) (*3–*4); and also argues that, since in this case the technicians whom the appellant claimed should have been called as witnesses were not aware the sample in question had been designated as "probable cause," their reports were not testimonial and so not subject to *Melendez-Diaz* (*5). In 2011, however, this ruling was set aside, and the case returned to the Air Force Judge Advocate General (JAG). 70 M.J. 358 (C.A.A.F. 2011).

[117] Williams v. Illinois, 132 S. Ct. 2221 (2012).

[118] S. Pac. Co. v. Jensen, 244 U.S. 205, 222 (1917) (Homes, J., dissenting). Holmes speaks specifically of the common law; but I believe the point holds more generally.

understood, however, it is a quite modest, though also a quite consequential, point:

- To say, as I have, that legal truths are in part constructed by judicial interpretations is *not* to say, *simpliciter*, that legal truths are made, and not, like natural-scientific truths, discovered. That would be to rely on a false contrast. The point is, rather, that unlike natural-scientific truths, legal truths become true only when some person or body makes them so; but of course, once they have been made true, that they are true is something to be discovered. (Before *Daubert* III, there was no true answer to the question, whether FRE 702 had superseded *Frye*; but after *Daubert* III, that *Frye* had been superseded federally was a true proposition that could be discovered by legal research.)
- To say, as I have, that courts' interpretations play a role in the social construction of legal truths is *not* to say that the law is whatever courts say it is. That would be a gross exaggeration. The point is, rather, that over the long haul an accumulation of individually small judicial interpretations and reinterpretations can play a significant role in refining, amplifying, extending, or restricting the application of statutes and precedents.[119]
- And to say, as I have, that judicial interpretations and reinterpretations involve something more than, and very different from, formal-logical reasoning is *not* to say that they can only be arbitrary and capricious. That would be to rely on another false contrast. The point is, rather, that the ongoing process of interpretation and reinterpretation calls, sometimes more and sometimes less successfully, on a whole raft of historical, moral, economic, and practical considerations.

5 THE NORMATIVE, THE LEGAL, AND THE MORAL

No, I haven't forgotten that, as I said earlier, legal truths are actually a sub-class of a special sub-class of truths about social institutions, those that concern the norms of this or that society. Now it is time—some may think it is well *past* time!—to think more carefully about the normative character of legal provisions.

[119] "Usually" because in special circumstances legal change may be, not gradual and incremental, but abrupt and radical: a point vividly illustrated by the plot of a recent best-selling legal thriller by Steve Martini, *The Rule of Nine* (New York: Harper, 2010), which turns on a scheme to blow up the Supreme Court and kill all nine of the Justices—so that a whole new Court will have to be appointed at once, and the legal landscape will change radically as a result.

What you have said, some might object, is all very well; but it doesn't even touch the most important question. You have been speaking at length about truths *about* legal provisions, I imagine such an objector complaining; but what about the truth *of* legal provisions? You seem to suggest, he might continue, that legal norms are just like rules of etiquette. But this can't be right. Rules of etiquette are pretty much wholly conventional; it makes no sense to say that society A, in which politeness demands that you clean your plate and belch as a sign of appreciation for the meal your host has provided, gets a principle of etiquette right, while society B, in which it is polite to leave a little food on your plate and rude to belch in public, gets it wrong. Legal norms, however, are *not* wholly conventional: they are principles about what is right or just, and must be judged by how well they conform to *real* justice, to the *true* account of what conduct is right and what wrong. But my imagined objector's argument relies on yet another false dichotomy.

In some languages, the same word is used for what in English we would call "law" and "right."[120] Perhaps this has contributed to the temptation to assimilate legal and moral norms. But to say that it is *morally wrong* to overburden your secretary with trivial or inappropriate tasks is one thing, and to say that it is *legally prohibited* is obviously quite another. In short, law is conceptually distinct from morality, and legal norms from moral norms. Morally bad laws are, nonetheless, laws.

So, though it strikes me as wrong-headed to speak of legal norms as being true or false, or even of the norms of some jurisdiction matching, or failing to match, some supposed ideal, trans-jurisdictional principles, I certainly allow that some legal systems, some legal provisions, and some legal rulings are morally better than others. To be sure, many legal norms—such as laws about what side of the road to drive on—are morally indifferent in themselves; there are very good prudential reasons for having some such rule, but *which* side of the road is chosen isn't a moral issue. Moreover, many kinds of morally bad behavior, such as being hurtful or inconsiderate to your spouse, your children, or your students, or buying "your" term paper from a commercial outfit that provides such things for a price,[121] or, etc., fall outside the scope of legal

[120] "*Derecho*" in Spanish; "*dereito*" in Portuguese; "*Recht*" in German; etc. (Of course, the English word "right" itself has more than one meaning: besides being the opposite of "left," as an adjective it may mean *either* "morally right" *or* "true, correct"; and as a noun, means "entitlement.")

[121] See Ed Dante, "The Shadow Scholar: The Man Who Writes Your Student Papers Tells His Story," *Chronicle of Higher Education*, November 12, 2010, available at http://chronicle.com/article/The-Shadow-Scholar/125329/ (describing how the author worked for such an outfit, churning out papers and even dissertations on a whole range of subjects for sale to students unable or unwilling to write their own).

regulation.[122] But some legal norms, such as Nazi laws disenfranchising Jews and confiscating their property,[123] or "Jim Crow" laws in southern US states, disadvantaging black people simply on account of their race,[124] are (by my lights, and I hope by yours too)[125] morally objectionable.

[122] Indeed, by my lights, a legal system that confines itself somewhat narrowly is better—I'm tempted to say, more civilized—than a legal system that takes it upon itself to regulate essentially private behavior, e.g., by making heresy, say, or adultery or homosexual relations, unlawful. (I might even say that legal systems can play a crucial role in establishing a boundary between public and private spheres.)

[123] Michael Stolleis, *The Law Under the Swastika: Studies in Legal History in Nazi Germany* (1994), trans. Thomas Dunlap (Chicago: University of Chicago Press, 1998), 12–21 summarizes the major legal changes under the Nazi régime: in 1933 Germany abolished political parties and ended federalism and the separation of powers, putting in place a "militarized and authoritarian centralized state" (13); then disenfranchised minorities and confiscated their property (14); imposed agricultural price controls and guaranteed markets (14); "cleansed" the judiciary by requiring that "[t]he basis for the interpretation of all legal sources [be] the National Socialist ideology" (14); passed the Law for the Prevention of Genetically Diseased Offspring in 1933, and the Blood Protection Law in 1935, forbidding marriage or sexual relations between Jews and non-Jews (17); regulated stock, cartel, and foreign currency laws (18); tried to rid itself of "useless" social welfare recipients through "euthanasia actions" and deportations to concentration camps (18); denied tax-exempt status to Jewish clubs, hospitals, religious orders, etc. (19); and introduced an expanded criminal law, granting special powers to the party and the SS, prohibiting the use of analogy (!), introducing alternative punishments, and enforcing laws retroactively (19–20). For other aspects of Nazi law, see Richard Lawrence Miller, *Nazi Justiz: Law of the Holocaust* (Westport, CT: Praeger, 1995); George J. Annas and Michael A. Grodin, *The Nazi Doctors and the Nuremburg Code: Human Rights in Human Experimentation* (New York: Oxford University Press, 1992).

[124] According to C. Vann Woodward, *The Strange Career of Jim Crow* (1955; revised ed., New York: Oxford University Press, 1966), the origin of the phrase "Jim Crow law" is lost in obscurity (7n). The extension of the term is also somewhat unclear. Woodward uses it to refer to the whole congeries of statutes that "lent the sanction of law to a racial ostracism that extended to churches and schools, to housing and jobs, to eating and drinking" and extended "to virtually all forms of public transportation, to sports and recreations, to hospitals, prisons, and asylums, and ultimately to funeral homes, morgues, and cemeteries" (*id.*). However, Charles S. Mangum, *The Legal Status of the Negro* (Chapel Hill, NC: University of North Carolina Press, 1940), while providing a detailed review of the statutes and cases concerning the relation of white and colored races since the Civil War—including civil rights, education, property rights, labor law, public transportation law, charitable and penal institutions, marriage, jury selection, voting, etc.—restricts the term "Jim Crow law" specifically to laws forbidding "any carrier to which such laws apply to transport white and colored passengers in the same vehicle or the same portion thereof" (181). (Hence the name "Freedom Riders," for those, black and white, who rode side by side in buses as a protest against racial segregation.) In "Laws of Racial Identification and Racial Purity in Nazi Germany and the United States: Did Jim Crow Write the Laws That Spawned the Holocaust?", *Southern University Law Review*, 30 (2002–03): 1–13 (which provides a useful brief comparison of the two), Bill Ezzell conjectures that Jim Crow laws may have provided "a ready-made set of time-tested racial legislation" (13) that influenced Nazi racial laws.

[125] The qualification is intended in part as an expression of moral fallibilism, and in part as an acknowledgment that others' moral sensibilities may be very different from mine. For

Though I have nothing like a fully-developed ethical theory to offer, I think, as the previous paragraph reveals, that moral claims *are* capable of truth and falsity. I don't, however, believe that what moral claims are true and what false is something we can know a priori: on the contrary, I think James was right when he described working out what rules and social arrangements are morally better and what worse as no less fallible an investigative process than discovering the laws of physics.[126] And Dewey, I believe, made a significant step forward when he argued that what we need to figure out is not, as James thought, how best to satisfy the most wants, but how best to satisfy the most needs: what moral rules and social arrangements, that is, are genuinely conducive to human flourishing.[127] For what is good or right for humans to do, as I have written elsewhere, cannot be entirely divorced from what is good for humans.[128]

So I don't believe legal norms are purely conventional, like rules of etiquette;[129] but neither do I think we should judge a legal system or a legal decision by how it measures up to some abstract ideal of justice—or that judicial interpretation is, or should be, invariably a matter of taking the law in the morally best direction.

First of all, it's not clear to me that the idea of a uniquely morally-best, ideally-just legal system is even viable; while some legal systems are clearly-enough morally better than others, some resist any such simple comparison—often, there will be no clear ordering of different ways of balancing the competing interests and demands that any legal system must accommodate.

example, a recent press report in which an Iranian official defended stoning on the grounds that "[m]ore than 50% … may not die" leaves me acutely aware how utterly and bafflingly alien another society's moral ideas may be to someone like myself. Jay Solomon and Farnaz Fassihi, "Iran Rights Envoy Assails U.N. Censure—Official Defends Stoning, Arrests, as General Assembly Committee Condemns Crackdown by Tehran," *Wall Street Journal*, November 19, 2010, available at http://online.wsj.com/article/SB10001424052748703374304575623040167164392.html.

126 William James, "The Moral Philosopher and the Moral Life" (1891), in James, *The Will to Believe and Other Essays in Popular Philosophy*, eds. Frederick Burkhardt and Fredson Bowers (Cambridge, MA: Harvard University Press, 1979), 141–72.

127 John Dewey, *The Quest for Certainty* (New York: Capricorn Books, 1929), chapter 10.

128 Susan Haack, "Six Signs of Scientism" (2012), in *Putting Philosophy to Work* (note 9 above), 117. (I am well aware, of course, that this leaves some tough questions—for example, what's morally wrong with cruelty to animals—unanswered.)

129 It might be thought that even some rules of etiquette may be appraised as morally better or worse. (Think of feminist criticisms of such practices as a man's opening the door and allowing a woman to pass first.) But when we criticize rules of etiquette that reflect underlying assumptions about gender, class, caste, etc., it is really the underlying assumptions that are at issue. It is worth noting, though, that in colloquial speech (while "impolite" is reserved for breaches of etiquette) "rude" often has a broader meaning; and that, when it conveys "disrespectful," "hurtful," takes on a moral role.

Moreover, a legal system is only one of the many, interrelated institutions by which modern societies are organized, and in some instances will need to be assessed, not in isolation, but as part of the larger whole: whether a system of tort law treats manufacturers and consumers fairly, for example, or unjustly disadvantages one over the other, may be answerable only if we also take into account the role and scope of the relevant regulatory bodies. Not to mention that, however morally admirable legal provisions may be in principle, if they are embedded in a legal system that is too overburdened, too slow, too inefficient, or too unwieldy to function adequately in practice—or so corrupt that its morally-admirable provisions are applied in a distorted way—the result may be not to enhance, but to impede, human flourishing.

Second, our moral assessments are fallible, and our foresight limited; so that legal changes made with the best of moral intentions sometimes turn out to have unintended and morally undesirable consequences.[130] Every legal system, and many legal decisions, will involve complicated and sometimes agonizingly difficult balancing of a welter of competing demands and interests—demands and interests almost all worthy of *some* weight, but not all mutually satisfiable. An ethical fallibilist like myself will be comfortable neither with appeals to the judgment of a hypothetical superhuman judicial Hercules, nor with simple reliance on individual human judges' seat-of-the-pants decisions.[131] To the extent that a legal system succeeds in gradually and raggedly fumbling its way towards morally better resolutions, it will more likely be because a whole variety of decent legislators and judges, each with his or her own legal, moral, political, economic, etc., priorities, along with a whole raft of other actors—attorneys and legal scholars, and a larger concerned public—all contribute, from their different perspectives, to the evolution of intelligently-crafted laws that enable human flourishing.[132]

[130] Trying to protect children from sexual predators, for example, many jurisdictions imposed residency restrictions (see note 76 above). One consequence has been that in many areas there is nowhere sex offenders can live when they are released from prison—except, for example, under the bridge to which Miami-Dade probation officers sometimes direct them, and which some even list as their legal address. All across the country, it seems, such well-intentioned efforts have not only condemned many sex offenders, after they have served their time, to a life of utter squalor, but have also made the public at large, if anything, less safe. Catharine Skipp and Arian Campo-Flores, "A Bridge Too Far," *Newsweek*. August 3, 2009, 41–46. See also, more generally, Richard G. Wright, "Introduction: The Failure of Sex Offender Policies," in Wright, ed., *Sex-Offender Laws* (note 76 above), 1–16.

[131] The attentive reader will notice that implicit in what I have said here is a criticism both of Professor Dworkin and of Judge Posner, who I believe have more in common than either supposes. But this is not the place to make that argument explicit.

[132] This is not to say that laws always or inevitably evolve in a morally-better direction; as I argued in "On Legal Pragmatism: Where Does 'The Path of the Law' Lead Us?" *American Journal of Jurisprudence* 50 (2005): 71–105, there can be *no* guarantee of that.

I anticipate one more objection: that, unless law and morality are more intimately connected than I have allowed, it is impossible to explain the normative force of law. As I see it, however, if we conceive of law and morality as *too* intimately connected, it will be impossible to explain what is *distinctively* normative about the law. This is a complicated matter; but here are some first steps towards an explanation:

- Of course, any law[133] carries with it a legal obligation on those within its jurisdiction to comply. Moreover, if detection of and imposition of penalties for violations are sufficiently probable, then rational people in that jurisdiction also have a prudential reason to comply.
- And of course some laws—e.g., laws against murder, cruelty to children, fraud, etc.—prohibit actions which are morally deplorable as well as legally forbidden; and here a moral obligation coincides with, and reinforces, the legal obligation to comply.
- Moreover, even with laws that in themselves have no moral force at all, there can be an indirect moral obligation to comply. For human flourishing requires, *inter alia*, allowing people as much freedom as possible to pursue their own projects and aspirations without getting in the way of others' pursuing their, perhaps very different, projects and aspirations; and in any society of any complexity, this is impossible without the security and predictability that the rule of law provides. So there are moral reasons to comply even with morally-indifferent laws.
- In the case of morally bad laws, however—laws that enjoin behavior which is morally deplorable, or that forbid behavior which is morally good or simply morally neutral—while there is a legal obligation to comply, there is no moral obligation; except, I would argue, a moral obligation to try to get such laws changed or, in egregious cases, to break or circumvent them. (It is precisely this that gives rise to those extraordinarily difficult questions about when civil disobedience, or even revolution, is morally justified.)

~

The attentive reader will probably have noticed not only how often I have quoted Holmes, but also how much my ethical thinking is informed by James's and Dewey's work, and how marked my *penchant* for ferreting out and disabling false dichotomies—perhaps, even, that my account of how legal

133 Exactly what makes a provision a law is another question, but not one I can take on here.

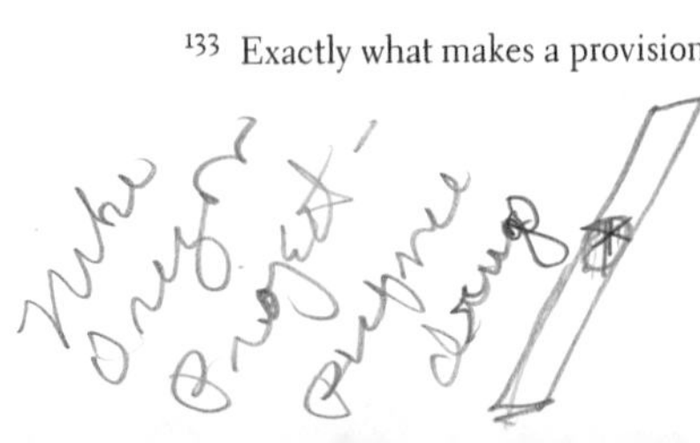

truths are made has some affinity with James's thoughts about truth more generally,[134] and my account of social reality with Peirce's pragmaticist amplification of Duns Scotus's definition of the real.[135] As this suggests, my developing legal philosophy is, indeed, best classified as a kind of neo-classical legal pragmatism.[136] But in philosophy, as George Santayana reminded us, "partisanship is treason."[137] I find the ideas developed here persuasive, *not* because they are pragmatist but because—well, because, as best I can tell, they are *true*.

[134] But I certainly don't hold that legal, or any other, truths are, as James suggests, made true by our verifying them.

[135] Peirce, *Collected Papers* (note 14 above), 5.405–10, and in *Writings: A Chronological Edition*, eds. Peirce Edition Project (Indianapolis, IN: Indiana University Press, 1982–), 3: 271–76 (1878). See also Haack, "Die Welt des Unschuldigen Realismus" (note 66 above), §3.

[136] The qualification "neo-classical" is intended to distinguish my position from, for example, what Richard Posner thinks of as pragmatism, and from a host of other misconceptions. See Haack, "On Legal Pragmatism" (note 131 above), and "The Pluralistic Universe of Law: Towards a Neo-Classical Legal Pragmatism," *Ratio Juris* 21, no. 4 (2008):453–80.

[137] George Santayana, *The Life of Reason* (1910; 2nd ed., New York: Charles Scribner's Sons, 1922), vol. 1, 110 (from a description of Bishop Berkeley as "a party man in philosophy").

Cases Cited

Prior and/or subsequent rulings in the same case that are referred to separately in the essays are designated by "I," "II," "III," etc. (e.g., "*Daubert* I," "*Daubert* II"). Different proceedings in the same case that are referred to separately in the essays are designated by the topic for which they are cited (e.g., "*Soldo*—Bradford Hill"). Cases that have the same name but are from different jurisdictions are designated by the jurisdiction (e.g., "United States v. Brown (California)").

CASES CITED: UNITED STATES

Abbott Labs. v. Sindell: see Sindell v. Abbott Labs.

ACLU v. Allegheny Cnty., 842 F.2d 655 (3d Cir. 1988), *aff'd in part, rev'd in part*, 492 U.S. 573 (1989), *remanded to* 887 F.2d 260 (3d Cir. 1989) (unpublished table decision)

Addington v. State, 546 S.W.2d 105 (Tex. Civ. App.), *rev'd*, 557 S.W.2d 511 (Tex. 1977), *vacated*, 441 U.S. 418, *remanded to* 588 S.W.2d 569 (Tex. 1979)

Addington v. Texas: see Addington v. State

Ahearn v. Fibreboard Corp., 162 F.R.D. 505 (E.D. Tex. 1995), *aff'd sub nom. In re* Asbestos Litig., 90 F.3d 963 (5th Cir.), *rehearing en banc denied by* 101 F.3d 368 (5th Cir. 1996), *vacated sub nom.* Flanagan v. Ahearn, 521 U.S. 1114 (1997), *on remand sub nom. In re* Asbestos Litig., 134 F.3d 668 (5th Cir. 1998), *rev'd sub nom.* Ortiz v. Fibreboard Corp., 527 U.S. 815, *remanded by* 527 U.S. 1031, *on remand sub nom. In re* Asbestos Litig., 182 F.3d 1013 (5th Cir. 1999)

Allegheny Cnty. v. ACLU: see ACLU v. Allegheny Cnty.

Allen v. United States, 588 F. Supp. 247 (D. Utah 1984), *rev'd on other grounds,* 816 F.2d 1417 (10th Cir. 1987), *cert. denied,* 484 U.S. 1004 (1988)

Allison v. McGhan Med. Corp., 184 F.3d 1300 (11th Cir. 1999)

Ambrosini v. Labarraque: see Ambrosini v. Richardson-Merrell Inc.

Ambrosini v. Richardson-Merrell Inc., Civ. No. 86-278, 1989 WL 298429 (D.D.C. June 30, 1989), *aff'd sub nom.* Ambrosini v. Labarraque, 946 F.2d 1563 (D.C. Cir. 1991) (unpublished table decision; for text of decision *see* 1991 WL 101512), *supplemented by* 966 F.2d 1464 (D.C. Cir. 1992), *remanded to sub nom.* Ambrosini v. Upjohn Co., Civ. A. No. 84-3483 (NJH) 1995 WL 637650 (D.D.C. Oct. 18, 1995), *rev'd sub nom.* Ambrosini v. Labarraque, 101 F.3d 129 (D.C. Cir. 1996), *cert. denied sub nom.* Upjohn Co. v. Ambrosini, 520 U.S. 1205 (1997)

Ambrosini v. Upjohn Co.: see Ambrosini v. Richardson-Merrell Inc.

Andrews v. State, 533 So. 2d 841 (Fla. Dist. Ct. App. 1988), *review denied,* 542 So. 2d 1332 (Fla. 1989) (unpublished table decision), *abrogation recognized by* Hadden v. State, 690 So. 2d 573 (Fla. 1997) (*Frye* test, not a relevancy standard as used in *Andrews,* is the proper standard for admitting novel scientific evidence in Florida)

Arabie v. Citgo Petroleum Corp., 49 So. 3d 529 (La. Ct. App. 2010), *aff'd in part, rev'd in part,* 89 So. 3d 307 (La. 2012)

Barefoot v. Estelle, 697 F.2d 593 (5th Cir.), *aff'd Dist. Ct.,* 463 U.S. 880, *reh'g denied,* 464 U.S. 874 (1983), *superseded by statute,* 28 U.S.C. § 2253 (1996) (codifying the certificate of appealability requirements in habeas corpus cases)

Barrel of Fun, Inc. v. State Farm Fire & Cas. Co., 739 F.2d 1028 (5th Cir. 1984), *abrogation recognized by* United States v. Posado, 57 F.3d 428 (5th Cir. 1995) (recognizing that the 5th Circuit's per se rule against admitting polygraph evidence did not survive Daubert v. Merrell Dow Pharm., Inc., 509 U.S. 579 (1993)

Bartley v. Euclid, Inc., 158 F.3d 261 (5th Cir. 1998) ("I"), *vacated by* 169 F.3d 215 (5th Cir.) ("II"), *on reh'g* 180 F.3d 175 (5th Cir. 1999) ("III")

Bauer v. Bayer A.G., 564 F. Supp. 2d 365 (M.D. Pa. 2008)

Berry v. City of Detroit, 25 F.3d 1342 (6th Cir. 1994), *cert. denied,* 513 U.S. 1111 (1995)

Berry v. CSX Transp., Inc., 709 So. 2d 552 (Fla. Dist. Ct. App.), *review denied,* 718 So. 2d 167 (Fla. 1998)

Bichler v. Eli Lilly & Co., 436 N.Y.S.2d 625 (App. Div. 1981), *aff'd*, 436 N.E.2d 182 (N.Y. 1982)

Bickel v. Pfizer, Inc., 431 F. Supp. 2d 918 (N.D. Ind. 2006)

Bitler v. A.O. Smith Corp., 391 F.3d 1114 (10th Cir.), *clarified on reh'g*, 400 F.3d 1227 (10th Cir. 2004), *cert. denied sub nom.* White-Rodgers v. Bitler, 546 U.S. 926 (2005)

Blum v. Merrell Dow Pharm., Inc., 1 Pa. D. & C.4th 634 (Phila. Cnty. Ct. 1988) ("I"), *rev'd*, 560 A.2d 212 (Pa. Super. Ct. 1989) ("II"), *aff'd*, 626 A.2d 537 (Pa. 1993) ("III"), *remanded to* 33 Phila. Cnty. Rep. 193 (1996) ("IV"), *rev'd*, 705 A.2d 1314 (Pa. Super. 1997) ("V"), *aff'd*, 764 A.2d 1 (Pa. 2000) ("VI")

Bonnichsen v. United States, 969 F. Supp. 628 (D. Or. 1997), *appeal after remand* 217 F. Supp. 2d 1116 (D. Or. 2002), *aff'd and remanded by* 357 F.3d 962 (9th Cir.), *amended and superseded by* 367 F.3d 864 (9th Cir. 2004)

Bradley v. Brown, 852 F. Supp. 690 (N.D. Ind.), *aff'd*, 42 F.3d 434 (7th Cir. 1994)

Brim v. State, Nos. 93-00860, 93-00863, 93-00864, 1995 WL 92712 (Fla. Dist. Ct. App. Mar. 8, 1995), *withdrawn and superseded on reh'g in part by* 654 So. 2d 184 (Fla. Dist. Ct. App. 1995), *disapproved in part by* 695 So. 2d 268 (Fla. 1997), *appeal after remand*, 779 So. 2d 427 (Fla. Dist. Ct. App. 2000), *after remand*, 827 So. 2d 259 (Fla. Dist. Ct. App. 2002), *review denied*, 839 So. 2d 697 (Fla. 2003) (unpublished table decision)

Brock v. Merrell Dow Pharm., Inc., 874 F.2d 307 (5th Cir.), *modified on reh'g*, 884 F.2d 166 (5th Cir.), *reh'g denied by* 884 F.2d 167 (5th Cir. 1989), *cert. denied*, 494 U.S. 1046 (1990)

Brown v. United States (New York): see United States v. Brown (New York)

Bruesewitz v. Wyeth, Inc., 508 F. Supp. 2d 430 (E.D. Pa. 2007), *aff'd*, 561 F.3d 233 (3d Cir. 2009), *aff'd*, 131 S. Ct. 1068 (2011)

Burleson v. Glass, 268 F. Supp. 2d 699 (W.D. Tex. 2003), *aff'd sub nom.* Burleson v. Tex. Dep't of Criminal Justice, 393 F.3d 577 (5th Cir. 2004)

Burleson v. Tex. Dep't of Criminal Justice: see Burleson v. Glass

Burton v. Wyeth-Ayerst Labs., 513 F. Supp. 2d 719 (N.D. Tex. 2007)

Caraker v. Sandoz Pharm. Corp., 188 F. Supp. 2d 1026 (S.D. Ill. 2001)

Carlson v. Gen. Elec. Co.: see Schudel v. Gen. Elec. Co.

Carmichael v. Samyang Tires, Inc., 923 F. Supp. 1514 (S.D. Ala. 1996), *rev'd*, 131 F.3d 1433 (11th Cir. 1997), *rev'd sub nom.* Kumho Tire Co. v. Carmichael, 526 U.S. 137 (1999)

Castillo v. E.I. du Pont de Nemours & Co.: see E.I. du Pont de Nemours & Co. v. Castillo

Cedillo v. Sec'y of Health & Human Servs., No. 98-916V, 2009 WL 331968 (Fed. Cl. Feb. 12, 2009), *reconsideration denied by* 2009 WL 996299 (Fed. Cl. Mar. 16, 2009), *aff'd*, 89 Fed. Cl. 158 (2009), *aff'd*, 617 F.3d 1328 (Fed. Cir. 2010)

Celotex Corp. v. AIU Ins. Co. (*In re* Celotex Corp.), 196 B.R. 973 (Bankr. M.D. Fla. 1996)

Chapin v. A & L Parts, Inc., 732 N.W.2d 578 (Mich. Ct. App.), *appeal denied by* 733 N.W.2d 23 (Mich.), *reconsideration denied by* 737 N.W.2d 774 (Mich. 2007)

Chaulk by Murphy v. Volkswagen of Am., Inc., 808 F.2d 639 (7th Cir. 1986)

Chikovsky v. Ortho Pharm. Corp., 832 F. Supp. 341 (S.D. Fla. 1993)

Christophersen v. Allied-Signal Corp., 902 F.2d 362 (5th Cir. 1990), *superseded by* 939 F.2d 1106 (5th Cir. 1991), *cert. denied*, 503 U.S. 912 (1992), *abrogated by* Daubert v. Merrell Dow Pharm., Inc., 509 U.S. 579 (1993)

Cloud v. Pfizer Inc., 198 F. Supp. 2d 1118 (D. Ariz. 2001)

Cnty. of Allegheny v. ACLU: see ACLU v. Allegheny Cnty.

Commonwealth v. Melendez-Diaz, 870 N.E.2d 676 (Mass. App. Ct.) (unpublished table decision; for text of decision *see* 2007 WL 2189152), *review denied by* 874 N.E.2d 407 (Mass. 2007), *rev'd*, 557 U.S. 305 (2009), *remanded to* 921 N.E.2d 108 (Mass. App. Ct.), *review denied by* 925 N.E.2d 864 (2010) (unpublished table decision)

Commonwealth v. Rompilla, 653 A.2d 626 (Pa. 1995), *denial of post-conviction relief aff'd*, 721 A.2d 786 (Pa. 1998), *habeas corpus granted in part sub nom.* Rompilla v. Horn, No. CIV.A.99-737, 2000 WL 964750 (E.D. Pa. July 11, 2000), *aff'd in part, rev'd in part*, 355 F.3d 233 (3d Cir.), *reh'g denied by* 359 F.3d 310 (3d Cir. 2004), *rev'd sub nom.* Rompilla v. Beard, 545 U.S. 374 (2005), *appeal after new sentencing hearing sub nom.* Commonwealth v. Rompilla, 983 A.2d 1207 (Pa. 2009)

Cook v. United States, 545 F. Supp. 306 (N.D. Cal. 1982)

Cooper v. Lafler: see People v. Cooper

Coppolino v. Florida: see Coppolino v. State

Coppolino v. State, 223 So. 2d 68 (Fla. Dist. Ct. App. 1968), *appeal dismissed*, 234 So. 2d 120 (Fla. 1969), *cert. denied*, 399 U.S. 927 (1970)

Cordoba v. United States: see United States v. Cordoba

CSX Transp., Inc. v. Berry: see Berry v. CSX Transp., Inc.

CSX Transp., Inc. v. McDaniel: see McDaniel v. CSX Transp., Inc.

Daniels v. Lyondell-Citgo Ref. Co., 99 S.W.3d 722 (Tex. App. 2003)

Daubert v. Merrell Dow Pharm., Inc., 727 F. Supp. 570 (S.D. Cal. 1989) ("I"), *aff'd*, 951 F.2d 1128 (9th Cir. 1991) ("II"), *vacated*, 509 U.S. 579 (1993) ("III"), *remanded to* 43 F.3d 1311 (9th Cir.) ("IV"), *cert. denied*, 516 U.S. 869 (1995) ("V")

DeLuca v. Merrell Dow Pharm., Inc., 131 F.R.D. 71 (D.N.J. 1989), *rev'd*, 911 F.2d 941 (3d Cir. 1990), *remanded to* 791 F. Supp. 1042 (D.N.J. 1992), *aff'd*, 6 F.3d 778 (3d Cir. 1993) (unpublished table decision), *cert. denied*, 510 U.S. 1044 (1994)

DePyper v. Navarro, No. 83-303467-NM, 1995 WL 788828 (Mich. Cir. Ct. Nov. 27, 1995), *aff'd*, No. 191949, 1998 WL 1988927 (Mich. Ct. App. Nov. 6, 1998)

Discepolo v. Gorgone, 399 F. Supp. 2d 123 (D. Conn. 2005)

Dolan v. Gen. Pub. Utils. Corp.: see *In re* TMI (Three Mile Island) Litig. Cases Consol. II

Donnelly v. Lynch, 525 F. Supp. 1150 (D.R.I. 1981), *aff'd*, 691 F.2d 1029 (1st Cir. 1982), *rev'd*, 465 U.S. 668, *reh'g denied*, 466 U.S. 994 (1984)

Downs v. Perstorp Components, Inc., 126 F. Supp. 2d 1090 (E.D. Tenn. 1999)

Dukes v. Wal-Mart Stores, Inc., 222 F.R.D. 137 (N.D. Cal. 2004), *aff'd*, 474 F.3d 1214 (9th Cir.), *superseded by* 509 F.3d 1168 (9th Cir. 2007), *aff'd in part, rev'd in part on reh'g en banc*, 603 F.3d 571 (9th Cir. 2010), *cert. granted in part*, 131 S. Ct. 795 (2010), *rev'd*, 131 S. Ct. 2541, *remanded to* 659 F.3d 801 (9th Cir. 2011)

Dunn v. Sandoz Pharm. Corp., 275 F. Supp. 2d 672 (M.D.N.C. 2003)

Ealy v. Richardson-Merrell, Inc., Civ. A. No. 83-3504, 1987 WL 18743 (D.D.C. Oct. 1, 1987), *rev'd*, 897 F.2d 1159 (D.C. Cir.), *cert. denied*, 498 U.S. 950 (1990)

E.I. du Pont de Nemours & Co. v. Castillo, Nos. 96-2486 & 96-2489, 1999 WL 71598 (Fla. Dist. Ct. App. 1999), *withdrawn and superseded by* 748 So. 2d 1108 (Fla. Dist. Ct. App. 2000), *quashed by* 854 So. 2d 1264 (Fla. 2003)

E.I. du Pont de Nemours & Co. v. Robinson: see Robinson v. E.I. du Pont de Nemours & Co.

E.I. du Pont de Nemours & Co. v. Stanton: see *In re* Hanford Nuclear Reservation Litig. ("Group B")

Eli Lilly & Co. v. Hymowitz: see Hymowitz v. Eli Lilly & Co.

Estate of George v. Vt. League of Cities & Towns Prop. & Cas. Intermunicipal Fund, Inc., No. S0182-07 CnC, 2008 WL 7541745 (Vt. Super. Ct. 2008), *aff'd*, 993 A.2d 367 (Vt. 2010)

Estate of Gonzales v. Hickman, ED CV 05-660 MMM (RCx), 2007 WL 3237727 (C.D. Cal. May 30, 2007)

Estates of Tobin *ex rel.* Tobin v. Smithkline Beecham Pharm., Civil No. 00-CV-0025-Bea, 2001 WL 36102161 (D. Wyo. May 8, 2001)

Everson v. Bd. of Educ. of Ewing Twp., 39 A.2d 75 (N.J. Sup. Ct. 1944), *rev'd*, 44 A.2d 333 (N.J. 1945), *aff'd*, 330 U.S. 1, *reh'g denied*, 330 U.S. 855 (1947)

Ferguson v. Hubbell, 26 Hun 250 (N.Y. Sup. Ct. Gen. Term 3d Dep't 1882), *rev'd*, 97 N.Y. 507 (1884)

Ferguson v. Riverside Sch. Dist. No. 416, No. CS-00-0097-FVS, 2002 WL 34355958 (E.D. Wash. Feb. 6, 2002)

Fitzpatrick v. State, 900 So. 2d 495 (Fla. 2005)

Flanagan v. Ahearn: see Ahearn v. Fibreboard Corp.

Flanagan v. State, 586 So. 2d 1085 (Fla. Dist. Ct. App. 1991), *approved in part by* 625 So. 2d 827 (Fla. 1993)

Flores v. Johnson: see Flores v. State

Flores v. State, 871 S.W.2d 714 (Tex. Crim. App. 1993), *cert. denied*, 513 U.S. 926 (1994), *denial of habeas corpus aff'd sub nom.* Flores v. Johnson, 210 F.3d 456 (5th Cir.), *cert. denied*, 531 U.S. 987 (2000)

Flores v. Texas: see Flores v. State

Florida *ex rel.* Bondi v. U.S. Dep't of Health & Human Servs., 780 F. Supp. 2d 1256 (N.D. Fla.), *clarified by* 780 F. Supp. 2d 1307 (N.D. Fla.), *aff'd in part, rev'd in part*, 648 F.3d 1235 (11th Cir. 2011), *aff'd in part, rev'd in part sub nom.* Nat'l Fed'n of Indep. Bus. v. Sebelius, 132 S. Ct. 2566 (2012)

Frye v. United States, 293 F. 1013 (D.C. Cir. 1923), *superseded by rule*, Fed. R. Evid. 702, *as stated in* Daubert v. Merrell Dow Pharm., Inc., 509 U.S. 579 (1993)

Fuesting v. Zimmer, Inc., 421 F.3d 528 (7th Cir. 2005), *vacated in part on reh'g by* 448 F.3d 936 (7th Cir. 2006), *cert. denied*, 549 U.S. 1180 (2007), *remanded to* 594 F. Supp. 2d 1043 (C.D. Ill. 2009), *aff'd*, 362 F. App'x 560 (7th Cir. 2010)

Gannon v. United States, 571 F. Supp. 2d 615 (E.D. Pa. 2007), *aff'd*, 292 F. App'x 170 (3d Cir. 2008)

Gen. Elec. Co. v. Ingram: see *In re* Paoli R.R. Yard PCB Litig.

Gen. Elec. Co. v. Joiner: see Joiner v. Gen. Elec. Co.

Gen. Motors Corp. v. Grenier, 981 A.2d 524 (Del.), *remanded sub nom. In re* Asbestos Litig., C.A. No. 05C-11-257 ASB, 2009 WL 1034487 (Del. Super.

Ct. Apr. 8, 2009), *aff'd sub nom.* Gen. Motors Corp. v. Grenier, 981 A.2d 531 (Del. 2009)

Gen. Pub. Utils. Corp. v. Abrams: see *In re* TMI (Three Mile Island) Litig. Cases Consol. II

Gilbert v. DaimlerChrysler Corp., No. 227392, 2002 WL 1767672 (Mich. Ct. App. July 30, 2002), *rev'd,* 685 N.W.2d 391 (Mich. 2004), *reh'g denied,* 691 N.W.2d 436 (Mich.), *cert. denied,* 546 U.S. 821 (2005)

Gilmore v. N. Pac. Ry. Co., 18 F. 866 (C.C.D. Or. 1884)

Godsey v. State, 989 S.W.2d 482 (Tex. App. 1999)

Grady v. Frito-Lay, Inc., No. GD 95-5934, 2000 WL 33436367 (Pa. Ct. C.P. Apr. 3, 2000), *rev'd,* 789 A.2d 735 (Pa. Super. Ct. 2001), *appeal granted in part,* 800 A.2d 294 (Pa. 2002), *rev'd in part,* 839 A.2d 1038 (Pa. 2003), *on remand,* No. GD 95-5934, 2004 WL 5162652 (Pa. Ct. C.P. Dec. 21, 2004)

Grassis v. Johns-Manville Corp., 591 A.2d 671 (N.J. Super. Ct. App. Div. 1991)

Grimes v. Hoffmann-LaRoche, Inc., 907 F. Supp. 33 (D.N.H. 1995)

Haft v. Lone Palm Hotel, 83 Cal. Rptr. 312 (Ct. App. 1969), *vacated by* 478 P.2d 465 (Cal. 1970)

Haggerty v. Upjohn Co., 950 F. Supp. 1160 (S.D. Fla. 1996), *aff'd,* 158 F.3d 588 (11th Cir. 1998) (unpublished table decision)

Hall v. Baxter Healthcare Corp., 947 F. Supp. 1387 (D. Or. 1996)

Hall v. United States: see United States v. Hall

Hankey v. United States: see United States v. Hankey

Hardiman v. Davita Inc., No. 2:05-CV-262-JM, 2007 WL 1395568 (N.D. Ind. May 10, 2007)

Havner v. Merrell Dow Pharm., Inc.: see Merrell Dow Pharm., Inc. v. Havner

Hazlehurst v. Sec'y of Health & Human Servs., No. 03-654V, 2009 WL 332306 (Fed. Cl. Feb. 12, 2009), *aff'd,* 88 Fed. Cl. 473 (2009), *aff'd,* 604 F.3d 1343 (Fed. Cir. 2010)

Henricksen v. ConocoPhillips Co., 605 F. Supp. 2d 1142 (E.D. Wash. 2009)

Hymowitz v. Eli Lilly & Co., 518 N.Y.S.2d 996 (Sup. Ct. 1987), *aff'd,* 526 N.Y.S.2d 922 (App. Div. 1988), *aff'd,* 539 N.E.2d 1069 (N.Y.), *cert. denied,* 493 U.S. 944 (1989)

Illinois v. Gates: see People v. Gates

In re "Agent Orange" Prod. Liab. Litig., 597 F. Supp. 740 (E.D.N.Y. 1984), *aff'd,* 818 F.2d 145 (2d Cir. 1987), *cert. denied sub nom.* Pinkney v. Dow

Chemical Co., 484 U.S. 1004, *remanded sub nom. In re* "Agent Orange" Prod. Liab. Litig., 689 F. Supp. 1250 (E.D.N.Y. 1988)

In re Asbestos Litig. (Delaware): see Gen. Motors Corp. v. Grenier

In re Asbestos Litig. (Texas): see Ahearn v. Fibreboard Corp.

In re Bextra & Celebrex Mktg. Sales Practices & Prod. Liab. Litig., 524 F. Supp. 2d 1166 (N.D. Cal. 2007)

In re Breast Implant Litig., 11 F. Supp. 2d 1217 (D. Colo. 1998)

In re Celotex Corp.: see Celotex Corp. v. AIU Ins. Co.

In re Fosamax Prods. Liab. Litig., 645 F. Supp. 2d 164 (S.D.N.Y. 2009)

In re Hanford Nuclear Reservation Litig., No. CY-91-3015-AAM, 1998 WL 775340 (E.D. Wash. Aug. 21, 1998), *rev'd*, 292 F.3d 1124 (9th Cir. 2002) (collectively "Group A")

In re Hanford Nuclear Reservation Litig., 497 F.3d 1005 (9th Cir. 2007), *amended and superseded by* 521 F.3d 1028 (9th Cir.), *amended and superseded by* 534 F.3d 986 (9th Cir.), *cert. denied sub nom.* E.I. du Pont de Nemours & Co. v. Stanton, 555 U.S. 1084 (2008) (collectively "Group B")

In re Jensen, 152 N.Y.S. 1120 (App. Div.), *aff'd sub nom.* Jensen v. S. Pac. Co., 109 N.E. 600 (N.Y. 1915), *rev'd*, 244 U.S. 205 (1917), *superseded by statute*, Longshoremen's and Harbor Workers' Compensation Act, Pub. L. No. 69-803, 44 Stat. 1424 (1927)

In re Joint E. & S. Dist. Asbestos Litig., 758 F. Supp. 199 (S.D.N.Y.), *reargument denied by* 774 F. Supp. 113 (S.D.N.Y.), *reconsideration denied by* 774 F. Supp. 116 (S.D.N.Y. 1991), *rev'd*, 964 F.2d 92 (2d Cir. 1992), *remanded* to 827 F. Supp. 1014 (S.D.N.Y. 1993), *rev'd*, 52 F.3d 1124 (2d Cir. 1995)

In re Lockheed Litig. Cases, 23 Cal. Rptr. 3d 762 (Cal. Ct. App.), *review granted and superseded by* 110 P.3d 289 (Cal. 2005), *review dismissed*, 192 P.3d 403 (Cal. 2007)

In re Neurontin Mktg., Sales Practices, & Prods. Liab. Litig., 612 F. Supp. 2d 116 (D. Mass. 2009)

In re Paoli R.R. Yard PCB Litig., 35 F.3d 717 (3d Cir. 1994), *cert. denied sub nom.* Gen. Elec. Co. v. Ingram, 513 U.S. 1190 (1995), *appeal after remand sub nom. In re* Paoli R.R. Yard PCB Litig., 113 F.3d 444 (3d Cir. 1997)

In re Peterson, 253 U.S. 300 (1920)

In re Phenylpropanolamine (PPA), 2003 WL 22417238 (N.J. Super. Law Div. July 21, 2003)

In re Propulsid Prods. Liab. Litig., No. 1355, 2000 WL 35621417 (J.P.M.L. Aug. 7, 2000)

In re Rezulin Prods. Liab. Litig., 369 F. Supp. 2d 398 (S.D.N.Y. 2005)

In re Silicone Gel Breast Implant Prods. Liab. Litig. (MDL 926) (Alabama), No. CV 92-P-10000-S, 1996 WL 34401813 (N.D. Ala. May 31, 1996), *amended by* 1996 WL 34401762 (N.D. Ala. June 10, 1996), *subsequent determination by* 1996 WL 34401763 (N.D. Ala. June 13, 1996), *vacated in part by* 1996 WL 34401764 (N.D. Ala. Aug. 23, 1996), *supplemented by* 1996 WL 34401766 (N.D. Ala. Oct. 31, 1996)

In re Silicone Gel Breast Implants Prods. Liab. Litig. (California), 318 F. Supp. 2d 879 (C.D. Cal. 2004)

In re Stand 'N Seal Prods. Liab. Litig., 623 F. Supp. 2d 1355 (N.D. Ga. 2009)

In re TMI (Three Mile Island) Litig. Cases Consol. II, 911 F. Supp. 775 (M.D. Pa. 1996), *aff'd*, 193 F.3d 613 (3d Cir. 1999), *amended by* 199 F.3d 158 (3d Cir.), *cert. denied sub nom.* Gen. Pub. Utils. Corp. v. Abrams and Dolan v. Gen. Pub. Utils. Corp., 530 U.S. 1225 (2000)

In re Trasylol Prods. Liab. Litig., No. 08-MD-01928, 2010 WL 1489734 (S.D. Fla. Mar. 8, 2010) ("In re *Trasylol*—Parikh")

In re Trasylol Prods. Liab. Litig., No. 08-MD-01928, 2010 WL 1489730 (S.D. Fla. Mar. 19, 2010) ("In re *Trasylol*—Derschwitz")

In re Viagra Prods. Liab. Litig., 572 F. Supp. 2d 1071 (D. Minn. 2008) ("In re *Viagra* I")

In re Viagra Prods. Liab. Litig., 658 F. Supp. 2d 936 (D. Minn. 2009) ("In re *Viagra* II")

In re Vioxx Prods. Liab. Litig., 360 F. Supp. 2d 1352 (J.P.M.L. 2005) ("In re *Vioxx*—§ 1407 Centralization")

In re Vioxx Prods. Liab. Litig., 401 F. Supp. 2d 565 (E.D. La.), *reconsideration denied by* MDL No. 1657, 05-4046, 2005 WL 3541045 (E.D. La. Dec. 6, 2005) ("In re *Vioxx*—Plunkett/Experts")

In re Vioxx Prods. Liab. Litig., 239 F.R.D. 450 (E.D. La. 2006) ("In re *Vioxx*—Rule 23 Certification")

In re W, 291 N.Y.S.2d 1005 (App. Div. 1968), *aff'd sub nom. In re* W. v. Family Ct., 247 N.E.2d 253 (N.Y. 1969), *rev'd sub nom. In re* Winship, 397 U.S. 358, *mandate conformed to sub nom. In re* W. v. Family Ct., 262 N.E.2d 675 (1970)

In re W v. Family Court: see *In re* W

In re Winship: see *In re* W

Isely v. Capuchin Province, 877 F. Supp. 1055 (E.D. Mich. 1995)

Jaros v. E.I. DuPont: see *In re* Hanford Nuclear Reservation Litig. ("Group A")

Jensen v. S. Pac. Co.: see *In re* Jensen

Johnston v. United States, 597 F. Supp. 374 (D. Kan. 1984)

Joiner v. Gen. Elec. Co., 864 F. Supp. 1310 (N.D. Ga. 1994) ("I"), *rev'd*, 78 F.3d 524 (11th Cir. 1996) ("II"), *rev'd*, 522 U.S. 136 (1997) ("III"), *remanded to* 134 F.3d 1457 (11th Cir. 1998) ("IV")

Jones v. Owens-Corning Fiberglas Corp., 672 A.2d 230 (N.J. Super. Ct. App. Div. 1996)

Kaminski v. State, 63 So. 2d 339 (Fla. 1953) (on rehearing), *appeal after remand* 72 So. 2d 400 (Fla.), *cert. denied sub nom.* Kaye v. Florida, 348 U.S. 832 (1954)

Kannankeril v. Terminix Int'l, Inc., 128 F.3d 802 (3d Cir. 1997)

Kaye v. Florida: see Kaminski v. State

Keegan v. Minneapolis & St. Louis R.R. Co., 78 N.W. 965 (Minn. 1899)

Kelo v. City of New London, No. 557299, 2002 WL 500238 (Conn. Super. Ct. Mar. 13, 2002), *aff'd in part, rev'd in part*, 843 A.2d 500 (Conn. 2004), *aff'd*, 545 U.S. 469, *reh'g denied*, 545 U.S. 1158 (2005)

Kitzmiller v. Dover Area Sch. Dist., 400 F. Supp. 2d 707 (M.D. Pa. 2005)

Kokoraleis v. Gilmore: see People v. Kokoraleis

Krutsinger v. Pharmacia Corp., No. 03-CV-0111-MJR, 2004 WL 5508617 (S.D. Ill. May 20, 2004)

Kumho Tire Co. v. Carmichael: see Carmichael v. Samyang Tires, Inc.

Lafler v. Cooper: see People v. Cooper

Landrigan v. Celotex Corp., 579 A.2d 1268 (N.J. Super. Ct. App. Div. 1990), *rev'd*, 605 A.2d 1079 (N.J. 1992)

LeBlanc v. Chevron USA, Inc., 513 F. Supp. 2d 641 (E.D. La. 2007), *vacated and remanded by* 275 F. App'x 319 (5th Cir. 2008), *on remand to* Civil Action No. 05-5485, 2009 WL 482160 (E.D. La. Feb. 25, 2009)

Lederle Labs. v. Toner: see Toner v. Lederle Labs.

Lemon v. Kurtzman, 310 F. Supp. 35 (E.D. Pa. 1969), *rev'd*, 403 U.S. 602, *reh'g denied*, 404 U.S. 876 (1971), *remanded to* 348 F. Supp. 300 (E.D. Pa. 1972), *aff'd*, 411 U.S. 192 (1973)

Lewis v. Airco, Inc., No. A-3509-08T3, 2011 WL 2731880 (N.J. Super. Ct. App. Div. July 15, 2011)

Liberty Univ., Inc. v. Geithner, 753 F. Supp. 2d 611 (W.D. Va. 2010), *vacated*, 671 F.3d 391 (4th Cir. 2011), *cert. denied*, 133 S. Ct. 60, *cert. granted and judgment vacated*, 133 S. Ct. 679 (2012), *aff'g district court sub nom.* Liberty Univ., Inc. v. Lew, No. 10-2347, 2013 WL 3470532 (4th Cir. July 11, 2013)

Liberty Univ., Inc. v. Lew: see Liberty Univ., Inc. v. Geithner

Lofgren v. Motorola, Inc., No. CV-93-05521, 1998 WL 299925 (Ariz. Super. Ct. June 1, 1998)

Lynch v. Donnelly: see Donnelly v. Lynch

Lynch v. Merrell-Nat'l Labs., 646 F. Supp. 856 (D. Mass. 1986), *aff'd*, 830 F.2d 1190 (1st Cir. 1987)

MacPherson v. Buick Motor Co., 145 N.Y.S. 462 (App. Div. 1914), *aff'd*, 111 N.E. 1050 (N.Y. 1916)

Maiorana v. Nat'l Gypsum Co.: see *In re* Joint E. & S. Dist. Asbestos Litig.

Mancuso v. Consol. Edison Co. of N.Y., Inc., 967 F. Supp. 1437 (S.D.N.Y. 1997)

Manko v. United States, 636 F. Supp. 1419 (W.D. Mo. 1986), *aff'd in relevant part*, 830 F.2d 831 (8th Cir. 1987)

Matt Dietz Co. v. Torres: see Torres v. Matt Dietz Co.

McCullock v. H.B. Fuller Co., 981 F.2d 656 (2d Cir. 1992), *appeal after remand* 61 F.3d 1038 (2d Cir. 1995)

McDaniel v. CSX Transp., Inc., 955 S.W.2d 257 (Tenn. 1997), *cert. denied*, 524 U.S. 915 (1998)

McLean v. Ark. Bd. of Educ., 529 F. Supp. 1255 (E.D. Ark. 1982)

Mead v. Holder, 766 F. Supp. 2d 16 (D.D.C. 2011), *reh'g denied sub nom.* Seven-Sky v. Holder, No. 11-5047, 2011 WL 1113489 (D.C. Cir. Mar. 17, 2011), *aff'd*, 661 F.3d 1 (D.C. Cir. 2011), *cert. denied*, 133 S. Ct. 63 (2012)

Melendez-Diaz v. Massachusetts: see Commonwealth v. Melendez-Diaz

Merrell Dow Pharm., Inc. v. Havner, 907 S.W.2d 535 (Tex. App. 1994), *rev'd*, 953 S.W.2d 706 (Tex. 1997), *cert. denied*, 523 U.S. 1119 (1998)

Merrell Dow Pharm., Inc., v. Oxendine: see Oxendine v. Merrell Dow Pharm., Inc.

Metabolife Int'l, Inc. v. Wornick, 72 F. Supp. 2d 1160 (S.D. Cal. 1999), *aff'd in part, rev'd in part*, 264 F.3d 832 (9th Cir. 2001)

Milward v. Acuity Specialty Prods. Grp., Inc., 664 F. Supp. 2d 137 (D. Mass. 2009), *rev'd*, 639 F.3d 11 (1st Cir. 2011), *cert. denied sub nom.* U.S. Steel Corp. v. Milward, 132 S. Ct. 1002 (2012)

Minn. Mining & Mfg. Co. v. Atterbury, 978 S.W.2d 183 (Tex. App. 1998)

Mitchell v. United States: see United States v. Mitchell

Mobil Oil Corp. v. Bailey, 187 S.W.3d 265 (Tex. App. 2006)

Moore v. Ashland Chem., Inc., 126 F.3d 679 (5th Cir. 1997), *aff'd District Court on reh'g*, 151 F.3d 269 (5th Cir. 1998), *cert. denied*, 526 U.S. 1064 (1999)

Muscarello v. United States: see United States v. Cleveland

Nat'l Bank of Commerce v. Associated Milk Producers, Inc., 22 F. Supp. 2d 942 (E.D. Ark. 1998), *aff'd*, 191 F.3d 858 (8th Cir.), *reh'g denied*, 1999 U.S. App. LEXIS 26485 (8th Cir. 1999)

Nat'l Fed'n of Indep. Bus. v. Sebelius: see Florida *ex rel.* Bondi v. U.S. Dep't of Health & Human Servs.

Nelson v. Tenn. Gas Pipeline Co., No. 95-1112, 1998 WL 1297690 (W.D. Tenn. Aug. 31, 1998), *aff'd*, 243 F.3d 244 (6th Cir.), *cert. denied*, 534 U.S. 822 (2001)

Nenno v. Dretke: see Nenno v. State

Nenno v. Quarterman: see Nenno v. State

Nenno v. State, 970 S.W.2d 549 (Tex. Crim. App. 1998), *habeas corpus denied sub nom.* Nenno v. Dretke, No. Civ.A.H 02 4907, 2006 WL 581271 (S.D. Tex. Mar. 7, 2006), *appeal dismissed sub nom.* Nenno v. Quarterman, 489 F.3d 214 (5th Cir. 2007), *cert. denied*, 552 U.S. 1281 (2008), *overruled by* State v. Terrazas, 4 S.W.3d 720, 727 (Tex. Crim. App. 1999) ("*Nenno* is overruled to the extent it decides Art. 38.22, Sec. 6 [of the Code of Criminal Procedure] applies only to custodial statements")

Newman v. Brent, Civ. No. 97-1647(TFH), 1998 U.S. Dist. LEXIS 10476 (D.D.C. July 8, 1998)

Nonnon v. City of New York, 897 N.Y.S.2d 671 (Sup. Ct. 2009) (unpublished table decision; for text of decision *see* 2009 WL 2045427), *aff'd*, 932 N.Y.S.2d 428 (App. Div. 2011)

N.Y. & Erie R.R. Co. v. Winans: see Winans v. N.Y. & Erie R.R. Co.

O'Gara v. United States, 560 F. Supp. 786 (E.D. Pa. 1983)

Ornelas v. United States: see United States v. Ornelas-Ledesma

Ortho Pharm. Corp. v. Wells: see Wells v. Ortho Pharm. Corp.

Ortiz v. Fibreboard Corp.: see Ahearn v. Fibreboard Corp.

Oxendine v. Merrell Dow Pharm., Inc., 506 A.2d 1100 (D.C. 1986) ("I"), *on subsequent appeal* 563 A.2d 330 (D.C. 1989) ("II"), *cert. denied*, 493 U.S. 1074 (1990), *appeal after remand* 593 A.2d 1023 (D.C. 1991) ("III"), *appeal after remand* 649 A.2d 825 (D.C. 1994) ("IV"), *remanded to* Civ. No. 82-1245, 1996 WL 680992 (D.C. Super. Ct. Oct. 24, 1996) ("V")

Paralyzed Veterans of Am. v. McPherson, No. C 06-4670 SBA, 2008 WL 4183981 (N.D. Cal. Sept. 9, 2008)

People v. Collins, 438 P.2d 33 (Cal. 1968)

People v. Cooper, No. 250583, 2005 WL 599740 (Mich. Ct. App. Mar. 15, 2005), *appeal denied*, 705 N.W.2d 118 (Mich. 2005) (unpublished table decision), *habeas corpus conditionally granted sub nom.* Cooper v. Lafler, No. 06-11068, 2009 WL 817712 (E.D. Mich. Mar. 26, 2009), *aff'd*, 376 F. App'x 563 (6th Cir. 2010), *vacated*, 132 S. Ct. 1376 (2012)

People v. Gates, 403 N.E.2d 77 (Ill. App. Ct. 1980), *aff'd*, 423 N.E.2d 887 (1981), *rev'd*, 462 U.S. 213, *reh'g denied by* 463 U.S. 1237 (1983)

People v. Kokoraleis, 547 N.E.2d 202 (Ill. 1989), *habeas corpus denied sub nom.* United States *ex rel.* Kokoraleis v. Dir. of Ill. Dep't of Corr., 963 F. Supp. 1473 (N.D. Ill.), *aff'd sub nom.* Kokoraleis v. Gilmore, 131 F.3d 692 (7th Cir. 1997), *cert denied*, 525 U.S. 829, *reh'g denied*, 525 U.S. 1034 (1998)

People v. Pizarro, 12 Cal. Rptr. 2d 436 (Ct. App. 1992), *appeal after remand* 123 Cal. Rptr. 2d 782 (Ct. App. 2002), *vacated by* 3 Cal. Rptr. 3d 21 (Ct. App. 2003), *appeal after remand* 158 Cal. Rptr. 3d 55 (Ct. App. 2013)

People v. Williams, 895 N.E.2d 961 (Ill. App. Ct. 2008), *aff'd in part, rev'd in part*, 939 N.E.2d 268 (Ill. 2010), *aff'd*, 132 S. Ct. 2221 (2012)

People v. Wright, No. 261380, 2006 WL 2271264 (Mich. Ct. App. Aug. 8, 2006)

Perry v. Novartis Pharm. Corp., 564 F. Supp. 2d 452 (E.D. Pa. 2008)

Perry v. United States, 755 F.2d 888 (11th Cir. 1985)

Phillips v. E.I. Dupont de Nemours & Co.: see *In re* Hanford Nuclear Reservation Litig. ("Group B")

Pick v. Am. Med. Sys., Inc., 958 F. Supp. 1151 (E.D. La. 1997)

Pinkney v. Dow Chemical Co.: see *In re* "Agent Orange" Prod. Liab. Litig.

Plunkett v. Merck & Co.: see *In re* Vioxx Prods. Liab. Litig. ("In re *Vioxx*—Plunkett/Experts")

Powell v. Texas, 392 U.S. 514, *reh'g denied*, 393 U.S. 898 (1968)

Prohaska v. Sofamor, S.N.C., 138 F. Supp. 2d 422 (W.D.N.Y. 2001)

Rains v. PPG Indus., Inc., 361 F. Supp. 2d 829 (S.D. Ill. 2004)

Ramirez v. State, 542 So. 2d 352 (Fla. 1989) ("I"), *appeal after remand* 651 So. 2d 1164 (Fla. 1995) ("II"), *appeal after new trial* 810 So. 2d 836 (Fla. 2001) ("III")

Reilly v. United States, 665 F. Supp. 976 (D.R.I. 1987), *motion denied*, 682 F. Supp. 150 (D.R.I.), *certified question answered by* 547 A.2d 894 (R.I.), *aff'd in part, remanded in part*, 863 F.2d 149 (1st Cir. 1988)

Richardson v. Richardson-Merrell, Inc., 649 F. Supp. 799 (D.D.C. 1986), *aff'd*, 857 F.2d 823 (D.C. Cir. 1988), *cert. denied*, 493 U.S. 882 (1989)

Robinson v. E.I. du Pont de Nemours & Co., 888 S.W.2d 490 (Tex. App. 1994), *rev'd*, 923 S.W.2d 549 (Tex. 1995)

Robinson v. Garlock Equip. Co., No. 05-CV-6553-CJS, 2009 WL 104197 (W.D.N.Y. Jan. 14, 2009)

Robinson v. United States, 533 F. Supp. 320 (E.D. Mich. 1982)

Rogers v. Sec'y of Health & Human Servs., No. 94-0089 V, 1999 WL 809824 (Fed. Cl. Sept. 17, 1999)

Rompilla v. Beard: see Commonwealth v. Rompilla

Rompilla v. Horn: see Commonwealth v. Rompilla

Rosen v. Ciba-Geigy Corp., 892 F. Supp. 208 (N.D. Ill. 1995), *aff'd*, 78 F.3d 316 (7th Cir.), *cert. denied*, 519 U.S. 819 (1996)

Ruiz Troche v. Pepsi Cola of P.R. Bottling Co., 177 F.R.D. 82 (D.P.R. 1997), *rev'd*, 161 F.3d 77 (1st Cir. 1998)

Sanderson v. Int'l Flavors & Fragrances, Inc., 950 F. Supp. 981 (C.D. Cal. 1996)

Sargent v. Mass. Accident Co., 29 N.E.2d 825 (Mass. 1940)

Savage v. Union Pac. R.R. Co., 67 F. Supp. 2d 1021 (E.D. Ark. 1999)

Sch. Dist. of Abington Twp. v. Schempp.: see Schempp v. Sch. Dist. of Abington Twp.

Schempp v. Sch. Dist. of Abington Twp., 201 F. Supp. 815 (E.D. Pa. 1962), *aff'd*, 374 U.S. 203 (1963)

Schudel v. Gen. Elec. Co., 120 F.3d 991 (9th Cir. 1997), *cert. denied*, 523 U.S. 1094 (1998), *appeal after remand* 35 F. App'x 481 (9th Cir.), *cert. denied sub nom.* Carlson v. Gen. Elec. Co., 537 U.S. 887 (2002), *abrogated by* Weisgram v. Marley Co., 528 U.S. 440 (2000) (holding that Court of Appeals may enter judgment as a matter of law upon determining that trial court erred in admitting evidence, and after excising such evidence, there remains insufficient evidence to support the jury's verdict)

Scopes v. State, 278 S.W. 57 (Tenn. 1925)

Selman v. Cobb Cnty. Sch. Dist., 390 F. Supp. 2d 1286 (N.D. Ga. 2005), *vacated and remanded by* 449 F.3d 1320 (11th Cir. 2006)

Seven-Sky v. Holder: see Mead v. Holder

Shahzade v. Gregory, 923 F. Supp. 286 (D. Mass. 1996)

Sindell v. Abbott Labs., 149 Cal. Rptr. 138 (Ct. App. 1978), *vacated*, 607 P.2d 924 (Cal.), *cert. denied sub nom.* Abbott Labs. v. Sindell, 449 U.S. 912 (1980)

Smith v. Rapid Transit, Inc., 58 N.E.2d 754 (Mass. 1945)

Snyder v. Sec'y of Health & Human Servs., No. 01-162V, 2009 WL 332044 (Fed. Cl. Feb. 12, 2009), *reconsideration denied by* 2009 WL 764611 (Fed. Cl. Mar. 16, 2009), *review denied by* 88 Fed. Cl. 706 (2009)

Soldo v. Sandoz Pharm. Corp.:

No. 98-1712, 2003 WL 22005007 (W.D. Pa. Jan. 16, 2002) ("*Soldo*—Bradford Hill")

244 F. Supp. 2d 434 (W.D. Pa. 2003) ("*Soldo*—falsifiability")

No. 98-1712, 2003 WL 22005007 (W.D. Pa. Jan. 16, 2002) (court-appointed experts required to file reports as part of the record) and 244 F. Supp. 2d 434 (W.D. Pa. 2003) (two court-appointed experts agree; one disagrees)

S. Pac. Co. v. Jensen: see *In re* Jensen

State v. Spann, 529 A.2d 1039 (N.J. Super. Ct. Law Div. 1987), *on appeal* 563 A.2d 1145 (N.J. Super. Ct. App. Div. 1989), *aff'd*, 617 A.2d 247 (N.J. 1993)

Summers v. Tice, 190 P.2d 963 (Cal. Dist. Ct. App.), *vacated by* 199 P.2d 1 (Cal. 1948)

Sutera v. Perrier Grp. of Am., 986 F. Supp. 655 (D. Mass. 1997)

Tehan v. United States *ex rel.* Schott: see United States *ex rel.* Shott v. Tehan

Thomas More Law Ctr. v. Obama, 720 F. Supp. 2d 882 (E.D. Mich. 2010), *aff'd*, 651 F.3d 529 (6th Cir. 2011), *cert. denied*, 133 S. Ct. 61 (2012)

Tobin v. Smithkline Beecham Pharm.: see Estates of Tobin *ex rel.* Tobin v. Smithkline Beecham Pharm.

Toner v. Lederle Labs., 779 F.2d 1429 (9th Cir. 1986), *certified question answered by* 732 P.2d 297 (Idaho), *answer to certified question conformed to by* 828 F.2d 510 (9th Cir.), *amending its original opinion* 831 F.2d 180 (9th Cir. 1987), *cert. denied*, 485 U.S. 942 (1988)

Torres v. Matt Dietz Co., No. 4,521, 2005 WL 4890697 (Tex. Dist. Ct. May 10, 2005), *rev'd*, 198 S.W.3d 798 (Tex. Ct. App. 2006)

Trammel v. United States: see United States v. Trammel

Truax v. Corrigan, 176 P. 570 (Ariz. 1918), *rev'd*, 257 U.S. 312 (1921)

Turpin v. Merrell Dow Pharm., Inc., 736 F. Supp. 737 (E.D. Ky. 1990), *aff'd*, 959 F.2d 1349 (6th Cir.), *cert. denied*, 506 U.S. 826 (1992)

Underwager v. Salter, No. 92-C-229-S, 1994 WL 242173 (W.D. Wis. June 4, 1993), *aff'd*, 22 F.3d 730 (7th Cir.), *cert. denied*, 513 U.S. 943 (1994)

United States *ex rel.* Kokoraleis v. Dir. of Ill. Dep't of Corr.: see People v. Kokoraleis

United States *ex rel.* Shott v. Tehan, 337 F.2d 990 (6th Cir. 1964), *vacated*, 382 U.S. 406, *reh'g denied*, 383 U.S. 931 (1966)

United States v. Bonds: see United States v. Yee

United States v. Brown (Michigan), 557 F.2d 541 (6th Cir. 1977)

United States v. Brown (New York), No. 05 Cr. 00538 (JBR) (S.D.N.Y. June 18, 2008) (transcript of bench ruling from Southern District Reporters), *aff'd*, 374 F. App'x 208 (2d Cir. 2010), *cert. denied*, 131 S. Ct. 619 (2010)

United States v. Carucci, 33 F. Supp. 2d 302 (S.D.N.Y. 1999)

United States v. Cleveland, 106 F.3d 1056 (1st Cir. 1997), *aff'd sub nom.* Muscarello v. United States, 524 U.S. 125 (1998), *abrogated by* Bailey v. United States, 516 U.S. 137 (1995) (interpreting the term "use" in the context of a federal firearm statute more narrowly than the *Cleveland* court); *superseded by statute*, Criminal Use of Guns, Pub. L. No. 105-386, 112 Stat. 3469 (1998)

United States v. Cordoba, 104 F.3d 225 (9th Cir. 1997), *remanded to* 991 F. Supp. 1199 (C.D. Cal. 1998), *aff'd*, 194 F.3d 1053 (9th Cir. 1999), *cert. denied*, 529 U.S. 1081 (2000)

United States v. Downing, 753 F.2d 1224 (3d Cir.), *remanded to* 609 F. Supp. 784 (E.D. Pa.), *aff'd*, 780 F.2d 1017 (3d. Cir. 1985)

United States v. Glynn, 578 F. Supp. 2d 567 (S.D.N.Y. 2008)

United States v. Hall, 93 F.3d 1337 (7th Cir. 1996), *remanded to* 974 F. Supp. 1198 (C.D. Ill. 1997), *aff'd*, 165 F.3d 1095 (7th Cir.), *cert. denied*, 527 U.S. 1029 (1999), *post-conviction relief dismissed*, No. 10-cv-1353, 2010 WL 4876191 (C.D. Ill. Nov. 18, 2010)

United States v. Hankey, 203 F.3d 1160 (9th Cir.), *cert. denied*, 530 U.S. 1268 (2000)

United States v. Havvard, 117 F. Supp. 2d 848 (S.D. Ind. 2000), *aff'd*, 260 F.3d 597 (7th Cir. 2001)

United States v. Hines, 55 F. Supp. 2d 62 (D. Mass. 1999)

United States v. Isaac, 134 F.3d 199 (3d Cir. 1998) (on rehearing)

United States v. Kilgus, 571 F.2d 508 (9th Cir. 1978)

United States v. Llera Plaza, Nos. CR. 98-362-10, 98-362-11, 98-362-12, 2002 WL 27305 (E.D. Pa. Jan. 7, 2002) (opinion designated as 179 F. Supp. 2d 492 was withdrawn) ("I"), *vacated and superseded on reconsideration by* 188 F. Supp. 2d 549 (E.D. Pa. 2002) ("II")

United States v. Mitchell, 199 F. Supp. 2d 262 (E.D. Pa. 2002), *aff'd*, 365 F.3d 215 (3d Cir.), *cert. denied*, 543 U.S. 974 (2004), *habeas corpus denied*, Civil Action Nos. 05-cv-823, 96-cr-407-1, 2007 WL 1521212 (E.D. Pa. May 21, 2007)

United States v. Ornelas-Ledesma, 16 F.3d 714 (7th Cir. 1994), *appeal after remand*, 52 F.3d 328 (7th Cir.) (unpublished table decision; for text of decision *see* 1995 WL 230342), *cert. granted in part by* 516 U.S. 963 (1995), *vacated by* 517 U.S. 690, *on remand to* 96 F.3d 1450 (7th Cir. 1996) (unpublished table decision; for text of decision *see* 1996 WL 508569)

United States v. Paiva, 892 F.2d 148 (1st Cir. 1989)

United States v. Poehlman:
No. 2:05-CR-38-1 (D. Vt. Mar. 16, 2005) (Plea Agreement)
No. 2:05-CR-38-1 (D. Vt. June 29, 2005) (Judgment in Criminal Case)

United States v. Skrede, No. 2009-09, 2009 WL 4250031 (A.F. Ct. Crim. App. Nov. 23, 2009), *review granted in part*, 69 M.J. 176 (C.A.A.F. 2010), *decision set aside by* 70 M.J. 358 (C.A.A.F. 2011)

United States v. Solomon, 753 F.2d 1522 (9th Cir. 1985), *superseded by rule*, Fed. R. Evid. 702, *as stated in* Daubert v. Merrell Dow Pharm., Inc., 43 F.3d 1311 (9th Cir. 1995)

United States v. Starzecpyzel, 880 F. Supp. 1027 (S.D.N.Y. 1995)

United States v. Thomas, No. CRIM CCB-03-0150, 2006 WL 140558 (D. Md. Jan. 13, 2006)

United States v. Trammel, 583 F.2d 1166 (10th Cir. 1978), *aff'd*, 445 U.S. 40 (1980)

United States v. Yee, 134 F.R.D. 161 (N.D. Ohio 1991), *aff'd sub nom.* United States v. Bonds, 12 F.3d 540 (6th Cir. 1993), *reh'g denied sub nom.* United States v. Yee, 1994 U.S. App. LEXIS 3679 (6th Cir. 1994)

Upjohn Co. v. Ambrosini: see Ambrosini v. Richardson-Merrell Inc.

USGen New England, Inc., v. Town of Rockingham, 862 A.2d 269 (Vt. 2004)

U.S. Steel Corp. v. Milward: see Milward v. Acuity Specialty Prods. Grp., Inc.

Virginia *ex rel.* Cuccinelli v. Sebelius, 728 F. Supp. 2d 768 (E.D. Va. 2010), *vacated*, 656 F.3d 253 (4th Cir. 2011), *cert. denied*, 133 S. Ct. 59 (2012)

Wal-Mart Stores, Inc. v. Dukes: see Dukes v. Wal-Mart Stores, Inc.

Walz v. Tax Comm'n, 292 N.Y.S.2d 353 (App. Div. 1968), *aff'd*, 246 N.E.2d 517 (N.Y. 1969), *aff'd*, 397 U.S. 664 (1970)

Wells v. Ortho Pharm. Corp., 615 F. Supp. 262 (N.D. Ga. 1985), *aff'd in part, modified in part, and remanded*, 788 F.2d 741 (11th Cir.), *reh'g denied*, 795 F.2d 89 (11th Cir.) (unpublished table decision), *cert. denied*, 479 U.S. 950 (1986)

West v. Randall, 29 F. Cas. 718 (C.C.D.R.I. 1820) (No. 17,424)

White-Rodgers v. Bitler: see Bitler v. A.O. Smith Corp.

Wiggins v. Corcoran: see Wiggins v. State

Wiggins v. Smith: see Wiggins v. State

Wiggins v. State, 597 A.2d 1359 (Md. 1991), *habeas corpus granted sub nom.* Wiggins v. Corcoran, 164 F. Supp. 2d 538 (D. Md. 2001), *rev'd*, 288 F.3d 629 (4th Cir.), *cert. granted in part sub nom.* Wiggins v. Smith, 537 U.S. 1027 (2002), *rev'd*, 539 U.S. 510 (2003)

Williams v. Commonwealth, 360 S.E.2d 361 (Va. 1987), *cert. denied*, 484 U.S. 1020 (1988), *habeas corpus denied sub nom.* Williams v. Warden of Mecklenburg Corr. Ctr., 487 S.E.2d 194 (Va. 1997), *grant of habeas corpus rev'd in part sub nom.* Williams v. Taylor, 163 F.3d 860 (4th Cir. 1998), *stay granted by* 526 U.S. 1048 (1999), *rev'd*, 529 U.S. 362 (2000)

Williams v. Illinois: see People v. Williams

Williams v. Long, 585 F. Supp. 2d 679 (D. Md. 2008)

Williams v. Taylor: see Williams v. Commonwealth

Williams v. Virginia: see Williams v. Commonwealth

Williams v. Warden of Mecklenburg Corr. Ctr.: see Williams v. Commonwealth

Wilson v. Merrell Dow Pharm., Inc., 893 F.2d 1149 (10th Cir. 1990)

Winans v. N.Y. & Erie R.R. Co., 30 F. Cas. 269 (C.C.N.D.N.Y. 1856), *aff'd*, 62 U.S. 88 (1858)

Ybarra v. Spangard, 146 P.2d 982 (Cal. Dist. Ct. App.), *vacated by* 154 P.2d 687 (Cal. 1944)

CANADA

R v. Mohan, [1994] 2 S.C.R. 9 (Can.)

R. v. J. (J.-L.), [2000] 2 S.C.R. 600 (Can.)

ENGLAND

Alsop v. Bowtrell, (1619) 79 Eng. Rep. 464 (K.B.); (1619) Cro. Jac. 541

Byrne v. Boadle, (1863) 159 Eng. Rep. 299 (Ex.); 2 H. & C. 722

Folkes v. Chadd, (1782) 99 Eng. Rep. 589 (K.B.); 3 Doug. 157

R v. Doheny, [1997] 1 Crim. App. 369 (Eng.)

The Trial of the Earl of Pembroke, (1678) 6 Cobb. St. Tr. 1310. (K.B.) (Eng.)

ITALY

Cass. Pen., sez. IV, 13 Dicembre 2010, n. 43786

MEXICO

Conocimientos Científicos. Características que deben tener para que pueden ser tomados en cuenta por el juzgador al momento de emitir su fallo, Suprema Corte de Justicia [SCJN] [Supreme Court], Semanario Judicial de la Federación y Su Gaceta, Novena Época, tomo XXV, Marzo de 2007, Tesis Aislada 1a. CLXXXVII/2006, Página 258 (Mex.)

Statutes, etc., Cited

CONSTITUTION CITED: UNITED STATES

Art I, § 8, cl 3 (Commerce Clause)

Art I, § 8, cl 18 (Necessary and Proper Clause)

Amend I (Establishment Clause)

Amend IV (Search and Seizure Clause)

Amend VI (Confrontation Clause)

ACTS & STATUTES CITED: UNITED STATES

(i) Federal

28 USC § 1407 (2006) (multidistrict litigation)

Espionage Act: see Sedition Act

Megan's Law, 42 USC §§ 13701 (note), 14071(d) (1994 & Supp 1996), repealed by the Adam Walsh Child Protection and Safety Act of 2006 § 129, Pub L No 109-248, 120 Stat 587, 600

National Childhood Vaccine Injury Act of 1986, Pub L No 99–660, 100 Stat 3743, 3755-84, codified at 42 USC §§ 300aa-1–300aa-34

National Swine Flu Immunization Program of 1976, Pub L No 94-380, 90 Stat 1113, codified at 42 USC § 247b (j)-(l), repealed by § 928, Pub L No 97-35, 95 Stat 357, 569 (1981)

Patient Protection and Affordable Care Act, Pub L No 111-148, 124 Stat 119 (2010)

Sedition Act, Pub L No 65-150, 40 Stat 553 (1918) (amendment to the Espionage Act of 1917), repealed by Pub Res No 66–64, 41 Stat 1359 (1921)

Suits and Costs in the Courts of the United States Act of 1813, 3 Stat 19, 21

Swine Flu Immunization Program: see National Swine Flu Immunization Program

Toxic Substances Control Act, Pub L No 94-469, 90 Stat 2003, 2025 (1976), codified at 15 USC § 2605(e)

(ii) State

Delaware:

11 Del Code Ann § 851 (Mitchie Supp 2012)

Florida:

Act of June 4, 2013, Chapter 2013-107, Laws of Florida, to be codified at Fla Stat §§ 90.702, 90.704, available at http://laws.flrules.org/2013/107

Fla Stat § 316.193 (driving under the influence; penalties)

Jimmy Ryce Involuntary Civil Commitment for Sexually Violent Predators' Treatment and Care Act (Jimmy Ryce Law), 1998 Fla Laws 98-64, as amended, codified at Fla Stat § 394.910 et seq.

Minnesota:

Minn Stat Ann § 609.53 (West 2009)

Missouri:

Mo Ann Stat § 570.080 (Vernon 1999 & Supp 2012)

New Jersey:

Megan's Law, NJ Stat Ann §§ 2C:7-1 to -19 (West 2005) (the 1994 statutes (§§ 2C:7-1 to -11) and the 2001 statutes (§§ 2C:7-12 to -19) were designated as "Megan's Law" by 2001 NJ Sess Law Serv 167 § 8 (West))

Tennessee:

1925 Ten Pub Acts 27 (Anti-Evolution Act)

Texas:

Texas Code of Crim Proc Ann art 37.071 (Vernon 2006 & Supp 2012)

Model Laws: United States

Model Penal Code § 223.6(2) (ALI 1962), in 10A *Uniform Laws Annotated* 561 (West Group 2001)

COURT RULES CITED: UNITED STATES

(i) Federal

FRCP 23 (class actions)
FRCP 42 (consolidation; separate trials)
FRCP 53 (appointment of "Special Masters")
FRE 102 (purpose and construction)
FRE 103 (rulings on evidence, e.g., plain error rule)
FRE 104 (preliminary questions, e.g., questions of admissibility generally)
FRE 106 (remainder of or related writings or recorded statements)
FRE 402 (general admissibility of relevant evidence)
FRE 403 (excluding relevant evidence for prejudice, confusion, waste of time, or other reasons)
FRE 407 (subsequent remedial measures)
FRE 702 (testimony by expert witnesses)
FRE 706 (court-appointed expert witnesses)
FRE 902 (evidence that is self-authenticating)

(ii) State

Michigan:
Mich Rule Evid 702

Michigan Supreme Court, "Rule 702. Testimony by Experts" and "Staff Comment to 2004 Amendment," in *Michigan Rules of Court—State* ([Eagan, MN?]: Thomson/West, 2008), 587.

Pennsylvania:
Pa Rule Evid 702

ADMINISTRATIVE MATERIALS CITED: UNITED STATES

Environmental Protection Agency (EPA), Guidelines for Carcinogen Risk Assessment, 51 Fed Reg 33992 (1986)

STATUTES CITED: FOREIGN

Colombia

Código de Procedimiento Penal [CPP] art 422

Bibliography

Adrogue, Sofia, "The Post-*Daubert* Court: 'Amateur Scientist' Gatekeeper or Executioner?" *Houston Lawyer* 35 (1998): 10–16.

Aitken, Colin, Paul Roberts, and Graham Jackson, *Fundamentals of Probability and Statistical Evidence in Criminal Proceedings: Guidance for Judges, Lawyers, Forensic Scientists and Expert Witnesses* (London: Royal Statistical Society, 2010).

Allen, Arthur, *Vaccine: The Controversial Story of Medicine's Greatest Lifesaver* (New York: W. W. Norton, 2007).

Allen, Michael E., *Florida Criminal Procedure* (Eagan, MN: Thomson Reuters, 2010).

Allen, Ronald J., "A Reconceptualization of Civil Trials," *Boston University Law Review* 66 (1986): 401–37. Reprinted in Tillers and Green, eds., *Probability and Inference in the Law of Evidence*, 21–60. [Page references are to the reprinted version.]

——."Expertise and the *Daubert* Decision," *Journal of Criminal Law & Criminology* 84, no.4 (1994): 1157–75.

Altman, Lawrence K., "For Science's Gatekeepers, a Credibility Gap," *New York Times*, May 2, 2006, F1.

American Bar Association, *Guidelines for the Appointment and Performance of Defense Counsel in Death Penalty Cases*, Guideline 10.7, 76 (revised ed., Feb. 2003), available at http://www.fjc.gov/public/pdf.nsf/lookup/DPen0709.pdf/$file/DPen0709.pdf.

American Medical Association, http://www.ama-assn.org/ama/pub/physician-resources/medical-ethics/code-medical-ethics.page.

American Society for Microbiology, http://www.asm.org/index.php/governance/code-of-ethics.

Andrewes, A., "The Growth of the Athenian State," in John Boardman and N. G. L. Hammond, eds., *Cambridge Ancient Histories* (Cambridge: Cambridge University Press, 1983), III, Part 3, *The Expansion of the Greek World, Eighth to Sixth Centuries B.C.*, chapter 43, 360–91.

Angell, Marcia, "Is Scientific Medicine for Sale?" *New England Journal of Medicine* 342 (2000): 1516–18.

Angier, Natalie, "High Court to Consider Rules on Use of Scientific Evidence," *New York Times*, January 2, 1993, 1, available at ProQuest Historical Newspapers The New York Times (1851–2003).

Annas, George J., and Michael A. Grodin, *The Nazi Doctors and the Nuremburg Code: Human Rights in Human Experimentation* (New York: Oxford University Press, 1992).

Anonymous, *The Sacco and Vanzetti Case: Transcript of the Record of the Trial of Nicola Sacco and Bartolemeo Vanzetti in the Courts of Massachusetts and Subsequent Proceedings*, 1920–27 (Mamaroneck, NY: Paul P. Appel, 1969).

Aristotle, *Metaphysics*, trans. W. D. Ross, in Richard McKeon, ed., *The Basic Works of Aristotle* (New York: Random House, 1941), 689–935.

Armitage, Peter, "Bradford Hill and the Randomized Controlled Trial," *Pharmaceutical Medicine* 6 (1992): 23–37.

——. "Austin Bradford Hill" (version 3), *StatProb: The Encyclopedia Sponsored by Statistics and Probability Societies* (n.d.), available at http://statprob.com/encyclopedia/AustinBradfordHILL.html.

Armstrong, David, "Bitter Pill: How the *New England Journal of Medicine* Missed Warning Signs in Vioxx—Medical Weekly Waited Years to Report Flaws in Article That Praised Pain Drug—Merck Seen as 'Punching Bag,'" *Wall Street Journal*, May 15, 2006, A1, A10.

Austen, Jane, *Pride and Prejudice* (1813), in *The Works of Jane Austen* (London: Spring Books, 1966), 171–343.

Austin, J. L., "On Truth," *Proceedings of the Aristotelian Society, Supplement* 24 (1950): 111–28. Reprinted in Urmson and Warnock, eds., *Philosophical Papers of J. L. Austin*, 85–101, and in George Pitcher, ed., *Truth* (Englewood Cliffs, NJ: 1950), 18–31.

——. "Performative Utterances" (from a talk given on BBC Radio, 1956), in Urmson and Warnock, eds., *Philosophical Papers of J. L. Austin*, 220–39.

——. *Sense and Sensibilia* (Oxford: Clarendon Press, 1962).

Avery, Oswald T., Colin M. MacCleod, and Maclyn McCarty, "Studies of the Chemical Nature of the Substance Inducing Transformation in Pneumococcal Types," *Journal of Experimental Medicine* 79 (1994):137–58.

Ayala, Francisco J., and Bert Black, "Science and the Courts," *American Scientist*, 81 (June 1, 1993): 230–39.

Ayer, A.J., *Language, Truth and Logic* (London: Victor Gollancz Ltd., 1936).

——., ed., *Logical Positivism* (New York: Free Press, 1959).

Ayer, A. J., "Truth, Verification and Verisimilitude," in Schilpp, ed., *The Philosophy of Karl Popper*, vol. 2, 684–92.

Bacon, Francis, *The Advancement of Learning* (1605), in Basil Montagu, ed., *The Works of Francis Bacon* (London: William Pickering, 1825), vol. II.

Bailar, John C., "Reliability, Fairness, Objectivity and Other Inappropriate Goals in Peer Review," *Behavioral and Brain Sciences* 14 (1991): 137–38.

Bailey, Linda A., Leon Gordis, and Michael D. Green, "Reference Guide on Epidemiology," in Federal Judicial Center, *Reference Manual on Scientific Evidence*, 1st ed., 123–80.

Bandow, Doug, "Keeping Junk Science Out of the Courtroom," *Wall Street Journal*, July 26, 1999, A23.

Barry, John M., *The Great Influenza: The Epic Story of the Deadliest Plague in History* (New York: Penguin Books, 2004).

Bartlett, Robert, *Trial by Fire and Water: The Medieval Judicial Ordeal* (Oxford: Clarendon Press, 1986).

Beecher-Monas, Erica, and Edgar Garcia-Rill, "Genetic Predictions of Future Dangerousness: Is There a Blueprint for Violence?" *Law & Contemporary Problems* 69 (2006): 301–41.

Begley, Sharon, "Despite Its Reputation, Fingerprint Evidence Isn't Really Infallible," *Wall Street Journal*, June 4, 2004, B1.

——. "Science Journals Artfully Try to Boost Their Rankings," *Wall Street Journal*, June 5, 2006, B1, B8.

Begley, Sharon, and Adam Rogers, "War of the Worlds: There Are No Little Green Men on Mars. But There Are Some Very Hostile Fellows on Earth Debating Whether There Was Life on the Red Planet," *Newsweek*, February 10, 1997, 56–58.

Behe, Michael J., *Darwin's Black Box: The Biochemical Challenge to Evolution* (New York: Free Press, 1996).

Benedict, Jeff, *No Bone Unturned: The Adventures of a Top Smithsonian Forensic Scientist and the Legal Battle for American's Oldest Skeletons* (New York: HarperCollins Publishers, 2003).

"Bendectin: FDA Approved Drugs," available at http://www.fdaapproveddrugs.us/bendectin.html.

Bentham, Jeremy, *A Treatise on Judicial Evidence*, ed. M. Dumont (1825; Littleton, CO: Fred B. Rothman and Co., 1981).

——. *Rationale of Judicial Evidence* (London: Hunt and Clarke, 1827; New York: Garland, 1978). (5 vols.)

Berenson, Alex, "Merck Admits a Data Error on Vioxx," *New York Times*, May 3, 2006, C1, available at 2006 WLNR 9291555.

Berger, Margaret, "Lessons from DNA: Restriking the Balance Between Finality and Justice," in Lazer, David, ed., *DNA and the Criminal Justice System: The Technology of Justice*, 109–131.

Bergmann, Gustav, *Philosophy of Science* (Madison, WI: University of Wisconsin Press, 1957).

Bernstein, Alan, "Crime Lab Scandal Leaves Prosecutor Feeling Betrayed: Owmby Says Sutton Case Tests Faith in Justice System," *Houston Chronicle*, May 16, 2003, 23.

Bernstein, Richard B., "Introduction," in Bernstein, ed., *The Constitution of the United States with the Declaration of Independence and the Articles of Confederation* (New York: Barnes and Noble, 2002), 5–25.

Bero, Lisa A., et al., "The Publication of Sponsored Symposiums in Medical Journals," *New England Journal of Medicine* 327 (1992): 1135–40.

Berry, John M., *The Great Influenza* (New York: Penguin Books, 2004).

Beyea, Jan, and Daniel Berger, "Scientific Misconceptions among *Daubert* Gatekeepers: The Need for Reform of Expert Review Procedures," *Law & Contemporary Problems* 64 (2001): 327–72.

Billings, John Shaw, "Literature and Institutions," *American Journal of Medical Science* 72 (1876): 439–80.

Black, Bert, Francisco J. Ayala, and Carol Saffran-Brinks, "Science and Law in the Wake of *Daubert*: A New Search for Scientific Knowledge," *Texas Law Review* 72, no.4 (1994): 715–802.

Black, Henry Campbell, *Black's Law Dictionary* (St. Paul, MN: West Publishing Co., 6th ed., 1990).

Black, Max, "Probability," in Paul Edwards, ed., *The Encyclopedia of Philosophy* (New York: MacMillan Publishing Co. Inc., and the Free Press, 1967), vol. 6, 464–79.

Bombadier, Claire, et al., "Comparison of Upper Gastrointestinal Toxicity of Rofecoxib and Naproxen in Patients with Rheumatoid Arthritis," *New England Journal of Medicine* 343, no.21 (2000): 1520–28.

Bondurant, Stuart, Virginia Ernster, and Roger Herdman, eds. *Safety of Silicone Breast Implants* (Washington, DC: National Academies Press, 2000) (e-book, available at http://www.nap.edu/catalog/9602.html).

Bone and Cancer Foundation, "Osteonecrosis of the Jaw (ONJ)," available at www.boneandcancerfoundation.org.

Bonetta, Laura, "The Aftermath of Scientific Fraud," *Cell* 124, no.5 (March 10, 2006): 873–75.

Boole, George, *The Laws of Thought* (1854; reprinted New York: Dover, n.d.).

Borghetti, Jean-Sébastien, "Litigation on Hepatitis B Vaccination and Demyelinating Disease in France: Breaking Through Scientific Uncertainty in France," in Diego Papayannis, ed., *Uncertain Causation in Tort Law* (Cambridge: Cambridge University Press, forthcoming).

Boyer, Peter J., "Annals of Justice: DNA on Trial," *New Yorker*, January 17, 2000, 42–53.

Bradley, F. H., *Ethical Studies* (London: Henry S. King and Co., 1876).

——. *Appearance and Reality: A Metaphysical Essay* (Oxford: Clarendon Press, 1895).

——. *Essays on Truth and Reality* (Oxford: Clarendon Press, 1914).

Brent, Robert L., "Bendectin: Review of the Medical Literature of a Comprehensively Studied Human Nonteratogen and the Most Prevalent Tortogen-Litigen," *Reproductive Toxicology* 9, no.4 (1995): 337–49.

——. "Litigation-Produced Pain, Disease, and Suffering: An Experience with Congenital Malformation Lawsuits," *Teratology* 16, no.1 (1997):1–13.

——. "Response to Dr. Stuart Newman's Commentary on an Article Entitled 'Bendectin: Review of the Medical Literature of a Comprehensively Studied Human Nonteratogen and the Most Prevalent Tortogen-Litigen,'" *Reproductive Toxicology* 13, no.4 (1999): 245–53.

——. "Bendectin and Birth Defects: Hopefully, the Final Chapter," *Birth Defects Research* Part A, 67, no.2, (2003): 79–87.

Bresalier, Robert S., et al., "Cardiovascular Events Associated with Rofecoxib in a Colorectal Adenoma Chemoprevention Trial," *New England Journal of Medicine* 352 (2005): 1092–102.

——. et al., "Correction" (to "Cardiovascular Events Associated with Rofecoxib in a Colorectal Adenoma Chemoprevention Trial"), *New England Journal of Medicine* 355 (2006): 221.

Bridgman, Percy W., "The Struggle for Intellectual Integrity" (1933), in Bridgman, *Reflections of a Physicist*, 361–79.

——. "On 'Scientific Method'" (1949), in Bridgman, *Reflections of a Physicist*, 81–83.

——. *Reflections of a Physicist* (New York: Philosophical Library, 2nd ed., 1955).

Broad, William, and Nicholas Wade, *Betrayers of the Truth* (New York: Simon and Schuster, Touchstone Books, 1982).

Brodin, Mark S., "Behavioral Science Evidence in the Age of *Daubert*: Reflections of a Skeptic," *University of Cincinnati Law Review* 73 (2005): 862–943.

Broun, Kenneth S., et al., eds., *McCormick on Evidence* (St. Paul, MN: Thomson/West, 2006) (2 vols.).

Brown, Harvey (Judge), "Eight Gates for Expert Witnesses," *Houston Law Review* 36 (1999): 743–882.

Bryant, Dianne, et al., "How Many Patients? How Many Limbs? Analysis of Patients or Limbs in the Orthopedic Literature: A Systematic Review," *Journal of Bone and Joint Surgery* 88 (2006): 41–45.

Brynner, Rock, and Trent Stephen, *Dark Remedy: The Impact of Thalidomide and Its Revival as a Vital Medicine* (Cambridge, MA: Perseus Publishing, 2001).

Burnham, John C., "The Evolution of Editorial Peer Review," *Journal of the American Medical Association* 263 (1990): 1323–29.

Butler, Samuel, *The Way of All Flesh* (1903; New York: American Library, 1998).

Campbell, Terence W., and Demosthenes Lorandos, *Cross Examining Experts in the Behavioral Sciences* ([Eagan, MN?]: West/Thomson Reuters, September 2012).

Capron, Alexander Morgan, "*Daubert* and the Quest for Value-Free 'Scientific Knowledge' in the Courtroom," *University of Richmond Law Review* 30 (1996): 85–108.

Carey, Benedict, "Researcher Pulls His Name from Paper on Prayer and Fertility," *New York Times*, December 4, 2006, A15.

Carruth, Russellyn S., and Bernard D. Goldstein, "Relative Risk Greater than Two in Proof of Causation in Toxic Tort Litigation," *Jurimetrics* 45 (2001): 195–209.

Carter, K. Codell, "Koch's Postulates in Relation to the Work of Jakob Henle and Edwin Krebs," *Medical History* 29 (1985): 353–74.

Cecil, Joe S., et al., "Assessing Causation in Breast Implant Litigation: The Role of Science Panels," *Law & Contemporary Problems* 64 (2001): 139–90.

Center for the Renewal of Science and Culture, "The Wedge Strategy," available at www.kcfs.org/Fliers_articles/Wedge.html.

Cha, Kwang Y., et al., "Does Prayer Influence the Success of In Vitro Fertilization-Embryo Transfer? Report of a Masked, Randomized Trial," *Journal of Reproductive Medicine* 46 (2001): 781–87.

Chadbourn, James H., ed., *Wigmore on Evidence* (Boston: Little, Brown and Company, 1981).

Chan, An Wen, et al., "Empirical Evidence for Selective Reporting of Outcomes in Randomized Trials," *Journal of the American Medical Association* 291 (2004): 2457–65.

Chan, Effie J., Note, "The 'Brave New World' of *Daubert*: True Peer Review, Editorial Peer Review, and Scientific Validity," *NYU Law Review* 70 (1995): 100–134.

Chang, Kenneth, "Dwarf Planet, Cause of Strife, Gains 'The Perfect Name,'" *New York Times*, September 15, 2006, A20.

Cheseboro, Kenneth J., "Galileo's Retort: Peter Huber's Junk Scholarship," *American University Law Review* 42 (1993): 1637–1726.

Clifford, William Kingdon, "The Ethics of Belief" (1877) in Clifford, *The Ethics of Belief and Other Essays*, eds. Leslie Stephen and Frederick Pollock (London: Watts & Co., 1947), 70–96.

Cohen, L. Jonathan, *The Provable and the Probable* (Oxford: Clarendon Press, 1977).

Cole, Simon, "What Counts for Identity? The Historical Origins of the Methodology of Latent Fingerprint Identification," *Science in Context* 12 (1999): 139–72.

——. "Grandfathering Evidence: Fingerprint Admissibility from *Jennings* to *Llera Plaza* and Back Again," *American Criminal Law Review* 41 (2004): 1189–1276.

Committee on Model Jury Instructions of the Judicial Council of the Eleventh Circuit, *Eleventh Circuit Pattern Jury Instructions (Criminal Cases)* ([Eagan, MN?]: West/Thomson Reuters, 2010.)

Committee on Science, Engineering, and Public Policy, Panel on Scientific Responsibility and the Integrity of the Research Process, National Academy of Sciences, *Responsible Science: Ensuring the Integrity of the Research Process* (Washington, DC: National Academy Press, 1992) (2 vols.).

Cooper, William [H. S. Hoff], *The Struggles of Albert Woods* (1952: Harmonsdsworth, Middlesex, UK: Penguin Books, 1966).

Connors, Edward, Thomas Lundgren, Neal Miller, and Tom McEwen, *Convicted by Juries, Exonerated by Science*, National Institute of Justice (NIJ) Research Report (June 1996).

Counts, George S., and Nucia Lodge, *The Country of the Blind: The Soviet System of Mind Control* (Boston: Houghton Mifflin, 1949).

Couzin, Jennifer, and Katherine Unger, "Cleaning Up the Paper Trail," *Science* 312 (2006): 38–43.

Crick, Francis, *What Mad Pursuit: A Personal View of Scientific Discovery* (New York: Basic Books, 1988).

Dante, Ed, "The Shadow Scholar: The Man Who Writes Your Student Papers Tells His Story," *Chronicle of Higher Education*, November 12, 2010, available at http://chronicle.com/article/The-Shadow-Scholar/125329/.

Darwin, Charles, *Selected Letters on Evolution and Origin of Species: With an Autobiographical Chapter*, ed. Francis Darwin (New York: D. Appleton and Company, 1893; reprinted New York: Dover, 1958).

David, Marian Alexander, *Correspondence and Disquotation: An Essay on the Nature of Truth* (New York: Oxford University Press, 1994).

Davidson, Donald, "Truth and Meaning," *Synthese*, 17 (1967): 304–23. Reprinted in Davidson, *Inquiries into Truth and Interpretation*, 17–36.

——. "What Metaphors Mean," *Critical Inquiry*, 5, no.1 (Autumn 1978): 31–47. Reprinted in *Inquiries into Truth and Interpretation*, 245–64.

——. *Inquiries into Truth and Interpretation* (Oxford: Clarendon Press, 1984, 2nd ed., 2001).

——. "A Nice Derangement of Epitaphs," in Ernest Lepore, ed., *Truth and Interpretation* (Oxford: Blackwell, 1986), 433–46.

Davidson, Richard A., "Sources of Funding and Outcomes of Clinical Trials," *Journal of Genera. Internal Medicine* 1 (1986): 155–58.

Davis, Percival, and Dean Kenyon, *Of Pandas and People* (Dallas, TX: Haughton Publishing Co., 3rd ed., 1993).

Davis, Theodore H., Jr. and Catherine B. Bowman, "No-Fault Compensation for Unavoidable Injuries: Evaluating the National Childhood Vaccine Injury Compensation Program," *University of Dayton Law Review* 16, no.2 (2010): 48–54.

Davis, Wendy, "The Immune Response," *ABA (American Bar Association) Journal* (October 2010): 48–54.

"De-*Daubertizing* Economic Damages Evidence," LostCompensation.com (January 2006), http://web.archive.org/web/20060522210711/http://www.lostcompensation.com/newsletters/v3_i1_2006.html.

de Finetti, Bruno, "La prévision: Ses lois logiques, ses sources subjectives," *Annales de l'Institut Henri Poincaré* 7 (1927): 1–68. In English translation by Henry E. Kyburg, Jr., in Kyburg and Smokler, eds., *Studies in Subjective Probability*, 93–158.

Delgado, Richard, "Beyond *Sindell*: Relaxation of Cause-in-Fact Rules for Indeterminate Plaintiffs," *California Law Review* 70 (1982): 881–908.

DeLoggio, Loretta, "Beyond a Reasonable Doubt: A Historical Analysis," *New York State Bar Journal* (April 1986): 19–25.

de Waal, Cornelis, *On Pragmatism* (Belmont, CA: Wadsworth, 2005).

Dershowitz, Alan M., "Casey Anthony: The System Worked," *Wall Street Journal*, July 7, 2011, A15.

Dervan, Lucian E., and Vanessa A. Edkins, "The Innocent Defendant's Dilemma: An Innovative Empirical Study of Plea Bargaining's Innocence Problem," *Journal of Criminal Law and Criminology* 103, no.1 (2013): 1–47.

DES Litigation Report, "Denial of Expert Witness Testimony Violates *Daubert*, Appeal States" (December 8).

Dewey, John, "The Problem of Truth" (1911), in Larry M. Hickman and Thomas M. Alexander, eds., *The Essential Dewey* (Indianapolis, IN: Indiana University Press, 1998), vol. 2, 101–30.

——. *The Quest for Certainty* (New York: Capricorn Books, 1929).

——. *Logic: The Theory of Inquiry* (New York: Henry Holt, 1938).

Doll, Richard, "Cancer," in Leslie John Witts, ed., *Medical Surveys and Clinical Trials: Some Methods and Applications of Group Research in Medicine* (London: Oxford University Press, 2nd ed., 1964).

Doll, Richard, and Austin Bradford Hill, "Smoking and Carcinoma of the Lung: Preliminary Report," *British Medical Journal* 2 (4682) (September 30, 1950): 739–48.

Drazen, Jeffrey M., "COX-2 Inhibitors—A Lesson in Unexpected Problems" *New England Journal of Medicine* 352 (2005): 1131–32.

Eccles, John C., "The World of Objective Knowledge," in Schilpp, ed., *The Philosophy of Karl Popper*, vol. 1, 349–70.

Editorial, "Is Science Really a Pack of Lies?" *Nature* 303 (1983): 361.

——. "Islam and Rape," *Wall Street Journal*, August 2006, A6.

——. "A Real Vaccine Scare," *Wall Street Journal*, October 16–17, 2010, A16.

Egilman, David, Joyce Kim, and Molly Biklen, "Proving Causation: The Use and Abuse of Medical and Scientific Information inside the Courtroom—An Epidemiologist's Critique of the Judicial Interpretation of the *Daubert* Ruling," *Food and Drug Law Journal* 56 (2003): 223–50.

Ellsworth, Laura E., "Court-Appointed Experts in State and Federal Courts: From Hens-Teeth to High Priests," *Pennsylvania Bar Association Quarterly* 71 (October 2000): 172–79.

Environmental Protection Agency (EPA), *Guidelines for Carcinogen Risk Assessment* (March 2005), available at http://www.epa.gov/ttnatw01/cancer_guidelines_final_3-25-05.pdf.

Epstein, Lee, and Gary King, "Empirical Research and the Goals of Legal Scholarship: The Rules of Inference," *University of Chicago Law Review* 69 (2002): 1–133.

Epstein, Robert, "Fingerprints Meet *Daubert*: The Myth of Fingerprint 'Science' Is Revealed," *Southern California Law Review* 75 (2002): 605–58.

Erichson, Howard M., "Mass Tort Litigation and Inquisitorial Justice," *Georgetown Law Journal* 87 (1999): 1983–2004.

Evans, Alfred S., "Causation and Disease: The Koch-Henle Postulates Revisited," *Yale Journal of Biology and Medicine* 49 (1976): 175–95.

Ezzell, Bill, "Laws of Racial Identification and Racial Purity in Nazi Germany and the United States: Did Jim Crow Write the Laws That Spawned the Holocaust?" *Southern University Law Review* 30 (2002–03): 1–13.

Fabro, Sergio, Robert L Smith, and Richard T. William, "Toxicity and Teratogenicity of Optical Isomers of Thalidomide," *Nature* 215 (July 15, 1967): 296.

Faigman, David L., "To Have and Have Not: Assessing the Value of Social Science to Law as Science and Policy," *Emory Law Journal* 38 (1989): 1005–95.

——. "The Law's Scientific Revolution: Reflections and Ruminations on the Law's Use of Experts in Year Seven of the Revolution," *Washington and Lee Law Review* 57 (2000): 661–84.

Fairweather, Abrol, and Linda Zagzebski, eds., *Virtue Epistemology: Essays on Epistemic Virtue and Responsibility* (New York: Oxford University Press, 2001).

Fallon, Eldon E., Jeremy T. Grabill, and Robert Pitard Wynne, "Bellwether Trials in Multi-District Litigation," *Tulane Law Review* 82 (2008): 2323–67.

Federal Judicial Center, *Reference Manual on Scientific Evidence* (Washington, DC: Federal Judicial Center, 1st ed., 1994).

——. *Reference Manual on Scientific Evidence* (Washington, DC: Federal Judicial Center, 2nd ed., 2000).

——. *Manual for Complex Litigation, Fourth* (St. Paul, MN: Thomson West, 2004).

Federal Judicial Center/ National Research Council, *Reference Manual on Scientific Evidence* (Washington, DC: National Academies Press, 3rd ed., 2011).

Feinstein, Alvan R., "Scientific Standards in Epidemiologic Studies of the Menace of Everyday Life," *Science* 242, no. 4883 (December 2, 1988): 1257–63.

Feldman, Richard, and Earl Conee, "Evidentialism," *Philosophical Studies* 48 (1985): 15–34.

Fellows, Jeffrey L., et al., "ONJ in Two Dental Practice-Based Research Network Regions," abstract available at http://www.ncbi.nlm.nih.gov/pubmed/21317245.

Fenner, G. Michael, "The *Daubert* Handbook: The Case, Its Essential Dilemma, and Its Progeny," *Creighton Law Review* 29 (1996): 939–1089.

Ferrer Beltrán, Jordi, *La valoración racional de la preuba* (Barcelona: Marcial Pons, 2007).

Feyerabend, Paul K., *Against Method: Outlines of an Anarchistic Theory of Knowledge* (London: New Left Books, 1978).

Finkelstein, Michael O., and William B. Fairley, "A Bayesian Approach to Identification Evidence," *Harvard Law Review* 83, no.3 (1969–70): 489–517.
Finley, Lucinda M., "Guarding the Gate to the Courthouse: How Trial Judges Are Using Their Evidentiary Screening Role to Remake Tort Causation Rules," *DePaul Law Review* 49 (1999–2000): 335–76.
Fisher, George, "Green Felt Jungle: The Story of *People v. Collins*," in Richard Lempert, ed., *Evidence Stories* (New York: Foundation Press, 2006), 7–28.
Flamm, "Bruce, The Columbia University 'Miracle' Study: Flawed and Fraud," *Skeptical Inquirer* 28 (September/October 2004): 25–31.
Florida Standard Jury Instructions in Criminal Cases ([Tallahassee, FL?]: The Florida Bar/LexisNexis, 7th ed., 2009).
Florida Standard Jury Instructions in Civil Cases ([Tallahassee, FL?]: The Florida Bar/LexisNexis, 2nd ed., 2010).
Food and Drug Administration, "FDA approves Diclegis for pregnant women experiencing nausea and vomiting," *FDA News Release* (April 8, 2013), available at http://www.fda.gov/NewsEvents/Newsroom/PressAnnouncements/ucm347087.htm.
Forbes, "Many Researches Break the Rules: Study," http://http://web.archive.org/web/20061017154742/http://www.forbes.com/forbeslife/health/feeds/hscout/2006/04/13/hscout532110.html (April 13, 2006).
Forrest, Barbara, and Paul R. Gross, *Creationism's Trojan Horse: The Wedge of Intelligent Design* (New York: Oxford University Press, 2004).
Fradella, Henry F., "From Insanity to Beyond: Diminished Capacity, Mental Illness, and Criminal Excuse in the Post-*Clark* Era," *University of Florida Journal of Law and Public Policy* 18, no.1 (2007): 7–91.
Frankel, Marvin F., "The Search for Truth: An Umpireal View," *University of Pennsylvania Law Review* 123, no.5 (1975): 1031–59.
Frankfurter, Felix, *The Case of Sacco and Vanzetti: A Critical Analysis for Lawyers and Laymen* (Boston: Little, Brown and Company, 1927).
Frápolli, María-José, "The Logical Enquiry into Truth," *History and Philosophy of Logic* 17 (1996): 179–97.
Frayn, Michael, *Headlong* (New York: Picador, 1999).
Freedman, David A., and Philip B. Stark, "The Swine Flu Vaccine and Guillain-Barré Syndrome: A Case Study in Relative Risk and Specific Causation," *Law & Contemporary Problems* 64 (2001): 49–62.
Freedman, Neal D., et al., "Cigarette Smoking and Subsequent Risk of Lung Cancer in Men and Women: Analysis of a Prospective Cohort Study," *Lancet Oncology* 9, no.7 (July 2008): 649–56, available at http://www.thelancet.com/journals/lanonc/article/PIIS1470-2045(08)70154-2/fulltext.
Friedman, Lawrence M., *A History of American Law* (New York: Simon and Schuster, 1973).
Friedman, Lee M., "Expert Testimony, Its Abuse and Reformation," *Yale Law Journal* 19 (1910): 247–257.
Friedman, Lee S., and Elihu D. Richter, "Relationship between Conflict of Interest and Research Results," *Journal of General Internal Medicine* 19, no.1 (January 2004): 51–56.
Friedman, Paul J., "Correcting the Literature Following Fraudulent Publication," *Journal of the American Medical Association* 263 (1990): 1416–19.

Galanter, Marc, "The Vanishing Trial: An Examination of Trials and Related Matters in Federal and State Courts," *Journal of Empirical Legal Studies* 1, no.3 (November 2004): 459–70.

García-Berthou, Emili, and Carles Alcaraz, "Incongruence between Test Statistics and P Values in Medical Papers," *BMC Medical Research Methodology* 4, no.13 (2004): 1–5.

Gardner, Martin J. and Jane Bond, "An Exploratory Study of Statistical Assessment of Papers Published in the *British Medical Journal*," *Journal of the American Medical Association* 263 (1990): 1355–57.

Garner, Bryan A., ed., *Black's Law Dictionary* (St. Paul, MN: Thomson Reuters, 9th ed., 2009.)

Genetic Home Reference, "Acute promyeloctytic leukemia," available at http://ghr.nlm.nih.gov/condition/acute-promyelocytic-leukemia.

Genewatch UK, *The Police National Database: Balancing Crime Detection, Human Rights and Privacy*, available at http://www.genewatch.org/uploads/f03c6d66-a9b354535738483c1c3d49e4/NationalDNADatabase.pdf (January 2005).

Gerontological Society of America, http://www.geron.org/Membership/code-of-ethics.

Gettier, Edmund, "Is Justified True Belief Knowledge?" *Analysis* 23 (1963): 121–23. Reprinted in Pojman, ed., *Theory of Knowledge: Classical and Contemporary Sources*, 142–43.

Givens, Richard A. (updated by Kevin Shirey), *Manual of Federal Practice, 2010 Cumulative Supplement* (New Providence, NJ: LexisNexus, 2010).

Glaberson, William, "Juries, Their Power under Siege, Find Their Role Is Being Eroded," *New York Times*, March 2, 2001, A1.

Godwin, Jean, "Wigmore's Chart Method," *Informal Logic* 20, no.3 (2000): 223–43.

Golan, Tal, *Laws of Men and Laws of Nature: The History of Scientific Expert Testimony in England and America* (Cambridge, MA: Harvard University Press, 2004).

Goldberg, Cary, "Judges' Unanimous Verdict on DNA Lessons: Wow!" *New York Times*, April 24, 1999, A10.

Goldman, Alvin I., "What Is Justified Belief?" in George Pappas, ed., *Justification and Knowledge* (Dordrecht, the Netherlands: Reidel, 1979), 1–21.

——. *Epistemology and Cognition* (Cambridge, MA: Harvard University Press, 1986).

——. "Two Concepts of Justification," in James Tomberlin, ed., *Philosophical Perspectives, 2: Epistemology* (Atascadero, CA: Ridgeview, 1988), 51–70.

——. *Knowledge in a Social World* (Oxford: Clarendon Press, 1999).

Goldstein, Bernard D., and Mary Sue Henifin, "Reference Guide on Toxicology," Federal Judicial Center, *Reference Manual on Scientific Evidence*, 1st ed., 181–220.

——. "Reference Guide on Toxicology," in Federal Judicial Center, *Reference Manual on Scientific Testimony* (Washington, DC: Federal Judicial Center, 2nd ed., 2000), 401–38.

Goldstein, Rebecca, "The Popperian Soundbite," in John Brockman, ed., *What Have You Changed Your Mind About? Today's Leading Minds Rethink Everything* (New York: Harper Perennial, 2009), 8–10.

Goodman, Nelson, "The New Riddle of Induction," in Goodman, *Fact, Fiction, and Forecast* (1954; 2nd ed., Indianapolis, IN: Bobbs-Merrill, 1965), 59–83.

Goodwin, Robert J., "The Hidden Significance of *Kumho Tire v. Carmichael*: A Compass for Problems of Definition and Procedure Created by *Daubert v. Merrell Dow Pharmaceuticals, Inc.*," *Baylor Law Review* 52 (2000): 603–46.

Gottesman, Michael H., "From *Barefoot* to *Daubert* to *Joiner*: Triple Play or Double Error?" *Arizona Law Review* 40 (1998): 753–80.

Gradmann, Christoph, "Heinrich Hermann Robert Koch," *Encyclopedia of Life Sciences*, available at http://www.els.net/WileyCDA/ElsArticle/refId-a0002493.html (Wiley, 2001).

Graham, Michael, *Federal Rules of Evidence in a Nutshell* (St. Paul, MN: West Publishing, 6th ed., 2003).

——. *Evidence* (St. Paul: Thomson/West, 2nd ed., 2007).

Grattan-Guinness, Ivor, "Truths and Contradictions about Karl Popper," *Annals of Science* 59 (2002): 89–96.

Gravitz, Lauren, "Biology's Image Problem," *Rockefeller University Scientist* 1 (Spring 2006): 1, 10–12.

Green, Michael D., "Expert Witnesses and Sufficiency of Evidence in Toxic Substances Litigation: The Legacy of Agent Orange and Bendectin Litigation," *Northwestern University Law Review* 86, no.3 (1991–92): 643–99.

——. *Bendectin and Birth Defects: The Challenges of Mass Toxic Substances Litigation* (Philadelphia, PA: University of Pennsylvania Press, 1996).

Green, Michael D., D. Michal Freedman, and Leon Gordis, "Reference Guide on Epidemiology," Federal Judicial Center, *Reference Manual on Scientific Evidence*, 2nd ed., 333–400.

——. "Reference Guide on Epidemiology," Federal Judicial Center/National Research Council, *Reference Manual on Scientific Evidence*, 3rd ed., 549–632.

Greenland, Sander, "Relation of Probability of Causation to Relative Risk and Doubling Dose: A Methodologic Error That Has Become a Social Problem," *American Journal of Public Health* 89, n.8 (1998): 1166–69.

——. "The Need for Critical Appraisal of Expert Witnesses in Epidemiology and Statistics," *Wake Forest Law Review* 39 (2004): 291–310.

Grisham, John, *The King of Torts* (New York: Doubleday/Dell, 2003).

Gross, John, ed., *The Oxford Book of Aphorisms* (New York: Oxford University Press, 1983).

Grover, Dorothy, *A Prosententialist Theory of Truth* (Princeton, NJ: Princeton University Press, 1992).

Grubin, Don, and Lars Madsen, "Lie Detection and the Polygraph: A Historical Review," *Journal of Forensic Psychiatry & Psychology* 16 (2005): 357–69.

Haack, Susan, *Deviant Logic* (Cambridge: Cambridge University Press, 1974; 2nd expanded ed., under the title *Deviant Logic, Fuzzy Logic: Beyond the Formalism* Chicago, IL: University of Chicago Press, 1996).

——. *Philosophy of Logics* (Cambridge: Cambridge University Press, 1978).

——."Do We Need 'Fuzzy Logic?'" *International Journal of Man-Machine Studies*, 11 (1979): 425–45. Reprinted in Haack, *Deviant Logic, Fuzzy Logic*, 232–42.

——."Is Truth Flat or Bumpy?" in D. H. Mellor, ed., *Prospects for Pragmatism* (Cambridge: Cambridge University Press, 1980), 1–20. Reprinted in Haack, *Deviant Logic, Fuzzy Logic*, 243–58.

——. *Evidence and Inquiry: Towards Reconstruction in Epistemology* (Oxford: Blackwell, 1993); expanded 2nd ed., *Evidence and Inquiry: A Pragmatist Reconstruction of Epistemology* (Amherst, NY: Prometheus Books, 2009).

——. "Knowledge and Propaganda: Reflections of an Old Feminist," *Partisan Review* LX, no.4 (1993): 556–64. Reprinted in Haack, *Manifesto of a Passionate Moderate,* 123–36.

——. "Multiculturalism and Objectivity," *Partisan Review* LXII, no. 3 (1995): 397–405. Reprinted in Haack, *Manifesto of a Passionate Moderate,* 137–48.

——. "Preposterism and Its Consequences," *Social Philosophy and Policy* 13, no.2 (1996): 296–315, and in Ellen Frankel Paul, Fred B. Miller, and Jeffrey Paul, eds., *Scientific Innovation, Philosophy and Public Policy* (Cambridge: Cambridge University Press, 1996), 296–315. Reprinted in Haack, *Manifesto of a Passionate Moderate,* 188–208.

——. "Reply to BonJour," *Synthese* 112, no.1 (1997): 25–35.

——. "A Foundherentist Theory of Empirical Justification," in Pojman, ed., *The Theory of Knowledge: Classical and Contemporary Sources,* 2nd ed., 1998, 283–93.

——. "Confessions of an Old-Fashioned Prig," in Haack, *Manifesto of a Passionate Moderate,* 7–30.

——. *Manifesto of a Passionate Moderate: Unfashionable Essays* (Chicago: University of Chicago Press, 1998).

——. "Staying for an Answer: The Untidy Process of Groping for Truth," *Times Literary Supplement* (July 9, 1999):12–14. Reprinted in Haack, *Putting Philosophy to Work,* 35–46.

——. "The Same, Only Different," *Journal of Aesthetic Education,* 36, no.3 (2002): 34–39. Reprinted in *Internationale Zeitschrift für Philosophie,* 2002, no.1 (2002): 18–22, and in Haack, *Putting Philosophy to Work,* 47–52.

——. "Realisms and Their Rivals: Recovering Our Innocence," *Facta Philosophica* 4, no.1 (2002): 67–88.

——. *Defending Science—Within Reason: Between Scientism and Cynicism* (Amherst, NY: Prometheus Books, 2003).

——. "Coherence, Consistency, Cogency, Congruity, Cohesiveness, &c.: Remain Calm! Don't Go Overboard!" *New Literary History* 35, no.2 (2004): 167–3. Reprinted in Haack, *Putting Philosophy to Work,* 69–82.

——. "An Epistemologist among the Epidemiologists," *Epidemiology* 15, no.5 (September 2004): 51–52. Reprinted in Haack, *Putting Philosophy to Work,* 195–98.

——. "Fallibilism and Faith, Naturalism and the Supernatural, Science and Religion," in Stefano Moriggi and Elio Sindoni, eds., *Dio, la natura e la legge* (Milan: Angelico/Mundo X, 2005), 143–54. Reprinted in Haack, *Putting Philosophy to Work,* 199–208.

——. "Formal Philosophy: A Plea for Pluralism," in John Symons and Vincent Hendricks, eds., *Formal Philosophy* (New York: Automatic Press/V.I. P., 2005), 77–98. Reprinted in Haack, *Putting Philosophy to Work,* 235–50.

——. "On Legal Pragmatism: Where Does 'The Path of the Law' Lead Us?" *American Journal of Jurisprudence* 50 (2005): 71–105.

——. "The Ideal of Intellectual Integrity, in Life and Literature," *New Literary History* 36, no.3 (2005): 359–73. Reprinted in Haack, *Putting Philosophy to Work,* 209–20.

——. "The Unity of Truth and the Plurality of Truths," *Principia* 9, no.21 (2005): 87–100. Reprinted in Haack, *Putting Philosophy to Work*, 53–68.

——. "On Legal Pragmatism: Where Does 'The Path of the Law' Lead Us?" *American Journal of Jurisprudence* 50 (2005): 71–105.

——. "Introduction: Pragmatism, Old and New," in Susan Haack and Robert E. Lane, eds., *Pragmatism, Old and New: Selected Writings* (Amherst, NY: Prometheus Books, 2006), 15–68.

——. "The Integrity of Science: What It Means, Why It Matters," in *Etica e Investigação nas Ciências da Vida—Actas do 10º Seminàrio do CNECV* (2006): 9–28. Reprinted in Haack, *Putting Philosophy to Work*, 121–40.

——. "On Logic in the Law: 'Something, but Not All,'" *Ratio Juris* 20, no.1 (2007): 1–31.

——. *Putting Philosophy to Work: Inquiry and Its Place in Culture* (Amherst, NY: Prometheus Books, 2008; 2nd, expanded ed., 2013). [Page references are to the 2nd ed., 2013.]

——. "Of Truth, in Science and in Law," *Brooklyn Law Review* 73, no.3 (2008): 895–1008.

——. "The Pluralistic Universe of Law: Towards a Neo-Classical Legal Pragmatism," *Ratio Juris* 21, no.4 (2008): 453–80.

——. "The Whole Truth and Nothing but the Truth," *Midwest Studies in Philosophy* XXXIII (2008): 20–35.

——. "'Know' Is Just a Four-Letter Word," in Haack, *Evidence and Inquiry*, 2nd ed., 301–31.

——. "The Growth of Meaning and the Limits of Formalism, in Science and Law," *Análisis Filosófico* XXIX, no.1 (2009): 5–29.

——. "Six Signs of Scientism" (first published, in Chinese and in Spanish, in 2010), *Logos & Episteme* III, no.1 (2012): 75–95. Reprinted in Haack, *Putting Philosophy to Work*, 105–20.

——. "Cracks in the Wall, A Bulge under the Carpet: The Singular Story of Religion, Evolution, and the US Constitution," *Wayne Law Review* 57, no.4 (2011):1303–32.

——. "Erkendelsesteori: hvem har brug for det?" ("Epistemology: Who Needs It?"), *Kritik* 200 (2011): 26–35. Also appeared, in Italian translation by Carlo Penco, under the title "Epistemologia: Chi Ne Ha Bisogno?" *Epistemologia* XXXIV (2011): 268–88. [English version available from the author.]

——. "Six Signs of Scientism," *Logos & Episteme* 3, no.1 (2012):75–95. Reprinted in Haack, *Putting Philosophy to Work*, 105–20.

——. "Técnicas forenses, ciencia impulsada por litígios y el problema de los incentivos perversos: Lecciones a partir de la saga *Ramirez*," in Monica María Bustamente Rúa, ed., *Derecho probatorio contemporáneo: Prueba cientifica y técnicas forenses* (Medellín, Colombia: Universidad de Medellín, 2012), 333–40. [English version available from the author.]

——. "Out of Step: Academic Ethics in a Preposterous Environment," in Haack, *Putting Philosophy to Work*, 251–68.

——. "Just Say 'No' to Logical Negativism," in Haack, *Putting Philosophy to Work*, 179–94.

——. "Die Welt des Unschuldigen Realismus," in Markus Gabriel, ed., *Der Neue Realismus* (Berlin: Suhrkamp, forthcoming).

Hacking, Ian M., *The Emergence of Probability* (Cambridge: Cambridge University Press, 1975).

Hailey, Arthur, *Strong Medicine* (London: Pan Books, 1984).

Haller, Christine, and Neal L. Benowitz, "Adverse Cardiovascular and Central Nervous System Events Associated with Dietary Supplements Containing Ephedra Alkaloids," *New England Journal of Medicine* 343 (2000): 1833–38.

Hand, Learned, "Historical and Practical Considerations Regarding Expert Testimony," *Harvard Law Review* 15 (1901): 40–58.

Hanlon, Michael, "Is This Proof of Life on Mars? The Meteorite That May Finally Have Resolved the Great Mystery," *Daily Mail* (London, UK), February 10, 2006, 40.

Hansen, Mogens Herman, *The Athenian Democracy in the Age of Demosthenes: Structure, Principles, and Ideology*, trans. J. A. Cook (Oxford: Blackwell, 1991).

Hazard, Geoffrey C., Jr., John L. Gedid, and Stefan Sowle, "An Historical Analysis of the Binding Effect of Class Suits," *University of Pennsylvania Law Review* 146 (1998): 1849–1948.

Heidegger, Martin, *Frage nach dem Ding* (1935–36), in Heidegger, *Gesamtausabe* (Frankfurt am Main: Vittorio Klostermann, 1984), vol. 41, ed. Petra Jaeger, 1–254.

Heilbrun, Robert, *Offer of Proof* (New York: Harper Torchbooks, 2003).

Heinzerling, Lisa, "Doubting *Daubert*," *Journal of Law & Policy* 14 (2006): 65–83.

Hempel, Carl G., "Studies in the Logic of Confirmation," *Mind* 54 (1945): 1–26, 97–121. Reprinted in Hempel, *Aspects of Scientific Explanation*, 3–46.

——. "Empiricist Criteria of Cognitive Significance: Problems and Changes" (adapted from "Problems and Changes in the Empiricist Criterion of Meaning," *Revue Internationale de Philosophie* 11 [January 1950]: 41–63, and "The Concept of Cognitive Significance," *Proceedings of the American Academy of Arts and Sciences* 80, no.1 [1951]: 61–77), in Hempel, *Aspects of Scientific Explanation*, 99–119.

——. "Postscript (1964) on Cognitive Significance," in Hempel, *Aspects of Scientific Explanation*, 120–22.

——. *Philosophy of Natural Science* (Englewood Cliffs, NJ: Prentice-Hall, 1966).

——. "The Irrelevance of the Concept of Truth for the Critical Appraisal of Scientific Theories" (originally published under the title "Il significato del concetto de verità per la valuazione critica delle teorie scientifiche," *Nuova Civiltà delle Macchine* VIII, no.4 [32] [1990]: 7–12); in William R. Shea and Antonio Spadafora, eds., *Interpreting the World* (Canton, MA: Science History Publications, 1992), 121–29. Reprinted in Richard Jeffrey, ed., *Selected Philosophical Essays [by] Carl G. Hempel* (Cambridge: Cambridge University Press, 2000), 75–84.

Henneckens, Charles H., et al., "Self-Reported Breast Implants and Connective Tissue Diseases in Female Health Professionals: A Retrospective Cohort Study," *Journal of the American Medical Association* 275, no.8 (1996): 616–21.

Hershey, A. D., and Martha Chase, "Independent Functions of Viral Protein and Nucleic Acid in Growth of Bacteriophage," *Journal of General Physiology* 36 (1952): 39–56.

Hill, Austin Bradford, *Principles of Medical Statistics* (London: Lancet, Ltd., 1937; 9th ed., 1971).

——. "The Statistician in Medicine" (Alfred Watson Memorial Lecture), *Journal of the Society of Actuaries* 88, no.II (1962): 178–91.

——. "The Environment and Disease: Association or Causation?" *Proceedings of the Royal Society of Medicine* 58 (1965): 295–300.

Hill, Austin Bradford, and I. D. Hill, *Bradford Hill's Principles of Medical Statistics* (London: Edward Arnold, 1991).

Hill, Kevin P., et al., "The ADVANTAGE Seeding Trial: A Review of Internal Documents," *Annals of Internal Medicine* 149, no.4 (August 19, 2008): 251–58.

Himes, Charles F., "The Scientific Expert in Forensic Procedure," 135 *Journal of the Franklin Institute* 135, no.6 (1893): 407–436.

Hinkle, Robert L., Chair, Advisory Committee on Evidence Rules, memorandum to Honorable Lee H. Rosenthal, Chair, Standing Committee on Rules of Practice and Procedure (May 6, 2009), United States Courts, available at http://www.uscourts.gov/uscourts/RulesAndPolicies/rules/jc09-2009/2009-09-Appendix-E.pdf.

Holmes, Oliver Wendell, Review of Langdell, *A Selection of Cases on the Law of Contracts*, 2nd ed. (1880; in Novick, ed., *Collected Works of Justice Wendell Holmes*, vol. 3, 102–04).

——. *The Common Law* (1881), in Novick, ed., *The Collected Works of Justice Holmes*, vol. 3, 109–324.

Holmes, Oliver Wendell "Speech at a Dinner Given to Chief Justice Holmes by the Bar Association of Boston" (1900), in Novick, ed., *The Collected Works of Justice Holmes*, vol. 3, 498–500.

Horrobin, David F., "The Philosophical Basis of Peer Review and the Suppression of Innovation," *Journal of the American Medical Association* 263 (1990): 1438–41.

Horton, Richard, "Expression of Concern: Non-Steroidal Anti-Inflammatory Drugs and the Risk of Oral Cancer," *Lancet* 367 (2006): 196.

——. "Retraction – Non-Steroidal Anti-Inflammatory Drugs and the Risk of Oral Cancer: A Nested Case-Control Study," *The Lancet* 367 (2006): 382.

Horwich, Paul, *Truth* (Cambridge, MA: Blackwell, 1990).

——. *From a Deflationary Point of View* (Oxford: Clarendon Press, 2004).

Howell, Thomas J., ed., *Cobbett's Complete Collection of State Trials and Proceedings for High Treason and Other Crimes and Misdemeanors from the Earliest Period to the Present Time* (London: R. Bagshaw, 1810), 34 vols.

Huber, Peter, "Junk Science in the Courtroom," *Valparaiso Law Review* 26 (1992): 723–55.

——. *Galileo's Revenge: Junk Science in the Courtroom* (New York: Basic Books, 1993).

Humes, Edward, *Monkey Girl: Evolution, Education, Religion, and the Battle for America's Soul* (New York: Ecco, 2007).

Humphrey, George F., "Scientific Fraud: The McBride Case," *Medicine, Science, and the Law* 32 (1992): 199–203.

Humphrey, George F., "Scientific Fraud: The McBride Case – Judgment," *Science Law* 34 (1994): 299–306.

Husni, Ronak, and Daniel L. Newman, *Muslim Women in Law and Society* (New York: Routledge, 2007).

"If It Walks Like a Fish . . .," *Newsweek*, April 27, 2007, 8.

Interlandi, Janeen, "An Unwelcome Discovery," *New York Times*, October 22, 2006 § 6 (Magazine), 98.

International Agency for Research on Cancer, "Some Thyrotropic Agents," *IARC Monographs on the Evaluation of Carcinogenic Risks to Humans* (Lyon, France: World Health Organization, vol. 79, 2001), 145–59, available at http://www.drugs.com/monograph/doxylamine-succinate.html.

——. "Preamble" to "A Review of Human Carcinogens," *IARC Monographs on the Evaluation of Carcinogenic Risks to Humans* (Lyon, France: World Health Organization, vol. 100, 2008).

International Early Lung Cancer Action Program Investigators, "Women's Susceptibility to Tobacco Carcinogens and Survival after Diagnosis of Lung Cancer," *Journal of the American Medical Association* 296, no.2 (2006): 180–84.

International Union of Biochemistry and Molecular Biology, http://www.iubmb.org/index.php?id=155.

Ionnadis, John P. A., "Contradicted and Initially Stronger Effects in Highly Cited Clinical Research," *Journal of the American Medical Association* 294 (2005): 218–28.

Ito, Takumi, Hideki Ando, and Horoshi Handa, "Teratogenic Effects of Thalidomide: Molecular Mechanisms," *Cell and Molecular Life Sciences*, available at http://link.springer.com/article/10.1007/s00018-010-0619-9 (2011).

Jaffe, Louis L., "*Res Ipsa Loquitur* Vindicated," *Buffalo Law Review* 1, no.1 (1951): 1–15.

Jaffee, Leonard R., "Of Probativity and Probability: Statistics, Scientific Evidence, and the Calculus of Chances at Trial," *University of Pittsburgh Law Review* 46 (1984–85): 925–1083.

James, Fleming, Jr., "Contributory Negligence," *Yale Law Journal* 62, no.1 (1953): 691–735.

James, William, "The Moral Philosopher and the Moral Life" (1891), in James, *The Will to Believe and Other Essays in Popular Philosophy*, eds. Frederick Burkhardt and Fredson Bowers (Cambridge, MA: Harvard University Press, 1979), 141–72.

——. "Philosophical Conceptions and Practical Results," *University Chronicle* (University of California, Berkeley) 1 (September 1898): 287–10; reprinted in James, *Pragmatism*, 255–70.

——. *Pragmatism* (1907), eds. Frederick Burkhardt and Fredson Bowers (Cambridge, MA: Harvard University Press, 1975).

——. *The Meaning of Truth* (1909), eds. Frederick Burkhardt and Fredson Bowers (Cambridge, MA: Harvard University Press, 1975).

Jamieson, Allan, and Scott Bader, "Got a Match, Guv?" available at http://www.barristermagazine.com/archive-articles/issue-49/got-a-match,-guv.html (2011).

Janin, Hunt and André Kahlmeyer, *Islamic Law: The Sharia from Muhammad's Time to the Present* (Jefferson, NC: McFarland and Company, 2007).

Johnson, Phillip E., *Darwin on Trial* (Washington, DC: Regnery Gateway, 1991; 2nd ed., Downers Grove, IL: Intervarsity Press, 1993).

Judicial Committee on Model Jury Instructions for the Eighth Circuit, *Manual of Model Criminal Jury Instructions for the District Courts of the Eighth Circuit* ([Eagan, MN?]: West/Thomson Reuters, 2011).

Judson, Horace Freeland, *The Eighth Day of Creation: Makers of the Revolution in Biology* (New York: Simon and Schuster, 1979).

——. "Structural Transformations of the Sciences and the End of Peer Review," *Journal of the American Medical Association* 272 (1994): 92–94.

Jurs, Andrew, "Judicial Analysis of Complex and Cutting-Edge Science in the *Daubert* Era: Epidemiological Risk Assessment as a Test Case for Reform Strategies," *Connecticut Law Review* 42, no.1 (2009): 49–100.

——. "Balancing Legal Process with Scientific Expertise: Expert Witness Methodology in Five Nations and Suggestions for Reform of Post-*Daubert* U.S. Reliability Determinations," *Marquette Law Review* 95, no.4 (2012): 1329–1415.

Kabat, Geoffrey C., Anthony B. Miller, and Thomas E. Rohan, "Reproductive and Hormonal Factors and Risk of Lung Cancer in Women: A Prospective Cohort Study," *International Journal of Cancer* 120, no. 10 (2007): 2214–20.

Kadane, Jay, and David Schum, *A Probabilistic Analysis of the Sacco and Vanzetti Evidence* (New York: John Wiley and Sons, 1996).

Kadri, Sadakat, *The Trial: A History, From Socrates to O. J. Simpson* (New York: Random House, 2005).

Konstantin Kakaes, review of Roger Weins, "*'Red Rover': Inside the Story of Robotic Space Exploration, from Genesis to the Mars Rover Curiosity*," *Washington Post*, May 10, 2013, available at http://articles.washingtonpost.com/2013-05-10/opinions/39164164_1_rover-curiosity-chemcam-previous-rovers.

Kaplan, John, "Decision Theory and the Factfinding Process," *Stanford Law Review* 20 (1968): 1065–92.

Kaye, David H., "Do We Need a Calculus of Weight to Understand Proof beyond a Reasonable Doubt?" in Tillers and Green, eds., *Probability and Inference in the Law of Evidence*, 129–45.

Kaye, David H., and David A. Freedman, "Reference Guide on Statistics," *Reference Manual on Scientific Evidence*, 3rd ed. (Washington, DC: National Academies Press, 2011), 211–302.

Keeton, W. Page et al., *Prosser and Keeton on the Law of Torts* (St. Paul, MN: West Publishing Co., 1984).

Keiter, Mitchell, "Just Say No Excuse: The Rise and Fall of the Intoxication Defense," *Journal of Criminal Law & Criminology* 87, no.2 (1997): 482–520.

Kevles, Bettyann Holtzmann, *Naked to the Bone: Medical Imaging in the Twentieth Century* (New Brunswick, NJ: Rutgers University Press, 1997).

Keynes, John Maynard, *A Treatise on Probability* (London: MacMillan and Co., Ltd., 1921).

Khanna, Roma, and Steve McVicker, "Police Chief Shakes Up Crime Lab; 2 Officials Quit, Others Disciplined," *Houston Chronicle*, June 13, 2003, A1.

——. "HPD Ignored Warnings, Ex-Lab Man Says: Retired Official Says He Cited 'Train Wreck,'" *Houston Chronicle*, June 23, 2003, A1.

Kierkegaard, Søren, *Journals* (1846), in Alexander Dru, ed., *A Selection from the Journals of Søren Kierkegaard* (New York: Oxford University Press, 1938).

Klein, Marc S., "Expert Testimony in Pharmaceutical Product Liability Actions," *Food, Drug, and Cosmetic Law Journal* 45, no.4 (1990): 393–442.

Knightley, Phillip, Harold Evans, Elaine Potter, and Marjorie Wallace, *Suffer the Children: The Story of Thalidomide* (New York: Viking, 1979).

Koertge, Noretta, "Popper and the Science Wars" (lecture for the Summer School on Theory of Knowledge, Madralin, Warsaw, August 16–31, 1997), available at http://www.indiana.edu/~koertge/PopLectI.html.

Kozinski, Alex, "Brave New World," *University of California Davis Law Review* 10 (1996–97): 997–1101.

Krause, Daniel A., John G. McCabe, and Joel D. Lieberman, "Dangerously Misunderstood: Representative Jurors' Reaction to Expert Testimony on Future Dangerousness in a Sexually Violent Predator Trial," *Psychology, Public Policy, and Law* 198, no.1 (2012): 18–49.

Kreuzer, Michaela, et al., "Hormonal Factors and Risk of Lung Cancer in Women?" *International Journal of Epidemiology* 32, no.1 (2003): 263–71.

Krimsky, Sheldon, *Science in the Private Interest* (Lanham, MD: Rowman and Littlefield, 2003).

Kronick, David A. "Peer Review in 18th-Century Scientific Journalism," *Journal of the American Medical Association* 263 (1990): 1321–22.

Kuhn, Thomas S., *The Structure of Scientific Revolutions* (Chicago: University of Chicago Press, 1962).

Kyburg, Henry E., Jr., and Howard E. Smokler, eds., *Studies in Subjective Probability* (New York: Wiley, 1964).

Lakatos, Imre, "Falsification and the Methodology of Scientific Research Programmes," in Imre Lakatos and Alan Musgrave, eds., *Criticism and the Growth of Knowledge* (Cambridge: Cambridge University Press, 1970), 91–195.

Lakoff, George, "A Cognitive Scientist Looks at *Daubert*," *American Journal of Public Health* 95 (2005): S114–20.

Landsman, Stephan, "Of Witches, Madmen, and Product Liability: An Historical Survey of the Use of Expert Testimony," *Behavioral Science and Law* 13, no.2 (1995): 131–57.

Langdell, Christopher Columbus, *A Selection of Cases on the Law of Contracts, with a Summary of the Topics Covered by the Cases* (Boston: Little, Brown, 2nd ed., 1879).

Larson, Edward J., *Trial and Error: The American Controversy over Creation and Evolution* (New York: Oxford University Press, 3rd ed., 2003).

Law Commission Report No.325, "Expert Evidence in Criminal Proceedings in England and Wales" (March 21, 2011) (London: The Stationery Office, 2011); also available at http://www.official-documents.gov.uk/document/hc1011/hc08/0829/0829.pdf.

Laudan, Larry, "Science at the Bar—Causes for Concern," *Science, Technology, and Human Values* 7, no.41 (1982): 16–19. Reprinted in Ruse, ed., *But Is It Science?* 351–55.

——."The Demise of the Demarcation Problem," in Robert S. Cohen and Larry Laudan, eds., *Physics, Philosophy, and Psychoanalysis* (Dordrecht, the Netherlands: D. Reidel Publishing Company, 1983), 111–27. Reprinted in Ruse, ed., *But Is It Science?* 337—50.

Lazer, David, "Introduction," in David Lazer, ed., *DNA and the Criminal Justice System: The Technology of Justice*, 3–12.

Lazer, David, ed., *DNA and the Criminal Justice System: The Technology of Justice* (Cambridge, MA: MIT Press, 2004).

Legal Information Bulletin, Bruesewitz v. Wyeth, Inc. (09–152), available at http://topics.law.cornell.edu/supct/cert/09-152.

Lempert, Richard, "The New Evidence Scholarship: Analyzing the Process of Proof," in Tillers and Green, ed., *Probability and Inference in the Law of Evidence*, 61–102.

Letzing, John, "A California City Is Tweeting—Chirping, Actually—in a Big Way," *Wall Street Journal*, January 17, 2012, A1, A12.

Lévesque, Linda, James M. Brophy, and Bin Zhang, "Time Variations in the Risk of Myocardial Infarction among Elderly Users of Cox-2 Inhibitors," published electronically at http://www.cmaj.ca/ (May 2, 2006) and, abridged, in *Canadian Medical Association Journal* 174, no.11 (May 23, 2006): 1563–69.

Levi, Edward, *Introduction to Legal Reasoning* (Chicago: University of Chicago Press, 1949).

Levin, Morton L., Hyman Goldstein, and Paul R. Gerhardt, "Cancer and Tobacco Smoking: A Preliminary Report", *Journal of the American Medical Association* 143, no.4 (1950): 336–38.

Lewis, Sinclair, *Arrowsmith* (1925; New York: Signet Classics, 1998).

Lock, Stephen, *A Difficult Balance: Editorial Peer Review in Medicine* (London: Nuffield Provincial Hospitals Trust, 1985).

Lock, Stephen, and Jane Smith, "What Do Peer Reviewers Do?" *Journal of the American Medical Association* 263 (1990): 1341–43.

Locke, John, *The Conduct of the Understanding*, in *Posthumous Works of Mr. John Locke* (London: A. and J. Churchill, 1706), 1–137.

Long, Ray, and Monique Garcia, "Quinn Expected to Sign Death Penalty Ban," *Chicago Tribune* (March 8, 2011), available at http://articles.chicagotribune.com/2011-03-08/news/ct-met-quinn-death-penalty-0309-20110308_1_death-penatlty-error-and-incompetence-capital-punishment.

Louisell, David W., and Christopher B. Mueller, *Federal Evidence* (Rochester, NY: Lawyers Co-operative Publishing Co., 1977–81) (5 vols.).

Lustre, Alice B., Annotation, "Post-*Daubert* Standards for Admissibility of Scientific and Other Expert Evidence in State Courts," *ALR* (*American Law Reports*) 5th, 90 (2001) 453–545.

Lysaght, Pamela, *Michigan Legal Research* (Durham, NC: Carolina Academic Press, 2006).

Mach, Ernst, "On the Principle of Conservation of Energy" and, especially, "On the Principle of Comparison in Physics," in *Populärwissenschaftlich Vorlesungen* (Leipzig, 1894), trans. Thomas J. McCormack, *Popular Scientific Lectures* (La Salle, IL: Open Court, 1943), 137–85 and 236–58.

Maitland, Frederic William, *The Forms of Action at Common Law*, eds. A. H. Chaytor and W. J. Whittaker (Cambridge: Cambridge University Press, 1909).

Maloney, Frank, "Gregor Johann Mendel O.S.A.," available at http://astro4.ast.vill.edu/mendel/gregor.htm.

Mangum, Charles S., *The Legal Status of the Negro* (Chapel Hill, NC: University of North Carolina Press, 1940).

March, Astara, "Drug Revived to Fight Morning Sickness," *Nurse Week* (October 11, 2000), available at http://web.archive.org/web/20011121155605/http://www.nurseweek.com/news/00-10/1011morn.asp.

Marcin, Raymond B., "Searching for the Origin of Class Action," *Catholic University Law Review* 23, no.3 (1974): 515–24.

Marquéz-Garbán, Diana C., et al., "Estrogen Receptor Signaling Pathways in Human Non-Small Cell Lung Cancer," *Steroids* 72, no.2 (February 2007): 135–43.

Martini, Steve, *Undue Influence* (New York: G. P. Putnam, 1994).

——. *The Rule of Nine* (New York: Harper, 2010).

Martinson, Brian C., et al., "Scientists Behaving Badly," *Nature* 435 (2005): 737–38.

Maugh, Thomas H., III, "Probe Enters Mars Orbit," *Los Angeles Times*, March 11, 2006, A12.

Maxwell, Simon R. J., and David J. Webb, "Cox-2 Selective Inhibitors – Important Lessons Learned," *Lancet* 365 (2005): 449–51.

MayoClinic.com, "Post-traumatic stress disorder (PTSD)," available at http://www.mayoclinic.com/health/post-truamatic-stress-disorder/DS00246.

McCormick, Charles T., *Handbook of the Law of Evidence* (St. Paul, MN: West Publishing Co., 1954).

McCutchen, Charles W., "Peer Review: Treacherous Servant, Disastrous Master," *Technology Review* 94 (1991): 28–51.

McGarity, Thomas O., "Our Science Is Sound Science and Their Science Is Junk Science: Science-Based Strategies for Avoiding Accountability and Responsibility for Risk-Producing Products and Activities," *Kansas Law Review* 52, no.4 (2004): 897–937.

McGettigan, Patricia, and David Henry, "Cardiovascular Risk and Inhibition of Cyclooxygenase: A Systematic Review of the Observational Studies of Selective and Non-Selective Inhibitors on Cyclooxygenase," *Journal of the American Medical Association* 296, no.2 (October 4, 2006), 1633–44.

McQuiston, John T., "Prosecutor Says DNA Evidence May Free Man," *New York Times*, December 1, 1992, B7.

——. "Man Freed after a DNA Test Is Sentenced in a Second Rape," *New York Times*, October 24, 1997, B4.

McVicker, Steve, and Roma Khanna, "3 Say Chief Knew of Lab Woes; Bradford Says Some Disgruntled Employees Trying to Discredit Him," *Houston Chronicle*, June 22, 2003, A1.

——. "93 HPD Lab Cases under Scrutiny: Investigator's New Report Raises Figure from 27," *Houston Chronicle*, May 11, 2006, B1.

Medawar, Peter, "Science and Literature," *Encounter* XXXII, no.1 (1969): 15–23.

Medical News Today, "*New England Journal of Medicine* Damaged by Its Conduct over Vioxx, Says Former Editor of *British Medical Journal*," available at www.medicalnewstoday.com/medicalnews.php?newsid=46831 (July 9, 2006).

MedicineNet.com, "Definition of Acute Promyeloctytic Leukemia," available at http://www.medterms.com/script/main/art.asp?articlekey=19758.

Mellor, D. H., "The Popper Phenomenon," *Philosophy* 52 (1977): 195–202.

Mercier, Louis-Sébastien, *Tableau de Paris* (revised ed., Amsterdam, the Netherlands: 1782–88) (12 vols.).

Merriam-Webster, *Webster's Ninth New Collegiate Dictionary* (Springfield, MA: Merriam-Webster Publishing, 1991).

Merriam-Webster Dictionary Online, http://www.merriam-webster.com/.

Merton, Robert, "Science and Democratic Social Structure," in Merton, *Social Theory and Social Structure* (Chicago: Free Press of Glencoe, 1949), 307–16.

Michaels, David, and Celeste Monforton, "Manufacturing Uncertainty: Contested Science and the Protection of the Public's Health and Environment," *American Journal of Public Health* 95 (2005): S39–48.

Mill, John Stuart, *A System of Logic, Ratiocinative and Inductive: Being a Connected View of the Principles of Evidence and the Methods of Scientific Investigation* (1843; 8th ed., London: Longman, Green, 1970).

Millay, Edna St. Vincent, "Justice Denied in Massachusetts," in *The Buck in the Snow and Other Poems* (New York: Harper and Brothers Publishers, 1928), 32–33.

Miller, Richard Lawrence, *Nazi Justiz: Law of the Holocaust* (Westport, CT: Praeger, 1995).

Mills, Clarence A., and Marjorie Mills Porter, "Tobacco Smoking Habits and Cancer of the Mouth and Respiratory System," *Cancer Research* 10, no.9 (1950): 539–42.

Mills, Steve, "What Killed Illinois' Death Penalty?" *Chicago Tribune*, March 10, 2011, available at http://articles.chicagotribune.com/2011-03-10/news/ct-met-illinois-death-penalty-history/20110309_1_death-penalty-death-row-death-sentence.

Mnookin, Jennifer, "Fingerprints: Not a Gold Standard," *Issues in Science and Technology* 20 (fall 2003): 47–54.

Molière, *Le Bourgeois Gentilhomme* (1670). ["Molière" was the stage name of actor Jean-Baptiste Poquelin.]

Mossman, Brooke T., George Klein, and Harald zur Hausen, "Modern Criteria to Determine the Etiology of Human Carcinogens," *Seminars in Cancer Biology* 14 (2004): 449–52.

Nance, Dale, "Two Concepts of Reliability," American Philosophical Association, *Newsletter on Philosophy and Law* (Fall 2003): 123–27.

National Institute of Neurological Disorders and Stroke, "Guillain-Barré Syndrome Fact Sheet," available at http://www.ninds.nih.gov/disorders/gbs/detail_gbs.htm.

National Institutes of Health, "Post-Traumatic Stress Disorder," available at http://www.nimh.nih.gov/health/topics/post-traumatic-stress-disorder-ptsd/index.shtml.

National Science Panel, *Silicone Breast Implants in Relation to Connective Tissue Diseases and Immunologic Dysfunction* (November 30, 1998), available at http://www.fjc.gov/BREIMLIT/SCIENCE/report.htm.

Neilson, George, *Trial by Combat* (London: Williams and Norgate, 1890).

Nesson, Charles, "The Evidence or the Event? On Judicial Proof and the Acceptability of Verdicts," *Harvard Law Review* 98, no.7 (1984–5): 1357–92.

——. "Peremptory Challenges: Technology Should Kill Them?" *Law, Probability and Risk* 3 (2003): 1–12.

Neville, Julie A., et al., "Errors in the *Archives of Dermatology* and the *Journal of the American Academy of Dermatology* from January through December 2003," *Archives of Dermatology* 142 (2006): 737–40.

Neufeld, Peter J., "The (Near) Irrelevance of *Daubert* to Criminal Justice and Some Suggestions for Reform," *American Journal of Public Health* 95 (2005): S107–13.

Newman, Stuart A., "Dr. Brent and Scientific Debate," *Reproductive Toxicology* 13, no.4 (1999): 241–44.

——. "A Response to Dr. Brent's Commentary on 'Dr. Brent and Scientific Debate,'" *Reproductive Toxicology* 13, no.4 (1999): 255–60.

Novick, Sheldon M., ed., *Collected Works of Justice Holmes* (Chicago: University of Chicago Press, 1995) (3 vols.).

O'Keefe, Patricia, and Jyoti Patel, "Women and Lung Cancer," *Seminars in Oncology Nursing*, 24, no.1 (February 2008): 3–8.

Oldenburg, Henry, *Correspondence of Henry Oldenburg*, translated and edited by A. Rupert Hall and Marie Boas Hall (Madison, WI: University of Wisconsin Press, 1966) (3 vols.).

Olding, Alan, "Popper for Afters," *Quadrant* 143, no.12 (December 1999): 19–22.

Oliver, Lisi, *The Beginnings of English Law* (Toronto: University of Toronto Press, 2002).

O'Malley, Kevin F., et al., eds., *Federal Jury Practice and Instructions: Civil* (Eagan, MN: West Group, 5th ed., 2000, and Supplement 2010).

——. et al., eds., *Federal Jury Practice and Instructions: Criminal* (6th ed., Eagan, MN: Thomson/West, 2008, and Supplement 2010).

Ordronaux, John, "On Expert Testimony in Judicial Proceedings," *Journal of Insanity* 30, no.3 (1874): 312–22.

Osmond, Daniel H., "Malice's Wonderland: Research Funding and Peer Review," *Journal of Neurobiology* 14, no.2 (1983): 95–112.

Osteogenesis Imperfecta (OI) Foundation, "What Is Osteonecrosis of the Jaw?" available at http://www.oif.org/site/DocServer/Osteonecrosis_of_the_Jaw.pdf.

Overbye, Dennis, "Astronomers in Quandary over Pluto's Planet Status," *New York Times*, August 23, 2006, A20.

Oxford English Dictionary Online, http://www.oed.com.

Panel on Scientific Responsibility and the Integrity of the Research Process, National Academy of Sciences, *Responsible Science: Ensuring the Integrity of the Research Process* (Washington, DC: National Academy Press, 1992), vol. I.

Papineau, David, "The Proof is in the Disproof," review of Malachi Haim Hacohen, *Karl Popper: The Formative Years*, *New York Times Book Review*, November 12, 2000, available at http://www.nytimes.com/books/00/11/12/reviews/001112.12papinet.html.

Pardo, Michael, "Estándares de prueba y teoría de la prueba," in Carmen Vázquez, ed., *Estándares de prueba y preuba científica: Ensayos de epistemología juridical* (Barcelona: Marcial Pons, 2013), 99–118.

Park, Roger, and Michael Saks, "Evidence Scholarship Reconsidered: Results of the Interdisciplinary Turn," *Boston College Law Review* 47 (2005–06): 949–1031.

Peirce, Charles Sanders, *Collected Papers*, eds. Charles Hartshorne, Paul Weiss, and (vols. 7 and 8) Arthur Burks (Cambridge, MA: Harvard University Press, 1931–58). References are by volume and paragraph number.

——. *Writings: A Chronological Edition*, eds. Peirce Edition Project (Indianapolis, IN: Indiana University Press, 1982–). References are by volume and page number.

Perlin, Michael L., *The Jurisprudence of the Insanity Defense* (Durham, NC: Carolina Academic Press, 1994).

Peterson, Joseph L., and Anna S. Leggett, "The Evolution of Forensic Science: Progress Amid the Pitfalls," *Stetson Law Review* 36, no.3 (Spring 2007): 621–60.

Pfeiffer, Mark P., and Gwendolyn L. Snodgrass, "The Continued Use of Retracted, Invalid Scientific Literature," *Journal of the American Medical Association* 263 (1990): 1420–23.

Carl V. Phillips and Karen J. Goodman, "The Missed Lessons of Sir Austin Bradford Hill," *Epidemiologic Perspectives & Innovations*, 1, no.3 (October 4, 2004), available at http://archive.biomedcentral.com/1742-5573/content/1/1/3.

Planetsave, "Mars Rover Curiosity—NASA's Rover Gearing Up For Second Ever Rock Drilling And Sampling On Mars," May 12, 2013, available at http://planetsave.com/2013/05/12/mars-rover-curiosity-nasas-rover-gearing-up-for-second-ever-rock-drilling-and-sampling-on-mars/.

Plato, *Republic*, trans. G. A. Grube, revised by C. D. C. Reeve (Indianapolis, IN: Hackett Publishing Company, 1992).

Poehlman, Eric T., et al., "Changes in Energy Balance and Body Composition at Menopause: A Controlled Longitudinal Study," *Annals of Internal Medicine* 123 (1995): 673–76.

"Pointer Rules Federal Science Panel Not Tainted by Payments to Panelist," *Medical-Legal Aspects of Breast Implants* 7, no.5 (April 1999): 1, 4, 5.

Pojman, Louis J., ed., *Theory of Knowledge: Classical and Contemporary Sources* (Belmont, CA: Wadsworth, 2nd ed., 1998).

Polanyi, Michael, *Science, Faith, and Society* (Cambridge: Cambridge University Press, 1946).

Pollack, Wendy, "Legal Demands Take Time from Scientists' Real Work," *Wall Street Journal*, January 27, 2007, A5.

Pons' Globalwörterbuch Deutsch-Englisch (Stuttgart: Klett, and London: Collins, 1983).

Pope, Tara Parker, "New Study Reassures Most Users of Hormones," *Wall Street Journal*, April 4, 2007, A1, A12.

Popper, Karl R., *The Logic of Scientific Discovery* (first published in German in 1934; English edition, London: Hutchinson, 1959).

——. *The Open Society and Its Enemies* (1945; revised ed., Princeton, NJ: Princeton University Press, 1950).

——. "Philosophy of Science: A Personal Report," in C. A. Mace, ed., *British Philosophy in Mid-Century* (London: George Allen and Unwin, 1957), 155–91 (not included in the second edition, 1966). Reprinted under the title, "Science: Conjectures and Refutations" in Karl R. Popper, *Conjectures and Refutations*, 33–65.

Popper, Karl R., "Truth, Rationality, and the Growth of Scientific Knowledge" (1963), in Popper, *Conjectures and Refutations*, 215–50.

Popper, Karl R., "Addenda: Some Technical Notes," in Popper, *Conjectures and Refutations*, 377–413.

——. *Conjectures and Refutations: The Growth of Scientific Knowledge* (London: Routledge and Kegan Paul, 1963).

——. "On the Theory of the Objective Mind" (1968), in Popper, *Objective Knowledge*, 153–90.

——. "Two Faces of Common Sense: An Argument for Commonsense Realism and against the Commonsense Theory of Knowledge" (from a talk given in 1970), in Popper, *Objective Knowledge*, 32–105.

——. "Toleration and Intellectual Responsibility" (lecture delivered at the University of Tübingen, 1981), in Popper, *In Search of a Better World: Lectures and Essays from Thirty Years,* trans. Laura J. Bennett (London: Routledge, 1992), 188–203.

——. "Conjectural Knowledge: My Solution of the Problem of Induction," *Revue Internationale de Philosophie* 25ᵉ année, no. 95–6, fasc. 1–2 (1971): 167–97. Reprinted in Popper, *Objective Knowledge,* 1–33.

——. "Comments on Tarski's Theory of Truth," in Popper, *Objective Knowledge,* 319–40.

——. *Objective Knowledge: An Evolutionary Approach* (Oxford: Clarendon Press, 1972).

——. "Ayer on Empiricism and against Verisimilitude," in Schilpp, ed., *The Philosophy of Karl Popper,* vol. 2, 1100–14.

——. "Natural Selection and Its Scientific Status" (1977), in David Miller, ed., *The Pocket Popper* (London: Fontana, 1983), 239–46.

——. *Unended Quest* (La Salle, IL: Open Court, 1979) (first published in Schilpp, ed., *The Philosophy of Karl Popper,* vol. 1, 3–181).

Posner, Richard, *Frontiers in Legal Theory* (Cambridge, MA: Harvard University Press, 2001).

Posner, Richard A., "Against the Law Reviews," *Legal Affairs* (November/December 2004): 57–58.

Psychology Today, "Post-Traumatic Stress Disorder," available at http://www.psychologytoday.com/basics/post-traumatic-stress-disorder.

Quayle, Dan, "Agenda for Civil Justice Reform in America," *University of Cincinnati Law Review* 60 (1992): 997–1007.

Quine, W. V., *Quiddities* (Cambridge, MA: Harvard University Press, 1987).

——. *Pursuit of Truth* (Cambridge, MA: Harvard University Press, 1992).

——. "Reactions," in Paulo Leonardo and Marco Santambrogio, eds., *On Quine* (Cambridge: Cambridge University Press, 1995), 347–61.

Quinton, A. M., "The Foundations of Knowledge," in Bernard Williams and Alan Montefiore, eds., *British Analytical Philosophy* (London: Routledge and Kegan Paul, 1966), 55–86.

Ramsey, Frank Plumpton, "Facts and Propositions" (1927), in Ramsey, *The Foundations of Mathematics and Other Logical Essays,* ed. Richard B. Braithwaite (London: Routledge and Kegan Paul, 1931), 138–55.

——. *On Truth: Original Manuscripts (1927–29) from the Ramsey Collection at the University of Pittsburgh,* eds. Nicholas Rescher and Ulrich Majer (Pittsburgh, PA: University of Pittsburgh Press, 1991).

Ray, Wayne A., et al., "COX-2 Selective Non-Steroidal Anti-Inflammatory Drugs and Risk of Serious Coronary Heart Disease," *Lancet* 360 (October 5, 2002): 1071–73.

Read, C. Stanford, letter to Smith Ely Jelliffe (February 3, 1921), in *Papers of Smith Ely Jellife,* 1866–1940 (on file with Library of Congress, Washington, DC, Box 16).

Regnier, Thomas, "*Barefoot* in Quicksand: The Future of 'Future Dangerousness' Predictions in Death Penalty Sentencing in the World of *Daubert* and *Kumho,*" *University of Akron Law Review* 37, no.3 (2004): 467–507.

Relman, Arthur, "Moscow in January," *New England Journal of Medicine* 302 (1980): 523.

Rennie, Drummond, "Guarding the Guardians: A Conference on Editorial Peer Review," *Journal of the American Medical Association* 256 (1986): 2391–92.

——. "Editorial Peer Review: Its Development and Rationale," in *Peer Review in Health Sciences*, eds. Fiona Godlee and Tom Jefferson (London: BMJ Publishing Group, 2nd ed., 2003).

Reno, Janet, "Message from the Attorney General," in Connors, Lundgren, Miller, and McEwen, *Convicted by Juries, Exonerated by Science*, iii–iv.

Rescher, Nicholas, *The Coherence Theory of Truth* (Oxford: Clarendon Press, 1973).

Rescher, Nicholas, and Ulrich Majer, "Editors' Introduction" to Ramsey, *On Truth*.

Resnick, Judith, "From 'Cases' to 'Litigation,'" *Law & Contemporary Problems* 5 (1991): 6–68.

Risinger, D. Michael, Mark P. Denbeaux, and Michael J. Saks, "Brave New 'Post-*Daubert* World'—A Reply to Professor Moenssens," *Seton Hall Law Review* 29 (1998): 405–90.

Risinger, D. Michael, et al., "Bayes Wars Redivivus—An Exchange," *International Commentary on Evidence* 8, no.1, ISSN (Online) 1554–4567, DOI: 10.2202/1554–4567.1115 (November 2010).

Rochon, Paula, et al., "A Study of Manufacturer-Supported Trials of Non-Steroidal Anti-Inflammatory Drugs in the Treatment of Arthritis," *Archives of Internal Medicine* 154, no.2 (January 24, 1994): 157–63.

Rodricks, Joseph V., and Susan H. Reith, "Toxicological Assessment in the Courtroom: Are Available Methodologies Suitable for Evaluating Toxic Tort and Product Liability Claims?" *Regulatory Toxicology and Pharmacology* 27 (1998): 21–31.

Rogers, Adam, "Come In, Mars," *Newsweek*, 19 August, 1996, 56–57.

Roll-Hansen, Nils, *The Lysenko Effect: The Politics of Science* (Amherst, NY: Humanity Books, 2005).

Rorty, Richard, *Philosophy and the Mirror of Nature* (Princeton, NJ: Princeton University Press, 1979).

——. *Objectivity, Relativism and Truth* (Cambridge: Cambridge University Press, 1991).

——. "Trotsky and the Wild Orchids," *Common Knowledge* 1, no.3 (1992): 140–53.

Rothman, Kenneth, *Modern Epidemiology* (Boston: Little, Brown, 1986).

Rubin, Carl R., and Laura Ringenbach, "The Use of Court Experts in Asbestos Litigation," *Federal Rules Decisions* 137 (1999): 35–52.

Rumsfeld, Donald H., US Secretary of Defense, Department of Defense, News Briefing (Febrary 12, 2002), transcript available at http://www.defense.gov/transcripts/transcript.aspx?transcriptid=2636.

Ruse, Michael, *Darwinism Defended: A Guide to the Creation/Evolution Controversies* (London: Addison-Wesley Publishing Company, 1982).

——. "Expert Witness Testimony Sheet," McLean v. Arkansas (1982), in Ruse, ed., *But Is It Science?* 287–306.

——. "A Philosopher's Day in Court," in Ruse, ed., *But Is It Science?* 13–35.

Ruse, Michael, ed., *But Is It Science? The Philosophical Question in the Creation/Evolution Controversy* (Amherst, NY: Prometheus Books), 1996.

Russell, Bertrand, "The Philosophy of Logical Atomism" (1918), in Russell, *Logic and Knowledge*, 177–281.

——. "On Propositions: What They Are and How They Mean" (1919), in *Logic and Knowledge*, 283–320.

——. *Human Knowledge, Its Scope and Limits* (New York: Simon and Schuster, 1948).

——. *Logic and Knowledge: Essays 1901–1950*, ed. Robert C. Marsh (New York: Capricorn Books, 1956).

RXList.com, Clinical Pharmacology, available at http://www.rxlist.com/cgi/generic2/transscop_cp.htm.

Sand, George, letter to Armand Barbes, 1867, in Gross, ed., *The Oxford Book of Aphorisms*, 228.

Sanders, Joseph, "From Science to Evidence: The Testimony on Causation in the Bendectin Cases," *Stanford Law Review* 46, no.1 (1993): 1–86.

——. *Bendectin on Trial: A Study of Mass Tort Litigation* (Ann Arbor, MI: University of Michigan Press, 1998).

——. "Science, Law, and the Expert Witness," *Law & Contemporary Problems* 72, no. 1 (2009): 63–90.

Sanders, Joseph, and Michael D. Green, "Admissibility versus Sufficiency: Controlling the Quality of Expert Witness Testimony in the United States," forthcoming in Diego Papayannis, ed., *Uncertain Causation in Tort Law* (Cambridge: Cambridge University Press, forthcoming).

Santayana, George, *The Life of Reason* (1910; 2nd ed., New York: Charles Scribner's Sons, 1922) (5 vols.).

Savage, Leonard J., *The Foundations of Statistics* (New York: Wiley, 1954).

Schiller, Ferdinand Canning Scott, "The Making of Truth," in Schiller, *Studies in Humanism* (New York: MacMillan, 1907), 179–203.

Schilpp, Paul A., ed., *The Philosophy of Karl Popper* (La Salle, IL: Open Court, 1974) (2 vols.).

Schmeck, Harold M. Jr., "Swine Flu Program Brings $10.7 Million in Claims," *New York Times* Global Edition, February 5, 1977, 8.

Schonberger, Lawrence B., et al., "Guillain-Barre [*sic*] Syndrome Following Vaccination in the National Influenza Vaccination Program, United States 1976–1977," *American Journal of Epidemiology* 110, no.2 (1979): 105–23.

Schreck, Robert, Lyle A. Baker, George P. Ballard, and Sidney Dolgoff, "Tobacco Smoking as an Etiologic Factor in Disease. Part I: Cancer," *Cancer Research* 10, no.1 (1950): 49–58.

Schrager, Sarina and Beth E. Potter, "Diethylstilbestrol Exposure," *American Family Physician* 69, no.10 (May 15, 2004), available at http://www.aafp.org/afp/2004/0515/p2395.html.

Schum, David, "A Review of the Case against Blaise Pascal and His Heirs," *Michigan Law Review* 77 (1979): 446–63.

——. *Evidential Foundations of Probabilistic Reasoning* (New York: John Wiley and Sons, 1994).

Schwartz, Adina, "A Systemic Challenge to the Reliability and Admissibility of Firearms and Toolmark Identification," *The Columbia Science & Technology Law Review* VI (2005): 1–42.

Schwarzer, William W., "Settlement of Mass Tort Actions: Order out of Chaos," *Cornell Law Review* 80 (1995): 837–44.

Seidemann, Ryan M., et al., "Closing the Gate on Questionable Expertwitness Testimony: A Proposal to Institute Expert Review Panels," *Southern University Law Review* 33, no.1 (2005): 29–91.

Sellars, Wilfrid, "Scientific Realism or Irenic Instrumentalism?" in Robert Cohen and Marx Wartofsky, eds., *Boston Studies in Philosophy of Science* (New York: Humanities Press, 1965), 171–204.

Severn, Bill, *The Roaring Twenties: Prohibition and Repeal* (New York: Julian Messner, 1969).

Shawcross, William, "Turning Dollars into Change," *Time* 150, no.9, September 1, 1997, 48–57.

Shephard, Thomas H., "'Proof' of Human Teratogenicity," *Teratology* 50 (1994): 97–98 (letters section).

Sial, Omar, and Sahar Iqbal, *A Legal Research Guide to Pakistan*, available at http://www.nyulawglobal.org/globalex/pakistan.htm.

Sinclair, Upton, *Boston* (New York: A. C. Boni, 1928).

Singer, Peter, "Discovering Karl Popper," *New York Review of Books* 21, no.7, May 1, 1974, 22–8.

Skipp, Catherine, and Arian Campo-Flores, "A Bridge Too Far," *Newsweek*, August 3, 2009, 46–51.

Skolnik, Andrew, "Key Witness against Morning Sickness Drug Faces Scientific Fraud Charges," *Journal of the American Medical Association* 263 (1990): 1468–73.

Skrabanek, Petr, and James McCormick, *Follies & Fallacies in Medicine* (Glasgow, Scotland: Tarragon Press, 1989; reprinted Amherst, NY: Prometheus Books, 1990).

Skyrms, Brain, *Choice and Chance: An Introduction to Inductive Logic* (Belmont, CA: Dickenson, 1966; 4th ed., Independence, KY: Cengage, 1999).

SmartJury, available at http://web.archive.org/web/20030216122804/ http://www.smartjury.com/.

Smith, Richard, "Peer Review: Reform or Revolution?" *British Medical Journal* 315 (1997): 759–60.

Snow, John, *On the Mode of Communication of Cholera* (London: John Churchill, 1855) (reprinted, with other material, in *Snow on Cholera* [Cambridge, MA: Harvard Medical Library, 1936]).

Soifer, Valerii N., *The Tragedy of Soviet Science*, trans. Leo Gruliow and Rebecca Gruliow (New Brunswick, NJ: Transaction Press, 1994).

Solomon, Daniel H., et al., "Relationship between Selective Cyclooxygenase-2 Inhibitors and Acute Myocardial Infarction in Older Adults," *Circulation* 109 (2004): 2068–73.

Solomon, Jay, and Farnaz Fassihi, "Iran Rights Envoy Assails U.N. Censure—Official Defends Stoning, Arrests, as General Assembly Committee Condemns Crackdown by Tehran," *Wall Street Journal*, November 19, 2010, available at http://online.wsj.com/article/SB10001424052748703374304575623040167164392.html.

Solomon, Scott D., et al., "Cardiovascular Risk Associated with Rofecoxib in a Colorectal Adenoma Prevention Trial," *New England Journal of Medicine* 352, no.11 (2005): 1071–80.

Sox, Harold C., and Drummond Rennie, "Research Misconduct, Retraction, and Cleansing Medical Literature: Lessons from the Poehlman Case," *Annals of Internal Medicine* 144 (2006): 609–13.

Speiser, Stuart M., Charles F. Krause, and Alfred W. Gans, *The American Law of Torts* (Rochester, NY: The Lawyers' Cooperative Publishing Co., and San Francisco, CA: Bancroft-Whitney Co., 1983–) (10 vols.) [vol. 6, cited in the text, appeared in 1989].

Starkie, Thomas, *A Practical Treatise of the Law of Evidence* (Philadelphia, PA: T. & J. W. Johnson, 7th ed., 1842) (2 vols.).

Starrs, James, "*Frye v. United States* Restructured and Revitalized: A Proposal to Amend Federal Rule of Evidence 702," *Jurimetrics Journal* 26 (1986): 249–59.

State Justice Institute, *A Judge's Deskbook on the Basic Philosophies and Methods of Science: Model Curriculum* (March 1999).

Stevenson, Charles, "The Emotive Meaning of Ethical Terms" (1947), in Morris Weitz, ed., *20th-Century Philosophy: The Analytic Tradition* (New York: Free Press, 1966), 237–53.

Stewart, Thomas, and Arthur Hayes, *The World's Most Famous Court Trial: State of Tennessee v. John Thomas Scopes* (1925), ed. Leonard W. Levy (New York: Da Capo Press, 1971).

Stolleis, Michael, *The Law Under the Swastika: Studies in Legal History in Nazi Germany* (1994), trans. Thomas Dunlap (Chicago: University of Chicago Press, 1998).

Story, Joseph, *Commentaries on the Constitution of the United States* (Boston, MA: Hilliard, Gray & Co., and Cambridge, MA: Shattuck & Co., 1833) (3 vols.).

Stove, David, *Popper and After: Four Modern Irrationalists* (1982), reprinted under the title *Anything Goes: Origins of the Cult of Scientific Irrationalism* (Paddington, Australia: Macleay Press, 1999).

——. "Cole Porter and Karl Popper: The Jazz Age in the Philosophy of Science" (1991), in Stove, David, ed., *Against the Idols of the Age*, ed. Roger Kimball (New Brunswick, NJ: Transaction Press, 1999), 3–32.

Stratton, Kathleen, Donna A. Almario, and Marie C. McCormick, eds., *Immunization Safety Review* (Washington, DC: National Academies Press, 2003).

Sudbø, John, et al., "Non-Steroidal Anti-Inflammatory Drugs and the Risk of Oral Cancer: A Nested Case-Control Study," *Lancet* 366 (2005): 1359–66.

Sun, Marjorie, "Peer Review Comes under Peer Review," *Science* 224 (1989): 910–12.

Suppe, Frederick, *The Semantic Conception of Scientific Theories and Scientific Realism* (Urbana, IL: University of Illinois Press, 1989).

Tarski, Alfred, "The Concept of Truth in Formalised Languages" (originally published in Polish in 1933), trans. J. H. Woodger, in Tarski, *Logic, Semantics, Metamathematics* (Oxford: Clarendon Press, 1956), 152–278.

——. "The Semantic Conception of Truth" (1944), reprinted in Herbert Feigl and Wilfrid Sellars, eds., *Readings in Philosophical Analysis* (New York: Appleton-Century-Crofts, 1949), 52–84.

Taruffo, Michele, *La semplice verità: Il guidice e la costruzzione de fatti* (Rome: Editora Laterza, 2009).

Terry, Karen J. and Alissa R. Ackerman, "A Brief History of Major Sex Offender Laws," in Richard G. Wright, ed., *Sex-Offender Laws*, 65–98.

Tesoriero, Heather Won, "Vioxx Study Correction May Add Pressure to Merck's Defense," *Wall Street Journal*, June 27, 2007, A2.

——. et al., "Vioxx Settlement for $4.85 Billion Largely Vindicates Merck's Tactics," *Wall Street Journal*, November 11, 2007, A1, A5.

Thayer, James, *Select Cases on Evidence at the Common Law* (Cambridge, MA: C. W. Sever, 1892).

Thomas, Evan et al., "The JFK-Marilyn Hoax," *Newsweek*, June 6, 1997, 36.

Thomas, Leno, L. Austin Doyle, and Martin J. Edelman, "Lung Cancer in Women: Emerging Differences in Epidemiology, Biology, and Therapy," *Chest* 128, no.1 (2005): 370–81.

Thompson, William C., "A Sociological Perspective on the Science of Forensic DNA Testing," *University of California Davis Law Review* 30 (1997): 1113–36.

Thompson, William C., and E. L. Schumann, "Interpretation of Statistical Evidence in Criminal Trials: The Prosecutor's Fallacy and the Defense Attorney's Fallacy," *Law and Human Behavior* II, no.3 (1987): 67–87.

Tillers, Peter, and Eric D. Green, eds., *Probability and Inference in the Law of Evidence: Uses and Limits of Bayesianism* (Dordrecht, the Netherlands: Kluwer, 1988).

Topp, Michael Miller, ed., *The Sacco and Vanzetti Case: A Brief History and Documents* (New York: Palgrave/Macmillan, 2005).

Tribe, Laurence, "Trial by Mathematics: Precision and Ritual in the Legal Process," *Harvard Law Review* 84 (1971): 1329–93.

Turow, Scott, *Reversible Errors* (New York: Warner Vision Books, 2002).

Twining, William, "What Is the Law of Evidence?" in Twining, *Rethinking Evidence* (Oxford: Blackwell, 1990), 178–218.

Unamuno, Miguel de, "Verdad y vida," in *Mi religión y otros ensayos breves* (1910; Madrid: Espasa-Calpe, S. A., 4th ed., 1964), 16–22.

Understanding Evolution: Your One-Stop Source for Information about Evolution, available at http://evolution.berkeley.edu/.

United States Department of Health, Education, and Welfare, *Smoking and Health Report of the Advisory Committee of the Surgeon General*, Public Health Service Publications No. 1103 (Washington, DC: 1964).

United States Department of Health and Human Services News, No. P80–45 (October 7, 1980).

Urmson, J. O., and Geoffrey Warnock, eds., *Philosophical Papers of J. L. Austin* (Oxford: Clarendon Press, 1961).

Vaccine News Daily, "Supreme Court to decide if vaccine makers can be sued," available at http://vaccinenewsdaily.com/news/212259-supreme-court-to-decide-if-vaccine-makers-can-be-sued/.

Vail, Andy, and Elizabeth Gardener, "Common Statistical Errors in the Design and Analysis of Subfertility Trials," *Human Reproduction* 18, no.5 (2003): 1000–04.

Van Fraassen, Bas C., *The Scientific Image* (Oxford: Clarendon Press, 1980).

Vázquez, Carmen, "Entrevista a Susan Haack," *Doxa* 36(2013): 573–86.

Vázquez, Carmen, ed., *Estándares de prueba y preuba científica: Ensayos de epistemología jurídical* (Barcelona: Marcial Pons, 2013).

von Mises, Richard, *Probability, Statistics and Truth* (London: Allen and Unwin, 2nd revised English edition, 1928).

Wade, Nicholas, and Choe Sang-Hun, "Human Cloning Was All Faked, Koreans Report," *New York Times*, January 10, 2006, A1.

Walker, Laurens, and John Monahan, "Scientific Authority: The Breast Implant Litigation and Beyond," *University of Virginia Law Review* 86 (2000): 801–33.

Walker, Ralph Charles Sutherland, *The Coherence Theory of Truth: Realism, Anti-Realism, Idealism* (New York: Routledge, 1989).

Watson, James D., and Francis Crick, "Molecular Structure of Nucleic Acids: A Structure for Deoxyribonucleic Acid," *Nature* 171 (April 25, 1953): 737–38.

Weed, Douglas, "Epidemiologic Evidence and Causal Inferences," *Hematology/Oncology Clinics of North America* 124, no.4 (2000): 797–807.

Weiner, Barbara A., "The Insanity Defense: Historical Development and Present Status," *Behavioral Sciences and the Law* 3, no.1 (1985): 3–35.

Weinstein, Jack B., *Individual Justice in Mass Tort Litigation: The Effect of Class Actions, Consolidations, and Other Multiparty Devices* (Evanston, IL: Northwestern University Press, 1995).

Weller, Ann C., "Editorial Peer Review in U.S. Medical Journals," *Journal of the American Medical Association* 263 (1990): 1344–47.

Whewell, William, *Philosophy of the Inductive Sciences* (1840), in *Selected Writings of William Whewell*, ed., Yehuda Elkana (Chicago: University of Chicago Press, 1984), 121–259.

Wigmore, John Henry, *The Principles of Judicial Proof as Given by Logic, Psychology, and General Experience as Illustrated in Judicial Trials* (1913; 5th ed., Littleton, CO: Fred B. Rothman & Co., 1981).

Wilde, Oscar, *The Importance of Being Earnest* (1895) in *The Plays of Oscar Wilde* (New York: H. S. Nichols, 1914), 105–228.

Wile, Timothy P., and Marc A. Werlinsky, *West's Pennsylvania Practice Driving under the Influence* (St. Paul, MN: Thomson/West, 2006–07 ed.).

Wilford, John Noble, "Fossil Called Missing Link from Sea to Land Animals," *New York Times*, April 6, 2006, A1.

Williams, C. J. F., *Being, Identity and Truth* (Oxford: Oxford University Press, 1992).

——. *What Is Truth?* (Cambridge: Cambridge University Press, 2009).

Wilson, Adam, "The Law Commission's Recommendation on Expert Opinion Evidence: Sufficient Reliability?" *Web Journal of Current Legal Issues* 3 (2011).

Wilson, E. O., *Consilience: The Unity of Knowledge* (New York: Knopf, 1998).

Winslow, Ron, and Shirley S. Wang, "More Vytorin Bad News Hits Merck, Schering," *Wall Street Journal*, July 22, 2008, B1, B2.

Winstein, Keith J., "Boston Scientific Stent Study Flawed," *Wall Street Journal*, August 14, 2008, B1, B6.

Wittgenstein, Ludwig, *Tractatus Logico-Philosophicus* (London: Routledge and Kegan Paul, 1922).

Woodward, C. Vann, *The Strange Career of Jim Crow* (1955; revised ed., New York: Oxford University Press, 1966).

Wright, Charles Alan, and Peter J. Henning, *Federal Practice and Procedure* (Eagan, MN: Thomson Reuters, 4th ed., 2009), vol. 2A.

Wright, Richard G., ed., *Sex-Offender Laws: Failed Policies, New Directions* (New York: Springer, 2009).

Wright, Richard G., "Introduction: The Failure of Sex Offender Policies," in Wright, ed., *Sex-Offender Laws*, 1–16.

Wynder, Ernest L., Evarts A. Graham, "Tobacco Smoking as a Possible Etiologic Factor in Bronchiogenic Carcinoma: A Study of 684 Proved Cases," *Journal of the American Medical Association* 143, no.4 (May 27, 1950): 329–36.

Wysocki, Bernard, Jr., "Scholarly Journals' Premier Status Is Diluted by Web," *Wall Street Journal*, May 23, 2005, A1, A8.

Yankauer, Alfred, "Who Are the Peer Reviewers and How Much Do They Review?" *Journal of the American Medical Association* 263 (1990): 1338–40.

Yates, Janelle, "Nausea and Vomiting of Pregnancy: Q&A with T. Murphy Goodwin," *OBG Management* 16, no.8 (August 2004): 54–67.

Yeazell, Steven C., *From Medieval Group Litigation to the Modern Class Action* (New Haven, CT: Yale University Press, 1987).

Zagzebski, Linda, *Virtues of the Mind* (New York: Cambridge University Press, 1996).

Ziman, John M., *Public Knowledge* (Cambridge: Cambridge University Press, 1968).

——. "Information, Communication, Knowledge," *Nature* 224 (1969): 318–24.

Zuckerman, Harriet, and Robert K. Merton, "Patterns of Evaluation in Science: Institutionalism, Structure, and Functions of the Referee System," *Minerva* 9 (1971): 66–100.

Zur Hausen, Harald, "Papilloma Viruses in the Causation of Human Cancers – A Brief Historical Account," *Virology*, 384 (2008): 260–65.

——. "Viruses in Human Cancers," *Current Science* 81, no.5 (2001), 523–27.

Glossary

AAAS: American Association for the Advancement of Science. Produces *Science* and other science-related publications; hosts scientific conferences and meetings; and undertakes activities that "promote science to the public" and raise awareness of "major issues that affect the scientific community." The AAAS website is available at http://www.aaas.org/. See also **CASE Project.**

AEU: Analytic Epistemologists' Union. A coinage of mine, used here to refer to those who classify themselves professionally as specialists in epistemology, or in some sub-field of epistemology.

***allocatur*:** "It is allowed"; used in Pennsylvania to refer to permission to appeal. See Bryan A. Garner, ed., *Black's Law Dictionary* (St. Paul, MN: Thomson Reuters, 9th ed., 2009), 88. See also ***certiorari*.**

APA: American Psychiatric Association. A medical association founded in 1844, now representing more than 33,000 psychiatric physicians from the US and elsewhere. Publishes the *Diagnostic and Statistical Manual* (*DSM*) classifying mental disorders, of which the fifth edition appeared in May 2013. The APA website is available at http://www.psychiatry.org/about-apa--psychiatry.

APL: Acute Promyelocytic Leukemia. A cancer of the bone marrow that causes immature white blood cells ("promyelocytes") to accumulate, leading to a shortage of normal white and red blood cells and platelets. APL accounts for approximately 10% of acute myeloid leukemia cases, and affects roughly one in 250,000 people in the US. It is not inherited, but is caused by a "translocation" or exchange of material between certain chromosomes after conception. See Genetic Home Reference, "Acute promyeloctytic leukemia," available at http://ghr.nlm.nih.gov/condition/acute-promyelocytic-leukemia; MedicineNet.com, "Definition of Acute promyelocytic leukemia," available at http://www.medterms.com/script/main/art.asp?articlekey=19758.

CASE Project: A project of the AAAS (see above), providing a list of qualified experts on scientific subjects on whom courts could call; its goal is to "assist[] federal and state judges, administrative law judges and arbitrators in identifying highly qualified scientists, engineers, and healthcare professionals to serve as scientific experts." See http://www.aaas.org/spp/case/case.htm. The project now (2013) seems to be defunct, though the CASE website is still available. See Andrew Jurs, "Balancing Legal Process with Scientific Expertise: Expert Witness Methodology in Five Nations and Suggestions for Reform of Post-*Daubert* U.S. Reliability Determinations," *Marquette Law Review* 95, no.4 (2012): 1329–1415, 1413.

CDC: Centers for Disease Control and Prevention, a federal agency that maintains several departments concerned with occupational safety and health, travelers' health, vaccines and immunizations, diseases and conditions, and health data and statistics. The CDC website is available at www.cdc.gov.

***certiorari* (abbreviated as "*cert.*"):** means "to be more fully informed," and refers to a general appellate remedy also known as a *writ of certiorari*. The US Supreme Court uses *certiorari* to review most of the cases it decides to hear. See Bryan A. Garner, ed., *Black's Law Dictionary* (St. Paul, MN: Thomson Reuters, 9th ed., 2009), 258.

constructive empiricism: (in philosophy of science) the view that, although theoretical statements in science are genuine statements, and are either true or else false, the goal of science is not truth, but only empirical (i.e., observational) adequacy. See Bas C. Van Fraassen, *The Scientific Image* (Oxford: Clarendon Press, 1980); Frederick Suppe, *The Semantic Conception of Scientific Theories and Scientific Realism* (Urbana, IL: University of Illinois Press, 1989), chapter 11. See also **instrumentalism**.

Critical Common-sensism: (in philosophy of science) refers to the view that inquiry in the sciences is continuous with everyday empirical inquiry. See Susan Haack, *Defending Science—Within Reason: Between Scientism and Cynicism* (Amherst, NY: Prometheus Books, 2003).

Critical Rationalism: (in philosophy of science) refers to Karl R. Popper's approach, understood as holding that science is a rational enterprise, and that what makes it so is its openness to criticism. See Karl R. Popper, *The Logic of Scientific Discovery* (1934; English edition, London: Hutchinson, 1959); and *Conjectures and Refutations: The Growth of Scientific Knowledge* (London: Routledge and Kegan Paul, 1963). See also **deductivism**; **falsificationism**; **Logical Negativism**.

***Daubert* factors:** the indicia of (legal) reliability of proffered expert scientific testimony given in the "flexible list" in the Supreme Court's ruling in *Daubert*: "whether [the testimony] can be (and has been) tested"; "whether the theory or technique has been subjected to peer review and publication"; "the known or potential error rate"; "[w]idespread acceptance [in the relevant scientific community]." Sometimes also taken to include a fifth factor, "the existence and maintenance of standards controlling [a] technique's operation." Daubert v. Merrell Dow Pharm., Inc., 509 U.S. 579, 593–94 (1993) ("*Daubert* III"). An additional "*Daubert* factor" sometimes added to the list, whether the scientific work appealed to is "litigation-driven," derives from Judge Kozinski's 1995 ruling in *Daubert* IV, on remand from the Supreme Court. Daubert v. Merrell Dow Pharm., Inc., 43 F.3d 1311 (9th Cir. 1995) ("*Daubert* IV").

***Daubert* trilogy:** refers to the three Supreme Court rulings on expert testimony: Daubert v. Merrell Dow Pharm., Inc., 509 U.S. 579 (1993) (interpreting Federal Rule of Evidence 702, on the admissibility of expert scientific testimony); Gen. Elec. Co. v. Joiner, 522 U.S. 136 (1997) (ruling that the standard of review for such evidentiary rulings remains abuse of discretion); Kumho Tire Co. v. Carmichael, 525 U.S. 137 (1999) (ruling that *Daubert* applies to non-scientific as well as to scientific expert testimony).

deductive logic: logic of deductive validity. An argument is deductively valid if and only if there is a necessary connection between premises and conclusion; i.e., it is such that it is impossible for the premises to be true and the conclusion false (including the limit case of logical truths, which follow deductively from any premises or none). See Susan Haack, *Philosophy of Logics* (Cambridge: Cambridge University Press, 1978), chapters 1 and 2. See also **inductive logic**.

Deductivism: (in philosophy of science) refers to Karl R. Popper's approach, since it holds that the only logic required in scientific inference is deductive—most importantly, *modus tollens*, the mode of inference used when a theory is falsified. See also **Critical Rationalism**; **deductive logic**; **Falsificationism**; **Logical Negativism**; ***modus tollendo tollens***.

demarcation, problem of: (in philosophy of science) refers to the problem of how to demarcate science from non-science. See Karl R. Popper, *The Logic of Scientific Discovery* (1934; English ed., London: Hutchinson, 1959), 34–39; Larry Laudan, "The Demise of the Demarcation Problem" (1983), in Michael Ruse, ed., *But Is It Science? The Philosophical Question in the Creation/Evolution Controversy* (Amherst, NY: Prometheus Books, 1996), 337–50; Susan Haack, *Defending Science—Within Reason: Between Scientism and Cynicism*

(Amherst, NY: Prometheus Books, 2003), 114–16, and "Six Signs of Scientism" in *Putting Philosophy to Work: Inquiry and Its Place in Culture* (Amherst, NY: Prometheus Books, 2nd ed., 2013), 105–20.

DES: diethylstilbestrol, a drug used to prevent miscarriage. DES was found to cause reproductive cancers in some of the adult daughters and sterility in some of the adult sons born to the women who had taken it. See Sarina Schrager and Beth E. Potter, "Diethylstilbestrol Exposure," *American Family Physician* 69, no.10 (May 15, 2004), available at http://www.aafp.org/afp/2004/0515/p2395.html.

EPA: Environmental Protection Agency. Federal agency conducting research, monitoring, standard-setting, and enforcement activities to ensure protection of the natural environment—air, water, and land. Founded in 1970. The EPA website is available at http://www.epa.gov.

Falsificationism: (in philosophy of science) refers to Karl R. Popper's approach, since it holds that scientific theories can neither be verified (shown to be true) nor confirmed (shown to be probably true), but can only be falsified (shown to be false, if they are false). See also **Critical Rationalism**; **Deductivism**; **Logical Negativism**.

FDA: Food and Drug Administration. Federal scientific, regulatory, and public-health agency overseeing most food products (except meat and poultry), human and animal drugs, therapeutic agents of biological origin, medical devices, radiation-emitting products for consumer, medical, and occupational use, cosmetics, and animal feed. Dates, in its modern form, from the passage of the Federal Food and Drugs Act of 1906. See http://www.fda.gov/AboutFDA/WhatWeDo/History/default.htm.

FRCP: Federal Rules of Civil Procedure. Rules governing procedure in civil cases in US district courts. First enacted in 1938. The ongoing Committee on Rules of Practice and Procedure was created in 1958, and has subsequently amended these rules on a regular basis, most recently in 2010. The FRCP do not apply to suits in state courts, but many states base their procedural rules on the federal rules. See "Current Rules of Practice and Procedure," available at http://www.uscourts.gov/RulesandPolicies/rules/current-rules.aspx; "Rules of Civil Procedure," available at http://legal-dictionary.thefreedictionary.com/Federal+Rules+of+Civil+Procedure.

FRE: Federal Rules of Evidence. Rules governing the introduction of evidence in legal proceedings, both civil and criminal, in federal courts. Signed into law in 1975. Among the modifications made since that time were changes to FRE 702 and 703, governing the admissibility of expert testimony, made in 2000. The FRE do not apply to suits in state courts; but the rules of many states have been closely modeled on these provisions. See http://www.law.cornell.edu/rules/fre/.

GBS: Guillain-Barré Syndrome, a disorder (normally affecting around one in a hundred thousand people) in which the immune system attacks the peripheral nervous system, leading to weakness and tingling, increasing in severity and in severe cases producing complete paralysis. Surgery or vaccinations can trigger the syndrome. See "Guillain-Barré Syndrome Fact Sheet," available at http://www.ninds.nih.gov/disorders/gbs/detail_gbs.htm.

Gettier Paradoxes: refers to purported counter-examples given by Edmund Gettier in 1963 to the traditional philosophical definition of knowledge as justified true belief. (Subsequent purported counter-examples devised by others in response to proposed modification of the definition to accommodate the original counter-examples are sometimes referred to as "Gettier-type" paradoxes.) See Edmund Gettier, "Is Justified True Belief Knowledge?" *Analysis* 23 (1963): 121–23; Susan Haack, "'Know' Is Just a Four-Letter Word," in Haack, *Evidence and Inquiry* (1993; 2nd ed., Amherst, NY: Prometheus Books, 2009), 301–31.

"grue" paradox: "grue" is a neologism introduced by Nelson Goodman, defined as applying to all things examined before time *t* if and only if they are green but to other things just in case they are blue. The paradox is that "the prediction that all emeralds subsequently examined [i.e., examined after *t*] will be green and the prediction that they will be grue are alike confirmed by evidence statements describing the same observations." See Nelson Goodman, "The New Riddle of Induction," in Goodman, *Fact, Fiction, and Forecast* (1954; 2nd ed., Indianapolis, IN: Bobbs-Merrill, 1965), 59–83.

iff: if and only if.

IDT: Intelligent Design Theory. The thesis that many biological structures, from mammalian hair to hemoglobin, are so complex that they could not have been produced by an accumulation of small mutations, but must be the result of intelligent design. Proponents of IDT claim that this is a scientific theory; critics see it, rather, as a religious idea masquerading as science. See Phillip E. Johnson, *Darwin on Trial* (Washington, DC: Regnery Gateway, 1991; 2nd ed., Downers Grove, IL: Intervarsity Press, 1993); Michael J. Behe, *Darwin's Black Box: The Biochemical Challenge to Evolution* (New York: Free Press, 1996); Barbara Forrest and Paul R. Gross, *Creationism's Trojan Horse: The Wedge of Intelligent Design* (New York: Oxford University Press, 2004).

inductive logic: logic of inductive strength. An argument is inductively strong if and only if, though it is not deductively valid, it is such that it is (not impossible, but) unlikely or improbable that the premises be true and the conclusion false. It is controversial, however, whether inductive strength is a matter of form rather than content. I believe the "grue" paradox shows it is not. See Brian Skyrms, *Choice and Chance: An Introduction to Inductive Logic* (1966; Independence, KY: Cengage, 1999). See also **deductive logic**; **"grue" paradox; inductivism.**

inductivism: (in philosophy of science) refers to approaches which hold either that scientific theories are arrived at by inductive reasoning, or that—though the process of discovering a scientific theory is not a matter of inference—the process by which scientific theories are confirmed is a matter of inductive logic. See also **Deductivism**; **inductive logic**.

instrumentalism: (in philosophy of science) the view that theoretical "statements" in science are not really genuine statements at all, and so are neither true nor false, but only tools or instruments for making observational predictions. See Ernst Mach, "On the Principle of Conservation of Energy" and "On the Principle of Comparison in Physics," in *Populärwissenschaftlich Vorlesungen* (Leipzig, 1894), trans. Thomas J. McCormack, *Popular Scientific Lectures* (La Salle, IL: Open Court, 1943), 137–85 and 236–58.

JAMA: *Journal of the American Medical Association.*

JMOL: Judgment as a Matter of Law. This includes both directed verdicts (where a judge takes the verdict out of the jury's hands) and judgments *n.o.v.* or "notwithstanding the verdict" (where a judge overrides a verdict the jury has already brought in). See Richard A. Givens (updated by Kevin Shirey), *Manual of Federal Practice, 2010 Cumulative Supplement* (New Providence, NJ: LexisNexus, 2010), §7.51, 790–91. See also ***n.o.v.***

laconicism: used here to refer to F. P. Ramsey's account of truth (more commonly, but inaccurately, known as the "redundancy theory").

Logical Negativism: used here to refer to Karl R. Popper's philosophy of science, because, by contrast with Logical Positivist approaches, it is thoroughly negative. See also **Critical Rationalism**; **Deductivism**; **Falsificationism**; **Logical Positivism**.

Logical Positivism: approach to philosophy initiated in the early 1920s by the "Vienna Circle" of philosophers, scientists, and mathematicians. Central themes were the "Verification Principle," according to which statements that aren't purely logical or mathematical have cognitive meaning only if they are empirically verifiable; and that the meaning of empirical statements is to be understood in terms of their verification conditions. See Alfred J. Ayer, ed., *Logical Positivism* (New York: Free Press, 1959). Since theoretical statements in science cannot be verified by observation, some Logical Positivists favored **instrumentalism**, while others developed various forms of **inductivism**. See also **Logical Negativism**.

Modus tollendo tollens **("*modus tollens*," for short):** the rule of deductive logic licensing inferences from premises of the form "if A then B," and "not-B" to a conclusion of the form "not A." See also: **deductive logic**; **Deductivism**; **Falsificationism**.

MMR: mumps, measles, and rubella (German measles). MMR vaccine was suspected of causing autism; but the work that suggested this is now known to have been fraudulent. See Andrew Wakefield et al., "Ileal-Lymphoid-Nodular Hyperplasia, Non-specific Colitis, and Pervasive Developmental Disorder in Children," *The Lancet* 351 (February 28, 1998): 637–41; Editors of the *British Medical Journal*, "Wakefield Article Linking MMR Vaccine and Autism Was Fraudulent," *British Medical Journal* 342 (2011): 64–66.

necessary and sufficient conditions: A is a necessary condition for B if B can't be the case unless A is, i.e., if B then A; for example, a necessary condition of a number's being greater than 100 is that it is greater than 1 (if $n > 100$, then $n > 1$). A is a sufficient condition for B if, if A is the case, then B is too, i.e., if A then B; for example, a sufficient condition of a number's being greater than 100 is that it is greater than 101 (if $n > 101$, then $n > 100$).

NEJM: *New England Journal of Medicine.*

n.o.v.: *non obstante veredicto* ("not withstanding the verdict"). A "judgment *n.o.v.*" refers to a judgment entered by the court for one party even though a jury verdict has been entered for the opposing party. See Bryan A. Garner, ed., *Black's Law Dictionary* (St. Paul, MN: Thomson Reuters, 9th ed., 2009), 219–20. See also **JMOL.**

ONJ: osteonecrosis of the jaw. A rare dental condition in which there is dead bone in the upper or lower jaw. Bisphosphonates (used for the treatment of osteoporosis, e.g., in Fosamax) have been suspected of causing ONJ in a small number of patients. See Osteogenesis Imperfecta (OI) Foundation, "What Is Osteonecrosis of the Jaw?" available at www.oif.org; Bone and Cancer Foundation, "Osteonecrosis of the Jaw (ONJ)," available at www.boneandcancerfoundation.org; Jeffrey L. Fellows, et al., "ONJ in Two Dental Practice-Based Research Network Regions," abstract available at http://www.ncbi.nlm.nih.gov/pubmed/21317245.

PAHs: polycyclic aromatic hydrocarbons. A class of organic compounds made up of two or more closed benzene rings arranged in various configurations, often by-products of combustion, but also of the degradation of biological materials. Because PAHs are carcinogenic at relatively low concentration, information about them can be found at, for example, "Toxic Substances Hydrology Program," available at http://toxics.usgs.gov/definitions/pah.html. Here, however, their relevance is that the discovery of PAHs in a Martian meteorite prompted the conjecture that there was once bacterial life on Mars. See Adam Rogers, "Come In, Mars," *Newsweek*, 19 August, 1996, 56–57.

PCBs: polychlorinated biphenyls. A broad class of man-made organic compounds, not found in nature but manufactured (in the US, under the trade name "Arcolor"). Used as coolants and lubricating fluids for transformers and capacitors, stabilizing components in flexible coating for electrical wiring and electronic components, pesticide extenders, flame retardants, oil-based paint, adhesives and tapes, carbonless copy-paper, etc. The commercial usefulness of PCBs was based largely on their chemical stability, including low flammability, and their electrical insulating properties; but this chemical stability is also responsible for their persistence in the environment. Most PCB mixtures are highly toxic: PCBs have been shown to cause cancer and a variety of other ill effects on the immune system, the reproductive system, the nervous system, and the endocrine system. PCB production has been banned in the US since 1977. See http://www.atsdr.cdc.gov/toxfaqs/tf.asp?id=140&tid=26 http://www.epa.gov/epawaste/hazard/tsd/pcbs/about.htm; http://www.dhs.wisconsin.gov/eh/ChemFS/fs/PCB.htm.

Pragmatism: refers here to the classical pragmatist tradition in philosophy, initiated by discussions between C. S. Peirce and William James at the Metaphysical Club in Cambridge, Massachusetts, in the early 1970s; carried on by John Dewey and (in philosophy of mind) by George Herbert Mead; and represented, in legal philosophy, by Oliver Wendell Holmes, an early member of the Metaphysical Club. See Susan Haack, "Introduction: Pragmatism, Old and New," in Susan Haack and Robert E. Lane, eds., *Pragmatism, Old and New: Selected Writings* (Amherst, NY: Prometheus Books, 2006), 15–68; and "On Legal Pragmatism: Where Does 'The Path of the Law' Lead Us?" *American Journal of Jurisprudence* 50 (2005): 71–105. See also **Pragmatic Maxim**.

Pragmatic Maxim: Both Peirce and James insisted that Pragmatism was not a body of philosophical doctrine, but rather a method of doing philosophy, the method embodied in the Pragmatic Maxim, according to which the meaning of a concept consists in its experiential consequences. (From the beginning, however, Peirce and James differed in how they interpreted this connection, and over time these differences would become more marked.) See C. S. Peirce, "How to Make our Ideas Clear," *Collected Papers*, eds. Charles Hartshorne, Paul Weiss and (vols. 7 and 8) Arthur Burks (Cambridge, MA: Harvard University Press, 1931–58), 5. 388–410 (1878); William James, "Philosophical Conceptions and Practical Results," *University Chronicle* (University of California, Berkeley) 1 (September 1898): 287–310; reprinted in James, *Pragmatism*, 255–70; and, for a useful summary, Cornelis de Waal, *On Pragmatism* (Belmont, CA: Wadsworth, 2005), chapters 1 and 2. See also **Pragmatism.**

PTSD: post-traumatic stress disorder. A psychological reaction after a traumatic event such as violence, military combat, rape, torture, etc. Symptoms include uncontrollable recurrent memories of the event, flashbacks, nightmares, and severe anxiety. See National Institutes of Health, "Post-Traumatic Stress Disorder," available at http://www.nimh.nih.gov/health/topics/post-traumatic-stress-disorder-ptsd/index.shtml; MayoClinic.com, "Post-Traumatic Stress Disorder (PTSD)," available at http://www.mayoclinic.com/health/post-truamatic-stress-disorder/DS00246; *Psychology Today*, "Post-Traumatic Stress Disorder," available at http://www.psychologytoday.com/basics/post-traumatic-stress-disorder.

RR > 2: short for "relative risk greater than 2" or, equivalently, "more than doubled risk." Used by epidemiologists when subjects exposed to some drug or toxin S are more than twice as likely to develop a disease or disorder D as those not so exposed.

scare quotes: quotation marks used to distance the writer from commitment to the appropriateness of the word or phrase inside, as in "the University has instituted an 'inquiry' into this scandal, but of course the upshot is bound to be a whitewash." (Sometimes called "sneer quotes" or—because, in speech, people sometimes "draw" them in the air with two fingers of each hand—"air quotes.")

SSA: Supervisory Special (FBI) Agent.

tautology: has a technical sense in logic, but as used here means a trivial verbal truth, a statement that says the same thing twice.

teratogen: substance that causes birth defects (from the Greek "*teras*," monster).

***t* table:** the "*t*-statistic" indicates how far away an estimate is from its expected value, relative to the standard error. See David H. Kaye and David A. Freedman, "Reference Guide on Statistics," *Reference Manual on Scientific Evidence*, 3rd ed. (Washington, DC: National Academies Press, 2011), 211–302, 300–01.

Index

Books in the Series (continued from page iii)

Cane: *Atiyah's Accidents, Compensation and the Law*

Clarke & Kohler: *Property Law: Commentary and Materials*

Collins: *The Law of Contract*

Cowan: *Housing Law and Policy*

Cranston: *Legal Foundations of the Welfare State*

Dauvergne: *Making People Illegal: What Globalisation Means for Immigration and Law*

Davies: *Perspectives on Labour Law*

de Sousa Santos: *Toward a New Legal Common Sense*

Dembour: *Who Believes in Human Rights? The European Convention in Question*

Diduck: *Law's Families*

Fortin: *Children's Rights and the Developing Law*

Glover-Thomas: *Reconstructing Mental Health Law and Policy*

Gobert & Punch: *Rethinking Corporate Crime*

Goldman: *Globalisation and the Western Legal Tradition: Recurring Patterns of Law and Authority*

Haack: *Evidence Matters: Science, Proof, and Truth in the Law*

Harlow & Rawlings: *Law and Administration*

Harris: *An Introduction to Law*

Harris, Campbell & Halson: *Remedies in Contract and Tort*

Harvey: *Seeking Asylum in the UK: Problems and Prospects*

Hervey & McHale: *Health Law and the European Union*

Holder & Lee: *Environmental Protection, Law and Policy*

Jackson & Summers: *The Internationalisation of Criminal Evidence*

Kostakopoulou: *The Future Governance of Citizenship*

Lewis: *Choice and the Legal Order: Rising above Politics*

Likosky: *Law, Infrastructure and Human Rights*

Likosky: *Transnational Legal Processes*

Maughan & Webb: *Lawyering Skills and the Legal Process*

McGlynn: *Families and the European Union: Law, Politics and Pluralism*

Moffat: *Trusts Law: Text and Materials*

Monti: *EC Competition Law*

Morgan & Yeung: *An Introduction to Law and Regulation: Text and Materials*

Norrie: *Crime, Reason and History*

O'Dair: *Legal Ethics*

Oliver: *Common Values and the Public–Private Divide*

Oliver & Drewry: *The Law and Parliament*

Picciotto: *International Business Taxation*

Probert: *The Changing Legal Regulation of Cohabitation, 1600–2010*

Reed: *Internet Law: Text and Materials*

Richardson: *Law, Process and Custody*

Roberts & Palmer: *Dispute Processes: ADR and the Primary Forms of Decision-Making*

Rowbottom: *Democracy Distorted: Wealth, Influence and Democratic Politics*

Scott & Black: *Cranston's Consumers and the Law*

Seneviratne: *Ombudsmen: Public Services and Administrative Justice*

Stapleton: *Product Liability*

Stewart: *Gender, Law and Justice in a Global Market*

Tamanaha: *Law as a Means to an End: Threat to the Rule of Law*

Turpin & Tomkins: *British Government and the Constitution: Text and Materials*

Twining: *General Jurisprudence: Understanding Law from a Global Perspective*

Twining: *Globalisation and Legal Theory*

Twining: *Human Rights, Southern Voices: Francis Deng, Abdullahi An-Na'im, Yash Ghai and Upendra Baxi*

Twining: *Rethinking Evidence*

Twining & Miers: *How to Do Things with Rules*

Ward: *A Critical Introduction to European Law*

Ward: *Law, Text, Terror*

Ward: *Shakespeare and Legal Imagination*

Wells & Quick: *Lacey, Wells and Quick: Reconstructing Criminal Law*

Zander: *Cases and Materials on the English Legal System*

Zander: *The Law-Making Process*

http://www.bu.edu/law/faculty/scholarship/workingpapers/2011.html

http://ssrn.com/abstract=1793973

What category did you put pt in → 50% who still had Ca cells in its body or the 50% who were Ca free.
What were the grounds for so deciding on behalf / pt.

What was your purpose for seeing pt.
Since do not see / or hear / or feel much during a tretmt — not much experiential stuff going on:

can't see the radiation field / rays) or cottage
can't see the organs to which the rays are directed
see pt's skin

Since can't see, plan + its implementation take on more importance than the actual "doing" or the "conducting of" the tretmt.

B 248

BU School / law

Negligence, Causation, + Incentives for Care

BU Sc / Keith N Hylton

Hingham MA

BU School of law working paper 11-15